THE
Great
Movie Stars

The Independent Years 3

Also by David Shipman:

THE GREAT MOVIE STARS 1: The Golden Years
THE GREAT MOVIE STARS 2: The International Years
BRANDO
A PICTORIAL HISTORY OF SCIENCE FICTION FILMS
THE GOOD FILM AND VIDEO GUIDE
CAUGHT IN THE ACT: Sex and Eroticism in the Cinema
MOVIE TALK: Who Said What About Whom in the Movies
THE STORY OF THE CINEMA

THE
Great
Movie Stars

The Independent Years 3

DAVID SHIPMAN

LITTLE, BROWN AND COMPANY

BOSTON   NEW YORK   TORONTO   LONDON

First U.S. Edition

ISBN 0-1316-78489-3

10 9 8 7 6 5 4 3 2 1

Printed in Great Britain

The Stars of The Golden Years . . .

Abbott and Costello
Don Ameche
Fatty Arbuckle
George Arliss
Jean Arthur
Fred Astaire
Mary Astor
Lew Ayres
Lucille Ball
Tallulah Bankhead
Theda Bara
John Barrymore
Richard Barthelmess
Freddie Bartholomew
Warner Baxter
Wallace Beery
Constance Bennett
Joan Bennett
Jack Benny
Ingrid Bergman
Elisabeth Bergner
Joan Blondell
Humphrey Bogart
Clara Bow
Charles Boyer
Louise Brooks
Jack Buchanan
Billie Burke
James Cagney
Eddie Cantor
Madeleine Carroll
Lon Chaney
Charlie Chaplin
Ruth Chatterton
Maurice Chevalier
Claudette Colbert
Ronald Colman
Gary Cooper
Cicely Courtneidge
Joan Crawford
Laird Cregar
Bing Crosby
Bebe Daniels
Marion Davies
Bette Davis
Olivia de Havilland

Dolores del Rio
Marlene Dietrich
Richard Dix
Robert Donat
Melvyn Douglas
Marie Dressler
Irene Dunne
Deanna Durbin
Nelson Eddy
Douglas Fairbanks
Douglas Fairbanks Jr
Frances Farmer
Alice Faye
Gracie Fields
W.C. Fields
Errol Flynn
Henry Fonda
Joan Fontaine
George Formby
Kay Francis
Clark Gable
Greta Garbo
John Garfield
Judy Garland
Greer Garson
Janet Gaynor
John Gilbert
Lillian Gish
Paulette Goddard
Betty Grable
Cary Grant
Ann Harding
Cedric Hardwicke
Jean Harlow
Will Hay
Helen Hayes
Rita Hayworth
Sonja Henie
Katharine Hepburn
Wendy Hiller
Valerie Hobson
Bob Hope
Miriam Hopkins
Leslie Howard
Walter Huston
Betty Hutton

Emil Jannings
Al Jolson
Boris Karloff
Buster Keaton
Ruby Keeler
Alan Ladd
Veronica Lake
Hedy Lamarr
Dorothy Lamour
Elissa Landi
Harry Langdon
Charles Laughton
Laurel and Hardy
Vivien Leigh
Harold Lloyd
Margaret Lockwood
Carole Lombard
Myrna Loy
Paul Lukas
Ida Lupino
Jeanette MacDonald
Aline MacMahon
Fred MacMurray
Fredric March
Herbert Marshall
Mary Martin
The Marx Brothers
James Mason
Jessie Matthews
Joel McCrea
Victor McLaglen
Ray Milland
Carmen Miranda
Maria Montez
Robert Montgomery
Grace Moore
Frank Morgan
Paul Muni
Anna Neagle
Pola Negri
Ramon Novarro
Merle Oberon
Margaret O'Brien
Laurence Olivier
Lilli Palmer
Mary Pickford

Walter Pidgeon
Dick Powell
Eleanor Powell
William Powell
Tyrone Power
George Raft
Luise Rainer
Claude Rains
Basil Rathbone
Michael Redgrave
Ralph Richardson
Paul Robeson
Edward G. Robinson
Flora Robson
Ginger Rogers
Will Rogers
Mickey Rooney
Rosalind Russell
George Sanders
Norma Shearer
Ann Sheridan
Sylvia Sidney
Ann Sothern
Barbara Stanwyck
Anna Sten
James Stewart
Margaret Sullavan
Gloria Swanson
Robert Taylor
Shirley Temple
Franchot Tone
Spencer Tracy
Claire Trevor
Lana Turner
Rudolph Valentino
Conrad Veidt
Erich Von Stroheim
Anton Walbrook
John Wayne
Johnny Weissmuller
Orson Welles
Mae West
Diana Wynyard
Loretta Young
Robert Young
Roland Young

The Stars of The International Years . . .

Anouk Aimée
June Allyson
Dana Andrews
Julie Andrews
Pier Angeli
Eve Arden
Alan Arkin
Arletty
Richard Attenborough
Lauren Bacall
Anne Bancroft
Brigitte Bardot
Alan Bates
Anne Baxter
Warren Beatty
Barbara Bel Geddes
Jean-Paul Belmondo
William Bendix
Claire Bloom
Ann Blyth
Dirk Bogarde
Shirley Booth
Ernest Borgnine
Marlon Brando
Charles Bronson
Mel Brooks
Yul Brynner
Ellen Burstyn
Richard Burton
James Caan
Michael Caine
Leslie Caron
Jack Carson
Jeff Chandler
Cyd Charisse
Julie Christie
Montgomery Clift
James Coburn
Sean Connery
Joseph Cotten
Jeanne Crain
Broderick Crawford
Tony Curtis
Zbigniew Cybulski
Linda Darnell
Danielle Darrieux
Doris Day
James Dean
Sandra Dee
Alain Delon
Catherine Deneuve
Diana Dors
Kirk Douglas

Paul Douglas
Faye Dunaway
Clint Eastwood
Edith Evans
Mia Farrow
Fernandel
José Ferrer
Edwige Feuillère
Peter Finch
Albert Finney
Louise Fletcher
Jane Fonda
Glenn Ford
Jean Gabin
Ava Gardner
Betty Garrett
Vittorio Gassmann
Mitzi Gaynor
Ben Gazzara
Elliott Gould
Gloria Grahame
Farley Granger
Stewart Granger
Kathryn Grayson
Sydney Greenstreet
Joan Greenwood
Alec Guinness
Gene Hackman
Julie Harris
Richard Harris
Kathleen Harrison
Rex Harrison
Laurence Harvey
Susan Hayward
Audrey Hepburn
Charlton Heston
William Holden
Judy Holliday
Celeste Holm
Trevor Howard
Rock Hudson
Tab Hunter
Glenda Jackson
Glynis Johns
Celia Johnson
Van Johnson
Jennifer Jones
Louis Jouvet
Danny Kaye
Howard Keel
Gene Kelly
Grace Kelly
Kay Kendall

Deborah Kerr
Burt Lancaster
Angela Lansbury
Mario Lanza
Jack Lemmon
Jerry Lewis
Gina Lollobrigida
Sophia Loren
Peter Lorre
Shirley MacLaine
Gordon MacRae
Anna Magnani
Jayne Mansfield
Jean Marais
Dean Martin
Lee Marvin
Giulietta Masina
Marcello Mastroianni
Walter Matthau
Victor Mature
Dorothy McGuire
Steve McQueen
Melina Mercouri
Toshiro Mifune
Ann Miller
Hayley Mills
John Mills
Robert Mitchum
Marilyn Monroe
Yves Montand
Agnes Moorehead
Kenneth More
Jeanne Moreau
Michèle Morgan
Robert Morley
Patricia Neal
Paul Newman
David Niven
Kim Novak
Maureen O'Hara
Ryan O'Neal
Tatum O'Neal
Peter O'Toole
Geraldine Page
Gregory Peck
Anthony Perkins
Gérard Philipe
Sidney Poitier
Jane Powell
Elvis Presley
Robert Preston
Vincent Price
Anthony Quinn

Raimu
Robert Redford
Lynn Redgrave
Vanessa Redgrave
Oliver Reed
Lee Remick
Debbie Reynolds
Thelma Ritter
Jason Robards
Cliff Robertson
Gail Russell
Jane Russell
Margaret Rutherford
Robert Ryan
Eva Marie Saint
Maximilian Schell
Romy Schneider
Paul Scofield
George C. Scott
Jean Seberg
George Segal
Peter Sellers
Omar Sharif
Simone Signoret
Alastair Sim
Jean Simmons
Frank Sinatra
Rod Steiger
Barbra Streisand
Elizabeth Taylor
Rod Taylor
Terry-Thomas
Gene Tierney
Richard Todd
Jean-Louis Trintignant
Liv Ullmann
Peter Ustinov
Alida Valli
Raf Vallone
Vera-Ellen
Monica Vitti
Robert Walker
Clifton Webb
Raquel Welch
Tuesday Weld
Richard Widmark
Cornel Wilde
Esther Williams
Shelley Winters
Natalie Wood
Joanne Woodward
Jane Wyman
Susannah York

The Stars of The Independent Years . . .

Alan Alda
Woody Allen
Ann-Margret
Dan Aykroyd
Kim Basinger
Tom Berenger
Jacqueline Bisset
Klaus Maria
Brandauer
Jeff Bridges
Matthew Broderick
Geneviève Bujold
Carol Burnett
Stockard Channing
Chevy Chase
Cher
Glenn Close
Kevin Costner
Tom Cruise
Willem Dafoe
Ted Danson
Daniel Day-Lewis
Robert De Niro
Gérard Depardieu

Danny DeVito
Matt Dillon
Michael Douglas
Richard Dreyfuss
Robert Duvall
Sally Field
Colin Firth
Harrison Ford
Jodie Foster
Michael J. Fox
Richard Gere
Mel Gibson
Tom Hanks
Daryl Hannah
Rutger Hauer
Goldie Hawn
Barbara Hershey
Dustin Hoffman
Paul Hogan
Anthony Hopkins
Bob Hoskins
Holly Hunter
William Hurt

Diane Keaton
Michael Keaton
Kevin Kline
Kris Kristofferson
Jessica Lange
Victor Lanoux
Shelley Long
Rob Lowe
Madonna
John Malkovich
Steve Martin
Bette Midler
Liza Minnelli
Rick Moranis
Eddie Murphy
Bill Murray
Jack Nicholson
Philippe Noiret
Nick Nolte
Al Pacino
Dolly Parton
Sean Penn
Valerie Perrine

Michelle Pfeiffer
Richard Pryor
Christopher Reeve
Burt Reynolds
Mickey Rourke
Theresa Russell
Marianne Sägebrecht
Arnold Schwarzenegger
Tom Selleck
Maggie Smith
Sissy Spacek
Sylvester Stallone
Meryl Streep
Patrick Swayze
John Travolta
Kathleen Turner
Jon Voight
Denzel Washington
Sigourney Weaver
Robin Williams
Bruce Willis
Debra Winger
James Woods

Introduction

In today's cinema, Hollywood has regained its former eminence – which is not to say that art-houses are not finding foreign films to show; but the high quality of television in many countries has caused a shrinkage in local film industries. In 1989 foreign markets returned no less than 43 per cent of total revenues to the American film companies.

Accompanying this trend is the phenomenon of increased costs. In 1980 the average cost of a studio feature was $9,300,000, and this had increased to $18,500,000 in 1988 and to $23,500,000 the following year. In addition to this the studio will spend a further huge sum on prints and advertising – reckoned until recently at an average $10 million on movies with a good chance at the box-office, but going as high as $54,700,000, in the case of *Dick Tracy* (which, added to the budget of $46,500,000 worked out at a total of $101,200,000; but since it only took $34,000,000 at the American box-office, the loss was considerable).

It is an old rule of thumb that a film must recover its cost at the American or domestic box-office (the figures used in this book, unless otherwise stated), but the reader may add on the estimated budgets for publicity and prints, bearing in mind that the more popular the film is expected to be the more likely it is to open 'wide', that is, at as many cinemas as possible. (On the other hand, some films open wide in a ploy to get as many people in before word gets out that they are really bad.)

In 1980 returns from theatres represented 80 per cent of revenues worldwide, but by 1990, with the growth of the video industry, this figure has shrunk to as little as 30 per cent. Thus while a failure at the American box-office will mean red ink in the ledger, results from overseas and sales of video cassettes may eventually reveal a very different picture.

The high fees paid to talent by the movie industry have been sufficiently discussed as to be not worth repeating here, but it should be borne in mind – in considering the resurrection of the movie-star after a period in which many starless pictures raked in huge grosses – that it is now easier to open a big-budget film with high-profile talent than one of medium-budget with 'names'.

I have paid particular attention to fees and financing, with budgets listed where known. The profit or loss on any given movie will usually be found under the name of the star most likely to have been responsible for box-office success; but there are cross-references where more than one star player is concerned.

In this volume I have not taken into account the box-office positions of the stars during the last few years, simply because it seems to me that there are too few of them shuffling for top place – as opposed to the couple of hundred stars during the Golden Years of Hollywood.

Finally, I cannot leave the subject without mentioning the power of the agents, which exceeds that of the studio heads in the old days. By common consent, Mike Ovitz of CAA (Creative Artists Agency) is the most powerful man in Hollywood; the other agencies with the most prestigious list of clients are William Morris and ICM (International Creative Management). Eric Pleskow of Orion Pictures explained the situation thus: 'We are all fishing in a relatively small pond. There are never enough talented writers, directors or stars. The agents influence the creative personnel about their career choices.'

They are also responsible for getting them huge fees, which also convey power. In 1985 Jane Wyman observed that 'even Clark Gable didn't dare complain if he didn't like his working conditions. Today the actors demand a chauffeur and a limo before they've read the script.'

It seemed only natural that there should be a *Great Movie Stars Volume 3*. When the idea was first mooted I suggested calling it simply 'Today's Players', since there were very few people capable of drawing cinemagoers into theatres. That has now changed, enabling me to pick one hundred stars of the eighties and nineties who I think are important for one reason or another: in the event I stopped at 92. I wrote each entry more-or-less in order of importance, which meant that almost a dozen people were in competition for the three final places: two or three of them disqualified themselves by coming into prominence only in this last year, but with the others I did not wish to play God, nor favour one actor above another.

Each individual entry follows the pattern of the previous two volumes, except that I have tended less to begin with a long summary of each artist's appeal – simply because many of the stars do not have careers long enough for that appeal to be clearly established; but I have also found it more rewarding to make each entry a narrative than to form an assessment as before. I was, incidentally, warned by many people that this book would be much less satisfying to write than the other two, but if anything I found it otherwise – partly because today's stars are less remote than those of the past, and partly because the films they have made are in my immediate consciousness. The essential facts about background and so on are followed by a detailed filmography. Each feature, then, is listed in chronological order except where stated. The dates used are those of the first known preview or public showing, with all ensuing titles belonging to that year – until the next date. Again, it should be remembered that by the time the film is shown the star may have worked on the stage or in television, and that if you are relating the dates to box-office results, a December release will not show much response in that respect until the following year. I have not tried to be exhaustive on the matter of stage and television credits – except in the case of tele-films and mini-series, which appear chronologically in their order of transmission. For reasons of space – and clarity – I have not sought to differentiate between a tele-film shown over two nights or a series shown over several. The preamble above on costs and profits explains why I have paid particular attention to them, with figures taken from 'Variety' unless explained otherwise; but it is the *New York Times* (8 July 1990) which provided the figures of $3–8 million as the cost of films made for television. If I have been more selective on awards and Oscar nominations (but not where the Oscar statuette itself is concerned) it is because awards have proliferated in recent years, while a nomination is not necessarily a factor in success.

All English titles are given as they appeared in the listed credits (except, again for clarity, in omitting the commas sometimes used); and I have used the original titles in French, German, Italian and Spanish. Films from other countries are usually given in the original and the best-known English title. A list of title-changes is given at the end of the book, including some featured as 'aka' in the text; but it is not possible to follow the vagaries involved in retitling tele-films.

I was helped by many people in writing the previous two volumes. My thanks on this occasion are due to three: Tony Sloman, Richard Chatten and Fons Castermans, each of them as stimulating as they are knowledgeable; and thanks are also due to the many periodicals and newspapers quoted, all mentioned by name in the text.

David Shipman
November 1990

ACKNOWLEDGEMENTS

Grateful acknowledgement is made to the many critics, authors and journalists who are quoted in this book – also to their publishers. Thanks, too, to the newspapers and magazines that have been more than helpful.

For picture research, grateful thanks is given to Howard and Ron Mandelbaum at Photofest, New York. Kind permission was also given by Columbia Pictures, Cannon, Paramount, the Rank Organisation, Orion, Palace, Vestron, 20th Century-Fox, MGM/UA, Paramount, Goldcrest, Warner Bros., Handmade Films, Films LaTour, Films Ariane, Carolco, Imagine Films, Lucasfilms, Amblin Entertainment, Merchant-Ivory, Working Title, Walt Disney, Universal, Weintraub Entertainment, Unifrance and the British Film Institute. Photos from the author's own collection have also been used.

ALAN ALDA

Impish, amiable, wry in humour and modestly likeable, Alan Alda is almost the only movie actor to have a fruitful film career after a long stint in a television series with which he was indelibly associated (Ted Danson and Tom Selleck are the others).

He was born in New York City in 1935, the son of the actor Robert Alda, whose Hollywood career had most notably included playing George Gershwin in *Rhapsody in Blue*. As a boy he was stricken with polio, in his teens he studied at Fordham University, and he enjoyed a spell in Europe while his father was making *La Donna più Bella del Mondo* in Italy in 1955. Alda made his first stage appearance in 1953 and first appeared on Broadway in 1959 in 'Only in America'; his breakthrough came with a long run in 'The Owl and the Pussycat' as a mild-mannered man bothered by a hooker living in the same house. He had a similar role, Charlie Cotchipec, in 'Purlie Victorious' (61), a look at contemporary black struggles in the South as tales of the Uncle Tom days are updated. Ossie Davis wrote it as a vehicle for himself and his wife, Ruby Dee. They, Alda and Godfrey Cambridge all repeated when it was filmed as *Gone Are the Days!* (63), but the supposedly more accessible title was no help at the box-office, and an obviously low budget did nothing to improve the situation.

Alda spent the next years in television, returning to the cinema as George Plimpton (who wanted to play himself) in the *Paper Lion* (68), that is, the sports-writer who diversified himself into the matters he wrote about. It did little for Alda, who dipped to third billing, after David Niven and Faye Dunaway, with *The Extraordinary Seaman* (69), playing a fatuous, well-meaning naval accountant who is not of much use when shipwrecked. Alda, whose later career would find him adept at playing contented mediocrities, did a superb job this first time out, but the direction of John Frankenheimer, once a talent to watch, was not persuasive enough in bringing audiences in. In *The Moonshine War* (70) Alda supported villainous Richard Widmark, playing a chum who has a cache of the stuff, whisky. He starred in the next two, but neither was of much interest: in *Jenny* he was a hip movie-maker who marries a pregnant Marlo Thomas (hoping to make the breakthrough from TV to movies – but in vain) to avoid being drafted to Vietnam; and in *The Mephisto Waltz* (71) he was a failed concert pianist who gets caught up in diabolism when the soul of a successful one (Curt Jurgens) enters his body; Jacqueline Bisset co-starred as his wife. In the British-made (but set in

New England) *To Kill a Clown* (72) he was a crippled Vietnam officer who becomes a reincarnation of Baron Zaroff, setting his hounds on Blythe Danner and husband Heath Lamberts. Alda's method-bound acting was not a distinct asset in any of these disappointing credits.

Earlier that year (the British film was shot in 1971, but had difficulty getting bookings) he had guest-starred in Truman Capote's 'The Glass House' for television, playing a professor convicted for manslaughter after attacking the careless driver who had killed his wife. Once inside, he pits himself against brutal, homosexual Vic Morrow, with seldom a prison cliché missed along the way. Alda put all of his heart into the role, as he was wont to do, but under Tom Gries's direction the result was rather blah, and the piece did little business when released theatrically overseas. Alda was in another TV movie, *Playmates*, a title which referred to two chums dating each other's ex-wife (the other was Doug McClure). In *Isn't It Shocking?* (73), also for TV, he was an untried small-town sheriff. Television had already offered him the role of 'Hawkeye' Pierce in 'M-A-S-H' (which Donald Sutherland had played in the film version, and which on the box became an extension of Larry Gelbart, who wrote the series). Cunning, resourceful, irreverent and right-minded, Hawkeye became a national icon, winning Alda an Emmy; he won another

Neil Simon is statistically the most successful playwright ever to write for Broadway, and apart from adapting his comedies for films, he has written original screenplays – with mixed results in both cases. California Suite (78) belongs to the former breed, and was by way of being a follow-up to Plaza Suite. The result was decidedly mixed, with four separate stories to tell, including this one, in which a divorced couple meet up again to exchange insults about New York, where she lives, and California, which he prefers. There was a zinger in every line, but too many of them. They were, however, expertly delivered by Alan Alda and Jane Fonda.

for directing some of the series, which ran from 1972 to 1983. He was said to be getting $75,000-$100,000 per episode. He had also turned to writing, for a TV series in 1975 which did not run, 'We'll Get By'. A television film in which he played the convicted murderer, Caryl Chessman, *Kill Me If You Can* (77), alerted him to the fact that there was more to life than Hawkeye, so he made a long-delayed return to the big screen in a role turned down by Burt Reynolds: *California Suite* (78), playing Jane Fonda's ex-husband, each of them tossing off so many Neil Simon zingers that the total effect was nil. He again needed all his comedy expertise to give point to a bland two-hander, *Same Time Next Year* with Ellen Burstyn, both of them married with three kids and meeting up once a year to revive old passions. We're spared the annual rendezvous, to find them at five-year intervals, against a changing America: and be thankful for that. Both films were based on long-running Broadway hits, which must be why they seemed worth doing: but with the encouragement of Martin Bregman, his agent and now his film producer, he was to take his career gently into a new dimension.

The Seduction of Joe Tynan (79) ably demonstrated the skill honed in playing Hawkeye, though it was less a comedy than a look at the lurid life available to senators in Washington, especially those with ambition and not too many scruples. He also did himself a favour by writing the script, which

went as under-rated as his performance, leaving us with the impression that Joe Tynan is not so much an all-time heel as a jolly good fellow. Jerry Schatzberg directed, but thereafter Alda would helm his own scripts, to agreeable results. His taste for writing was also put to good effect in *The Four Seasons* (81), a pleasing entertainment about the friendship of three couples, in which he and Carol Burnett were well matched, with a nice taste for sharing each other's jokes. Maybe he did not restore Hollywood comedy to the wit of its great days, but he was slyly observant, as he proved again with *Sweet Liberty* (86), which he directed and wrote, playing an unworldly professor caught up with the egos of movie-making (including those of Michael Caine, Michelle Pfeiffer and Bob Hoskins) when his novel about the American Revolution is filmed in his own home town. Alda again deserted his nice guy persona to play an insufferably conceited (and bearded) stockbroker in *A New Life* (88), adjusting to just that after he and his wife (Ann-Margret) divorce. These four Alda vehicles took respectively $9,400,000, $27,100,000, $7,600,000 (on a $14 million budget), all for Universal, and $3,600,000 for Paramount. Two of them must accordingly be reckoned financial failures, which is sad, for this was a time when 'anything goes' comedies seemed all that the industry could offer – or Woody Allen.

Alda acted in one of Allen's better films, *Crimes and Misdemeanors* (89) and was inventive and very funny playing his brother-in-law, an egotistical, platitude-spouting television producer: the New York critics voted him their Best Supporting Actor, which may have been why he decided not to return to television, as announced. In 1990 he was to have supplied a one-hour pilot, scripted by him, for a series about a middle-aged man experiencing a series of crises. He said he was too busy in films, and in the meantime had scripted, directed and starred in one, *Betsy's Wedding* (90), as the father of Molly Ringwald, who is marrying Dylan Walsh; the rivalry between the two sets of parents as to which can throw the showiest wedding turns into tribal warfare. It's a touching, rich film, taking in mid-life problems and managing to say much on the messiness of bourgeois marriages which was not said in two similar films of the past, *Father of the Bride* and Altman's *A Wedding*. The movie took over $18 million in its first month, which must have been gratifying to Alda and Bregman, who had moved him over to Disney for this occasion.

Alda is married (since 1957) to Arlene Weiss, a former concert clarinet-player, with three grown-up daughters; the family lives in

After years of playing Hawkeye in 'M.A.S.H.', Alan Alda returned to the big screen in a series of gently satirical comedies which he wrote as vehicles for himself, most of which he also directed. He put much of his knowledge of film-making into Sweet Liberty *(86), in which he played a historian bewildered by the cast and crew shooting a version of his novel about the American Revolution.*

New Jersey, from which he commuted to Hollywood weekly when shooting 'M-A-S-H'. He does not care for Hollywood life and says that he is particular about what he does: the five films he wrote and starred in are ample demonstration of this. Some may think that any one of these civilized entertainments is worth the whole of Mr Allen's over-rated oeuvre.

WOODY ALLEN

Woody Allen is adept at one-liners. An evening with Woody Allen is like a Woody Allen movie, according to one young lady who years ago had a date with him at the Russian Tea-Room – amusing at first, but wearing thin, since they're all the same joke: put-downs of himself. Oh, he is eloquent on himself – on how it feels to be an insecure, Jewish, manic-depressive, weedy little schlemiel, carrot-topped, bespectacled, prune-faced and totally unattractive to the opposite sex. He is thus in a privileged position to make jokes about the battle of the sexes; he can be bright on the pretensions of certain New York intellectuals, as who couldn't? One day he may make a joke about something else.

'There is a tendency to compare my films to Chaplin and Keaton,' he told Kathleen Carroll of the 'Sunday News'. 'You can't compare. I'm working 40 years later. I'm a product of television and psycho-analysis. There's no similarity . . . It's tough being compared to old masters. What happens is you're a product of those comedians you liked.' The one he liked most was Bob Hope: 'I used to deliver like him. In fact, I feel I have characteristics in common with Hope. We're both cowards, womanizers, egotistical, vain. Hope was not a clown in the sense of Chaplin or Keaton. He was the guy next door, the man from the electric company. You really believed him.' You will remember Allen in *Annie Hall*, struggling with lobsters or offering Diane Keaton birthday gifts: and you may wonder why he could not think up for himself one-tenth of the business that Hope's writers used to think up for him.

He was born (Allen Stewart Konigsberg) in Flatbush, New York, in 1935, and grew up an addict of baseball and comic-books; at fifteen he started studying movies and vaudeville at the Flatbush Theater, which encouraged him to write his own jokes: he mailed them to newspapers, and saw them printed – a consolation for being thrown out of New York University and the City College of New York. He married: Harlene Rose (1954–9) and actress Louise Lasser (1966–9), and during this period rose from one-liners for various performers – Herb Schriner, Peter Lind Hayes – to collaborating on the Sid Caesar TV show. Encouraged by his agents, Charles Roffe and Jack Rollins (later the producers of his movies) he worked on a stand-up act, tried out originally in small clubs in Greenwich Village, and, by his own admission, very much in the shadow of Mort Sahl; by the mid-60s he was contributing to the 'New Yorker' and in demand on late-night chat shows. He also wrote a film-script, *What's New, Pussycat?* (65), about a guy (Peter O'Toole) having trouble with girls and psycho-analysis, and he played his best friend, who worked in a strip joint: it was directed in Paris by the British Clive Donner, whose frenzied pacing tried to disguise the fact that the jokes were one-liners. Next, out of a 1964 Japanese film, *Kizino Kisi*, Allen and friends made *What's Up, Tiger Lily?*, and he appeared in it to explain that he was dubbing it into English to turn it into effect a James Bond parody: an offbeat idea, promisingly done. For 'an absurd fee, quite out of proportion to the size of my role' he was in another Bond spoof, *Casino Royale* (67): 'I never saw the film, but my loved ones tell me it was a uniquely ghastly experience.' Yes, but he had the sole funny scene – alas, at the beginning.

He was ambitious – for reasons abundantly clear from his 'humour' – and he planned a double attack on show business: a play, 'Play It Again, Sam', about a schmuck who is hung up on old movies and his inability to make it with pretty girls, and a film, *Take the Money and Run* (69), about a schmuck forever bungling attempts at robberies. He wrote and acted in both, and directed the latter (after considering Jerry Lewis for that job); the play was a qualified success, but although the film lost money, it brought him a three-picture contract with United Artists, with budget limitations but carte blanche. Also at this time appeared *Don't Drink the Water* with Jackie Gleason and Estelle Parsons, based on another play by Allen. *Bananas* (71) had the same theme as Harold Lloyd's *Why Worry?* – an innocent caught up in a banana republic revolution – and it was about one-tenth as funny.

Paramount filmed *Play It Again, Sam* (72), and under the direction of Herbert Ross it was a brighter moment among the year's films; but repeating his role of the sad sap Allen couldn't avoid self-pity (unlike Lloyd and Keaton, who also made us doubt that they'd really get the girl at the end). The title alone, *Everything You Always Wanted To Know About Sex*, should have gained him wider recognition, and this formless, seven-part satire did show a considerable advance – unlike the slapstick

Mouse into mountain: a mild comedy, Annie Hall (77) *became a very popular film, due to some nice people like Tony Roberts and Diane Keaton. Between them is their co-star, writer and director, Woody Allen. In Joan Didion's famous essay on Allen's self-absorption and woozy cultural values she suggested that 'the paradigm in these recent Woody Allen movies is high school'; there is a scene in this one when he takes Roberts and Keaton on a nostalgic trip to his own schoolyard.*

Sleeper (73), in which he awoke after two hundred years to cope with the future. Equally dire was *Love and Death* (75), an attempt to parody 'War and Peace', and other Russian novels. Allen then appeared in *The Front* (76), written and directed by Martin Ritt and Walter Bernstein respectively. They were among several participants who had been blacklisted by the entertainment industry during the McCarthy period – which is its subject. Allen is a night cashier who becomes a front for several writers, notably Michael Murphy, and who thereby becomes involved with a comic (Zero Mostel), who finds suicide the only solution to being refused work. The film is calm enough about its high-pitched situations, and very funny when 'American-ism' is being explained by someone from a Government 'front' organization calling itself the Freedom Information Agency.

We might pause to look at some of the figures earned by these movies. The first Allen vehicle to take serious money was *Play It Again, Sam*, with $5,700,000. Then: *Everything You Always Wanted to Know About Sex But Were Afraid to Ask*, $8,800,000; *Sleeper*, $8,200,000; *Love and Death*, $7,300,000; and *The Front*, $4,900,000. In other words Allen had created a following, boosted perhaps by cinemagoers curious about him, although he was eighth at the box-office in 1975 and ninth in 1976. His films were helped in that they were oases of light in deserts of cinema gloom

and gore, but it was not till *Annie Hall* (77) that one went through the roof, when it took $19 million (on a budget of $3 million). Outside his homeland his reception had been mixed, but the world loved Annie (Diane Keaton, his consistent co-star) and the schmuck who loved her. On Oscar night, the film swept the board: Best Picture, and Oscars to Allen for Best Direction (incredibly) and, with Marshall Brickman, Best Screenplay from another source. A contender was *The Goodbye Girl*, which was contrived while *Annie Hall* told it like it was: but in most other respects it was all that Allen's film tried to be, particularly in respect of charm and humour.

However, the Oscars (even if he preferred blowing jazz in New York to attending the presentation ceremony) encouraged a serious film in which he did not appear: *Interiors* (78). Interviewed on British television on this, he was, said Julian Barnes in the 'New States-man', 'all too twitchily out of touch with his own ambitions, and all too enthusiastically in touch with his limitations.' On this evidence, Barnes went on, Allen was 'a serious and intelligent funny man . . . a lightweight and trite serious man. And when it comes to discussing *Interiors* [he] didn't inspire much confidence. He talked naively of "creating ambiguity and ambivalence" in the film, because he admired such qualities in Bergman and Kafka; the idea that complicated artists might actually be simplifying in order to reach the point at which they nevertheless still seem complicated to us didn't appear to have struck him . . . By the end of the interview, Allen's charming disclaimers – "I do think that it's a respectable failure . . . I do think it shows some ability to work in that style" – had come to sound like rousing arrogance.'

Annie Hall, Interiors and box-office status (No. 6 in 1977) notwithstanding, Allen needed a new pitch, but he stuck to the old one in *Manhattan* (79), reaping generally excellent notices, and a 'Time' magazine cover which carelessly reckoned him 'A comic genius'; in that journal Richard Schickel noted the 'list of the things and people that make life worth living' which is offered in the film – including Flaubert, Groucho Marx, Mozart, Cézanne and Satchmo – and suggested as the prime omission Allen himself, 'somebody who belongs on anyone's short list of today's essential cultural clarifiers and consolations.' In theory, this media-made comic is hard to dislike: he's a loser, a mild little man aware of his failings, and so feeble-looking as to be pitiable. That he evokes a strong response is due to the fact that his films are invariably about himself. He asks us to take a stand, while coming on so humble, self-aware and self-deprecatory as to deny a battle: he needs to be liked, in compensation for the lack of looks and virility he would dearly and clearly love to have. Success – writing, directing and starring in his own movies – isn't enough; he needs our love in compensation, and it is boring to have it sought so pleadingly. Even Chaplin didn't do that.

The novelist Joan Didion had also noted that list and she used it in an attack on Allen as a sick symptom of American culture: '[It] is modishly eclectic, a trace wry, definitely okay with real linen; and notable, as *raisons d'être* go, in that every experience it evokes is essentially passive. This list of Woody Allen's is the ultimate consumer report . . . it suggests a subworld rigid with apprehension that they will die wearing the wrong sneakers [or] preferring "Madame Bovary" [to Allen's choice, "A Sentimental Education"].' Worried by such attacks, Allen offered an apologia, *Stardust Memories* (80), about a famous director of minority-taste comedies who is regarded by his fans as 'a genius'. 'I'm not talking about my stupid little films,' he says modestly. He is shot at the end, but it turns out to be an illusion, a flashback to the time when he dreamed of making fake magic (i.e. tricks) before growing up to be a perpetrator of real magic, one of the most famous directors in the world. And what about those beautiful women? Woody does not get slag, but beauties in the form of Charlotte Rampling and Marie-Christine Barrault. 'What's he worried about?' someone asks (oh, the irony!). 'He has the greatest gift of all. The gift of laughter.' Well, not here. 'Life you can't control,' he says. 'Only art and masturbation. Two areas in which I am expert', but then we expect one jerk-off joke. 'If I related to a Greek mythological figure it would not be Narcissus. Who would it be? Zeus' – and in this case the audience got there first. And: 'Here's a joke I put in my pictures and always take out. I thought the Goldberg Variations were what Mr and Mrs Goldberg did on their wedding night.' In other words, the ego is now so big that we are offered cast-off jokes, presumably as an insight into the Allen brain.

He said later that this was the favourite of his films, perhaps in response to the critical reception, which hovered near 'self-absorbed' ('New York Times') and 'mean-spirited' ('Variety'). In Britain, another novelist, Peter Ackroyd, used his film column in the 'Spectator' to point out that the film 'has that knowingness combined with irony that passes among cut-price intellectuals as a constituent of a thoroughly modern sensibility. The conventional references are all here – Schopenhauer, suicide, psychiatry, like cheap goods at a white elephant sale held in New

York. It is a peculiar feature of Allen's films that he thinks it enough to mention something to persuade people that he understands it. In this sense he represents the fine point of American culture, which might be defined as the triumph of vulgarity over barbarism. When he can think of nothing to say, he says it.' Ackroyd concluded: 'He tries to intellectualize without being intelligent, to be witty without first being perceptive. In the process, he is too willing to trust his audience not to get bored – in other words, he expects them to be as interested in himself as he is. Here he has made a fundamental mistake: one tires quickly of his second-hand insights, his borrowed culture, and his self-conscious naivety.' In the US, in an extended review only marginally kinder, John Simon noted the cribs from Buster Keaton and Antonioni, and the many from Bergman and Fellini: 'The film has been called Woody Allen's *8½*, but it is too dumb for that; it is really his *Juliet of the Spirits*.' And in mentioning the joke about art and masturbation Simon concludes that there is no doubt that Allen 'has difficulty figuring out which is which'.

From this nadir, Allen could only rise, but he did not do so with 'The Floating Light Bulb', a Broadway play which managed an exceedingly modest run (without him). He decided he might retrieve his position as an American guru with some more borrowings from Bergman: for *A Midsummer Night's Sex*

Manhattan (79) tried, between typically knowing jokes ('When it comes to women, I get the August Strindberg award') to set down some of the angst associated with the place which gives the piece its title. Allen played a television writer who, tired of the rubbish he is required to turn out, wants to become a novelist and who, when his wife leaves him, starts an affair with teenager Margaux Hemingway, left, whom he thinks should leave him – for her own sake.

Comedy (82) is a retread of *Smiles of a Summer Night*. It starts beautifully, as a turn-of-the-century pastoral, with fair jokes, but it strains as it pushes towards a truly horrible ending. The old adage about 'a little learning' was seldom more effectively demonstrated, as the film contravenes much of what we know about behaviour back then, though this does not necessarily refer to a parody of the sex scenes in the most recent version of *The Postman Always Rings Twice*. Allen played the host, a Tatiesque failed inventor, and Mary Steenbergen is his wife; among the guests, as a professor's wife, is Mia Farrow – Allen's muse from then on and the mother of two of his children.

However, Allen did take those criticisms to heart – to judge from his next three films. *Zelig* (83) may be a one-joke film, and it may not be too original – since TV comics had been spoofing old movies for a generation now – but this is a cod documentary, set mainly in the 30s, about a man with so little personality (autobiography again?) that he can be re-interpreted by the famous (Saul Bellow, Susan Sontag) and serve as the subject of countless old newsreels since his ability to change his appearance and personality brings him into conflict or harmony with the major figures of the time. Technically, the simulation of old newsreels when unreal, as it were, is flawlessly done, and if not very funny it is sweet and likeable. These two adjectives will serve for *Broadway Danny Rose* (84), probably his best picture, with pathos and wistfulness happily replacing the old ego-jokes. Allen plays a New York Uriah Heep, an agent of no clout whatsoever, who finds himself a Mafia target while squiring the doxie (Farrow) of his only name-client to a booking

on the Borscht-belt. He wrote and directed, but did not appear in, *The Purple Rose of Cairo* (85), in which a waif-wife (Farrow) falls in love with her screen idol, who promptly descends from the screen to sweep her off her feet: borrowings again from Keaton (*Sherlock Junior*) and a reprise, in the last reel, of that theme that movie-makers provide us poor cinemagoers with, magic. That is not, after all, untrue, and the film proves yet again that if Allen would only take longer on his scripts – and perhaps permit a collaborator, as Hollywood would have insisted upon in its great days – he might achieve a masterpiece.

Let us look again at Allen's box-office record, with the budgets, where known, in brackets: *Manhattan*, $17,500,000; *Stardust Memories*, $4,100,000 ($10 million); *A Midsummer Night's Sex Comedy*, $4,500,000 ($7 million); *Zelig*, $6,800,000 ($6,500,000); *Broadway Danny Rose*, $5,356,000 ($8 million); and *The Purple Rose of Cairo*, $5,075,000 ($13 million). The first two and the fourth of these were in unfashionable monochrome; the third boasted if not an all-star cast, a host of names, but nothing otherwise is clear, though undoubtedly these figures were studied by Orion, who had taken Allen on when his faithful producers – Jack Rollins, Charles H. Joffe – left United Artists. *Hannah and her Sisters* (86) provides us with our answers, for it had both colour and a name-cast (Farrow, Michael Caine, Barbara Hershey, Max von Sydow, etc.), for it received almost unanimously fine reviews; they would be partly why the film did very nicely at $18,200,000 ($9 million). The film examined a large family – Allen knew much about these, since Farrow had a multitude of children and siblings – and he himself played Farrow's ex-spouse, a TV writer-producer who drops out of the rat race when hypochondria takes his very soul.

Allen had recently observed that all of his films had fallen short of his hopes for them, and that he had been sustained only by his reviews. These were only fair-to-middling on *Radio Days* (87), a nostalgic look at growing up in Queens in the 40s, when the stars of the air ruled the waves. It cost $16 million and took only $6,400,000. Orion had been long resigned to the fact that Allen, like Garbo at MGM before him, was a prestige item who might just provide them with a box-office hit, but his position looked dangerously assailable when two all-name angst-ridden dramas, *September* and *Another Woman* (88), disappeared without even aspiring to recover their costs of approximately $10 million each. *New York Stories* (89) was more bad news (see Nick Nolte), even if Disney was the loser and Allen's segment of this three-part film was

Allen and his muse and mistress (they have several children between them), Mia Farrow, a breathless, rather twee actress whom he has successfully used in all of his movies since 1982 to date. Here they are, as a divorced couple in Hannah and her Sisters *(86), his one big 'commercial' film of this period.*

much liked. It was his first appearance before the camera since *Hannah . . .*, at ease as ever doing his old schtick as an attorney whose overbearing Jewish mother does not want him to marry a Gentile (Farrow).

Crimes and Misdemeanors, for Orion, returned him to the all-name familiar round of family crimes and show business misdemeanours, but was somewhat more serious than most of his work. When the marriage of a distinguished opthalmologist (Martin Landau) is threatened because his mistress (Anjelica Huston) wants a show-down with his wife (Claire Bloom), his shady brother (Jerry Orbach) arranges for a convenient murder. This strand of the plot managed to be schematic, pretentious and unconvincing at the same time, despite a fine performance by Landau, but it has a glorious sub-plot about one of life's losers, Allen, an unsuccessful director of documentaries, who is almost terminally jealous of his odious brother-in-law (Alan Alda), a television producer whose sitcoms have made national fame. Because of this part alone, this is Allen's most satisfying film since *Broadway Danny Rose*, but, as 'Variety' predicted, the film did not break Allen's 'losing streak': a wicket handover of $7 million ($13 million, or $20 million, with the cost of prints and advertising) did not suggest that he is anything but yesterday's man. It was widely thought that Orion would not care to renew when his contract expired in 1990. It was a unique deal, requiring him to make at least one film a year, without any interference providing that he brought it in on a specified, usually low budget (and when there are names in the cast they are usually there for the prestige of being in an Allen film). However, Orion did renew for another three years.

Allen has left his mark on his era, if less indelibly than the admirers of *Annie Hall* and *Manhattan* might allow – for a score or more of very personal movies have yielded perhaps ten memorable moments, and that doesn't begin to compare with Keaton (Buster) or even Bob Hope. That might change again, however, with another of the very few films in which he has served only as a performer, Paul Mazursky's *Scenes From a Mall* (90), in which he and Bette Midler are an unhappily married couple. After that: *Alice*, with himself directing Ms Farrow again.

ANN-MARGRET

Ann-Margret is a big-busted, full-lipped, zesty redhead. She has lots of pep and pizazz, and she pouts. The first ten years of her screen career were a no-no.

She was born Ann-Margret Olsson in 1941 in Stockholm. Her father, an electrician, left for the US the following year and four years later mother and child joined him – in Willmette, Illinois.

While at college she took to singing with a combo, and was encouraged to give up her studies and try her luck with a professional band. At sixteen she sang on Ted Mack's 'Original Amateur Hour' and three years later was with a lounge act in Las Vegas. George Burns saw her and decided that her sexy, youthful appearance could provide him with some strong jokes for his act. So did his friend Jack Benny: and as a result of appearing with him on television, and singing, she was offered a record contract by RCA and a film contract by 20th-Century-Fox. However, her first Hollywood movie was under the auspices of United Artists, playing Bette Davis's European-bred daughter in *Pocketful of Miracles* (61), Frank Capra's remake of his own *Lady for a Day*. It was a saccharine performance, and she was hardly better in the wretched (except for Alice Faye) remake of *State Fair* (62), as the gold-digger who seduces the son (Bobby Darin). She was like the campus tease, eager, blatant, projecting that old 40s sexiness without its saving fake innocence. 20th-Century-Fox decided not to keep her, as their series of youth-oriented musicals – often with Tommy Sands – were proving a drag at the box-office.

Columbia, however, signed her for its transcription of a Broadway musical, *Bye Bye Birdie* (63), a small-town satire on pop singers that was inspired by the fuss surrounding Elvis Presley's call-up. Jesse Pearson was the boy and Ann-Margret his steady girl, to whom he is to give a farewell kiss on 'The Ed Sullivan Show'. This was a second musical lacking any charm, though Ann-Margret certainly had 'fire' – the word of George Sidney, who directed *Birdie*. She was effervescent. She was vibrant. She was what is known as nubile. One critic who had disliked her watched *Birdie* on TV many years later to decide what it was about her he had disliked. He decided: everything. Hollywood remained impressed, and MGM signed her to a deal, starting with *Viva Las Vegas* (64), as the rich girl Elvis Presley follows to that burg after spotting her at a filling-station. Sidney again directed, on a modest budget, and he could not have been too happy to return under these circumstances to the studio where he had directed *Annie Get Your Gun*, *Show Boat* and *Kiss Me Kate*.

In 1964 TOA (the Theater Owners of America) voted her 'Star of the Year' – an honour previously voted to Cary Grant, Gregory Peck, John Wayne, Doris Day, Jerry Lewis, Deborah Kerr, Rock Hudson, James

Ann-Margret, old- and new-style. Left, in The Cincinnati Kid *(65), as the sexy, frustrated wife of the much older Karl Malden, putting the make on Steve McQueen and, right, in* 52 Pick-Up *(86), as the wife whose political ambitions are thwarted when her husband is involved in a scandal. The years between the two films show a growth in skill and talent – and glamour – which has not been sufficiently recognised.*

Stewart, William Holden, Danny Kaye (Julie Andrews won the following year). She was eighth-ranked at the box-office. 'Variety' reported on the state of her contracts: a firm commitment at Universal for six pictures at $1½ million plus participation; three more for MGM, at $150,000 plus 10 per cent, $200,000 plus 12 per cent, and $250,000 plus 15 per cent; four more for 20th; three more for Columbia; plus one each for United Artists and Frank Sinatra Enterprises. At Universal she was the *Kitten With a Whip*, playing 'the unsympathetic lead with a display of over-acting' ('Variety'), and at 20th one of *The Pleasure Seekers*, along with Pamela Tiffin and Carol Lynley – both of whom outclassed her in this remake of *Three Coins in the Fountain* with music and Madrid settings. Both flopped; indeed, she had been in only two modest hits – *Birdie* and the Presley pic. *Kitten* was never shown in Britain. It began to dawn on Hollywood that the huge publicity campaign was not working: people who tried this 'Swedish meatball' did not go back for a second helping. Universal mucked about with *Bus Riley's Back in Town* (65) to give her more footing and a more refined image – and in the process William Inge took his name off the credits. The 'MFB' still liked the film but thought the star 'as a predatory bitch is about as provocative as a kitten pretending to be a sexy lioness'.

Such reviews provoked an attempt to change the image, so she played Alain Delon's hysterical wife in *Once a Thief/Les Tueurs de San Francisco*. Critics were no kinder, so she was back as a sexpot in *The Cincinnati Kid*, battling for Steve McQueen with Tuesday Weld – who also outclassed her. She was no more interesting in a weak comedy with Louis Jourdan, set in the fashion world, *Made in Paris* (66), nor in George Sidney's *The Swinger*, where, having abandoned her usual image for one reel, she proceeds to imitate – even more archly – another sexpot for the rest of the picture. Predictably, there was little kudos going for anyone in the remaking of *Stagecoach*, but Ann-Margret came in for most schtick, partly because she offered such little value in a role to which Claire Trevor had given thrust and bite. Ann-Margret offered only a sympathetic floozi-ness, and since the original was, anyway, based on 'Boule de Suif' it might have worked if the director, Gordon Douglas, had encouraged her to do more than moon around. There was a role in a Dean Martin adventure requiring sexy girls, *Murderers' Row*, and then nothing for it but Italy. She was, said 'Time' magazine later, 'a has-been and a joke to the industry'. She, apparently, blamed her managers for exploiting her sex-appeal the wrong way. In 1967 she married a television actor, Roger Smith (of '77 Sunset Strip'), and he and a new agent, Allan Carr, took over her career.

Meanwhile, in Italy, she did two comedies with Vittorio Gassmann, *Il Profeta* (67) and *Il Tigre/The Tiger and the Pussycat*, the latter a stale piece in which she seduced him from wife Eleanor Parker. Still in Italy, she met her match in Laurence Harvey, *Rebus* (68), and played with the equally quiescent Rossano Brazzi in *Sette Uomini e Un Cervello*. The *Tiger* film got a few US bookings; otherwise Americans could see her only on TV and in night-clubs – until Avco-Embassy put her into a motor-bike picture, *C.C. and Company* (70), co-produced and written by her husband. Then Stanley Kramer gave her another film chance, as Anthony Quinn's student mistress in *RPM* (71). A bigger surprise was to find her in *Carnal Knowledge*, as Jack Nicholson's disillusioned mistress. Indeed, director Mike Nichols was reputedly sceptical when she was suggested to him (he had considered Jane Fonda and Dyan Cannon, among others). He tested her; and directed her so well that she got reviews. Perhaps it was surprise; as the critic of the 'Washington Post' wrote, 'Eight million other girls could have played the part as adequately'. Her career took a leap; but the film did nothing to help her two previous movies, which flopped around the same time.

In *The Train Robbers* (73) she hires John Wayne to retrieve the gold said to have been stolen by her husband, now gone to the great corral in the sky; in *Un Homme est Mort/The Outside Man* she is the LA bar girl who is supposed to hide hit-man Jean-Louis Trintignant. If, after reams of publicity, the best you can do is support in a medium-budget French movie, you might as well give up. Instead, Ann-Margret went back to the clubs: 'When I finish a show, I really feel that I have communicated with people, and have done what I really wanted to do . . . Before, all I was doing was going on the set in the morning. I'd go to work in the dark, and come home in the dark. I'd just come home and eat and go to bed, for months and months and months. The more you become a loner, the more you become introverted.' In truth, the good offers had stopped coming and she was tired of poor notices; she said years later that after working with Laurence Harvey in *Rebus* she wanted to give it all up. In 1973, while rehearsing in Lake Tahoe, she fell 22 feet from a platform, fracturing her face in five places, her jaw and an arm. After a mere ten weeks' hospitalization, with her face wired up inside to heal without scarring, she made a comeback in a televised stage show which was well rated.

She planned to play film star Frances Farmer in a movie based on her autobiography, 'Will There Really Be a Morning?', for her husband purchased the rights, but nothing came of this.

Hollywood did not renew its interest, but Britain's splashy Ken Russell thought her ideal for his rock opera originated on records by The Who, *Tommy* (75), as Tommy's mother. The boy was blind, deaf and dumb; she was his mother, ageing from youthful innocence to hard and greedy middle age. Her notices were the most cautiously warm she had yet received, and her next film showed a further improvement: she looked stunning and smiled sexily – both of which were within her armaments factory, if over used. What she had acquired was style – in the wrong movie, perhaps, and in an impossible role, as the girl who translates Bruce Dern's novel into Italian. It was certainly a terrible movie, wonderfully titled *Folies Bourgeoises* (76) or, in English, *Twist*. Claude Chabrol, who directed, wrote the screenplay with Norman Enfield, and on internal evidence the French and English spoke their own language while filming, for later dubbing was necessary. That is not why it is bad. Its subject is infidelity, which had given this director some of his richest films, and the novelty here is that it is not clear which affairs are real and which imagined. But it is unconvincing. There was another offer from Britain: *Joseph Andrews* (77), as Lady Booby, in whose service Joseph (Peter Firth) grows up and who, after he rejects her advances, pursues him with much determination. The film recalled – from afar – *Tom Jones*, also based on a novel by Henry Fielding and also directed by Tony Richardson, who hoped to revive his flagging career by returning to this writer. Such players as John Gielgud, Peggy Ashcroft, Jim Dale and Pauline Jameson were, like audiences, overcome by the onslaught of an enervating vulgarity. When Ann-Margret has to remind us of the eating scene in *Tom Jones* it is impossible to feel sorry for Richardson in his decline. She had a similar role in a very different movie, *The Last Remake of Beau Geste*, but you would be forgiven if you confused the two a few weeks later, for this too had an all-name cast scampering around in period costume. She was Lady Flavia, young wife to old Sir Hector (Trevor Howard), involved in the disappearance of the Blue Water and then sleeping with anybody who might help her to get it back. The two Geste brothers were Michael York and Marty Feldman, who directed and co-wrote the script. The younger Ann-Margret might have deserved these films, but the present one did not – nor a third disaster which could not be salvaged by some other classy talents: *The Cheap Detective* (78). These included Peter

Falk, playing the lead in this spoof of old Bogart movies written by Neil Simon and directed by Robert Moore. All the ladies encountered oozed mystery, including Ann-Margret as wife and then widow of millionaire Sid Caesar.

Ann-Margret accordingly had her best Hollywood chance in a good while when she played the ex-girlfriend of Anthony Hopkins in *Magic*, rekindling their affair despite the fact that she has now married. Richard Attenborough directed, in Hollywood, and during filming a candid-camera shot of a bedroom scene found its way to a magazine called 'High Society Celebrity Skin'; one of Ann-Margret's breasts was visible and she sued, but the judge found against her for her decision to do the scene in the first place. She was, he said, 'a woman who has occupied the fantasies of many film fans over the years and who chose to perform unclad.' The film did not 'perform' and neither did the next two: *The Villain* (79) aka *Cactus Jack*, with Kirk Douglas and Arnold Schwarzenegger, type-cast again as a man-hungry beauty, and *Middle Age Crazy* (80), as the perfect wife deserted by Bruce Dern for a younger woman (Deborah Wakeham). She had another fine chance in Hal Ashby's *Lookin' to Get Out*, doing just that with Jon Voight, both fugitives with gambling debts in Las Vegas; but the film sat on the shelf till 1982, when it found few admirers. As with the Simon/Bogart film, *The Return of the Soldier* (82), she was in competition with two other actresses, in a role which barely exists, the cousin through whose eyes the action is seen. These were Julie Christie, miscast as the bad-tempered wife, and Glenda Jackson as the mistress whom Alan Bates preferred: but Ann-Margret in her few scenes took the picture. *I Ought to be in Pictures* was another Simon script, directed by the reliable Herbert Ross, with Walter Matthau as a broken-down screenwriter visited by his long-lost daughter (Dinah Manoff). Once again it was a picture no one ought to have been in, but Ann-Margret, as Matthau's girlfriend, was terrific, again lifting the film in her few appearances, showing common sense and care. She had become a radiant screen presence.

Perhaps this splendour came naturally with maturity; she herself observed that her brush with death had made her into a different kind of performer, though more likely years of bad reviews had taught her that she had been coming on too strong – because of inexperience and lack of confidence. Whatever it was, she had become what she had formerly tried much too hard to be, an exciting talent. She had, also, chosen carefully once the good offers had returned. Who wouldn't have wanted to work with Voight, or Matthau or

Hopkins? But luck had been against her. So she turned to television – or rather, television drama, since she had continued to perform as singer-dancer in that medium. Luck was now with her, for there came her way *Who Will Love My Children?* (83), horribly titled but well scripted – by Michael Bortman – a factual tale of an Iowa farmer's wife trying to find homes for her ten children because she knows she is dying, and because she knows that they cannot be entrusted to her alcoholic husband (Frederic Forrest). John Erman directed, and he was to guide her through one of the really big ones, *A Streetcar Named Desire* (84), adapted both from Tennessee Williams's play and the screenplay he had written for the 1951 movie; i.e. it utilized the cinematic devices of the movie while reinserting the aspects of the original which the censor had forbidden at the time. Williams had asked Ann-Margret to play the role, and since he was dead by the time of the telecast, one can only imagine him smiling benignly from heaven. The suitor and the sister, Randy Quaid and Beverly d'Angelo, improved on their predecessors, grinning ninny and a highly charged, sexy woman; Treat Williams, faced with memories of Brando, makes of Stanley a lithe, ordinary Joe with the hots for his wife; and although Ann-Margret is less theatrical than Vivien Leigh, she manages the conventions of seduction better than the desperation. At the same time Blanche's nymphomania is under-stressed, so that anyone coming to the piece for the first time must wonder why it seemed so sensational in 1948; attitudes to sex have changed so much since then that Erman did not help the piece by setting it in an undefinable present. He helped, however, his star to Emmy nominations on both occasions.

For cinemas Ann-Margret did two more promising movies which did not quite make it: Bud Yorkin's *Twice in a Lifetime* (85), as the widow who consoles Gene Hackman when he finds he doesn't like turning fifty or his marriage; and John Frankenheimer's *52 Pick-up* (86), as Roy Scheider's politically ambitious wife, who might be compromised when he is blackmailed with a video of himself and a young lady in bed, from an Elmore Leonard novel. She appeared in a mini directed by Erman, *The Two Mrs Grenvilles* (87), based on fact, as a Copacabana showgirl who marries above her station and is loathed by her mother-in-law, a lady who stands by her when she is indicted for her husband's murder because she does not wish society to know that the marriage was unhappy. The older Mrs Grenville was played by Claudette Colbert at her most stylish, but Ann-Margret yielded nothing to her in what was overall a lush,

Let's take another look at the later Ann-Margret, who bears a strong claim to be considered the most improved actress in the whole history of motion pictures. Here she is, fourth from the left, in a publicity still issued in connection with Alan Alda's comedy of divorce, A New Life (88) – and there he is, bearded in the centre. The others are Hal Linden, Veronica Hamel, John Shea and Mary Kay Place, all of them nice people to have around.

enjoyable melodrama. Movies again were not kind: *A Tiger's Tale*, written and directed by Peter (Kirk's son) Douglas, as the mother of a teenage daughter, whose boyfriend falls in love with her; and Alan Alda's *A New Life* (88) – each of them discovering that after divorcing. She has worked infrequently since, because her husband has contracted myasthenia gravis, a debilitating muscular disease.

DAN AYKROYD

'I've never wanted to be a solo act,' said Dan Aykroyd. 'My strength is in collaboration. I enjoy the feeling of kinship with an ensemble.' It has paid off handsomely. He has also said that his style, as such, was influenced by 'great TV performers like Jackie Gleason, Lucille Ball, Desi Arnaz, Red Skelton, Phil Silvers', most of whom managed to be shrill and bland at the same time. Maybe he should have looked to Jack Benny.

He was born in 1952 in Ottawa, where his father was Assistant Deputy Minister of Transport. He was expelled from his Catholic seminary; later he studied sociology at Carleton University, where he began writing and performing sketches. From there he went to Toronto to perform with the Second City improvizational comedy troupe and was seen

by John Belushi, scouting for talent for 'National Lampoon Radio Hour' and its touring offshoot, 'The Lemmings'. He took Belushi to the Club 505, an after-hours haunt which he himself described as 'sleazy', and which he managed on the side. With Belushi he was asked to join 'Saturday Night Live' when it began in 1975, along with Jane Curtin, Gilda Radner, Harold Ramis, Bill Murray and Chevy Chase. The programme, which originally went out on NBC at 11.30 p.m., soon found favour, not least for Aykroyd's impersonations of Nixon and Carter; his 'Weekend Update' was popular, as was Beldar, the patriarch of an alien family trying to assimilate into American society. He teamed with Chase on 'Ex-Police', who shot first and asked questions later; with Steve Martin as immigrants whose attempts to hip were desperately muddled; and with Belushi as 'The Blues Brothers', crooked white soul-men in shades and fedoras. During this period he returned to Canada to appear in *Love at First Sight* (77), which did little for him – nor did *Mr Mike's Mondo Video*, which collected a few 'SNL' fans on its equally few outings.

His film career may be said to have begun when Steven Spielberg cast him in *1941* (79), his attempt to do for the war what *It's a Mad* (4) *World* had done for treasure-hunts. If the thing had a hero it was Treat Williams, and Aykroyd was his chum, a belligerent, lame-

Soon he won't have much to smile about: Dan Ackroyd as the wealthy and self-satisfied young broker in Trading Places *(83), whose employers and benefactors will reduce him to penury for the sake of a joke. It couldn't have happened to a nastier guy, and the film has some difficulty in making us sympathise with him as he sinks to the gutter.*

Bill Murray, left, Dan Ackroyd and Harold Ramis, right, in Ghostbusters *(84), a somewhat loud and successful comedy in which they set out to rid New York of some of its finest phantoms.*

brained sergeant. The cost was so great that Universal and Columbia shared the risk – $32 million, more than the cost of combined output of those two studios in 1941; and every film they made then, or in any other year, has to be more entertaining than this horrendous mess. It does not entirely waste time, for it is not common to see a film fail as lavishly as this at every turn. It took $23,400,000 in its first weeks, before dropping rapidly out of sight. Belushi was also in the cast, and the two of them teamed up to recreate *The Blues Brothers* (80), part-written by Aykroyd, here trying to reunite their band to raise money for their old orphanage. In the process they all but level Chicago, an orgy of destruction which brought the cost to $30 million for a return of $32,100,000. Foreign reviews killed any prospect of further profits, though it did develop a cult following in some countries. The Belushi–Aykroyd double-act then made them *Neighbors* (81), with newcomer Dan and his nympho wife (Cathy Moriarty) interrupting the peaceful suburban life of John and his wife (Kathryn Walker). John G. Avildsen directed from a screenplay credited to Larry Gelbart, but any respect they may have had for Thomas Berger's original novel was hidden under a jokiness more suitable to Belushi's two alma maters, 'National Lam-

poon' and 'SNL'. The film took $17,100,000 in the US but did a belly-up everywhere else.

In life Belushi was the wild one; fame had sent him on a roller-coaster of drink and drugs which ended with an overdose in 1982. Aykroyd led the funeral parade in black leather and jeans on his Harley Davison. He declined work and television for a while, uncertain whether he could make it as a single. He was talked into making a movie, and when it took only $5,540,000, *Doctor Detroit* (83) seemed to suggest that he wouldn't. Michael Pressman directed from a story by Bruce Jay Friedman about a nerdy professor who becomes involved with ladies of the night and their protectors. His leading lady was Donna Dixon, whom he married about the time the film came out. Top-billed but surrounded by some other major talents – Eddie Murphy, Don Ameche, Ralph Bellamy, Denholm Elliott – he was in his element in John Landis's *Trading Places*, as the obnoxious young broker fed, almost literally, to the wolves for a joke. Although the occasion was a personal success for Murphy, Aykroyd came in for some praise and was for the first time seen widely abroad. *Twilight Zone the Movie* was an attempt to revamp for the big screen four segments from Rod Serling's television series. Among the four directors was Landis, who also did the prologue in which a driver (Albert Brooks) scares his passenger, till hitch-hiker Aykroyd offers to show him something truly frightening. The *Ghostbusters* (84) were himself, Bill Murray and Harold Ramis, with Ivan Reitman directing. Aykroyd played a not unfamiliar role, the college-trained pedant, in this case called Dr Raymond Stantz. He also worked on the script, and said later, 'No one has ever approached a ghost comedy – and there've been many, everyone from Abbott and Costello to the Bowery Boys – with any reality before and there is a basis of reality in [this].' Yes, and it was about one-tenth as funny as *The Ghost Breakers* of 1940.

He also said, apropos his co-stars: 'What we did was interlock and interweave the training we got from the three main comedy institutions in America – "Second City", "SNL" and "National Lampoon". Combining our kind of comedy with a special effects picture, you've got two of the ingredients American audiences have responded to most strongly in the last few years. We knew it would be successful.' And it was (see Bill Murray). The special effects films, when popular, have been so precisely because they are not television; and the 'comedy institutions' have been popular, less from any merit than as reaction to the soulless factory-line sitcoms which Aykroyd grew up with – to which may be added the influence of some outside maverick talents

such as Lenny Bruce and Monty Python. 'I write comedy and action adventure', Aykroyd went on. 'Once I realized there were people out here in Hollywood who would finance the visions, I let my writing free-associate. I think there may be a time for chamber comedy, perhaps when the audience is older, but for now you gotta be outside, you gotta have movement, action, effects, big budgets. Hey, why not?'

He did a guest spot in *Indiana Jones and the Temple of Doom* (84), as the pilot who bails out leaving Indy asleep, and another as Jeff Goldblum's self-satisfied colleague at the beginning of *Into the Night* (85). Landis directed both this and *Spies Like Us*, in both cases persuading other film-makers, chiefly directors, to put in cameo appearances. Aykroyd was one of the credited writers of the second, and like *Ghostbusters* it had been prepared before Belushi's death with him in mind. In the event Chevy Chase partnered him, as guys who think they're spies but are in fact decoys. It was also another of this decade's attempts to get some mileage out of a Crosby/Hope type relationship. He was teamed with Tom Hanks in *Dragnet* (87), again to very big business (see Chase and Hanks respectively). But on his own it was another matter: Michael Ritchie's *The Couch Trip* (88) found him as an escaped con who becomes locum for a radio shrink, Charles Grodin, who takes time off to relish his own nervous breakdown but returns with murder in mind on learning that Aykroyd is having an affair with his wife. Like Walter Matthau, in an extended cameo as a spokesman for plant liberation, Grodin is really a foil. The three of them played in contrasting comic styles, with Aykroyd at his most inventive, if restrained, but the public did not respond, for it returned only $4,600,000 of its investment, confirming Aykroyd's belief that his screen persona worked only when in partnership. Someone, like Mike Ovitz of CAA, was working very hard to make him a star, which he officially was – and he was certainly getting a star salary. Someone, anyway, decided that a replay of *Neighbors* was needed, so here was Aykroyd again being arrogant and making life difficult in *The Great Outdoors*, for John Candy, standing in for Belushi. It returned $20 million on a $24 million investment, making it one of the most successful American films of the year: but when Universal sent it direct to video in most foreign territories, it showed that he still had not broken out.

After doing poorly in the States (see Chase), *Caddyshack II* shared the same fate, but Aykroyd had only a guest role. He was an eccentric boffin who marries an android (Kim Basinger), a fact which he has to keep secret, in the charming *My Stepmother Is an Alien*. It cost $20 million and took only $5,300,000, despite moderately good reviews – and 'officially' the reason was that it was up against *Twins* that season. Columbia distributed, having taken over from the troubled Weintraub Entertainment Group, who had looked to this film for financial help. And Columbia itself looked to *Ghostbusters II* (89) after several lean years, including its period under the aegis of David Puttnam, when that gentleman had upset Aykroyd by trying to force him to accept Cyndi Lauper as his leading lady in *Vibes*, and then had dumped him from the project when he refused. *Ghostbusters II* was the tonic Columbia needed, even if it took (see Murray) only just over half of the original. Following Reitman's experience with *Twins*, the participants took a percentage.

The film underlined the fact that Aykroyd had a public only when fully stretched in teamwork. He wanted to stay the course and accordingly loaned support to a prestigious project but one of doubtful box-office appeal, Bruce Beresford's *Driving Miss Daisy*. He worked for scale, to help keep the budget to $8 million for this version of an off-Broadway play by Alfred Uhry, who also wrote the screenplay. It examined the relationship of a Southern Jewish woman (Jessica Tandy) and her black chauffeur (Morgan Freeman) over thirty years — what we might call the Civil Rights era. It was not an easy relationship, but she discovers in the end that she respects him, since, despite a few attempts to prove otherwise, he always knew his place. This affectionate but rather cute homily managed to win an Oscar for Best Film, despite the fact that Beresford had not even been nominated; and a Best Actress Award for the veteran Tandy. Aykroyd was nominated for Best Supporting Actor for playing her son, rather oddly, since neither his accent nor the ageing make-up were at all convincing. Oscar's attention brought financial rewards: the film opened in December, and 'Variety' did not dare to predict, as it usually does, the eventual outcome. It took only $1 million during the first month of release, which in other circumstances might have sent it direct to video; but by July 1990 it had taken over $105 million.

Long delayed, Bob Clark's *Loose Cannons* (90) eventually limped into view, to be gunned down by the press, a dreadful cop comedy costarring Gene Hackman. A few weeks later Warners announced a comedy for Christmas to star Aykroyd, Chase and John Candy, i.e. the three (cf. Murphy, Williams, Martin) who had failed to make any headway in the overseas market. It was later announced that the title would be *Valkenvania*, that the cast would also include Peter Aykroyd and Demi Moore. Dan Aykroyd would also be writing and directing what is described as a 'paranoid fantasy', as a married couple (Chase, Moore) lose their way and are sentenced to death by an aged judge – one of the two roles played by Aykroyd.

A writer said in 'Film Review' in 1988: 'Dan Aykroyd has had more hilarious leading men than your average comedienne. Count them: John Belushi, Bill Murray, Eddie Murphy, Chevy Chase, Tom Hanks, and, soon, John Candy. In his current opus, *The Couch Trip*, Aykroyd is surrounded by comics acting their manic hearts out, while he plays straight man yet again. He's goofy, occasionally whacky, but he's never very funny; not *Steve Martin* funny, not *Bill Murray* funny. Humour, of course, is in the eye of the funny bone, and I may be overlooking one of the twentieth century's great comic geniuses. If so, I'm sorry. But Dan Aykroyd doesn't make me laugh. His films are OK – damn it, you'd have to be a fridge not to gurgle at at least *some* of *Ghostbusters*, *Trading Places* and *Dragnet*, but Aykroyd himself is getting a reputation as something of an amusing guy. And I don't get it.'

KIM BASINGER

In 'Show Magazine' in 1970 Lou Valentino wrote, speaking of the Golden Days (as he called them), 'And the women! Will we ever again see their likes on the screen? Raquel Welch and Ann-Margret are trying very hard, but how can they possibly measure up to Ann Sheridan at her peak?' Twenty years on we are still asking that question, and what have we got? Kim Basinger, that's what we've got. And her lookalikes. She can, on occasion, glow, and she does not reject the suggestion that she, too, is a sex-symbol: 'That expression has been scratched around and gotten a bad rap lately – but it's a classic term and belongs to some legends. If some people assume that's what I am, that's a huge compliment. You entertain people in different ways. People tell me I was such a clown in *Blind Date* or so sexy in *9½ Weeks*. So whether you're seen as a clown or a sex-symbol, it doesn't matter. Some people like me and some don't – it's in the eye of the beholder. Me, I call myself a people actress.' Ann Sheridan also rejected that sexy image, 'the Oomph Girl', but you remembered her. Ms Basinger should be so lucky.

She was born in Athens, Georgia, in 1953, the third of five children of Swedish, German and Cherokee Indian stock; their father was president of his own finance and investment company. Given her flair for entertaining the family, her love of movies and of beauty parades, he made her enter the town's Junior Miss pageant, which she won. She was also the state's Miss Breck (as her mother had been) – a beauty contest organized by Breck shampoos – and was chosen to go to New York for the finals, which she won. She was invited to join Eileen Ford's model agency, which she did after a brief stint at the University of Georgia. She did not care for modelling, and, after all, she had boasted from childhood that she was going to be 'the biggest movie star and singer in the world'. The only place to achieve that was in Hollywood, so one day in 1976 she took herself off in a jeep with a fellow model, Dale Robinette, who was a client of the agent Martin Gage. He introduced her to Gage, who thought her 'gorgeous'; within two weeks she was in 'Starsky and Hutch'. She 'was always a smart cookie,' he said later, while her brother Mick was quoted as saying, 'She was just hell-bent on where she was going, and nothing was going to stop her. She's tough as nails, she really is.' She appeared regularly on television, in such shows as 'Charlie's Angels', 'Gemini Man', 'The Bionic Woman' and 'The Six Million Dollar Man'. In 1977 she starred opposite Lou Antonio in a short-lived series, 'Dog and Cat', as a sassy but inexperienced cop. She became better known in some telemovies: *The Ghost of Flight 401* (78) with Ernest Borgnine in the title-role, an apparently factual tale following a crash in the Everglades in 1972; *Kate: Portrait of a Centerfold*, as Katie, a Texas beauty queen trying for Hollywood stardom by way of a dodgy model agency, with Vivian Blaine and Tab Hunter; *From Here to Eternity* (79), in the Donna Reed role in this mini and the series that followed; and *Killjoy* (81), top-billed in this hospital-set mystery, as the wealthy board chairman's daughter.

She had appeared in a cinema movie earlier that year, *Hard Country*, directed by David Greene and co-starring Jan-Michael Vincent as her Texas boyfriend, more interested in having a good time than settling down, so she plans to go to LA to become an air hostess. Her make-up man was Ron Britton, a score of years her senior, and they were married before the film came out (in 1980). Gage withdrew some time later, on the grounds that Britton could now give the lady the '24 hours a day' attention she needed. In *Mother Lode* (82) she and Nick Mancuso confront an evil Charlton Heston (there was also a good one, since this was a double role) in the Canadian wilderness, coming to blows when they believe him to be a murderer. The battle did not help the picture, which disappeared as

quickly as the one before. She tested for *Frances* and *The Postman Always Rings Twice*, both of which went to Jessica Lange, and with no offers coming in agreed to pose for 'Playboy'. 'I need a film right now,' she said, 'an international film. If the film isn't available, I'll do it through the pictures.' She was warned that she would ruin her career, but these soothsayers had reckoned without James Bond. Bond girls were seldom expected to be more than decorative and it certainly would not hurt to have her splashed all over the 'Playboy' cover as '007's New Woman'. Before the spread was published she began work on *Never Say Never Again* (83), decorative indeed as the mistress of Klaus Maria Brandauer, who tries to sell her in a North African slave-market after she's defected to Bond (Sean Connery).

When the 'Playboy' pictures appeared, James L. Brooks offered the role of Debra Winger's friend, then a bigger role, in *Terms of Endearment*, but she accepted what was a firmer offer from Blake Edwards. Thus in *The Man Who Loved Women* she was one of Burt Reynolds's women, preferring to chew on his pubic hair than his moustache – whenever, that is, her husband, a Texas oilman, isn't looking. She did what she was required to do – including getting glued to the carpet – with such confidence that it was clear that she would be heard from again quite quickly, despite the film's failure. And she was, in *The Natural* (84), as the girl whose lovemaking with Robert Redford leaves him too exhausted to be much good once he gets out on the baseball field. Sam Shepard recommended her to Robert Altman when he came to film his play *Fool for Love* (85), because the expected choice of co-star – Miss Lange – was pregnant at the time. Shepard himself played opposite her, two down-home Southern lovers who can't get it together and can't let go. She was supposed to be sexy but shopworn, which meant shovelling her hair out of her eyes much of the time, an action which lent extra tedium to the occasion. She played a similar role in very different circumstances (taking over from Dominique Sanda) in *9½ Weeks* (86), except that they are strangers when they meet – he was played by Mickey Rourke – and their explicit sexual pleasures take place in the most chic designer settings, in New York. Rourke's insistence on a sado-masochistic relationship, watching her for instance while she masturbates, was seen from his point of view, even if the film retained the perspective of Elizabeth McNeill's novel. Its makers clearly hoped for some of the controversy that had attended the opening of *Last Tango in Paris* some years before, but a strange thing happened – or

Mickey Rouke and Kim Basinger in 9½ Weeks *(86), a title which refers to the duration of their affair. It was swell while it lasted, as well as experimental – which was one of the reasons why the film became notorious: but it lasted less than 9½ days in many cinemas and did hardly better on video.*

Kim Basinger in My Stepmother Is an Alien *(88), which also did poorly at the box-office, but at least the 'New York Times' like her: '[she] reveals unfailingly sound instincts for comedy. Enchantingly eccentric, outfitted in a series of outstandingly funny costumes, Miss Basinger ought to be more than enough to make the film interesting. But unfortunately, she's not alone. And the romantic scenes between Miss Basinger and Mr Aykroyd play like a game of What's Wrong With This Picture?' (Janet Maslin).*

perhaps not, given the ever-growing power of critics: they pronounced, and the public stayed away. A disastrous box-office performance (see Rourke) indicated that even the curious hardly turned up. So if the film and its players achieved notoriety, it was muted – though Basinger was happy with it, if not with the emasculated version of the American final cut (by MGM/UA; it had local distribution in most foreign markets). She 'became an actress in my own eyes . . . I did what I wanted to do emotionally.'

She played a lady in peril in *No Mercy*, mistress of the villain (Jeroen Krabbe), taken hostage by the hero (Richard Gere), but lacked the vulnerability to make the role work. Blake Edwards thought Basinger, after first considering Madonna, capable of bringing back screwball comedy, so he sent her and Bruce Willis on a *Blind Date* (87). This revived the classic formula of the Carole Lombard–Fred MacMurray films, in which a scatty, independent female liberates a buttoned-up, nine-to-five male; but Edwards, in another of his mirth-free miscalculations, could not find a way of liberating Basinger herself unless she had had too much to drink.

It was a performance of stridency rather than charm, but was the only film she had yet made to come close to recovering its budget (see Willis). *Nadine* with Jeff Bridges and *My Stepmother Is an Alien* (88) with Dan Aykroyd were both failures (in the latter she replaced yet another actress originally cast, Shelley Long), but Basinger was finally to make a film which would take more at the domestic box-office than the cost of its budget – thanks to Sean Young, who fell off a horse not long after shooting began: this was *Batman* (89), in which she screamed more than any screen heroine since Fay Wray. By overacting, Jack Nicholson rose above the Special Effects, and by integrity Michael Keaton stayed level-pegging; but Basinger went down for the count.

Late in 1989 she and her husband parted, with much publicity as to who would get custody of their menagerie of cats and dogs. She parted with her agents, the mighty CAA, arguing that the roles she had been getting she had obtained without their help. One she sought was at 20th-Century-Fox, *Sleeping With the Enemy*, but she wanted co-star approval, which Fox refused to grant, as the role was unlikely to attract a major box-office actor; Julia Roberts got the part. Basinger will be seen in *The Marrying Man* (90), written by Neil Simon, with Alec Baldwin for Disney, and has been offered $3 million for a sequel to *9½ Weeks*; but, said the report, she is not returning calls.

vice. For cinemas, he made his debut in *The Sentinel*, a daft dip into the diabolical directed by Michael Winner, whom Berenger described as 'one of the strangest people I've ever met' – though that may be pique because his major scene was cut from the final print. He appears well down the credits, listed as 'Man at end', and he did not come on till the end of *Looking for Mr Goodbar*. You were not, however, likely to miss him, whether parading in black bra and garter belt, quarrelling with his black boyfriend or sniffing amyl nitrate while trying to get it up with Diane Keaton.

He also spent most of his next film chiefly naked, though strictly in the cause of straight A sex if, on occasion, on the floor: *In Praise of Older Women* (78), directed by George Kaczender from the autobiographical novel by Stephen Vizinczey, who with good reason loathed the result. Berenger later said the film was hard work because they had to make up for lost time when Bibi Andersson left the cast, to be replaced by Karen Black. His own inexperience cannot be disguised in the general incompetence, but he is a sturdy centre as he seduces anything in skirts from Vienna to Montreal by way of Budapest. He had something of the charisma of Hollywood's leading men of the past. Paramount Pictures Television obviously thought so, for they gave him the lead in an important four-hour mini, *Flesh and Blood* (79), based on the bestseller by Pete Hamill. He played streetwise Bobby,

TOM BERENGER

When Tom Berenger smiles out of his studio stills he seems a sweet-tempered gentle man; but there are others in which he stares out at us disdainfully, with his mouth twisted cruelly. That suggests a wide range, which he effortlessly has; but even in villainy he can seem lost, wistful.

He was born in 1949 in Chicago of Irish stock. His father was a printer and he himself expected to follow him into that profession until he acted in 'Who's Afraid of Virginia Woolf?' while studying at the University of Missouri. He went to New York to study acting, going to work professionally in such plays as 'The Rose Tattoo', 'Electra' and 'A Streetcar Named Desire' (in Milwaukee and Tokyo). His exceptional looks brought him the role of the heartthrob on a daytime soap, 'One Life to Live', which in turn brought him an offer of a small role in a telefilm, *Johnny We Hardly Knew Ye* (77), directed by Gilbert Gates and based on John F. Kennedy's first steps into politics after concluding war ser-

In Praise of Older Women (78) is not a film anyone of sensibility would care to remember, but it was the first leading role for Tom Berenger, who gave a more than promising performance as a young man whom the ladies find irresistible – and vice-versa.

who makes it to the top of the prizefight racket, pausing on the way for affairs with a TV reporter (Kristin Griffith) and his own mother (Suzanne Pleshette). It was a personal triumph for him and for many years his favourite role; he said in 1983 that he might be in middle-age before he got another one as good. Still, he seemed set on a movie career with *Butch and Sundance: The Early Years*, in Paul Newman's old part, with William Katt in the one played by Robert Redford. William Goldman had again worked on the script (by discussing it with Allan Burns, to whom it is credited), and although Berenger had reservations about it he liked both him and the director, Richard Lester, 'so organized and disciplined'. The film's trouble was that it was not about anything beyond the joky relationship between the two outlaws. When the first reviews and returns were in, 20th-Century-Fox dropped it like a hot potato – in Berenger's opinion because they had made so much money from *Star Wars* that they were looking for a tax write-off. Promising to make up for the disappointment was *The Dogs of War* (80), adapted from a bestseller by Frederick Forsyth and directed by John Irvin (fresh from his success with the BBC's *Tinker Tailor Soldier Spy*). He played a fellow mercenary to the top-billed Christopher Walken, both of them involved in West African politics, but his part was cut in Britain, where the film was made, and further for American audiences. Helen Shaver, who had the third biggest role, as his wife, did not appear at all in either version.

There can be little sympathy with his involvement in *Oltre la Porta* (82) – not, that is, if he had seen any of the other films of this director, Liliana Cavani; he was flattered to know that she had asked Milos Forman for advice on casting and he had loaned her a cassette of *Flesh and Blood*. Cavani used him for his innocence, he explained, as an American engineer working in Marrakesh who is puzzled by the hatred between his girlfriend (Eleonora Giorgi) and her father (Marcello Mastroianni). The film hardly travelled. *Eddie and the Cruisers* (83) were a 60s rock group who disappeared spectacularly when their leader headed his car into the sea: one reporter believes the truth is not so simple and tracks down the present-day Eddie. Berenger observed that he had loved the script before the several rewrites, and that he had jumped at the chance of playing two ages. He would do this again in Lawrence Kasdan's *The Big Chill*, though in the end Kasdan did not use the flashbacks he had filmed. He was one of the old university friends gathered at the house of Glenn Close and Kevin Kline, the one who had been a radical orator but is now

a nice but narcissistic television private eye, moustached like Tom Selleck. He was praised by the press, along with the others, and it was a major credit, but it actually did little for his career. It did better for his private life. A lady called Lisa was the real-estate agent handling the locations, and when she became Berenger's second wife (in 1986), she did so in the grounds of the house used in the film.

He was next due to appear opposite Terri Garr in Michael Apted's *Firstborn*, but was in an auto accident and was replaced by Peter Weller. The film had no success at all, but neither did the two he did, chiefly because the writers and directors concerned had not got the weight for the job. *Fear City* (84) was as sleazy as the Times Square area in which it was set, with Berenger as an ex-boxer running a series of strip-joints whose performers are being picked off by a maniac intent on cleaning up the town; Rae Dawn Chong was one of them, loved by Berenger but drawn to her own sex, and Billy Dee Williams was the cop in charge of the case. *Rustlers' Rhapsody* (85) was advertised by a tagline which fairly describes it: 'The singing cowboy. To a lawless land he brought truth, justice, fancy riding and some wonderful outfits.' Hugh Wilson wrote and directed (riding high after *Police Academy*). Berenger's own notices for these two were good to excellent, but he was dead at the box-office. Later he admitted that there were three years when he couldn't get work, which would seem to be true if Paramount had delayed release of his last film and if we discount a seven-hour Sidney Sheldon mini, *If Tomorrow Comes* (86), which he surely did in desperation. He and Madolyn Smith disported themselves over London, New York, Amsterdam, the East and West coasts of America and much of the Côte d'Azur, falling in love and stealing jewels.

'I got to the point when I wasn't depressed about my career any more; I just didn't care.' His agent had surrendered to cocaine and his manager to alcohol, so he replaced them. But rescue came from Oliver Stone, who puts talent before box-office clout when casting: *Platoon* was his autobiographical account of the Vietnam war, with Sergeant Barnes (Berenger) in charge of the platoon which massacres the inhabitants of a native village. In his account of the filming Stone wrote: 'He's a quiet actor with the moral stamina and possible longevity of a Fredric March or Spencer Tracy. He buries his natural personality so well in his parts that, even in films like *The Big Chill*, people don't see the original stamp and tend to overlook him. Here I want him to play someone with evil in his heart, but play him with an understanding . . . from watching his coiled performance

I think many people at the end of the film will think he has been wronged by Charlie Sheen, Willem Dafoe, and destiny.' Berenger was surely impressive, but his evil seems fictional – unlike, say, Sean Penn in *Casualties of War* later, who was only a few stops up from a moron. The film won a Best Picture Oscar and reinstated Berenger, who was offered *Someone to Watch Over Me* (87) when its director, Ridley Scott, saw it in rough cut. Scott's film was a thriller with Berenger as a working-class cop from Queens whose marriage is in danger when he falls for the socialite witness (Mimi Rogers) he has been assigned to protect. The film did not succeed in breaking Scott's bad box-office run and returned only $4,500,000 of its $17 million budget.

Of the several stars whose career dipped in the 80s, Berenger was the strongest of those talents who returned at the end of the decade. And he chose carefully. Roger Spottiswoode directed *Shoot to Kill* (88), co-produced and part-written by Daniel Petrie Jr (who had scripted *Beverly Hills Cop*). It co-starred Sidney Poitier in a tale of a city cop (Poitier) and a mountain guide locked together, often in enmity, as they plough through a rugged mountainous terrain in search of a killer and a party led by the guide's girlfriend (Kirstie Alley). The film did well, making back $12,500,000 of its $15 million budget, but not well enough to avoid a retitling for overseas, *Deadly Pursuit. Be- trayed* had an even better director, Costa-Gavras, and a clever leading lady, Debra Winger, but neither player was able to bring dimension to unconvincing characters, a brave little FBI lady and the redneck farmer she sleeps with in order to uncover the Fascist group to which he secretly belongs. This time: $12 million recovered of its $19 million cost. *Last Rites* was the first thriller since *I Confess* predicated on the fact that a priest is bound by silence not to reveal what he has heard in the confessional, but in this case he is unsure of the truth and torn by divided loyalties, since he has family links to the Mafia. Donald P. Bellisario, creator of 'Magnum, P.I.', wrote this holy unlikely story, which made back only $100,000 of $16 million budget, though it has to be said that a troubled and yet quiescent MGM/UA was doing little to sell its films during this period. A baseball story, *Major League* (89) was not ill named, for the return this time was $21,500,000 on a budget of $12 million. Berenger was the veteran player with dodgy legs playing alongside some goofballs and neophytes. The director was David Ward, better known as a scriptwriter, and he and Berenger did not get on: 'He treated me like I knew nothing. Most of the cast felt the same. He was so inexperienced. I nearly walked off the set. It's the only time I felt like quitting.' He also had a guest role as a gung-ho recruiting sergeant in *Born on the Fourth of July*, directed by Vietnam vet Oliver Stone.

In the meantime he had decided to stray from the Hollywood mainstream by filming with Alan Rudolph, and *Love at Large* (90) found him playing a bumbling private eye hired by a mysterious lady (Anne Archer) to track down her lover, while also employing another (Elizabeth Perkins) to spy on him. He then played an amnesiac in *Shattered* with Greta Scacchi, once announced for William Hurt and Sissy Spacek, and then he did *The Field*, in Ireland for director Jim Sheridan, as the catalyst. It is not a large role, but they asked him and he said yes, for supporting parts rid him of the onus of carrying a film, while he also enjoyed being part of an ensemble cast (though this is not). He then went to Brazil to do a film once meant for Paul Newman, *At Play in the Fields of the Lord* (91) written by Hector Babenco (who is also directing) and Jean-Claude Carrière from the novel by Peter Matthiessen. Saul Zaentz is producing, a guarantee of quality, and most cinemagoers would be happy to find Berenger on the receiving end of many such offers. He said: 'I don't have ambition like I used to. I've done it all, I feel like I'm there. If I wanted to I could retire in about four years . . . If they don't want me, I don't care.' So all right: but because Richard Gere and John Travolta are at present enjoying enormous hits, it would be our loss if Berenger were lower in the pecking order.

JACQUELINE BISSET

She was, said 'Newsweek' in 1977, 'an image of primal beauty. Which is appropriate, since she is the leading candidate for that place of honor in our fantasy life, the Screen's Most Beautiful Woman.' This did not make her, the piece went on, 'the Best Actress or the Biggest Star', but she might have become one of these. She chose badly. Few stars have chosen more ineptly. She started as a nice-looking ornament and then embarked on a series of films which no one went to see – well, there was an occasional good one, when it was clear that she had developed into someone very special. Good looks on their own are of no help: not only had she learnt to act, but she had presence. Furthermore, she was radiantly sexy and when she wanted to she could be as mysterious as any of the screen's great sirens. It says much about her magic that she still went on choosing badly but is still around to tell the tale.

She was born in Weybridge, Surrey, in 1944, to a Scottish doctor and a half-French mother who had cycled to the coast when the Germans invaded in 1940 to embark on one of the last boats leaving for Britain. She studied ballet, but decided that she was not meant for that, and after a spell at the *lycée* in London began modelling. That led to a small role in *The Knack* (65), standing in a queue behind Rita Tushingham. She applied for a small role in *Cul-de-Sac* (66), which Polanski promised her was hers if she could slim down a little. She did, and thus played, billed as Jackie Bisset, a silent part as one of the enigmatic visitors to the isolated ménage of Donald Pleasance. After another brief role in *Arrivederci Baby*, which starred Tony Curtis, she auditioned for a role in *Two for the Road* (67), that of a girl who is about to bed Albert Finney when she discovers she has chicken-pox. Director Stanley Donen explained that he cast her because he needed someone stunning to make it convincing if Finney was going to be unfaithful to Audrey Hepburn. She was one of the several beauties gracing the dire James Bond spoof, *Casino Royale*, in a scene with Peter Sellers, sweetly called Miss Goodthighs. That encouraged her to seek her fortunes in Hollywood, where she was awarded a seven-year contract calling for ten films with 20th Century-Fox, who gave her a leading role opposite James Brolin in a B-picture, *The Cape Town Affair*, actually filmed in that city and a remake of *Pick-Up on South Street*, when the part had been played by Jean Peters, that of an innocent involved in other people's espionage. To do the film she turned down George Cukor after a series of tests (for a film that was never made), not realizing how eminent he was; and she recalled that when they worked together later, 'the matter lay unspoken between us.'

Nothing else happened, so she returned to Europe and in France starred in *La Promesse* (68), as the mysterious English mistress of the disturbed young hero (Jean-François Maurin), who passes her off as the daughter of a wartime colleague. 20th sent for her to test for a role opposite Michael Sarrazin, with whom she began a relationship which lasted seven years. The film was made, but 20th delayed release till after the première of *The Detective* with Frank Sinatra. His wife, Mia Farrow, had originally been cast, but the marriage was breaking up and he accepted Bisset as a substitute, as the girl who comes to him complaining that she does not believe that her husband committed suicide. She loathed Los Angeles, but applied for a resident's permit because it looked as though she would have an American career after all; and, as she said later, she was emotionally committed. The film with Sarrazin, *The Sweet Ride*, then appeared, to evoke only ridicule as she made her first entrance from the sea, having lost her bikini-top, to be raped by a motor-cyclist – and it would have been even sillier, she maintained, if filmed as originally planned, when she would have been raped by the whole gang. Certainly she looked luscious throughout the rest of the absurd proceedings, which concerned some surfers in Malibu, but it was her participation in *The Detective* which brought her a good part, as Steve McQueen's girlfriend in *Bullitt*. If a new star had arrived, no one was permitted to know it – certainly not with *The First Time* (69), in which she was again a mysterious English girl, initiating an American teenager into the joys of sex after his buddies have fantasized about her doing the same with them. Having died in the States, the film had the indignity of being retitled *You Don't Need Pajamas at Rosie's* for the foreign market. She was better exposed in the all-star *Airport* (70), as the stewardess pregnant by Dean Martin and not knowing whether or not she wants an abortion. Edith Head, who designed the costumes, said that Bisset had 'one of the greatest bodies I've ever worked with. But besides that she is rather the opposite, because she is so damned intelligent.' Anyone who has read other interviews with Miss Head will know that this was not a quality she expected to find in actresses.

Someone, somewhere, knew she was potential star material, for she had had top-billing in *The First Time* and so she had again in *The Grasshopper*, a title which referred to her as a showgirl, going from man to man while married to a black footballer (Jim Brown), to final disillusion, probably her best performance to date. She remained a lower-case femme fatale in a rip-off of *Rosemary's Baby* called *The Mephisto Waltz* (71), as Alan Alda's wife, with which she and 20th called it quits. At this point, with money draining away in some spectacularly unsuccessful films, no studio wanted to be obliged to pay contract players, especially as in that uncertain climate they did not know what to do with them. Bisset and Sarrazin did another dumb film together, *Believe in Me*, he as a partygoing intern happily into amphetamines and she as a children's book editor who for love goes down the same dangerous path. She returned to Britain to make *Secrets*, playing a dissatisfied wife who finds renewed pleasure in her husband (Robert Powell) after being screwed by a Swedish industrialist (Per Oscarsson) while wearing his wife's clothes and wandering about London with a strange young man

(Martin C. Thurley). Back in Hollywood she wanted to *Stand Up and Be Counted* (72), a fashion journalist who returns to Denver to get caught up in the Women's Lib movement, but as directed by Jackie Cooper the film was closer to soap opera; the second-billed Steve Lawrence played a selfish executive being mean to her chum Loretta Swit. And then she finally got one high-class credit – though the film itself was hardly better than those she was used to – when John Huston chose her to play Paul Newman's illegitimate daughter in *The Life and Times of Judge Roy Bean*. This was better: it was the first time since *Airport* that she had co-starred with someone with box-office pull, which she certainly did not herself possess. *The Thief Who Came to Dinner* (73) was another such, for Ryan O'Neal had appeared in some popular films: but this was not another of them, and Bisset was wasted as a bankrupt socialite getting her kicks from knowing that he's a crook.

François Truffaut wrote to her time and again to persuade her to appear in *La Nuit Americaine*, but the reason she did not answer, it transpired later, was that her agent had not forwarded the letters because she did not want her to work with Truffaut. There may be several opinions about Truffaut's contribution to films – after his dazzling start – but he was well regarded, and this film turned out to be a big success on the art-house circuit as *Day for Night*, without having much to offer on its subject-matter, the making of movies. Clearly another of his filmed collection of memoirs, it was as small as his own personality, on view therein as a film director. Bisset played a British-born Hollywood actress who had just recovered from a nervous breakdown – and the character, if not the illness, was based on Julie Christie, whom Truffaut had directed in *Fahrenheit 451*. Bisset received by far her best notices to date, thus proving her agent wrong, and we should note in passing that this is the only time her name was linked to Christie's, which is to say that despite some similarities – both are British, well-bred, sexy and beautiful – they do not seem to have been in line for the same roles. But since Christie had an Oscar and box-office clout it has to be that she turned down some of the films Bisset made. Bisset remained in Paris to co-star with Jean-Paul Belmondo in Philippe de Broca's *Le Magnifique*, both of them in double-roles, he as a timid writer who becomes a dare-all adventurer in the films he imagines, and she as the English neighbour who becomes the heroine of his dreams. In both roles she was even more entrancing than in Truffaut's film.

The films which followed were varied but not destined to keep her high in the public's

mind: Sidney Lumet's *Murder on the Orient Express* (74), in which she and Michael York had little to do among the all-star murder suspects; Peter Collinson's disregarded modern-dress remake of *The Spiral Staircase* (75) with Christopher Plummer, as the deaf-mute heroine; Maximilian Schell's *Der Richter und sein Henker/End of the Game*, which did not cross frontiers, despite the presence of her and Jon Voight; Luigi Comencini's *La Donna della Domenica* (76) with Marcello Mastroianni, as another murder suspect, a woman whose marital status does not prevent her from collecting lovers as others collect stamps; and J. Lee Thompson's *St Ives* with Charles Bronson, as the double-crossing darling of an old man (John Houseman). The future promised better. *The Deep* (77) was directed by

The Deep (77) offered little in the way of plot – or, rather, what there was didn't exactly assault anyone's brain: but who cared as long as Jacqueline Bisset was wandering around like this?

Peter Yates from a bestseller by the man who had written *Jaws*, while *The Greek Tycoon* (78) would give her the chance to play a thinly-disguised Jackie Kennedy Onassis to Anthony Quinn in the title-role. In the event both were laughed off the screen by the critics, although she herself was well received in the first of these, looking sumptuous as she wandered about with bits of clothing clinging to her damp body. No one commented on her actual acting, but then who could act in junk like this? She was George Segal's ex-wife and an intended murder victim in *Who is Killing the Great Chefs of Europe?*, which proved that comedy was not exactly her forte – at least not under this director, Ted Kotcheff; after a domestic drama in Italy made by the feminist director, Armenia Balducci, *Amo Non Amo* (79) with Schell, she made one of her worst films, *When Time Ran Out . . .* (80). The time ran out, actually, for Irving Allen, who had produced one too many 'disaster' films – and the old devil volcano is about to explode in this one, in derisory special effects. The name-cast was headed by Paul Newman, and anyone hoping that he and Bisset would team well would have to wait till another occasion; it included Barbara Carrera, described by 'Playboy' three years earlier as 'so blindingly beautiful that she may well become a contender for the title unofficially held by Jacqueline Bisset as Hollywood's number-one love goddess.'

That did not happen, but not because Bisset was doing much to retain it. She was making *Inchon* (81) – for the understandable reason that it gave her a chance to work with Laurence Olivier, and because shooting was arranged around her schedule; but, as she admitted later, it was so bad that it was the one of her non-Hollywood films which she regretted making. She did at last something positive for her career: she produced *Rich and Famous*, a remake of *Old Acquaintance*, which she said she had never seen, so we may suppose she learnt about it from the reviews of *The Turning Point*, which had been inspired by it. Robert Mulligan directed for four days, but was not getting on with Bisset and her co-producer; so when filming resumed after a Screen Actors Guild strike he was replaced, at MGM's suggestion, by George Cukor, who at eighty-two (this would be his last film) still found 'a witty, intelligent script irresistible'. So many movies of this period fed off the films of the past without understanding them, but Cukor, of course, did. The dishy men graphically coupling with the Bisset character – Hart Bochner, David Selby and an eighteen-year-old messenger – underlined the essentially trashy nature of this enterprise, but it was often fun as it traces the relationship between an acclaimed novelist (Bisset) and the sort of bestselling writer (Candice Bergen) who gets invited on 'The Merv Griffin Show'. Bisset said that she adored working with Cukor and Bergen, but ruefully admitted that the film had not done well. Perhaps the trouble was that few cinemagoers associated her name with 'class', which this film had – but despite its title that was a quality missing from *Class* (83). Or if you prefer a better pun it was provided by the 'New York Daily News', which said, 'You can skip *Class*.' As directed by Lewis John Carlino, it had aspirations to be the *Graduate* of the 80s, with a Dustin Hoffman-lookalike, Andrew McCarthy, as the boy willing to be seduced by this Mrs Robinson, Bisset. 'Do you prefer to go up . . . or down?' she asks him in an elevator, but that was not to what she was referring. It is reassuring to learn that the script as filmed was not the one she agreed to do, but the excuse that she did this movie because she had been off the screen for a while does not forgive it.

However, a splendid credit awaited her: the wife of the drunken consul (Albert Finney) in Huston's *Under the Volcano* (84), even if she had little to do but act concerned, which offered no difficulty. She was not entirely well cast in the Anglo-German *Forbidden* (85) as a countess who sheltered a Jew (Juergen Prochnow) throughout the war and became a force in the Berlin underground: the role,

Rich and Famous (81) was an updating of Old Acquaintances, *in which Bette Davis was a moderately successful serious writer and Miriam Hopkins a friend who writes fabulously popular, but trashy bestsellers. It was no secret that the two stars loathed each other, while Bisset (here) and Candice Bergen, in this version, enjoyed working together. Maybe if they had hated each other this might have had the bite of the earlier version.*

which was based on fact, needed a Jane Fonda or an Anne Bancroft, for Bisset seemed to be acting on whim rather than from any conviction. The film, though inadequate to the story it told as directed by Anthony Page, was nevertheless a sound credit; it played some cinemas in Europe but in a preproduction deal went direct to television in the States. Bisset stayed in that medium: a lavish three-hour *Anna Karenina*, in the title-role, with Paul Scofield as Karenin and Christopher Reeve as Vronsky; and *Choices* (86), as George C. Scott's second wife, discussing abortion with the daughter of his first, who is also pregnant. *High Season* (87) was filmed in Greece and financed in Britain by what would seem to be more people than actually went to see it on its brief foray into cinema showings; Bisset and James Fox were on fine form as a divorced couple – she a photographer and he a sculptor – around whom swarm some rather dreary ex-pats, as written up by Clare (who also directed) and Mark Peploe. Both of them have worked with Antonioni and Bertolucci, but on their own they are much closer to the latter. Back in the US, Bisset starred in a soapy David L. Wolper mini-series for ABC, *Napoleon and Josephine: a Love Story* (87) with Armand Assante as her Bonaparte. Said John Leonard in 'New York' magazine, 'Although she knows how, she isn't asked to act; she's asked to show off, and so she does.' Bisset returned to France to star in Nadine Trintignant's *La Maison de Jade* (88), playing a lady of a certain age who is seduced by a younger man (Vincent Perez) who subsequently sends her over the moon till she suspects that he is cheating on her.

She said at this time, 'Everyone dreams of getting the roles Meryl Streep gets. I would love to be paid like a star in a starry film. I do ask too much money, but then I wind up in some low-budget production because I like the role. What is important from now on is to not be ashamed of the films I make.' She should not have said that, for she promptly made *Scenes From the Class Struggle in Beverly Hills* (89) – for the director Paul Bartel, because she found Bruce Wagner's script 'outrageous'. She played a former sitcom queen planning a comeback while burying her husband and coping with various house-guests and servants with seduction on their minds. Explained Bartel, 'What I was aiming for was something between "The Marriage of Figaro" and Buñuel's *The Discreet Charm of the Bourgeoisie*,' which is something else better left unsaid. After that, *Wild Orchid* (90) could only be an improvement; Mickey Rourke co-starred and Bisset, who originally turned down the role, accepted after Anne Archer withdrew. That will be

followed by *The Maid* (91), filmed in Paris with Martin Sheen.

For some years she lived with the financier Victor Drai, who uprooted himself from France to be with her in LA, but the man in her life for some time has been the Russian ballet dancer who defected, Alexander Godunov, who has also appeared in films. She said in 1984: 'My private life is at about the best point it's been in years. And I'm as far from tying the proverbial knot as I've ever been.' But let Stanley Donen have the last word: 'She doesn't have a bizarre personality, as Marilyn Monroe did, which seems to strike people's fancy. Jackie doesn't make a caricature of herself like some screen goddesses, which they then used in their movies rather than a characterization. She hasn't aimed at being notorious like Elizabeth Taylor. Had she behaved in a more infamous way she would have been a much more saleable lady for the movies.'

KLAUS MARIA BRANDAUER

As a world star, Klaus Maria Brandauer has only one problem: his accent. It is not a new one as far as continental actors are concerned. Only one, Charles Boyer, achieved a long star career in Hollywood, though Anton Walbrook was successful in Britain for a while. A more recent outstanding German-speaking actor, Maximilian Schell, won an Oscar in Hollywood but has had to work in a dozen countries to keep his career going – as have Max von Sydow and Erland Josephson, both introduced to us in the films of Ingmar Bergman. The pity of it is that Brandauer is a superb actor – imaginative, electrifying, versatile; the pity of it is that world audiences may have to be content to experience his talent intermittently.

He was born in 1944 in Alt Aussee, a village in the Salzkammergut region of Austria, where his first experience of his future profession was limited to a mobile projector which turned up weekly with a film. His family moved to Germany when he was ten, when he learnt to speak proper German and to see movies and television regularly. He always wanted to be an actor and studied at the Stuttgart Academy of Music and Dramatic Art for three years, leaving at the age of nineteen when offered a job with the Türingen Landestheater. He also married a fellow student, Karin Müller, who is now a television director. She came from the same village as Brandauer, and it is there they now live, in a house described by one writer – Stephen Schiff in the 'Observer' – as 'a nonstop bacchanal', with a rotating cabal of painters, directors, actors and home-town pals eating and drinking till the small hours. The same article refers to Brandauer's offstage energy and excitability, while being eloquent on 'his famous tantrums'.

His first major role was in Düsseldorf, supporting Elisabeth Bergner in 'The Madwoman of Chaillot', and after that he appeared in Munich, Hamburg, West Berlin and Zürich. En route he encountered Fritz Kortner, a formidable predecessor whose exceptional performances (on screen, for instance, in *Der Mörder Dimitri Karamazoff*) may have influenced him; Kortner encouraged him, but told him that he could always do better. Brandauer broke into films in English, in *The Salzburg Connection* (72), directed by Lee H. Katzin from a novel by Helen McInnes, playing a double agent, Anna Karina's brother, who aids the hero, Barry Newman, an American lawyer on vacation in Austria. He was billed third, but the film's complete failure caused him to concentrate on theatre, with an occasional sortie into television.

He had already gravitated to the Burgtheater in Vienna and he remained there for the next few years, playing, among other roles, Don Carlos, Romeo, Petrucchio, Tartuffe, Figaro and Hamlet. He does not care for modern theatre and directs only occasionally, for 'it's not a job, but a profession'. He returned to the screen when the Hungarian director István Szabó invited him to play the title-role in *Mephisto* (81), filmed in German, the story of an actor who loses his principles as he becomes the most respected actor in Nazi Germany. '*Warum?*' he cries at the end, trapped in the spotlight, '*Ich bin ein Schauspieler. Ich bin nur ein Schauspieler.*' It is also about a world turned topsy-turvy, with a man of over-riding arrogance in the centre of it. He is called Hendrik Höfgen, and is a thinly-disguised Gustav Gundgens, who married Erika Mann, daughter to Thomas Mann and sister to Klaus Mann, the author of the novel on which this film is based. All three men were homosexual, but this film gives Gundgens/Höfgen a negro mistress; while at the same time Brandauer plays a man of eclectic temperament, a law unto himself. The film's success made him world famous and brought dozens of offers from Hollywood, all to play SS men. He declined them all. He was also called 'an intellectual sex symbol' by 'Vanity Fair', which caused him to comment later: 'In the beginning these comments made me very nervous. You have no influence . . . Anna Magnani was for me a fantastic woman and for someone else an ugly actress.'

He finally accepted the role of the boyish

Klaus Maria Brandauer in István Szabó's fine, feisty Mephisto *(81), a German-Hungarian co-production which made his name on the international scene – which was inevitable, given his versatility and the vibrancy of his screen personality.*

villain, missile-meister Maximilian Largo, in *Never Say Never Again* (83), Sean Connery's final outing as James Bond: the two men play a game with computers which is not exactly a battle of wits, but Brandauer has no scene with von Sydow, who plays his boss. Irving Kershner, who directed, said that Brandauer is 'an intellectual, a full, rich person – and you don't find that often with actors. And he's so quick and unpredictable. He has that animal vitality, that magnetism in the eyes and the way he moves – I would imagine women find him devastating.' Brandauer announced that he would next star in *A Patriot for Me*, based on the play by John Osborne, but instead he made *Colonel Redl* (85) – *Redl Ezredes/Oberst Redl* – which acknowledges that play as one of its sources. Redl came from humble Jewish stock, which he hid as he rose to high rank in the Imperial army, becoming head of Intelligence; along the way the Russians got wind of his homosexuality and used it to blackmail him into handing over military secrets. Speaking later of his fascination with Osborne's play, Brandauer pointedly avoided explaining why he and Szabó preferred not to film it; the play has Redl as an unrepentant gay man while he has become bisexual in the film, which makes a certain nonsense of the plot, while his treachery seems less pressing as the film tries hard for analogies between the Austro-Hungarian Empire and the Soviet bloc as it then was. Where *Mephisto* was all passion and fire this is stately and controlled, with Brandauer subtly different as another hollow, vain, ambitious man. He was the captain of *The Lightship*, facing up to Robert Duvall (q.v.) and a few months later he was more

Brandauer in Burning Secret *(88), as the dashing, mysterious baron whose friendship with a youngster leads to an affair with his mother, and disillusion for the boy. Stefan Zweig's story had been memorably filmed by Robert Siodmalk in 1933, for which this one – apart from Brandauer's contribution – offered little in its place.*

widely seen as the baron (and, briefly, his twin brother) unfortunate enough to marry Karen Blixen (Meryl Streep) in *Out of Africa*. The role required him to do little more than look cunning, but once the baroness has shuffled him off in favour of Robert Redford, the film simply dies, drained of any true *raison d'être*. Sydney Pollack, who directed, was another to comment on Brandauer's appeal: 'I think what women find erotic about him has something to do with menace. Along with the mischief in the eyes, there's something dark and dangerous.' The reverse of the bland Mr Redford, in fact.

Brandauer was an outrageous Nero in an otherwise dull and overlong *Quo Vadis?*, filmed for television in Italy, mainly in English, with a cast including Frederic Forrest and von Sydow; then he did an American film about boxing, *Streets of Fire* (86), directed by Joe Roth, as a Soviet champion banned from the sport because of his Jewish origins. In the US he coaches a young Irishman and a black, to seek revenge on Russia when its team arrives in New York. The film had only a mild success, and Columbia, which had world rights in the third of the Szabó-Brandauer trilogy, *Hanussen* (88), seemed reluctant to do much with it, perhaps because it was little more than a replay of *Mephisto*. This time the protagonist was a corporal, wounded in World War I, who becomes to believe in himself as a magician, hypnotist and even clairvoyant, a man wavering between talent, phoniness and political compromise – with the new Nazi party, which alternately uses him and distrusts him. Brandauer played another German baron in the Anglo-American *Burning Secret*,

dallying with Faye Dunaway, a guest at the same hotel – a liaison discovered by her twelve-year-old son, to consequent disillusion. Andrew Birkin directed, from a short story by Stefan Zweig, which as *Brennendes Geheimnis* had made a moody romantic drama for Robert Siodmak in 1933 – with Willi Forst in the role now played by Brandauer. Birkin's several changes included changing the baron from a narcissistic womanizer to a war-scarred veteran whose interest in the boy is in inverse proportion to the original, where he used him only to gain the interest of the mother. It was hard to think the lukewarm notices undeserved, especially as Brandauer's otherwise galvanizing presence seemed muted in the scenes with Dunaway, perhaps because of tension on the set.

In France he was one of a large international cast celebrating the tercentenary of a remarkable event at great expense, *La Révolution Française* (89) – celebrated at such length, in fact, that it was divided into two, *Les Années Lumières* and *Les Années Terribles*. It was not, however, a celebration which attracted the French public. Brandauer was Danton. He was then scheduled to appear in *The Children* and *The Hunt for Red October*, but ceded his roles respectively to Ben Kingsley and Sean Connery. Instead he directed and starred in *Georg Elser-einer aus Deutschland* or *Seven Minutes* in English, with reference to the incident in 1939 when Elser plotted to assassinate Hitler in a Bavarian beerhall. Brandauer will be seen acting with Connery again in *The Russia House* (90); also made but not yet shown are a film directed by

Bernhard Wicki, advertised as *Spider's Web* in the trade press, and a new version of *White Fang* (91), to be followed by *Becoming Colette*, filmed in Paris.

During this period of world fame Joseph Papp invited him to play Hamlet in New York, but Brandauer decided that his accent disqualified him. He has said: 'I'm happy as long as I'm working with intelligent people that I can learn something from. I'm rather like a vampire in that way . . . You have to live your role, to become the person you portray. On film I exist as the character 24 hours a day . . . Acting is the wrong word. I don't believe in acting. You do something as if it was true. You have to always keep your eyes and heart open to the world around you, to make it true. With acting I need a partner. [He] might even be the camera and the cameraman behind it, but a partner has to be there. I am happiest when the director is my partner, like István Szabó. In *Out of Africa* Sydney Pollack had a wonderful style of working where all the time I had the feeling that I was doing what I wanted. But in reality he provoked or manipulated me. A true partner!'

JEFF BRIDGES

Jeff Bridges was in movies for over a decade before stardom came, and that was partly because he chose the wrong parts – or else they did not allow him to do what he does best, to embody the average guy who is slow in thought and quick in action. Now, the word 'average' is a give-away: you would never have called Wayne or Cooper or Tracy 'average' – though, like them, Bridges has a distinctive voice, low and thin, which never seems to strive for the unexpected cadences on which it alights. This is hardly the heroic age in movies: no Bengal Lancers, no cavalry leaders . . . but it was clear a while back that Bridges had developed that charisma the big screen likes so much. He had also become a very good actor, adept with a witty line, and always relaxed, natural but, withall, vulnerable. Observing once that he was probably not 'bankable', he said, 'I've got mixed feelings about it. I'd like to get a crack at the great scripts, but I think of myself more as a character actor. I'm afraid to get typecast in one role. Look what happened to my dad.'

Dad is Lloyd Bridges, a second-plan leading man of the 40s; in Jeff's view, once his father was cast in the television series 'Sea Hunt' he was offered few varied roles thereafter. His mother was also an actress, Dorothy Simpson. He was born in Los Angeles in 1949, and at the age of four months played a crying baby held by Jane Greer in *The Company She Keeps* (50), because his mother happened to be visiting the studio at the time. At the age of eight he made the first of several appearances alongside his father in 'Sea Hunt', as did his brother Beau, his elder by eight years. At the age of fourteen he toured with his father in 'Anniversary Waltz' and later he studied with Uta Hagen in New York; he also returned to television briefly in 'The FBI'. But he regards himself as 'sort of drifting into acting; it was like going into the family business. My real training was with Dad . . . [I] began doing films while I was doing seven years' military service in the Coast Guard reserve. Dad had encouraged us without being too pushy, and managed to open a few doors for us, but it was only after I'd done about ten movies that I made a serious decision to make it my career; till then I though I might become a musician or a painter, because every time I finished a film, I'd be exhausted and feel like never acting again.'

His first film was for television, *Silent Night Lonely Night* (69), which starred Lloyd Bridges and Shirley Jones in the roles played on Broadway by Henry Fonda and Barbara Bel Geddes. They were two lonely people, married to others, who come together at Christmas; Jeff played his father in a flashback sequence. His big screen debut was in Paul Bogart's *Halls of Anger* (70), as a student, and for Bogart he did a film for TV, *In Search of America* (71), playing a high school dropout who in 1928 persuades his parents (Carl Betz, Vera Miles) to do just that, travel across the country by Greyhound Bus. He played another student in Bogdanovich's *The Last Picture Show*, seducing Cybill Shepherd at second attempt, only she would have preferred the better-off Randy Quaid. The success of the film did everyone concerned much good, including Bridges, who was nominated for Best Supporting Actor. He was noticed by John Huston, who cast him as the up-and-coming prizefighter taken up by an older one, a has-been (Stacey Keach), in *Fat City* (72), a decrepit town in northern California. He later observed that he learned from Huston that acting was not about feeling comfortable. In Robert Benton's *Bad Company* he was a knowing and unprincipled young hick fleeing the Civil War and teaming up with Barry Brown to rob banks. Benton's attempt to revitalize the Western by showing its inhabitants as mean, turning to crime as a means of survival, was not appreciated by the public, but Stephen Farber in the 'New York Times' liked Bridges: '[he] is another kind of classic American hero – Peck's Bad Boy, the teen-age con-artist, an insolent Huck Finn on the range, with a Brer Rabbit shrewdness to

Fat City *(72) was a return to form for the director John Huston after a fallow period, a tale of small-time prizefighters in a Californian town. It showed not only that Huston was one of the few veterans to adapt to the movies' more sophisticated new techniques, but as able to get strong, individual performances as he had in directing Bogart, Greenstreet et al in* The Maltese Falcon. *Here are Stacey Keach, left, as the older boxer who takes the young one, Jeff Bridges, under his wing.*

keep away from the wolves . . . Jeff Bridges gives the kind of assured, magnetic, irresistible performance that used to turn actors into overnight stars.'

Bridges had a more expected failure with Lamont Johnson's tedious exercise on the pitfalls of fame, *The Last American Hero* (73), as Junior Jackson, who quits Pappy's moonshine business to become a stock-car driver; the real Junior was technical adviser and Valerie Perrine was the groupie who falls for Bridges. He turned down a chance to appear in John Frankenheimer's filmed-theatre, *The Iceman Cometh*, till Johnson reminded him that it would give him the chance to work with some of the masters of his trade – Fredric March, Lee Marvin, Robert Ryan. And he was with Ryan again in *Lolly-Madonna XXX* aka *The Lolly-Madonna War*, feuding with him in this cautionary hillbilly tale as one of the several sons of patriarch Rod Steiger. After that quartet Bridges needed a success, and it was provided by *Thunderbolt and Lightfoot* (74), which launched the directorial talent of Michael Cimino on an unsuspecting

world. Cimino also wrote it, drawing on other and better buddy-buddy/road movies; the interplay between thief Eastwood and drifter Bridges is entirely predictable, with dour, silent Clint taking a lot of lip from the sassy, chirpy Bridges. 'I like you,' says Bridges intently, before procuring for him and getting into drag: but we see them screwing the girls to prove they aren't gay. Bridges promptly found himself in an even worse movie, Frank Perry's simple-minded modern Western, *Rancho De Luxe* (75), with himself and half-Indian Sam Waterston as rustlers, 'free' spirits, pitted against a vicious cattle baron (Clifton James). Thomas McGuane wrote the script.

Bridges was no luckier with a better film, *Hearts of the West*, which did so badly that it was retitled *Hollywood Cowboy* for some markets; it was more entertaining than both *The Great Waldo Pepper* and *Nickelodeon*, other recent films also dealing with the makers of Silent movies. Rob Thompson's original screenplay was little more than an update of *Merton of the Movies*, and Bridges was most engaging as the Merton character. Two more good films punctuated this dismal record: Bob Rafelson's *Stay Hungry* (76) and John Guillerman's *King Kong*. In the first, Bridges is the darling of the Birmingham (Alabama) country club set, rejecting its values as he finds 'real' ones at the Olympic Spa Gymnasium (whose inmates include Sally Field and Arnold Schwarzenegger); in the second he is the stowaway paleontologist who knows of the giant Kong. Both are men with dreams, and both characters need a player with a strong sense of humour. It looked as though Bridges was coming into his own, but in fact Rafelson's film was only a cult success and *King Kong* was widely thought to be the flop critics predicted it would be (when in fact it took $36 million on an outlay of $24 million). Bridges certainly did himself no favours with his next choice, however, Lamont Johnson's *Somebody Killed Her Husband* (78), the 'her' being Farrah Fawcett-Majors making her bid for big screen stardom; he took billing after her, playing a clerk in Macy's toy department who writes children's stories in his spare time. She illustrates same, which means romance till they try to discover who made her a widow.

Winter Kills (79) had been started in 1976; not only did the money run out, but one of the executive producers was shot dead and another went to jail. Writer-director William Richert was working from a *roman-à-clef* by Richard Condon, who described the result as a 'highly colored comic-book version' of his original. Condon's starting point was the assassination of President Kennedy, plus the character of his father. Thus: Bridges played a man who opens up a whole can of worms in seeking to discover who murdered his brother, the US president. Though surrounded by many fine talents (Toshiro Mifune, John Huston, Eli Wallach), Bridges was unable to help this film make any headway at the box-office, and it went unshown in many countries. It is by far from being the total disaster which is *The American Success Company* aka *Success*. During that break in filming, Bridges followed Richert to Munich, for this supposed comedy in which he is a wimpish muck-muck with an American credit card company in Germany; his wife is playing around with a different type, all flash and dazzle, so Bridges buys himself a gangster suit and returns to his wife pretending to be his double. Very, very few people went to this movie because few cinemas were willing to show it: something similar happened to *Heaven's Gate* (80) – at least after the first week, after the reviews were in. It could not have been worse than *Success*, but Cimino was trying very hard to make it so, and with

a great deal more money. A clean-shaven Kris Kristofferson had the biggest role, while a bearded Bridges got off lightly, 'also starring' as the immigrant's storekeeper: indeed, he was lucky, since Cimino had originally wanted him for the larger role played by Christopher Walken.

Filming took so long that Bridges could not appear with brother Beau in Walter Hill's *The Long Riders*, exec-produced by James and Stacey Keach, who also worked on the script and appeared in the film along with the Quaid and Carradine siblings; Jeff observed later that he wasn't sorry, for there was something gimmicky about the casting. *Heaven's Gate* was in fact shot in the same Montana valley as *Rancho De Luxe*, during the making of which Bridges had met his wife Susan; they bought the whorehouse built for Cimino's movie and converted it into a home where they live part of the year; they have three daughters.

Bridges' penchant for choosing badly went into abeyance with *Cutter and Bone* (81), Ivan Passar's strange, affectionate and original film about a horribly wounded Vietnam veteran (John Heard) who develops a fixation on an oil tycoon he believes to be a murderer. Heard was Cutter and Bridges was Bone, his feckless Santa Barbara chum who fancies himself as a stud. Both actors were fine, but without box-office clout: the film did no better under the changed title by which it is more usually known, *Cutter's Way*. Despite these calamities, someone at Disney thought Bridges had potential as an action man, so he was set down among the video games of the computerized *Tron* (82), which succeeded in being worse than *Heaven's Gate* and even less comprehensible as written and directed by Steven Lisberger; it cost $21 million and by dint of Disney hype took over $15 million. Bridges' troubles were not over: partnered with Sally Field (he was her stuffed-shirt second husband) and James Caan in *Kiss Me Goodbye* it was clear that audiences did not want to make their acquaintance in the first place.

By this time there may have been only one person in Hollywood who believed that Bridges still had potential as a star actor: Taylor Hackford, whose success with *An Officer and a Gentleman* was of such proportions that he had carte blanche. And what he wanted to do was remake *Out of the Past* with Bridges in Robert Mitchum's old role, now star footballer on the Los Angeles team, but still caught in a dangerous web as spun by some people as ruthless as they are rich – including perhaps the lady owner of the team, played by Jane Greer, who had been the mysterious heroine of the earlier film. *Against*

All Odds (84), as this one was called, was an excellent thriller, taking in over $10,500,000 at the box-office on a $13 million investment; it also demonstrated that the American cinema had found, or refound, a star. John Carpenter immediately cast him as an alien, the *Starman*, the film for which Columbia had turned down *E.T. The Extra-Terrestrial* – which is to say, they already owned this property and thought the stories too much alike. Certainly Bridges was more attractive than the E.T. – and more lovable, which was the point of the movie, for Karen Allen falls in love with him and wants to save him from the scientists who wish to examine and perhaps extinguish him. Carpenter observed that 'if audiences didn't like Starman, they weren't going to like the movie. I needed someone who could handle the physical requirements of the role, but who could also project warmth and vulnerability. Jeff was the perfect guy. He is a chameleon. He's rugged and vulnerable, but he's also a child-man. Look at his smile. It's full of little secrets.' Bridges played with jerky movements, slurred speech – a teddy bear, but also a zombie, the

sort of role for which they might have cast a zombie-like actor. It was simply one of the most endearing performances of the decade, and his Oscar nomination stood him in good stead when the film returned only $13,800,000 of its $22 million cost.

Bridges consolidated his late-won position with a superb performance as the rather arrogant publisher defended on a wife-murder charge by Glenn Close in *Jagged Edge* (85), a nail-biting thriller which returned almost $17 million on a cost of $15 million. A second thriller died that year after receiving feeble notices: Hal Ashby's *8 Million Ways to Die* (86), which cost $18 million and took only $500,000. Bridges was an alcoholic ex-cop whose protection is sought by a high-priced hooker who wants to get rid of her pimp; Rosanna Arquette is the loose lady who accompanies him on his journey through the mayhem. *The Thanksgiving Promise* starred brother Beau, who also directed for Walt Disney Television; both parents are also in the cast and Jeff pops up in an unbilled bit as a neighbour.

Jane Fonda was the alcoholic in Sidney

The deceptive ease of Jeff Bridge's playing may be one reason why he has not always received just acclaim for his work, but he was much praised for his taxing role in Starman *(84), as a creature from another planet. With him is Karen Allen, also on fine form as the lonely woman who protects him – and falls in love with him.*

Another first-rate Bridges credit was The Fabulous Baker Boys *(89), and this time there were two of them, for his brother Beau, left, played his brother in the picture, which concerned two pianist-enterainers of decidedly second-rank quality.*

James Stewart, he is as near as this generation can get to sharing their integrity. But it is a measure of this film's failure that it is virtually the first of its kind to persuade us that it is the other side which has a stronger case than our hero. Paramount eventually released, to find a return of $10 million on their books.

Alan K. Pakula wrote and directed a thoughtful semi-autobiographical comedy, *See You in the Morning* (89), examining the effect of divorce on three people – Bridges (who plays a psychiatrist), Farrah Fawcett (as she now is) as his wife and Alice Krige as the widow with whom he falls in love: fairly lethal reviews shot that one down, and it returned only $2,200,000 of its $17 million budget. At least everyone liked *The Fabulous Baker Boys*, in which Jeff and Beau played road-house pianists whose act enjoys a new popularity when they employ Michelle Pfeiffer as vocalist. The point about the Baker boys is that they are anything but fabulous – just doing a nine-to-five job that isn't, Beau the family man and Jeff the philanderer. Novice director Steve Kloves was to be in charge of his own screenplay, which was why several Hollywood studios passed: 20th-Century-Fox said yes, to see an $8 million return on a $13 million budget, which was not entirely encouraging for a film so warmly received, but since in truth it ran out of steam before the end, word-of-mouth may not have been as encouraging as it might have been. Just after Tom McGuane had worked with Bridges in *Rancho De Luxe* he wrote a script which took this long to get to the screen: *Cold Feet*, in which he played a cowboy; Bridges did an unbilled bit as a bartender. He was also seen in *Texasville* (90), Bogdanovich's long-delayed sequel to *The Last Picture Show*, described by 'Variety' as the 'non-adventures' of an oil-tycoon, the role played by Bridges. It's a terrible movie, proving that what Cybill Shepherd never had, she still hasn't got. He's also set to play a disc-jockey in *The Fisher King* with Robin Williams.

He also writes songs, one of which was used on the soundtrack of the 1969 movie, *John and Mary*.

MATTHEW BRODERICK

Matthew Broderick is second-generation show business, but that it is not the usual albatross, since he does not look at all like his father James, who was – after all – a character actor, one of distinction if not a star, like Henry Fonda, or a well-known leading man like Lloyd Bridges.

He was born in New York in 1962, to a mother who was also in the business, directing

Lumet's *The Morning After*, but he was again an ex-cop, the dumb lug who hangs around, feeling sorry for her, but ready to dare all when she needs help in solving a murder. The film's rentals were fine at $12 million, but that was still $5 million less than the cost. It's Kim Basinger who witnesses murder in Robert Benton's *Nadine* (87), and he's the two-bit loser of a husband she's about to divorce: this was considerably lighter than Bridges' other recent thrillers – as was reflected in the returns, which were a mere $2,500,000 on a $12 million budget. As for *Tucker: The Man and his Dream* (88), that went into production without a distributor, despite a budget of $23 million (including the $1 million reckoned to be Bridges' fee at this time). The second half of the title was equally a reference to producer-director Francis Coppola, who for years had wanted to make this biopic on Preston Tucker, who in the immediate post-war period patented and manufactured an automobile of revolutionary design, till brought low because the 'Big Three' in Detroit were determined to drive him out of business. From Capra onwards Hollywood has always made us care about the pioneers and prophets done in by big business and/or politicians: and if Bridges, under interrogation, is not as persuasive as Gary Cooper or plays in New York. He grew up in Greenwich Village and in theatres, which encouraged an early desire to act, but when, at the age of seven, he was offered a role in a play in which his father was appearing – in Stockbridge, Mass. – he chickened out. For his secondary studies he chose the Walden School because its facilities included a good theatre, and he continued studying acting – with Uta Hagen – after completing his courses. With the HB Studio group he made his professional appearance, alongside his father, in Horton Foote's play 'Valentine's Day' (79). He also appeared in an episode of 'Lou Grant', virtually his only appearance in a show done expressly for that medium. He thought his big chance had come when Martin Ritt chose him to play opposite Sally Field in *No Small Affair*, but the project was cancelled after three weeks' filming. Against the advice of his agent he decided to take the role of the teenager who is adopted by drag queen Harvey Fierstein in 'Torch Song Trilogy' off-Broadway, which won him fine notices and a couple of awards; but he had left the cast before it moved to Broadway. Neil Simon auditioned him with a view to playing his alter ego in 'Brighton Beach Memoirs', which he did, and Simon also cast him as Marsha Mason's son in *Max Dugan Returns* (83). His father, who died at the age of 55 in 1982, had recommended him to agree to audition for *WarGames*, but when Martin Brest (then to direct) asked him to test, his father advised him to look instead at the rushes of the Simon film. Thus he was cast as a teenage computer expert who stumbles by chance on a plan to start a nuclear war, which he must prevent – an unattractive idea, as directed by John Badham (who had taken over from Brest) and in the event a tedious one, as bland as *Dr Strangelove* had been acrid, if not vicious. Still, it was popular on its home ground, at least, where it pulled a mighty $36,500,000 (budget: $12 million).

He went into the second part of Simon's autobiographical trilogy, 'Brighton Beach Memoirs', and then travelled south to Waxahachie, Texas, posing as a fictional town after having served as itself, more or less, in *Places of the Heart* and *Tender Mercies*. *1918* (85) was like them, an autobiographical piece, the seventh of Foote's nine plays about the Robedaux family, with his daughter, Hallie Foote, playing a character based on his own grandmother. There is some truth and niceness here, but not enough, as directed – amateurishly – by Ken Harrison. Broderick played a Robedaux brother-in-law, inspired to join up after watching *Hearts of the World*; he also reports a gambling debt and a girlfriend who wants an abortion before jumping ship while training as a merchant seaman. While

playing with spirit and a sense of character, he hardly seemed the type for such matters, but of the cast only he and Ms Foote seemed real professionals. The film opened the same month as *Ladyhawke*, which at $21 million had cost twenty-one times as much, if not more. Broderick played the young hero, a thief, in this medieval fantasy directed by Richard Donner with Michelle Pfeiffer and Rutger Hauer also being decorative. (The take was $7,900,000.) Seesawing, Broderick appeared in a Showtime presentation of Athol Fugard's play, *Master Harold . . . and the Boys* and returned to Foote and Harrison for an old role in *On Valentine's Day* (86), which after minimal exposure in cinemas was shown on PBS's 'American Playhouse' with *1918* as *Story of a Marriage*, but preceding it, as this was set in 1917.

Up, up again, to enjoy *Ferris Bueller's Day Off* – from school, that is, playing truant and racing about in a chum's dad's Ferrari for one of writer-director John Hughes's teen wish-fulfilment fantasies which, muddled though it was, realized audience fantasies to the tune of $28,600,000, on a budget of $12 million. You thought he had it made? Try *Project X* (87), a title referring to a US military scheme to train chimps to fly aircraft simulators, with inexperienced Broderick in charge and befriending a special chimp called Virgil, who can communicate in sign language. Jonathan Kaplan directed this mild $18 million fantasy, which went to video in most overseas markets after returning only $7,700,000 on its home ground. These were big sums of money to tie up in a young actor of no proved appeal, but

Matthew Broderick in WarGames (83), a fable about a youthful computer expert who stumbles upon some mighty state secrets. It was meant to be an Awful Warning, but Dr Strangelove it wasn't. Still, the young star was on fine form – and was well-supported by Ally Sheedy, left.

Broderick growing up – or almost, in Ferris Bueller's Day Off *(86), left, and* Biloxi Blues *(88), both of which celebrated the joys of, well, growing up. In the first he went joy-riding in a borrowed auto, and in the second, as a young army recruit, he learnt about sex – which may account for the smile.*

as in the case of Michael J. Fox the industry knew that young audiences were looking for young heroes. Like Fox, Broderick looked much younger than his years, so it is surprising that he did not play his stage role in the 1986 *Brighton Beach Memoirs*: Jonathan Silverman did. Broderick, however, did apppear in the much more successful sequel, *Biloxi Blues* (88), though looking far too young either to join the army or to be deflowered. Mike Nichols has a better feeling for the period – World War II – than Gene Saks in the earlier film, and his pacing is infinitely better. *Memoirs* cost $18 million and *Blues* $20 million, and they made back respectively $6,300,000 and $21 million; neither, however, did well overseas.

In 1987 Broderick was on vacation with Jennifer Grey, daughter of Joel Grey and a fellow-member of the cast of *Ferris Bueller*, when his hired BMW crashed head-on with a Volvo in which two women died. Broderick, who suffered a broken leg, and Grey were the only witnesses, and he was unable to say whether he had forgotten for the instant that in Ireland one drives on the left. He was charged with reckless driving, which could have carried a prison term of five years, but in the event was fined only £100 after pleading guilty *in absentia* to a reduced charge of careless driving. 'Ferris Bueller's Let Off' screamed the 'New York Post', which disregarded the fact that Broderick was a markedly careful driver and that he had been shattered by the accident. Ms Grey, incidentally, went on record with her opinion of him: 'You don't ever feel when you're with him that you're with an *actor*. I mean this in the best way. Actors tend to be unbearable. Matthew reads comic books instead of scripts.' So did Mickey Rourke, though whether he was asked to do so is unrecorded: 'In ten years' time people like him who haven't worked tables, shined shoes and driven taxis will have had no experience of life, other than their life as actors, to draw on,' to which Broderick responded, 'I think that's valid and you certainly have to be aware of it.' (He might instead have pointed to Montgomery Clift, also an actor from his teens, and one better than Rourke will ever be.)

Broderick refused offers for several months, but agreed to appear in *Torch Song Trilogy*, undoubtedly to help Fierstein get backing, since what Hollywood interest there was meant either removing the sex or having the role played by Richard Dreyfuss or Dustin Hoffman, both of whom told Fierstein he must play on screen the role he had written for himself. Broderick did not play his stage role, that of the boy adopted by the gay couple, but the youngster who is injured in a brawl while watching Fierstein's drag act and who later moves in with him, only to be killed by queer-bashers. If a delicate performance, the character comes across as little more than a wimp. The film belongs, when Fierstein will let it, to Brian Kerwin as the laid-back bisexual schoolteacher who does not care who gets hurt as long as he gets his jollies. Paul Bogart directed. The film, which cost approximately $7 million, took only $2,500,000, while two for Tri-Star were only going to make red ink in the ledgers, *Family Business* (89) and *Glory* – which opened in New York within a day of each other to compete for the Christmas trade. The former was a caper comedy thriller with Dustin Hoffman (q.v.) and Sean Connery; the latter was a serious drama about the celebrated black regiment, the 54th Union Army Infantry, which fought in the Civil War, with Broderick as its colonel. Well-intentioned and well-directed in the battle scenes by Edward Zwick, it did not avoid the stereotyping that has plagued military movies since they began. The film cost $21 million and was expected to take in something over $7 million.

Broderick did have a big success with *The Freshman* (90), as a film student who becomes a part-time delivery boy to a Mafia boss, one whom the young guy thinks too much like Don Corleone in *The Godfather*, and here was Brando with Broderick, spoofing his own performance in that movie. This one took over $21 million in just over eleven weeks. Next up for Broderick should be the last part of Simon's trilogy, *Broadway Bound* (91).

GENEVIÈVE BUJOLD

She is an almond-eyed beauty who has grown in stature with the years, bringing intelligence and warmth to too many films in themselves lacking those qualities.

Geneviève Bujold was born in Montreal in 1942 to a French-Canadian family who sent her to the best Catholic schools, where any thespian opportunities were limited to making loyal greetings to visitors. She studied at the Montreal Conservatoire d'Art Dramatique, but left before taking her diploma to join a company touring 'Le Barbier de Seville'. She joined another company, Rideau Vert, and began to be seen on television. She made her film debut in a small role in René Bonnière's *Amanita Pestilens* (62), and followed it with the star role in 'Geneviève', an episode of *La Fleur de l'Age* (64), neither of which travelled. In 1965 Rideau Vert played in Moscow and Paris, where Alain Resnais saw her play Puck in Shakespeare's 'Le Songe d'une Nuit d'Été' and engaged her to play the pro-Spanish student with whom Yves Montand has a passionate affair, and whose activist actions are to involve him deeply: *La Guerre est Finie* (66). It was seen the world over, but she remained in France to make Philippe de Broca's loopy *Le Roi de Coeur* with Alan Bates, as the only virgin in the brothel. She was also a tight-rope walker, but then, it was that sort of film. Louis Malle engaged her to play one of the several beauties in love with Jean-Paul Belmondo, *Le Voleur* (67), specifically the cousin whose father has forbidden her to marry him.

She returned to Canada to star in *Entre la Mer et l'Eau* for Michel Brualt, who had directed her in *La Fleur de l'Age*, and *Isabel* (68), in which she returned home to cope with some distinctly bizarre happenings. That

Geneviève Bujold in the movie in which the world first noticed her, Alain Resnais's eloquent La Guerre est Finie *(66).*

The Tudor dynasty was not one which the movies could ignore, and its members have been variously represented by Marion Davies, Flora Robson, Nova Pilbeam, Charles Laughton and Bette Davis. The last memorable occasion – if not cinematically – was Anne of the Thousand Days *(69), in which Richard Burton was a rather glum Henry VIII and Geneviève Bujold the second of his six wives, Anne Boleyn.*

brought her the Best Actress award at the Festival of Toronto and marriage to its director, Paul Almond (she had earlier been wed for 18 months to a biology student). She also appeared on television in Anouilh's *Roméo et Jeanette*, Ibsen's *Maison de Poupée* and *Crime et Châtiment*. On American television she was Shaw's *Saint Joan*, but it was not that but *Isabel* which wakened the interest of Hal Wallis, looking for a young actress to play Anne Boleyn, *Anne of the Thousand Days* (69), opposite Richard Burton's Henry VIII. He ranted and roared while she cajoled and wept, a role written as a cipher and not sufficiently well directed – by Charles Jarrott – to disguise the fact that she was far too modern. Universal had considered the role important enough to sign her to three more pictures, but she returned instead to Canada to made *Act of the Heart* (70) for her husband, as a fanatically religious farm-girl who falls in love with a priest (Donald Sutherland). She also appeared in a short, *Marie-Christine*. Wallis and Universal wanted her back to play the title-role in *Mary Queen of Scots*, but she refused, probably on the grounds that a natural Anne Boleyn was not a natural Mary Stuart. She declined other offers from Universal, who sued for $750,000.

Rather than pay it, she returned to Europe to become one of *The Trojan Women* (71),

Cassandra, for director Michael Cacoyannis. Katharine Hepburn, Vanessa Redgrave and she sank, though Irene Papas as Helen launched a thousand ships, if in intensity rather than looks. There may have been duller, more ragged interpretations of the play by Euripides since it was first produced 2,400 years ago, but if so posterity has been mercifully spared them. Bujold had expected the film to do much for her, given the subject and the company she kept; but the reverse was the case. She returned to Canada to do two films: *Journey* (72), directed by her husband, as a girl trying to discover her true identity by voyaging back in time; and Claude Jutra's 19th-century gothic pastiche, *Kamouraska* (73), as the unhappy wife of a drunkard/lecher, deciding to murder him with the connivance of her childhood sweetheart/lover/doctor (Richard Thomas). It played only a few dates in the US, to demonstrate that Bujold was not a name to conjure with, even among the art-house crowd. Her marriage was over, so after a trip to Britain to tape 'Caesar and Cleopatra' for Southern Television with Alec Guinness she returned to Hollywood to resuscitate her career. Universal could have had her sent to jail, but they came to an arrangement by which they used her in the name-heavy *Earthquake* (74), as the widow who dallies with Charlton Heston while his

after a prologue in Europe. James Caan and Bujold, a baker's daughter who becomes a photographer, made an attractive couple. She had never been seen to better advantage, however, than in *Coma* (78), written and directed by Michael Crichton – from a novel by Robin Cook – for a chilling hour or so. Bujold was junior surgeon at a Boston hospital, utterly at home as one of those maddening heroines who risk a thousand perils to get at the truth. Still, no one can be lucky all the time, and she was incarcerated in a Richmond mental home in *Murder by Decree* (79), a rotten thriller with Christopher Plummer as Sherlock Holmes and James Mason as Dr Watson.

Charles Jarrott, now directing an occasional film for Disney, chose her to play a missionary in *The Last Flight of Noah's Ark* (80) in which she, a pilot (Elliott Gould), some kids and two Japanese soldiers unite for preservation work in the Pacific. She returned to Canada to be directed by Almond again in what may be his worst film, *Final Assignment*, as a television reporter who tackles the KGB because the Russians are conducting experiments on schoolchildren. She made her telefilm debut in a gothic horror tale, *Mistress of Paradise* (81), as a northern wife ill at ease in the Natchez mansion of her Southern husband (Chad Everett). At this point she suffered severely from depression, and took the usual Hollywood method to counter it, which meant an eventual spell for detoxification in a special clinic. In 1982 she became a mother for the second time, returning to the screen as a nun who has an affair with a priest (Christopher Reeve). Oh, come on! The film was called *Monsignor* (82). She was a social worker running a rape crisis clinic in *Tightrope* (84), in danger from the murderer with whom detective Clint Eastwood identifies.

Simultaneously she found her most sympathetic director, Alan Rudolph, for whom she would do perhaps her best work, beginning with *Choose Me* (84), one of his reflective studies of life in Los Angeles; Bujold played a TV personality dispensing sexual and psychological advice who herself is in urgent need of same, especially after beginning an affair with a drifter (Keith Carradine). *Trouble in Mind* (85) was less successful – and she had a smaller role as the owner of Wanda's café, but she was beautifully matched with Kris Kristofferson. In *The Moderns* (88) Rudolph moved to Paris and back to the 20s for another of his arabesques, with Keith Carradine as an unsuccessful artist on the fringe of expatriate society and Bujold as a gallery owner. The *Dead Ringers* were twins, both played by Jeremy Irons, and she was the drug-addicted, masochistic actress who sleeps

Bujold, like most stars of her generation, has been in any number of films which tried her and the audiences' patience, but Coma *(77) was an excellent thriller. She played a doctor attempting to solve a mystery in the hospital.*

wife, Ava Gardner, looks the other way. She went to Paris to be Belmondo's leading lady in de Broca's *L'Incorrigible* (75), and then did another unwilling assignment under her Universal pact, as Robert Shaw's beloved in *Swashbuckler* (76), which was an attempt to revive that genre for a new generation; but Shaw and James Goldstone's inept direction ensured that it was only a shadow of the great heroes and heroics of the past.

Bujold's career really began moving again with a derivative, mediocre thriller, *Obsession* (76), written by Paul Schrader and directed by Brian De Palma. Amid a welter of kidnappings and other disappearances Bujold was wife to both Cliff Robertson and the Italian who resembles her almost twenty years on. A generation not weaned on Hitchcock liked it. She was notably effective, as she was again when Jack Lemmon and she were *Alex and the Gypsy*, a weary California bail bondsman and she an eccentric, excitable ex-flame whom he can't get out of his mind or his hair. Said 'Variety': 'Bujold is in that unique category of actress who can be forgiven any botched job of casting or performance.' Forgiveness was in order on *Un Autre Homme une Autre Chance/ Another Man Another Woman* (77), on the part of writer-director Claude Lelouch, who had too soon revamped *Un Homme et une Femme*, setting it in the American old West with both of them after going to their fertility clinic. David Cronenberg co-wrote and directed this above-average horror film, which was made in Bujold's native land. She played a mother in a telemovie, *Red Earth White Earth*, with a prodigal son (Timothy Daly) and problems with belligerent Indians. *False Identity* (90) was a low-budget thriller co-starring Stacey Keach as a stranger in town, with Bujold in a familiar role, as a radio reporter – one who knows something about a Vietnam veteran who was murdered years ago. Though by no means a bad movie, it was hardly what this fine actress deserves: may she have better material in the next two, *Secret Places of the Heart* with Charles Dance, and *Les Noces de Papier*.

CAROL BURNETT

'I'd like to thank the world for Carol Burnett,' said one of her writers when presented with an Emmy Award in 1973. Millions of others have felt the same way, both before and since. Most of her work has been in television, and much of it is in syndication. If you come across her by chance – which is unlikely, since you are more likely to have scoured the schedules for a repeat – you may be struck anew by her skill, particularly in its precision and its timing. She is an incomparable artist.

San Antonio, Texas, was her birthplace in 1933, but she grew up in Hollywood, where her mother was a studio publicity writer and her father manager of a movie theatre, in which she worked part-time as an usherette. She was educated at Hollywood High and UCLA, where she majored in theatre arts. There she met Don Saroyan (cousin to the writer), whom she married; together they went to New York to break into show business, which is interesting in view of her subsequent career – for most young hopefuls go in the opposite direction. Via summer stock and industrial shows she got a job in television, in 1955, as the girlfriend of Jerry Mahoney, the dummy of ventriloquist Paul Winchell. In 1956 she played the girlfriend of Buddy Hackett in a short-lived sitcom, 'Stanley', but she first became noticed on Jack Paar's late night show, when she sang a song from her cabaret act, 'I Made a Fool of Myself over John Foster Dulles'.

This was strictly small-scale cabaret, in the Village, but she was spotted also one night by Joe Hamilton, producer of Garry Moore's morning show. He signed her for several appearances and later made her a regular on Moore's evening show. He also married her and became her manager, which created a small scandal since both were already married

(he had eight children already, and Burnett would become the mother of three girls). She first appeared on the New York stage as the tomboy princess in 'Once Upon a Mattress', originally off-Broadway, and began collecting the myriad trophies which have been targeted in her direction ever since, in this case 'The Most Outstanding Comedienne of the Year' from the American Guild of Variety Artists. She won her first Emmy for her mimicry on the Moore show and her second of many for an episode of 'Twilight Zone' (62). In Kansas City in 1961 and in Dallas in 1963 she starred in 'Calamity Jane', adapted from the Doris Day movie, which she would also do in a television version. Meanwhile, she made her first movie, *Who's Been Sleeping in My Bed?* (63), as Elizabeth Montgomery's meddling room-mate, complicating her romance with Dean Martin. Given that she was not an outstanding beauty, she might have remained in Hollywood, type-cast as the heroine's wise-cracking best friend. But she didn't.

She said later that she found movie-making slow and boring: 'I take my hat off to movie actors who know just how big or small emotionally they should be, filming out of sequence as they are. I just really wasn't prepared for that kind of work. I got sleepy. I was just sitting around. I missed the audience, and working with the characters.' But the real reason to eschew movies was another triumph on television, the very special Special with Miss Andrews, 'Julie and Carol at Carnegie Hall', and the chance of starring on Broadway in a musical with a score by Jules Styne, 'Fade In Fade Out', a spoof of Hollywood – something she would very soon be doing regularly. It had the weakest score (and book) of several outstanding Styne musicals of this period, and its run was limited – partly because of exhaustion, because she was also appearing in a weekly television revue with Bob Newhart and Caterina Valente, 'The Entertainers'. She also suffered from a recurring neck injury first sustained while doing a Neil Simon sketch in the Moore show, 'The Last Woman on Earth', in the title-role, jumping over a sofa on learning that Cary Grant is on the phone. There were legal complications over her departure from the show, but when she returned to it briefly the following year its potential to still pull audiences was slim.

The hour-long 'The Carol Burnett Show' made its bow in 1967 and for eleven years brought her and CBS huge audiences, hefty Nielsens and more Emmys. Among the sketches most popular were those with a dissatisfied Southern housewife, a dumb secretary and a charwoman; but best loved were her parodies of old Hollywood movies, 'The

Doily Sisters', 'Went With the Wind' and 'Double Calamity', and others in which she played Mildred Fierce and Dora Desmond. She also guested on other shows, while extra-curricular television work included 'Julie and Carol at Lincoln Center' (71), '6 Rms Riv Vu' (74) with Alan Alda, from the Broadway play; and 'Twigs' (75), also from Broadway, in four roles – three sisters and her mother. In 1972 she repeated her performance in *Once Upon a Mattress* for TV for the second time, having done it in black and white in 1964. She also returned to the stage in LA in both 'Plaza Suite' (71), and in 'I Do I Do' with Rock Hudson – in each case with runs of two to four weeks which were 'just about the right amount of time to work at night, and then I don't want to do it any more because I like to be home.' She still hankered after movies, and with her power would have insisted on longer rehearsals to cut down the waiting. She also pointed that she got up at nine a.m. to do her own show, instead of five as it would be if filming. The scripts submitted to her she characterized as 'Daughter of the Fuller Brushwoman', adding, 'Why bother? There's nothing to prove.' Still, she had been movie-struck since childhood and liked to think she would have been offered a screen musical had they still been in fashion. And oh the waste! Listen to the poignancy and point of her version of 'I'm Still Here' in the 1985 recording of 'Follies'.

It was Walter Matthau who brought her back to the screen. He telephoned her. 'I didn't know him very well, and usually when a movie star calls someone in TV they want you to do a benefit or something': thus *Pete 'n' Tillie* (72), a sort-of *Love Affair* for the 70s. Says Tillie: 'When you've reached my age, and your friends are beginning to worry you, blind dates are a way of life.' That is how she and Matthau meet; they marry and survive his infidelities, but cannot overcome the fatal illness of their son. Martin Ritt, not an experienced director of light comedy, does well in the first half because he has two players who have a genius for it; but he falters badly as the piece becomes serious. Burnett commented: 'I wish I could do it again, mainly because I didn't feel I was human enough in it. It's tough to fight an image that's built up over the years. People were expecting me to come on screen swinging from a chandelier and I think I was inhibited by that, to the point of underplaying Tillie by stifling myself. She could have had more personality. But it was a happy experience.' She had a supporting role in another Matthau movie, *The Front Page* (74), but it was a good one, and who would turn down the chance to work also with Jack Lemmon and director Billy Wilder? But

Carol Burnett in Who's Been Sleeping in My Bed? *(63), which marked her movie debut. Later, on television, she made fun of old movies. She didn't make fun of this one. She never even mentioned it.*

this was Wilder in a lost, vulgar mood, with Burnett too strident as Molly, the two-bit whore from Division Street.

As she made the last of her TV series she returned to the cinema, as the mother of the bride in Robert Altman's *A Wedding* (78), which was much less incisive and much less funny than an old British movie on the same subject, *Quiet Wedding*. Complications abound. Of a large cast, only Burnett supplied the missing qualities. A month later she was seen in a telemovie, produced by her husband for CBS, *The Grass is Always Greener over the Septic Tank*, about a New York couple – the husband was Charles Grodin – who leave the city's clamour behind for the peace of the suburbs. Burnett had always said that she would never turn to drama, but a middle-aged lady has a right to change her mind: and very moving she was, too, in *Friendly Fire* (79), based on the true story of war activist Peg Mullen, a country woman determined to discover the real facts about her son's death in Vietnam; Ned Beatty played her husband in a telefilm which was voted an Emmy for Outstanding Drama. That was for ABC, but Burnett returned to CBS for *The Tenth Month*, produced by her husband and written and directed by Joan Tewkesbury, from the novel by Laura Z. Hobson. Burnett played an ageing divorcée who after an affair with a famous pianist (Keith Michell) decides to keep the child which results.

Altman brought her back to the big screen with *Health* (80), top-billed over such movie names as Lauren Bacall, James Garner and Glenda Jackson. She played a government representative attending a convention on health in St Petersburg, Florida, proving yet again that she could do more with a look or a line than any woman living – in the first few reels, that is, before the piece begins spiralling rapidly towards the unwatchable. *The Four Seasons* (81) was an altogether happier experience for herself and moviegoers. She played the wife of Alan Alda, a couple with the taking habit of liking to laugh together. He also wrote and directed, returning Hollywood comedy to its old civilized level. It would be great if on other occasions he had Burnett to interpret his lines, for her handling of them is a gilt-edged asset. It's a beautiful performance, but when Universal wanted to campaign for an Oscar nomination she retorted that she was 'okay, no gem'. However, another film that year, *Chu Chu and the Philly Flash*, wasted her, as a show business has-been involved with government secrets, and another major talent, Alan Arkin, whose wife wrote the script. The lady finally got her wish to appear in a screen musical, but despite its

Carol Burnett in an unexpectedly thoughtful mood in a scene from The Four Seasons *(81), in which she played the wife of Alan Alda, who also wrote and directed the picture.*

long run on Broadway and John Huston in the director's chair, *Annie* (82) was not up to much. She played Miss Hannigan, the drunken, domineering head of Little Annie's orphanage, rightly seeing that the only thing to be done with her role was to camp it up. Her intonations and expressions were the nearest it came to entertainment. She was drunk again for some of *Life of the Party: the Story of Beatrice*, a telefilm on the life of that Mrs O'Reilly who founded the first recovery house for drunken women after having her own life saved by Alcoholics Anonymous. Lloyd Bridges co-starred, Lamont Johnson directed, and the piece was written by one of Burnett's longtime writers, Mitzie Welch, who produced it along with her husband.

During this period Burnett also appeared on stage in 'Same Time Next Year' with Dick Van Dyke in Los Angeles and Burt Reynolds in Florida. The question as to why an artist of her standing would want to appear in *Between Friends* (83) must be asked. Because she can stop being Carol the clown and play a mature woman, the sort whose lover asks, 'Have you ever had your toes sucked?' which was what he then proceeds to do? HBO presented this soap opera about the problems of the menopause. Elizabeth Taylor played the new best friend, who also doesn't realize how miserable she is till they get drunk together. Watching it, no amount of booze could prevent any intelligent viewer from being entirely miserable. Or perhaps she wanted to star opposite a genuine movie queen, Taylor, who for once was not eclipsed by a superior talent (but where she is concerned, is there any other kind?). With Altman directing, she (will some people never learn?) and Amy Madigan appeared in a one-hour telefilm, *The Laundromat* (86), about two lonely women who make friends in an all-night such. Burnett's last major work to date was in a six-hour mini, *Fresno* (86), which sent up soaps. She was the matriarch, and the fine Dabney Coleman her arch-rival. Reception was mixed, with some spectators revelling in the deliberate idiocies, while others felt it could have been better and quicker done in the context of Burnett's old movie spoofs.

In 1988 the Museum of Broadcasting paid a special tribute to the 'standard-bearer of the comedy/variety tradition in television', called 'The Many Worlds of Carol Burnett'. Gratifyingly, it proved how much of her work had survived, including a recent Special, 'Carol, Carl, Whoopi and Robin', respectively herself, Reiner, Goldberg and Williams. Even more tantalizing was a compendium of excerpts from her TV series, including sketches with Lucille Ball, Martha Raye, Joan Rivers and Lily Tomlin, funny ladies all. After admitting that she has made a splendid album of songs with Raye, it has to be said that she is so far ahead of the others because she shows a Fieldsian (W.C.) and Marxian (Groucho) disdain for the modern workaday world as well as the fantasy worlds she parodies, yet always with an underlying kindness. She once said, about her TV show, 'Our guidelines are: if the sketch reads funny, do it; if it reads preachy without being funny, don't do it. Our intention is that it should be funny first. If there's a message underlining it, and it's still funny, that's peachy. But if it's just hammering people over the heads about something, forget it.' In 1990 she began a 30-minute Saturday evening show for NBC, 'Carol and Company'.

Also in 1990 'Variety' reported that she was interested in taking over the lead in the Broadway revival of 'Gypsy', in which TV's Tyne Daly had magnificently obliterated memories of Ethel Merman in the original production, TV commitments permitting. Arthur Laurents, librettist and director of the revival, favoured Daly in a projected video version, rather than Bette Midler or Barbra Streisand in a remake of the 1962 film with Rosalind Russell. But Burnett in 'Gypsy': doesn't that just toast your toes?

And so as the sun sets slowly in the West we say farewell to a lady who doesn't need the money and doesn't need the work; but movies need someone as talented as this. Couldn't they make up for lost time?

STOCKARD CHANNING

Just when we all despaired of seeing an interesting new girl on the screen, Stockard Channing hove into view. The film itself was one of several attempts to resurrect the 20s and 30s, and it – The Fortune – was not good; but it was the only one of these films with a heroine who fitted into the period. Channing had the crisp, dry delivery of Myrna Loy or Miriam Hopkins – and almost alone of her generation she had the right style: she had poise, authority and attack. She looks a little like Elizabeth Taylor crossed with a chipmunk: and she was the best thing to happen to Hollywood in an age.

She was born in New York in 1944, of wealthy parents (father was in shipping) and educated at Radcliffe: it was there that she began to act, and when she left she was with repertory companies in New York, Boston and Washington. She took her stage name from her own surname, suppressing a Susan, and adding the surname of her first husband, an investment broker; her second husband

was a professor of Slavic languages; and she is now married to David Debin, who partners her in her production company, Little Bear. However, to return to her early career, we must note one film role, in The Hospital (71), where she can be glimpsed as one of the nurses. Later in the year she was in the chorus of a musical version of 'Two Gentlemen of Verona', and she understudied the lead – which she played in the Los Angeles production: that led to another bit part, in Up the Sandbox, starring Barbra Streisand, but that got left on the cutting-room floor. Small roles in TV led to a starring one in The Girl Most Likely To . . . (73), playing an ugly duckling who sets out for revenge after plastic surgery. She went after the role in The Fortune (75), but the director, Mike Nichols, was not at first interested: he found her useful, however, for reading the script with the stars, Jack Nicholson and Warren Beatty, and finally cast her.

It was apparent – it could not be missed – that here was a star, and MGM cast her in a leading role, in Dandy, the All American Girl (76): she played an automobile thief loved by a lawyer, Sam Waterston – a rotten idea not well made by Jerry Schatzberg. Shown at the Cannes Film Festival, it was agreed that everything was right about Channing, and everything, otherwise, wrong with the movie. It was withdrawn for tinkering, retitled Sweet Revenge – to emerge and die. The Big Bus did not fare much better; as directed by James Frawley, it was that 'rarity . . . a successfully sustained parody' (David Robinson in 'The Times') – of Hollywood's disaster movies. Audiences clearly feared the elephantitis of The Great Race or It's a Mad (4) World, and it was their loss: they missed Channing being

Stockard Channing made an auspicious movie debut in The Fortune (75), *as an heiress latched on to by two bumbling conmen, Jack Nicholson (here) and Warren Beatty. Beatty has persuaded her that she is in love with him, and while they both fall in love with her they find her more than a match for any of their schemes.*

stunning as the stewardess, especially in the cod Bogart–Bacall exchanges with the driver (Joseph Bologna). With three flops, Channing needed help, and after a TV movie, *Lucan* (77), and some theatre roles in LA, she placed her career in the hands of a flamboyant Hollywood agent, Allan Carr, who put her into *Grease* (78), which he had a hand in producing. It was only a supporting role – as the most 'liberated' of the girl students – but she was generally thought to be either the best thing about the movie or the only reason for seeing it. Concurrently she could be seen among some other lovelies in *The Cheap Detective*, as that gentleman's loyal secretary; and that was followed by *The Fish That Saved Pittsburgh* (79), as an astrologist who helps a basketball team to victory. Keeping her career moving, Carr signed her to a five-year contract with CBS, guaranteeing $2 million, starting with a TV movie, *Silent Victory: The Kitty O'Neill Story*, a biopic of a deaf stunt woman, and her own series, 'Just Friends'.

In 1980 she took over the lead in a Broadway play, 'They're Playing Our Song', and in 1984 she took over from Liza Minnelli in a musical, 'The Rink'; betweenwhiles her stage work included appearing opposite Burt Reynolds in the last of three one-act plays at the Burt Reynolds Dinner Theater, Jupiter in Florida, and co-starring with Irene Worth in 'The Golden Age' in Washington. Success in films continued to elude her: she supported

Kate Nelligan and Judd Hirsch in *Without a Trace* (83), playing a New York couple – based on fact – whose child disappears on the way to school; she played Nelligan's best friend. And that was a title which could apply to *Safari 3000*, a spoof action film with David Carradine made in 1980, test-shown by MGM in 1982 and released to cassette in 1984. She did not need to worry, for New York was hers: she and Jim Dale received marvellous notices for a revival of 'A Day in the Death of Joe Egg', which she had done earlier in Williamstown, Mass., with Richard Dreyfuss. The production transferred upwards from off-Broadway and brought her the Tony Award as 1985's Best Actress. Michael Tuchner's *Not My Kid* (85) was a predictable malady-of-the-week TV movie with Channing and George Segal as a well-to-do-couple who discover that their teenage daughter is a drug addict. The best the big screen could offer was the role of another best friend, Meryl Streep's, in *Heartburn* (86). Channing later told 'Premiere' magazine that she would have been 'terrific' in the Streep role, and Streep's agent is probably the only person in the world who would disagree. Channing took off while making it for a better role in Peter Medak's *The Men's Club*, but it was the men's film – they included Roy Scheider, Treat Williams, Harvey Keitel, David Dukes and Richard Jordan. Their names, however, were not enough to get this piece more than a minimal release.

She turned profitably to television, playing a teacher on both occasions: *The Room Upstairs* (87), falling in love with fellow-boarder Sam Waterston, and *Echoes in the Darkness*, a mini-series, falling in love with fellow teacher Peter Coyote before being murdered. She was 'terrific', said 'Variety', and the piece itself was much praised, as co-produced and written by Joseph Wambaugh from his own novel, based in turn on some events in Philadelphia in 1979. Still in that medium, she made the hour-long *Tidy Endings* (88) with Harvey Fierstein, the two of them quarrelling over which of them grieves most over their dead husband/lover. *A Time of Destiny* (89) was another unfortunate movie credit, in a supporting role as William Hurt's sister: she did it, she said, to get the chance to work with him. *Staying Together* did not change her cinema fortunes: it concerned a family and she was a righteous, ambitious woman who has an affair with one of its members. Returning to television, she was second-billed as a colleague of attorney Brian Dennehy in *Perfect Witness* with Aidan Quinn, who played witness to a contract killing. Also at this time she was one of the rotating casts in A.R. Gurney's two-character

As Ms Channing lost star roles in movies – usually by appearing in many unworthy of her – she found that whenever she appeared on stage rave notices inevitably followed. 1990 was therefore a big year for her, for not only did she triumph in one of off-Broadway's biggest-ever successes, 'Six Degrees of Separation', but she returned to Hollywood to star opposite Beau Bridges in Out of It. *The 'New York Times' thought it reason enough to celebrate.*

play, 'Love Letters': her partner was John Rubinstein and she was, said John Simon in 'New York' magazine, 'magnificent, with her dancing eyes, her mouth as moldable as Plasticine, her desperate hopefulness and disconsolate humor.' (Among the others who appeared in the piece were George Segal, Jason Robards and Elaine Stritch, William Hurt, Blythe Danner, Christopher Reeve, Kathleen Turner, Treat Williams and Kate Nelligan, Richard Thomas and Swoozie Kurtz, Julie Harris and Colleen Dewhurst and Josef Sommer.) Remaining on the stage she was the out-of-town lead in Neil Simon's 'Jake's Women' (90), but the reception for the play was so poor that it did not reach Broadway. *The Applegates* was a science fiction comedy which was only moderately received.

But the good news is that after having another big success in New York, off-Broadway in 'Six Degrees of Separation', she was again to star in a Hollywood picture, Arthur Hiller's *Married to It* (91), with Beau Bridges and Cybill Shepherd.

No one in their right mind would want to see Chevy Chase's first two movies, but his third, and the one in which he came to prominence, was Foul Play *(78) with Goldie Hawn. She played an innocent who has something wanted by some ruthless killers, and Chase was the cop who started to help her after she has survived their first attempt on her life. At this point in the film the killers seem to have the upper hand . . .*

CHEVY CHASE

'I'm Chevy Chase . . . and you're not,' he said on 'Saturday Night Live', and it sounded wonderful. This bland, amiable guy had made it to networked television and he was famous: all those schmucks out there should be so lucky!

This lucky schmuck was born in 1943 to a well-to-do family in New York. He was educated at Bard College and after graduating made a name for himself as a comic writer with 'Mad' magazine and the 'National Lampoon'; he wrote for the Smothers Brothers and Alan King, among other television shows, and contributed to the National Lampoon's 'Lemmings', an off-Broadway debut in which he made his acting debut. He also collaborated with a college friend, Ken Shapiro, who had begun to dabble with videotape recorders, and he appeared in Shapiro's 'Channel One', a collection of sketches on video which was shown in an old theatre on the East Side in 1967. These also played the campuses. By 1973 Shapiro had gathered enough tax shelter money to transfer the best of these, *The Groove Tube* (74), to film. The money involved was $400,000, which was to become over $9 million in receipts, perhaps because it mined a hitherto-unacknowledged American taste for excremental humour. No major American movie star ever had a less promising start; *Tunnelvision* (76) was no improvement, a supposed satire on the television

programmes of the future. Then 'Saturday Night Live' came to national fame and with it the opportunity to co-star with John Belushi, another of its regulars, in *National Lampoon's Animal House*. But Belushi and Chase did not hit it off, reputedly because Chase was more popular. Chase had only done himself a favour, for he immediately found an infinitely more attractive film for his debut as a leading man, *Foul Play* (78), as the cop protecting the mortally threatened Goldie Hawn. He was tall, personable and pleasant, school of Burt Reynolds – not quite a romantic hero, not yet quite a clown, either.

The film did well, but he was unable or unwilling to capitalize on the favourable impression he had made: at least he was off the screen for two years, if returning in three films almost simultaneously: *Caddyshack* (80) directed by Harold Ramis, *Oh Heavenly Dog!* and *Seems Like Old Times*, listed chronologically but also in rising order of merit. The first of them, in fact, is awful, an *Animal House*-like mix set in and around a country club, with Chase as a wealthy, eccentric golfer; that the film took over $20 million was generally reckoned to be due to Rodney Dangerfield, who as a vulgar-suited guest was reckoned to be its sole saving grace. The second had Chase as a private eye returning to earth as a dog – the famous Benji – in order to uncover his murderer; it took $3,750,000. The third was a reunion with Goldie Hawn, playing her ex-husband in Neil Simon's script, and it did very

little business at all. It was, however, a masterpiece compared with *Under the Rainbow* (81), which imagined what the Munchkins mights be doing after leaving the set of *The Wizard of Oz*. Chase, looking depressed, played an FBI man guarding a ducal German couple staying at the same hotel. The result almost broke Orion, for it brought back only $8,400,000 on a budget of $18 million. Shapiro's *Modern Problems*, with Chase as an air traffic controller who develops telekinetic powers, was no better, but it managed $14,800,000 on a much lower budget.

Whether Chase had a cinema following remained open to doubt, and the problem was not solved by *National Lampoon's Vacation* (83) and its huge box-office haul of $61 million. As directed by Ramis and written by John Hughes, it was another abysmal collection of wheezes built around a trip taken by Chase (an inventor of food additives), wife Beverly D'Angelo and their kids. Chase was revealed as having less comic persona than anyone since Harold Lloyd, but at least Lloyd had a series of brilliant gags. Chase brought little, too, to William Friedkin's *Deal of the Century*, playing an arms dealer who gets caught up with a young widow, Sigourney Weaver: this time a $15 million budget brought back a return of $4,900,000. So quite a lot was riding on an unashamed star vehicle,

Fletch (85), directed by Michael Ritchie from a screenplay by Andrew Bergman from a novel by Gregory Mcdonald. Well, if every dog has his day, this was Chase's. As the usual foolishly bold reporter we've always had in movies, he faces death a number of times, lying and cheating to get the information he wants; when lied to in turn or told something he already knows, he has a cool: 'Is that so?' Chase does little, but he does it delightfully, mugging much less than, say, Red Skelton or Danny Kaye, two predecessors of attractive appearance but little individual personality. The film cost $15 million and took $24,500,000. *National Lampoon's European Vacation* cost $19 million and took $25,600,000. He put in a guest appearance in *Sesame Street Presents: Follow That Bird*, and to complete a good year, *Spies Like Us* – the other one was Dan Aykroyd, a companion from 'Saturday Night Live' – cost $22 million and took $30,500,000.

But there was a snag: of these, only *Fletch* did well overseas, and as *National Lampoon's Vacation* had done badly overseas, its European ditto went direct to video in most markets. The *Three Amigos* (86) were Chase, Steve Martin and Martin Short, directed down South by John Landis for some goodish spoofing: but as some of the gags recalled Hope and Crosby it was a shame that Martin and Chase were some light-years behind. It cost $25 million and took $19,400,000 – but someone must have had doubts about Europe, for the amigos lost their pants for the ads there and had their gun-belts around their garters. Chase did a cameo in *The Couch Trip* (88) playing a father having trouble with a condom, but was then involved in more traditional Hollywood humour, the horrors of bucolic life: except *Funny Farm* wasn't funny – certainly not to the Warner accountants, noting that its $19 million cost returned only $11,900,000. It was the first of Chase's new contract with Warners, which was non-exclusive but gave them first refusal of any project he wanted to do. *Caddyshack II*, bereft of Dangerfield, cost $20 million and took only $6,200,000. Chase had only a guest role – as the club's laid-back owner, but the industry noticed that he featured prominently in the art-work of the ads. Warners did not bother to open these films in most markets and sent them direct to video. Chase had received warm notices the first time he played Fletch, but these were denied to him on *Fletch Lives* (89), which cost $18 million and took $17,800,000. Set in deepest Dixie, it was, said the 'Independent', not a patch on the earlier film and 'nothing more than a vehicle for Chase's half-cocked wisecracks [which] can be added to the sorry list of films which gave no hint of his early promise'. *National Lampoon's Christmas Vacation* cost $27 million and took $42,000,000 – but that was only $2 million more than the budget once the cost of prints and advertising had been added. And there was still very little income from overseas. Warners, who produced, signed Chase again for three more films, and announced that the first of them would be a comedy to co-star Aykroyd for Christmas 1990. Aykroyd was another whose popularity in the international market left very much to be desired. It had taken Steve Martin and Robin Williams a while to crack the international market, and after they had done so, two other comedies equalled their American success overseas: *Twins* and *Three Men and a Baby* had names in Schwarzenegger and Tom Selleck, but neither was noted as a comedian – and neither film was expected to do well abroad. That they did well everywhere seemed a good augury for another Chase–Aykroyd male-bonding comedy. However, Chase will have to be on his best *Fletch* form if he is to compete with Martin or Williams.

CHER

Cher was five when she knew that she wanted to be famous. She achieved it before she was twenty, as a singer. Almost twenty years on she made it as an actress, but she gives the impression that if performing deserted her she would make it as a freak. Each outfit she wears in public is more outlandish than the last; she has to go to new depths of outrageousness to make us stare, to shock us. It has been maintained that she is only a competent actress but seems much better than that, for her outfits have prepared us for an absolute disaster when she appears in some big screen fiction.

She was born Cherilyn Sarkissian in 1946 in El Centro, California, to a troubled childhood – fatherless, peripatetic – and at sixteen she dropped out of school. Shortly afterwards she met Sonny Bono and they were married in 1964. As Sonny and Cher, they sang in nightclubs and had a record, 'I Got You, Babe', which sold over three million copies. They sang it again in *Good Times* (67), directed by William Friedkin (his first feature), a bizarre thing in which they played themselves and fantasized about the movies in which they would be appearing. The hint was lost on Hollywood, but two years later, AIP, not renowned for its fastidiousness, accepted a script by Bono and allowed him to produce it: *Chastity* (69), so called because that is the name the lady has given herself – ironically, we may suppose – since she sleeps around indiscriminately and does a spell in a Mexican brothel, where she has a sweaty session with the lesbian madam. When not making love she is talking dirty, moralizing or hitching around Arizona. The film was not exactly a crowd-pleaser, but it provided a name for their daughter. Gee, they were certainly fond of the name 'Chastity'.

In 1971 CBS began 'The Sonny and Cher Comedy Hour', which ran for several seasons, till they divorced rather noisily. A second, brief, marriage, to Gregg Allman brought a son, but neither she nor Sonny made it as solo performers, so they were briefly reunited. 'The Sonny and Cher Show' for CBS in 1976 failed to run, but she now began to enjoy success on records and in clubs. In 1981 she claimed that she was making $325,000 a week but could not meet her debts; she suddenly realized that she loathed performing in Las Vegas and went to New York to gain recognition as an actress.

In 1974, between marriages and when her companion was the Warners executive David Geffen, she optioned *The Enchanted Cottage*, presumably hoping to play the Dorothy McGuire role. Nothing came of this, and she did not become an actress till Robert Altman auditioned her in 1981 for an off-Broadway production he was directing, 'Come Back to the Five and Dime, Jimmy Dean, Jimmy

Nichols saw it and offered her the role of Meryl Streep's lesbian friend in *Silkwood* (83). Her fee was $250,000 and when it brought her an Oscar nomination as Best Supporting Actress, that rose to $1 million (so said 'People' magazine, noting that when Tom Conti's fee went from $100,000 to $1 million after his nomination – for *Reuben Reuben* – there were no takers). At least, that is what she was paid for *Mask* (85), playing the biker mother of a hideously disfigured teenager (Eric Stoltz). These characters, based on real people, had been touchingly written by Ann Hamilton Phelan, with Cher initially protective, independent and unorthodox. She brought a fire to the role and never played for sympathy, but was never more than two-dimensional. She and the director, Peter Bogdanovich, were not on speaking terms when they took the piece to the Cannes Film Festival, where she was voted Best Actress.

She turned down the Diane Keaton role in *Baby Boom* and that played by Theresa Russell in *Black Widow* because she thought she was not right for them. When offered the part of one of *The Witches of Eastwick* (87) who taunt Jack Nicholson she indicated that she wished for another one – that for which Susan Sarandon had already been cast. There was a last-minute switch, and Sarandon took the smaller role because, as she explained, 'the legal complications were too ghastly'. Peter Yates cast her as the public defender who with Washington lobbyist Dennis Quaid investigates on behalf of murder *Suspect* Liam Neeson, a deaf-mute. This took only $8 million at the box-office, but Norman Jewison's *Moonstruck* gave Cher a second hit, chalking up over $34 million or $3 million more than *Witches*. She played a freelance accountant, a divorcee, who shocks her Italian family by falling in love with the freewheeling brother (Nicolas Cage) of her dullish fiancé (Danny Aiello). As written by an off-Broadway playwright, John Patrick Shanley, it was affectionate and funny, winning six Oscar nominations as against the superior *Roxanne*, which did not get one. Cher's performance brought her the Best Actress Oscar (and the same from BAFTA), which was deserved inasmuch as everyone was rooting for her and the unprepossessing Cage to have a happy ending; but nothing she did suggested a successor to Bette Davis.

An Oscar and two big successes made her a power to deal with in movieland. *Mermaids* (90) was delayed because of her illness, and she was allowed to choose Emily Lloyd to play her daughter. Frank Oz, who had replaced Lasse Hallstrom as director, recast Lloyd's role with Winona Ryder, because he thought it should be played by an American; but when

Cher is one of those stars who is a star because that is what she wanted to be. She has, however, given some pleasing performances, notably in Mask (85), as the biker-mother of a horribly-disfigured (by illness) teenage son.

Dean'. She played one of several women celebrating the twentieth anniversary of Dean's death. She was the blowsy one who in Altman's film version, *Come Back to the Five and Dime, Jimmy Dean, Jimmy Dean* (82) does imitations of the McGuire Sisters with Sandy Dennis. The film was taken from both of them by a very stylish Karen Black. Mike

And she won an Oscar for Moonstruck *(87), in which she falls in love with Nicolas Cage, here, when actually engaged to his brother. Lillian Gish was expected to be nominated (for* The Whales of August*) but wasn't, causing her to comment something to the effect that she didn't like being beaten by Cher.*

he and Cher did not get on, he was replaced by Richard Benjamin. She has a 'housekeeping' deal at Columbia, and may do *Pincushion* (91) there: it was due to go with Jamie Lee Curtis, directed by John Carpenter, but when Cher expressed an interest it was put on hold. And she is due to play Pat Montgomery, the wife of rodeo announcer Cy Taillon; she has bought the book about them written by their daughter, Cyra McFadden. When she toured in concerts in 1990, 'Variety' reported that although audiences were paying $40 top, they spent one-third of the evening watching her on a large video while she changed her costume.

GLENN CLOSE

Close is all class. She has looks, charisma and talent. Movies could do with a few more like her – or not, as the case may be. Think of almost any of today's female Hollywood leads, and you can think of another one or more, looking almost exactly like each other But no one comes close to Close. Like Katharine Hepburn she is of good New England stock, but it is another New England-born actress that she most admires: 'Bette Davis . . . because she wasn't trying to please people. She didn't say "Love me." She had the courage to play unattractive characters with only the hope that people understand them in the end.' Her two most celebrated performances so far have been as the most unlikeable ladies, belying the serenity of her earlier roles. It must be remembered that she came to films comparatively late, but so far has had some choice roles. Let us hope she gets many more before she has to play mothers.

She was born in 1947 in Greenwich, Connecticut, to a doctor's wife. When she was five, her parents went as medical missionaries to Zaire and she was sent to boarding schools in Connecticut and Switzerland. While still in her teens she joined a pop group, 'Up the People', which sang of traditional values while all the others were protesting; the group travelled to most military installations in the US and all over the world. After five years, she said, 'I came out of it spiritually bereft and realizing that I had to start from scratch.' She enrolled at the College of William and Mary in Williamsburg, Virginia, to study speech and drama, and on graduating in 1974 was a last-minute replacement for Mary Ure, then about to star in New York in Congreve's 'Love for Love'. Back to back the same company was

The World According to Garp (82) was too offbeat to enjoy a great success – but it was, for one thing, much more intelligent and entertaining than the novel on which it was based. It also introduced us to Glenn Close, who played mother to another player who has come a long way since then, Robin Williams.

offering revivals of 'The Member of the Wedding' and 'The Rules of the Game'. She made her Broadway debut as Mary Tudor in Richard Rodgers's unsuccessful musical about Henry VIII, 'Oh Henry!', with Nicol Williamson; she was also in 'Crucifer of Blood', 'A Streetcar Named Desire' (as Stella) and 'King Lear' (as Cordelia). Television offered her good roles in two movies, starting with *Too Far to Go* (79), based on some John Updike stories with Michael Moriarty and Blythe Danner as a couple whose marriage is breaking up; Close was the other woman. The film was given a couple of theatrical bookings but did not make it on that territory. The other film was *Orphan Train*, which starred Jill Eikenberry as a social worker who took some deprived children across the US in 1894. She was playing – and singing – the wife of 'Barnum' on Broadway when she was seen by the director George Roy Hill, who offered her the role of the mother in *The World According to Garp* (82). It was in one way a splendid start, for she played a dedicated feminist with several eccentricities, but some spectators believed that she must be getting on to play Robin Williams's mother.

Lawrence Kasdan chose her to play perhaps the most important female role in *The Big Chill* (83) – the hostess, wife to Kevin Kline and mistress of the dead Alex, and the saddest, most introspective person gathered that weekend. She was Ted Danson's wife in a bold telefilm, *Something About Amelia* (84), coping when he confesses to have sexually abused their teenage daughter, and she was Robert Duvall's wife in *The Stone Boy*, the story of another sad family, but this time suffering bereavement. She opted out of taking a role in *The Bostonians* (the one

Vanessa Redgrave eventually took), because she had been offered another, in *The Natural*, as the girl who had been Robert Redford's childhood sweetheart. She was flattered that Redford wanted her, she said later, but her decision had been a mistake: it was better to take a 'rich' role in a 'little' film than an unworthy one in a big-budget production; she did not find much collaboration from the director, Barry Levinson, but thought the result much better than she had anticipated. Yes, and her presence was one of the few pleasures in that vainglorious picture. She also dubbed the voice of Andie McDowell, thought to sound too transatlantic as a British girl in *Greystoke: The Legend of Tarzan Lord of the Apes*. During this time there were two showy stage roles, in an adaptation of Nathalie Sauret's 'Childhood', in which she had to spend much of her time on the stage alone, and in 'The Singular Life of Albert Nobbs', in drag because she wants to get a job as a waiter. On Broadway she starred opposite Jeremy Irons in Tom Stoppard's 'The Sure Thing', in a role turned down by Meryl Streep and which brought her a Tony award, and she was in Michael Frayn's 'Benefactors' with Mary Beth Hurt and Sam Waterston.

Movies were ready to top-bill her: in *Maxie* (85), in which she was the prim private secretary to the bishop of San Francisco who finds her body inhabited by a raucous movie star of the roaring twenties. Close did not seem entirely happy in the second role – whose screen image, incidentally, was borrowed from some of Carole Lombard's Silent films. Despite these two special ladies it was a whimsy which strained for its scanty jokes, with a particularly strong and sympathetic performance by Mandy Patinkin as Close's confused husband. If few people heard of it, the situation was reversed with *Jagged Edge*, though she was not the original choice for the role. That was probably Meryl Streep, though the screenwriter, Joe Eszterhas, declined to name her when he discussed the actress who wanted a dozen major changes to his work. Normally, he said, the studio would side with the star, but in this case the producer, Marton Ransohoff, agreed with him. They and we were lucky to get Close, playing a smart San Francisco lawyer who elects to sleep with a client (Jeff Bridges) whom she is defending for murdering his wife. As a thriller, it was equally smart, as was *Fatal Attraction* (87), in which the lawyer (Michael Douglas) is consultant to the publisher for whom she works: a brief fling is just that to him, but to her it is her whole life – and a life is what she is prepared to take to get him back. It's a situation where she's always ahead, while he squirms – and it was a superb role for her, moving from charm to pity to neurosis, sometimes within the same scene. She smiled as she had always smiled and caressed her words, but there was poison in both as she sought to bully or humiliate the man into submission. She said she might not have accepted the role if the original script had had the present ending, borrowed from *Les Diaboliques* (written by Nicholas Meyer and not James Dearden, the credited screenwriter); it was substituted after a disappointing preview – though it is clearly superior, with Close committing suicide and leaving clues incriminating Douglas as her murderer. The film did big business in Japan (as everywhere), and was brought back some months later with the original ending, when it did even better.

During this period she saw the Royal Shakespeare Company's production of 'Les Liaisons Dangereuses' – the novel by Choderlos de Laclos, as adapted for the stage by Christopher Hampton. She thought the role of the Marquise so good that she was prepared to take it on after the RSC cast returned to London: but the Shubert Organization reported that Close was not a box-office attraction and chose to close the play rather than re-cast it. This was three weeks before *Fatal Attraction* opened, i.e. after *Jagged Edge* had made her a name to be reckoned with. Hampton recommended her for the film

Ms Close as Maxie *(85), a 20s flapper reincarnated in a modern housewife. Most whimsies start well and then fall off because they don't know where to go: this went in the other direction, but – the players aside – it was hard to sit through till some strong scenes towards the end.*

Glenn Close and John Malkovich as the scheming aristocrats in Dangerous Liaisons *(88), one of the few successful historical films of the last few years: that the original dramatic version was acclaimed in both London and New York did the film no harm at all.*

version, retitled *Dangerous Liaisons* (88), after the rights were sold to Lorimar. To simplify: the Marquise has lost her lover to the chaste Cecile (Uma Thurman), so she asks a notorious philanderer, Valmont (John Malkovich), to seduce the girl: the two plot for their own sexual satisfaction, in the course of which they destroy the young people and then themselves. Close was 'chilling' said David Ansen in 'Newsweek', 'in a performance of

controlled venom, she's superb.' 'Nothing Miss Close has done before approaches the richness and comic delicacy of her elegant performance' wrote Vincent Canby in the 'New York Times'. Peter Travers in 'People' thought it was one 'to become widely celebrated'. The whole was equally well-received, but you may be forgiven if you think it so goddam busy being tasteful that it lacked eroticism. And it was much more professional than anything director Stephen Frears had done to that point. Also, it was made at a time when period subjects had long been out of fashion, and with a cost of $17 million it did extremely well with a take of $15,500,000. A much better director, Milos Forman, was working on his own version of the book, *Valmont*, before Lorimar came on the scene; he and his backers had every reason to suppose that theirs would be the better of the two, but when it opened almost a year later there was hardly a critic who agreed: lethal reviews destroyed much hope of people wishing to see this subject twice, and it went under at just $400,000 on a budget of $33 million.

Close herself did not have a success with *Immediate Family* (89), in which she and James Woods play a infertile couple who adopt a baby – and except for *Maxie* the lightest film of her career; it cost $14 million and took just $2,100,000. After that, *Reversal of Fortune* (90), in which she plays Sunny Von Bulow, the heiress who has been in a coma since her Danish husband allegedly administered drugs and so the cause of long legal battles over his guilt, the division of the estate, etc. Jeremy Irons plays Von Bulow in the movie, which was generally well received. Then, Zeffirelli's *Hamlet*, as Gertrude, with Mel Gibson in the title-role and Alan Bates as Claudius. She discussed two films with David Puttnam, of which the first will be *Meeting Venus* (91), directed by István Szabó, a comedy about the staging of an international opera in Paris; she plays a temperamental diva and is dubbed by Kiri Te Kanawa. The second film was said to be *House of the Spirits*, based on the novel by Isabel Allende, with William Hurt. She will be seen on television in a Hallmark Hall of Fame presentation, *Sarah Plain and Tall*.

She has a daughter, Annie Maude, born in 1987, whose father, John Starke, is a producer whom Close met while making *The World According to Garp*.

KEVIN COSTNER

Sometimes they creep up on you, the new movie idols. You've seen their names on cassettes in the video stores – almost always in flops you've never heard of; you may have caught them in early supporting roles on television. After almost a dozen films of no distinction someone took a chance with Kevin Costner – but that did not mean, in the 80s, that he was here to stay. He can now look back on a short string of successes – and most people would like him to stay. Some of the male stars of the last two decades have been a bit freakish, and Costner looks comfortably ordinary at worst. At best, he reminds you of the leading men of the 30s – which is to say that he lacks the aggression notable in some of the post-war idols. He's a nice-looking guy, and he shares with another such, Jeff Bridges, a low, reedy voice which can get a lot of mileage out of intonation. He does well with a wry stare, a shy smile; the touch of raffishness (because of the sex scene) in *No Way Out* was not unattractive. Short-back-and-sides may be as essential to him as to Steve McQueen, because he stops being interesting when his hair is longer. When asked whether today's stars were as individual and attractive as those of the past he replied, 'Most are interchangeable . . . I don't think you could confuse Clark Gable with Cagney.'

He was born in Lynwood, a suburb of Los Angeles, in 1955, but his father's position with the electricity company found the family on the move throughout his childhood. He was a business major at California State University, Fullerton, where he met his wife Cindy. Returning from their honeymoon on the same plane as Richard Burton, he approached him for advice about an acting career. Exactly a month later he quit his job in marketing and found a lowly administrative job with a small studio in Hollywood: if he was going to take out trash, he said, at least it would be movie trash. His college friends were buying houses, his wife was Snow-White at Disneyland, and he and his new friends were dreaming of careers in movies. Or in his case, he said, going for interviews. In 1981 he was given a small role in *Frances*, but it was left on the cutting-room floor. His clean good looks got him the role of one of six fraternity students in *Night Shift* (82) and his youth that of a fond newly-wed on a cruise honeymoon in *Table for Five* (83). John Badham offered him a leading role in *WarGames*, but he chose instead to play the dead husband in Lawrence Kasdan's *The Big Chill* – and that in the end was all he did play, for Kasdan cut all the flashback scenes in which he had appeared, as jarring to the rest of the film. *Testament* was so favourably received when it was aired on the PBS 'American Playhouse' that it received some cinema bookings; it concerned one small-town family which survives a nuclear bomb, and starred Jane Alexander and William Devane, with Costner prominent among the supporting cast.

His first lead was in a low-budget thriller, *Stacy's Knights* (84) aka *Winning Streak*, which starred Andra Millian as a law student who takes to gambling and who declares war on the casinos when Costner, her streetwise lover and mentor, is killed. Better – and equally unseen – was *Fandango* (85), made under the auspices of Steven Spielberg by Kevin Reynolds, on whose student film, *Proof*, it was based. Costner was one of four college buddies going on a long bender before facing up to marriage and the Vietnam War. Kasdan and Badham both then gave Costner a second chance – Kasdan with *Silverado*, in which Costner is Scott Glen's younger brother, whom he rescues from jail, and Badham with *American Flyers*, written by Steve Tesich, about two brothers (the other was David Grant) engaged in a gruelling bicycle marathon. *Sizzle Beach USA* (86) was produced by Troma, a New York company which specializes in exploitation junk with absurd titles (*Rabid Grannies*, *Surf Nazis Must Die*): it found Costner involved with three girls sharing a house near Malibu, and it continued his habit of making films – the one exception was *Silverado* – which disappeared without trace. And since we are in that recondite area, mention must be made of two films made before, but shown after, he became very famous. The first is *The Gunrun-*

ner, a tawdry tale of gang warfare in Montreal in the 20s; when it surfaced in 1989 Costner observed that he didn't know that it had even been finished. Also going direct to video at this time was *Chasing Dreams*, a baseball story in which he had only one scene. And in late 1987 Universal released in Europe and elsewhere *Amazing Stories*, a collection of three episodes based on Spielberg's unsuccessful television series of the same name. Costner was in 'The Mission', playing the captain of a Flying Fortress on a bombing mission during the war. It was at this time, late 1986, that he went after the role that Nicolas Cage played in the Coens' *Raising Arizona*. The previous year he had turned down the role of the sergeant in *Platoon* (which went to Tom Berenger), because of possible distress to his brother, who had been in Vietnam. It is less clear why he rejected the role Jeff Bridges played in *Jagged Edge*, which would surely have brought him stardom two years earlier.

He was not too happy about his career, but consoled himself with the thought that the buzz came from within, 'from directors wanting to use me.' One who did was Brian De Palma, looking for someone to play Eliot Ness (the role played by Robert Stack in the 1960s television series of the same name) in *The Untouchables* (87). It was the real-life Ness, special agent of the Treasury, who in the 20s cleaned up Chicago. The picture was a considerable advance on anything De Palma had

The Untouchables *(87) was one of the best of several fine thrillers of the decade, marking a big advance for the director, Brian De Palma. It also marked the arrival at stardom for Kevin Costner, who played gangbuster Eliot Ness, here seen leading a raid on one of Al Capone's warehouses.*

And if Costner was a very welcome new star, he also managed to appear in some very good films – and none was better than Field of Dreams *(89), which was about a man who had the courage to make his dreams come true.*

from the publishing world to the Pentagon. Only the basic idea was kept from Kenneth Fearing's novel: a man has an affair with the mistress (Sean Young) of his boss (Gene Hackman) and is a witness when he murders her; told to investigate he discovers that he is the chief suspect. He was much more sympathetic in this Johnny-on-the-spot role than the rather smug Ray Milland. The film cost $15 million and took $15,500,000. He had another good one with *Bull Durham* (88), about a baseball groupie (Susan Sarandon) who every year selects a player to receive her sexual favours. Costner wasn't the player, but his mentor, who steps between the two for a sparky fight with the girl. Ron Shelton directed, and the film scored a home run with $21,900,000 at the box-office. Costner was at pains to point out that *Field of Dreams* (89) was not his second consecutive film about baseball: it was about a farmer who wanted a baseball field in his back yard. He's a man with a crazy dream, and Costner had just the edge to suggest the obsession. His scenes with a magisterial James Earl Jones, playing a reclusive author (based on J.D. Salinger in Ray Kinsella's original novella) converted to the cause, have a sweetness and strength missing from Hollywood's recent whimsies – but then these have tended to the grotesque, e.g. *Gremlins*. For many people this film evoked *It's a Wonderful Life*, but as directed by Phil Alden Robinson, it had a spirit closer to the innocent-men-with-dreams films of the 20s. Costner observed that this was the third consecutive movie he had made which had had difficulty finding backing. It cost $16 million and Universal were so wary of the twin dangers of baseball and whimsy – both box-office risks – that they sold off the foreign theatrical rights, leaving them with an outlay of only $5 million, plus ad costs. The return in the US was a heavenly $30,300,000.

He took a risk with his new-found popularity by playing an unsympathetic character in *Revenge* (90), an ex-Navy pilot having a passionate affair with the wife of his chum Anthony Quinn, who is inclined, when he finds out, to take ruthless revenge: but that risk was justified, for the film to date has taken over $15 million. He was also Executive Producer, and therefore saw this updating of *One-Eyed Jacks* through a stormy post-production. He said, 'I hope that when people look in the paper and see my name they'll say, "There's always a story in his work, there's always come out of the movie feeling something.' His fee at this time is said to be $3 million per film. He directs, as well as stars in *Dances With Wolves*, a Western for Orion, with whom he has a deal for two further pictures, announced

done up to that time, but David Mamet, who wrote the clever script, later said that he loathed the 'Odessa Steps' sequence ('borrowed' from Eisenstein) used at the climax. Costner, who was paid $800,000 for the role, got top-billing, but was bolstered by two names who received guest credits – Sean Connery, playing a cop helping in the good fight, and Robert De Niro, who was Al Capone. Their box-office insurance was needed, for the film cost $30 million. It took $36,900,000. Its producer, Art Linson, said: 'Kevin had just the combination of innocence, enthusiasm, earnestness and leading-man looks we were looking for. He's one of a small group of actors who fit the bill for middle-American, middle-thirties, leading-man parts. That means Kevin Costner could get very rich.'

What he got immediately was another excellent movie – another thriller – *No Way Out*, a remake of *The Big Clock*, directed by Roger Donaldson, with the action transferred as *Mick*, a life of the Irish patriot Michael Collins (originally a project for director Michael Cimino at Nelson/Columbia and *American Sportsman*. However, he will first appear in *Prince of Thieves* (91), one of three films about Robin Hood announced simultaneously. The script of this one was apparently in better shape than the other two, and once Morgan Creek/Warner Bros had signed Costner to the lead the prospects for the two rivals was much lessened; at this writing it seems as though one will be made as a telefilm and the other abandoned.

TOM CRUISE

It is not entirely clear why Tom Cruise should have streaked so far ahead of his brothers in the brat-pack, though luck would have something to do with it. In an article on this group of actors, written before Cruise hit it really big, 'New York' magazine called him 'The Hottest of Them All'. Perhaps there was something in the climate. 'It's just Tom Cruise doing his thing,' said one young lady of *Cocktail*, to which the reply must be that he hasn't got one. Clark Gable had a thing, so did James Cagney and Gary Cooper. He is their heir. If they are looking down, you can bet they're surprised.

He was born in Syracuse, New York, in 1962, the third of four children and the only boy – all of them sufferers from dyslexia in varying degrees. His father was an electrical engineer whose work took him to various parts of the country; but the parents were divorced when Tom was eleven, when his mother took them to live in Louisville; when she remarried they relocated to Glenn Ridge, New Jersey. Cruise hesitated between the Church (he studied for a year at a Franciscan seminary) and the sports-field as the scene of his future endeavours, but decided on the stage after playing the role of Nathan Detroit in 'Guys and Dolls' in high school. He bussed tables in New York till Franco Zeffirelli auditioned him for a role as one of the fellow-students of the teenage lovers in his vacuous *Endless Love* (81). That enabled him to get another small role, as a side-kick in *Taps*, to an aggressive cadet at military school, David Shawn, but while rehearsing, the director, Harold Becker, decided to promote him to the role of Shawn. Cruise felt that because his own role had already been enlarged, and since the whole set-up was so new to him, he should refuse, till it was pointed out that they were not going to beg him to play it. It was a showy role, for Shawn becomes deranged before being shot by the National Guard. This

brought him offers to play other psychotic youngsters, but to avoid type-casting he accepted a more 'sensitive' role, the lead in *Losin' It* (83), called *Tijuana* while in production, which probably tells you more about it than you would want to know: if not – well, the title applies to him, one of three teenagers on a spree. He later referred to it as his 'cable classic'.

Auditioning for Francis Coppola for *The Outsiders*, he told him that he wanted to work for him, to which the answer must be, Yes, but not in this particular film, a bilious teen pic from a novel by S.E. Hinton. Coppola decided to film it after receiving a letter from a school in Fresno saying that he had been nominated to turn it into a movie. The story gives them – the rival gangs, the Greasers and the Socs (set back in the 60s) – 'a kind of beauty and nobility,' boasted the director, presumably referring to the fact that a couple of the members quote Robert Frost and go into a deserted church to read 'Gone With the Wind'. There is nothing intrinsically wrong with trying to make mythic heroes out of young punks, and it could be claimed that those playing them were later to attain mythic status: for billed above Cruise were (in order) C. Thomas Howell, Matt Dillon, Ralph Macchio, Patrick Swayze, Rob Lowe and Emilio Estevez, the brat-pack in its first flowering. Cruise put himself in the hands of Hollywood's biggest agency, CAA, and found himself in another hymn to teenism, *Risky Business*, about an adolescent who has Adventures while his parents are away, mainly of a sexual variety, for a hooker (Rebecca De Mornay) moves in to turn the family mansion into a fancy brothel. Cruise pitched his bewildered innocent somewhere between lumpishness and 'gee whiz' wistfulness, which gave a touch of class to the opportunistic whole, which also benefited from a joyous dance to celebrate parent-free freedom in his jockey-shorts. The film took $28,500,000, but from his point of view *All the Right Moves* was not too well named, for its rental figure clocked in at $8 million. He played a high school football player locked in conflict with his hot-headed coach (Craig T. Nelson). Before either of these came out Cruise auditioned for Paul Newman, who was looking for someone to play his son in *Harry and Son*, but he decided that he was too young. The role was played by Robby Benson, of whom little has been heard since: 'I saved your career, kid,' Newman said later to Cruise.

Legend (85) proved to be a decisively wrong move, as Cruise limned 'a woodland boy in harmony with nature's magic', one in love with a princess (Mia Sara) in this pseudo-

Grimm tale of evil wizards and hobgoblins. When Errol Flynn played Robin Hood, his producers knew exactly what qualities they wanted him to project, but this director, Ridley Scott, seemed only interested in his special effects. Cruise went down with the ship, an epic of mistaken malarkey, which arrived in the US after much trimming and a new score after Europe (it was made in Britain) had rejected it. 20th-Century-Fox were the losers in those territories, and Universal in the States: they had combined to meet the huge budget of $30 million, of which American distribution returned only $6,100,000. That was not, of course, Cruise's fault, for what's a fella to do when confronted with material like this? The film took over a year to make and was produced by Arnon Milchan, whose *The King of Comedy* also lost a packet. It was reported that Cruise's salary had gone to over $1 million after *Risky Business*, and while he was making *Legend* it was reported that he now had casting approval and script consultation. When he was first offered *Top Gun* (86), he agreed to do it only if the script was improved, and while waiting for a new one he visited the Naval Fighter Weapons School in Miramar, California (where the film was set), for ideas. He also asked for some new sequences to be shot after filming was finished, but it was never quite clear what plot there was beyond the fact that a military instructress (Kelly McGillis) makes it with a maverick cadet because he's doing strange, wonderful things over the Indian Ocean in his MIG fighter and she's using his knowledge because she wants to get on. 'This gives me a hard-on,' says one cadet during a lecture on MIG tactics, and as directed by Tony Scott (Ridley's brother) this was entirely the film's attitude to the weaponry on view. It sold glamour, and audiences bought it, which with Stallone ramboing on and sabres being rattled in the White House seemed to reflect a return to America's hawkish values after the shame of Vietnam. Hoping for another *Officer and a Gentleman* and looking at the producers' track record, which included *Beverly Hills Cop* and *Flashdance*, Paramount had budgeted it at $14 million. It took $79,400,000, the year's most popular film, with over $20 million more than its nearest rival, *The Karate Kid Part II*.

The Color of Money was directed by Martin Scorsese and featured Paul Newman playing the same character that he had done years earlier in *The Hustler*, a poolroom champ. Here, he emerges from retirement to teach young Cruise the tricks of the trade. The piece is nicely made and played, but beyond a portrait of a certain underbelly of America it all adds up to no more than an anecdote, so

it said much for the drawing-power of the two stars that it returned Disney $24,400,000 on an $18 million investment. Roger Donaldson's *Cocktail* (88) was hardly more substantial, feather-brained stuff, little different from many a Silent Screen outing about a determined youngster on the make – Cruise, tending bar while studying business on the side. He's given a mentor (Bryan Brown) and an on-off affair with a rich girl (Elizabeth Shue) – oh yes, and super values, walking out on the woman keeping him because she won't give him a job, spurning the advances of his best friend's wife and insulting the rich girl's father when he tries to pay him off. The script (by Heywood Gould, from his novel) had been hanging around Hollywood for some years, and was unenthusiastically accepted by Disney, who thought the result might be like *The Graduate*, and they 'didn't want to make a dark movie'. It might have been harsher, but not with Smiling Jim – for apart from a not unengaging perkiness it was hard to see what more Cruise had to offer. But someone had done something very right, at least commercially, for the film cost $17 million and took $36,400,000.

Cruise had made it while waiting to begin *Rain Man*, which was delayed till Dustin Hoffman thought the script right. He and Cruise played brothers, long separated, who are reunited when Cruise – playing a salesman of expensive imported cars – decides that he, and not the 'dummy' brother, should receive their father's legacy. Though Hoffman won an Oscar, Cruise had the more interesting character, and he coasted beautifully with it, to another big financial success (see Hoffman). Cruise was paid $3 million, half of Hoffman's fee, but he had told his agent that he wasn't concerned with money and that his career would be in fine shape if he could only work with the best scripts and directors.

One of the best contemporary directors has to be Oliver Stone, who in 1987 was paired with Cruise for a project which never got off the ground, *Tom Mix and Pancho Villa*. Stone had a screenplay deposited at Universal, which he had once planned to do with Al Pacino; Stone had come a long way since then, and the studio's new head, Tom Pollock, told him that they would do *Born on the Fourth of July* (89) if he could bring it in 'real cheap', yet with a major star. Stone considered Sean Penn, Charlie Sheen and Nicolas Cage along with Cruise, who shared with the film's real life protagonist, Ron Kovic, his Catholicism, his working-class background and his drive – as David Puttnam once put it, 'Cruise has got an incredible want-to-be about him, and deservedly so.' Kovic had been wounded in Vietnam and reduced to being

Tom Cruise's route to superstardom: 1) as the youngster in Risky Business *(83), who has a field-day at the family mansion while his parents are on vacation, and ends up dancing in his underwear on the sofa 2) as the fighter pilot in* Top Gun *(86) 3) as the young entrepreneur learning to mix a wicked one in* Cocktail *(87) 4) and as the greedy auto salesman who learns to love his estranged, autistic brother in* Rain Man *(88).*

This doesn't look much like the young man on the preceding page, but Oliver Stone's Born on the Fourth of July *(89) proved Cruise to be a terrific actor when he wanted to be. He looked like himself at the beginning of the film, and this shows him after he has been horribly mutilated in Vietnam, and now a passionate campaigner against the War.*

bound to a wheelchair – and certainly Cruise was perfectly cast as an all-American boy who goes to serve in Vietnam for the most patriotic of motives. He returns, wounded, in the same mood, but as he faces life as a semi-vegetable he becomes anguished and bitter about life, finding salvation in campaigning against that war and perhaps war in general. His pilgrimage to rebirth is very moving, and, said Richard T. Jameson in New York's 'Seven Days', 'Tom Cruise has a big share in that victory. There's growing conviction that his performance was the best thing about *Rain Man*: his work as Ron Kovic should ensure he's never again classified as merely an up-scale Rob Lowe.' David Denby in 'New York' magazine called it 'a powerful and heartbreaking piece of work dominated by Cruise's impassioned performance', while in Britain, Derek Malcolm of the 'Guardian' said: 'Of course, he is naturally very good in the early scenes, where he has to play the country boy turned war hero. But the second half of the film is a huge test for him, and he survives it triumphantly. He doesn't even look the same healthy, clean-cut boy we knew before.' The film cost $18 million ($4 million more than Universal intended) and to date has taken over $70 million. Cruise lost the widely-tipped Oscar to Daniel Day-Lewis, but won a Golden Globe: and no one who saw the televised ceremony would forget the look of joy on Kovic's face as the award was announced.

Cruise's achievement put him on the cover of most of the nation's magazines, who were in no doubt that he was now Hollywood's biggest star, able to command $8 million per film; but, well you can't have everything, his two-year marriage to the actress Mimi Rogers was over. And *Days of Thunder* (90), a reunion with the director and producers of *Top Gun*, a film about auto-racing, was not well received – with more than one critic complaining that it was just *Top Gun* on wheels, with no hint in Cruise's performance that his last movie had established him as a major talent. There was consolation for him, however: his huge fee had helped push the budget to $55 million, and the film would take over $81 million in its first three months – though it was expected to drop sharply thereafter. With some of 1990's bumper crop of movies doing much better, Cruise was somewhat less 'hot' than a year earlier. But he was probably still the most sought-after star of all. He turned down *Edward Scissorhands*, which went to Johnny Depp, and one of the leads in *Backdraft*. But he was said to be doing Stone's movie about Jim Morrison of *The Doors* (though he himself didn't); *Rush*, in which he will play the husband of a female cop; *Innocent Millionaire*, directed by Peter Weir from Stephen Vizinczey's novel; *Such Good Men* with Michelle Pfeiffer; and *What Makes Sammy Run?*, directed by Sidney Lumet. Or some of these, anyway.

WILLEM DAFOE

Interviewers are agreed that Willem Dafoe is a confident, contented man. 'I do like my face,' he told one of them. 'I really do. I can't be coy about that, and I feel fine saying it because I had nothing to do with it. It was a gift. I like it because it's changeable, you know? . . . I don't think I have a clear picture of how I look, and I don't think anyone else does. And that's wonderful.' In some stills he is as handsome as any Hollywood idol of the past, but most of the time he looks different, reflecting his versatility. And that, more than looks, is what cinemagoers want in the post-Brando era.

He was born in Appletown, Wisconsin, in 1955, the son of a surgeon and a nurse and one of eight children. He studied drama at high school, but decided that his classes had little to do with theatre, so he dropped out and joined an experimental group in Milwaukee, Theatre X, which toured in Europe as well as the States. To make ends meet, he got a job binding 'Penthouse' magazine, but in 1978 took off for New York, 'for the possibility of making a living as an actor. That's all I really wanted.' What he did not want was to work on or off Broadway, since he did not like what he saw there. He joined another avant-garde troupe, the Wooster Group, whose work he did not totally understand, but he found it exciting. It was run then and now by Elizabeth LeCompte, the mother of his son. ('No one can say we're not a union.') He began in films with an unbilled walk-on in *Heaven's Gate* (80) and then was the vicious head of a gang of bikers in Kathryn Bigelow's *The Loveless*, which seems to have had some scattered showings three years later. A similar fate seems to have befallen *New York Nights*, a soft-porn modernized version of 'La Ronde', with Dafoe staying dressed for a minute role as a boyfriend in the final episode, 'The Financier and the Debutante'. He played a guy in a phone booth in Tony Scott's *The Hunger* (83), undoubtedly pleased to be in a horror film, because Boris Karloff was one of his heroes.

His break came when he was offered the lead in John Mark Robinson's *Roadhouse 66* (84), stranded in a small Arizona town with rich Judge Reinhold, with whom he had hitched a lift. It passed almost unnoticed, however, but a week later he turned up in Walter Hill's *Streets of Fire* as another biker, a malevolent leather-jacketed thug who kidnaps rock star Diane Lane. Seemingly type-cast, he was a psychotic counterfeiter and killer, second-billed in William Friedkin's panorama of car chases, *To Live and Die in LA* (85), either of which would have been preferable to

Willem Dafoe as the sergeant determined on justice in Platoon *(86), Oliver Stone's impassioned drama about the Vietnam war. It also won an Academy Award as Best Picture, which may be why Oscar is always so fascinating, since it was a very different thing from the anodyne* Out of Africa, *which took that award the previous year.*

watching this picture. With others of the Wooster Theater Group he was in Ken Kobland's *The Communists are Comfortable* (and Three Other Stories), a 16 mm experimental film, a tribute to film-maker Hollis Frampton and writer Clifford Odets, who had been a second father to Kobland, who also wrote and directed. It was shown at the Collective for Living Cinema in New York, and then at the Berlin Festival, which exhausted its limited audience. It was Dafoe's last minority film.

He became well known after Oliver Stone tested him and cast him in *Platoon* (86) as Sergeant Elias, who is determined that the truth be told about the slaughter of civilians in Vietnam. Stone was later to say: 'There's this saintly quality to him. He's a gentle soul, he has a big heart. But the thing about Willem is that his judgement is not as refined as some other actors I know, because he has such a voracious curiosity. He's an experimentalist, and for that reason I think he'll do a proportion of clinkers in his time. He's gonna make mistakes. But he's gonna grow. And what he does will always be interesting.' Well, yes and no. *Off Limits* (87) contained an interesting, tense, Dafoe performance, but the film itself was standard action fare as he and fellow-cop Gregory Hines arrive in Saigon to investigate the murder of six prostitutes. Why should the American military police be concerned? Because each of the victims had had a child by an American soldier. After failing in the US, the film was retitled *Saigon* for foreign markets. 'It's not my favourite,' said Dafoe tersely. 'The people making it didn't quite give the director what he needed to make it and it really fell apart.'

His best chance yet came when Martin Scorsese chose him to play Jesus in *The Last Temptation of Christ* (88) – not Scorsese's first choice, but then the project had been around for years. As early as 1982 Paramount had accepted a second-draft script, but then watched *The Right Stuff* go over budget and feared this would do the same, as it was to be made far from control, first in Israel and then in Morocco; the studio also began receiving hate-mail. Scorsese managed to trim the budget from $16 million to $7 million, but Paramount pulled out. He tried to get financing in France, to no avail, but once Universal agreed to distribute, Cinéplex Odéon brought forth a loan and the film was made for a modest $6,700,000, which did not permit a name star. Attempts to ban it and picket it attracted huge queues for the first few days, but business fell off disastrously, and the film took only $3,740,000 – which must be good news for the idiots and bigots who tried to ban it. For this interpretation, from the novel by Nikos Kazantzakis, is as valid for our times as is anything in the history of religious art. It is persuasive that this is what happened in Israel almost 1988 years ago; it is honest and

courageous, and so what if Christ was an exhibitionist and St Paul an opportunist? As for Christ's 'blasphemous' yearning for Mary Magdalene during the Crucifixion, who in this day and age would deny that any human being is also a sexual being? And if he were not human, might he not wonder about the most pleasurable experience available to mankind? Dafoe trod carefully through this, which was made with high competence rather than inspiration, but that was just what was needed.

Mississippi Burning also provoked some controversy – about whether it was historically accurate and whether it was wise to resurrect the Mississippi murder case of 1964 involving three Civil Rights workers, especially when all whites are seen to be such bigots. Except, that is, the two FBI agents – the liberal, intellectual, bespectacled Dafoe and the genial, hot-headed man, also from the South, Gene Hackman. The film took $15 million, just $300,000 more than it cost, but the next Dafoe film was a gigantic success: *Born on the Fourth of July* (89), which was not Dafoe's film but Tom Cruise's. Or rather, director Oliver Stone's. Dafoe had the larger of the two cameo roles (Tom Berenger did the other), as the paraplegic drowning in Tequila who befriends Cruise – a friendship which goes foully and foolishly wrong as they act out their frustration and bitterness on each other. This

It took Martin Scorsese a long time to bring The Last Temptation of Christ *(88) to the screen, but it was worth the struggle, for it offered for this generation many new insights into the most famous story ever told; and although Dafoe's Jesus may be the most flawed of all the screen Christs, he was also the most sympathetic – if that's what Jesus is meant to be.*

was Dafoe again physically transformed, and so he was in *Triumph of the Spirit*, the true story of a Jewish-Greek man who survived Auschwitz because he won his boxing-matches instead of losing them. Originally offered a supporting role, he demanded the lead – of Arnold Kopelson, who had produced *Platoon*. Salamo Arouch, in the film played by Dafoe, was in fact the consultant. Robert M. Young directed, on location in the concen-tration camp, but with results not entirely as gruelling as they might have been. 'People may not want to see it but they know they are going to have to,' said Kopelson, who was proved quickly wrong. They were going to have to only if the press told them to do so, which they did not, in generally respectful reviews. Produced and distributed indepen-dently, it cost $15 million and took only $200,000 at the box-office.

Wanting to play a villain again, Dafoe did so in *Wild at Heart* (90), 'malignantly charis-matic' (said 'Variety'), as one who is sexually and physically a threat to the anti-establishment hero, Nicolas Cage. He perhaps enjoyed working with director David Lynch, renowned for his grotesque films, and he wanted to work with John Waters, known if not renowned for his tacky comedies. Thus he was one of several names in *Cry-Baby*, as a hateful prison guard. (In *Wild at Heart* Dafoe sported a hommage-to-Waters pencil-line moustache.) Next up: *Flight of the Intruder*, with Danny Glover. Not next up: *Arrive Alive*, in which he should have played a hotel detective. Indeed, he was doing so on loca-tions in Florida, when the decision was made to inject more slapstick. Dafoe decided that this was not his style, and left amicably. Six days later, Paramount pulled the plug on the picture.

TED DANSON

One critic, reviewing *Dad*, said that Ted Danson was the best light comedian in the world – which was tempting providence, since Jack Lemmon was also in the film. Would anyone settle for the second best light come-dian in the world? For some years now his bartender – formerly owner – of 'Cheers' has delighted millions. Sam Malone is ever-hopeful, ever-optimistic, a jock with a big head, a big heart and an itchy prick. He has had a big yen for both his leading ladies, Shelley Long and Kirstie Alley, both uppity dames in their different ways, but he has always been ready to overlook that when they show signs of admitting what he knows to be true, that he is irresistible. Lemmon is the

Not Sam the barman from 'Cheers', whom we all know and love, but Ted Danson in his first movie, The Onion Field *(79), pre-'Cheers', as the cop who is brutally murdered in the first reel.*

most outstanding of his predecessors in a line going back to William Powell – but no further, since we are talking about the Sound era when their vowels and consonants can wander over a veritable glissando; at the same time Danson can be witty with his hands, his eyes, his chin.

He was born in 1947 in San Diego, the son of a naval officer and brought up chiefly in Flagstaff, Arizona. He was educated at Stan-ford University, where he discovered theatre, and went on to the Carnegie Mellon Univer-sity in Pittsburgh, where he graduated in drama. His first New York appearance was in 'The Real Inspector Hound', and he gained experience with Joseph Papp's Shakespeare in the Park before appearing in two television soaps, 'The Doctors' and 'Somerset'. In 1978 he became teacher and manager at the Actors Institute; he also married and decided to move to Los Angeles. 'You only move to LA for one reason,' he said later. 'To make it. That's when I confronted ambition.' He log-ged a nice little credit almost immediately, when Joseph Wambaugh chose him to play the partner-policeman who is killed at the beginning of *The Onion Field* (79). There followed a television movie in which he starred, and another in which you were unlikely to forget him: *Once Upon a Spy* (80), as a chess and computer expert who is lured by a glamorous secret agent (Eleanor Parker) into working for a demented genius (Christ-opher Lee) bent on destroying the world; and *The Women's Room*, as the caddish husband ditched by an emancipated Lee Remick. He has a small but crucial role in Lawrence Kasdan's *Body Heat* (81), as the volatile Jewish cop who is instrumental in William

Hurt's undoing. *Creepshow* (82) was directed by George A. Romero from four tired horror stories by Stephen King, with Danson in the episode 'Something to Tide You Over', as a man buried up to his neck in sand by his mistress's jealous husband. Then came 'Cheers', the Boston bar, with its fun and freshness – the latter quality stemming partly from the fact that its writers and producers (who were often the same) wanted new faces to match the new angles they were bringing to the sitcom business.

It has kept him busy for several months every year ever since, though he has made an occasional movie: *Cowboy* (83) for television, starring James Brolin, in a supporting role as a crippled ex-rodeo performer; *Something About Amelia* (84), also for TV, as a supposedly married man whose wife (Glenn Close) has to face that their daughter is not lying when accusing him of incest; Alan Sharp's *Little Treasure* (85), as an American bum helping a stripper (Margot Kidder) to find the money her father (Burt Lancaster) buried in Mexico years before; and, for television, *When the Bough Breaks*, as a child psychologist drawn out of seclusion after the death of a child molester in his office. He produced the last of these, one of the two titles to bear witness to the fact that he is a member of an organization called 'Futures for Children'. He

is the founder of another, 'The American Oceans Campaign', because he lives by the sea and 'your kids can't go swimming in it because it's full of junk and toxics . . . You realize – without being too noble about it – that you want to do something.' He added that 'Cheers' paid immensely well, 'now', an indication that he was well rewarded for signing again after his five-year contract was up – for almost certainly it could not have survived the loss of both Ms Long and him. 'It is a good show,' he agreed, but, 'Why am I self-critical? I mean I have my basic actor-guilt that I'm living in Los Angeles, and I pick up the "New York Times" and see people I know are doing serious theatre.' He added that most of his next batch of movies were 'career-choices' rather than anything he was burning to do, and that it wasn't for a couple of years more that he considered he had the 'weight' for a leading man.

One of the movie roles he had done was to escape from Sam's 'nice-guy' image, and he did so again in *Just Between Friends* (86), as husband to Mary Tyler Moore and lover of career woman Christine Lahti, contentedly enjoying the favours of both till they meet up and become friends without knowing how much they have in common. *A Fine Mess* had started out as a remake of Laurel and Hardy's *The Music Box* with Burt Reynolds, but when

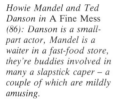

Howie Mandel and Ted Danson in A Fine Mess *(86): Danson is a small-part actor, Mandel is a waiter in a fast-food store, they're buddies involved in many a slapstick caper – a couple of which are mildly amusing.*

Reynolds and Blake Edwards parted after the failure of *The Man Who Loved Women*, it changed considerably. It is not a homage or even a rip-off, but, 'It's as if you took the Marx Brothers, Laurel and Hardy and every great comedy star of that era, and put them in a blender' (Edwards). None of them would have looked quite so great in this well-titled movie, which features a racehorse, a piano and car chases. Danson plays a small-part actor who starts off the whole chase when he overhears two crooks plotting; he does sometimes rise above his material, unlike his amiable co-star, Howie Mandel. The reception of neither of these films suggested that Danson was one of those television stars who could draw audiences away to the big screen, so when he broke from 'Cheers' that year he stayed with the small one, again also as producer: *We Are the Children* (87), as a TV newsman who falls in love with a doctor (Ally Sheedy) newly arrived at a clinic for the starving in Ethiopia.

When Disney came to film *Three Men and a Baby* they used their usual cunning casting sense: Tom Selleck and Steve Guttenberg were big or biggish names, associated with a light approach to their material; Danson might not mean as much to cinemagoers, but his comic experience would make them and the film look better. Thus he became the vain, philandering TV actor whose enigmatic warning lands them with the baby, to cause them much confusion when he returns from filming. The film was a gigantic hit (see Selleck), which brought Danson the Victor Lanoux role in the remake of *Cousin Cousine*, called simply *Cousins* (89), now a teacher of ballroom dancing. Isabella Rossellini was the lady, facing the fact with him that their spouses are having an affair and, although attracted, unwilling – for a while – to do anything about it. The result, written by Stephen Metcalfe and directed by Joel Schumaker, was one of the funniest comedies in a while, and deserved to do better than its tidy $9,400,000 (on a $13 million budget). *Dad* was the one with Lemmon, and Danson was his son, showing a sudden filial concern when the old boy is taken ill. It was great to see them together – till sentimentality engulfs them, as devised and directed by Gary David Goldberg (making his movie debut after working on television's 'Family Ties'). With a surer hand the film would surely have made back more than its $10 million (on a $19 million budget).

Next up: *Three Men and a Little Lady* (90), a sequel. Meanwhile, there is always 'Cheers' which, miracle of miracles, is virtually as fresh and funny now as when it started – as is reflected in the 1990 Emmy nominations (including one for Danson, his seventh: and

this time he won, the Outstanding Actor in a Comedy Series) and its usual position as one of the top rated programmes across the country.

Danson and Sean Young in Cousins *(89), 'a joyful romantic comedy from Paramount about the changing lives and loves of two families' – at least, that's how Paramount's publicity described it. The reality was something else.*

DANIEL DAY-LEWIS

Laurence Olivier died in 1989, just as Kenneth Branagh was launching the film of *Henry V*, which he wrote and directed, and in which he starred. The coincidence made some journalists, especially in the US, wonder whether Branagh was the new Olivier. Then, when Branagh's performance was nominated for the annual awards at the end of the year he seldom looked like being strong competition against Daniel Day-Lewis. For *My Left Foot* this second young British actor swept all before him. This is not to say that Day-Lewis is the next Olivier, for which over the years there have been many failed claimants. Certainly it does not now look likely that Day-Lewis will seek greatness on the stage, as Olivier did. But it would seem that we have a chameleon of an actor, one gifted with sensitivity and authority. Because of his looks and the Oscar won while so young he may become a leading romantic actor in Hollywood – if that is what he and Hollywood want (and with the British film industry in its depressed state let us at least hope he will dazzle us with his versatility from there). But the closest analogy with Olivier is one that both actors probably would have appreciated – that other actors are in awe of him.

His antecedents augured well for his profession. His mother is Jill Balcon, herself an actress and the daughter of Michael Balcon, the British film producer; his father was Cecil Day-Lewis, the Oxford professor and Poet Laureate. Daniel was born in 1957, probably

The changing face of the man who may be the best young actor on the screen today. Above, Daniel Day-Lewis as the gay punk in My Beautiful Laundrette *(85), right, as the English-born, New York-based art dealer in* Stars and Bars *(87), and opposite page, as the tormented human 'vegetable', Christy Brown, in* My Left Foot *(89), which brought him an Oscar for the year's Best Actor.*

in London, though one studio hand-out says Ireland, and the actor certainly prefers to be considered Irish–Jewish rather than English. Another studio biog states that he spent his childhood summers in Mayo and Connemara. Cecil Day-Lewis's political views were left-wing, so the boy was sent to a local primary school till he was eleven, when his parents' worries about his accent made them pack him off to a public school in Sevenoaks. He soon left, to make for his sister's school, Bedales, where he was allowed to stay and where he developed skills as a cabinet-maker. He also acted well enough in school plays to impress his mother who, in any case, was not without connections, so that he had a small role as an upper-class delinquent in *Sunday, Bloody Sunday* (71). In 1972, after his father's death, he had a spell in a mental hospital. At fifteen he was with the National Youth Theatre, after which he studied at the Bristol Old Vic school and was one of the three students annually transferred to that company's theatre, where he played in 'Edward II', 'Look Back in Anger' and 'Dracula', among others. He had a small speaking part in *Gandhi* (82), and he toured for the RSC as Romeo before taking over the lead in 'Another Country' from Rupert Everett. He left that to take on a goodish movie role in *The Bounty* (84), as the foppish First Mate replaced by Mel Gibson on the outward voyage.

His film break came when he heard about *My Beautiful Laundrette* (85), a modestly budgeted film to be made with the co-operation of Channel 4. Day-Lewis wrote to the director, Stephen Frears, to say that if he didn't get the role he would break his legs. (They had originally met when he auditioned for the role of playwright Joe Orton in *Prick Up Your Ears*, which was postponed and eventually filmed with Gary Oldman.) Day-Lewis explained later that the letter was meant to prove that anyone wanting that part so badly 'deserved it [and] it may have convinced [him] that my exterior hid some aggression' – for the role was that of a south London punk who has an affair with the Pakistani owner of the laundrette who is a schoolchum, Gordon Warnecke. The film's reception was out of all proportion to its modest virtues, but there were hardly any virtues in *A Room With a View* (86), which was curiously accepted as a masterpiece by some critics. A manhandling of E.M. Forster's novel by the deadly duo of director James Ivory and writer Ruth Prawer Jhabvala, it abounded in anachronisms and showed not the least understanding of either the text or the period – except in Day-Lewis's performance, *even* when he was sharing the screen with a miscast Helena Bonham-Carter.

He played her fiancé Cecil Vyse, with all his snobbishness, pretension and condescension. The two films were seen in the US almost simultaneously, which did him a great deal of good, but he played a third supporting role in another low-budget prestige number, the Anglo-French *Nanou*, directed by Conny Templeman. Nanou (Imogen Stubbs) is a tiresome English student who drifts into an almost masochistic existence with a French factory-worker and political activist; Day-Lewis is the ex-boyfriend who goes to visit and might perhaps persuade her to leave. He virtually erupts into the torpor of the thing, quite funny as a certain sort of gauche, intense Englishman: when he leaves, the film dies with him. It was not widely seen.

As much may be said of the next two. He ceded his role in *Withnail and I* to Richard E. Grant when offered the lead in an important Hollywood film, *The Unbearable Lightness of Being* (88). It was actually made in France with a distinguished team assembled by producer Saul Zaentz (himself a winner of two recent Best Picture Oscars, for *One Flew Over the Cuckoo's Nest* and *Amadeus*) – photographer Sven Nykvist, Buñuel's writer Jean-Claude Carrière, who had penned the screenplay with the director Philip Kaufman, from a novel by Milan Kundera set in Prague in 1968. Day-Lewis played a brain surgeon whose life, to put it simply, is complicated by his philandering. A rich, dark film, it was also almost three hours long: neither Day-Lewis nor Lena Olin meant a light at the American box-office and the film returned only $4,500,000 on a $17 million investment. It had long since gone from cinemas when the National Society of Critics in the US voted it the Best Film of the Year. *Stars and Bars* cost $8 million and returned only $100,000, though it has to be said that it was one of those films Columbia made during David Puttnam's aegis which was slagged off after he left. Pat O'Connor directed from William Boyd's novel and script about a middle-aged (only he wasn't any longer) English chappie set down in Dogpatch as represented by darkest Georgia in order to buy a Renoir from rube Harry Dean Stanton. It moved from Peter Arno to Charles Addams with confidence, the grotesques over-playing neatly and Day-Lewis underplaying beautifully in the midst of them, revealing himself the most promising British light comedian since Rex Harrison.

While at a party in Dublin with O'Connor he met Noel Pearson, who was planning to film *My Left Foot* (89) in partnership with Jim Sheridan, another Irish theatre man; Sheridan wrote the script with Shane Connaughton, the only one of the three with cinema experience. Day-Lewis received this through the post and

agreed to take the part before financing was completed. Granada Television came in when it looked like falling through, to a total which was the equivalent of $2 million. For few people regarded the result as having any box-office appeal. The film was based on the autobiography of Christy Brown, a victim of cerebral palsy whose frustrations were somewhat relieved when he learnt to paint with his foot. No matter that the real Christy Brown was generally an unsympathetic character, the film is about the triumph of the human spirit, as a creature given up as a vegetable or a cretin struggles to transform himself. An episodic script follows Christy from birth to marriage, often movingly – and perhaps never more so than in his youth when the family finally gets professional help in coping. Fiona Shaw plays the therapist, who was to encourage him also to read the classics, a step towards writing his memoirs and national fame. Those making the film were determined that it would, above all, be about a Dublin working-class family – being Catholic, it is large, and in the heart of it is the 'misfit'. Day-Lewis also learnt to paint with his foot, and his exhausting preparations for the role included studying victims of the disease at first hand for eight weeks. It is an extraordinary performance, never demanding sympathy though strong in humour, and always alive to the anger, frustration, despair and bitterness. As the boy Christy, Gary O'Conor is also

exceptional, with further outstanding performances by Ray McAnally as the resentful, uncomprehending father and Brenda Fricker as the passive mother, observing quietly at the end that *she* had always understood Christy.

Day-Lewis went on to do *Eversmile New Jersey*, an American independent production directed by Carlos Sorin, which cast him as an American dentist motorcycling through Patagonia to make the locals more aware of the virtues of dentistry. He accepted the role because he had caught Sorin's only previous film (*The King and his Movie*) at the London Film Festival, and he described this one as 'a kind of religious allegory. Mad, absolutely barmy.' Immediately afterwards he accepted an invitation to return to the National Theatre (where he had already done 'The Futurist', as Mayakovsky) to play Hamlet, which he did to warm but not outstanding notices. He did not know the play well, and found resonances with his own life – a famous father who died (after a long illness) when he was young, to whom he was not close and to whom he felt himself to be a disappointment. At one performance when the Ghost appeared in the Bedchamber scene, Day-Lewis left the stage, overcome with terror. His breakdown was diagnosed as due to overwork and he considered giving up acting. (The role was taken over at a later date by Ian Charleson, who had already spent some time at the National, and for whom this production had originally been planned.)

The reception of his last two films could hardly have cheered him. *Eversmile New Jersey* was regarded as virtually unshowable, and *My Left Foot* was turned down by the Cannes Film Festival. It was popular in Ireland but it disappeared in Britain at a speed of knots and was available on video two weeks later. Derek Malcolm of the 'Guardian' called Day-Lewis's performance 'exceptionally good' and observed that 'the great plus about the film is that it dares to be funny as well as moving'. The American notices, however, were even more enthusiastic and for him a personal triumph: 'a towering performance – fierce, witty and moving' said Peter Travers in 'Rolling Stone'. At the end of the year he began to pick up almost every award going for the year's Best Actor, including citations from the critics in London, New York and Los Angeles. In the Oscar stakes his chief competitor was not Branagh, but Tom Cruise, also playing a role in which he was confined to a wheelchair – and Cruise had the advantage of being in a film widely admired and popular, *Born on the Fourth of July*. But it was Day-Lewis who went up on the podium to collect the Best Actor Oscar, to the delight of the Academy. He was also Best Actor for

BAFTA, making this a remarkable series of awards which kept the film running on both sides of the Atlantic. Before the Oscars (Miss Fricker was voted Best Supporting Actress) the film had taken over $7 million in the US; a month later it had taken another $4 million. Day-Lewis was expected to be offered his pick of roles, but six months later had announced only one job, production executive on *Orlando*, from Virginia Woolf's novel, partly to enable director Sally Potter to find financing. The story of an individual who changes sex over the centuries does not seem like ideal screen material, and Ms Potter's previous feature, *The Gold Diggers*, hardly inspires confidence. In late 1990 he signed a two-picture deal with 20th Century-Fox, a new version of *The Last of the Mohicans* (91) and Martin Scorsese's *The Age of Innocence*.

ROBERT DE NIRO

In 1977, 'Newsweek' had no doubt: having listed Robert De Niro's film roles, it found him 'all of these characters and more. It is this astonishing variety and authenticity of his characterizations that make him, at 33, the most exciting young American actor on the screen, the one with the greatest potential to combine superstardom with extraordinary creative ability. More than that' – it went on – 'De Niro is the heir apparent to the post of American Cultural Symbol once occupied by Marlon Brando and the late James Dean. As Brando and Dean did . . . De Niro seems to embody the conflicting, questing energies of his generation, the generation coming to young maturity in the fragmented 70s.' (De Niro himself once observed that Brando and Dean were 'the best actors in the past', along with Spencer Tracy, Montgomery Clift, Kim Stanley and Geraldine Page.)

De Niro was born in New York City in 1943, the son of parents who were both painters and who separated not long after he was born. At school he appeared in Chekhov's 'The Bear'; and he studied acting with Stella Adler and others. He appeared in workshop productions and off-off Broadway, and did TV commercials; he was an extra in Marcel Carné's *Trois Chambres à Manhattan* (65). An open call for a movie, *The Wedding Party* (66), brought him a small role, $50, and acquaintance with one of its directors, Brian De Palma, who used him again in *Greetings* (68), slightly less amateurish but equally an underground effort: its subject was the young, and its hero a draft-evader. He was also one of several weekend guests at the Long Island home of a film editor in *Sam's Song* (69), a feeble venture which received a few isolated showings. Cannon later bought it on the strength of De Niro's presence, finally issuing it in 1979 after seven years on the shelf, much of it now reshot and retitled *The Swap*. It remained unshowable.

Shelley Winters, who had met De Niro briefly when he studied at the Actors' Studio, chose him to play the role of her slow-witted, drugged-up son in *Bloody Mama* (70), and she got him into an off-Broadway play she had written, 'One Night Stands of a Noisy Passenger', as a hippie; De Palma cast him again, in *Hi Mom!*, as its hero, a Vietnam veteran who makes porno flicks and gets into Revolt. De Niro's exposure, however in *Bloody Mama* led to other offers in main-line movies: *Born to Win* (71), Ivan Passar's tale of heroin addiction, with George Segal; *Jennifer on My Mind*, another daft story about drugs, written by Erich Segal; and *The Gang That Couldn't Shoot Straight*, a Mafia comedy. He played an Italian con-man, kleptomaniac and professional cyclist, which in this rendering became an all-time creep, and he was billed fifth, above the title; but the film itself was to be so inept as to be unwatchable.

De Niro came into his own co-starring with Michael Moriarty in *Bang the Drum Slowly* (73), John Hancock's superior version of Mark Harris's baseball novel; they played team-mates and not-alike friends, with De Niro as the fatally ill ask-for-little catcher. The New York critics voted him Best Supporting Actor, but the film was not a success; however, a certain cachet attached to Martin Scorsese's first major film, *Mean Streets*, in which De Niro and Harvey Keitel were back-street boys bumming around together and getting drunk together. Hollywood had turned down the project – De Niro was not yet bankable – and the producer had raised the $480,000 cost from friends in his home town, Cleveland; after its success at the New York Film Festival, Warners bought it – but found that people did not want to come and see it, presumably because between the violence and the swearing nothing intelligible could be perceived going on.

The hype on De Niro started when he was cast in *The Godfather II* (74) as that gentleman, previously Marlon Brando, as a young man. He won a Best Supporting Oscar, and the film itself won others, including Best Picture and Best Director: but its performance at the box-office was poor in comparison with both its predecessors and other Oscar winners of recent years. The public this time must have decided what was going on was not really of much significance, but the film was of epoch-making importance compared with Scorsese's *Taxi-Driver* (76), with De Niro in

the title-role, a mesmerizing performance by any standard, and a winner for the New York Critics that year. The cab-driver is a loner, and by sheer attention to detail, De Niro has built up idiosyncrasies, filling the gaping holes left by writing and director; but long before he goes berserk and the thing becomes a bloodbath you know it isn't going anywhere. De Niro's next three films succeeded in actually being worse – and *Novecento/1900* may well be the worst ever made: at four and a half hours, even in its cut version, it certainly bores for a longer length of time than most films. This epic by Bernardo Bertolucci purports to tell the story of two Italians from birth to the end of the Second World War – the rich one (De Niro) and his friend, the poor one (Gérard Depardieu). Since what happens to them bears no relation to life but seems

Baseball on the screen has not always had its adherants, and there was no great welcome for John Hancock's Bang the Drum Slowly *(73), based on the novel by Mark Harris. For one thing, it was much too downbeat, as it told of the friendship between two members of the team, Michael Moriarty and, here, Robert De Niro as the simpleton catcher.*

culled from the worst excesses of D.W. Griffith and De Sade – with the aid of a child's primer on Marx – it was an industry headache and an audience turn-off: after switching from studio to studio it opened in several European countries as two separate films – of which the second only did 40 per cent of the business of the first, a pattern repeated when it belatedly turned up in the US and Britain. De Niro's landowner was amused and self-effacing, and in the circumstances he cannot be blamed for giving the same performance in the title-role of *The Last Tycoon*, which also suffered from inadequate direction and writing – by Elia Kazan and Harold Pinter respectively – which reduced Scott Fitzgerald's brisk novel about a Hollywood producer to a film about, well, nothing. Pinter did not even have the wisdom to use Fitzgerald's draft-plan for the latter part of the unfinished book, and Sam Spiegel, producing, was too much in awe of him to insist. Kazan, who does not regard the result as one of 'his films', took the job on at the last moment as a favour to Spielberg, when Mike Nichols quit. At that point the lead had not been cast, as Spielberg wanted Jack Nicholson and Nichols preferred Dustin Hoffman: Kazan convinced Spielberg that De Niro would be better than either. He was to record later: 'Bobby was the only actor I know who wanted to rehearse on a Sunday.' Myrna Loy also paid a tribute: 'I think De Niro is wonderful, so contained in his acting, in such total control. I saw him play Thalberg. I *knew* Thalberg, and he *was* Thalberg'.

In 1975 he began filming *Bogart Slept Here*, written by Neil Simon and directed by Mike Nicholls, but production was halted after ten days due to internal dissension (Simon: De Niro is 'dynamite. But he has a different rhythm from the one in which I write'): retitled *The Goodbye Girl* and rewritten, De Niro's role was played by Richard Dreyfuss. The old studio control was missed also in Scorsese's haphazard *New York, New York* (77), an attempt to repeat the formula of *Orchestra Wives*, only telling it like it really was. Since what it really was was two and a half hours of rowing and yelling between a saxophonist (De Niro) and his vocalist wife (Liza Minnelli) audiences again stayed away, despite massive publicity. It cost $8 million but took only $6 million at the box-office. The critic John Simon had long been an admirer of De Niro's acting: it was 'inspired' in *Bang the Drum Slowly*, 'extraordinary' in *The Godfather II*, 'impeccable' in *Taxi-Driver*, 'perfection itself' in *The Last Tycoon*, but on this occasion he wrote: 'De Niro apparently decided that maniacal drivenness was the only thing that could be played in his part; he may have been right, but . . . he quickly becomes

grating.' Another comment on the actor was made by Georgie Auld, the film's technical adviser, notably involved in teaching him to 'play' the sax: 'Bob asked me ten million questions a day. He got to be a real pain in the ass.' The cast included Diahanne Abbott, whom De Niro had married in 1976 (they have since split up); and despite the film's failure De Niro was voted the tenth draw at the box-office.

The Deer Hunter (78) was another horror. As the Pennsylvania steelworker who goes to Vietnam and back, De Niro sustains the excessive three hours' running time, though even he cannot make sense of the notorious Russian roulette scene or some chases which would seem unlikely done by Errol Flynn. Michael Cimino's flaccid but flamboyant direction caused the budget to double during production, to $14 million, but it brought him an Oscar and there was another for Best Picture, a contributory factor in the film's earning $27,435,000 at the box-office. Some sections of the press disliked it, though these were seldom the film critics but the war correspondents who had been in Vietnam. In the 'Spectator', Richard West called it 'a travesty of the war and an insult to those who fought in it', while in the 'New York Times', Gloria Emerson wrote, 'Cimino has cheapened and degraded the war as no one else has' – and that newspaper reprinted an attack by John Pilger in the 'New Statesman', claiming that the film 'and its apologists insult the memory of every American who died in Vietnam'.

In the midst of the controversy De Niro was reunited with Scorsese for a pet project, *Raging Bull* (80), to play the prize-fighter Jake La Motta in this movie based on his autobiography. It takes him from unprincipled slob and World Champion to the days when he is trading on his former celebrity. De Niro pigged out to get the size of the middle-aged La Motta, and therefore may be said to have joined the other winners of Best Actor Oscars for playing plain or handicapped. He is impressive throughout, but he cannot help us to see into La Motta, handicapped as he is by script and direction which are verismo but not much else – they certainly lack any insight into the man or the milieu. The film cost $17 million and took only $10,111,000, despite De Niro's Oscar. It was reissued in 1990, when it topped the poll of American critics asked to name the best film of the decade, but the box-office figure proved that the public was not curious enough to turn up to see whether it agreed or not. De Niro was much happier playing a worldly monsignor in Ulu Gosbard's murder mystery, *True Confessions* (81), and he was brilliant in Scorsese's *The King of*

Comedy (83). Indeed, this may still be his best performance – a rather moronic New Yorker who dreams of being a television star, facing every adversity in 'Playboy'-recommended colour-co-ordinated clothes with the smile of a real creep. The film took a mere $1,200,000 at the box-office on a budget of $19 million, most of it provided by Arnon Milchan, an Israeli entrepreneur who had produced some other films or been their financial guarantor, including 'Masada' for television. He had originally approached Scorsese about a life of Moshe Dayan, but they eventually settled on this script, which Scorsese admitted he had considered 'too simple, too superficial' when he had first read it. Just so, but surely he could have given it some verisimilitude by showing that a TV station is as hard to get into as Fort Knox?

With another pretentious European director, Sergio Leone, De Niro got himself into yet another disaster, *Once Upon a Time in America* (84), in which the director sought to demonstrate all his fantasies about gangsters or at least the gangster movies of the past. De Niro played one of them, coincidentally Jewish. The director commented: 'I don't consider Bob so much an actor as an incarnation of the character he is playing. Until he feels like that, he can't go on the set. We have the same defects. We are precise in detail, and share an obsession with perfection.' Their reward was a return of $2,500,000 on a $30 million budget. De Niro agreed to play the impresario Sol Hurok in a grandiose co-production between the US and the USSR, *Pavlova, a Woman for All Time*, but that came to nothing. With reason, he looked at his box-office record and decided that he should try to make a popular film and play a character with whom audiences could identify, so he and Meryl Streep were *Falling in Love*, but the figures (see Streep) showed that they were not the couple for that, at least as far as audiences were concerned. He then had two further failures, both British and ambitious, but Terry Gilliam's *Brazil* (85) has some magnificent things in it – and if Gilliam had only cut, especially towards the end, when banality seems to nudge into what is already overlength, it might have been a great picture. It takes place in some undefined future at Christmas, mainly in a cavernous department store and a government department, neither much like those we know, and the central character is a mild unambitious bureaucrat (Jonathan Pryce) whose virtues are the trigger for his destruction. De Niro, who wanted to work with Gilliam, accepted a guest-role as a free renegade spirit who is therefore an enemy of the state. The $15 million budget was shared by 20th Century-Fox, who released in

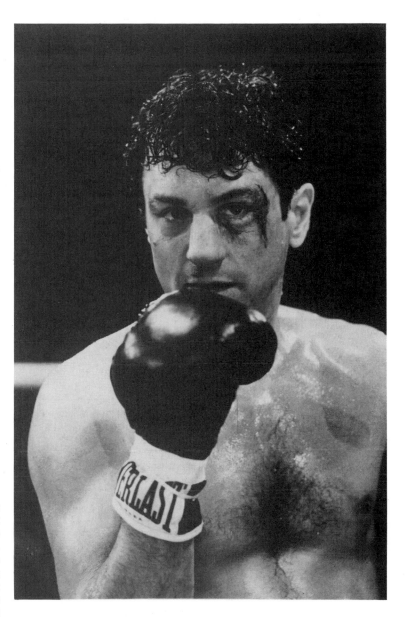

De Niro losing a fight, maybe, but winning an Oscar, certainly: Scorsese's study of Jake La Motta, Raging Bull *(80).*

Britain, and Universal, who declined to do so in the US after studying the British returns. They decided to open it in Los Angeles, to qualify it for Oscar nominations, but only after Gilliam had taken ads in the trade press demanding to know when they were going to release it. When the critics in that city voted it the year's Best Film, Universal was encouraged to ship out more prints, but the American take was still under $4,500,000 – another disappointment for Arnon Milchan, who produced.

The other film was *The Mission* (86), a study of the conflict between the Jesuits and the state in a remote part of South America in the eighteenth century. Jeremy Irons represented the former and De Niro, as an army captain, the latter. Roland Joffe directed from a script by Robert Bolt, with Goldcrest putting up the bulk of the $24,500,000 budget (with Warners, who were releasing, in for $5 million). It was epic all right, as it needed to be at that price, but it was difficult to tell whether it was anything else – and so decided the great American unwashed, who coughed up only a total of $8,300,000 to sample it. According to David Puttman, who produced, De Niro was startled when he told him that he did not think him right for the role; when De Niro queried a line, Puttnam observed that if it took more than his last five films combined it would still end up in the red. The film's editor, Jim Clark, said, 'With De Niro, you don't cut him – you *mine* him. You have to seek out the performance because it varies so.'

Around the same time De Niro played a Cuban–American drug-dealer off-Broadway in 'Cuba and the Teddy Bear', which transferred to Broadway a few months later, playing to virtual capacity throughout its limited run. He was then offered the role of Al Capone in De Palma's *The Untouchables* (87), a re-run of the old television series in which government agent Eliot Ness brought about the downfall of the Chicago mobster. The role of Capone was subsidiary to that of Ness, and De Niro declined it at first, if not for that reason. Indeed, his next film would mark the fourth consecutive time he has played little more than guest roles; he once said that he was not entirely happy to carry a film. Bob Hoskins was signed, but in the meantime Paramount's researchers discovered that few of the potential audience knew of Ness, but they were familiar with Capone. So the Capone role was beefed up and De Niro's agent agreed to a reduced fee of $2 million. Hoskins was paid off to the tune of $200,000 and De Niro ceded his role in *Ironweed* to Jack Nicholson. De Niro, who had tried to get under the skin of La Motta, did his utmost again as Capone, ordering his wardrobe from those who had supplied Capone with his clothes, including silk underwear. The result was a memorable study in sleek brutishness, articulate and vain, but the film still belonged to the two actors with bigger roles, Kevin Costner, who played Ness, and Sean Connery. The result (see Costner) was still De Niro's only successful film since *The Deer Hunter*. He chose to play another supporting role, in Alan Parker's diabolic thriller, *Angel Heart*, as Lucifer – smiling, expansive, enigmatic in his three scenes – in contrast to Mickey Rourke's fidgety hero. Research on this occasion meant reading biographies of the evil men of history, while for his appearance he sported a beard and a ponytail. He said once that disguise was

a mixed blessing: 'In a way it's covering up, but in another way it's the only way you can let yourself go, so it's an odd contradiction. To be able to see yourself straight on, it's hard.' The director said of him, 'When De Niro walks on the set, you can feel his presence, but he never behaves like a movie star, just an actor. And when he acts, his sheer concentration permeates the whole set.' But, he observed, 'I'm not sure I could work with him on an entire film; it would be too much of an exhausting experience. De Niro would constantly ask questions on the set, and then ring me up every day with new possibilities and ideas. His involvement was phenomenal.'

He turned down the lead in Scorsese's *The Last Temptation of Christ*, because he could not relate to it. He was also looking for something to prove him a box-office actor, and considered *Big* for a while: but he settled on *Midnight Run* (88), a thriller about a bounty-hunter employed to bring in for reckoning a mild accountant who has embezzled $15 million from a Mafia man. In the latter role the director Martin Brest wanted either Robin Williams or Charles Grodin, but since the film was going to cost over $20 million – in the event it cost $30 million – Paramount wanted either Dustin Hoffman or Cher, who couldn't see the role with a sex-change. Universal, however, told Brest to go ahead with whom he pleased and he chose Grodin, who had had a somewhat hazardous career as a leading actor. On this occasion he was superb, teaming with De Niro to make the best buddy movie in ages, always surprising in its twists. De Niro was on top form, gliding in, having chipped away his old intensity to find the humanity and the laughs in this seemingly dour and bitter man. He 'is not, to put it mildly, the American actor most closely associated with laughter,' Adam Mars-Jones wrote in the 'Independent'. 'When he renounces the intensity that is his trademark, as he did for instance, in [that] lamentable romantic vehicle with Meryl Streep, it is easy to forget that he is a world-class actor at all. He played a comic, true, in *The King of Comedy*, but an unfunny one; that was the joke (if any). And he was funny in *Brazil*, but that was a cameo part, and by the time he appeared on the screen, his director had created a refracted universe where everything was funny, though very little bearable. But . . . his playing [here] is genuinely funny . . . he lets the part build as a whole, so that it is cumulatively funny, instead of cashing in laughs the moment his credit is good for them.' Neither actor was nominated for an Oscar, and this was the year when Hoffman won for *Rain Man*.

Two more faces of De Niro: above, fattened up to play Al Capone in The Untouchables *(87) with Kevin Costner, and left, slimmed down, you might say, in* We're No Angels *(89), with Sean Penn as fellow-convicts masquerading as priests.*

De Niro found himself another complex role in *Jacknife* (89), a Vietnam vet whose extrovert exterior constantly hides bloody memories, and who embarks on an affair with the sister (Kathy Baker) of a wartime buddy (Ed Harris), which is too much for him. This actor had always been intelligent about his appearance, wanting to change for the role but not to be unrecognizable: he sported curls and a huge moustache, but once again to an unappreciative public. The film cost $10 million and took only $2,200,000. De Niro exec-produced the witless *We're No Angels*, directed by Neil Jordan from a screenplay by David Mamet, based in turn on a Paramount picture of 1955 with Humphrey Bogart: De Niro and Sean Penn played escaped convicts who disguise themselves as priests, but not with skill. 'At times they seem to be aping Laurel and Hardy,' wrote Adrian Turner in '20/20' magazine, 'at others, Lenny and George in *Of Mice and Men*. De Niro gives an A–Z of facial expressions in what must be his worst performance to date.' 'De Niro,' said New York's 'Seven Days', 'as often when he is playing clods, is so excessively pleased with himself that he leaves the audience behind.' *Stanley and Iris* (90), which followed hard upon, had equally fine people behind the camera – Martin Ritt as director and Harriet Frank Jr and Irving Ravetch as the writers. Jane Fonda was the co-star, as a recently widowed mother who takes under her wing De Niro, whose literal illiteracy is both a safeguard and a matter of shame. In the same 'Seven Days' magazine, Richard T. Jameson wrote that the stars 'commit a cardinal sin in conspicuously scaling down their stellar wonderfulness in the name of honoring their resolutely mundane characters. This is a variation of the liberal masochism that used to lead Paul Newman and Joanne Woodward, back in the 70s, to subvert their natural attractiveness in order to sever the glum "honesty" of [some] kamikaze missions . . . How selflessly we give of ourselves, these stars seem to be saying, to be true to these proletarian bodies.'

We're No Angels, which cost $22 million, took only $5 million; *Stanley and Iris*, with a similar budget, did even less well. De Niro was said to be getting $4–5 million per film, but the cumulative losses on his films since *New York New York* amounted to almost $150 million. The public now knew what the industry had been aware of for years – that the man commonly regarded as America's best film actor was without any box-office clout. This had been concealed as long as he had worked with such erratic talents as Leone, Bertolucci, Cimino and (on occasion) Scorsese, but in recent years he had made

pictures for directors usually able to turn them out to please both public and press. He could count on the prestige he brought with him to obtain star roles, but the situation would become uncertain if his notices were no longer unanimously favourable. So with that consideration in mind he went from project to project almost non-stop: Scorsese's *Goodfellas*, playing Mafia boss Jimmy the Gent; *Awakenings* with Robin Williams; and *Guilt by Association*, with which producer Irwin Winkler turned director.

The Scorsese was the first to open, an overlong and factual tale of Mafia life in New York 1955–80, with Ray Liotta playing a neophyte to De Niro's boss. Acclaimed at the Venice festival, it was equally warmly received in the US, where it took over $17 million in its first two weeks. The film with Williams is directed by Penny Marshall and concerns a doctor who wakes up a patient who has been vegetating for years, whilst Winkler's movie concerns the Hollywood blacklisting of the 50s; De Niro plays a film director. Both these pieces followed *Goodfellas* into the autumn cinema schedules.

Conceivably he also wished to change his image, from being a markedly reclusive actor to a high profile producer. Late in 1989 he announced the formation of his own production company, Tribeca Film Center, with fourteen projects already under way. Some were already under development at Universal, Warner Bros, Columbia and Arnon Milchan's New Regency Films, while for the moment Tri-Star had first refusal on the others. Those most closely involving De Niro himself were: *Thunderhearts*, a drama about an FBI agent who becomes a victim of prejudice while examining his ethnic (i.e. Indian) roots, which he would produce; *Tales of the Bronx*, which he would direct; *The Battling Spumonti Brothers*, to co-star him and Danny De Vito; and *Gold Lust*, with Dustin Hoffman as his co-star.

De Niro's Tribeca Film Center is home not only to his company but any others which wish to use its post-production facilities; its space also houses a fashionable restaurant in which De Niro can frequently be seen. Meanwhile, instead of making any of the projects listed above he joined the cast of *Backdraft* (91), supporting the already-signed leads, Kurt Russell and William Baldwin. Announced to follow that are a remake of *Cape Fear, Mad Dog and Glory* and *The Mistress*, the last-named for Tribeca.

GÉRARD DEPARDIEU

Gérard Depardieu is outsize in every way – if not especially tall, bulky, and with energy to spare whether on the set or in a room. He is given to playing slobs and tearaways, perhaps because he can relate best to them; but being also a fine actor he can be disciplined – and he has a larger range than at first appears. He is to foreign audiences what only two actors before him have been – Jean Gabin at the time of the Popular Front and Jean-Paul Belmondo during the era of the Nouvelle Vague: the one actor to represent the Frenchman. You may say that Gabin echoed the pessimism of his era and Belmondo the insouciance of a new breed of film-makers, but in fact all three can be recognised as masters of their craft.

Neither Gabin nor Belmondo was interested in Hollywood fame (though Gabin made two films there during the war) – nor is Depardieu, who has turned down many offers from the US. But there the difference ends, for Depardieu wants to work in the United States for the experience. He likes being an international name. He also likes Britain, or at least its actors and writers, though his fondness for the country and its people is filtered through his fascination with the age-old rivalry with France. He also loves movies. Asked once what cinema means to him, he replied, 'Belmondo, Lino Ventura, Yves Boisset', which is to say the picture-houses of the *grands boulevards*. But he added the names of Claude Miller and Gerard Zingg to represent the *cinémas d'art et essaie* on the Rive Gauche. He has kept faith with these opposing aspects of moviegoing.

He is the third of six children of an illiterate metal-worker who left his native village for a factory in Châteauroux, in central France, where Depardieu was born in 1948. He found himself in constant conflict at school, and at the age of twelve ran away from home, allegedly to see the sea. Later, at Cannes, he was boat-hand and beach-boy, but in the meantime he made a living by pilfering and flogging black-market Scotch from American air bases. At fifteen a chance meeting with an itinerant actor, Michel Pilorge, at the railway station in his home town took him to Paris, where he studied for nine months with the Théâtre National Populaire. He also met there Elisabeth Guignot, seven years his senior, whom he married when he was twenty-one. Two days after leaving the TNP, he was given two days' work on a short directed by Roger Leenhardt, *Le Beatnik et le Minet* (65), and that led to a role in Agnès Varda's *Christmas Carol*, which was abandoned during production. Jean-Laurent Cochet, with

whom he studied, gave him a role in a revival of 'Boudu Sauvé des Eaux', and years later he told an English journalist, 'I was Boudu. I *am* Boudu! Not just the screwing and the destruction but also the attempted suicide' – but alas, for the record, he played the student and not Boudu. He toured with this and then was featured in a television series, 'Rendez-vous à Badenberg', and while making it he met Rufus and Romain Bouteille, with whom he would do cabaret at the Café de la Gare for six months. Among the other plays he did were 'Les Garçons de la Bande', 'Une Fille dans ma Soupe' and 'Galapagos' (71), for which he got rave notices, drawing the attention of the movie industry to him. The director Michel Audiard offered Depardieu and Romain Bouteille small roles in *Le Cri du Cormoran le Soir au-dessus des Jonques*, a starring vehicle for Michel Serrault and Bernard Blier, based on a novel by Evan Hunter.

A meeting with the novelist Marguérite Duras brought an offer to appear in *Nathalie Granger* (72), which she also wrote and directed. Lucia Bose and Jeanne Moreau played haggard zombies (though that was not the intention), whose dreary ménage is enlivened by the arrival of Depardieu as a travelling salesman, bewildered by what he sees before him, and his fifteen-minute explosion into the action may well have been as spontaneous as it seems. It was the film's only good idea – indeed its only idea – so Duras brought him back at the end, a prospect which might just have prevented audiences deserting *en masse*. He has remained faithful to Duras and her minimal cinema over the years and when asked why by a dumbfounded 'Ciné-Revue', he replied it was because she is a friend – which to anyone chancing upon one of her films would not seem sufficient reason. But he was now in steady demand for small roles, usually as a bad 'un: *Le Tueur*, which starred Jean Gabin; Jacques Deray's *Un Peu de Soleil dans l'Eau Froide*, from a Françoise Sagan novel, with Claudine Auger and Marc Porel;

L'Affaire Dominici with Gabin, fifth-billed; *Au Rendez-vous de la Mort Joyeuse* (73), directed by Juan Luis Buñuel (Luis's son), with Françoise Fabian and Jean-Marc Bory, a mystery set in an isolated house; José Giovanni's *La Scoumone* with Belmondo; Pierre Tchernia's *Le Viager* with Serrault; René Allio's *Rude Journée pour la Reine* with Simone Signoret; Giovanni's *Deux Hommes dans la Ville* with Gabin; and Tchernia's *Les Gaspards* (74), as a postman.

This last was an important part, as was the one in Alain Resnais's *Stavisky* with Belmondo, in which he was the inventor of the 'Matriscope': but before this was shown he was starred, along with Patrick Dewaere, in Bertrand Blier's *Les Valseuses*. The two of them played petty crooks, having adventures, which consisted of, among other things, Depardieu sodomizing Dewaere, the two of them taking turns to make love to Miou-Miou and initiating Isabelle Huppert into the delights of sex after she has stolen her mother's car for them. After rejoining Duras for *La Femme du Ganges* he played a young boxer temporarily working with Yves Montand in Claude Sautet's *Vincent, François, Paul et les Autres*. Though for a while he would not always command star-billing, it was his last supporting role (except when he chose to do a cameo part). Claude Goretta's *Pas si Méchant que Ça* (75) found him at the centre of events, as cheerful ne'er-do-well husband and father who rallies himself to try and save the family furniture business. Jacques Rouffio's *Sept Morts sur Ordonnance* was the tale of a small-town surgeon (Charles Vanel) who tries ruthlessly to get rid of a rival (Michel Piccoli); Depardieu played one who had been similarly destroyed some years earlier.

The next two found him again up to his waist in sexual irregularities. In Barbet-Schroeder's *Maîtresse* (76) he falls madly in love with a leather-dressed dominatrix (Bulle Ogier) who services masochist clients, one of whom requires him to urinate upon him. This was a positively healthy movie when compared with Marco Ferreri's *L'Ultima Donna*, in which he was a young engineer who picks up Ornella Muti when his wife leaves him: he is, he tells her, so enthralled with his prick that he masturbates instead of making love to her, but when her disillusion proves too great he slices it off with an electric knife. Both films, perhaps it is needless to say, found their way into the international market. That was not a fate awarded to one which Depardieu did between them, Serge Gainsbourg's *Je t'Aime Moi Non Plus*, but Depardieu had only a walk-on, done as a joke. He travelled to Italy for Bernardo Bertolucci's ghastly epic, *Novecento*, to play the peasant-born chum of

Robert De Niro – oh, and they loved each other so much, but just in case we worried about that (again) they share the same girl later in the action. He was better employed (but only just) in André Téchiné's foolish *Barocco*. Here again he was a boxer, who after a garish night-on-the-town with his mistress (Isabelle Adjani) is gunned down; she then falls in love with his murderer – who looks just like him, for the very good reason that Depardieu played that role as well. Francis Girod's *René la Canne* (77) told of the wartime adventures of a cop (Piccoli) and a bum (Depardieu). It was a box-office disaster, but was still seen by more people than went to a couple directed by Duras, *Baxter Vera Baxter* and *Le Camion*. Sanity was restored to audiences, if not to Depardieu, by Claude Miller's engaging homage to *Rebecca, Dites-lui que je l'Aime*, in which he was a mystery man with a château in the French Alps; during the week he works in town (unlike Maxim de Winter), where a fellow-lodger (Miou-Miou) throws herself at him, with all manner of consequences.

Because no one else would do so, he produced Claude Zingg's *La Nuit Tous les Chats Sont Gris*, in which he was a village philanderer whose exploits are recounted by an English writer (Robert Stephens). The result was like a rip-off of Resnais's worst film (*Providence*), and it fared even worse with press and public: Depardieu later said that the subject was dear to his heart and that he would not be discouraged from producing again, despite his difficulty in finding a distributor. Blier's opportunistic *Préparez vos Mouchoirs* found Depardieu and Dewaere again sharing a woman – Dewaere's wife (Carol Laure) – amid other idiosyncratic, but not tedious, activities. Like Depardieu's previous collaboration with this director, this found a greeting abroad, and abroad was where Depardieu found himself for two festival oddities (no one else, at least, was anxious to show them): Peter Handke's *Die Linkshändige Frau*, made in Germany, in a cameo as a 'man in T-shirt' in this minimal drama about a disintegrating marriage, and Ferreri's English-language *Ciao Mascio/Bye Bye Monkey* (78), filmed in New York, with Marcello Mastroianni; and he did another guest appearance in Switzerland, in Daniel Schmid's *Violanta*, a tale of a village matriarch (Lucia Bose). After these three fruitless journeys Depardieu found himself back in France, in a solid commercial job which was also to demonstrate his widening range, Rouffio's entertaining but artificial *Le Sucre*, as a big wheel on the Bourse not averse to a little larceny. He was the leader of the dog people in Alain Jessua's semi-SF *Les Chiens* (79) with

Victor Lanoux, and simultaneously one of several names (Dewaere, Annie Girardot, Marcello Mastroianni, Fernando Rey, Alberto Sordi) involved in the biggest traffic jam of all time, Luigi Comencini's frenetic *L'Ingorgo*. The year finished even more horribly with Blier's *Buffet Froid*, in which he drew a switch-blade on Michel Serrault in the Métro in reel one, virtually the only incident in the entire enterprise which anyone could either sympathize with or understand. In Italy he made *Temporale Rosy* (80) for Mario Monicelli, again playing a prize-fighter, if now retired, who falls in love with a lady wrestler (Faith Minton).

It was at a low point, therefore, that he was offered two excellent films, Resnais's *Mon Oncle d'Amérique* and Maurice Pialat's *Loulou*. The first was a haunting memory piece about three young people (the others: Roger Pierre, Nicole Garcia) and how their lives touch, with Depardieu as a boy from bigoted farming stock who becomes a wealthy businessman. The second was one of Pialat's cries against the difficulty of living, with Depardieu as a petty hood obsessed with making a bourgeois girl (Huppert), who goes off the rails for love of him. Depardieu was tremendous in both, but if he was more at home in a *blouson noir* than an executive suit, that was perhaps part of his appeal. Both were big successes for film-makers the French public had not always admired, and the same might be said of François Truffaut and *Le Dernier Métro*, a tinny little epic set during the Occupation which vanquished both his two better, previous films in virtually every category at the annual César ceremony. Depardieu was among those prized, as Best Actor. He played a newcomer to Catherine Deneuve's drama company, a secret member of the Resistance, with whom she falls in love while hiding her husband in the cellar. Depardieu knew that these were three major credits, but he was also aware that these were chiefly prestige items. Accordingly he accepted supporting roles in Claude Zidi's comedy, *Inspecteur La Bavure*, as a gangster to the police chief of Coluche, and Claude Berri's *Je Vous Aime* (81), as a former lover, a saxophonist/singer, to the confused heroine, Deneuve. He was billed above Deneuve, but below Yves Montand, in Alain Corneau's *Le Choix des Armes*, in which the two men were crooks in unholy alliance. Depardieu returned to Truffaut for *La Femme d'à Côté*, in which he resumes an old affair with his neighbour's wife (Fanny Ardant) under the very noses of their spouses, sleepwalking through his role – perhaps to disguise the fact that it was soap opera, even to the unintentional laughs.

There was genuine laughter to be had with *La Chèvre* (82), written and directed by Francis Veber, and teaming Depardieu with Pierre Richard, respectively a private eye and a sad sack who doesn't know that he is: Richard's employer has sent them to find his kidnapped daughter on the premise that his ineptitude will lead him to the same fate as her. Said David Denby in 'New York' magazine: 'Depardieu, who moves with the force of an angry locomotive, rushes through slapstick violence without looking left or right; the rest of the time, he is required to express indignation, something that few actors can do without turning into a prig. But even in this brutal straight-man role, Depardieu is a great film actor and a great film star.' Also seen overseas was *Le Retour de Martin Guerre*, best described as an idea whose time had come, as directed by Daniel Vigne and written by him and Jean-Claude Carrière, with no acknowledgement to the recent book on the same subject. Both concern the disappearance, in the 16th century, of a husband, and the man (Depardieu) who returns and is exposed as an impostor against the wishes of the wife (Nathalie Baye). As a reconstruction of past events the film is mild, but it is an effective mystery, with a towering, imaginative performance by Depardieu. He did another thriller, Girod's *Le Grand Frère*, in a double role, importantly as a man used by a sly Arab boy after he has seen him kill another (Jean Rochefort) – in vengeance, let it be said, after being left to die in the jungle when they were in the Légion. This year ended on a high note, in the title-role of *Danton*,

Depardieu in the title-role of Andrzej Wajda's Danton *(82), which perhaps got closer to the experience of living through the French Revolution and the subsequent Terror than any of the many other films on the subject.*

written by Carrière from a Polish play for Andrzej Wajda – who went on record as admiring Depardieu's performance, though to others it was over-familiar, finickety in its boorishness. It tended to diminish the occasion, a vivid account of some matters pertaining to the Revolution, but not the superb Robespierre of Wojciech Pszoniak, admittedly dubbed into French. For the record, many regarded the film as an analogy for current events in Poland.

Depardieu was a stevedore in *La Lune dans le Caniveau* (83), hoping to escape from his grotty environment when the ritzy Nastassia Kinski comes looking for her drunken brother in the city's low dives. Taking his clue from *Mon Oncle d'Amérique*, in which the Depardieu character identified with Gabin, that is whom director Jean-Jacques Beineix has him play here, in a mistaken facsimile of *Quai des Brumes*. The actor was among the many who disliked the result, claiming that it failed to catch the spirit of David Goodis's original novel. Veber's *Les Compères* was the welcome follow-up to *La Chèvre*, with Richard and Depardieu as ex-lovers whom Annie Duperey individually persuades is the father of her missing son, so that they will go in search of him. Corneau's *Fort Saganne* (84) was a big one, a three-hour epic with Depardieu as the enigmatic peasant-born legionnaire who finds fulfilment in the desert, as

well as love with Deneuve. He played the title-role and directed, rather lumpishly, *Le Tartuffe*, from Molière's play, doing better as its hypocritical protagonist; and he was on top form again in Philippe Labro's *Rive Droite Rive Gauche*, as a dangerously successful lawyer whose career and marriage have staled till he meets a divorcée (Nathalie Baye). Indeed, he seemed unstoppable, giving Pialat another big success with *Police* (85), as a racist, sexist and violent top cop who behaves like a romantic schoolboy after beginning an affair with the girlfriend (Sophie Marceau) of a Tunisian drug-trafficker. After that, he needed a comedy, and he found it with Vigne's *Une Femme ou Deux*, playing an obsessed archeologist who mistakes Sigourney Weaver for the head of an American foundation financing his discoveries. Television's Dr Ruth Westheimer – played the real chief, but neither her presence nor that of Weaver managed to get the film more than isolated screenings in the territories where they were known. And that was no great loss, even to Depardieu-watchers, for on this outing he was 'coy and tame' (Denby).

Tenue de Soirée (86) begins with a butch burglar (Depardieu) picking up a bourgeois couple (Miou-Miou, Michel Blanc): she is sexy and the guy mouse-like. Our expectations are upended when it turns out that he wants to initiate him into the delights of men loving men. At the end all three are in frocks and make-up looking for clients, and along the way sodomy and fellatio have been abundantly celebrated. Few today would object to that, but what is repellent is the rampant misogyny. Both Depardieu and the director, Blier, have rejected the accusations that Blier is a misogynist, though it was apparent to many others from his first film onwards. Or, says Depardieu, look at Ingmar Bergman, who has also been accused of misogyny, which is avoiding the fact that Bergman is a film-maker of genius – which Blier is light-years from being, on this or any other showing.

Depardieu redeemed himself by appearing in one of his most ingratiating films – and, indeed, it would be one of the greatest successes ever in the international market: *Jean de Florette*, directed by Claude Berri from a film and novel by Marcel Pagnol. In the title-role, Depardieu's hunchbacked city boy has a self-destructive decency, an extraordinary niceness, as he struggles to farm an inherited smallholding without benefit of a spring. His own wife played his wife, and there were in the film two other outstanding performances, by Yves Montand and Daniel Auteuil as the peasant villains of the piece. Depardieu was not in the sequel, *Manon des*

Jean de Florette (86) and its sequel Manon des Sources *were the most popular French films in foreign markets for two generations, and perhaps more. Depardieu was in the first of these only because he died at the end – as we supposed he might, being a good man whose sacrifices and hard work to farm his carnation plantation seem virtually self-destructive. A superb performance, too, by Yves Montand and Daniel Auteuil in both films.*

Sources, named after the 1952 original, in which the events of this film were disposed of in ten minutes' conversation. That does not make *Jean de Florette* redundant or take anything from the millions who have loved Berri's two films: but anyone who has seen Pagnol's own film is likely to think that Berri has changed too much, and for the worse – notably in making Jean's daughter Manon a fey mountain girl instead of a smart Parisian for the men to ogle and the woman to despise. After a reunion with Veber and Richard for another harum-scarum comedy, *Les Fugitifs*, he returned to Pialat for *Sous le Soleil de Satan* (87), based on a novel by Georges Bernanos which emerges in this treatment as complex and unyielding. Depardieu was a priest who doubts his calling, Pialat himself played his superior and Sandrine Bonnaire the woman who would shape Depardieu's fate. He was to say later that great acting – De Niro, Brando, Laughton and 'sometimes' Hoffman – 'is to let your life escape you. Of keeping things that simple'. This picture of Pialat's was his own favourite of his films, 'very classic, very simple, like a movie by Dreyer'.

He and Catherine Deneuve, abandoned by her husband, are thrown together on a rainy night on a motorway layby, *Drôle d'Endroit pour une Rencontre* (88), but what followed was not so much droll as dull, as it followed these two people in crisis for a couple of days. It was a first feature for François Dupeyron, and to help him get it financed the two stars involved their own production companies, as well as taking no salary for a percentage of the profits – which were not so lucrative.

Isabelle Adjani was *Camille Claudel* and he was her philandering lover, the sculptor Auguste Rodin, in Bruno Nuytten's grim, overlong biography. That was followed by Claude Zidi's love story, *Deux* (89), in which he is a musician and the girl (Marushka Detmers) an employee of the estate agent selling him a concert hall. *Trop Belle pour Toi* was his fifth film for Blier, more acceptable than some as it casts Depardieu in midlife crisis, turning from his sleek wife (Carole Bouquet) to his dumpy new secretary (Josiane Balasko) – but hardly a better movie than those by Blier which had preceded it. Still, as Christopher Tookey remarked in the 'Sunday Telegraph', Balasko is erotic, and 'Depardieu is no less watchable, becoming gloomier and gloomier as his sex-life gets better and better. For much of the film he wanders round with hunched shoulders, like a moose in a cardboard suit.' But oh dear: what of Resnais's English-language *I Want to Go Home?* Better just to record that Jules Feiffer wrote it, and that Depardieu plays a professor who falls in love with the daughter of comic-strip artist Adolph Green. Conversely, *Cyrano de Bergerac* (90) was a triumph for him and director Jean-Paul Rappeneau, and to judge from its reception at the Cannes Festival, where he was voted Best Actor, should return its $15 million (equivalent) investment – which would have been much higher had it not been shot in Hungary, where costs are still low. He goes from this to Peter Weir's *Green Card*, about a forty-year-old Frenchman bewildered by America, and then to Berri's *Uranus*, with Philippe Noiret. And that will be followed by another English-language film, *Welcome to Vevay* (91), with Kirk Douglas. He plans to return then to the theatre, to play in 'Gilles de Rais', which he regards as preparation to tackle Macbeth and Othello. Also at this time he bought Kenneth Branagh's *Henry V* for distribution in France, while other companies hesitated – and because he admired it; and is producing Satyajit Ray's *Branches in the Trees*. 'Ray is a visionary, a great auteur,' he said, for which he may be forgiven his transgressions with Blier and Duras.

DANNY DEVITO

At five feet, Danny DeVito is an unlikely star, but then he is not a tragedian. It may be a case of Pagliacci, though it is rage he says which is inside him, not tears. He's a funny guy, sweet-faced, mild-mannered, though he is excellent at playing obnoxious or foul-tempered characters. He seems to have mileage, but then, as he says himself, 'the competition is pretty flimsy for roles around five feet.'

He was born in 1944 of Italian stock on both sides, in Asbury Park, New Jersey, where his father was a small-time entrepreneur (a candy store, dry cleaner's, pool hall). Young DeVito first acted in a school play, as St Francis of Assisi, and liked the experience enough to train at the American Academy of Dramatic Art. After graduating, he auditioned numerous times without success in New York and Los Angeles, when he arrived on a one-way ticket in 1967, was no kinder. He worked as a night janitor and did so again after regaining New York, till a former professor at the AADA found some stage work for him. It was during this period that he first met Michael Douglas – and Rhea Perlman, whom he would marry in 1981 after ten years of being together. He got a movie role, in *Lady Liberty* (71), which starred Sophia Loren: but it was a minute one. Still, as he said, he got a trip to Italy out of it. Douglas recommended him for a part in *Scalawag* (73), a Douglas family enterprise, and that got him to Yugoslavia, where it was filmed. Kirk Douglas starred and directed, as a pirate, with DeVito seventh-billed as one of the crew, Flyspeck. The film was a disaster and, like the Loren film, is omitted from most DeVito filmographies, as is also *Hurry Up or I'll be Thirty*, in which he supported John Lefkowitz as a young Brooklyn boy on the make in Manhattan. He was in an off-Broadway production of 'One Flew Over the Cuckoo's Nest', which first established him, but 'The Shrinking Bride', in which he starred, was only too well named, for it closed on the opening night.

Michael Douglas, who had seen the play, meanwhile invited him to repeat his performance in *One Flew Over the Cuckoo's Nest* (75), which he was producing; as the diminutive

Danny DeVito in The Jewel of the Nile *(85), as the comic villain. In the earlier film of the series,* Romancing the Stone *(85) he had been less comic, more villainous. In this one he even buddy-buddies up with the hero for a while – but in the ensuing high spirits it did not seem to matter.*

(obviously), playful Martini, DeVito was well noticed. He applied to the American Film Institute for a grant to make a short, *Minestrone*, written and directed by himself and Perlman, which they took successfully to the Cannes Film Festival. Another short, *The Sound Sleeper*, again demonstrated a liking for the macabre, which would characterize much of his later screen work. He played a small role as one of several Assistant Directors in a horrible send-up of Hollywood in the 20s, *The World's Greatest Lover* (77), produced, directed and written by Gene Wilder, who also had the effrontery to play the lead. DeVito became a national figure the following year when he was signed on to play the despatcher in 'Taxi', a vain, dictatorial and malicious little man whom the other characters loved to hate. It ran until 1983, by which time Perlman had joined him in fame, as the waitress Carla in 'Cheers'. DeVito's film credits during this period are best forgotten: *Valentine* (79), made for television, with Mary Martin and Jack Albertson as oldsters fleeing from their families and encountering various kind people, including him; and *Going Ape!* (81), in which Tony Danza stands to inherit a fortune by looking after some orang-utans. (It was directed by Jeremy Joe Kronsberg, who as a writer had teamed Clint Eastwood with said animal in *Every Which Way But Loose*.)

DeVito's rise to the top of the Hollywood heap began when he played Shirley MacLaine's self-opinionated suitor in *Terms of Endearment* (83): it was not a large role, but he made it clear that they deserved each other (for at this point in the plot we had only witnessed her pretensions). Michael Douglas cast him as one of the hamfisted comic villains, Ralphie, in *Romancing the Stone* (84), a second very popular movie, but he was then in the failed gangster spoof, *Johnny Dangerously*; Michael Keaton and Joe Piscopo starred, with DeVito as one of several bad lots wheeling around them, a corrupt District Attorney. Television offered him his first star role in a film and the chance to direct: *The Ratings Game*, in which he was a New Jersey trucking tycoon who intends by fair means or foul (and mostly the latter) to become a big noise in television. Perlman played his girlfriend, and this was the first film made especially for the Movie Channel. Reunited with Douglas for a sequel, *The Jewel of the Nile* (85), Ralphie has become as much companion as enemy, but even at his friendliest he could not resist any chance to double-cross. *Head Office* (86) was a wasted credit, a shapeless comedy about high finance with Judge Reinhold which went speedily to video, as did *Wise Guys*, who were he and Piscopo, not smart enough to cheat their boss (Dan

Hedaya), a petty hood. The latter has his revenge by setting each up to bump the other off: Brian De Palma directed, to prove that comedy was not his forte.

DeVito had his best movie chance yet with *Ruthless People*, this time cast above Reinhold, who with his wife (Helen Slater) kidnaps the wife (Bette Midler) of DeVito, who doesn't want her back. Indeed, in the opening sequence he is telling his mistress that he had planned to have the woman murdered that afternoon – and why not? since he had married her only for her money. DeVito had some splendid looks of glee and cunning, but one wondered what Walter Matthau might have made of the role, since Matthau is a light comedian of genius, while DeVito is only a major talent. Disney produced, and that company handed DeVito a second star role alongside Richard Dreyfuss in Barry Levinson's delightful *Tin Men* (87), as rivals but not friendly ones – in fact, after their autos collide they are each other's *bêtes noires* till DeVito's wife (Barbara Hershey) comes between them, as it were. He had another big one with *Throw Momma from the Train*, which features a scene from *Strangers on a Train*, a viewing of which suggests to DeVito that his Creative Writing professor (Billy Crystal) should exchange a murder with him, for he wants to be rid of his monstrous mother (Anne Ramsey) – because the prof had recommended him to see it in the first place. The producer, Larry Brezner, said he could see DeVito's cherubic face as the right one for one particular joke in the plot, and that he asked him to direct because he had so many ideas on how the film should be done. There was only one mistake in the direction, that DeVito makes his character too much a sweet innocent, a disappointment after the unpleasant role he had taken in *Tin Men*; but the film, which cost $14 million, took $27,800,000 at the box-office.

Still, he was a low-down cunning critter in *Twins* (88), till twin brother Arnold Schwarzenegger proves that being good can be better, and it certainly (see Arnold) paid off at the box-office. And the noise made at the turnstiles by *The War of the Roses* was considerable, with no clashes. DeVito was not only reunited with Kathleen Turner and Douglas, from his two adventure romps, but James L. Brooks, one of the writer-producers of 'Taxi': for Brooks's Gracie Films made this movie, which DeVito directed, as well as playing the Roses' divorce lawyer. Next he will star in *Other People's Money* (91), directed by Norman Jewison, from Jerry Sterner's play. After that, he is due to direct and star in *Hoffa*, as Hoffa's sidekick, after which he will do *Charo*.

MATT DILLON

Matt Dillon has a lean and hungry look, which suits the rather disenchanted youngsters he plays. Something has been said about his being the latest representative of the breed that started – God help us all! – with James Dean. He deserves better, if not (yet) much better.

He was born in a suburb in northern New York in 1964, into a large middle-class Irish-American family. He was a sickly child, but made up for that fact in adolescence when, quite by chance, he became a movie actor. Casting director Vic Ramon was working on a film for Jonathan Kaplan, *Over the Edge* (79), about bored suburban kids who take to drugs, vandalism and worse; so he took himself on a tour of local educational establishments. In Mamoroneck High School he found Dillon, skulking in a corridor because he had cut class: the boy, at fourteen, seemed ideal for one of the spaced-out adolescents of Kaplan's film. Testing him, Ramon decided that he 'had everything' and he quit casting to manage his career. Like the best-remembered of Dean's three films, *Rebel Without a Cause*, Kaplan's film was loaded against the parents in favour of the young ones. It had nowhere near the same success – haven't there been too many movies about the anguish of youth? – and although Dillon, billed third, was noticed, it did not make him a star. Nor did *Little Darlings* (80), in which he was a boy from a nearby camp who is pursued by Kristy McNichol because there is a bet on as to whether she or Tatum O'Neal is the first to lose her virginity. To that end she gets him drunk and is annoyed when he goes to sleep; then, when he's willing and ready the silly goose prevaricates. And so on. After that, anything would be less tiresome, and Tony Bill (in his directing debut) made one of the more pleasing teen pics, *My Bodyguard*, in which Dillon was the school bully, Chris Makepeace his shrimpish victim and Adam Baldwin the possibly dangerous fellow-student who undertakes to protect him, Makepeace.

Ramon did not try to push Dillon into any unsuitable movie, but bided his time: stardom of sorts came when he was chosen to play the lead in the film with which the Disney company tried to change its image, *Tex*. Taken from one of the novels by S.E. Hinton of proven appeal to teens, it told of a no-hoper (Dillon) being cared for, after a fashion, by his ill-tempered brother. Tim Hunter directed, to little avail, for the film did not break Disney's then-run of failures. Nor was much heard of *Liar's Moon*, written and directed by David Fisher, in which he was

'If we ain't got each other, we ain't got nothing' was the motto of the gang in The Outsiders *(83). From left to right: Emilio Estevez, Rob Lowe, C. Thomas Howell, Matt Dillon, Ralph Macchio, Patrick Swayze and Tom Cruise. None of them exactly shone in it, neither was it either much praised or popular – so it wasn't a real stepping-stone to stardom for any of them, as their next films mostly showed, but it was certainly a happy coincidence.*

poor once again, but in love with a rich girl (Cindy Fisher). But Hinton recommended him to Francis Coppola when he was filming *The Outsiders* (83), as one of the chief of them, the cheeky, supposedly experienced Dallas. Because he was better known than some of the others (Tom Cruise, Patrick Swayze, etc.) he was reputedly paid three times more than the other outsiders, and Coppola chose him for the lead in *Rumble Fish*, also from a Hinton novel, as the deprived Tulsa teenager Rusty-James who hero-worships his older brother, Motorcycle Boy (Mickey Rourke). Said Hinton: 'Matt is exactly the kind of kid I write about. Of course, he's a much more complex person than any of my characters, but he has facets of all of them. He has a sweet side, which was good for *Tex*, and that streetwise thing that got him through Dallas in *The Outsiders* and a funny charming cockiness that's perfect for Rusty-James.'

It could be argued that Coppola's two trashy, sentimental, overheated movies made teenagers much less acceptable as movie heroes, but most of the youngsters who took part in them were much in demand for other roles as teen protagonists. Dillon's key to the big time was *The Flamingo Kid* (84), Garry Marshall's engaging movie about a Brooklyn boy in 1963 who gets to move in the Long Island smart set when his girlfriend's father (Richard Crenna) takes a shine to him. He, you see, came from the same background and 'got on', so he's prepared to give the kid a helping hand: not pleased is Dad (Hector Elizondo), who thinks he's getting above himself. Dillon observed that the character as written was not too interesting, but could be made so if given an individuality with what he wore and how he looked. He played with a certain intensity, a broad grin and a furrowed brow, not yielding the screen to the more experienced older actors, both (see above) at their best. The movie did modestly well at the box-office. Dillon was known for it and for being one of the 'brat-pack', which he didn't care for: he knew some of the so-called others, he admitted, because he had acted with them, but he did not hang out with them

In Dillon's case stardom came with The Flamingo Kid (84), left, in which he played a youngster unsure of his direction in life – a description which also may be applied to the drug addict of Drugstore Cowboy (89). The film, however, showed a new maturity in his acting.

– it was, anyway, 'a media-invented thing'. He had a second goodish film with Arthur Penn's thriller, *Target* (85), in which he and his father (Gene Hackman) search over half of Europe for Mama (Gayle Hunnicutt), who had been kidnapped. *Rebel*, however, was pretty disastrous, a wartime story set in Australia, with Dillon as a wounded GI who deserts when he falls in love with a nightclub singer. Nor was *The Big Town* (87) much improvement, with Dillon as a country boy who comes to Chicago back in the 60s and learns to be a big time operator under the tutelage of a gambling couple (Bruce Dern, Lee Grant). The original director left after two days' work and was replaced by the inexperienced Ben Bolt (son of playwright Robert Bolt), who, Dillon said later, did as well as he could under difficult circumstances.

Kansas (88), filmed in Texas, was a further failure, with Dillon as a psychopathic ex-con hooking up with a hitchhiker (Andrew McCarthy) who is persuaded to help him rob a bank. *Bloodhounds of Broadway*, with Madonna, did nothing to change Dillon's losing streak. He now seemed to be the one big new/young star who hadn't made it, and he commented that that was perhaps because he lived in New York (in a hotel) and because he hated publicity (he particularly loathed being described as a sex symbol). Whatever his talent, he needed a good movie, and it was provided by *Drugstore Cowboy* (89), co-written and directed by Gus Van Sant, set in Portland, Oregon, in the 70s, and concerning a couple so 'out' from drugs – the girl was Kelly Lynch – that they can't work, and thus do petty drugstore heists to get more of same. The film was based on a novel by James Fogle, himself apparently an unrepentant addict: everything is seen, therefore, from the point of view of Dillon's character, and in demonstrating this Dillon showed more intelligence and humour than in his previous screen work. His career was renewed thereby, and Dillon was signed up by James Dearden for his remake of *A Kiss Before Dying* (90) which was horribly filmed the first time round. If this version is faithful to Ira Levin's novel it will give Dillon's career a further lift.

MICHAEL DOUGLAS

Ol' Kirk's kid. It took him much, much longer than it did Dad to make it to the front, but he may well be the better actor.

Michael was born to Kirk Douglas and his English actress wife Diana Dill in New Brunswick, New Jersey, in 1944. His parents divorced when he was eight, and he left Los Angeles to live with his mother in Westport, Connecticut. He went to military academy and spent some of his childhood summers on his father's movie sets, and later he was assistant director on *Lonely are the Brave* (62), *Heroes of Telemark* (65) and *Cast a Giant Shadow*. 'I saw enough of my father's household,' he said later, 'to know how the business can control your life without your even being aware of it – you have to keep something for yourself.' But his experience on these three films made him decide to be an actor, and he studied drama at the University

of California till – a true child of the 60s – he dropped out 'to experiment with life'; he pumped gas for a while in Westport and with his mother's encouragement became involved with the National Playwrights' Conference in Connecticut. He took acting classes again in New York and had some small parts off-Broadway as 'M.K. Douglas'. He appeared with Teresa Wright in the highly-acclaimed 'The Experiment' on CBS television and was her son in *Hail Hero* (69), which just happened to be directed by David Miller, who had helmed *Lonely are the Brave*. CBS, which produced, in its brief foray into cinema movies, announced that he had been selected from two hundred applicants, but few heard of the film anyway. Arthur Kennedy was the father, and Douglas was a hippie who enlists to fight in Vietnam in a war he doesn't believe in. In 'Newsweek', Joseph Morgenstern called it a movie about 'life, love, death, age, youth and cowflap'.

Steve McQueen's company, Solar, gave Douglas another star role, as a young Californian professor who buckles down to a labouring job, in Missouri, in his summer vacation: *Adam at Six A.M.* (70), which went unreleased in most countries. His father's company produced *Summertree* (71), in which he was a young music student anxious to avoid the Vietnam draft despite the objections of his parents (Barbara Bel Geddes, Jack Warden). It was a role he had originated in Connecticut, but when Ron Cowen's play moved to off-Broadway he was replaced by David Birney. Marginally more popular was Disney's *Napoleon and Samantha* (72), in which he befriended two kids who run away with their pet lion. On television, he was son to Ben Gazzara and Elizabeth Ashley, bothered *When Michael Calls*, for Michael had been lost to them some fifteen years before. Also for that medium he was Karl Malden's young college-educated partner in a cop thriller, *The Streets of San Francisco*. That became an hour-long series which ran from 1972 to 1976. For Douglas it was a way of learning, of overcoming his self-consciousness before the camera, and he likened it to the experience of summer stock. He also directed two episodes. In 1977 he married Diandra Murrell Luker.

During this period he left the streets of San Francisco to produce a movie, *One Flew Over the Cuckoo's Nest* (75), based on a play (based on a novel) which his father had done on Broadway; Kirk Douglas had bought the movie rights, but when he couldn't get backing he turned it over to Michael. The film's success brought renewed attention to Michael, who was offered a role in a movie. This was Michael Crichton's chilling *Coma* (78), and he was the nice lover of its heroine,

Geneviève Bujold, but also capable of seeming to be part of the conspiracy against her. When he was sent the script of *The China Syndrome* (79) as a result of producing *One Flew Over the Cuckoo's Nest*, he knew that he had another major movie on his hands. He put together a package of himself, Jack Lemmon, Jane Fonda (whose company gets a co-producer credit, partly because her role, intended for Richard Dreyfuss, was hardly defined when she agreed to take part) and director James Bridges, whom he had first known as writer of *When Michael Calls*. Douglas played a freelance newscaster who joins Fonda in bucking the system to expose a leak at a nuclear power station. Since most of the piece takes place there, Columbia had not much, visually, to use in publicity, so they concentrated on the three stars gazing earnestly at the camera. The two producers look proudly it, and they had much to be proud about, since the film has much that must be said on several important matters, not least the conflict that can arise between money and responsibility. The film cost almost $6 million, and after the previews, the studio decided to spend half as much again to promote it. It took $25,300,000, making Douglas one of the hottest producers in the business, for the two films he had made in that capacity had been liked by both the press and the public.

He chose instead to return to acting, because he liked the script of *Running* when he received it from Canada. He played a shoe-salesman who opts to train for the Olympic Games to restore his self-esteem after his job and his marriage have fallen apart. The film was little seen outside Canada and it had cost only $3,650,000, but Douglas negotiated deals in the US with Universal, ABC television and cable which put it well into profit ($5,500,000) without consideration of its Canadian earnings – for which he was rewarded with a credit as 'Executive Producer' (which he has since had removed). *It's My Turn* (80) was, however, a turn for the worse, as 'Playboy' put it. Claudia Weill directed from a first screenplay by the novelist Eleanor Bergstein which was pretentious and empty; Jill Clayburgh played a brilliant professor of mathematics who leaves her lover (Charles Grodin) to attend her mother's new wedding, where she meets her new stepfather's son (Douglas). Few went to see it, and the rather better *The Star Chamber* (83) was hardly more popular – perhaps because it was too predictable as directed by Peter Hyams from a novel by Roderick Taylor. Douglas played an idealistic young judge who is drawn into a clandestine society of top legal people whose aim is to punish criminals who have been acquitted on some technicality. Sharon Gless,

Michael Douglas and Jane Fonda in The China Syndrome *(79), co-producers of the film, which cast them as an investigative news team checking out some probably lethal happenings at a nuclear power plant.*

who played his wife, was later to say that he was 'one of the most intense actors I have ever worked with. I suppose it takes that kind of self-confidence and focus to get out of the shadow of somebody like his father. But I wonder if he doesn't drive himself too hard. He isn't easy to get to know. He's not a talker or a smiler, or someone to exchange easy banter with.'

He did not seem to be the ideal action adventurer, and that was a role in which he now cast himself: *Romancing the Stone* (84). He had been trying to find a serious script of the same quality as the two which he had produced, and when one failed to materialize he decided to go to the other extreme, making a piece of pop entertainment. When the film was compared with *Raiders of the Lost Ark*, he confessed himself irritated, because he had had the script for five years. He chose Robert Zemeckis to direct and Kathleen Turner to co-star: together they clambered through the jungles of Colombia, and though he was preferable to his father at his most determined, you could not be blamed for thinking he might be better occupied. He is not in the class of Errol Flynn, who brought charm and bravado to his tales of derring-do: Douglas, in contrast, is a schmuck to whom things happen. 20th-Century-Fox, which backed the film, were putting all their might behind *Rhinestone* and *Johnny Dangerously* that season, but the public decided that it was Douglas's film they wanted to see: it made $36 million in the domestic market. Money must be a factor in discussing *A Chorus Line* (85), based on what is in many ways the most successful-ever Broadway musical. For one thing, it ran for fifteen years, 1975–90. Universal paid $5,500,000 for the film rights in 1976, but it was to change hands – to go to Embassy and thus Columbia, when Coca-Cola, who owned that company, decided to add Embassy to its movie holdings. The result cost $27 million, in an age when movie musicals were firmly believed to be dead: and by taking only $9,800,000 it did little to confound the pessimists. Blamed for the failure was the director, Richard Attenborough, perhaps because he was both British and perceived to be square. Several American directors had looked at the material without seeing it as a viable movie, partly because it is little more than a series of rehearsals for a Broadway show, with some flashy numbers fleshed out by monologues from the chorus line. Attenborough could certainly have brought more pizzazz, but perhaps what was missing most was any premise of the part the Broadway theatre plays in New York mythology. As the director of the show, growling from the darkness of the stalls, Douglas sounded like his father; but in close-up he was much more sympathetic, and sufficiently strong in personality to flesh out a character written only as a cipher. *The Jewel of the Nile*, released at the same time, was a sequel to *Romancing the Stone*: lighter, and altogether more entertaining, it cost $21 million and took just a little more than its predecessor – $36,500,000. The comic villain was again played by Danny DeVito.

The film, however, which consolidated Douglas's popularity was *Fatal Attraction* (87), in which he played a lawyer who has an idle fling with a publisher (Glenn Close); he is married, and then he discovers that not only will she not let go, but is psychotic as well. Fiendishly clever (at least, till the threatened family start leaving doors unlocked), as directed by Adrian Lyne and written by James Dearden, it cost $14 million and took $70 million. And Douglas had a second big success that year, with *Wall Street*, which had a budget of $19 million and a take of $20 million. Oliver Stone, fresh from winning an Oscar for *Platoon*, was the director, and there was a certain amount of tension between him and Douglas over the latter's performance. He plays a financial wheeler-dealer, Gordon Gekko, with a lot of power and few ethics – role-model for the picture's young hero, played by Charlie Sheen (another second-generation actor, incidentally). In an era of financial scandals in high places, Gordon Gekko's name took on a life beyond the film, and since he had many different and elegant braces it was only right that men's fashion designer Alan Fusser was the first person to be thanked in the credits (*Wall Street* brought braces back into fashion). It would seem that Stone cast Douglas in the role in the hope that he would play in his father's aggressive, self-confident manner – at least, he has said that that was what he wanted from the actor. Douglas himself says that he resisted taking roles which were like any that his father had played, but the piece has a happy ending: he carried off the Oscar for the Year's Best Actor. The award, however, did result in some strain between the two Douglases – for Kirk never won one. 'I just happened to be in the right place at the right time,' said Michael. 'My dad *is* jealous about it. Somewhat. It's mingled with his pride in me.'

In 1986 he had made a deal with Mercury Entertainment to produce two films for HBO, but nothing more was heard of this till Mercury announced that they needed 'to introduce new flexibility into the arrangement so that Michael can pursue the opportunities he has now.' These would establish Douglas as one of the most successful actors in Hollywood: *The War of the Roses* (89) and *Black Rain*. The first reunited Douglas and Miss Turner – and DeVito, who was also directing, but it was a far cry from their earlier films together, for the Roses were a couple at daggers drawn when their marriage breaks up; it was said to be a comedy, but there was little to laugh about in the second half of the film. Ridley Scott directed the other one, in which Douglas is a maverick New York cop who, on an assignment in Japan, teams up with the Yakuza (the Japanese Mafia). The budget on the first was $25 million and it did a handsome $40 million for 20th-Century-Fox; the respective figures for Paramount are $30 million and $22,500,000 – not a disastrous loss.

In May 1990, Columbia dropped, or did not renew, its 'first refusal' agreements drawn up by Dawn Steel in her tenure at the studio with such names as Madonna, Pierce Brosnan, Molly Ringwald, Diane Keaton and Richard Gere. Douglas was among the most prominent survivors, along with Sally Field, Cher and Jane Fonda; but his next movie would be for 20th-Century-Fox, *Shining Through* (91), a romantic spy thriller with Melanie Griffith.

After that, *Basic Instinct*, with some basic disagreements between Douglas and director Paul Verhoeven on one hand, and writer Joe Ezterhas and producer Irwin Winkler on the other – with both of these last-named leaving the project. Mention was also made of *The Fugitive*, based on the old television serial, but that will now be made with Alec Baldwin replacing Douglas.

Around this time he said: 'I didn't always think of myself as leading man material. Not in that almost superhuman sense that Kirk Douglas was, and is, a leading man. I knew I wasn't conventionally goodlooking . . . Those charismatic personalities, in my opinion, are a thing of the past. I think my father was one of the last of them. I'm thinking of people like Garbo and Gable, and all those extraordinary people from the 30s and 40s. The people other people would line up round the block to see *any* film they appeared in. I don't think that exists any more. Now, with myself, or others, it depends on the story, the character you're playing, the other actors. And so I pay real close attention to all of that. Especially a strong script.'

Michael Douglas as Gordon Gekko in Wall Street *(87), for which he won an Oscar – after the director, Oliver Stone, had persuaded him that that he should play the role in the assertive manner of his father.*

Andy Garcia, left, and Douglas in Ridley Scott's thriller, Black Rain *(89), in which they are a top New York police team sent to Japan on a dangerous assignment.*

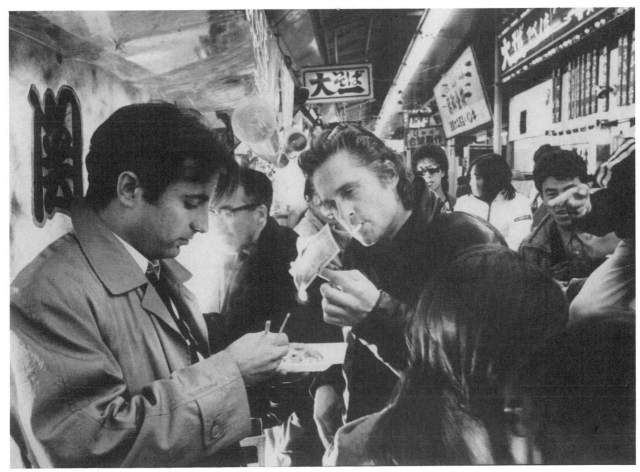

RICHARD DREYFUSS

When Richard Dreyfuss collected his Oscar for *The Goodbye Girl*, he could not help betraying some of the characteristics he had shown in an earlier film, *The Apprenticeship of Duddy Kravitz* – a certain, shall we say? pushiness, a certain lack of modesty. With it – which was why the Oscar was such a popular one – is a beaming charm rare among his generation of actors, and 'energy that just flies off the screen', as it was put by Neil Simon, who wrote *The Goodbye Girl*. He doesn't, he went on, 'fall into any of the usual acting categories. He's not a handsome-man type like Redford or a dramatic-actor type like Pacino or De Niro. Rich can do anything – and he is funnier than any of them.'

He was born in Brooklyn in 1947, and he made his stage debut at the age of nine at the West Side Jewish Center in Beverly Hills. His family had moved there, and he graduated from there; he also studied at San Fernando Valley State College and spent two years as a clerk in an LA hospital, because he had registered as a conscientious objector in the Vietnam War. Never having any doubts that he would be an actor, he acted wherever and whenever he could – off-Broadway, TV, and once at the Playboy Club in New York with a comedy group which was fired after one show for insulting the customers. In films he started with one line each in *The Graduate* (67) and *Valley of the Dolls*, progressing to slightly larger roles in *The Young Runaways* (68), which was about Chicago hippies, with Dreyfuss as a cocky car-thief, and *Hello Down There* (69), which had songs, dolphins, Tony Randall and Janet Leigh. Among much work for the small screen was *Two for the Money* (72), a cop thriller which starred Robert Hooks. He was first seen in a big screen role in *Dillinger* (73), as Baby Face Nelson, but he had already made *American Graffiti*, which followed aimless youth around one small Californian town one fine summer day (and night). As directed by George Lucas, their junketings were mild but entertaining, and their company ingratiating – especially Dreyfuss as the would-be loner, secret and yet open, modest and yet conceited, and always humorous. The film was a huge, huge success, and led to the lead in a Canadian film, *The Apprenticeship of Duddy Kravitz* (74), which is 'What Makes Sammy Run?' transferred to Montreal, its hero – as his Uncle Ben says – 'a little Jewboy on the make'. *The Second Coming of Suzanne*, made earlier, quickly disappeared.

When he saw *Duddy Kravitz*, he was so appalled by his own performance that he decided that he would never be offered work again. He considered, therefore, that he should take whatever was offered next, and never did a wiser thing. *Jaws* (75) had been a bestselling novel about shark-hunting, and as directed by Steven Spielberg it had a strong narrative drive; blessed with the biggest promotion budget in Universal's history, it became the biggest-grossing film in Hollywood's history – and that was due in no short measure to the performances of Roy Scheider as the worried police-chief and Dreyfuss as the (bearded and be-spectacled) oceanographer. Dreyfuss achieved an ambition to play Cassius in 'Julius Caesar' in New York for Joseph Papp – but briefly, for it was cancelled in rehearsal, which led, he says, to a breakdown. He was no luckier on *Inserts*, on which he was associate producer: he played an old-time movie-star eking out a living directing porno movies – but neither the press nor public was also very interested. There was an offer from TV, to play an Israeli colonel in the all-star *Victory at Entebbe* (76), which played cinemas overseas. It was not, in those venues, a success, but the next one was, and a high-budget one – Spielberg's *Close Encounters of the Third Kind* (77), which though thematically and morally a mess was a dazzling cinema experience; Dreyfuss was a hard hat who becomes obsessed with UFOs. It was easy to overlook him amid the hardware; but impossible – as the Academy voters proved – in *The Goodbye Girl*, as aspiring actor and unwilling lodger to Marsha Mason, the two of them falling into a love affair as calculated as anything in today's movies – but as touching and funny as it is rare. The film took $49,893,000 for Rastar, giving him (if we ignore *Inserts*, which got little distribution) three giant movie hits in a row. Their popularity did not extend to him, however, if we are to believe the mere $6,256,000 taken by *The Big Fix* (78), despite warm notices for the film, which he co-produced, and himself personally: '[it] delivers what is for him a particularly relaxed and confident performance', said 'Variety'. Jeremy Paul Kagan directed this twisty private-eye thriller, in which Dreyfuss is a Jewish investigator who discovers that disillusionment with 60s radicalism is at the root of the mayhem. In 1979 he played Iago in Central Park.

The casting of Bob Fosse's autobiographical *All This Jazz* was said to be a nightmare when originally announced, for the leading character was bisexual: Dreyfuss dared to tread where many others had refused, but left by mutual agreement after two weeks because he could not handle the choreography, to be replaced by Roy Scheider. By the time the film was finished, all hints of deviance were gone, while the time was nigh when leading

Richard Dreyfuss and Marsha Mason, who was then Mrs Neil Simon, in The Goodbye Girl *(77), for which he won his Best Actor Oscar. The reviews were no better than usual for one of Simon's films, but the public soon discovered that they liked this one even better than most of the others.*

Dreyfuss in trouble in The Big Fix *(78) – but he's a dectective, so more than a match for one of LA's finest.*

stars would play gay men. Returning to Rastar, he played a piano-teacher who decides he wants to win *The Competition* (80), being rather nasty to young Amy Irving before falling in love with her. That film took $7 million, and for the same company he was due to appear in *Burr*, based on Gore Vidal's novel, but the project was cancelled. He turned down *Arthur* and instead appeared in *Whose Life Is It Anyway?* (81), a drama about euthanasia which had been a big hit in London and New York – not a cheery subject, but he has a merry quip for every occasion. He manages a few teary scenes without becoming maudlin, and holds the film together: the trouble was, it was not worth holding as directed by John Badham and written by Brian Clark (author of the original play) and Reginald Rose. Not a cliché was missed – neither was the fact that the Dreyfuss role was little but show-off: so when the film failed dismally his career nose-dived. He was regarded by the industry as arrogant and difficult; and he did himself no good at all when his Mercedes convertible went into a tree in October 1982 and he was found to be in possession of cocaine. He himself said that he had begun the downward path by becoming addicted to amphetamines while working in hospital to avoid the draft; in this case he was let off, provided he attended a rehabilitation centre. In 1983 he married a television writer, Jeramie Rain, who will be known to readers of Bob Woodward's biography of John Belushi, 'Wired'.

Various projects came to nothing, of which the most consistent was *Benya the King* in France for director Aleksander Petrovic with Isabelle Adjani, but after one postponement it was cancelled. He returned to the stage, doing 'A Day in the Death of Joe Egg' for a month with Stockard Channing in Williamstown, Mass., and he was on Broadway in 1983 in 'Total Abandon'. He finally got a movie job at 20th-Century-Fox, carrying no salary but with a participation: *The Buddy System* (84), in which he is a school caretaker who is also a struggling writer with a glamorous mistress. The film cuts away from him constantly to a single mother (Susan Sarandon), and by the time they eventually meet and hop in the sack what audiences there were had long ago gone to sleep. It was not so much bad as grindingly mediocre, and those territories where it did not even make it to video could count themselves lucky. For Dreyfuss, however, it was the way back. He said: 'The night I received the Academy Award I looked out into the faces of the audience and I didn't feel like a member of the community. I decided I wanted to be' – and he accordingly made an agreement with Columbia for four films, each to be done as his last one, with no salary but with a participation. Nothing happened. He appeared in Los Angeles in a play about a man with Aids, 'The Normal Heart' at the time that he finally had (after almost two years) a new film coming out: *Down and Out*

in Beverly Hills (85). The director, Paul Mazursky, was an admirer, and he had invited Dreyfuss to play Bette Midler's husband, the coat-hanger manufacturer who on a whim invites a bum (Nick Nolte) to move in. Whatever pretensions to class the piece possessed were all in Dreyfuss's performance. He has a way of moving and standing which exudes self-satisfaction, but his impish, quizzical expressions ensure that we like the man; and his timing was beautiful. The film's success (see Midler) meant that Dreyfuss again had his pick of offers – especially at Disney, where the film was made.

He played a cameo role in Rob Reiner's *Stand By Me* (86) as the middle-aged writer recalling the events of one summer when he and some schoolfriends went to explore the woodlands of Oregon. There were two for Disney: Barry Levinson's sprightly, affectionate *Tin Men* (87), battling it out, literally, with rival salesman Danny DeVito in Baltimore in 1963, and Badham's *Stakeout*, a comic-cop tale in which he had Emilio Estevez as his (much younger) partner. The first cost $15 million and took $11,200,000; the second cost $14 million and took $24,600,000. The box-office appeal – which was middling – of *Nuts* would be due to its top-billed star, Barbra Streisand, who chose Dreyfuss to be her (bearded) lawyer in the picture, one reluctant to take her case but, once retained, very caring. Dreyfuss had liked his three pictures for Disney but did not care for the next, a revamp of *The Prisoner of Zenda*, *Moon Over Parador* (88): 'It should have been a lot funnier,' he said. 'Everyone looks a little tight-assed in that film.' The public did not care for it either, chalking up only a $5 million return on its $20 million cost. Mazursky co-wrote and directed it, and it is neither better nor worse than others on his fairly dismal record – if with a smarter idea than some, when an unsuccessful actor (Dreyfuss) is employed to impersonate a recently deceased dictator in a Caribbean republic. He played a cab-driver who becomes a compulsive gambler in *Let It Ride* (89), which he did not care for either: 'I thought we were making a rude, funny, edgy, impolite, make-you-nervous kind of comedy – which we weren't successful in when we shot it.' Paramount was not happy with it, he added: they certainly did not show it to New York's critics, a ploy which might have helped it to return as much as $2,100,000 of its $18 million.

For a while it seemed he was about to begin *Men*, a remake of Doris Dorrie's German film, with that lady again in command; it was to have been produced for Lorimar, whose head, Bernie Brillstein, was described in the trade press as Dreyfuss's 'management client'.

Dreyfuss again as a cop, with Emilio Estevez, left, as his partner, in a comedy thriller, Stakeout *(87), in which they search a murderer by spying on his voluptuous girlfriend.*

Lorimar, however, were having financial difficulties and Dreyfuss began *Dinosaurs* for Tri-Star, with Elliott Gould co-starring, but it was abandoned due to 'creative disagreement' between Dreyfuss and the director, Mark Rydell. Tri-Star sought to have Dreyfuss made liable for all expenses, to which he responded by seeking a 'judicial ruling' claiming that he was not responsible, and demanding $3,500,000 against 10% of the 'adjusted gross receipts' (which was presumably his fee). The suit was quickly settled in his favour, and the film was started again with Gene Hackman and Mikhail Baryshnikov.

He returned to Spielberg for *Always*, a remake of *A Guy Named Joe* which the director had long planned – an odd choice for a movie, since even wartime sentiment could not excuse the original, in which a dead pilot returns as a ghost to guide a younger one after his girlfriend has recovered from grief by falling in love with him. This had been updated, so that it no longer concerned sorties over the Pacific, but fighting forest fires from the air; Holly Hunter played the girl. Dreyfuss and Spielberg had discovered a common love of the original while making *Jaws*, which additionally Dreyfuss credits with having taught him how to court women. He could not have felt too happy with his participation in this version, for poor reviews included little enthusiasm for his own performance. 'On screen he has a smugness that is as far as can be imagined from Spencer Tracy's persona' said Adam Mars-Jones in the 'Independent', 'and a crucial inability to let the material breathe.' The film cost $31 million and is expected (by 'Variety') to return only $20 million.

Dreyfuss's fee at this time was said to be $4 million per film, but he agreed to a salary of only $75,000 when he replaced Sean Connery in *Rosencrantz and Guildenstern Are Dead* (90), after Connery changed his mind and the money-men got cold feet. For this was 'minority' cinema, as written and directed (his debut in that capacity) by Tom Stoppard, from his lauded play about two of the minor players in 'Hamlet'. It had, and has in this version, as much tension, cohesion and finesse as the foolish dreams most of us have on first awakening, but Gore Vidal (as president of the jury, and who should have known better) championed it at the Venice Festival, where its Grand Prix was roundly booed by the prize-night audience. Dreyfuss played the king, Claudius if you like, or the head of the strolling players, billed after the actors playing R and G, Gary Oldman and Tim Roth. He played another supporting role in *Postcards From the Edge*, released simultaneously, as the doctor who cures drug-addicted Meryl Streep – playing Carrie Fisher, some say, though others claim that Ms Fisher's novel is not as autobiographical as all that (certainly Shirley MacLaine, playing Streep's mother, says she is not Debbie Reynolds, who is Fisher's mother). Dreyfuss also appears in *Once Around* (91), a May-September romance which reunites him with Holly Hunter, directed by Lasse Hallstrom, the Swedish director whose spurious *My Life as a Dog* had received acclaim in some – indeed, many – quarters; Hallstrom had originally intended to do it with Dustin Hoffman, and he left *Mermaids* when the chance came to make it with Dreyfuss. At one point Dreyfuss was to have appeared in a remake of the French *Romuald et Juliette*, with Colette Serreau again directing, but that was cancelled. Instead he will star in *What About Bob?*, directed by Frank Oz, with Bill Murray co-starring. In 1990 this busy actor fronted a series for Fox television, 'American Chronicles', and he bought the rights to 'The Proud and the Free', Howard Fast's 1949 novel about the American Revolution. Brave man, this Dreyfuss, or else he hasn't heard what happened to *Revolution* (see Pacino).

ROBERT DUVALL

Robert Duvall had been a supporting player for almost two decades when he was nominated for the Best Actor Oscar in *The Great Santini*. The award went to Robert De Niro for *Raging Bull*. 'Had I lost to the other three nominees,' observed Duvall, 'I'd have said "bullshit".' (They were John Hurt in *The Elephant Man*, Jack Lemmon in *Tribute* and Peter O'Toole in *The Stunt Man*.) He said, during the same conversation, that he did not admire Olivier because he was 'too stylized'. On another occasion he said that he had seen Lee J. Cobb and Spencer Tracy in the same movie, but preferred Tracy because he was more natural. In his own gallery of admirable screen portrayals Duvall comes at us with nothing between himself and us but his emotion which, because he is a master of his craft, is always under control. He has intensity only when he needs it. He is not a star in the old sense, but he may be the best living American actor.

He was born in San Diego, California, in 1931, the second of three sons of a rear-admiral. His mother, an amateur actress, encouraged an interest in drama, which he studied at Principia College in Illinois. In 1953 after two years in the army he headed to New York for more acting classes, with Sandy Meisner at the Neighborhood Playhouse, supporting himself by dishwashing, driving trucks and with a spell as a postal clerk. One of his first professional roles was as March-banks in 'Candida' (58); among some scores of other performances in stock (mainly in Belleport, Long Island) and off-Broadway he was in 'The Days and Nights of Bee Bee Fenstermaker', 'Call Me By My Rightful Name' and 'A View From the Bridge'. He said later that the combination of thinning hair and not knowing which role he would be playing till just before rehearsal forced him into becoming a character actor. Among the works he appeared in at the Playhouse was one by Horton Foote, who was so impressed that he recommended him to director Robert Mulligan when he was commissioned to write the screenplay of *To Kill a Mocking-Bird* (62). The role was a small but crucial one, Boo Radley, the local 'looney' who is the chil-dren's pet bogeyman. That led to solid employment as a supporting player: *Captain Newman M.D.* (63), as an officer in a catato-nic trance; *Nightmare in the Sun* (65), a co-star venture for John Derek and his then wife, Ursula Andress, with him and Richard Jaeckel as bikers; and *The Chase* (66) as a prissy vice-president of a bank. He was in a television film, *Fame is the Name of the Game*, a remake of *Chicago Deadline*, with Anthony Franciosa in Alan Ladd's old role as a fearless reporter (this became a series, with Gene Barry and Robert Stack rotating with Fran-ciosa in the leading role). Duvall's other work in this medium included, among others, 'Route 66', 'The Naked City', 'The Defen-ders' and 'Outer Limits'. He returned to New York to appear opposite Lee Remick in 'Wait Until Dark'; he said later, referring to *Night-mare in the Sun*, 'I had begun to think I had made a great mistake in going to Hollywood. My life had been tied to New York, but it's not possible to do the two things in America, because of the geography. The theater is in New York, the cinema is three thousand miles away in California. You can't commute. The sunshine just gets to you. They say that if you don't get out of Los Angeles within a month of arriving, you never leave.'

Well, back there, then, he appeared with James Caan in *Countdown* (68), a dopey drama about the Russian–American space race directed by Robert Altman before he hit his stride; Caan was an astronaut and Duvall his tough instructor. There were small roles in those that followed: *The Detective*, as a anti-gay sidekick of the closet queen (Tony Musante) who is the villain of the piece; *Bullitt*, as a cab-driver, fifth-billed and a small role, but essential to the plot; *True Grit* (69), as the leader of the gang out to get one-eyed John Wayne, and as good a bad man as you'll

ever get; and Francis Coppola's *The Rain People* with Caan, as a motor-cycle cop who tries to rape the heroine. These last four credits provided Duvall with as good a batch of movies as any supporting actor ever had, and if only the last was a box-office failure, it still trailed prestige. He had two further fine movies with Altman's *M-A-S-H* (70), as the sexually repressed officer who gets to make it with 'Hot Lips' (Sally Kellerman), and Paul Williams's *The Revolutionary*, as the old-hand activist who encourages Jon Voight in his anarchic aspirations. The first was a success, but the other was not. A protégé of Coppola, George Lucas, gave Duvall his biggest screen role to date, in *THX 1138* (71), developed from his (Lucas's) own student film: Warner Bros, who had offered development money on the strength of Coppola's record to date, demanded it back, for the result was virtually unshowable. Duvall played the title-role, an automaton living in some computerized Dys-topia. From that it must have been a relief to work even for Michael Winner, who directed him as a dirt-poor cowardly killer hiding away from *Lawman* Burt Lancaster.

The one that made the difference was Coppola's *The Godfather* (72) – that is, the one that made Duvall best known to the public at large, because of the film's success: he played the trusted *consigliere* or lawyer to the Mafia family, a courtier dancing attend-ance on crime tsar Brando. On *Tomorrow*, Duvall renewed acquaintance with Horton Foote, this time adapting a story by William Faulkner. The role, for which he was top-billed, was much too similar to Boo Radley, Duvall said later, adding that he was not sorry that the film failed, as he had quarrelled with the director, Joseph Anthony, over the edit-ing. Whatever, the result was relentlessly grim as Duvall, an almost catatonic handyman in a sawmill, falls unwillingly in love with the pregnant woman (Olga Bellin) for whom he is caring. Although two Westerns did better (obviously), neither was a commercial triumph: John Sturges's *Joe Kidd*, in which Duvall was evil again, as the landowner who employs Clint Eastwood to subdue the honest homesteaders, and Philip Kaufman's *The Great Northfield Missouri Raid*, as Jesse James to Cliff Robertson's Cole Younger. He played cops in both his films the following year: Tom Gries's *Lady Ice* (73), a caper thriller starring Donald Sutherland, which opened first in foreign markets, and Howard W. Koch's *Badge 373*, written by Pete Hamill from the exploits of real-life policeman Eddie Egan, played by the top-billed Duvall – while Egan supported him in a brief role as his superior. Both of these missed, but Duvall had a good one in John Flynn's *The Outfit*

(74), in the lead as a bank robber seeking revenge when released from bail. Coppola sent for him again for *The Conversation*, to play the sinister director whose tape causes Gene Hackman so much aggro; he was un-billed for his one scene, but chillingly effective. He had a second important assignment for Coppola, in his sequel, *The Godfather Part II*, playing the lawyer again. His salary was $135,000 plus a small percentage, which caused him to comment that he would become a millionaire if it did only half as well as the original (which it didn't: $30,700,000, as opposed to over $86,275,000). He declined to do *Nashville*, later observing that if you turn down Altman he doesn't ask you again. There were better roles to be had in two action thrillers, Gries's *Breakout* (75) and Sam Peckinpah's *The Killer Elite*. In the former his grandfather (John Huston) has had him imprisoned on a trumped-up charge, so his wife (Jill Ireland) hires a mercenary (Charles Bronson) to help him; in the second, moustached and with an oily smile, he pumps a couple of non-fatal bullets into James Caan, who accordingly wants revenge.

But he realized that he could be typed as an all-purpose villain, so he accepted more taxing roles in Lumet's *Network* (76), that of a shark-like television executive, and Nicholas Meyer's *The Seven-Per-Cent Solution*, Dr Watson to Nicol Williamson's Sherlock Holmes. Over the last three years he had directed and co-produced a documentary about redneck farmers in Nebraska (whom he had come to know while making *The Rain People*), but the result, *We're Not the Jet Set* (77) failed to make much impression. Nor did his other two films that year: Sturges's *The Eagle Has Landed* with Michael Caine, as a Nazi intelligence officer, and Gries's film about and with Cassius Clay/Muhammed Ali, *The Greatest*, a title which in no way described it: Duvall had only a cameo role. He played Olivier's grandson in Daniel Petrie's *The Betsy* (78), both of them automobile tycoons: he opted for soft villainy this time, the moustache pencil-thin and the smile merely queasy. He did another unbilled spot – five seconds as a priest on a swing – in Kaufman's *Invasion of the Body Snatchers*, and then did a role turned down by Gene Hackman, in Coppola's *Apocalypse Now* (79), a war-loving general. He had the temperament to play authoritative, bigoted men, and this one brought him a BAFTA award for Best Supporting Actor. He played another officer, a really high-ranking one, in *Ike: the War Years*, a mini-series about General Eisenhower for ABC television. His resemblance to Ike was closer than many others in biographical subjects.

The steps by which a supporting, or character, actor becomes a star are little trod, partly because the industry has traditionally put looks and youth before talent. The best exemplars before Robert Duvall are Humphrey Bogart and Lee Marvin. The public and critics recognised a star in Bogey long before Warners, who reluctantly bestowed stardom when other actors turned down roles which they let him play; in Marvin's case it took him almost two decades to attain star-billing, which he did mainly by being a memorable villain. In Duvall's case it was clear not long after he started that he was an exceptional actor – but it was not until The Great Santini *(79), above, that he had a large role to his measure. It was a role few leading actors wanted – for the man was a near-alcoholic bully with an opinion of himself shared neither by his fellow-officers or his family. Three years later, Duvall was to win a Best Actor Oscar for* Tender Mercies, *and there was an inevitability about that too, for it was one of those performances which, although quiet and controlled, would knock you between the eyes.*

He did a familiar part again in *The Great Santini*, but this time it was the star role in which his admirers had long hoped to see him. The occasion caused Vincent Canby in the 'New York Times' to say: 'Now it's about time to recognize Robert Duvall as one of the most resourceful, most technically proficient, most remarkable actors in America today . . . [Having just seen him in this film] I think he may be the best we have, the American Olivier.' 'The redoubtable Robert Duvall has played this role before', said David Denby in 'New York' magazine. 'Duvall has an ironclad forehead, a frightening shark's smile, paranoid eyes, and a lusterless, bullhorn voice that doesn't provide much shading or variety. He's an accomplished, powerful, uningratiating actor.' As Lt-Colonel 'Bull' Meechum, he describes himself to his family as 'the meanest, toughest, screamingest' and to his troops simply as 'God'; he's also considered by his C.O. to be virtually an alcoholic, but kept on by him because he's considered a good leader. For the film's sake he is seen through his son (Michael O'Keefe), as in Pat Conroy's autobiographical novel: but apart from Duvall the writer-director Lewis John Carlino has overheated matters, so that all Duvall's skill and energy cannot bring the piece to success. In his book, 'Adventures in the Screen Trade', William Goldman analyses one sequence with admiration – 'but most of all I blessed that great *character actor*, Robert Duvall' because the guy is a loser, and 'no major star would ever ever ever in this world play it.'

Ulu Grosbard's *True Confessions* (81) was based on a novel by John Gregory Dunne, who wrote the screenplay with his wife, Joan Didion. Duvall and Robert De Niro co-starred, playing brothers with combined attack and intelligence, the former as a cop and the latter a monsignor. Like that, *The Pursuit of D.B. Cooper* was also based on fact – an incident in 1971 when a man pulled a gun on a jet over Seattle and parachuted out, $200,000 richer. As directed by Roger Spottiswoode, the result is a half-hearted thriller, and it is hard to see what attracted Duvall to the role of the insurance investigator, unless it was top billing (over Treat Williams, as the Cooper character). As he says himself, 'You hope you can work three times a year – I like to work more – but something good only comes along maybe *once* a year.' The rest of the time he spends on his farm in Virginia.

Duvall and Foote teamed up to co-produce *Tender Mercies* (82), which Foote had written for him, utilizing his love of music – and in the film two of the songs sung by Duvall were also composed by him. He plays a drunk who, deserted by a chum, gets a job as handyman to a woman (Tess Harper) who runs a lonely run-down motel. The subject is only about his reformation, and all we have to worry about is whether he'll fall off the wagon. Universal were willing to put up only part of the budget and the rest came from Britain; an Australian, Bruce Beresford, was brought in to direct, and though the film demonstrates a fascination with that part of Texas in which it was set, it was not a happy shoot. There was friction between him and Duvall, who explained: 'Hell, I was just trying to tell him to leave me alone. Any director who never

asks you, "What do *you* think?", well, he's in trouble. The way I see it, an actor's job is to get off-camera as fast as possible.' The film opened to warm notices but little business – who wanted to see an alcoholic ex-C & W singer make eyes at a young widow? – so it went quickly to cable, which, knowing that it had something special, publicized it heavily: it took only just over $2,500,000 at the box-office, but most people had seen it by the time Duvall won his well-deserved and popular Best Actor Oscar.

Duvall had already done a film for HBO and Canadian television, *The Terry Fox Story* (83), in which he played the PR man from the Cancer Society who promoted Terry's run after he had been stricken by illness. Encouraged by Duvall's Oscar, some distributors showed it in cinemas in foreign territories – without success; nor was there a much warmer welcome for Duvall's second film as a director, *Angelo My Love*, the story of a New York gypsy hustler, which he also wrote and produced. *The Stone Boy* (84), with Glenn Close, deserved better but was little seen. That could not be said of *The Natural*, because it starred Robert Redford; Duvall had little more than a cameo as a leading sports-writer. The impetus given Duvall's career by the Oscar was further dissipated by *The Lightship* (85), an odd venture with a Williams–O'Neill-type hero reminiscing about his days at sea, when Dad (Klaus Maria Brandauer) gave transport to three strangers, all armed and dangerous. Duvall was fastidious and foplike as their leader, along with Brandauer creating some tension among the artificiality usually associated with this director, Jerzy Skolimowski. Most of it was filmed in Germany, as co-financed by CBS and Warner Bros, who managed to get it some festival exposure before sending it to TV in the US, where it attracted little attention. Little more was heard of *Belizaire the Cajun*, in which Duvall did another cameo, or *Hotel Colonial* (87), another curiosity. This was an Italian film made in Mexico with American money; John Savage co-starred with Duvall, who played a mysterious drug trafficker. Said the producer, 'No one lost money, but you lose something when a film flops.' These sorry credits are completed by *Let's Get Harry*, a routine action movie with Gary Busey and Duvall, as an experienced mercenary; it was directed by Stuart Rosenberg, who took his name off the credits, and after minimum exposure, it went to video.

Conceivably Duvall chose some of these subjects because they seemed appropriate to his new status. He said he chose *Colors* (88) because its director, Dennis Hopper, and his co-star, Sean Penn, were Hollywood outsiders

like himself. He and Penn played tough cops battling it out with the gangs of Los Angeles. The film was criticized for making the gangs seem glamorous, but that didn't harm the box-office, through which poured a nice $20,000,000 to Orion. And much was heard of *Lonesome Dove* (89), a 480-minute mini-series based on Larry McMurtry's Pulitzer-prize-winning novel, directed by the Austra-lian, Simon Wincer, from a screenplay by William D. Wittliff (also the executive pro-ducer and the writer of one of the last fine Westerns for the big screen, *Barbarosa*). Duvall played a retired Texas Ranger and Tommy Lee Jones is his partner, the stern leader of the horsemen, the role for which Duvall was originally approached: united, they hunt down the bad men and much else in this sprawling recreation of the Old West. Walter Goodman, reviewing it for the 'New York Times', said, 'Mainly, there is Robert Duvall, who makes a simple, sentimental creation seem complex, heroic, always human and altogether enjoyable. He must have read the book, for he is the embodiment of Mr McMurtry's style – easy-going yet taut, casual in emergency, stoical in disaster, never a melodramatic phrase or gesture even in a downpour of melodrama.' Motown spent $20 million on it for CBS, who had every reason

to be happy with the ratings. It also picked up eighteen Emmy nominations, which may be a record, but it won only one, which may be another sort of record.

The Handmaid's Tale (90) was directed by Volker Schlondorff from a novel by Margaret Atwood, which Harold Pinter had reworked for the screen, not happily: Duvall was the head of state security police in this grim tale of the future, with Faye Dunaway as his wife. He had hardly more than a cameo again in *A Show of Force*, as the somewhat squeamish boss of Amy Irving, playing a television newscaster. Few emerged well in the notices for *Days of Thunder*, least of all its star, Tom Cruise; it was generally reckoned that Duvall took the movie, as the grizzled manager of this racing driver, dispensing fatherly wisdom. To follow: *Convicts*, written by Horton Foote, with John Travolta and James Earl Jones and *Rambling Rose* (91), co-starring Laura Dern and her mother, Dianne Ladd.

SALLY FIELD

She was a cute, effervescent teenager who stayed in television far too long. If the Best Actress Oscar is any guide, she is a great

As a mature actor and without the secure hold on stardom that Bogart had, Duvall has limited chances. He seems to have decided that in a Hollywood chiefly interested in promoting action heroes his best bet is to go for good roles in films likely to be popular – such as Days of Thunder *(90), supporting Tom Cruise, right, as his manager in this auto-racing yarn. Cruise is on a summit of popularity undreamed of by Duvall, and that's Randy Quaid in the centre, but it was not he who stole the notices.*

actress, for she has two. Bette Davis had two, too, but then so have Elizabeth Taylor and Glenda Jackson. 'Sally is one of the best, perhaps *the* best, actress I've ever worked with,' said Martin Ritt, who directed her in *Norma Rae*. 'She's simply astounding.' Ritt, who has worked with Joanne Woodward, Patricia Neal, Lee Remick, Geraldine Page and Carol Burnett, may have felt a little defensive, since teenage television players do not usually turn into anything interesting. In this case, however, few would disagree with him. This is a small lady with a way of making small gestures, but with burning intensity. She has a Field Day with a certain sort of American lady, of the strength of which the pioneer women were made, no doubt. For many people she can do no wrong.

Sally Field and Burt Reynolds in the hit movie, Smokey and the Bandit *(77), described by him as 'a Saturday-afternoon-rainy-day movie that will make you laugh, feel good and have a lot of fun . . .' It was also a matter of luck, he added, since the script was terrible and 'we just improvised everything'. So now we know, for his indifference as she paraded her New York culture values in front of him made both of them funny, and a delightful team.*

She was born in Pasadena, California, in 1946 to a minor Paramount contract actress who later remarried – Jock Mahoney, one of the screen Tarzans of the 50s. When she was seventeen, her stepfather suggested that her low high-school grades might improve if she attended a workshop at Columbia Studios; on the second day a casting director from the studio's Screen Gems subsidiary asked her to audition, and as a result she became television's 'Gidget', as based on some popular movies about a teenage brat. It ran for a year, and when it was cancelled she was cast in a Western with Kirk Douglas and Robert Mitchum, *The Way West* (67), as a nubile youngster who cannot wait to offer her virginity to anyone wanting it. After that she became television's 'The Flying Nun' and she flew with it till 1970. She also married – her schoolgirl sweetheart, who became the father of her two sons; she also contracted to play in occasional shows of another popular series, 'Alias Smith and Jones'. Jackie Cooper, who had been the head of Screen Gems, played her father in her first film for television, *Maybe I'll Come Home in the Spring* (71), about a runaway who returns to find her parents quarrelling; mother was Eleanor Parker.

She made four more TV movies: *Marriage: Year One*, as an heiress whose medical student husband (Robert Pratt) insists that they live on his money; *Mongo's Back in Town*, a gritty crime tale with Telly Savalas and Joe Don Baker; *Home for the Holidays* (72), as one of the daughters of Walter Brennan, all of them in danger from a homicidal maniac; and *Hitched* (73), with Tim Matheson, as a frontier couple – he reprising his role in *Lock, Stock and Barrel* and she replacing Belinda Montgomery, who had played his wife in that. She did another series, 'The Girl With Something Extra' (1973–4). When she told her agent that she did not want to do any more television, he told her that she was not good enough for anything else. It was a time of turmoil, she has said, for she also left her husband; she had been studying with the West Coast branch of the Actors' Studio and believed that her work there had given her an 'underground' reputation. At any rate, a casting lady called her about talking to Bob Rafelson for a role in *Stay Hungry* (76), that of the gymnasium receptionist who becomes Jeff Bridges' mistress. She knew that she was good enough in it to risk another TV movie, *Bridger*, about that nineteenth-century mountain man who blazed a trail through the Rockies. There was yet another television film, *Sybil*, and it was this, rather than *Stay Hungry*, which made the difference: she played a woman of multiple personality, and stunningly, alongside Joanne Woodward as her psychiatrist. Woodward had earlier played a similar role on screen, and they worked marvellously together. Both were nominated for Emmy awards and Field won; Emmys also went to Best Production and Stewart Stern as Best Writer. The four-hour film was edited down for showings in cinemas abroad.

Field knew that she was now taken as a serious actress, but feared that she was like 'a munchkin', as she put it, in *Sybil*: so when Burt Reynolds asked her to co-star, she thought, 'Even if the film doesn't work, if *he* [being a macho star] thinks I'm attractive in it, other people will think so too.' They were also to start a much-publicized off-screen relationship. In *Smokey and the Bandit* (77), she was a New York dancer who on impulse has become engaged to a country boy but has changed her mind. There is a chemistry between her and Reynolds, as the 'bandit' who picks her up, and that may be because some of their scenes were improvised, as directed by Reynolds's chum, Hal Needham. The film took some mighty money, as Reynolds was then riding high – just as surely as *Heroes* proved that television's Henry Winkler wasn't going to make it in movies. Field again had marriage trouble – she couldn't get to her groom as she and ex-soldier Winkler squabble as they journey cross-country. This old movie standby was chiefly delightful for the lady's strong, funny performance, but she did not have a great deal to do in two more with Reynolds, *The End* (78) and *Hooper*, in both as his girlfriend, indifferent and ever-worrying respectively.

Ritt directed *Norma Rae* (79), working from a script by his old collaborators, Irving Ravetch and Harriet Frank Jr, based on a true story. According to Field herself, the title-role had been turned down by most of Hollywood's leading actresses, but once you see her in it, it is hard to imagine that anyone else was considered. She plays a girl working in a factory who marries, but who in the course of the tale becomes more than fond of a Jewish Union activist (Ron Leibman) from New York; the contrast between the city slicker and the hick girl is touchingly made, perhaps a contributory factor when Field's warm, feisty performance won her a Best Actress Oscar. She had got $50,000 for the film and this went up to $75,000 for *Beyond the Poseidon Adventure*, a 'disaster' movie, which wasted her and some other clever people; she was the ship's nurse. She had thought it a good idea to follow a serious film with a lighthearted adventure, but this, as she admitted, proved her wrong. *Smokey and the Bandit II* (80) was another fairly useless credit. Field did another revamp of *It Hap-*

pened One Night for Ritt, *Back Roads* (81), only this being the 80s she's a hooker and he an ex-prizefighter – Tommy Lee Jones, whom Field did not enjoy working with. Her chirpy persona sat easily on this tart-with-a-heart-of, and if you were lucky you did not think of Giulietta Masina; Field really is made of grittier stuff.

She made another excellent film, Sydney Pollack's *Absence of Malice*, likeable and sensitive as a Miami reporter who 'investigates' Paul Newman and then wishes she hadn't. It was the success she needed ($19,700,000, on a budget of $12 million) after the failure of her last one, but the box-office was sour again on *Kiss Me Goodbye* (82), Robert Mulligan's comedy about husband No. 1 (James Caan) who returns in spirit to mock husband No. 2 (Jeff Bridges). These three players, especially Ms Field, can play comedy – especially she – so it was a pity there was so little of it in the second half. Which may have caused the film's failure. In Robert Benton's autobiographical rural tale, *Places in the Heart* (84), she was again a determined woman coping with hardship, newly widowed in 1935. She won her second Oscar over stiff competition and as she collected it said, 'This means you really like me!', which was called gushing by some; but she explained later that her first Oscar had numbed her and the second overwhelmed her. Her fee was $1,500,000 and the film itself took a healthy $16 million at the box-office. She also remarried – producer Alan Greisman. She formed her own production company because, she said, she knew

Sally Field has won two Oscars, and given her predecessors in that respect – they include Luise Rainer, Elizabeth Taylor and Glenda Jackson – that is no guarantee of respectability. But her two award-winning performances, in Norma Rae *(79), left, and* Places in the Heart *(84), right, are both very winning – plucky, determined little women with heart and soul.*

exactly the sort of movies she wanted to make and she couldn't simply hope that projects would drop on her doorstep. She invited Ritt to direct *Murphy's Romance* (85), and if you ask what Ritt was doing at this period, it would seem to be perpetuating the art of Sally Field. Here was another of her plucky, bounce-back heroines, and only a curmudgeon would object, especially when partnered by a masterly James Garner: she was the new lady in town, a one-parent family, and he the town druggist, so much older than she that he is afraid to show his fondness for her. Doubtless helped by his Oscar nomination, the film did a nice $13,800,000 on a cost of $13 million. There were, however, few takers for Cannon's *Surrender* (87), written and directed by Jerry Belson, with Michael Caine and Steve Guttenberg as the other sides of the triangle: Caine was rich, famous and oft-married, and as she was none of these things there were supposed to be laughs along with the romance. Not laughing were Cannon, whose investment of $15 million returned only a mean $2,400,000. Field turned producer again for *Punchline* (88), also playing a New Jersey housewife determined to become a stand-up comic – in which she is coached by Tom Hanks. He said of her: 'This is a woman who has a facade that makes her very likeable. I'm not saying Sally isn't actually, truly likeable; she is . . . but she's also a sharp businesswoman and producer. I guess it's no secret that there were problems with [*Punchline*], but it became a hit, and that's also due to timing. Sally had a lot of say in when it got released, and knowing when to release your product is an art, I guess.' It was only a moderate hit, however, with a take of $10,200,000 on a budget of $17 million.

Steel Magnolias (89) was a success, with a neat $30 million on a budget of $22 million. The public was obviously curious about the cast, which included Dolly Parton and Shirley MacLaine; Field was top-billed, as a mother who loses her daughter (Julia Roberts) and so cares for her granddaughter. The Flying Nun is a grandmother? Tom Skerritt played her husband and Herbert Ross directed from a play by Robert Harling which from this version would not seem to be of merit. It was not pleasing to find Field bringing true emotion to phoney situations. She followed this with a true story, *Not Without My Daughter* (90), with Alfred Molina, playing an Iranian-American woman whose daughter is detained in the Middle East; the cost was $20 million to Pathé, who produced. This was to be followed by *Delirious* (91), with John Candy.

Field's Fogwood Productions was one of several individual agreements (see Michael Douglas) drawn up by Dawn Steel when she was supremo at Columbia – and it was one of the few which Columbia wished to renew in 1990: but Fogwood had the right to go elsewhere if the studio turned down any project, so *Conundrum* will be made by MGM/UA – while Fogwood would be relocated to Pathé. Two projects remain at Columbia, while there are developments at Universal, 20th-Century-Fox and Geffen. One of the Pathé films will be *Rough Justice*.

COLIN FIRTH

Britain has two very fine actors, both called Firth – Colin and Peter, who are not related. If the country still had a film industry – if, that is, the Thatcher administration had not tried (as with every other industry, it seems) to kill it off, both might take their place as the heirs to Donat, Mason and Guinness. Peter Firth has some impressive credits and was notably good in *Tess* and *Letter From Brezhnev*, but he is now in his thirties. Colin Firth has attracted more international attention and may find the parts he can play overseas. At present he seems to be, with Daniel Day-Lewis, the best young actor the British have.

He was born in 1960 near the Hamphire–Surrey border to academics – his father is a lecturer at King Alfred's College, Winchester, and his mother teaches comparative religion for the Open University. He was educated at state schools in Winchester, except for a year in St Louis when his father was on an exchange scheme. He contracted the acting bug while at infant school, playing Jack Frost in the annual pantomime. He tried to evade university by taking a job as tea-boy at the National Theatre, but his parents were firm – and to placate them he chose to study at the Drama Centre at Chalk Farm in north London because of its reputation as a hard school. He was always given the flamboyant roles and was to comment later that his career proper usually found him playing repressed or sensitive souls. Among the leading roles he took in his second year were Tartuffe, King Lear and Hamlet; and the last-named brought an offer to take over the leading role, the Guy Burgess character, in 'Another Country' (83), when Daniel Day-Lewis left the cast. The originator of the part, Rupert Everett, caught Firth's performance and recommended him for the role of Judd in the film version, *Another Country* (84), that is, his best friend – played in the original by Kenneth Branagh – since Everett was to repeat his stage performance. Julian Mitchell wrote the screenplay from his play and very fine it is, as it evokes the far-off days of English public schools when cricket and homosexuality were the chief preoccupations, as bounded by matters religious and military. It keeps till the end Guy's conversion to communism, as fitting for someone who has decided to live as an open gay; Judd is an open Red from the start, and he would seem to be the only hetero in the whole school. Firth's good nature and common sense contrasted well with Everett's petulance, and the whole, as directed by Marek Kanievska, was as successful on screen as on stage.

Firth returned to the play to finish the run and then took a role in another movie, *Nineteen Nineteen*, that of the young Paul Scofield, when he was a pupil of Freud. As directed by Hugh Brody and written by him and Michael Ignatieff, this was chiefly about a reunion of two ex-pupils – Maria Schell was the other – reminiscing with flashbacks. Produced by the BFI and Channel 4, this arid piece sat over a year on the shelf before finding deservedly few bookings late in 1985; in the meantime Firth had played Armand Duvall to Greta Scacchi's *Camille* (84) for CBS television. 'Incredible cast,' he said (it also included John Gielgud and Ben Kingsley, as the older Duvall), 'wonderful story, dreadful script'. He joined the National Theatre to play the lead in a version of Schnitzler, 'Another Country', and had important parts on British television, in a film, *Dutch Girls* (85) and a mini-series based on a novel by J.B. Priestley about the great days of the music halls, *Lost Empires* (86), which marked one of Olivier's last performances.

Although Warner Bros. agreed to distribute *A Month in the Country* (87), it was another of the 'little' films which seem to constitute the entire indigenous output, again made with the co-operation of Channel 4. Pat O'Connor directed, with a bias towards thoughts unspoken and feelings undisclosed, though at other points Simon Gray's screenplay does a clumsy job on J.L. Carr's novel. The film is at its most remarkable in its central double portrait of two veterans of the Great War, who in 1919 seek their own private missions in a Yorkshire churchyard. One (Kenneth Branagh) is excavating, a comfortable man who is not only a hero but a homosexual, the other (Firth), uncovering a wall-painting, is tortured by memories of 'over there'. Both actors are superlative, Branagh unselfishly so, as Firth has the longer, more disturbed role. Firth played 'Desire Under the Elms' at the Greenwich Theatre and was then cast in a much-discussed BBC movie, *Tumbledown* (88), as Robert Lawrence, the Scots Guards officer who had almost half of his brain blown away in the Falklands conflict, and who felt compelled to indict the British army brass for the mistakes made therein. While making it, he

Colin Firth in Another Country *(84), based on the West End success by Julian Mitchell. The title may refer to the past, as defined by L.P. Hartley in 'The Go-Between', from which no traveller returns – that of an English public school in the 30s. It may also refer to Russia, which was so attractive to the spy Guy Burgess, for the play was about him as a schoolboy. Firth played his best friend, seemingly the only straight male in the school.*

became obsessed with Argentina, so was pleased when an offer came to film there: *Apartment Zero* (89), in fact a British film, in English, written and directed by a local man, Martin Donovan, who had trained in Europe. Firth admitted that he was pleased with the result, 'because I expected not to be. Despite odd pretences the film has, ultimately I was pleased because I found it very truthful to the

Apartment Zero (89) was a movie for buffs, because its leading character was one with whom they could identify – a buff more buffish than the rest of them who ran his own cinema: enter Colin Firth.

experience I had in Argentina.' He played a bachelor who, lonely after his mother is taken to hospital, advertises for a lodger. What he gets is someone who is the antithesis of himself – a laid-back hunky American (Hart Bochner) who may be a mass murderer. He is irritated by Firth's old-maid fussiness, but basks in his adoration, which may or may not be sexual, and which in time may cause him to turn a blind eye to murder. The result is like a pastiche of *Psycho*, *Repulsion* and *The Servant* welded together, but because Firth plays one who is a movie-nut above all else, the blood-bolter'd bodies of the final sequences may be in his imagination. Because of the movie references, the film achieved a cult following, but it should be seen above all for Firth, wittily making his paranoia secondary to pedantry.

His biggest chance for international stardom arrived with the title-role in *Valmont*, Milos Foreman's version of 'Les Liaisons Dangereuses'; so far on screen less flamboyant than John Malkovich, the Valmont in the rival version, he is his equal at getting under the skin of his characters. He commented that Malkovich 'plays a lovable rogue . . . I don't', and on another occasion that the role no more belonged to Malkovich than Hamlet to Olivier; but he and his fellow-players were factors in a movie always compared unfavourably to the earlier version – at least in those countries in which Orion chose to open it. Among his co-stars was Meg Tilly, with whom he began a liaison of his own. Another foreign film in English, the Dutch *Wings of Fame* (90), may find as much favour as *Apartment Zero*. Directed by Otakar Votocek, it has the attractive whimsical idea of a confrontation after death of a murderer (Firth) and the over-the-hill matinée idol (Peter O'Toole) whom he has killed. Next up: *The Pleasure Principle*.

HARRISON FORD

'I want to be recognized for the job I do,' he said once, 'which is acting. I get paid money for that, not for being a movie star. The business of being a star and doing what's necessary to remain one, promoting yourself as a fascinating personality, is something I'm inadequate to do. I don't consider myself unique. I just work in the movie business.' The statement shows a realism entirely in keeping with his screen image, which is that of a nice guy – good looks, good manners, without the aura of such predecessors as Gable and Cooper. 'The most striking thing about him,' wrote Minty Clinch in 'Photo-

play', 'is his studied anonymity.'

He was born in 1942 in Chicago to an Irish Catholic father, an advertising executive, and a Russian Jewish mother. He was educated at Ripon College, Wisconsin, studying English and philosophy, but was expelled just three days before graduation. He married his college sweetheart, Mary, and got a job in summer stock in Williams Bay, not far away, playing leads in 'Damn Yankees' and 'Little Mary Sunshine'. But he wanted to be in movies, so they moved to California – to Laguna Bay, where he appeared in a production of 'John Brown's Body'. That led to an appointment with the head of Columbia's new talent programme; he was offered a seven-year contract, which included acting classes, instructions to wear his hair in an Elvis Presley pompadour and which started at $150 a week. He made his screen debut in *Dead Heat on a Merry-Go-Round* (66), as a bellboy delivering a telegram to James Coburn, and he had an uncredited walk-on in *Luv* (67), which starred Jack Lemmon. He moved up to twelfth on the cast-list of a dud Glenn Ford Western, *A Time for Killing* (76), but Columbia was not happy. After the first of these films one executive told him that when Tony Curtis first appeared on screen in an equally brief role, 'you knew that that was a star . . . You ain't got it, kid.'

He moved over to Universal on another seven-year contract and appeared in another Western, *Journey to Shiloh* (68); he was in various episodes of 'Gunsmoke', 'Ironside', 'The Virginian' and 'The FBI', but, he said later, Universal never really had 'the guts' to use him. He was usually cast as the sensitive younger brother. Well, he did look very young: in his next two films he played students: *Zabriskie Point* (70) on loan-out, and cut from the final print; and *Getting Straight*. After a TV Western starring Don Murray, *The Intruders*, he threw the towel in and took up carpentry because 'it was the only job I had the clothes for'; he was successful at it (he constructed a sun-deck for Sally Kellerman, a recording studio for Sergio Mendes), finding that movie people had a new respect for him. A friend he had made at Columbia, Fred Roos, called him to ask whether he would like to try for *American Graffiti* (73), which he was casting: Ford said that with his self-respect restored he found it much easier to feel confident when meeting the director, George Lucas. Thus Ford became the out-of-town guy in the cowboy hat who picks up one of the girls and challenges one of the boys (Paul Le Mat) to a race at the end. He was offered scale – $485 per week – for the role, but said that he could make more than that as a carpenter, and anyway, he had a wife and two children to support. Yeah, well, they responded, the budget would not permit them to go to more than $500.

Roos recommended him for a role in Francis Coppola's *The Conversation* (74), that of Robert Duvall's henchman; it was a nothing part, he said, until he realized that he could play it as a homosexual with a crush on his boss. Returning to television, he had a good role in *James A. Michener's 'Dynasty'* (76) and a lesser one in *The Possessed* (77), about exorcism in a girls' school. He was also in a special for Stanley Kramer, 'Justice: the Court Martial of Lieutenant Calley'. Roos rang him again about *Star Wars*, but warned that Lucas had said he wanted new faces. Among the others most seriously being considered were Nick Nolte, William Katt, Christopher Walken and the black actor Glynn Turman. As it happened, Coppola's production designer, Dean Tavoularis, had commissioned Ford to build a new entrance to Coppola's office, and he was working on it when Lucas chanced along and asked him to read for the role, 'just as a favour'. And as a favour, Ford agreed to do so. Thus Ford was taken on to play IIan Solo, the mercenary/space captain who accompanies the hero (Mark Hamill). Carrie Fisher, who played the princess, said that she knew from the start that he would be a star 'of the order of Bogart or Tracy. I mean, you look at Harrison and you *listen*; he looks like he's carrying a gun, even if he isn't. I think he has qualities that disappeared into the pioneer West. You know that saying, "An actress is a little bit more than a woman; an actor is a little bit less than a man"? Well, that's except if it's Harrison Ford. He's this incredibly attractive male animal, in every sense of the word. This carpenter stud.' The film cost $10 million and was owned 60 per cent by 20th-Century-Fox and 40 per cent by Lucas and his partners, who would eventually share over $193 million (Ford was in for one-quarter of 1 per cent); at that time it was the highest-grossing film of all time (and is now beaten only by *E.T. The Extra-Terrestrial*).

Ford had already accepted an 'also starring' (i.e. under the title) role in *Heroes*, a star vehicle for Henry Winkler, whose old pal

Harrison Ford, right, in the first of his mega-hits, Star Wars *(77) – only he wasn't Harrison Ford in those days. Not as we know him now, anyway. On the left is Mark Hamill and that is Alec Guinness in the centre.*

Ford played – a Vietnam veteran now farming in Missouri. He played it with strength and a slight cookiness, plus a charm that he had not been allowed to use as Han Solo. He acted opposite Robert Shaw in the unsuccessful *Force Ten From Navarone* (78), in the role played in the original by Richard Harris, and for Coppola he played another military man in one crucial scene in *Apocalypse Now* (79), after turning down a bigger role. When Kris Kristofferson walked off the set of *Hanover Street*, Ford played his first romantic lead, as an American bomber pilot who falls in love, in wartime London, with Red Cross nurse Lesley-Ann Down. Unfortunately, wartime London, as conceived by writer-director Peter Hyams, seemed like a mythical city where the inhabitants aped the Brits at several removes. This was an overheated affair which did little business. Ford was luckier with Robert Aldrich's *The Frisco Kid*, as the gentle outlaw who tours the Old West with rabbi Gene Wilder – but not much luckier, since it took only $4,700,000 (cf. this year's reissue of *Blazing Saddles*, of which this was a fawning imitation). These films he made 'to consolidate his position, to get the billing', said Patricia McQueeney, his manager and agent then and since. 'You go in with high hopes, but he ran into trouble. One thing he learned is that an actor is really at the mercy of the director. Ever since he's been very careful about what directors he works with.' Ford's marriage broke up around this time, and when the divorce was final he married Melissa Mathison, one of the writers of *Star Wars*.

The Empire Strikes Back (80) was the first sequel of the many proposed to *Star Wars*, costing $32 million and taking over $141,600,000. Lucas had something else similar in mind – similar, that is, to the mindless adventures he had enjoyed on Saturday matinées as a kid. Steven Spielberg was to direct it for him and they had failed to find a star actor (they had settled on Tom Selleck, who wasn't free) till Spielberg saw *The Empire Strikes Back*. He contacted Ford immediately: 'Harrison was a remarkable combination of Errol Flynn in *The Adventures of Don Juan* and Humphrey Bogart in *The Treasure of the Sierra Madre*. He can be villainous and romantic all at once.' The role was of an academician who gets caught up in high (or, if you prefer, low) adventure, Indiana Jones. The title was *Raiders of the Lost Ark* (81); it cost $22 million and brought in $115,600,000. You might, however, be forgiven for preferring *Blade Runner* (82), which cost $27 million and took $14,900,000. That was not bad, given that this was a bleak, if not grim SF fantasy; Ford was a retired blade runner – i.e. a policeman trained to kill unruly androids on

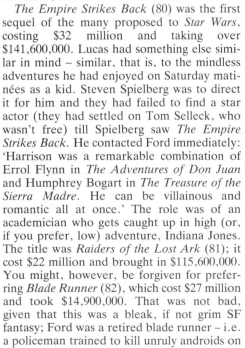

Ford in Ridley Scott's futuristic thriller, Blade Runner *(82), in which this ex-carpenter revealed himself as more than the block of wood most critics had thought him to be.*

sight. It was a role he was well equipped to play, and it confirmed him as the movies' greatest action icon: but one moment when he parodied Bogart suggested he might have more to offer.

He played Han Solo again in *Return of the Jedi* (83), with which that series unexpectedly folded, but not till making $168 million on a $32,500,000 outlay. *Indiana Jones and the Temple of Doom* (84): $109 million on a budget of $27 million. As his films crowded into the top ten money-makers of all time, Ford established a record which no actor had come near achieving – except Bing Crosby in the mid-1940s. But where Crosby was demonstrably popular, Ford was a rather remote figure. Indeed, 'People' magazine established that only 20 per cent of the public could recognise him from a photograph (but that was higher than some other much-touted names). He said: 'I had no ambition for [this] kind of status. I just wanted to make a living with a regular role in a television series. That was the most I hoped for.' He was no guarantee of box-office success. But he had,

The icon of the 80s: action heroes were all over the place, and no one was more everywhere – in global adventures and cinemas the world-over – than that academic archaeologist, Indiana Jones. Ford played him in Raiders of the Lost Ark *(81) and in two sequels, of which* Indiana Jones and the Last Crusade *(89), insert, was by far the better. For one thing, he was partnered by the magnificent Sean Connery, as his father, who managed to set-off new reserves of humour in Ford's playing.*

because of his percentage of the profits, become a very wealthy man. So what did he do? He started to make some decent pictures, proving in them that he was, after all, an actor.

Peter Weir's *Witness* (85) was an excellent thriller about a Philadelphia cop hiding out in the Amish community because he is a hunted man. It cost $12 million and took $28,500,000 – less than the season's other popular thriller, *Beverly Hills Cop*, also produced by Paramount, also with strong local colour, some weaknesses in the plot and an undoubted star. Ford had developed the charisma he had lacked. The handsome face looks loping, twisted; the hair is unruly, sometimes *en brosse*; the alligator mouth suggests humour, and for the first time that is in his playing. He still had a way to go so that you would never want to miss one of his films, like Cagney or Bogart; but like Eastwood and McQueen once they surfaced, nothing he did would be without interest. He was nominated for an Oscar, which consolidated his stardom. Spielberg said later: 'I don't think *Star Wars* really made him a star . . . I think he became a star somewhere in between *Raiders of the Lost Ark* and *Witness*. But I'm not even sure what a movie star is. Harrison just hasn't changed. In real life, he's a very plain and simple person. Harrison only became a movie star because Thomas Edison happened to invent the movie camera. I've seen him pick up a hammer and fix a set when the construction man's not there. I've seen him, during a shooting, drift off – he already knows how to play the scene, and I think he's just drifting away from all the fakery. He's planting a crop, or building a bookshelf in Wyoming.'

Confident that he could carry a film without Spielberg–Lucas special effects and derring-do, Ford chose to do *The Mosquito Coast* (86) for Weir, who had got backing after the success of *Witness*. Financing with Jack Nicholson had fallen through, and in this role Ford indicated that he shared a quality of the manic with Nicholson – which you would never have guessed from his Indiana Jones. Paul Schrader's screenplay, from Paul Theroux's novel, centres on an ingenious inventor, father of four, who turns his back on Massachusetts, a chump who wants a better world elsewhere. Trouble is, he chooses an inhospitable jungle and no amount of incident or character could make audiences believe that this was a wise decision. The film cost $25 million and took only $7,700,000. Its failure may be why Ford was not nominated for an Oscar, for he brings more shadings to the role than William Hurt did to his nominated role in *Children of a Lesser God*. Then he was *Frantic* (88) in Paris for Roman Polanski, because his wife has disappeared. The holes in the plotting, however, made the flaws of *Witness* insignificant: the public voted accordingly, and it took only $8,400,000 at the American box-office.

It was at this point that Ford decided to do a comedy, knowing that in *Working Girl* he has to stand by, or almost, as Melanie Griffith vies for Sigourney Weaver's job and then her beau (him). Mike Nichols directed and the piece took a splendid $28,600,000. Since it cost $28 million, that was not exactly good news. So it was Indy to the rescue. *Indiana Jones and the Last Crusade* (89) cost $36 million and mopped up $115,500,000. As it deserved to. Nothing could have saved the second of the series, which piled absurdity on absurdity, but for this third and last adventure – it was announced that there would be no more Indys – came a welcome injection of humour, especially in Ford's scenes with Sean Connery, playing his father. There wasn't a deal of wit and what there was they understated, but they made one of the most felicitous teams since Laurel and Hardy.

Ford is not the wealthiest actor ever, since many stars of the 1930s invested in real estate, the value of which rocketed. His percentages may have made him richer than Stallone; unlike him, Ford does not go public with his fees, but they are reckoned to be in the $7-8 million range and are reflected in the budgets of the later films. *Presumed Innocent* (90), based on the bestseller by Scott Turow, marked a terrific return to form for its director, Alan J. Pakula, with Ford on top form as a prosecutor assigned to investigate the murder of a colleague (Greta Scacchi): it's not quite a simple case, since he had been having an affair with her, as his wife (Bonnie Bedelia) very well knows. But simply a

Ford, right, in the film of Scott Turow's novel, Presumed Innocent *(90), with Raoul Julia, playing his defending counsel, and Bonnie Bedelia as his wife. Said Turow: 'I learned a lot watching that movie being made, including the business side which is deplorable, and the result is a film of which I'm proud and would choose as a favourite. Harrison Ford is as near as possible to the mental picture I had of Rusty Sabich when I wrote the book . . .'*

riveting thriller, which immediately became one of the biggest hits in a summer boasting the likes of *Dick Tracy, Days of Thunder, Die Hard 2* and *Total Recall*. Who wouldn't rather have this? Next along the line is *Regarding Henry*, which will reunite the team of *Working Girl*.

Mike Nichols, who will direct, made an interesting comment on Ford: 'Harrison is as good an example as I know of someone who has conquered the making of movies through a series of very sophisticated choices, including his personal life. Very successful actors pay an enormous price in shame for doing something that isn't quite serious enough, that isn't quite manly. It's why they do drink and do drugs, it's why they womanize. Harrison's rigor and practicality, his living with and for his family and staying out of any and all social life – his carpenter's approach to action – have somehow preserved him from the restlessness and self-dissatisfaction.'

JODIE FOSTER

Perhaps because she usually played 'grown-up', Jodie Foster never really seemed like a child actress; when she was interviewed she sounded as if she had been in the profession most of her life, which she has, but she spoke as an adult – one who had known no childhood. She left movies to study, and when she talked to the press after that period, she seemed much more appealing. She had also become a very fine actress.

She was born in Los Angeles in 1962, to a Hollywood publicist and divorcée, Evelyn Foster, one of four children; the only boy among them, Buddy, was a child actor doing commercials. When she was almost three she and her mother accompanied him to an interview because a babysitter was unavailable; she showed off, she said, and got a job – 'and never really stopped working from then on'. The job was having her *derrière* slightly exposed by a friendly puppy for Coppertan sun lotion, the first of many stints in commercials. There were acting jobs, irregularly, but whenever a little girl was needed, starting with 'Mayberry RFD' (68) and including 'My Three Sons' and 'The Courtship of Eddie's Father'. Mother eventually got for her exactly what *she* wanted, the lead in a Disney film, *Napoleon and Samantha* (72), as one of two children who run away with a pet lion; Johnny Whitaker was the other. Two brief roles followed, as the daughter of Raquel Welch in *Kansas City Bomber* and of the widow (Vera Miles) courted by James Garner in *One Little Indian* (73), which was also for Disney. But

she had a good part again in a singing *Tom Sawyer*, as sweetheart Becky Thatcher to Tom, who was played by young Whitaker. She was Elizabeth Henderson in a short-lived series, 'Bob and Carol and Ted and Alice', based on the film, after which she was in *Smile Jenny You're Dead* (74), the pilot for the series with David Janssen, 'Harry-O'. She was herself in another series, 'Paper Moon', when Tatum O'Neill declined to repeat her movie success, and then had her most important exposure yet for cinemas, in *Alice Doesn't Live Here Anymore* (74), as the precocious girl who provides distraction for Ellen Burstyn's son when they arrive in Tucson.

Her most important role yet was something else again, for few heard of the film concerned, *Echoes of a Summer* (76): she played a youngster seemingly impervious to the fact that she is fatally ill. Among those more visibly concerned was Richard Harris, who was her father as well as the producer. As the teenage (almost pre-teen) hooker in Scorsese's *Taxi Driver*, she first really made her

Jodie Foster as we first knew her and learnt not to love her, as the teenage hooker in Martin Scorsese's punishing Taxi Driver *(76).*

mark. The role required her to be extremely self-possessed, if not hard-boiled, and by all accounts did not require much acting. Still high profile, she played the vamp Tallulah, most at home in the underworld in *Bugsy Malone*: the gimmick of this horrendous movie was that the characters were kids in grown-up clothes, and singing kids at that. It was directed in Britain by a misguided Alan Parker, who thought he was making a 'fun' film; although he imported another American to play his hero, Scott Baio, it was considered British in the US market, which did not welcome it. She returned to Disney to experience a *Freaky Friday* with her mother, Barbara Harris, changing places for the day – an idea which did not work, since Harris played 'kooky' and Foster was renowned for being more mature than her years. There was much comment when she played *The Little Girl Who Lives Down the Lane* (77), since the little girl concerned is a natural killer. Stir in a child molester (Martin Sheen), a nude love scene with the child's crippled accomplice (Scott Jacoby), and you have a pretty repellent brew. Still and again, the powers-that-be at Disney did not think these antics would have alienated their very different audience, for they sent for her again – but to be a wrong-un this time, in *Candleshoe*, as the orphan Leo McKern uses to impersonate the missing granddaughter of a wealthy Englishwoman (Helen Hayes).

Little in Foster's work indicated that she would be inundated with offers, so Mother accepted two offers on the Continent – in Eric Le Hung's *Moi Fleur Bleue* (78) and Sergio Citti's *Il Cassotto*. Both, also, of course, enabled her to see foreign countries on travelling expenses, but the films themselves did not travel. Returning to the US she was the leader of the pack of *Foxes* (79), four girls in search of a good time if not a great one. They, their boyfriends and assorted parents were strictly for the birds, as the returns told the British producer and director, David Puttnam and Adrian Lyne respectively. Foster seemed incapable of showing any emotion beyond an extreme self-satisfaction, and she was only marginally better in a much better film, Robert Kaylor's *Carny* (80), which was the old one about the girl who comes between two friends. They were Gary Busey and Robbie Robertson, respectively the 'bozo' of the carnival and its trouble-shooter: and although the atmosphere of the milieu was strongly done, the film failed to find an audience. Foster said later that she had expected her career to peter out once she reached her late teens, but that it was a career that Mother had built instead of pushing her into whatever was offered. She had deliberately chosen roles for

her which were not typical teenagers, but 'people with real personalities and eccentricities'. She also said, 'I was never a typical teenager, and it means I have a lot of growing up to do', adding that while she could travel the world with a credit card she found it impossible to cope with daily chores like taking clothes to the cleaners. She was, however, very happy at Yale, where she studied Afro-American literature – though afterwards depression and a weight problem were to cause what one interviewer called 'tequila bouts'.

A prime role attended her come-back, a modern Trilby, a rock-singer, to Peter O'Toole's *Svengali* (83), even if it was only for the small screen. Cinemas saw her again, if not many of them, in *The Hotel New Hampshire* (84), written and directed much too faithfully by Tony Richardson from John Irving's crude attempt at an epic novel. Raped by the football jock worshipped by her homosexual brother, she has a wild night of love with another sibling (Rob Lowe) before discovering that lesbianism is a viable alternative: seems as though she had never been away. *Le Sang des Autres* is a good title, which *The Blood of Others* decidedly is not, though the latter would be technically correct, for this was an American telefilm – with French participation. Claude Chabrol directed from a screenplay by Brian Moore based on a novel by Simone de Beauvoir. Foster and Michael Ontkean as French Resistance workers proved to be unhappy casting, as was that of Sam Neill as a Nazi obsessed with her; but Stephane Audran, Micheline Presle and Jean-Pierre Aumont helped them over many a hill. *Mesmerised* (86) was another uneasy co-production, written and directed by Michael Laughlin from an original by Jerzy Skolimowski with financing from British, Australian and New Zealand sources. Set in the 19th century, it featured Foster as a virginal orphan who marries a wierdo (John Lithgow) and decides to murder him after years of deviant sexual anguish. After this little lot, the British-produced *Five Corners* (87) seemed like a return to normalcy, with Foster as a 1964 Bronx broad threatened by an ex-con schizoid (John Turturro), whom at one point she agrees to meet at midnight by a deserted swimming-pool, after which she has little to do but scream: Tony Bill directed from a screenplay by John Patrick Shanley, and it was a wasted credit for all of them. But then, as ye sow, so shall ye reap, and Foster found herself in a movie even more bizarre, even for her: *Siesta*, though the hapless Ellen Barkin had the leading role, as a daredevil stunt-artist wandering about Spain, wondering whether she is a murderess and running into many odd types, including Foster and Julian Sands as a Sloane Ranger couple. This was a first feature for a lady experienced in directing Madonna videos, Mary Lambert, who showed that movies provided an activity in which it would be unwise to encourage her. Foster is dead at the start of *Stealing Home* (88) and has bequeathed her ashes to a retired ball-player (Mark Harmon), who reminisces about the time he knew her as a babysitter and how, some years later, she initiated him into the pleasures of sex. This thing, which disappeared with rapidity, was written and directed by Steven Kampmann and Will Aldis.

Foster was to say later that her mother chose 95 per cent of her material when she was younger, but by now she had taken over. Mother still 'comes with me the first four weeks of shooting and she yells at whoever has to be yelled at and makes sure everything's taken care of, and about the fourth week she disappears, unless it's a problem shoot, and then she stays.' 'You have to keep working,' she admitted. 'For me, the fun part is being one of the scores of people in the film crew, all chipping away at one block, working to a common end. I'm a technician working within the framework of a film. That's why I don't belong to the school of actors who only look for juicy roles for themselves. I look for good films.' The only response to this is that she hasn't looked hard enough nor has she kept to a vow only to make subjects which touched on feminist issues or Civil Rights. Her box-office record as an adult was so dismal that she was probably not the first choice for *The Accused*, but as it turned out she was the right one. As written by Tom Topor and directed by Jonathan Kaplan, this was vitally sound on the subject of women's rights, as it handled the dangerous subject of gang-rape. Sarah (Foster) has a mouth like a truck-driver and lives in a trailer park with a dropout; just before the rape she had been drinking heavily and smoking pot, so her lawyer (Kelly McGillis), fearful of losing the case, settles for 'reckless endangerment' rather than 'sexual assault'. A furious Sarah cries that she hasn't been able to put her side of it, demanding respect, and the case eventually goes to court. Foster played the girl as perky but resigned to the fact that she was one of life's losers. She emerged as a major actress, and indeed her Oscar proved her the Best of the Year.

She had already made *Backtrack*, a thriller which she hated, partly because the distributor, Vestron, wanted to cash in on her Oscar: but the company was in financial difficulties and the film remains unshown. The only immediate consequence, therefore, of her

newly-won prestige was the lead in *The Silence of the Lambs* (90), but that was partly because she then chose to direct *Little Man Tate*, about a child genuis coping with the adult world; she also appears in it.

MICHAEL J. FOX

'Can you imagine how many squillions of letters we've had about Michael J. Fox?' asked one movie magazine, 'I've never seen anything like it.' Well, there aren't many other juve faves, are there? The movie stars of the golden age were curiously ageless. Hollywood knew that youth itself could be appealing, but on the other hand . . . once it fled, you started playing grandparents. So the stars were styled, costumed and made to act in a way which was mature but far from middle-aged. Until the lines began to show they were all permanently about thirty.

Foster, in the meantime, didn't do too much we could feel enthusiastic about, but then she came up with a performance in The Accused *(88), which put her up there with the Greer Garsons and the Grace Kellys, i.e. she won an Academy Award for it. She played, unlike those ladies, the victim – Hollywood does change – of a gang-rape.*

Mickey Rooney was obviously young, and so was James Dean. In the post-Dean/Presley era stars simply faded away – or, like Eastwood and Reynolds, old enough after a bit to be your grandfathers. As stars came back they were ageless in the old mould, like Harrison Ford, or honestly young, like Tom Cruise and Fox. 'He's hip, trendy and cool,' said one fanwriter hopefully. What he is is young – or, rather, young-looking. He is also only 5 feet 4 inches, but most winningly is quite different from his screen image, being altogether tougher and more colourful than the milquetoast characters he tends to play.

He was born in Edmonton, Alberta, in 1961, one of a family of five whose father was an army officer. He grew up chiefly in Vancouver, where he played rhythm guitar in a rock band for a while. He had acted before then, and did so again, in 'Witch of Westminster Crossing' (77) and a local series, 'Leo and Me', playing a ten-year-old. He dropped out of high school to appear in the Vancouver production of 'The Shadow Box', and supported Art Carney and Maureen Stapleton in the locally-made telemovie, *Letters From Frank* (79). He had already changed his own name slightly, in deference to an established Michael Fox. He might have become Michael A., since Andrew is his middle name, but he chose J. after Michael J. Pollard, an actor he admired. Having decided that if he was going to get anywhere in show business the place to be was Los Angeles, he headed south. He was 18. That helped, you see, in a Hollywood dedicated to making mindless teen pics, and Fox made his feature debut in one of the worst, *Midnight Madness* (80), a Disney-produced comedy about a college scavenger hunt. He also appeared in episodes of 'Trapper John M.D.' and 'Lou Grant' and in all of 'Palmerstown USA', which was somewhere between a mini and a series as created by Alex Haley. He was back in college for another nasty one, getting stabbed in *Class of 1984* (82), when psychotic student Timothy Van Patten goes on the trail of headteacher Perry King. In 1982 he was cast (not the first choice, but the casting director was sure he was the right one) as the son of Meredith Baxter Birney and Michael Gross in 'Family Ties', and it was he, rather than they, on whom the show conferred stardom as well as three Emmies. Expectedly, it was a generation gap sitcom, with the Keaton parents as ex-hippies and Alex (Fox) as the son who rejected all their values. He was a shallow guy who worshipped money and Ronald Reagan, but as played by Fox it was nevertheless hard to dislike him.

Despite the schedule he managed to fit in three movies for the small screen: *High School USA* (83), top-billed in a tame tale in which he and other TV teen players are pitted against parents and teachers – roles, in fact, for their predecessors of a generation ago; *Poison Ivy* (85), a summer camp comedy; and *Family Ties Vacation*, a spin-off of the series, in which the Keatons become involved with spies while Alex (Fox) is on a summer scholarship to Oxford. Fox's first two starring roles for cinemas were in fact premiered before this last was aired by NBC. The first to be made was the low-budget *Teen Wolf*, in which he discovered that he was a werewolf, which he didn't mind when it brought him popularity at school. It made $12,950,000, while the first to be shown, *Back to the Future*, was turning out to be one of the most popular films ever made. Steven Spielberg, who produced, had pencilled him in for the lead, but 'Family Ties' had indicated that he would not be free; the film started with Eric Stoltz (from *Mask*), but after five weeks' shooting, director Robert Zemeckis decided that the film was drifting, and he needed a replacement for Stoltz. Fox still was not free, but Spielberg was prepared to raise the budget to get the quality of innocence he wanted in Marty McFly: so Fox worked on 'Family Ties' from 10 till 6, when he reported to Universal to shoot from 6.30 to 2.30 a.m. The eventual cost was $22 million, but it took in $104 million in the US, with its popularity duplicated throughout the world. It was a once-in-a-lifetime thing, about a boy taken back in time to the 1950s, lovingly and amusingly re-created, to be witness to his parents' courtship, but with the added difficulty that his mother gets the hots for him. In an almost flawless entertainment the weak links were some members of the cast: there have been funnier mad professors than Christopher Lloyd and wetter nerds than Crispin Glover (Marty's father). Fox himself was likeable and capable, but little more.

Certainly the industry thought so, for *Light of Day* (87) only appeared spottily in foreign markets and then mostly after Fox's next two films. Admittedly it had not been well received at home, nor was it exactly an upbeat situation, as Fox and his sister (Joan Jett) have plenty trouble trying to make it as part of a rock band while their mother (Gena Rowlands) is dying of the Big C. Paul Shrader directed on locations in Cleveland, Ohio, and as ever in his films there are perceptions about the littleness of life which can be startling in mainstream cinema. This was Fox's first clash with a demotic role, smoking, drinking and reading 'Penthouse'. He was next a hick from the sticks – because 'I wanna make lots of money and I want an incredibly moving experience with a beautiful woman', or so he tells his mother in *The Secret of My Success*; Richard Jordan was the wicked uncle who gives him a job in the mailroom and Helen Slater the exec who provides the experience. Rastar-Universal invested $25 million in this, perhaps because the undernourished script was by the team which had written *Top Gun*: they were, anyway, rewarded with $30 million bounding back. Fox declined to do *Teen Wolf Too*, wisely, in view of the quality of the script, and the role went to his 'cousin', played by Jason Bateman. Instead, feeling he could not be lovable or endearing for ever, he took a role once mooted for Tom Cruise in James Bridges' *Bright Lights Big City* (88), written by Jay McInerney from his own autobiographical novel. So here is Fox screwing up, as a 'New York' magazine researcher so into cocaine and double vodkas that he exists in a spiral of depression and self-pity. Keifer Sutherland played his chum, a charming yuppie ad exec, equally committed to the drugs scene but more happily, and although one was billed above the title and the other below, those who saw the film in preview were convinced that Sutherland would emerge as the bigger star. That that didn't happen tells us something about something, for Fox's performance was poorly received – and rightly, for he is a void at the centre. Had the roles been reversed (or if Cruise had played the lead?) the film might have returned more than $8 million on its $25 million expenditure. He was good, however, if lightweight, as a nice, decent guy who is himself almost one of the *Casualties of War* (89), squaring up to a very nasty non-com (Sean Penn), but the grosses (see Penn) would seem to confirm that the public was not overly keen to see Fox in drama. Vincent Canby, incidentally, commented that Fox was 'a decent actor but not a very complex or expressive one', allowing Penn to dominate the film 'with his easy, self-assured grace of manner, his wariness, his old-fashioned cool'. It's not good for a movie on conscience and principle when a noble hero is overshadowed by a particularly brutal villain.

Back to the Future II (89) and *Back to the Future III* (90) were filmed back to back but released some months apart. Part II was generally panned, and in New York's 'Seven Days' Richard T. Jameson had some thoughts on the matter: in the first of the series, he said, 'Michael J. Fox's nimbleness, throwaway delivery, and vaguely dyspeptic air of preoccupation ideally suited the McFlyweight fantasy', but in the second, he concluded, 'Fox throws himself into an impressive variety of roles (Marty I, Marty II, Marty as a middle-aged loser, Marty's son *and* daughter) without ever quite finding his footing.' Conversely, Part III was warmly praised, especially for its

Michael J. Fox as Marty McFly in Back to the Future *(85), introducing 80s rock to a 1955 school prom, where it is distinctly unappreciated – except by the musicians. The gag was refined in Part II of the series, with two Martys on- or back-stage, but it seemed less funny*

Fox, lying down, as the good soldier seemingly eager for martyrdom in Brian De Palma's fine film about the war in Vietnam, Casualties of War *(89) with Sean Penn as the vicious corporal in charge of the expedition.*

utilization of the old West, with many unsatisfactory aspects of the Second Part now falling into focus, to make an entertainment almost as good as Part I. The cost of both these sections of the trilogy was $40 million, but while Part II had achieved a gross of $67 million after two months in release, Part III has so far taken $82 million during the same period.

In 1988 Fox married an actress, Tracey Pollan, just after 'Family Ties' finally came to an end – and apart from Ted Danson and 'Cheers' (a rather special case), there is no other example of an actor staying with a series after becoming a ranking movie star. But then: who needs the fickle movie public when he has the chained millions watching what had become just another pap sitcom? Next up is *The Hard Way* (90), a comedy in which he plays an actor researching the role of a cop, so he hangs around with a real one, James Woods. After *Doc Hollywood* (91) for Warners he starts a two-year contract with Universal. Fox may surprise us yet: he has said that if told to do one thing, he will do another, specifically saying that if recommended at this stage of his career not to do television, that is exactly what he will do. There is steel there, as his career demonstrates. But: 'I've tried a change of image,' he said in 1990, 'and I know that the *Back to the Future* movies are my biggest hits.' He added that he is prepared to do several sequels if the occasion arises. At eighteen, he headed for Lotus Land, where the big bucks are, and he is a millionaire several times over. Yeah, this fresh-faced kid. He didn't choose to go to London or any other city where he might, after a bit, have played Hamlet. So what's so wrong with that?

RICHARD GERE

Good looks have never hindered a film star, but they can make him suspect – as in the case, say, of Robert Taylor, who certainly did not owe his stellar position to any thesping ability. Those MGM executives who moulded Taylor's career remembered the mesmerizing effect of Valentino, and showcased Taylor so that he could bring in the sort of money to satisfy stockholders. Gere has had no studio to help him. He could not have achieved his position in an age of 'uglies' if he had only looks: his interviews indicate a man with an almost desperate regard to be taken seriously. He is handicapped by the fact that, like Valentino – with whom he shares both a self-absorption and sexual insolence – he is disregarded by men while their womenfolk adore him. There are worse things.

He was born in Philadelphia in 1949, the son of an insurance salesman, and raised in upstate New York. He studied philosophy at the University of Massachusetts, where he received his first acting experience, and he left there to do summer stock at the Provincetown Playhouse. He also worked with the Seattle Repertory Theater, appearing in, among others, 'Volpone', for which he also composed the music. He did a stint with a rock band and contributed to the score of 'Soon' (71), a rock opera in which he made his New York debut. It did not run, but it got him the role of Danny Zuko in 'Grease', which he later did in London. He was also on Broadway in 'Habeas Corpus', off-Broadway in Sam Shepard's 'Killer's Head' and in London and New York in the Young Vic's 'The Taming of the Shrew', as Christopher Sly. For television he was in 'Kojak', and around the same time he made his film debut in an excellent thriller starring Michael Moriarty and Yaphet Kotto, Milton Katselas's *Report to the Commissioner* (75), as a low-life type being interrogated, with beard, long hair and hippie hat. These came off when he played a state trooper, himself doing the investigating, in a TV movie, *Strike Force*, billed after Cliff Gorman and Donald Blakely: they were trying to bust a narcotics case in this pilot intended for a series. He had a scene-stealing role in the next, *Baby Blue Marine* (76), as the troubled veteran marine who gets the hero (Jan-Michael Vincent) drunk so that he can steal his clothes. In *Looking for Mr Goodbar* (77) it was the heroine (Diane Keaton) this time whom he picks up in a bar, offering her 'the best fuck' she ever had: she refuses the offer but accepts when they next meet, after which he does a wild dance wielding a knife and naked except for a jock-strap. It was clear that Gere had arrived.

Indeed, Gere fever was on: within a month he could be seen in Robert Mulligan's *Bloodbrothers* (78) and Terrence Malick's *Days of Heaven*. In the former he was the son of a large Italian family, wanting to go to college instead of following the family trade of electrician; in the latter he was the Chicago boy who allows his girl (Brooke Adams) to marry a farmer (Sam Shepard) for his money. Both were roles requiring sensitivity, but many viewers found Gere merely insipid; neither film was worth a light at the box-office. John Schlesinger's *Yanks* (79) was supposed to turn the trick for Gere, playing the soldier too noble to make a pass at the English girl (Lisa Eichhorn) with whom he has fallen in love. His next role would find him once again in competition with John Travolta.

Travolta had been in the chorus of 'Grease', but had been given Gere's role when they filmed it; *Days of Heaven* had been offered to Travolta first, while it was Gere's turn to

The Yanks (79) of John Schlesinger's film were not like the Yanks the British remembered: 'over-paid, over-sexed and over-here' (an expression first heard in a 1952 West End revue). Sex seemed secondary to love, for instance, and while the major had a discreet affair with the lady of the manor this Matt (Richard Gere) whose folks had a diner in Tucson, woos Jean (Lisa Eichhorn), whose family keeps the local grocers store. When he does eventually get to first base, he's too noble to go through with it. That's a Yank?

refuse *Moment by Moment*, which Travolta did. Travolta, as the bigger star, was offered *American Gigolo* (80) first, but his fee was considered too high. So Gere did it. This was another of writer-director Paul Schrader's examinations of the underbelly of society, and perhaps he had discovered that gigolos did exist in the good old US of A when researching *Taxi Driver* and/or *Hardcore*. Made for $5 million, it took $11,500,000 – a handsome sum for telling some unpalatable truths even

if, like Theda Bara, Gere could be redeemed by true love. Still, it was exactly the role he needed after his exposure in *Mr Goodbar*, shucking off his Armani suits or telling his latest paying lady that he's 'lying here with a hard-on and it's not ten o'clock yet. I'll have to hang-up and jerk-off.' He doesn't do fags or kinks, he claims – not, that is, unless pressured by his pimp. The film leaves blurred the crossover point for California gigolos, and there would be other hints in later Gere movies that he was not exactly immune to bisexuality, which in the early 1980s (before AIDS) added to his screen appeal, to women at least. He played a homosexual on Broadway, in Martin Sherman's play about being gay in Nazi Germany, 'Bent'.

Paramount put *An Officer and a Gentleman* (82) into production as a filler before a projected strike by the Directors' Guild; it cost $7 million and took over $55 million in rentals (then the largest sum in the company's history after *The Godfather*, *Star Trek* and two with Travolta, who had just done Gere another favour by turning this down). Gere in whites had something to do with this happy outcome, plus the fact that he's a born rebel buckling under the system while hoping to subvert it, in this case the deadly business of cadet-training. The audience had something to root for, for he's a working-class guy, and so is the girl (Debra Winger) for whom he falls. As written by Douglas Day Stewart and directed by Taylor Hackford, this was really a film about class, astute rather than sympathetic. Jim McBride's remake of the French movie, *Breathless* (83), was not a particularly good idea, even if the two films had in common only the idea of an aimless, amoral young hood who between petty jobs is screwing a pretty foreigner – here Valerie Kaprisky. Gere was not the first to be approached: Robert De Niro had dithered, Al Pacino and John Travolta were unwilling to trust themselves to an inexperienced director – but Gere agreed to McBride after meeting him. Instead of Belmondo's dour *je m'enfichism* we have Gere's smiling big star confidence; one ambled round Paris, the other drives flashy cars; Belmondo's idol was Bogart and Gere's is Jerry Lee Lewis, a very different kettle of fish. He, Gere, is seldom out of camera-range, preening, narcissistic – so much himself, of course, that it's a shame the public did not take to the persona so liberally offered. The film cost $7,500,000 and took just over $10,200,000.

The fall was swift, and *The Honorary Consul*, made for $11,800,000, took just over $3 million at the American box-office. It was not helped when a worried Paramount hastily retitled it *Beyond the Limit* at the last minute – or by the critics, who disliked this version of Graham Greene's novel as written by Christopher Hampton and directed by John MacKenzie. One who did admire it was Peter Ackroyd in the 'Spectator', although he didn't like Gere, 'perhaps best known for taking off his clothes'. As the exiled, meddling Paraguayan doctor from just over the border, Gere received a critical trouncing, but the joke was on the press, for he was supposed to be a shell, devoid of principles, feelings,

emotions, a man blown by the wind. He does not provide an interesting centre, but Michael Caine, in the title-role, does. They are both burnt-out cases, and this is one of the best screen Greenelands.

An unusual amount of bumbling and amateurism, copiously documented, brought *The Cotton Club* (84) to a budget of $51 million, a record then only beaten by *Annie* in American film history. All that concerns us here is the lead, which was originally offered to Al Pacino. Sylvester Stallone later accepted it, but was dropped when he doubled his original salary demand to $4 million. This was what Richard Pryor was asking, but only because he felt the film would be a disaster: his role went eventually to Gregory Hines, while for $2 million Gere checked in for the lead after several rewrites. Without him, the venture might have collapsed, which would have been no loss to anyone except the backers who, in any case, looked on in dismay as less than $3 million was returned at the box-office. Gere, moustached, played a cornet-player who becomes chauffeur and trouble-shooter to Dutch Schultz (James Remar), before being parlayed into a successful movie star specializing in gangster roles. A gloomy air of incompetence almost buried him and indeed the entire cast, except when Hines and brother Maurice were imitating the Nicholas Brothers. For Gere, incredibly, worse was to come.

It was called *King David* (85). After the failure of *The Greatest Story Ever Told*, Hollywood said farewell to one of its old staples, the religious epic, but Paramount, with its history of successful DeMilles, thought again after the world-wide popularity of Zeffirelli's TV *Jesus of Nazareth*. The first script was written in 1980; the one used is credited to James Costigan and Andrew Birkin, who came aboard with director Bruce Beresford in 1983. Beresford looked at the old religiosos, to learn or to confirm what to avoid – and there is no question that this film – beautifully filmed on location (in Italy) – is a vast advance on, say, the 1959 Oscar-laureated *Ben-Hur*, which was even duller. The public didn't mind dull movies if they had uplift. Here then are Old Testament warlords, plots, primitive history, much mumbling under beards: in their midst Gere goes for an intermittent British accent, but he is never big enough or resourceful enough to be at the heart of an epic. Most of the time he looks – as ever – petulant. The critics laughed as he stripped to his loincloth for another memorable movie dance (for bringing the Ark of the Covenant into Jerusalem). The image he had projected so far was unlikely to win him new fans in a Biblical epic, and the film went down at $2,500,000. It had cost $22 million.

It had never been hip to like a Gere movie, and *Power* (86) was badly mauled, though no better or worse than the other political movies of the 80s – indeed, since it was about the marketing of politicians, it was more instructive than most, considered in the light of Bush, Reagan and those who sought to make the wretched Thatcher more appealing. Sidney Lumet directed; Julie Christie and Gene Hackman were among those confronting Gere, moustached, with a natty line in braces and not a principle in sight. For huge fees he manipulated the campaigns of those seeking high office, and he was at his best. This film and *No Mercy* both cost $14 million and took $1,700,000 and $7 million respectively. Richard Pearce's film was a thriller, giving Gere the tough-guy role he needed, a Chicago cop who goes off to New Orleans to avenge his partner, but with little knowledge of how to set about it. *Beverly Hills Cop?* Well yes, but good, even if neither he nor Kim Basinger can make us care enough when they are menaced. Bogart was a tough guy, but Gere simply docs his schtick, which is to open his mouth like a fish and narrow his eyes. Two 1987 projects never came to fruition, *Witness to War*, which he was to co-produce, and *Yogi and Al*, a romantic comedy with Michelle Pfeiffer. He said himself that he could have got his career into high gear again by doing *American Gigolo II* or a sequel to *An Officer and a Gentlemen*, but because he was more interested in being an actor than a sex-symbol he never considered this. He returned quietly in *Miles From Home* (88), directed for Cinecom by Gary Sinise, formerly of Chicago's Steppenwolf Theater Company, from a screenplay by Chris Gerolmo, who also wrote *Mississippi Burning*. The plot tells of brothers (Gere, Kevin Anderson) who turn outlaw to save their farm from bankruptcy. Gere's performance, said Janet Maslin in the 'New York Times', 'incorporated more dilatory, decorative flourishes than are really needed, but its essential urgency comes through, as does its liveliness.' But these did not come through for enough people and the film did not make it to the million-dollar barrier at the box-office, so it is just as well that Gere's fee was a mere $150,000, plus 10% of the gross worldwide, but bookings were scarce.

But at the eleventh hour Gere bounded back – not once but twice, and within weeks of each other. First came Mike Figgis's showy police thriller, *Internal Affairs* (90), for Paramount, and then Disney's *Pretty Woman*. In neither was he too admirable, and getting the best reviews of his life it was conceded that he was most effective when playing not-nice characters. That would be an understatement to describe the pathologically bent cop-on-

the-beat he played in the first of these pictures – which concerns a policeman (Andy Garcia) examining corruption in his own force – who ruthlessly kills anyone who gets in the way of his becoming a real estate millionaire. He is the sort of man who needs women to feed his ego but whose preferred form of sex is sodomy, fully-clothed, and when discovered at it by an irate husband can only grin in a contemptuous way. Obviously, some people were not displeased, for the film took more than $26 million in its first two months on release. The Disney film is something else again. Garry Marshall, who directed, considered Gere's reputation for sullenness, his

After some ups and downs in his career, Gere returned with a double-whammy in 1990: in the thriller Internal Affairs, *top, as a corrupt street cop, here seen talking to William Baldwin on the right; and in a romantic comedy,* Pretty Woman, *as a corporate businessman who invites a hooker (Julia Roberts) to spend a week in his hotel penthouse. The public approved – mightily, for this became one of the most successful films ever made.*

limited ability and box-office status, coupled with the fact that his co-star, Julia Roberts, was little known: but 'I wanted two one hundred per cent beautiful people. But there are a lot of good-looking actors who can't act at all. The chemistry between the two stars is quite beautiful.' The remark suggests great confidence in the script, by J.F. Lawton, but Roberts, who was cast first, said that when she first saw it it was 'dark . . . and then they turned it into this delightful, funny, extremely different story.' It is still a slight one, about a wealthy corporate raider who picks up a hooker more or less on a whim, who treats her somewhat as Pygmalion did Galatea, while she falls in love with him. 'I appreciate the seduction scene' she tells him, 'but I'm a sure thing.' Does he fall in love with her? Roberts is a radiant, long-legged beauty who would make any man ache with longing, and a reserved Gere complements her splendidly (now grey-haired, but they gave him brown hair in the ads). This is a supreme example of a 'feel-good' movie (let us not forget Hector Elizondo as the hotel manager), budgeted (per 'Variety') at under $20 million, but with a $170 million domestic gross after four months in release and still going strong. It will be some years yet till Gere's fee slips as it did for *Miles From Home*. His next film will be for Akira Kurosawa, *Rhapsody in August* (91), in which he will play a Japanese–American pineapple grower who, married to an American, returns to Japan to see how it has changed. Kurosawa says he hopes to examine the different thinkings of both nationalities. Shoshiku will produce, and it is Kurosawa's first film wholly funded in Japan for more than a decade. Gere's salary was not reported, but in the few precedents for major names working in prestigious foreign films it is probable that he will work for a small fee upfront and a percentage of the world gross outside Japan. He is then due to start John Boorman's *Final Analysis*, which may be part of his new deal with Tri-star, signed in 1990 when his contract with its sister company, Columbia, expired.

Miss Roberts, along with model Cindy Crawford, is said to be the latest of his companions, but he never discusses his private life. He is a practising Buddhist and will discuss that, as many a journalist will tell you.

MEL GIBSON

Mel Gibson is a talented actor and a very lucky guy. Early in his career the public associated him with action adventures, and every time he does one his box-office stature increases. But unlike Stallone or Schwarzenegger he does not have to do them; unlike them, he can do other roles – and if these don't please the public he can always pick up his mace or sharpshooter again.

He was born in Peekskill, New York, in 1956, the sixth of eleven children, to a railroad brakeman and an Australian ex-opera singer. When his father was awarded compensation after an injury at work, he decided to use it to emigrate to Australia, specifically to remove the threat to the older boys of being drafted to Vietnam. Mel was twelve at the time, not pleased about the move, which was made worse by taunts from fellow-classmates in Australia. He enjoyed larking around the house, and one sister sent off an application on his behalf to the National Institute of Dramatic Art at the University of New South Wales, where he studied for three years. In his second year he was given a role in a low-budget surf movie, *Summer City* (77), as a layabout in search of a good time. He was not paid, he recalled, but was the only contributor involved not to get dire notices. On occasion he has said that its producer, Phil Avalon, recommended him to try for a role in *Mad Max* (79), but it has also been claimed that the prospective director, George Miller, saw *Summer City* and invited him to come to an audition. Miller was seeking some 'bad-looking people', and Gibson was in fact suffering from a beating-up in a pub the night before (or alternatively a street fight a week earlier), when some drunks set on him without provocation. The casting lady thought him sufficiently freaky to qualify for the role, and suggested he return after he was healed in case he still looked bad enough. Thus Gibson became Max, an ex-cop who in some strange future sees his wife and children killed, which makes him understandably mad and he sets off in revenge. The film, made for the equivalent of $300,000, was a big success in Australia and elsewhere, but the US distributor dumped it after re-dubbing it.

The film left unresolved the question of whether Gibson could act, and that was only partially proved in *Tim*, directed by Michael Pate from a novel by Colleen McCullough. He looked sensational – gleaming white teeth (he hardly stopped smiling), blue eyes, a mop of well-greased hair, a clear tanned skin stuffed into the briefest of cut-offs. He bounds along the beach like a colt, without artifice – and there is only one thing wrong with Tim. He is not, in the film's parlance, 'the full quid', which is to say that he is mentally retarded. He is taught to read by a middle-aged career spinster (Piper Laurie), who soon has Designs On Him. Even with these central perform-

ances – and Gibson, who adopted a splayed walk for the role, took Best Actor at the Australian Film Awards – the film is a mess, like a melon left to rot in the sun, oozing rancid syrup. He also put in an unbilled guest appearance as a mechanic who appears from under a car in *The Chain Reaction*, presumably as a joke or a favour, for the film's lead was Steve Bisley, with whom he had shared an apartment while they were studying drama together.

With two local box-office hits behind him he went into Tim Burstall's Kung-Fu war movie, *Attack Force Z* (81) with John Philip Law and Sam Neill, which he later refused to discuss. He plays an army captain in the Pacific in World War Two, leading his men through the jungle to find a crashed plane. But then he did get to star in Peter Weir's *Gallipoli*, which was made to show audiences of what the new Australian cinema was capable, as financed by two Australian tycoons in partnership, Robert Stigwood and Rupert Murdoch. As in *Chariots of Fire* (a coincidence?) the two heroes are runners – Gibson from the city (Perth) and Mark Lee from the country, the outback. The film had an admirable simplicity and when it eventually

Mel Gibson in the title-role, Mad Max *(79), retitled* The Road Warrior *for its not-too-successful US showings. But Warners, noting its huge success elsewhere in the world, did some careful marketing on the first sequel, and cannily put a lot of money into the second.*

gets to that shameful incident in the Great War which gives the film its title, it is all the more effective for not dwelling on the blood or the fear. Gibson, abrasive of tongue, showed that he had a big future, while his screen partner, Lee, was to languish in Australia, unseen on the international screen till 1988, when he played a senator's toyboy in a batty film extolling the gay life, *The Everlasting Secret Family*.

Gibson, meanwhile, had joined the State Theatre Company of South Australia, appearing in 'Romeo and Juliet', 'Waiting for Godot' and a local success, 'No Names No Pack Drill'; he also played Biff when Warren Mitchell repeated his Willy Loman in 'Death of a Salesman' (which Mitchell had played at the National Theatre in London). Gibson was already in demand by the television companies and had appeared in, among others, 'Cop Shop', 'The Sullivans', 'The Oracle' and 'Tickled Pink'. He agreed to do *Mad Max 2*, for which a breathless world seemed to be waiting. It was more of the same, and more expensive, costing the equivalent of $10 million. The cinema as dead-end: hardware and cardboard characters, as Max struggles with bikers anxious to hold on to what is left of the world's oil. Warner Bros. took distribution rights outside Australia, rechristening it *The Road Warrior* for those Americans who might just have heard of *Mad Max* – a film which was soon to enjoy a successful reissue on the strength of this, even if the US yield of $11,300,000 represents a cult following rather than wide popularity. Still, no Aussie film had done nearly as well in the US before. On the strength of it Peter Weir was able to get some backing from MGM for *The Year of Living Dangerously* (82), which had been developed under the auspices of the Australian Film Commission, but at $13 million was too expensive for a local company. Its subject is the world of the foreign correspondent, as taken from an autobiographical novel by C.J. Koch and written by him, Weir and David Williamson. It is set in Indonesia at the time the Communists attempted to overthrow Sukarno – vividly and intelligently, even as an Australian broadcaster (Gibson) falls for an attaché at the British embassy. She was played by Sigourney Weaver, and neither artist then meant enough in the international market for the piece to be more than a modest success. But at least Gibson's boyish, exuberant performance justified the hopes being made for him in the trade press.

He was then called upon to star in an expensive American epic, *The Bounty* (84), but that was only after Sting had turned down the role because of the length of the shooting schedule. The film itself had a troubled

history, having started as a pet project of David Lean, who left it when the producer, Dino de Laurentiis, balked at a budget of $80 million – for just one film, instead of the two originally planned by Lean and written by Robert Bolt (credited with the one used). Lean's choice for the role had been Christopher Reeve, and briefly, when Alan Bridges was to have replaced him, the choice fell on David Essex (who, disappointed, co-authored a West End musical on the subject which managed to run for a while). Producer Bernard Williams managed to reduce the budget to $25,000,000, partly by getting a less expensive director than Lean, the New Zealander Roger Donaldson. Donaldson did a first-rate job, but the film took less than $5 million at the American box-office – which may be because the public at large did not read the trade press and knew not of Gibson or Anthony Hopkins, who played Captain Bligh. More likely most people thought the story over-familiar, having seen the two previous film versions – *Mutiny on the Bounty* (1935 and 1962) – too often on television. This one is by far the best of the three, because it makes sense of the relationship between Bligh and Fletcher Christian, inasmuch as it is clear that the captain has a crush on Christian, an emotion which Christian exploits till he cannot have his own way, when he reacts like a petulant teacher's pet: the spat between the two is so sudden and so violent that the mutiny is in full flood before either is aware of it.

Hopkins said, 'He's in danger of blowing it unless he takes hold of himself,' meaning that the young man was doing too much, too soon. Gibson later agreed, saying, 'I was just trying to keep busy. Because you don't know what direction you're going in, the best thing to do is just to keep scrambling.' He made three films very quickly: *The River* with Sissy Spacek, playing a Tennessee farmer; *Mrs Soffel* with Diane Keaton, as an escaped convict in a doomed romance with her; and *Mad Max Beyond the Thunderdome* (85), more of same with a vengeance. The first two failed horribly, but a lot of people the world over were happy to see Max get mad again, and Warners, happy to budget Max to the tune of $18 million, saw a $17,900,000 return in the US alone. Gibson, bitten by the failure of two serious films and not entirely pleased by the success of one for which he had little sympathy, took a year off, which he spent with his wife (since 1980) Robyn, a former nurse, and their several children on their farm in South Australia. 'I had to clear my head,' he explained later. 'Hollywood is a seductive place for someone with an exuberant personality. I was in real danger of stepping off.'

He left behind a reputation for roistering, of being rude to the press, of temperament and an industry which regarded him as a spent force. Director Richard Donner, however, hoped there was enough madness still in him to play a crazy cop in *Lethal Weapon* (87), that is, one who apart from being a top marksman and a martial arts expert is reckless because he has nothing left to lose. Indeed, the cop's experience in Vietnam had left him virtually paranoic, in contrast to his partner, a family man, played by Danny Glover. These are talented actors playing stock characters, and the tale of tracking down drug-traffickers is told to an old formula. But there was big-heap bang-bang for those who liked that sort of thing, and they liked it to the tune of $29,500,000, on a budget of $15,000,000, of which $1 million went to Gibson.

Writer-director Robert Towne then cast him in a role meant originally for Warren Beatty in 1981. Thus Gibson became a drug dealer who wants to turn over a new leaf in *Tequila Sunrise* (88) but finds too much is against him – including somehow Kurt Russell as a onetime schoolchum, now a cop, out to get him. With Michelle Pfeiffer as the third co-star, the film cost $19 million and took $19,100,000. Towne said that Gibson 'has an intensity that can transform into a kind of ferocious innocence, He's like Gary Cooper in that way . . . He has courage. He's not just an actor trying to hang on to an audience the way a politician tries to maintain a constituency – and there are certain actors like that. You can look at Rambo as an example . . . He's a venturesome soul, a pure one. So it makes you trust him.' *Lethal Weapon 2* (89) redefines the word 'dumb', and you wonder why anyone bothered to make it. The answer would seem to be to take in $79,500,000 on a budget of $30 million, of which $4 million reputedly went to Gibson. Both he and Glover again rose above their material, and Joss Ackland made the best movie villain since Alan Rickman in *Die Hard*. He's dealing in drugs, of course, though a South African diplomat, and the film's sole point of interest is that this is an opportunistic replacement for the Russians who have been the baddies in every other Hollywood thriller of the last forty years.

While making the film Gibson told producer Rob Cohen and director John Badham that he wanted to play comedy. It so happened that they had time on their hands, later, when *The Hard Way* was postponed because Michael J. Fox was booked up for a year. They asked Universal if they had a likely script and although *Bird on a Wire* (90) needed adjustment it seemed ideal for Goldie Hawn and Gibson, who was between commit-

ments. She plays a hotshot lawyer and he an old lover whom she helps to escape from some crooks who aim to kill him because he turned state's witness. The film grossed more than $68 million in less than three months in release. Gibson reputedly received $7 million for *Air America*, in which he plays a cynical war-weary pilot flying opium to the Far East, which he justifies as being essential to the war effort – the Vietnam War, that is. The title refers to the CIA's proprietory airline, which used drug-money to finance the war. Roger Spottiswoode directed, from Christopher Robbins's 1979 book on the subject, and Robert Downey Jr co-starred. The film did $8 million in its first three days (as of this writing).

Allegedly Gibson put some of his own money into Franco Zeffirelli's *Hamlet*, and since he is working for scale we may be sure he is on a profit percentage. As it finished shooting he was offered one of the rival *Robin Hood*s, but left the field clear to Kevin

Gibson in Bird on a Wire *(90), forced to confront his past when a former girlfriend and a gang of killers catch up with him at the same time. The critics didn't care for it but the public loved it.*

Costner (q.v.) because he didn't want to do two films in tights consecutively. This *Hamlet*, by the way, began to look a much sounder box-office proposition when Gibson was voted the most popular star in the US in mid-1990. 'USA Today' polled the public on stars, asking to rate them from one to a hundred as to whether they would attract them to the cinema. Here are the top ten, with the voters' average rating: 1. Gibson (79) 2. Tom Cruise, Jack Nicholson (76) 4. Goldie Hawn (74) 5. Meryl Streep (71) 6. Kathleen Turner (68) 7. Bruce Willis, Eddie Murphy (67) 9. Michelle Pfeiffer, Arnold Schwarzenegger. It should be borne in mind, however, that Gibson was on high profile with the success of *Bird on a Wire* and with *Air America* about to open – and that, for instance, the public has shown a marked reluctance to see any of the last few films in which Streep has appeared.

TOM HANKS

He's been called the King of Comedy, but when told he was the successor to Cary Grant, he replied that he was 'awed, but it just isn't true' – because, he said, Grant's sort of sophisticated comedy was no longer being made. He said on another occasion that he would like to leave a body of work like Jack Lemmon's or James Stewart's, and well he may. He brings a similar intelligence to comedy, and like all the best screen comics, from Keaton to Steve Martin, he has a touch of the manic when obsessed. We're lucky to have him.

He was born in Concord, California, in 1956, where his father was a restaurateur. Five years later his parents were divorced; the youngest of the four children stayed with mother, but Tom and the two others moved around with father – who was always finding a reason for opening another restaurant. He was also married again, to a woman with eight children, and when he married for the third time, the family settled in Oakland. The last of several institutions of education was the California State University at Sacramento, where he became involved with student theatricals. The director, Vincent Dowling, cast him in his own translation of 'The Cherry Orchard' and invited him to perform at the Great Lakes Theater Festival, near Cleveland, where he played Grumio in 'The Taming of the Shrew' and, the following year, Proteus in 'Two Gentlemen of Verona'. In 1978, with another company member, Michael John McGann, he went to try his fortunes in New York, where he married an actress, Samantha Lewes. Most of 1979 was spent on unemploy-

ment benefits, but he did return to Cleveland to play a small part in 'Othello', and for $800 he played a small role – billed eighth – in a dreadful slasher movie, *He Knows You're Alone* (80), directed for the once-mighty MGM by Armand Mastroianni (Marcello's cousin). In Los Angeles he auditioned several times for ABC, who eventually starred him in 'Bosom Buddies', a sitcom in which he played an adman who spends most of the time in drag with a colleague because the only place they can afford to live is a ladies' hostel. It ran for two years, during which he also appeared on 'Taxi', 'Family Ties' and 'Happy Days', with Ron Howard, who thought him very funny as a Black Belt who returns to revenge himself on Fonzie, who had pushed him out of a swing in childhood. Hanks also starred in a telefilm, *Rona Jaffe's Mazes and Monsters* (82), in which he and three college friends indulge in medieval war fantasies. It was made in Canada, and Vera Miles played his mother.

He was still generally unknown when Howard, turned director, cast him and another such, Darryl Hannah, in *Splash* (84), after an audition and after the role had been turned down by several actors, including Michael Keaton (whom Howard had directed in *Night Shift*). Howard and his partner, Brian Grazer, had already peddled the subject to several studios before it was accepted by Disney – where, at that point, there was only confusion. After years of success with films aimed at the kiddie market, they had had a run of flops. Moving towards the adolescent market only proved them even more out of touch, so *Splash* was to be the first of some more mature subjects released under the Touchstone logo. Its heroine was a mermaid who pursues Hanks, met at Cape Cod, to New York: on dry land her tail becomes legs, and she's a great deal of bother to many people, not least him – because she likes to copulate. John Candy played his brother, both of them in the wholesale vegetable business, while Hanks and Hannah made a winning team – she all daffy innocence and he a mixture of dither and naivity, willingness and occasional inspired clowning. Despite the sex, it was hardly adult stuff, but when it took over $34 million – Disney's most successful film by far in ages – it did usher in a new era for the studio. Hanks's salary was $70,000.

Made before that was released was *Bachelor Party*, a much more desperate comedy in which Hanks was a carefree bus-driver whose animal-like chums are determined that his last few marriage-free hours shall be crammed with broads, booze and drugs. It took over $19 million, but *The Man With One Red Shoe* (85) saw little joy at $4,500,000. This remake of *Le Grand Blond avec une Chaussure Noire* gave Hanks little chance to be funny, as directed by Stan Dragoti, despite a good comic role as an innocent concert pianist caught up in the machinations of the CIA and the FBI. He had some fine chances, however, in Nicholas Meyer's *Volunteers*, as a useless student playboy who in 1962 elects to spend two years in the Peace Corps in preference to having some bones broken by the bookmaker to whom he owes a small fortune. Incongruous in white dinner-jacket in the Thai jungle, he lives by his creed: 'I'm very rich and I have certain rights', trying to bring 'civilization' to a village which doesn't want it. Reunited with John Candy, as a self-righteous member on the same mission, he doublecrosses him in Hope–Crosby style: but as Hanks himself remarked, 'The real problem is the third act. It's like, where's Dorothy Lamour?' Curiously, then, the chief female role was played by Rita Wilson, who became the second Mrs Hanks. Nevertheless or therefore or regardless, the film took $8,900,000. It was certainly better than *The Money Pit* (86), which was the pits, as produced by Steven Spielberg and directed by Richard Benjamin. Most critics compared it unfavourably to the film which inspired it, *Mr Blandings Builds His Dream House*, but what it really is is *Poltergeist* without the ghosts. Hanks and Shelley Long were the hapless couple trapped amid the falling masonry, which was liked enough to return $16,800,000 of its $20 million budget.

The two who had *Nothing in Common* were he and Jackie Gleason, playing his father, an unsuccessful salesman with a failed marriage – which is why he and Mother (Eva Marie Saint) are bothering him after he has avoided them for years. He is a Chicago ad man, on top of his job and with several ladies, 'funnier than Henny Yougman; but Hanks is not a gloater, not crappy and nasty like Bill Murray at his worst nor puckish and cheap like Chevy Chase. Those guys are comics; Hanks is a light-comedy romantic *actor*. He has springy legs, a curled mouth that makes him an obvious choice to play mashers, a serious forehead, and very large eyes. Even in the low, pandering *Bachelor Party*, he brought abundant wit to the role of a cynical make-out artist. And he demonstrated something else – a generosity to other actors' (David Denby in 'New York' magazine). Gary Marshall directed the film, which took a neat $13,500,000. Hanks should then have made *Night on the Town*, which was to have marked the American debut of the French director, Francis Veber. Instead, he played a straight romantic role in Moshe Mizrahi's *Every Time We Say Goodbye*, his only outright failure to date; he played an airman who, while recover-

ing from an accident in Israel, falls in love with a girl (Christina Marsillach) from a strict Sephardic Jewish family. Hanks accepted the role because he wanted variety in what he did; and, in fact, he asked to be in Universal's spoof *Dragnet* (87), because he was tired of getting the girl at the end, because he would 'play a cop who does things like slug people', and because he wanted to work with Dan Aykroyd. Their salaries were two reasons why the film cost $23 million; it took $30,900,000.

Even so, *Big* (88) was Hanks's breakthrough, the film with which audiences discovered that they loved him. The role, which had been declined by Harrison Ford and Robert De Niro, was exactly right for Hanks, who is much aware of his youthful appearance. A twelve-year-old boy in a moment of pique in a fairground wants to become grown

Tom Hanks in Big *(88), as the little boy who overnight finds himself a very big boy – but only physically. Two other comedies of the season had the same premise, but while they got nowhere fast this was very, and deservedly, popular.*

up; so he finds himself transformed in the morning to Hanks, a boy in a big body, singularly unequipped for any adult job – but because he can work a computer he gets a job in a toy factory, where his empathy with the little monsters to whom they cater leads to swift promotion. Hanks's understanding of the role was such that Janet Maslin in the 'New York Times' called him 'an absolute delight' while Gerald Clarke in 'Time' magazine said he 'emerged as one of Hollywood's top comic actors'. Penny Marshall (Gary's sister) directed an inventive script by Gary Ross and Anne Spielberg, and Hanks himself observed later that it was better than the other two concurrent films on the same theme, *Vice Versa* and *Like Father Like Son*. Both flopped, while *Big* took $52 million, making a huge profit on its $20 million budget. His fee at this time was reckoned to be around $1 million. The critics admired him again in *Punchline*, which he described as a love story between 'a very good stand-up comedian who is a horrible human being and a wonderful human being who is a horrible stand-up comedian'. He was the first of these, a mean-spirited, neurotic, self-centred guy, and Sally Field was the second. David Seltzer, who wrote and directed, said that he had created 'a character whose outward behaviour was rude and insulting, praying to find an actor with the courage to play it and the vulnerability lurking within. In Hanks, I found both. He's brilliant.' In the 'New York Times', Vincent Canby said that the film confirmed that here was 'a fine comic actor. He is full of nervous energy and has the talent to channel it properly' while Donna Britt in 'USA Today' said that 'Hanks has evolved into a comic actor who can seemingly do anything.' One thing he could not do was make audiences turn up this time in sufficient numbers (see Field). But Hanks was content: he had asked to do the role and later observed that it was not an easy film. 'It's grim and introspective, so I'm not sure you can expect it to make lots of money.'

Joe Dante's *The 'Burbs* (89) found Hanks in deepest Suburbia, holidaying at home and becoming obsessed with the idea that some neighbours are very strange. His fee for it was $3,500,000, bringing the budget to $17 million; it bettered that at the box-office by $300,000, which was not bad going for a rather harmless comedy. Roger Spottiswoode's *Turner and Hooch* was a cop comedy-thriller made for Disney, which partnered Hanks with an ugly mutt – because the dog is the sole witness to his master's murder. This did much better than Hanks's earlier film that year, making $34,200,000 on an $18 million budget. And making a similar amount in just four

Hanks in The 'Burbs *(89), another comedy which couldn't be accused of too much originality – the suburban man beset by new neighbours. But it had some agreeable moments.*

weeks (to date) was John Patrick Shanley's *Joe Versus the Volcano* (90), the tale of a nebbish guy with only three months to live and to whom some strange and wonderful things happen, including a trip to the South Seas and Meg Ryan in triplicate.

He said at this time: 'Right now, I'm hot. Next year I may not be. Comedy's a temperamental thing. As for the work I do, I don't think I'll have many real cracks at drama or playing any kind of comedy till I'm 40, at least. Like I said, my face is funny, and I have this image of a grown-up kid. But I'm not in much hurry to change it . . .' All the same, he was scheduled to do a remake of *Night and the City*, which could hardly be a load of laughs – but that was cancelled when Brian De Palma cast him in *The Bonfire of the Vanities*, based on Tom Wolfe's novel. William Hurt was the first choice to play the Wall Street bond-dealer, but was already committed to a film with Wim Wenders: still, who would mind being second choice when they are willing to pay you $5 million?

DARYL HANNAH

She's the other Hollywood blonde, the one who looks like Kim Basinger. Or is it the other way around?

She was born in Chicago in 1960 to parents who divorced when she was seven. Five years later her mother married again, and since

Jerry Wexler was chairman of Jupiter Industries, young Daryl and her brother and sister found that overnight they had moved into the moneyed classes, with trips to the Caribbean and Europe. There was a show-business connection, since her stepfather's brother was Haxell Wexler, the cinematographer. She wanted to be a dancer, and studied with Maria Tallchief, who had a school in Chicago, but she found the training too hard, too rigid. A viewing of *Singin' in the Rain* convinced her that her future lay in movies, so she joined the prestigious Goodman Theater, the only juvenile to be studying there at the time. At seventeen she went to Hollywood and managed to get a small role as a student in Brian De Palma's *The Fury* (78) with Kirk Douglas. When nothing else came along, she returned to Chicago, but the family knew Susan St James, who was able to offer advice about surviving in the Hollywood jungle. And, according to one interviewer, one of Daryl's friends, Jonathan Kaufer, a director and screenwriter, twice took her to lunch at Warner Bros. in Burbank in 1979, 'and both times she was hit on by directors.' She had further brief roles in *The Final Terror* (81), a decimate-the-students tale which also included in its cast Rachel Ward (with whom Hannah shared a flat at the time), and *Hard Country*, in which she supported the debuting Ms Basinger. Matters picked up considerably with a television movie, *Paper Dolls* (82), in which she and Alexandra Paul aimed to make it big as Junior Miss models as aided and abetted by their mothers, Joan Hackett and Jennifer Warren, plus a hammy Joan Collins as a top agent. A few months later Hannah was highly visible in *Blade Runner*, as a vicious, leather-clad 'replicant' being nasty to Harrison Ford, and she consolidated her position as a promising star (it would have been starlet in the old days) with Randal Kleiser's *Summer Lovers*. We do know that Kleiser saw Hannah in the Warner commissary as he was planning a follow-up to his successful *The Blue Lagoon*. The young lovers this time would be joined by a third, not for some deviate passion, but because it is accepted that the hot Mediterranean sun makes a man dissatisfied with only one sexual partner. The lucky boy was Peter Gallagher; Hannah and Valerie Quennessen, a French archaeologist, were the girls, and they disported themselves over much of Santorini, perhaps the most ravishing of the Greek islands – and unspoilt, a fact unchanged by this movie, which most people avoided.

This they did not get a chance to do with *Reckless* (84), since it was not widely booked. James Foley directed this teen pic in which she, Hannah, takes up with a wild boy (Aidan Quinn) from the wrong side of the tracks and finds that moving in the fast lane is more fun than the swing on the back porch. But a lot of people were to see, and love, *Splash*, which made Hannah famous – as well as Tom Hanks (q.v.), her co-star. This was the first 'adult' film for Disney, which did not wish to shell out large salaries, partly because many of the studio's (non-animated) successes in the past not been reliant on star names. In this case the two young players needed to have exceptional abilities, if not necessarily for acting *per se*: the film concerns a New York executive and a mermaid who is vulnerable and very loving. Curiously, the last screen mermaids date from 1948, Glynis Johns (in *Miranda*) and Ann Blyth (in *Mr Peabody and the Mermaid*), and though neither film is widely known today, they followed mythology, as Hannah needed to do, in being enigmatic and amorous. Yet Hannah's was an original performance, teaming her felicitously with Hanks. She was seen to much less advantage in her third film that year, *The Pope of Greenwich Village*, as Mickey Rourke's girlfriend, a Waspish blonde icon for his rage to rail against. In the book by Vincent Patrick, the character is an actress-cum-waitress, but in the screenplay, also by Mr Patrick, she has become an aerobics teacher – possibly due to the demand of the director, Stuart Rosenberg.

The Clan of the Cave Bear (86) was directed by Michael Chapman and written by John Sayles from Jean M. Auel's bestselling novel of life in the Cro-Magnon era. Using a combination of sign language, documentary commentary and subtitles, the film tries to communicate without the idiocies of previous movie excursions among the Neanderthals, but the result is equally lunatic, as little orphan Hannah begs her way into life with a new tribe, 'a girl trying to fit in and make a place for herself', as the publicity put it. Returning to her wide-eyed mermaid persona, Hannah intermittently suggested that the thing might have made a good comedy; instead, it made a dull nothing – which would include, virtually, its box-office figure of $1,500,000. It cost $18 million. Among its four executive producers were Peter Guber and Jon Peters, who after *The Witches of Eastwick*, *Rain Man* and *Batman* were regarded as the saviours of the American film industry; at this time they were delivering such other turkeys as *Who's That Girl?*, *The Legend of Billie Jean* and *Six Weeks*. From this one, with top-billing, it was not a descent to supporting Robert Redford and Debra Winger in *Legal Eagles*, especially as she had a colourful role as Redford's kookie client, whose irrational behaviour includes trying to bed him (and succeeding).

Darryl Hannah in the title-role of Roxanne *(87), understandably making men fall in love with her; and with Steve Martin in a scene from the film. For those who haven't seen it, it is a loose re-working of 'Cyrano de Bergerac', hence the nose.*

Her growing stature enabled her to be cast in two of the year's most important and most popular movies – and they were two of the best, too: Fred Schepisi's *Roxanne* (87), in the title-role, and Oliver Stone's *Wall Street*. The former demonstrates her inefficiency in comedy, but she looked the part marvellously and was well cast as a girl too dumb to realize that it's the long-nosed guy (Steve Martin) wooing her in place of his shy colleague (Rick Rossovich); and she was even more out of her

depth in the other film, as a cast-off of Gordon Gekko (Michael Douglas) who gets it on with his protégé (Charlie Sheen). Since Sean Young played Gekko's wife, the two ladies were sort-of rivals, and since Ms Young did not get on too well with Stone, at least one of her lines went to Hannah. After making this dangerous foray into the real world, Hannah was back where she belonged, as one of the *High Spirits* (88) – the most prominent one, however, of those haunting an Irish castle. When an American tycoon (Steve Guttenberg) prevents her husband (Liam Neeson) from murdering her a second time, she falls in love with him, which is inconvenient, since he is equally attracted, but believes an Experience with a ghost must lead to death; so he gives in . . . and much more besides, with nary a laugh along the way as written and directed by Neil Jordan. Guber and Peters were involved in this one, too, which cost the equivalent of $17 million to an American appreciation of only $3,500,000. Her fee at this time was said to be $600,000 per film.

Thus Hannah was much cooler property when she auditioned for a role in *Steel Magnolias* (89), that of Sally Field's fatally ill daughter. That went to the lesser-known Julia Roberts, with Hannah offered (after several readings) the consolation of another showy role, that of a bimbo with a failed marriage who is taken on by beautician Dolly Parton. Hannah, rightly, regarded this as a new departure, and was determined henceforward 'to find roles for myself that are more personality-orientated, more character-orientated', as she put it. Neither description applied to her role in *Crazy People* (90) as Dudley Moore's love interest. He plays a Madison Avenue executive sent to an institution – where he meets Hannah – for wishing to tell the truth in adverts, and he took over during filming, not being much in demand, from John Malkovich. Tony Bill's film was reasonably well received, but with Moore in the lead managed to take only $13 million in its first two months before dropping out of sight. Next for Hannah: Hector Babenco's *At Play in the Fields of the Lord* (90), co-starring Tom Berenger and John Lithgow, and *A League of Their Own*, a baseball drama with Laura Dern and James Belushi co-starring.

RUTGER HAUER

Rutger Hauer is the only Dutch actor to become an international star. Well, there was Philip Dorn, but he was hardly more than just another of Hollywood's leading men. Type-cast too long as a villain, Hauer has a talent and a personality which may continue to astonish us. The unpredictability of his bad guys and the trustworthiness of his heroes make him a valuable screen star.

He was born in 1944 in Breukelen, the Netherlands, into a theatrical family, whose profession he did not care to follow. At first, he ran away from home to join the merchant navy, but gave it up 'because everyone was stupid and I didn't think I was. I think it's stupid to be a grown-up male going from harbour to harbour, spending your time with hookers in bars.' He also joined the army, but managed to get himself discharged for 'psychological unfitness', and between whiles studied at drama school in Amsterdam, from which he was expelled. 'What I was really interested in was writing poetry and living the life of the streets,' he said later, but at that moment he headed for Switzerland to climb the mountains. While there (in 1967), he married (it lasted three months) and joined a theatre in Basle, as stagehand, gardener and heating engineer, an experience which renewed his interest in theatre. He returned to Amsterdam to resume his drama studies, and then spent five years with a repertory company in North Holland, during which time he translated a dramatized version of 'Of Mice and Men' and played Lenny in it. He clashed with the company's new manager, who told him to work in movies – and at this time he was recommended to director Paul Verhoeven by a friend, Gerard Soeteman, who had seen him in rep. 'He was a good-looking boy, very blond with blue eyes, and very sympathetic,' recalled Verhoeven, who tested him and gave him the leading role in a television adventure serial when his original choice, Carol van Herwijnen, became unavailable. 'Floris' (69) was a swashbuckler that almost every child in the country watched. Hauer continued to act on the stage and made his movie debut in a small role in an unimportant venture, *Repelsteeltje* (73).

But it was later that Verhoeven assigned him to the chief part in *Turks Fruit/Turkish Delight*, and Hauer decided to restrict his activities to the cinema. The film, produced by Rob Houwer from the bestseller by Jan Wolkers, was an ideal showcase for the young actor, who played a promiscuous sculptor remembering his stormy affair and marriage to one particular woman (Monique van de Ven). Its international reception was mixed, as might be expected when it turned up in some countries dubbed and cut, looking often like soft pornography.

It brought Hauer an offer to appear in *Pusteblume* (74), directed by Adrian Hove, in which Hauer is a sailor with a broken mar-riage in his past and many other women in his future, including a model who is murdered by a jealous girlfriend. It also brought the opportunity to play a leading role in *The Wilby Conspiracy* (75), as the Afrikaans pilot blackmailed by Michael Caine into flying him out of South Africa – partly because Caine's current girlfriend is his ex-wife. The film was not of a quality to ensure an international career, and in any case Hauer was working with Houwer and Verhoeven again in *Keetje Tippel*, based on three novelized memoirs written by Neel Doff, who after a long struggle surrendered her virginity and succumbed to prostitution in the 1880s. The film took a fairly rosy view of poverty and vice in the nineteenth century, and had an affecting heroine in Monique van de Ven. Hauer was second-billed, but was just one of several men in her life, in his case a bank-clerk who rejects her to marry his wealthy boss's daughter.

He starred again in *Het Jaar van de Kreeft*, directed by Herbert Curiel, as a rich playboy who showers presents on Willeke van Ammel-rooy but cannot make her love him. Then he was in support again, as an officer in the Dutch Colonial army, in Fons Rademaker's *Max Havelaar* (76), but this was a very prestigious picture based on the one undisputed Dutch literary classic, written in 1860 by Multatuli, and again autobiographical. The screenwriter was Gerard Soeteman (who had 'discovered' Hauer) and the star Peter Faber, coping with the problems of the Dutch administration of Java, again during the last century. Hauer did another German film, *Griechische Feigen*, which tells of a German girl (Olivia Pascall) trekking through Greece with a tape-recorder with which to record her amorous adventures, one of which is provided by Hauer. He himself later observed that the films he made in Germany were terrible, but that he had done them for the money – the equivalent of 100,000 gulden, as opposed to *Max Havelaar*, for instance, for which he was paid 5,000 gulden, or *Het Jaar van de Kreeft*, for which he got 25,000 gulden. Hauer had been out of work for over a year when Verhoeven offered him another leading role, in *Soldaat van Oranje/Soldier of Orange* (77), about the experiences of six students during the Occupation. He hesitated, because this was what he called a 'boy scout' character – as he later told the author of the autobiography on which it was based (and he agreed). Wim Verstappen's *Pastorale 1943* (78) was not dissimilar (except in tone: it was less concerned with heroism), but the character that Hauer played was different: he was an SS officer, proud, self-assured, not without humour and romantically inclined to fight for lost causes. His brother is in the Resistance, but it is Hauer who turns the trick for himself in the end, since the director was trying to question Dutch sentiment in the matter of the Occupation. Sylvia Kristel was also in the cast.

He then went off to Belgium to make *Femme Entre Chien et Loup/Een Vrouw Tussen Hond en Wolf* for director André Delvaux with Marie-Christine Barrault, as her husband in this drama set in an Antwerp suburb from 1940 to 1952 (with a concentration on the war period).

He returned for a reunion with Kristel, in *Knut Hamsen's Mysteries/Mysteries* (79), which also starred Rita Tushingham. Paul de Lussanet directed, Hauer co-produced and played a mysterious stranger who arrives on the Isle of Man to have a disquieting effect on many people, including the vicar's daughter. *Het Begon bij Tiffany* was a German telefilm, directed by Wolfgang Becker, about an incompetent crook (Hauer) who sets up his own bank – for illegal purposes – when his own robberies fail. Also at this time Rijk de Gooyer and Hauer were *Gripsta en de Gier* respectively, buddy cops, the steady married one and the boozing, womanizing bachelor. Verhoeven's *Spetters* (80) is a rites-of-passage tale concerned with several youngsters, most importantly the one who faces up to his repressed homosexuality after being raped – none of which had anything to do with Hauer, who had a supporting role as the boys' idol, a champion motor-cyclist.

Meanwhile, *Soldier of Orange* had been widely seen abroad, including a showing at the Seattle Film Festival. 'Variety' singled Hauer out for praise ('does a great job') and Hollywood made an offer, to play a role loosely based on Carlos the Terrorist in a Sylvester Stallone vehicle, *Nighthawks* (81). Said Hauer: 'I had a lot of problems on that film, principally with Stallone. I had to fight him all the time on the level of what I thought was good enough for the part and what what he thought was good enough. I was very angry . . . very aggressive, very alert, very awake. I don't think I've ever been more motivated or done better work.' At the same time he observed that with the simultaneous departure of himself, Verhoeven, Jeroen Krabbe and Sylvia Kristel (she to France; the others went to Hollywood), the Dutch cinema had virtually collapsed: 'We were accused of disloyalty and that sort of thing, but I don't accept it. To me, it's like children leaving home: if you want to grow, you have to move on.' His American career did not progress with a poor Franco–American biography, *Chanel Solitaire*, which was only too well named as far as audiences were concerned.

Hauer was tired of playing the bad man, so when offered another in The Osterman Weekend *(83) he asked for the role of the hero instead. Thus he was the host of a popular television interview show who becomes involved in a deadly game of double espionage.*

Marie-France Pisier played the couturier and Hauer was one of her lovers, a French playboy. He was the star of a five-hour mini-series, *Inside the Third Reich* (82), as the architect Albert Speer (on whose book it was based), which was fine for an actor now determined on an American career. But he attracted most attention at the time as a Germanic blond android in leather in *Blade Runner*, with him and his friend Daryl Hannah doing vicious things to Harrison Ford, though not without a hint of bisexuality from the pair of them. He was a French count married to Theresa Russell in *Eureka* (83), Nicholas Roeg's ghastly film based on the Harry Oakes affair (in fact, the son-in-law acquitted of the murder), and one which was hardly seen.

When proposed as the bad guy in Sam Peckinpah's *The Osterman Weekend*, he observed that he had had enough of villainy, so he turned the role down. He was then offered the hero, a TV investigative reporter who gets caught up in the schemes of the CIA and the KGB, and John Hurt was cast instead as the treacherous friend. Said Hurt: 'Rutger has an understanding of himself that I certainly haven't reached about myself.' He might have added that Hauer had also got himself on to the books of William Morris, one of the industry's most influential agencies. Philip Mora's *A Breed Apart* (84) found him

mons). It proved him an excellent action hero, but did not support the contention of its producer, Arthur Sarkissian, that it was 'a lineal descendant' of the old Steve McQueen TV series of the same name: on the contrary, it was the same old 80s formula action stuff being churned out with Stallone or Chuck Norris. He did not have their box-office clout, however, but unlike them he found something worthwhile to do, if only for television: *Escape from Sobibor*, as the Russian POW who organizes it. He then found something wonderful to do, and almost certainly was paid peanuts to do it: *The Legend of the Holy Drinker/La Leggenda del Santo Bevitore* (88), directed in English in Paris by an Italian, Ermanno Olmi, from a German novella, 'Die Legende des heiligen Trinkers' by Arthur Roth. Olmi is unquestionably a great film-maker, but then so were de Sica, Antonioni and Visconti, all of whom failed miserably on expensive international productions. Perhaps because Olmi had obstinately remained outside the Italian mainstream he was able to pull this off, a rare, mysterious fable about – well, what? Hauer, who was never better, plays a *clochard* handed 200 francs by a stranger, the start of a run of good fortune which brings happiness in the days before his death. Allegory is intended, and is marvellously pulled off.

It marked a new phase in Hauer's career, which would lead to more diversified work, including the Guinness commercials in Britain, a job his agent found for him when he explained that he needed money. These made him well known in Britain for the first time, which was just as well, as *Bloodhounds of Broadway*, made some years before, finally received a few test engagements before disappearing. Earmarked by the press as 'Madonna's latest flop', it also had in the cast Matt Dillon and Randy Quaid. Hauer played a gangster called The Brain. Playing in a film with Madonna cannot be the ambition of any responsible actor, so it was no wonder that Hauer returned to Europe. Still, why on earth would he also want to appear in a film for director Lina Wertmuller – if, that is, he had seen some of the others she had made? *On a Moonlit Night* (89) co-stars Faye Dunaway and Nastassia Kinski, with Hauer as a man who is HIV positive. It is 'unintentionally funny,' wrote David Stratton, reviewing it from the Venice Film Festival. *Blind Fury* found him as a blind Vietnam veteran who goes on a desperate mission to escort a small boy across the US to reunite him with his father. That he is also a martial arts expert suggests a rip-off of Zatoichi, the Japanese cinema's blind samurai, and why not? This was directed by an Australian, Philip Noyce, and Hauer went the other way up with *The*

Back on evil form again, Rutger Hauer in The Hitcher *(85), his most renowned study in villainy, in which he stalks the driver unlucky enough to have stopped to pick him up.*

top-billed again as another nice guy, a New Zealand conservationist in this tale of greed, with Kathleen Turner and Powers Boothe. But then there was another macabre role, *The Hitcher* (85), a demonic psychopath who stalks the poor driver (C. Thomas Howell) unfortunate enough to have given him a lift. He said of this role, which furthered his reputation, 'People have a hard time accepting that a villain has a heart. They need to make it easy. The whole trick is to show many sides when creating a memorable villain.' He was a medieval knight bent on revenge in Richard Donner's expensive and elaborate *Ladyhawke*, and he stayed unrewardingly in the past in Verhoeven's *Flesh & Blood*, as a mercenary. This was Verhoeven's first English-speaking film, a Dutch–American co-production for Orion, and with its range of accents and uncertain aim avoided none of the pitfalls of expensive 'international' movies; it was also excessively violent and sexist, defended by the director on the grounds that 'the Middle Ages were not a fairy-tale.' The two might have worked together again, for Verhoeven offered Hauer the lead in *Robocop*, but he turned it down (Peter Weller played it).

Wanted: Dead or Alive (87) found Hauer still in action, as an ex-CIA agent turned bounty-hunter, whose former boss hires him to track down an Arab terrorist (Gene Sim-

Blood of Heroes (90), made in Australia by an American, writer-director David Peoples, who had known Hauer since penning the screenplay of *Blade Runner*. This too is set in some dystopia of the future, with Hauer as the veteran head of a team of itinerant gladiators playing pick-up games of something called 'juggers'. Favourable reviews in the US do not seem to have turned Hauer's box-office fortunes.

He has done an Italian mini-series, *Maketub, The Law of the Desert* (90), and now has a home in the Netherlands with his second wife (since 1985, though they had been together then for many years). After that he is due to star in *The Castle* (91) with Omar Sharif and Glenda Jackson, about a knight returning from the Crusades. Although as ambitious as ever, he was not altogether starry-eyed about the American film industry, for he said once: 'There are so many rules in Hollywood. You need an agent, a press agent and sometimes a manager. And you don't have them because *you* need them, but because that's the way the game is played.'

GOLDIE HAWN

When Rowan and Martin's NBC show 'Laugh-In' first hit the air-waves in 1968, it was an immediate success not only because of its free-wheeling form – and not, probably, because of the patter-act of the stars – but because of the gifted team assembled round them. There was Ruth Buzzi – the only survivor of several seasons – Artie Johnson, Judy Carne, Joanne Worley, Henry Gibson, Lily Tomlin – and Goldie Hawn. Goldie flubbed her lines and giggled – a new version of that old standby, the dumb blonde, but she was pretty and mischievous. Above all, she did everything with a bland air of inconsequence which was fetching and very funny.

She was born in Washington in 1945, the daughter of a professional musician. She started ballet and tap lessons at three. At sixteen she made her professional debut as Shakespeare's Juliet with the Virginia Stage Company. She studied for two years at American University, dropped out at eighteen and started her own dancing school in her home town. She drifted from that to the chorus of 'Can-Can' during the New York World's Fair, then joined road companies of 'Kiss Me Kate' and 'Guys and Dolls'. She danced in Puerto Rico in the chorus-line, was a go-go dancer in New York, and worked in Los Angeles as a choreographer. She danced on TV in the Andy Griffith Show and was

seen by manager Art Simon, who signed her to an agreement. He got her a brief role (as Goldie Jean Hawn) in Disney's *The One and Only Genuine Original Family Band* (68) – one of the few Disney flops of this period.

He also sent her to audition for the 'Laugh-In'. The producer, George Schlatter, has said that her incompetence with lines was not feigned, that she was nervous, but that he recognized a quality in her which could be utilized. She became a favourite wherever the programme was aired, the most endearing of the regulars. Mike J. Frankovitch of Columbia signed her for a role in *Cactus Flower* (69), as the odd little girl who tries to kill herself when she thinks her lover (Walter Matthau) no longer wants her. It was, in fact, a comedy; she soon recovers, and tries to aid Ingrid Bergman, whom she thinks is his wife. There was no hesitation or doubt now about her lines; her daffiness was very appealing. Some observers compared her to Marilyn Monroe and Judy Holliday, but she was like them only in being vulnerable and good-natured. She won a Best Supporting Actress Oscar and married Gus Trikonis, screen-writer and director.

Frankovitch upped her to co-star billing opposite Peter Sellers in *There's a Girl in My Soup* (70), again as a waif – who moves in and takes care of that worldly gentleman. The success of the film was mainly due to her. Frankovitch starred her in two more movies: *$* (72), playing a kooky hooker who is Warren Beatty's accomplice, and *Butterflies Are Free*, another adaptation of a long-running play, as the young budding actress who stumbles into the life of blind Edward Albert. Both films failed, and Hawn-watchers worried, as she remained away from films: for films could not do without the one genuine young talent around. When she returned, she had put that in abeyance; but had discovered a genuine acting talent – both as the crazed young wife egging on her convict husband in *The Sugarland Express* (74), and as the Russian ballerina loved by American journalist Hal Holbrook in *The Girl From Petrovka*. As directed by Steven Spielberg, the former was a very fine thriller; the latter was a decent attempt at the impossible – an attempt to recreate the milieu of modern Russia. Neither did well, and Universal did not proceed with the third of a three-picture contract. On the other hand, from all standpoints except its sexual content, *Shampoo* (75) should have been minority cinema, but the sexual content was there, and so lots of people went to see it. Hawn was Beatty's girlfriend.

Again she was a hooker – out West – in *The Duchess and the Dirtwater Fox* (76), which also mired down the comic gifts of George

Segal; but a comedy-thriller with Chevy Chase (fresh from TV) proved just the thing – she was 'superb' in *Foul Play* (78), said 'Variety', 'This toned-down vulnerable image is just right and broadens extensively her future theatrical dramatic spectrum.' She almost did not get the role, which had been marked down for Farrah Fawcett – but it is unlikely that with her the film would have brought in a far from foul $27,500,000. Hawn had already contracted to do an Italian–US co-production, *Viaggio con Anita/Lovers and Liars* (79), in which she played a tourist romantically involved with a bank manager (Giancarlo Giannini); the director was Mario Monicelli, whose light touch had long left him, so that this black comedy was damply received when it eventually turned up in the States in 1981. In the meantime Hawn had confirmed her box-office situation with *Private Benjamin* (80), which she also exec-produced. Howard Zieff directed this sometimes bright, often inane, comedy about a Jewish princess who joins the army after losing her husband (Albert Brooks) while on the job on their wedding night. Much strain and multo message in the last part did not prevent the film from taking $34,400,000, which made it one of the most successful films in the history of Warners. $21,500,000 was the also pleasing take of *Seems Like Old Times*, which was on display a month later. Jay Sandrich directed this product of the Neil Simon laughter-machine which posed Hawn and husband Charles Grodin hiding her first, Chevy Chase, after he had been forced to rob a bank by some crooks. Did someone say strained? But at least it gave the star a chance to show that she could play something other than dreamy dumb blondes.

Best Friends (82) was a nice one with Burt Reynolds, but Hawn came a cropper with *Swing Shift* (84) – and among them might well be the credited director, Jonathan Demme, who publicly dissociated himself from the result, of which at least thirty minutes was the work of someone else. Only one writer is credited, though with a different name on the cassette cover – all for a poor little tale of a wartime marriage, with a feminist tinge when the wife goes to work in an aircraft factory. Hawn behaves so implausibly with a new man around that you wonder the neighbours did not write to the husband (Ed Harris) pronto. Someone seems to have realized that wartime separation and infidelity were painful, so this is not a comedy: but it is not anything else, either. It cost $16 million and took only $4,600,000, but for Goldie it was memorable, for the factory boss who woos and wins her was played by Kurt Russell, who has shared her life ever since. Her first marriage had

$ (72) – that's what they called it, though the press more sensibly printed it as Dollars, *obviously what you called it if you mentioned it – not that many did, for it wasn't exactly popular: the public was tiring of lookalike heist movies. Still, there were pleasing contributions from Goldie Hawn and Warren Beatty.*

What do you say to Goldie Hawn? Well, maybe 'A thousand welcomes', especially if she's in a nice, old-fashioned thriller like Foul Play (78), *with a nice, old-fashioned leading man, Chevy Chase.*

ended in 1976, with a payment to Trikonis of $75,000. She had two children by her second husband, rock star Bill Hudson (1976–81), and she has one by Russell. In 1989 she was fighting Hudson through lawyers, because he wanted to increase his minimal visiting rights to the children. Earlier she had observed that her two husbands could not cope with being Mr Hawn, and that divorce – while leading a career and caring for children – was 'devastating'. Certainly, seen in television interviews at this time she was hardly the Goldie of 'Laugh-In', but an intense, humourless and forceful woman.

Protocol was fashioned for her by Charles Myer, Nancy Meyers and Harvey Miller, who had written *Private Benjamin*; Buck Henry penned the actual screenplay and Herbert Ross directed. The story had Hawn as a cocktail waitress accidentally saving the life of a Middle East potentate, who decides that he wants her in his harem: and because the government has interests in his country, that is where they all want her to be. Until a last-ditch 'we-the-people' message, this is a very funny film, if only making back its $14 million cost with only $200,000 to spare. *Wildcats* (86) found our heroine so crazy about football that she progresses from teaching phys. ed. to coach, but to a team of high school scumbags. Michael Ritchie directed, again getting any laughs that were going. The film cost $15 million and took only $13,600,000, which is still respectable. Several reports speak of both these films as failures, but anyone might be pleased with their tallies. Warners did send this direct to cassette in many territories, but chiefly because American football was not expected to have much allure overseas. At the same time, Warners had produced all of Hawn's films since *Private Benjamin* with the exception of *Seems Like Old Times*, but the association came to an end with this one.

She attempted to widen her range in her next film, to play a rich bitch who changes character after falling *Overboard* (87) from her husband's yacht. He (Edward Herrmann) is glad to be rid of her, she has amnesia, and the carpenter (Russell) whom she had humiliated is determined to seek revenge by making her a drudge in his home. Gary Marshall directed for maximum impact but for only a $12,700,000 return on the $20 million budget. Hawn was off the screen for quite a while again, but, as she has pointed out, her absences were due to motherhood and her desire to make her marriages work. 'I watch fathers and mothers who don't take time with their children, and they have disastrous children' she said. Her return was a gladsome thing, at least as far as Universal were concerned, for *Bird on a Wire* (90) made a

company record by bringing in over $15 million in its first three days; and it went on to take over $70 million, despite luke-warm notices. Well, in the first place Hawn and Mel Gibson made an excellent team, and in the second they had a lot of fun, as a lawyer (her) and a gas-station attendant, her ex-lover, hiding from some crooks who catch up with him just as they meet again. Hawn's reaction to the hundred and one ensuing perils is to squeal or scream, which she does delightfully.

The film's success pleased her, for as she said, Hollywood was making far more comedies than a decade ago, 'And people still prefer to laugh at, or with, men than they do with women. If Carole Lombard or Judy Holliday came along today, no matter that those women were comic geniuses on a par with any man, they would have a rough time . . . Things have got more violent, raunchy and mean. Humour today is more mean-spirited and more bawdy, and there's a limit to how bawdy a woman can be on screen.' Her future, anyway, is secure: in 1989 she signed a contract with Disney calling for nine films, excluding any she already had in development elsewhere. She exec-produced *My Blue Heaven* with Steve Martin, after turning down the role Nora Ephron had written for her, that of a methodical district attorney – which Joan Cusack played (a thought: wouldn't Hawn and Martin have made a great team?). Then she co-produced *Crisscross* (91) and Chris Menges directed, the tale of a mother and son deserted by a Vietnam veteran. This is more serious than usual, but she has no intention of turning serious: '. . . not being able to do a Meryl Streep in *Sophie's Choice* and all those roles, I don't walk around with that chip. It just wasn't in the cards. My life just didn't go that way but I'm so grateful and thankful for the way it *did* go that I can't sit back and think "Don't they know I'm better than that?"'

Barbara Hershey

With two Best Actress awards in consecutive years at the Cannes Film Festival – for *Shy People* and *A World Apart* – Barbara Hershey has to be reckoned one of the screen's leading actresses. 'Twas not ever thus. She has come a long way, with many a bumpy ride, to be where she is today.

She was born in Hollywood in 1948 to a mother who was a Presbyterian from Arkansas and a Jewish father who wrote a racing column when not running his fashion shop. At home she was known as 'Sarah Bernhardt', because of her compulsion as soon as she got home to re-enact scenes from films she had seen. At Hollywood High School, where she studied drama, her teacher sent her to see an agent who knew that Screen Gems were looking for pretty teenagers of both sexes to appear in 'Gidget' (65) starring Sally Field, who said to her after she was taken on, 'If you need any help, I'll be here.' She was a regular in another series, 'The Monroes' (66–7), and subsequently appeared in 'Daniel Boone', 'Run for Your Life' and others. She broke into films, fourth-billed, as Brian Keith's teenage daughter in *With Six You Get Eggroll* (68), a possible obstacle to his marrying widow Doris Day. She was upped to third-billing in a Glenn Ford Western, *Heaven with a Gun* (69) as an ill-used Indian girl, and was top-billed as one of three adolescents (the others: Richard Thomas and Bruce Davison) enjoying a lyrical *Last Summer* before facing adulthood. As directed by Frank Perry and written by his then-wife, Eleanor (from a novel by Evan Hunter), it has an honesty composed of half-truths. The boys first meet her when she is tending a wounded seagull, which she kills after it has bitten her – and that was an action which, in life, she came to regret.

She had a smaller role in *The Liberation of L.B. Jones* (70), but it was directed by William Wyler – his last film, and not his best. Its subject was Civil Rights, its chief protagonist a lawyer (Lee J. Cobb) in a small Southern town, with Hershey as the wife of his nephew (Lee Majors). Robert Wise produced *The Baby Maker*, giving an undeserved first chance to debuting director James Bridges – though he would go on to better things. He also wrote it, an exploitive thing about a proper couple (Sam Groom, Collin Wilcox-Horne) who, unable to have a baby, hire a hippy couple (Hershey, Scott Glen, deep into sex and drugs) to do the necessary – only in doing it, the proper husband falls in love with the hippy girl. Her career lost momentum with Robert Mulligan's *The Pursuit of Happiness* (71), in which Michael Sarrazin is sent to jail for a petty offence, and Paul Williams's *Dealing: or the Berkeley-to-Boston Forty-Brick Lost-Bag Blues*, in which Richard F. Lyons is a Harvard law student happily into drug-dealing; in both she was the hero's lady. Then she was *Boxcar Bertha* (72), a lady who once existed, going around robbing and killing in the Depression era – but only, as this film has it, after some provocation, because of her left-wing views. Roger Corman produced this happy rip-off of *Bonnie and Clyde*, and Martin Scorsese, then at the start of his career, directed it. He claimed that he was looking less romantically at that time than the earlier film, and this one can certainly stand on its own feet – just. David Carradine played

Barbara Hershey in The Baby Maker *(70), in which she produces an heir for a bourgeois couple – breaking up two marriages in the process, her own and theirs, which they hadn't bargained for. This film served them right.*

the man who deflowers Bertha and who later becomes her companion-in-crime. He directed *Americana* as a vehicle for them both, with him playing a Vietnam veteran obsessed with reconstructing a carousel in a small town in Kansas: bold, vivid, melancholic, it tried to say something about the country during these years. Mainly filmed in 1973, it was not ready for showing till 1981, when it acquired only a cult following.

She had a son by Carradine, called Free, and even at this late date their live-in relationship (1969–75) raised some eyebrows. She also, remembering that bird she killed, rechristened herself Barbara Seagull, and it was under that name she went to the Netherlands to make a murky drama directed by Nikolai van der Heyde, *Angela*, which brought her the Best Actress award at the Berlin Festival. (For the US it was renamed *Love Comes Quietly*, but if it came at all, it was silently.) Her new name meant that she had to take a 50 per cent salary cut when she made Arthur Hiller's *The Crazy World of Julius Vrooder* (74), a failed comedy about a hospital of Vietnam veterans. She played the girlfriend of Richard Roundtree, 'the London underworld's leading forger and safecracker', in Menahem Golan's *Diamonds* (75) with Robert Shaw, a heist drama set mainly in Tel Aviv. In Britain, she was an American architectural student to the murderous Donald Pleasance in an abysmal comedy known variously as *A Choice of Weapons* (76), *Trial by Combat* and *Dirty Knight's Work*. It was clearly a time for change: and she became Barbara Hershey again. At some point Free was rechristened Tom, and when queried about this period in her life later, she merely said that she did not wish to discuss it. She also said: 'The transition I made from girl to woman was done in public, and it was a difficult time for me.'

Back in Hollywood, Hershey had an excellent role in an unsuccessful Western, *The Last Hard Men* (76), as Charlton Heston's daughter, but then she turned to television for a couple of years, though the first of these was shown in cinemas overseas, even if bookings were meagre: *Flood* with Robert Culp, an Irwin Allen disaster film, his first for TV; *In the Glitter Palace* (77), a murder mystery in which a lesbian (Hershey) drags in a lawyer (Chad Everett) to deal with a blackmailer; *Just a Little Inconvenience*, produced by and

starring Lee Majors, a tale of wounded war veterans; *Sunshine Christmas*, a sequel to the 1973 *Sunshine*, in which a footloose musician (Cliff DeYoung) returns to his roots with his adopted daughter, to fall in love with his childhood sweetheart (Hershey); and *A Man Called Intrepid* (79), a six-hour mini, co-starring with David Niven and Michael York in this (true) tale of espionage activities in the Second World War. 'From Here to Eternity' was a spin-off from another mini, in which Hershey's role had been played by Natalie Wood (Deborah Kerr in the original film); repeating from the mini was William Devane, who did not get on with Hershey during the series' run, 1979–80. *Angel on My Shoulder* (80) was a TV remake of the 1946 film with Peter Strauss in the Paul Muni role of a judge whose body is inhabited by a former gangster; Hershey had Anne Baxter's old role of his bewildered secretary-fiancée. She returned to cinemas belatedly, for *The Stunt Man*, filmed (in Canada) in 1978, was not shown till two years later: she played a movie queen loved by the director, a massively mannered Peter O'Toole. *Take This Job and Shove It* (81) was a tiresome, hopefully Capraesque comedy in which Robert Hays returns to his hometown to hot up an old-fashioned brewery; as his ex-girlfriend, Hershey might wisely have taken the title seriously.

For an actress who had started so promisingly, she had wasted almost a decade, just another journeyman player whom you might be glad to see, but you would not go out of your way. She herself said that *The Stunt Man* was her only challenging role in a while, and that it marked the turning point. But that distinction goes to the sort of role few major actresses would accept, a woman possessed by *The Entity* (82), constantly being raped by it and generally creating murderous havoc. Sidney J. Furie directed this horror movie, but what gave it some distinction, despite some loose ends, was the screenplay by Frank DeFelitta (from his novel). Plus Hershey's own performance, all the more effective for being understated. What she did next were two small roles, but they were in two classy, much-seen products: Philip Kaufman's *The Right Stuff* (83), based on Tom Wolfe's exhaustive study of the first astronauts, as the free-spirited wife of one of them, Sam Shepard; and Barry Levinson's *The Natural* (84), as the girl who makes an unsuccessful pass at Robert Redford before stripping to her scanties, shooting him and committing suicide. Whether planned or not, these two credits put Hershey's career on a very different footing, and though her next two movies were for TV, they were more interesting than most she had done: *My Wicked Wicked Ways . . . The*

After several years of downmarket credits Hershey's talent began to be used again by major directors – like Philip Kaufman, who cast her as one of the astronauts' wives in The Right Stuff *(83).*

Hannah had several sisters in Woody Allen's Hannah and Her Sisters *(86) and Hershey played one of them. Unfortunately for Hannah (played by Mia Farrow), her husband (Michael Caine) suddenly develops a middle-aged passion for Hershey.*

Legend of Errol Flynn (85), directed by Don Taylor, as Lili Damita, the first wife of Flynn (Duncan Regehr); and *Passion Flower* (86), directed by Joseph Sargent, set in Singapore, as a British-born wife who schemes with her new lover (Bruce Boxleitner) to kill her millionaire father (Nicol Williamson) or/and her philandering husband (John Waters). Doris Keating produced both films for CBS.

There followed two more Upper Case credits: Woody Allen's *Hannah and Her Sisters*, as the one of them Michael Caine gets the hots for, a reformed alcoholic living with an anti-social painter, Max von Sydow; and David Anspaugh's *Hoosiers*, as the repressed fellow-teacher and girlfriend of baseball coach Gene Hackman. Her best screen chance yet came when Levinson cast her in *Tin Men* (87), though it was a role subsidiary to the two men. She has to look ordinary enough to be a Social Security clerk who has nabbed only the unprepossessing Danny DeVito as her husband, and yet attractive enough for his rival, Richard Dreyfuss, an inveterate womanizer, to want to marry her. Her situation is poignant: she has a stable marriage, despite petty differences – and then she hasn't; and then Dreyfuss changes his mind. She has become a pawn – and has the most difficult of the three roles, which she plays touchingly. These were the sorts of parts she should have been playing years before: she enjoys playing complex roles and admitted she yelled with joy when she read the Allen script. Though she was much

admired in that film, it was probably *Tin Men* which finally propelled her to the front rank of screen actresses.

Andrei Konchalovsky wrote and directed *Shy People*, perhaps the best of his variable output. Jill Clayburgh played a liberated New York journalist visiting some distant relatives in backwoods Cajun country, including Hershey as a put-upon, but capable, badly ageing mother of four grown sons – *all* of whom play around with the journalist's daughter (Martha Plimpton), causing maternal anguish and unity. The cinematographer was Chris Menges, who was to turn to directing for the first time in his distinguished career: *A World Apart* (88), written by Shawn Slovo, is an autobiographical account of the time her mother (Hershey), a South African activist, was imprisoned. The film is better focused than some others on Apartheid on the brutality of the police and the absolute courage required of white activists; and if it propounds the beliefs of neither side, that is perhaps correct. Hershey conveys moral rectitude without fussiness, and as seen through the child's eyes, is somewhat reserved.

The Last Temptation of Christ came about because Hershey gave a copy of Kazantzakis's novel to Scorsese when they were making *Boxcar Bertha*: when she read in 1982 that he was to film it, she asked for the role of Mary Magdelene. He auditioned her several times over a three-month period – because, he said, he felt obligated to her and had to be certain that she would be right for the role. Paramount cancelled the project back then, but now that Scorsese was finally able to go ahead, with Willem Dafoe in the lead, he sent for Hershey, who is as good as everyone else in the cast, which is to say, very. In *Beaches* she co-starred with Bette Midler, playing a strait-laced San Francisco attorney who maintains a friendship with this very different lady over a period of years. Playing opposite Midler is Big Time, so it was rather surprising to see Hershey returning to TV, even if Brian Dennehy headed the supporting cast, as her lawyer when charged with an axe-murder, in *Killing in a Small Town* (90). It was not, however, surprising to find that she won an Emmy for her performance. To follow on the big screen: *Tune In Tomorrow*, as Aunt Julia returning to New Orleans which she left as a girl, to become embroiled in a romance with her nephew (Keann Reeves), *Defenseless* with Mary Beth Hurt and Sam Shepard; and *Paris Trout* (91), with Dennis Hopper and Ed Harris.

DUSTIN HOFFMAN

Everyone should be as lucky as Dustin Hoffman with *The Graduate*: his first (not quite, see below) film, and it made him world famous. 'Time' magazine put him on its cover (silver-plated success symbol) and wrote about him as the most representative of the new generation of actors (like, the most successful). 'Time' couldn't be wrong; in the old days that sort of coverage only happened to the Beautiful People. As far as Hoffman is concerned, you wouldn't notice him in a crowd of three.

He was born in Los Angeles in 1937, son of a furniture-designer. He studied for a bit as a doctor, then enrolled at the Pasadena Playhouse, but, like, he didn't like LA and went to New York to begin his career. He did odd jobs (typist, janitor, attendant in a mental ward) waiting to be discovered. He studied; he did sporadic TV shows, in bit parts; occasional stock; worked with the Community Theater in Fargo, North Dakota; and at one point gave it all up to teach acting. He finally was taken on to assist on an off-Broadway production of 'A View from the Bridge' with Jon Voight, and made his New York debut in 'Yes is for a Very Young Man' (60); then, also off-Broadway, made a dent as a hunch-backed German homosexual in 'Harry Noon and Night' (64). He was in 'Sergeant Musgrave's Dance,' but was canned after a week; but his performance in 'Journey of the Fifth Horse' (67), as a middle-aged Russian misanthrope,

brought him an award for the best off-Broadway actor. He was engaged for a lead in 'The Subject was Roses', but was hospitalized and lost it. His performance in the off-Broadway production of a British farce, 'Eh?', directed by Alan Arkin, brought him to the notice of Mike Nichols, looking for someone to play *The Graduate*. It was not his first film. He may be glimpsed in one scene of *The Tiger Makes Out* (67), and for a fee of $5,000 he had played a bumbling G-man in a Spanish-Italian cheapie made in Rome, with Cesar Romero, *Un Dollaro per Sette Vigliacchi*. Because of his success, it was dusted off and screened in the US in 1969 as *Madigan's Millions*.

The Graduate (67) was a tame tale, wryly funny, of a boy seduced by Mrs Robinson (Anne Bancroft), a member of his parents' generation, and what happens when she discovers he's in love with her daughter (Katherine Ross). The second half was both pointless and tasteless, but Hoffman represented every youth trapped for the first time in the adults' world, and the response of the world's youth catapulted him into superstar status. He had got $17,000 for it. He did a play on Broadway, 'Jimmy Shine', and earned $250,000 for his next movie, John Schlesinger's film of James Leo Herlihy's novel *Midnight Cowboy* (69), as the crippled oddball outcast befriended by the title-character, the would-be hustler, Jon Voight. He found the part easy: 'I mean, he was so sad, so grotesque, so loathsome. Ratso . . . there is so much you can do with a part like that.' He found his next part difficult: 'It's your leading man bit, right down the middle . . . And I do have this terrible suspicion that if I play myself . . . I'm going to be bloody boring. I mean, Brando can be Brando and it's – exciting, at least interesting.' He was not bloody boring, but he wasn't exactly exciting either, in this contemporary love-story with Mia Farrow, *John and Mary*. Nor were the grosses – contrary to expectations – very exciting. Hoffman's fee was $425,000.

So far, at no point had he looked like joining the ranks of those great, charismatic movie stars, though the publicity was so overwhelming that you might have thought so. His box-office rating was fine, fourth in 1969, sixth in 1970. A 20th executive commented in 1969: 'He may be an anti-star, but he sure gets superstar privileges.' He played an Indian fighter in Arthur Penn's *Little Big Man* (70), a conscientious and sometimes exciting account of some of the Indian wars, culminating in the Battle of Little Big Horn, based on a novel by Thomas Berger; the action required Hoffman to age over a hundred years, which brought a merry $15 million

A very successful story of seduction: Dustin Hoffman as The Graduate *(68), and Anne Bancroft as Mrs Robinson, a friend of his parents who has taken a fancy to him.*

From the start Hoffman showed a propensity for character roles, and in his second starring film played one which few young actors would have accepted, the sick, crippled society-reject, Ratso Rizzo: with Jon Voight in Midnight Cowboy *(69).*

tinkling into the box-office. Hoffman then played a pop singer with hang-ups, asking his shrink *Who is Harry Kellerman and Why Is He Saying Those Terrible Things About Me?*, but Harry Kellerman does not exist. The film was directed, at Hoffman's request, by an old friend of his New York days, Ulu Gosbard, and it shows a nice 'feel' for that city. Unfortunately, the screenplay by Herb Gardner preferred the whoosy to the satiric, and the result was Hoffman's first movie failure.

In Britain he replaced Cliff Robertson, who changed his mind at the last minute, in *Straw Dogs*, concerning a couple in a lonely house and hostile visitors without. Since this plot had been around since the early Silent days, the director Sam Peckinpah decided that the only way it might be sustained was to make it as gory as possible, not an achievement worthy of this director at his best. It was roundly attacked by the press, which did not spare Hoffman because, during filming, he had defended his decision to participate by liking 'Power, Money'. The film took $4 million and at the end of the year he remained No. 6 at the box-office. He meandered down to Italy to make a movie there with Pietro Germi directing, *Alfredo Alfredo* (73), playing a timorous young man who avoids one bad marriage only to make a worse one. An English-track version played the States, where the takings did not equal Hoffman's fee, said to be $1 million (but thought by trade sources, *pace* 'Variety', to be $50,000 plus expenses and a percentage). His fee for *Papillon* was $1,200,000 and that of Steve McQueen $2 million, and it has to be said that Hoffman earned it for his unclichéd playing of a long-term prisoner, secretive, self-absorbed and a renowned counterfeiter – the one McQueen befriends from self-interest. Franklin J. Schaffner directed from the supposedly autobiographical novel by Henri Charrière, with a then-high budget of $13 million and a return of $22,500,000. *Lenny* (74) announced itself as tribute to a man who was prosecuted for language and a way of life now accepted as normal, and it is part of the film's cleverness that we believe it as it ends – despite the fact that Julian Barry's screenplay is in no way a hagiography. Indeed it makes it clear that Lenny Bruce became famous with little talent while at the same time Bob Fosse's virtuoso direction otherwise bludgeons away on his recurrent theme, the destructive powers of show business. In the title-role Hoffman is pretty good, but as wife and mother respectively, Valerie Perrine and Jan Miner are pretty terrific. The film did $11,600,000 at the box-office.

Hoffman played his third consecutive real-life character, Carl Bernstein, in *All the President's Men* (76) with Robert Redford, who also produced, as the other of the two investigative journalists who helped to harry Nixon on the road from Watergate: spellbinding entertainment, and a deserved popular success at a take of $30 million. William Goldman, who wrote the screenplay, also authored *Marathon Man*, a much less elevating one as Hoffman, as a rather over-age student, is chased over unlikely New York locations – never thinking to call a cop – by a bunch of Nazis whom he till then treated with all the uncertainty with which he had once confronted Mrs Robinson. One of the Nazis was played by Laurence Olivier, whose frailty was of concern to all on the set, except apparently Hoffman, who insisted on putting him through a series of improvisations despite Olivier's expressed unwillingness to do so. Goldman, in his memoir, speculates on why the director, John Schlesinger, did not intervene, and implies that he knew Olivier was docile while being aware that it was necessary to keep his top-billed star happy. Others (not Goldman) have quoted Olivier's comment on Hoffman: 'Why doesn't the boy just act? Why must he go through all this storm and stress?' It was presumably worth it in box-office terms, for the film brought in $16,500,000, and Hoffman returned to the exhibitors' Top Ten list for the first time since 1972, at No. 5, but he was not in the first twelve listed in 'Box Office' magazine.

He signed a contract for two films with First Artists, though on slightly different terms from the other partners (McQueen, Streisand, Newman and Poitier); and he forfeited salary advances for the right to approve the final cut, and other 'artistic' advantages. Grosbard directed the first of these, *Straight Time* (78), though Hoffman originally had undertaken the task, but asked Grosbard to take over. In this one Hoffman played an ex-con – and, gee, nothing goes right for him. The piece sets itself up as an essay on the perils of parole, but ends up as the same old movie glamorizing criminals, if not crime. Hoffman expressed himself upset when it did not perform well at the box-office, taking only $4,200,000. Meanwhile, David Puttnam was producing *Agatha* (79), which concerned the disappearance in 1926 of the crime-writer Mrs Christie, a role to be played by Vanessa Redgrave. Hoffman telephoned Puttnam out of the blue to say that it was a terrific script and since he had to be out of the US 'for a week or so' (for marital reasons) would there be a role for him? Puttnam was in a dilemma because Rank, who had promised backing, had withdrawn on discovering that Colonel Christie, though long defunct, had been one of its directors and he was, by implication, the villain of the piece.

Hoffman would bring in not only First Artists but its distributor, Warner Bros, who were only too happy to have another film with Hoffman. But Hoffman also brought with him his own writer, Murray Schisgal, who proceeded to beef up Hoffman's part from the agreed cameo. It so happened that Hoffman's contract did not permit him to play anything but a leading role; so Puttnam left the project after referring to Hoffman as 'this worrisome American pest' – and Michael Apted, who directed, later described himself as 'stranded' with Hoffman, 'who is very difficult to deal with.' Redgrave found herself not only having to learn new dialogue but a co-star who refused to talk to her; Puttnam's biographer, Andrew Yule, quotes a journalist who visited the set, as finding it 'the most frenzied and bitter he had ever encountered'. The result was merely dull, with Hoffman popping up from time to time as the correspondent of an American newspaper and looking foxy, which he could do well enough.

He refused to post-dub on *Agatha*, at which point First Artists claimed that he had concluded his commitments to them in the least possible time, because he was anxious to move to more 'lucrative' work. He thereupon sued for $2 million in lost salary and $66 million for breach of contract. The company countersued, alleging that he had publicly disparaged the quality of the first film and had refused the final work on the other. He sought to control the final cut of *Agatha*, thus withholding its release, and they sought to prevent him from proceeding on his next project: neither was allowed, and nothing more was publicly heard of these matters. *Agatha* was released to dismal business, while the next movie, *Kramer vs Kramer*, became a personal triumph, bringing him Best Actor citations from the critics in New York and Los Angeles, as well as an Oscar; he also won a Golden Globe award, and when accepting it paid tribute to Jack Lemmon's 'great performance' in *The China Syndrome*. Furthermore, the film took $59,900,000, a large amount for a serious film. Its subject was divorce, as written and directed for the screen by Robert Benton from a novel by Avery Corman. Benton also was Oscared for Best Director and Best Film, and the result was superb, as Hoffman comes to terms with being a one-parent father and then defence witness when his ex-wife (Meryl Streep) sues for custody. His was beautiful acting, justifying his comments in a current interview: 'I'm not easy to work with. I demand certain things in my contracts. But if you don't insist on certain controls up front, you're in real trouble as an artist. If I'm going to spend two and a half years of my life on a project . . . then I've got

to be more than a puppet actor. I need, I really need, to be part of the creative process from start to finish.' He went on to say that he did not normally give interviews, 'but it's one way I can repay the director and producer, two quite decent people. They went overboard living up to the promises they made to me when I agreed to do the film. Not that we didn't have our differences . . . Benton helped us by shooting things in sequence, which is always the best way for an actor. There's not a whole lot of film-makers who really care what's best for the actors. Most of them are interested in what's the easiest shot to get, or the most convenient for the technicians or certainly what's least expensive.'

Hoffman's methods certainly paid off when *Tootsie* (82) became his second consecutive smash hit, taking $96,200,000 on a budget of $25 million. His percentage of the profits was reckoned to have brought him in $21 million. However, it was a comedy, and a pleasing one, about an actor who is not only unemployed but unemployable because he argues with everyone he works with: so he gets into drag and achieves stardom in skirts as a nurse in a wildly popular soap opera. The subject is handled with a discretion which recalls 'Charley's Aunt' and *Some Like It Hot* – and to critics' complaints that *Tootsie* is much less funny than the last named, you can say that Hoffman is not as expert a farceur as Lemmon. Since Hoffman's research is meticulous, it may be best not to enquire what he did to be Tootsie, but in that matter we may discuss one of the funniest scenes in the film, when Hoffman is angrily told by his agent that he

Hollywood claimed a maturity for itself in the seventies which was hardly justified by its output: between Five Easy Pieces *and* The China Syndrome, *at opposite ends of the decade, there was only a handful of serious films – but* All the President's Men *(76) was certainly one of them, and a very exciting movie, too, as two journalists set about discovering the truth behind the Watergate break-in. Hoffman and Robert Redford were the stars.*

cannot find him work, for the agent was played by Sydney Pollack, who also directed (after others had been involved, including Hal Ashby, Dick Richards – who produced – and Barry Levinson). He said later that he would work with Hoffman again only 'after a long rest', while Larry Gelbart who, with Schisgal, is credited with the screenplay, made it clear that that would be too soon. Bill Murray, who played Hoffman's room-mate, said: 'It was a *hell-ride*! I came to the set the first day and there was Pollack and Dustin arguing over everything and the whole crew was like in the other room. People get pretty tired making a movie, but Dustin's always got the juice. Well, he's not Dustin Hoffman because he's Joe Schmoe. He does every single take differently. I don't know how the hell they cut the movie! He virtually made seven films. He's always looking for material to push him to the limit. He's famous in New York for having twenty-five script-writers. You go to a dinner party, everybody's writing for Dustin.'

Hoffman might then have been in *Gorky Park*, but the producers balked at his fee of $5 million. So, pushing himself to the limit, he returned to Broadway as Willy Loman in Arthur Miller's 'Death of a Salesman' (84), to enthusiastic notices and business to match. Miller himself said that Hoffman was the best Willy that he had seen, because he was nearer the height which he had imagined – and because, although it is never mentioned, he is Jewish. And when it was filmed for CBS, *Death of a Salesman* (85) won Hoffman an Emmy and a Golden Globe award. Germany's prestigious Volker Schlöndorff was brought in at his request to ensure that this was a cinematic occasion, and he uneasily adopted sets which were by turns stylized and solid. The piece had lost none of its power, but its one weakness was its Willy, bringing too much of the stage with his relentless acting. He's no ham, neither does he demand the attention of, say, Burt Lancaster being quiet when he was in quality material, but his response is less intuitive than it should be in comparison with some superior talents around him (Charles Durning, Kate Reid, John Malkovich); it's a performance done with too much loving care.

He returned to the large screen with *Ishtar* (87) for a fee of $6 million, the same as his co-star and the film's producer, Warren Beatty. These fees, plus onerous location work and the demands of their director, Elaine May, pushed the budget to a frightening $55 million. When the film took only $7,700,000, Beatty blamed Puttnam, at that time head of Columbia, which produced it, because Puttnam had shown no interest in the film, which had started before he arrived. Clearly there was no love lost between Puttnam and Hoffman, but Puttnam's indifference should have been more welcome than the virulence of the critics. The film at least starts well, with Beatty and Hoffman as a second-rate cabaret act, singing their own songs; Hoffman is a successful Lothario and Beatty is trying to pick up tips because women aren't interested in him . . . But once they get caught up in intrigue when they play a date in a fictional Arab city, no amount of star power can disguise the fact that their badinage is far from the Hope–Crosby team they are emulating. Around this time Hoffman should also have been in *La Brava* (from a novel by Elmore Leonard) for Cannon, but he cancelled his contract when the preliminary trade ads featured his likeness, which he did not permit. He commented that if Cannon could get this wrong at the start, he did not expect to enjoy the experience to come. The film was not made, but *Angel Heart*, for which he was also announced, went ahead with Mickey Rourke. Other projects which Hoffman considered during this period were *The Yellow Jersey* (to be directed by Michael Cimino), *Ditto List* (from a screenplay by Nora Ephron), *Random Hearts* (based on the Air Florida disaster in Washington, DC, in 1982), *1968* (to be directed by Taylor Hackford), *Diamonds*, *My New Partner* (a remake of *Les Ripoux*, in the Philippe Noiret role), and a biopic of Harry S. Truman, none of which was made. Nor was *Stonybrook*, whose writer, Alan Shapiro, told 'Premiere' magazine that when Hoffman came aboard, 'it puts inordinate heat on a project. He's impulsive, doesn't think ahead. He could have been more aware of the impact he had. It was a nightmare.' The same article was eloquent on the others who had spent man-hours discussing these projects with Hoffman – though less time was apparently wasted on Barry Levinson's *Tin Men*, which Hoffman turned down, and *Dead Poets' Society*, which went ahead with Robin Williams because Disney was not too concerned with meeting Hoffman's demands.

In the meantime, Hoffman's agent, CAA, was concerned with him being thought of as an actor of the 60s, because of *The Graduate*, and it was also seeking – at the same time – a prestige success for a young client, Tom Cruise. Hoffman accordingly committed himself to a script he did like, *Rain Man* (88), and turned down *Midnight Run* while this venture was considered by Martin Brest, Steven Spielberg and Sydney Pollack – or, alternatively, Hoffman was considering them. Six writers came and went, and even more producers, till Levinson took on the job of directing, with a screenplay credited to Ronald Bass and Barry Morrow. Hoffman played an 'autistic savant', that is, someone highly developed mentally but deficient in other areas, including building normal relationships – which in the narrative most concerned his estranged brother, Cruise, who has leeched on to him for his fortune. The film cost $30 million and took a tremendous $86 million, in part helped by Cruise's box-office draw and Hoffman's (second) Best Actor Oscar. Hoffman's triumph might be considered in the light of the many Academy members unlikely to vote for him, plus the fact that anyone familiar with autistic patients could not have found the performance convincing.

Then, looking for new worlds to conquer, our hero decided to tackle Shakespeare in the Bard's birthplace, England. He contacted the former director of the Royal Shakespeare Company, Peter Hall, suggesting 'Hamlet'. It was not that he was too old (though he was), said Hall diplomatically, but that it was a very taxing role for someone untrained in verse-speaking. They discussed Malvolio and Angelo (in 'Measure for Measure'), but settled on Shylock in 'The Merchant of Venice' (89), which received respectful reviews – which, in truth, were more than it deserved. It transferred to New York, where the notices were warmer, but still of the opinion that the best thing about the production was the Portia of Geraldine James. Hoffman made a touching tribute when he took second billing to Sean Connery on *Family Business* – a major talent, certainly, but one with pulling power less than Hoffman, though the conjunction of a third name, Matthew Broderick, managed to bring in only $6 million on an $18 million outlay. They play three generations of one family, uneasily reuniting for one last caper – and very exciting it is when it comes. Perhaps it was a mite old fashioned as directed by Sidney Lumet and written, from his own book, by Vincent Patrick, but it was also very likeable. Hoffman was originally dissatisfied with some sequences and held up release until they were fixed. He put in a cameo appearance in *Dick Tracy* (90), as did several other names.

His next movie will be *Billy Bathgate* (91), directed by Robert Benson from a screenplay by Tom Stoppard based on the novel by E.L. Doctorow. That may be followed by *The Mario Brothers* with Danny DeVito as co-star, or *Hook*, a modernized version of 'Peter Pan' in which he will play Captain Hook and Robin Williams will be Peter's grandson. As of this writing, it seems that he will also appear as Hook in a version of Barrie's play to be filmed back-to-back. Steven Spielberg will direct. Hoffman was married to former ballerina Anne Byrne in 1969, and after their divorce in 1981 he married actress Lisa Gottesgen.

PAUL HOGAN

When Australia conquered the world, it was with a movie. And not even a very good movie. The perceptions the rest of us have about that far-off country are stereotyped: kangaroos, 'Waltzing Matilda', becorked-hats, Ocker types drinking lager and saying 'G'day'. The cities are as cosmopolitan and sophisticated as you'll find on the globe, but there's a certain truth to the rest of it. Cutting-through-the-crap it might be called. The Aussie is laid-back, square, loth to trust the priggish, supercilious Pom. What the Aussie is is what Paul Hogan got so exactly in his first major movie, but that may not be why he conquered the world.

The essence of Hogan – *le film, c'est lui* – is distilled in this comment on why he dislikes being interviewed: 'I was watching Madonna interviewed on TV recently and she got treated like she was the Queen or the Virgin Mary or something. It was such a load of crap that it wanted to make me throw up. Nothing is worse than seeing some little pop star who knows nothing about anything asked for her views on everything under the sun. She isn't going to bring about world peace. What has she got to say that really matters?'

He was born in Lightning Ridge, New South Wales, in 1940, the son of a soldier. He left school at fifteen and, in his own words, had dozens of jobs, because whenever he was bored he moved on to another: 'It's been fairly well recorded that I used to work on the Sydney Harbour Bridge as a rigger . . .' He married at eighteen and by the time he was twenty-two had had the first two of his children. At the age of thirty-two he entered a local TV talent contest, claiming to be a tap-dancing knife-thrower from the Outback. The show's producers thought he would be unconsciously funny at his own expense, but instead he was consciously funny at theirs. John Cornell, the Melbourne producer of 'A Current Affair', heard about him and sent a reporter to interview him on the bridge. Hogan ridiculed him, which so amused viewers that Cornell invited him to appear regularly on the show. Cornell also became his manager, encouraging him to his chief ambition, to break the stranglehold of British and American comedy on Australian television. It was at this time, 1972, that the Labour Party prime minister, Gough Whitlam, was preaching that the country had been outward-looking for too long. Thus Australian cinema flourished and 'The Paul Hogan Show' taught Australians to laugh at themselves. Seventy-five specials were produced in twelve years, eventually being syndicated to twenty-six countries. Cornell also kept tight control over

Paul Hogan in the role which made him world-famous, Mick 'Crocodile' Dundee. The smaller picture was issued in connection with the sequel, in which the love-interest was again Linda Kozlowski. Movie stars didn't have names like that in the old days.

the offers to do commercials; it was a deliberate policy to make Hogan known abroad by this method. In the US he represented, as it were, the Australian Tourist Commission – and he was happy to do these commercials for nothing, because American audiences became familiar with him. In Britain Hogan became known when he advertised Foster's lager. He made his movie debut in a minor role in *Fatty Finn* (80), financed by the Australian Children's Film Foundation, about street gangs in suburban Sydney. But he wanted movie stardom, and to that end made his dramatic debut in a TV series, 'Anzac: the War Down Under' (85).

Cornell always knew that Hogan should be on the big screen, but the scripts they received were never quite right. He considered that the idea should come from Hogan himself, perhaps built round the sort of Australian who would rid the country of its inferiority complex and at the same time be an unoffical ambassador. To a certain extent *'Crocodile' Dundee* (86) is Hogan's own TV persona, in itself not a million miles from Will Rogers, the country rube whose folk wisdom is deep-down common sense; long, lean and laconic. But mythology entered into it, as Hogan explained: 'The character is an attempt to give Australia a hero. It's a country desperately short of heroes. We haven't got a Daniel Boone or a Robin Hood. All we ever had was Ned Kelly, an Irishman with a bucket over his head who pulled a few unsuccessful robberies a long time ago.' To that end he went up to the Northern Territory to meet 'the guys living off the land who think that Darwin is pretty racy. Darwin, by the way, has a population of about 40,000! And the thought occurred to me that if they went to New York they'd have thought it was Mars. And then I wrote the story in three days.' He penned the screenplay with Cornell and Ken Shadie; the equally inexperienced (in cinema) Peter Faiman was set to direct. They were in agreement in wanting a 'feel good' movie, and it was chopped and changed after being tested with American audiences. Hogan's own taste ran to John Wayne, 'but I like Dundee, that's an important thing. I'd shove Sylvester Stallone aside to go up to the bar and buy him a drink.'

The film cost the equivalent of US$6 million, and was 65 per cent owned by Hogan and Cornell, with the actor due two-thirds of any profits and the producer the remaining third. Cornell waited till the film had broken the record (set by *ET*) for Australian box-office receipts before seeking an American deal. He started with 20th Century-Fox, since it was owned by Rupert Murdoch, whom he knew slightly; the studio did not return his call, and Warners turned the film down. Paramount took it and added the quotation marks to the title so that it would not be taken to be an animal movie. The company did not care to take international rights, which went to 20th Century-Fox.

Well, then. An American journalist (Linda Kozlowski) goes to the Outback to interview the legendary Mick J. 'Crocodile' Dundee, who is said to have wrestled with a croc and won. They have various adventures and then they go together to New York, where they have some more. He's an honest man amid the coke-heads, snobs, pimps and hookers. He uses his Outback skills on a couple of muggers (twice). He feels at home saying 'Howdy' to folks in the street, who think him odd. Why is it their cynicism is no match for his naivety? The result, in truth, is a piece put together by people of limited talent with the sorts of jokes which would just pass muster on a TV sitcom: yet it is very enjoyable – partly, it is true, due to its leading actor. In the US and Canada it was beaten at the box-office only by *Top Gun* and *The Karate Kid Part II*, when the year's figures were in, and when it peaked out at $70,227,000 it had overtaken the second of these; in Australia it blasted all existing box-office records to end at A$19,772,000.

A sequel was unquestionably called for, *'Crocodile' Dundee II* (88), with Cornell assuming the direction, after some friction on the first shoot. He and Hogan owned this one 100 per cent between them though it is likely Paramount invested in the US$15 million budget – for this company owned world rights, granted partly because of its brilliant opening campaign for the first film. In the US it took $49 million, and in Australia A$12,316,000, still the second most successful movie at the local wickets. That's still a sharp falling off, however, and the fact is that this is a quite dreadful movie, getting the Croc involved in a tired plot of drugs, which takes him from New York to the Outback instead of vice versa. Hogan and Kozlowski, so glowing in the first film, brought little feeling to their roles. It flopped on video, which is very revealing. Hogan had said from the start that there would be no third adventure for the Croc; his next film for Paramount is called *Almost an Angel* (90).

ANTHONY HOPKINS

These days, few British stage-trained actors can claim to be names on both sides of the Atlantic – or, if they are, it is more likely to be for their appearances on television. To Hollywood, anyway, there is no other British actor of Anthony Hopkins's generation who is also a dependable movie name.

He was born in Port Talbot in 1937, the son of a master confectioner and baker. When he won a scholarship to study at the Cardiff School of Music and Drama, it was the piano which engaged his endeavours. At the same time, 'I didn't know what I was thinking, but I wanted to become an actor . . . be notoriously famous and rich. Like (Richard) Burton, I suppose. There was no theatre in Port Talbot, but Burton had been an actor for some time, you see. All I had was a gift for mimicry.' So he imitated Burton; but after his two years' National Service, with the Royal Artillery, he went to the Library Theatre in Manchester as ASM, with the promise of a small role in 'The Quare Fellow'. When his services were dispensed with he studied at RADA for two years, afterwards working in rep in Leicester and Liverpool; during this period he was invited by Lindsay Anderson to make his London debut in a small role – Metellus Cimber – in his production of 'Julius Caesar' (64) at the Royal Court; Anderson also engaged him to sing a song in a pub in his short, *The White Bus*. At Hornchurch he played Dick Dudgeon in 'The Devil's Disciple' and Leontes in 'A Winter's Tale'. He auditioned for Olivier at the National, and played small roles for his first few months; he made headway in the company when he had to go on for Olivier in 'The Dance of Death', and he became known to London theatregoers when he played Andrei in 'Three Sisters' (67). As a result of that, Peter O'Toole invited him to test for the role of Richard in *The Lion in Winter* (68): he played him as sturdy and blunt, revealing a treacherous nature and effeminate only when under stress. He received £3,000 for three months' work, as opposed to £16 a week at the National; Olivier agreed to let him have time off, but his commitment to the National still overlapped with shooting – the start of the pressures which would eventually send him from the National. He also married – the actress Petronella Barker – but the marriage was soon in trouble and he was drinking heavily. It was feared that his career might follow the same pattern as Richard Burton's.

He tested, unsuccessfully, for a supporting role in *The Bridge at Remagen*, but had an effective one in *The Looking-Glass War* (69), from John Le Carré's novel, as a member of the British secret service. Tony Richardson invited him to play Claudius in his stagey, low-budget *Hamlet*, with a very mannered Nicol Williamson in the title-role, while Hopkins stayed with the classics for the BBC, Andrei again, and more Chekhov: Astrov in 'Uncle Vanya'. He also played Danton in a play of that name for television. *When Eight Bells Toll* (71) marked his first leading role in a movie, top-billed for £8,000: he was a secret serviceman again, naval rather than bureaucratic, searching for underwater bullion in a weak script by Alistair MacLean. The American producer, Elliott Kastner, clearly saw Hopkins as an international star, but this was not the film to achieve it. Rather to his surprise Hopkins was asked to return to the National, in leading roles: 'A Woman Killed by Kindness' and 'Danton's Death', but was forced to exchange his role in the next one with Christopher Plummer, who did not want to be a Brechtian Coriolanus. He became nationally famous when he played Pierre in the BBC's lavish twenty-hour mini, *War and Peace* (72). 'I worked very hard on it,' he said, 'and I learned a great deal. I'm here to find out what the job is about in the first place. I'm scared to death of cocking things up . . . There's a great deal of me in the part. We both make the same mistakes. We both have a two-sided nature, part gentle, part very violent.'

He added to his laurels by playing Petruccio at the Chichester festival and Macbeth at the National. He did a cameo as fellow-Welshman Lloyd George in Richard Attenborough's *Young Winston* and played opposite Claire Bloom in *A Doll's House* (73), a soft and indulgent Torvald. At the same time as he was rehearsing this, he was preparing to play Lloyd George again for the BBC and still acting Macbeth; after a row with the director of the last, Michael Blakemore, he walked out of the National. He was also rehearsing 'The Misanthrope' with director John Dexter, who 'was hammering me into the ground'; he would later work again with Dexter, because he was 'brilliant', but most of his interviews over a twenty-year period – he is calmer now – are diatribes against the power of the director, whether on screen or stage: 'What really scares me and worries me, makes me get very neurotic and voice these rather vicious opinions, is that I'm frightened all the time – I don't have that supreme confidence. I go to rehearsals in a nervous state, but I try to turn nervous instability into nervous energy. But when somebody comes along and uses that nervousness for their own sadistic gratification because they like to see someone squirm, then what is the point of working? I didn't come into this marvellous business of acting to be tortured.' Denis Quilley, a failed musical comedy star (only because British musicals are so dreadful), eventually took over Macbeth, one of a series of roles at the National which revealed his brilliant talent; he also inherited the role of Lopakhin in 'The Cherry Orchard' that had been earmarked for Hopkins. He said, 'Anthony is a fine actor but the timing of his departure caught us right on the hop and gave us the most horrendous problems. But I'm bloody grateful to be given the chance.' In 1973 Hopkins married for the second time – Jenni Lynton, who had been a secretary to the associate producer on *When Eight Bells Toll*.

He had a commitment to star opposite Ben Gazzara in the first-ever US mini-series *QB VIII* (74) as the Polish-born British doctor who sued him for libel – Gazzara, in fact, as a fictionalized Leon Uris, who had written an autobiographical novel when sued over 'Exodus'. There was a Hollywood offer, to play a cheery black-marketeer in *The Girl From Petrovka*, and another from Britain's

Anthony Hopkins in the two films he made in 1980. At the height of his Hollywood career, The Elephant Man, left, and A Change of Seasons, right – which is to say, he was then living in the US and pursuing movie stardom. He later decided to return to his roots, to do prestigious work in Britain, at the National Theatre and for BBC television. But, happily, Hollywood still needs him when it has a role for a major talent.

branch of United Artists to play a Scotland Yard man assigned to discover how and why an ocean liner has had dynamite secreted aboard: Richard Lester's disappointing *Juggernaut*. And the British branch of 'Reader's Digest' sponsored *All Creatures Great and Small*, after James Herriot's autobiographical novel had been a successful series for the BBC. Simon Ward played the Herriot role and Hopkins was his crabby but kindly older partner (roles played in the later sequel, *It Shouldn't Happen to a Vet*, by John Alderton and Colin Blakely). Towards the end of the year he starred on Broadway in Peter Shaffer's 'Equus', the National's great hit, directed by Dexter, playing the psychiatrist trying to understand an adolescent with a sexual fixation on horses. Richard Burton took over the role later in the run, on the tacit understanding that he would star in the film version, which he did, in a shaming performance way below the coruscating one which Hopkins had given. But Burton was the bigger film name. The plus for Hopkins was that he had decided that he did not want his career to echo Burton's, and for one thing he gave up drinking.

After Hopkins's stint in the play in New York, there were offers for three telemovies: *Dark Victory* (76), with him and Elizabeth Montgomery in the roles played in 1939 by George Brent and Bette Davis; *The Lindberg Kidnapping Case*, as Hauptmann, the illiterate German immigrant who was convicted of the crime; and the all-star *Victory at Entebbe*, as the Israeli prime minister. The first of these brought Hopkins his biggest fee yet, $80,000, and the second an Emmy for Best Actor. He was in another all-star effort, Attenborough's *A Bridge Too Far* (77), as a rather twittish lieutenant-colonel who learns to calm down in battle.

By this time he had not only quit drinking but had settled in Los Angeles, where he had a fine chance in Robert Wise's *Audrey Rose*, in fact premiered before the Attenborough film. In the movie Hopkins believes that a small child is the reincarnation of his own child and asks the parents (Marsha Mason, John Beck) for visiting rights. This proves a strong start to the piece, but once the child starts hallucinating it is like all the other films about diabolism: the dialogue, like the screams, is interchangeable. Bryan Forbes offered Hopkins a choice of roles in *International Velvet* (78), a crusty trainer or the riding master, which in the event went to Christopher Plummer. 'I needed the cash,' Hopkins explained later. He was then in Attenborough's American film, *Magic*, as a ventriloquist in what was an extended version of the Michael Redgrave episode of *Dead of Night*. Said Philip French in the 'Observer': 'Anthony Hopkins, a fine actor in danger of becoming an irritatingly mannered one, is crazy too soon and too obviously. In a recent Twitch report on British screen acting, he came out just behind Dirk Bogarde for quantity and marginally ahead for quality.' When 'Equus' was produced in Los Angeles he agreed to stage it as well as star, and he was Sartre's Kean for the BBC as well as Prospero on returning to LA in 1979. *Mayflower: The Pilgrims' Adventure* (79) found him as the captain in this telefilm, with Richard Crenna in opposition throughout the voyage.

But it was in back in Britain that Hopkins found the first cinema role to his measure, as the kindly and dedicated Dr Treves who both studies and protects *The Elephant Man* (80), till then a circus freak (John Hurt). Mel Brooks produced and David Lynch directed a piece which was more than a *succès d'estime*, and Hopkins's always halting movie career seemed to be finally moving when he turned up in *A Change of Seasons*, a comedy of infidelity with Shirley MacLaine as his wife, who takes a lover (Michael Brandon) after he has told her he has a paramour (Bo Derek). This is probably only remembered now by the participants, for the set became a battle-ground after MacLaine took to criticizing Hopkins's playing to the director Richard Lang (son of Fritz Lang). The film's failure, while it did not surprise Hopkins, persuaded him that he would never be one of Holly-wood's glories, and he turned his considerable talent elsewhere – to television in the US, for which he was Adolf Hitler in *The Bunker* (81), directed by George Schaefer, who had done *Mayflower*, and *Peter and Paul*, a four-hour mini, in which he played St Paul (Robert Foxworth was Peter). The first of these brought him another Emmy. For the BBC he was Othello in their Shakespeare series, directed by Jonathan Miller, and Allmers in 'Little Eyolf'.

Changing agents, he turned down *The Island*, which Michael Caine did, *Priest of Love*, as D.H. Lawrence, which was played by Ian McKellan, and he knew he would never be physically right as Gandhi, which Attenborough had often discussed with him. He prepared to play Captain Bligh in David Lean's remake of *Mutiny on the Bounty*, but the project was postponed and then cancelled. He did play another of Laughton's roles, Quasimodo, in *The Hunchback of Notre Dame* (82) for Columbia Pictures Television and Norman Rosemont, who specialized in TV versions of the classics, and turned down *Under the Volcano* (Albert Finney played the role) when the possibility of playing Bligh recurred. Either shoot, he commented, 'involved heat, humidity and mosquitoes'. Mel Gibson was to be Fletcher Christian and the director was Roger Donaldson, with whom Hopkins did not hit it off. The problems were exacerbated by the difficulties of shooting on location, but understandably enough Hopkins did not care for the director's habit of merely shouting instructions and then studying the video playback. Hopkins was also concentrating on his role, since Laughton had been legendary in it and Trevor Howard outstanding in the first remake. *The Bounty* (84) is the best of the three versions, not least because it is the only one to treat Bligh sympathetically; but then Hopkins is the best of the three Blighs, partly because the film suggests an unreciprocated homosexual dependency on Christian. Quentin Falk said in the 'Daily Mail': 'He establishes a much more rounded Bligh than any of his predecessors. No swaggering sadist, but by turns an ambitious, stubborn, petulant, puritanical and brilliant seaman desperate to get a job done. [He] dominates the film and his increasingly shrill frustration . . . is chillingly done.'

When the showings of these films did not bring in the hoped-for Hollywood offers, Hopkins embarked on increased activity, in most of which he reminded us why he was regarded as one of the leaders of his profession. He did a seven-week limited run of Pinter's 'Old Times' in New York, causing John Simon in 'New York' magazine to remind us: 'In a theater full of phonies, there is, I believe, none phonier than Harold Pinter, whose terminally specious "Old Times" is being revived at the Roundabout, insofar as a corpse can be revived . . .' In Europe Hopkins did two movies, both destined for American TV: *Arch of Triumph* (85), with Lesley-Anne Down (earlier Esmerelda to his Quasimodo), from the Erich Maria Remarque novel about refugees in pre-war Paris, in the roles played in the 1948 film by Ingrid Bergman and Charles Boyer; and *Mussolini: the Rise and Fall of Il Duce*, with Bob Hoskins (earlier Iago to his Othello) in the title-role, as his son-in-law Count Ciano. George C. Scott, starring in a rival project on the dictator, said, 'I think Hopkins is the best English-speaking actor today. The mantle of Olivier will rest on him if he doesn't get too commercial.' (Scott was one of Hopkins's 'American gods', along with Brando, Kim Stanley and Geraldine Page.) Which is precisely what he did do, though – when offered a six-hour mini based on Jackie Collins's junky bestseller, *Hollywood Wives*, he said simply, 'Why not?' And, as he told Collins, 'It's so nice to put on such lovely clothes and to walk around seeing all these pretty ladies.' He played a British-born movie director. He also appeared in a Levinson-Link telefilm, *Guilty Conscience*, as a philandering lawyer. (These four TV credits are listed in order of shooting, not transmission).

At this point he reached a decision: 'I thought maybe I should do it, if only to prove to myself I had the nerve.' This was to give up his home in Beverly Hills to return to the National Theatre, specifically to star in 'Pravda', a play by David Hare and Howard Brenton about a Murdoch-type newspaper proprietor. First he appeared at the Old Vic in a play by Schnitzler, 'The Lonely Road', and then, while at the National, he played Lear (86) and 'Antony and Cleopatra' (87) with Judi Dench. He reported that the National's director, Peter Hall, had charmed him into doing both in repertory, but he was miserable throughout the time — 'I would think back to when I walked out in 1973 and remember how exhilarated I was.' Ian McKel-

Ian later told him that there was nothing wrong in tackling two Shakespeares at the same time, but *no one* could do two of 'the big ones' simultaneously – which was reflected in his performances, which varied, despite overall warm reviews. But after all, he was back where his talent belonged. He played Guy Burgess in the BBC's *Blunt* (86) during this period, and was in two British-made movies, *The Good Father*, directed by Mike Newell, as a middle-aged man deprived of access to his son, and *84 Charing Cross Road* (87), as the bookseller who in the postwar period became pen-pal with a feisty New York literary type, played by Anne Bancroft (who had earlier been in both *Young Winston* and *The Elephant Man*, but on this third occasion their paths would yet again cross only fleetingly).

He played a mysterious and cynical Irish Republican, wearied after four years in the Flanders trenches, in *The Dawning* (88), which attracted little attention despite the additional presence of Jean Simmons and Trevor Howard. There was also a classy item for the BBC, *Across the Lake*, as the racing-driver Donald Campbell. *The Tenth Man* was based on a Graham Greene screen treatment (written while under contract to MGM in 1944) which had been forgotten until discovered in the company's vaults and published in 1985. Now filmed for television, Hopkins was a French lawyer who, condemned to death by the Germans, bargains with a deprived prisoner so that he will die in his place in order that his mother and sister can benefit from his, Hopkins's, wealth. He turned down the role of Peachum (because of his doubts about his singing ability) in the Cannon version of *The Threepenny Opera* – wisely, as it turned out; and he could not have been sorry when at the last minute German financiers pulled out of *The Beethoven Secret*, perhaps influenced by the artistic and commercial record of the putative director, Ken Russell. Hopkins's co-stars would have been Jodie Foster, Glenda Jackson and Charlotte Rampling – and the fact that there were so many women in Beethoven's life was certainly a well-kept secret. After playing a Welsh farmer bewildered by EEC regulations in the BBC's *Heartland* (89), he was the convict Magwitch (a role vacated by Stacy Keach after being convicted of drugs charges in Britain) in a mini for American television, a new version of *Great Expectations*. In a busy year he made his West End debut in 'M.Butterfly', as the French diplomat who had not known that his Chinese mistress was a transvestite till 'she' was arrested for espionage. Finally he was the manic Welsh director of an amateur drama group in *A Chorus of Disapproval*, directed by Michael Winner from a play by Alan Ayckbourn, two talents which deserved each other – or so the public thought, because it showed its own disapproval by staying away in droves, despite a cast including such other clever people as Prunella Scales, Jeremy Irons and Richard Briers.

He had left his West End play to take the Fredric March role in Michael Cimino's remake of *The Desperate Hours* (90), and to let him do that, the producers of *The Silence of Lambs* postponed its starting date. Also on the actor's agenda is a British film made in Mexico, *One Man's War* (91), and a third Merchant-Ivory bash at an E.M. Foster novel, *Howard's End*.

BOB HOSKINS

He's a character man. Nature made him thus. When you see a photograph you can (if you know him) hear his loud north London voice, not a pretty thing. But he does not always use his voice in that way; he can change, as varied an actor as films have ever seen. His work has a quality of rawness, of hurt, of awareness that suddenly this – fame, success – will disappear, for working-class actors like Hoskins seldom get to the top branches of show business. They may, in the clarified terms of British cinema, be clowns or comics, but never a leading man. Michael Caine is another exception, and in his case a look of surprise permeated his early performances. Hoskins is a more rounded performer, if usually cast in strong roles. In the US he has been compared to Edward G. Robinson and George C. Scott; comparisons in Britain would be to James Mason or Oliver Reed, both of whose careers were very different.

He was born in 1942 in Bury St Edmunds, Suffolk, to a bookkeeper and a school cook. He grew up in Finsbury Park, London, without showing much interest in any career. When he left school at sixteen he drifted through a series of jobs, including washing windows, driving a truck and being a Covent Garden porter; at one time he studied accountancy to follow in his father's footsteps. Acting happened by chance. He was waiting for a friend in the bar of the left-wing Unity Theatre – 'I was three parts pissed. We were going to a party. And this bloke comes round and says: "Right. You're next. Have you seen the script?" . . . And I got the leading part.' The play was 'The Feather Pluckers' (68); '. . . it was the part for a yob and it *was* me.' It also got him an agent. His first professional job was in 'Romeo and Juliet' (69); he has also played Richard III and King Lear, as well as

Pompey in 'Antony and Cleopatra' and Doolittle in 'Pygmalion'. He was also appearing on television, and there were a number of small roles in movies, starting with a good one in the film of Peter Nichols's *The National Health* (73), as one of the patients, a young man with socialist views and a penchant for visiting stately homes in his minibus. He was almost last on the cast-list of *Royal Flash* (75), with Alan Howard joining him there, but he headed way up to be one of the several Americans he would play in his career, the wheeler-dealer backer of the porno pic 'Boy Wonder' Richard Dreyfuss is making in *Inserts*.

He had met his wife, a drama teacher, at Unity, and with the break-up of his marriage he had a nervous breakdown. Verity Bargate, who ran the lunchtime theatre at the Soho Polytechnic, advised him as a friend to put his plots on paper instead of confiding in a psychiatrist. He wrote a play, 'The Bystander', which brought an offer from the BBC to star in a series, 'Pennies From Heaven', in which he was a rep selling sheet music in the thirties and getting in a bit on the side while away from his wife. With songs. Rubbishy and talentless in the writing, it was nevertheless a success, doubtless with people who didn't

know they had good tunes back then. Hoskins was thereafter in demand. On television he was in Somerset Maugham's play, *Sheppey*, and was in a series about the early days of movie-making, *Flickers*. In films he was a company sergeant major in *Zulu Dawn* (79) and then a gang boss, East-End style, in *The Long Good Friday* (80), one with a sprightly turn of phrase – often consisting of four-letter words, no apparent intellectual resources and an upper-class mistress (Helen Mirren). He sweats, is full of bluster and ruthless only when necessary; he is deeply attached to an ex-RAF pal who is gay, is wary of the highly-placed bent copper in his pay, and he shrugs off his deeply religious mother. The British cinema is not noted for its gangster films, but in the past some actors have done well as leaders of crime – Francis L. Sullivan, Griffith Jones, William Hartnell, Herbert Lom – but there was a whiff of greasepaint about their portrayals. Hoskins seemed to have walked off the street, easily inhabiting the now idle East End docklands, which he sees as a lucrative area for new activities. The film, written by Barrie Keefe and directed by John Mackenzie, was made independently and it became a *cause célèbre* when it was bought by Lew Grade's company, which proposed to make cuts and sell it direct to television. HandMade came to its rescue and got it some festival bookings – fortunately, for it was one of the most colourful British movies in a while. Chief among its virtues was Hoskins, who was not only a star but a *bona fide* one – as the reviews and the grosses (in Britain) proved. . .

He went to the National Theatre to play the villain, Bosola, in 'The Duchess of Malfi' (81) and Nathan Detroit in its long-delayed revival of 'Guys and Dolls', a role once earmarked by Olivier for himself (till the production was cancelled by a member of the Board while Olivier was abroad). On television he was Iago to Anthony Hopkins's Othello in Jonathan Miller's production for the BBC. In *Pink Floyd The Wall* (82), Alan Parker's indulgent, navel-gazing view of the life of a rock star (Bob Geldof), based on a rock album, Hoskins was one of the many manipulators, the manager. Mackenzie then called upon him to play the Argentinian police chief in *The Honorary Consul* (83) from Graham Greene's novel, with Michael Caine and Richard Gere, and Hoskins removed from cliché a role usually played as such, giving the character pride, ambition and a latent cruelty while still thinking of himself as a nice man. He was, however, rather tiresome as another top cop, of Scotland Yard, in *Lassiter* (84), aiming to put Tom Selleck inside but while doing so going way over the top in a poorly

Bob Hoskins as the East End crime boss in The Long Good Friday *(80), which proved that this rather unlikely star could carry a picture.*

written part. He was offered a role, again supporting Gere, in *The Cotton Club*. The film's director, Francis Coppola, called him out of the blue to ask him to play Owney Madden, owner of the club and an affable top mobster. Hoskins had shown he could play gangsters, while his Nathan Detroit had revealed that he did not have the usual English actor's strangulated American accent. He was harshly convincing, but as shooting dragged on for eight months, he discovered that he did not care for living in New York, and the result, he said, suffered because Coppola was 'fucked up' by his producer, Robert Evans.

He was one of several major actors doing cameos in *Brazil* (85), as one of two vicious workmen wrecking Jonathan Pryce's apartment, after which he was in two mini-series, the Australian *The 'Dunera' Boys*, about the European Jews travelling out on the ship of that name at the start of the war, and the Italian–American *Mussolini: the Decline and Fall of Il Duce*, in the title-role. *The Woman Who Married Clark Gable* (86) was an Anglo-Irish short film, a jape about a factory-worker (Hoskins) and his fantasizing wife. After that Hoskins did one of his most polished jobs as the screenwriter in Alan Alda's *Sweet Liberty*, a modishly bearded man who has made it big after writing continuities for commercials, but still an eager-beaver, if both cynical and sycophantic at the same time. Caine was in the cast, and he accepted a guest-role in Hoskins's next movie, *Mona Lisa*, so called, apparently, because every time Hoskins turns on the car radio it's playing Nat 'King' Cole's song of that name. We should be so lucky: what we get is a daft plot about a chauffeur who develops a hang-up about his passenger, a high-class black tart (Cathy Tyson) who is not about to return his interest since – it's unsurprisingly revealed – she's a lesbian. The director, Neil Jordan, had shown talent previously in *Angel*; his co-writer, David Leland, would go on to write an even more phony movie about prostitution, *Personal Services*. They were saved from disaster here by Hoskins, superb as the chauffeur, an ex-con, a loner who nevertheless enjoys swopping yarns with his mates. At this point he was due to return to the US to make *Strange Hearts* for director Louis Malle, but nothing came of this.

That may be because Hoskins was offered a bigger project, to play Al Capone in *The Untouchables*, but although the role was eventually played by Robert De Niro, he was still paid for it. He was a Catholic priest in Mike Hodges's *A Prayer for the Dying* (87) whose lips have to be sealed after an IRA gunman (Mickey Rourke) confesses to him, and he remained in Eire for Jack Clayton's *The Lonely Passion of Judith Hearne*, attracting the amorous attention of a fellow-guest, Maggie Smith, though in this case he sported an American accent since he had returned to the Old Turf after forty years' absence. HandMade, which produced, agreed to put up the money for Hoskins's own pet project, *The Raggedy Rawney*, which he directed and co-wrote from stories told him by his grandmother. This was essentially a tribute to the Romany way of life, incorporating a tale of a deserter who hides out with the tribe, of which Hoskins played the chief. Though shot in Czechoslovakia, the film was vague about where it was supposed to be set, which war the soldier was running from and even whether the wanderers were in fact gypsies in the first place. Hoskins's anti-war views may be shared by most of the world's population, but since not by all of it, they are always worth re-stating; but in this case they emerged as rather trite, which did not help matters. It was the third consecutive failure for Hoskins: there was controversy over the content of the Hodges film, which underwent changes after previews and was then badly received; the Clayton film, although it gave Hoskins the joy of working with Miss Smith, was too downbeat to get major play; but his own film was the greatest disappointment. Unveiled to scant enthusiasm at the Cannes festival in 1988, it received a few bookings in Britain the following year before being despatched to video. A quarrel between HandMade and Cannon over video rights – on the last two films – did not help matters.

Meanwhile, Hoskins made a film which almost everyone went to see: *Who Framed Roger Rabbit* (88), a blend of 40s *noir* elements and most of Hollywood's animated animals – and 'humans', if it comes to that. It was an idea whose time had come: director Robert Zemeckis thought again of Gary K. Wolf's novel, 'Who Censored Roger Rabbit?' after the success of *Back to the Future* for Steven Spielberg's Amblin Entertainment, while at this time Disney – which had seen and liked the material – approached Spielberg. Hoskins was *faute de mieux* the seedy Hollywood detective employed by the leaping lapin of the title, secondly because Zemeckis felt the film a tough enough assignment without having to worry about Hoskins's American accent, and firstly because few actors wished to co-star with a rodent. Zemeckis tested Hoskins, whose American accent has been called flawless by many Americans on more than one occasion; and while such stars as Paul Newman and Gene Hackman were mentioned, the already high budget might not (it depended) be able to encompass their

salary demands. The film eventually cost $53 million – one million of which went to Hoskins, probably more than he was worth as a draw, but in consideration of the perils and problems of working with colleagues who would not be painted in till later. Hoskins observed that he was 'the kind of actor who gets off on other people', so that he found it hard to act to space, but he was helped by Charlie Fleischer, who voiced Roger, and who was on set most of the time. He, Hoskins, was also on a percentage, but when asked to specify, retorted, 'Fuck off, you cunt, what are you, my accountant?' Disney marketing and positive reviews sent the gross spiralling to an unrabbitlike $81,240,000, making it one of the most successful films yet shown. Audiences did not see Popeye, Felix the Cat or Tom and Jerry, whose agents and/or owners demanded exorbitant fees, but they did get most of the Disney menagerie – and Warners received a copyright notice for their animated zoo, which was nicely timed, as during production Warners took over Disney's distribution in most overseas territories. All this and Industrial Light and Magic! The rabbit is ingratiating, wacky, feckless and never sentimental, and he has a grand fight-to-the-finish, with brilliant animation throughout by

Richard Williams, specially engaged by the canny Disney team for this special occasion. It is the humans who are disappointing, including a drab villain, Christopher Lloyd, and Hoskins himself, playing without charm or verve (he has energy, but that's not the same thing). Hoskins is scruffy, with frayed cuffs, whereas the point of the *noir* private eyes was that they had seen better days, and if their pants were threadbare they were still neatly creased – and their shirts, if scuffed, were still laundered. Even less felicitously for this *noir* re-vamp, the bar in which Hoskins hangs out is peopled by characters whom even Skid Row would have rejected. Still, only purists were complaining.

Having now made three films back to back, of which this last and the one he had directed had been particularly strenuous, Hoskins found himself counselled by his doctor to ease up or he would be dead within a year: in his own words, 'I was a complete physical wreck.' His second wife, Linda (whom he met in 1982), 'really laid down the rules. No more work. Don't read scripts. Stop the drinking and smoking. Cut down on food. Do I feel any better? No, I bloody don't. I'm longing for a pint and a fag.' A plan for a modern 'Candide', reunited with Keefe and Mackenzie, was mooted, and Hoskins remained away till *Heart Condition* (90), in which he was a bigoted detective forced to live with the fact that after a heart transplant an accomplished black lawyer (Denzel Washington) becomes his constant ghostly companion. It was written and directed by James D. Parriott, after many successes in television ('The Bionic Woman', 'The Incredible Hulk'), but was not sufficiently well received to be around for long. On the line: *Shattered*, with Tom Berenger, and *Mermaids*, in which he plays Cher's lover – for another $1 million. He said: 'I'm just happy doing it. The whole thing comes as a constant surprise and pleasure to me. If the script is good, then I get excited. If the money is brilliant but the words or characters aren't there, forget it.'

In September he began shooting a film in France, *The Favor, the Watch and the Very Big Fish* (91), with Natasha Richardson and Jeff Goldblum, which he followed with *The Projectionist*, made in Moscow. Then he is due to start on a film of Chekov's *The Cherry Orchard*, directed by Lindsay Anderson, with Maggie Smith and Alan Bates.

HOLLY HUNTER

Holly Hunter is only a little thing (5 feet 2 inches), but she's big in talent. It took her six years to make it to the top, and you wonder why it took so long.

She was born in 1958 in Conyers, Georgia, the daughter of a sports goods representative and the youngest of seven children. Her high school grades were not good enough to get her into the best drama schools, but she was confident of entry if permitted to audition: so she studied drama for four years at the Carnegie Mellon University in Pittsburgh. Within a month of arriving in New York to find work, she was one of the threatened youngsters in *The Burning* (81), the Miramax rip-off of *Friday the Thirteenth*. It was not a big part, but it was a start. She appeared off-Broadway in 'Battery' the same year, and in 'Weekend Near Madison'. She auditioned for Beth Henley's play 'The Wake of Jamey Foster' and was turned down; but on the way to the audition she had met Miss Henley in a lift, and was invited to take over one of the leading roles in another Henley play, 'Places of the Heart'. She did, after all, do the play for which she had auditioned, as well as two other Henley plays, 'The Miss Firecracker Contest' off-Broadway and 'Lucky Spot' in the Williamstown Theater Festival. Meanwhile, she had a small role in a telefilm with Jodie Foster, *Svengali* (83), and a larger one as a student in *An Uncommon Love*, third-

billed in this tale of a professor (Barry Bostwick) who falls in love with a pupil (Kathryn Harrold), only to discover that she works in a massage parlour. She was cut from most of *Swing Shift* (84) after the star, Goldie Hawn, and director, Jonathan Demme, had parted so acrimoniously, but was seen to advantage in a TV movie, *With Intent to Kill*, as the daughter of Karl Malden, who after her death hounds the man responsible on the grounds that his insanity plea had allowed him too short a time in an institution.

After a long run in Henley's 'Firecracker' play she had one of the leads, a Southern girl, in a prestigious telefilm directed by Volker Schlöndorff, *A Gathering of Old Men* (87), with sheriff Richard Widmark uncertain how to act when a racist white man has been killed by blacks. Even better, she got *Raising Arizona*, written for her by Joel and Ethan Coen, whom she had got to know when sharing an apartment years before with Frances McDormond – who had starred in their film *Blood Simple*. Equally original but less organized, this told of a mismatched couple – a petty thief (Nicolas Cage) and a police booking officer (Hunter) who steal one of quintuplets when they find they can't have a child of their own. Better still, she got *Broadcast News* because Debra Winger was pregnant. James L. Brooks had written it for Winger and as replacement had considered Sigourney Weaver, Judy Davis, Elizabeth McGovern, Christine Lahti and Elizabeth Perkins. He spent five months in auditions, before seeing Hunter at the request of the casting director just before auditions were due to begin. The role needed someone dynamic enough to become a wheeler-dealer in the competitive world of television, vulnerable enough not to know which of the two men (William Hurt, Albert

Miss Holly Hunter, and none other: a little lady who can sweep all before her.

Brooks) she loves, and yet while manipulating them have charm enough to make the audience care. The press and audiences welcomed a new star, and among the prizes was the Best Actress award from the New York critics. She had already made *End of the Line* (88), a down-home-folks tale of two Arkansas railroad workers who journey to Chicago to argue against the closure of their company. They were played by Wilford Brimley and Levon Helm, with Hunter as Brimley's daughter and Mary Steenbergen (who also produced) as Helm's wife: they were left behind, and the picture degenerated thereafter. Hunter, who was billed ninth, had Kevin Bacon as her boyfriend, while the remarkable cast also included Bob Balaban.

Hunter took off to tour southern Europe with a friend, and then did a course in art history in New York; in Los Angeles she starred in Sam Shepard's 'A Lie of the Mind'. In other words, the hottest little girl in films let matters cool down, She chose what she wanted to do and what she wanted to do was Henley's piece, now called just *Miss Firecracker* (89) – and here she was as the tramp of Yazoo City, Missouri, who enters the 4th of July beauty pageant in an effort to change her reputation. Now, Hunter had every reason to be grateful to Henley, but as transcribed to the screen this was superficial stuff. What she also wanted to do was a factual telemovie – because it dealt seriously with an important issue: *Roe vs Wade* concerned Ellen Russell (Hunter) who in 1970 decided to petition for an abortion, which was illegal in her home state of Texas. Amy Madigan played the lawyer and the piece won Emmy awards for Best Film and Best Actress, Hunter. And what she also wanted to do was take a supporting role in an independent picture, *Animal Behavior* – in the display ads billed fourth, under the title. 'Karen Allen and Armand Assante are falling in love' said those ads, 'but there's one thing standing in their way . . . Holly Hunter.'

Still, she knew the world's most successful film-maker, Steven Spielberg, wanted her to star opposite Richard Dreyfuss in *Always*, his remake of *A Guy Named Joe*, a film which should never have been made in the first place. Although Hunter is not at all like Irene Dunne, she is equally welcome on anybody's screen. Next she should be seen with Dreyfuss again in *Once Around* (90).

WILLIAM HURT

In 1987 in an interview the British actor Robert Powell spoke of his admiration for Laurence Olivier and Paul Newman. 'There are a lot of movie actors about these days,' he said, 'but there aren't many stars – with the possible exception of William Hurt.' Hurt wouldn't like that. 'I am not a star, I am an actor,' he said once. And: 'I am a character actor in a leading man's body.' On another occasion: 'I am not an actor. I'm just a man who likes acting'. And then: 'I am what I am. I am nobody. I don't exist. But the work exists. The work is more than the actor.' 'I've got a hunch that his creative life is an enormous part of his life,' said the director James L. Brooks. 'Everything else gets expressed by that and feeds into that, in some way.'

Joanna Pacula, who has also worked with him, observed, 'I think Bill has wonderful screen presence, but he is so introverted, tense and intellectual. That doesn't make him an easy actor to work opposite. He made me feel left out in the cold.' I never saw a man who could talk so long and so much. You'd be sitting there with Bill in the middle of nowhere, and he'd just knit those eyebrows and *go*. He gives a new definition to the word "intense".' After interviewing him, James Cameron-Wilson wrote: 'William Hurt is an intense man! He stares through you with those pale, cool blue eyes as if he was reading an autocue. He tries to explain his reason for *being*. He quotes Saul Bellow, talks about Albert Camus and Eugene O'Neill.' Tense. Intense. It hasn't hurt his work.

He was born in Washington DC in 1950, the son of a director of the Trust Territories for the State Department. He was brought up in Guam, Hawaii, Somaliland, Pakistan and New York, later graduating in theology from Tufts University. He knew by this time that he wanted to act: he studied drama first in London and then at the Juilliard in New York. After joining the Circle Repertory Theater in 1977, he began to make a reputation, in Corinne Jacker's 'My Life' (for which he won an Obie), 'Hamlet', 'The Runner Stumbles'; and he originated the role of Kenneth Talley in Lanford Wilson's 'The Fifth of July'.

He had good and bad luck on his first film, *Altered States* (80): he was chosen for the lead by Paddy Chayevsky, who wrote it; but it was directed by Ken Russell, who took over from Arthur Penn early in the troubled shooting. Hurt played a Harvard scientist whose researches result in becoming not a Mr Hyde but an ape. What with hallucinations and experiments, Russell himself went ape, discovering new excesses; Chayevsky took his name off the film, the cost mounted to $15 million, of which $12,500,000 was returned at the US box-office. Those who saw it were not encouraged to return to see Hurt in his second film,

Eyewitness (81), a reunion for director Peter Yates and writer Steve Tesich after their success with *Breaking Away*. Hurt, again top-billed, played a janitor who, questioned about a murder in his building, gets to meet a TV reporter (Sigourney Weaver) with whom he had been obsessed from afar. It was fine and should have done better; for some foreign territories it was retitled *The Janitor*. An even better thriller was *Body Heat*, ingeniously written by its director, Lawrence Kasdan, about an unsuccessful, mediocre Miami lawyer who begins an affair with a dangerous married lady (Kathleen Turner); her husband (Richard Crenna) doesn't get to stay alive much longer. Since the adulterous couple spend much of the time screwing, Hurt might have challenged Richard Gere over the next few years as the movies' No. 1 stud; and since he had made himself strikingly good-looking by dyeing his hair darker and growing a moustache, he might have aimed for old-time movie stardom. This, after all, was the film in which he made his mark. He looked in life as he did in *Eyewitness*, small, insignificant, wearing granny glasses. The film took $12,500,000, but Kasdan's *The Big Chill* (83) took almost twice that: Hurt was one of the weekend guests at the home of Glenn Close and Kevin Kline, a former phone-in psychologist now dealing in narcotics.

Between the two films he had returned to the Circle Rep to play the lead in Romulus Linney's 'Childe Byron' and a smaller role in 'The Diviners'. He played a Russian police detective in Michael Apted's *Gorki Park*, uneasily adapted (by Dennis Potter) from the bestseller by Martin Cruz Smith. It cost $14 million and the $6,300,000 it took was considerably more than it deserved. Hurt was no longer one of Hollywood's 'hot' actors, which may be why he chose to make his Broadway debut in David Rabe's 'Hurlyburly', which also featured Sigourney Weaver, Christopher Walken and Harvey Keitel. Hollywood certainly did not think he was helping his career when he went to Brazil to make *Kiss of the Spider Woman/Beijo de a Mulher Aranha* (85), especially as it consisted of little more than interplay between two prisoners, a revolutionary and a homosexual. A play based upon Manuel Puig's novel had had some international success and the film was to be directed by Hector Babenco, who had just won the Foreign Picture Oscar for *Pixote*. Burt Lancaster, who had extended his career by appearing in occasional prestige foreign productions, had agreed to play the gay man, the better of the two roles. When he withdrew because of his heart attack, Raul Julia, cast as the political prisoner, asked whether he could now play it; and when Babenco said he

William Hurt, actor extraordinaire, in three of the films which have brought him acclaim: Body Heat *(81), left, as the run-down lawyer who embarks on a steamy affair with a married woman;* Kiss of the Spider Woman *(85), as a homosexual prisoner – the performance which won him an Oscar; and* Children of a Lesser God *(86), as a teacher of deaf-mute pupils.*

wanted a bigger name, Julia suggested Hurt, who won a Best Actor Oscar for it. The question is, how do you play a gay? Well, this one was supposed to be flamboyant and effeminate, living in a fantasy world. So that was all right then.

The film made less than $7 million for Island Releasing, but it put Hurt back to the top of the Hollywood heap. And he was kept there by *Children of a Lesser God* (86), in which boy meets girl, boy loses girl, girl comes back to boy: but in this case the girl (Marlee Matlin) is a deaf-mute and the boy (Hurt) is a teacher of same. This adaptation of a Broadway play, hideously overlong, might have done nicely as a telefilm: it took over $12 million at the box-office and won Ms Matlin, herself a deaf-mute, a Best Actress Oscar.

When James L. Brooks had finished his screenplay for *Broadcast News* (87) he was prepared to wait till Hurt was free, because he needed someone who could cause a stir by just entering a room: 'You can't act that, you do that,' he explained. And the heroine (Holly Hunter) tells him, 'You're the classiest guy I know. The plot (to simplify) has her pulling strings so that he can find fame as a newscaster, dumping on the way an old colleague (Albert Brooks) who also is in love with her. Hurt's lithe, laid-back performance was his most attractive screen work to date, nicely matched by Miss Hunter: and if the film is taken from them by Mr Brooks, he has the most interesting character and the best lines. The film cost $20 million and took $24,900,000, not bad for a class job. Hurt has another such in his immediate future, but around here there appeared briefly the film made before *Broadcast News* – *The Time of Destiny*, press-shown in 1988 and given a few test-dates early in 1989 before going to video. The director Gregory Nava and producer Anna Thomas, also the writers, had previously collaborated on the over-rated *El Norte*, American independent art cinema at its worst – but maybe Hurt felt they could pull it off with this, a saga about a Basque family, whose no-good scion joins the army in order to kill the guy (Timothy Hutton) who eloped with his sister. Kasdan had a good one for him, *The Accidental Tourist* (88), based on Anne Tyler's novel, about (again, to simplify) an unenthusiastic travel-writer who moves in with an unlikely woman (Geena Davis) when his wife (Kathleen Turner) leaves him. The point of the man is that he goes through life letting things happen to him: Hurt had a wonderful role, he knew it, and he played it beautifully. One of the producers was John Malkovich, who observed that Hurt and Sean Penn were 'the two best young actors in America today.'

At this time he returned to the Circle Rep to appear in Joe Pintauro's 'Beside Herself'. He had already done his guest role in *I Love You to Death* (90), as a hippie trying to kill Kevin Kline – a performance not much appreciated. As a young man he was briefly married to actress Mary Beth Hurt, who herself later achieved success. Later liaisons included one with Ms Matlin, who persuaded him to undertake drying-out sessions at the Betty Ford Clinic in Rancho Mirage, California, and the Hazelden Clinic in Minnesota; a prior relationship with ballerina Sandra Jennings found her sueing for support of their son in 1988; the following year she sued for a share of his earnings as his common law wife, but the judge found in Hurt's favour – which must have been a mighty consolation, though he expressed himself incensed by press coverage of the case, which did his screen image no harm at all. In September 1990 he played the title role in Chekov's 'Ivanov' at the Yale Repertory Theatre, but without the warm notices to which he was accustomed.

He is due to appear in *To the End of the World* for Wim Wenders, a role meant for Willem Dafoe till a spiralling budget caused the backers to demand a bigger name, and then in *The Doctor* at Disney, replacing Warren Beatty – unless he himself changes his mind, for in August 1990 it was reported that he intended to become a priest.

DIANE KEATON

'La-dee-dah,' said Diane Keaton in *Annie Hall*, 'Wow' and 'Oooh' and 'Oh' and 'Right' and 'Yeah', putting them into various permutations. Her director and co-star, Woody Allen, had lived with her at one time, and we all suspected that the film was more autobiographical than they cared to admit in interviews. We didn't care, either, for it told us more than we needed to know; but since she won an Oscar for it we may say that this is the most valuable self-portrait of an Oscar-winner that we have. The film's success was surely due to her: seemingly spontaneous, healthy-looking, a free spirit bubbling with merriment – and occasional doubts. 'Wow. Right. Yeah. Oh. Wow.'

She was born in Los Angeles in 1946 and grew up in nearby Santa Ana; in school she played second lead in 'Little Mary Sunshine', which prompted her to apply for a scholarship to the Neighborhood Playhouse School of the Theater in Manhattan. From there she understudied in 'Hair' (68), and took over one of the leads – but refused to undress; it was at this time that she met Allen, when she appeared with him in his Broadway success, 'Play It Again, Sam' (69). Her first film role was in a comedy about a wedding, *Lovers and Other Strangers* (70), as the wife the groom's brother wanted to divorce. In *The Godfather* (72) she was the nice non-Italian girl who falls in love with one of his sons (Al Pacino); but she first made an impression on audiences as the wife Allen dreams of taking from friend Tony Roberts, in *Play It Again, Sam*. She read for Neil Simon's *The Heartbreak Kid*, and was, in his words, 'Dynamite, perfect', but director Elaine May wanted, said Simon, her daughter Jeannie Berlin in the film. She was with Allen again in *Sleeper* (73), playing a useless, sophisticated but basically likeable poetess, and was then Pacino's wife in *The Godfather Part II* (74). She was not, in that, very impressive, but some glimmerings of comic skill were apparent in the midst of Allen's self-conscious, amateurish cavorting – in, for instance, *Love and Death* (75): so she was cast as leading lady in two comedies with Elliott Gould, *I Will I Will for Now* (76), as the ex-wife with whom he gets together, and *Harry and Walter Go to New York*, as a crusading reporter of the 70s. The first found them an uneasy team and in the second she shouted a lot at Michael Caine; both flopped. She was in a play in New York, 'The Primary English Class', and then came *Annie Hall*, which brought her a Best Actress Oscar – against the heaviest competition in recent years – and a place in the box-office ten (actually, No. 9). Simultaneously audiences could see her in *Looking For Mr Goodbar*, as the teacher of deaf children whose night-time swinging in the Singles bars leads to her grisly end. After that, she returned to Allen, to his serious *Interiors* (78), again his idea of a poetess, one of the family sundered when parents (Geraldine Page, E.G. Marshall) part; and *Manhattan* (79), wife to his best friend in this roundelay.

She became romantically involved with Warren Beatty, both of them in *Reds* (81), she Louise Bryant to his John Reed, the American journalist who fervently approved of the Russian Revolution. She was not much like the real Bryant, and she proved not to have a personality able to sustain a movie running over three hours, but she had some touching moments, notably when telling a Senate committee that she did not believe in God. There was some discussion between their respective distributors, who did not want two Keaton movies on view in the same season: so *Shoot the Moon* (82) was delayed. In the event it had started out at 20th Century-Fox, but moved to MGM after one executive was quoted as saying: 'Who'd pay $2 million to Diane Keaton and $1.5 million to Albert

Finney?' The public felt the same way, for few went to Alan Parker's story of a strained literary marriage in Marin County: it took less than $4 million on a $12 budget. Keaton so much wanted to do *The Little Drummer Girl* (84) that she halved her usual fee and accepted only $1 million – to no avail, for there was only a chilly welcome for George Roy Hill's bland version of the John Le Carré novel, even though she was on form as a pro-Palestinian actress being used as an Israeli agent. And she was at her most restrained as *Mrs Soffel*, the wife of a prison governor who runs off with a convict (Mel Gibson); but Gillian Armstrong's film was too stark to appeal. Both films were in the $14–15 million range: they took respectively $3.7 million and less than $2 million.

Crimes of the Heart (86) wound up in the black, but at $10 million that was $1 million

Another Oscar-winner, Diane Keaton as Annie Hall, which was the title of the film and which was made in 1976. It was written for her, and directed by, Woody Allen, who also co-starred.

Ms Keaton in her first full-scale dramatic role, in Looking for Mr Goodbar *(77) – and she was looking in singles-bars for anyone good: in bed, that is. And much good did it do her! Dear old Hollywood: after all this time it still couldn't allow that promiscuity could have a happy ending.*

more than its cost; and it was one of several films which forced Dino De Laurentiis to quit movie-making after almost fifty years. He 'owed substantial points', as 'Variety' put it, as the actresses concerned had only taken $500,000 for their services with a view to profit participation. The others were Jessica Lange and Sissy Spacek, none of them erasing memories of Lizbeth Mackay, Mary Beth Hurt and Mia Dillon in the original New York production. Indeed, their performances on the stage as sisters may have been the reason why Beth Henley's derivative down-home drama won a Pulitzer prize; the three screen actresses played in differing styles, with Keaton making particularly little of the lonely, frustrated sister. Bruce Beresford directed, and that was a chore which Keaton took on with *Heaven* (87), some opinions on that place by people shortly expecting to arrive there, intercut with scenes from movies set there. She did not appear in this very personal project, which lost on even its small budget; nor was she in Bill Forsyth's first American feature, *Housekeeping*, having changed her mind at the last minute, to be replaced by a lesser name but a more interesting actress, Christine Lahti. Instead she appeared in Charles Shyer's *Baby Boom*, as a career-type yuppie whose life is changed when a baby is visited upon her. It did nicely, but there were few takers for Leonard Nimoy's *The Good Mother* (88), in which she was a single parent battling with ex-husband Liam Neesom (who accused her lover of sexually abusing their child), and even less for *The Lemon Sisters* (89), in which she was the asthmatic member of a singing trio in Las Vegas. Her mannerisms overwhelmed the performance, possibly because as co-producer she did not care to be restrained. The film actually appeared in 1990, after being trade-shown a year earlier, to take less than $3,500,000.

There were other off-camera activities, including a book of photographs, 'Reservations', and she had long been planning to produce a remake of *The Blue Angel*, with Madonna as the star at this time. Keaton directed – and very well – a 60-minute film for television, *The Girl With the Crazy Brother* (90), about coming to terms with a schizophrenic brother: CBS premiered it on a weekday afternoon at 4 p.m., and it deserved better than that. She then rejoined Coppola and Pacino for *The Godfather: the Continuing Story*, and had an affair with the latter, though that appears to be over now. One project was more certain: Joan Micklin Silver's *Running Mates*, in which she would play an old flame of womanizing Senator Dennis Hopper, who has been ordered to marry.

MICHAEL KEATON

Michael Keaton is an amiable actor whose successes may augur a long career. Clearly he can play the same roles as Tom Hanks, Tom Cruise, Bill Murray, Dan Aykroyd and others, but in today's Hollywood the more there are of them the more will be the roles tailored for them and then altered for someone else.

He was born in 1951 in Coraopolis, a suburb of Pittsburgh, Philadelphia, the youngest of seven children, in fact named Michael Douglas; but when show business beckoned there was already one of them, so he renamed himself on a whim after seeing a newspaper picture of Diane Keaton. As a child, he entertained the family with impressions of Elvis Presley; he had his first experience of the footlights while studying speech ('the vaguest thing I could major in') at Kent State University, with a comedy sketch he had worked up. But he dropped out, driving a cab and a truck for a while, and performing in the local Pittsburgh boîtes with Louis, the Incredible Dancing Chicken. In 1972, when he was 21, he was taken on by Pittsburgh's public television station, WQED, to work behind the camera; but during the three years he was there he managed to get in front of it often enough. Eventually, he decided to move to Los Angeles ('If I was going to starve, the weather at least should be good'), where he poured beer for a time, also keeping his hand in at the Comedy Store and the Second City Improvisational Workshop. He had one contact, a producer who used to work at WQED and who was now working on 'Maude'; he got Keaton a cameo as a reporter in one episode of that show. Norman Lear liked him and decided to feature him in a series, but it did not run, 'All's Fair' (76) with Bernadette Peters, as a presidential joke-writer. Mary Tyler Moore's variety show, 'Mary', employed him, but it lasted only three weeks; he returned to that lady's assistance on 'The Mary Tyler Moore Hour', which introduced him to Caroline McWilliams, to whom he was at one time married. He and Jim Belushi shared the leads of 'Working Stiffs' (79), a series in which they were janitors in Chicago. That was swiftly followed by 'Report to Murphy', which also did not run, but Keaton's profile was now high enough to get a movie offer – *Caveman*, which he declined (and it went to Randy Quaid). The sitcom world can be a small one, and two others who had made their name in one, 'Happy Days', Ron Howard and Henry Winkler, were respectively directing and starring in *Night Shift* (82), a comedy about two night janitors who turn the morgue in which they work into a brothel. This was a rotten premise, but it was good news all the way from then on, with Winkler's wimpish hero the most pleasing of his screen appearances – and wonderfully teamed with Keaton, a joyous extrovert.

It led to the lead in *Mr Mom* (83), at a salary of $300,000, which was five times more than he had been paid on his first movie. This one was directed by Stan Dragoti from a screenplay by John Hughes which is more than a glorified sitcom – and not original, either, for Harry Langdon had done the same plot in 1928, *The Chaser*, the one about the spouses who change places. Age-old situations renew themselves, for now we might see, as we could not back then, infidelity acted out: but Terri Garr, as the wife, clearly loves the stay-at-home husband, incompetent at the least household chore. When the film grossed $32 million, it confirmed Keaton as a star, bringing him a rise in salary to $1 million a picture. He turned down *Splash* in order to make Amy Heckerling's *Johnny Dangerously* (84), a poor gangster spoof enlivened by some of the performances, including Keaton's in the lead. He was later to say that the script of the finished film was not the one he had first read. As shooting ended, 20th-Century-Fox, who were distributing, offered him a four-picture contract in a deal rare at this time, but when the film took only $9,100,000, it somehow fell apart.

During this period Keaton had acquired a partner and business manager, Harry Colomby, who counselled him against doing *The Purple Rose of Cairo* (85) partly because the role was bland, but to work with Woody Allen, Keaton was prepared to take only a quarter of his usual salary. However, he was sacked after three days – reputedly at the insistence of the star, Mia Farrow. Keaton was playing the dream prince with whose screen image she falls in love, and was replaced – when Allen could not get Kevin Kline – by Jeff Daniels. Never mind: Ron Howard and the writers of *Night Shift* offered *Gung Ho* (86), a comedy about a small town which goes into shock when most of its inhabitants are thrown out of work by the closure of its automobile factory. Or, rather, it was about the culture shock experienced when one of them, Keaton, invited the Japanese to reopen it. That grossed a pleasing $15,500,000. but there were few takers for Robert Mandel's *Touch and Go*, in which Keaton was a self-centred ice-hockey star who gets involved with the unmarried mother (Maria Conchita Alonso) of a teenage delinquent who has mugged him. *The Squeeze* (87) managed $1 million, which was more than it deserved, a witless chase comedy about a con-man (the role 'most like me') and a detective

Michael Keaton talking his way in and out of trouble in Gung Ho (86), as the foreman of a closed auto factory who negotiates with a Japanese firm to take it over.

(Rae Dawn Chong) who unite to expose a rigged lottery prize. Thinking it too similar, he turned down *Stakeout*, but that turned out to be a big success.

Beetlejuice (88) was a grotesque comedy which raids *The Canterville Ghost* and *Blithe Spirit* without profit: a young couple (Alec Baldwin, Geena Davis) are killed, to return as spooks to their home, to find it refitted with every pretension known to interior design. They call upon Keaton, a mad-as-a-hatter ghost who claims to be a bio-exorcist, but whose main aim seems to be lechery. The director, Tim Burton, was of the school which believes that Special Effects take precedence over all else, and he is certainly prodigal with them: but when they are not tired they are not for the squeamish. Still, it had a certain energy, though one good scene – in which some haughty dinner guests go into a bump-and-grind routine to Harry Belafonte's 'Banana Boat Song' – cannot explain why it managed to take $33,200,000. Keaton came in after the rest of the film was shot for just three weeks' work, much of it improvised; he had realized, he said, that it was not essential to be likeable on the screen, and he therefore made his character as repellent as possible.

147

No one will need to be told who this is, will they? But there he is then, when out of his Batsuit, as millionaire Bruce Wayne, as he's about to fall heavily for a beautiful photojournalist, played by Kim Basinger. He is played by Michael Keaton and the film was made in 1989.

Though smeared with make-up which rendered him unrecognizable and billed sixth ('as Beetlejuice'), he found himself in demand again, and he chose, wisely, a serious role, but only after the director, Glenn Gordon Caron from television's 'Moonlighting', had told him he was the only one to play it. Caron, referring to Keaton's earlier work, said: 'He wasn't just funny – there was an ache in the performance, a sort of pain . . . this sense of self-destructiveness. It was the black Irish in him – with Keaton you get the sense that the abyss is as deep as the peaks are high. I thought – and everyone on the production thought – he'd be perfect. The only person who had doubts was Keaton. When I approached him, he said, "Those aren't the kind of movies I do." I said, "Maybe it's the kind of movie you *should* do." ' Thus, in *Clean and Sober*, which Tom Hanks had wanted to do, Keaton was a hotshot real-estate salesman who hides out in a rehabilitation centre to escape from the cops, not admitting to its head (Morgan Freeman) that he's as hooked on drink and drugs as the next man. The role was a veritable *tour de force* for Keaton, and in view of the fact that addiction is seldom box-office, the film took a neat $4 million. Keaton was on more familiar ground as one of Howard Zieff's *The Dream Team* (89), for this was comedy – and the others on the team were Christopher Lloyd, Peter Boyle and Stephen Furst, a quartet who lose their therapist while leaving their New Jersey mental home for a baseball match in New York. There, the folks are madder than they, which provided some exhilarating adventures, after a dubious start. Universal backed them, to the tune of $15 million, and saw $14,400,000 returned at the box-office.

Then came *Batman*, but before it opened it was revealed that Keaton's fee was now $3 million for a starring role and that he had a deal with Warners which gave that company first look at any projects. As it happened, Warners produced *Batman*, a Special Effects bonanza which they consigned to Burton to direct on the strength of *Beetlejuice* (after considering Ivan Reitman, Joe Dante and Steven Spielberg; at one time it was to be a comic *Batman* with Bill Murray). He insisted on Keaton, despite flak from the industry and Batman fans. The best that can be said for Keaton is that he holds his own, but that ain't hay when confronted with Jack Nicholson, doing his all as the villain, and having to act only with his eyes when encased in a black-leather fetishist outfit. He was only ordinary as Batman in civvies, as it were, the millionaire Bruce Wayne, but as the director said, 'The whole point is that he's *not* Arnold Schwarzenegger because, if he were, then why would he need to put on a Batsuit?' The gigantic success of the film (see Nicholson) established Keaton as one of Hollywood's major stars, but he was aware that there had been much pre-première criticism of his selection for it. Accordingly he chose to take a supporting role to show his versatility again; in John Schlesinger's *Pacific Heights* (91), billed third, as a reptilian tenant who not only manages to pay no rent, but also makes life impossible for the owners, Melanie Griffith and Matthew Modine. The film took over $15 million in its first two weeks. After that he is scheduled to do *One Good Cop*.

KEVIN KLINE

It's all there with this one: looks (especially when moustached, as he well knows), bravura, sensitivity, versatility, humour, danger, intelligence.

Kevin Kline was born in St Louis, Missouri, in 1947, of an Irish Catholic mother and a German Jewish father who was in the record business. He was educated by Benedictine monks and then at Indiana University, where he studied music till co-opted for a production of 'Macbeth': he had only a small role, as a bleeding sergeant, but he went on to study drama at the Juilliard School in New York. 'Growing up in the Sixties', he said, 'coming from a background which was middle-class and suburban, our paradigms were Paul Newman and Hud and James Dean. You know, alienated cool . . . Showing emotion was strictly taboo, so acting came as a great release, and that was part of its challenge. It made me feel very vulnerable.'

He joined John Houseman's Acting Company and toured with it, and made his debut with the New York Shakespeare Festival Company at the Delacorte in Central Park as a spear-carrier in 1970. Stardom would find him at the Delacorte, in 'Henry V', 'Richard III', 'Arms and the Man' (as Bluntschli), among others, but he started there as understudy to Raul Julia, Mack the Knife in 'The Threepenny Opera'. His Broadway debut was as the juvenile in 'On the Twentieth Century', which won him a Tony award. He returned to the Shakespeare Festival two years later to replace the unavailable Julia as the Pirate King in 'The Pirates of Penzance' (79), bringing to the role a winning combination of sexual charisma, foolishness and physical daring. Broadway had a leading man as it had not seen in years, and he won a second Tony.

He was up for the lead in Lawrence Kasdan's *Body Heat*, but lost it to William Hurt. He did get a flashy start in pictures

'Mr Kline gives the kind of bravura performance not often found in movies' said Vincent Canby in the 'New York Times', 'The best thing about I Love You to Death *is that it accommodates him without inhibiting him . . . Everything Mr Kline does is both too much and absolutely right. He speaks with the kind of broad, brilliantly elocuted Italian-American accent that recalls the linguistic skills of Laurence Olivier. He also manages to be both manic and laid back.' Here is Kline, left, in his first film,* Sophie's Choice *(82), a classy but dull picture which he galvanised into entertainment every time he was on the screen. So if Canby's comments apply to that, too, that cannot be said to be true of Richard Attenborough's* Cry Freedom! *(87), in which he gave a notably self-effacing performance as Donald Woods, the South African newspaper editor who gave his support to black activist Steve Biko.*

when director Alan J. Pakula cast him (before Meryl Streep) in his long-winded version of William Styron's bestseller, *Sophie's Choice* (82). He gave a dashing performance as the temperamental, drug-addicted, schizophrenic Jewish biologist with whom Streep is involved; but as he observed four films later, 'People have predicted for me on other films, "This movie will do *so* much you have no idea. You'll be a household name. All the Hollywood studios want [now] is Eddie Murphy, Robert Redford or Sylvester Stallone." You say, "We're doing Dostoevsky's early life", and they say, "Great, that's Sly". You say, "We see Dostoevsky as an overweight epileptic." They say, "He can play an epileptic."' Certainly Kline's movie career did not take off; it was not helped by the artistic and commercial failure of *The Pirates of Penzance* (83), directed by Wilford Leach in theatrical imitation of Joseph Papp's original Shakespeare Festival production. Kline was top-billed, over Angela Lansbury.

Kasdan remembered him and cast him in *The Big Chill*, not as the spaced-out Jewish reporter (which Kline wanted, and which Jeff Goldblum played), but as the affluent, agreeable, respected husband of Glenn Close, the couple hosting this reunion of old friends (among whom was Jobeth Williams, with whom Kline was romantically involved). Kasdan wrote a role for him in his Western, *Silverado* (85), procrastinating where buddy Scott Glenn is all for action. Kline thought the role based on himself, but Kasdan explained: 'I didn't say I was writing *you* into the movie. I said I've written a character that I think *you* can play well.' Kline's magnetism was for the first time really shown on screen, and he may have been the first film cowboy to show fear since William S. Hart. He was top-billed over several other names later to achieve prominence (including Kevin Costner and Danny Glover), but this did not benefit him when the film failed to establish that there was still a market for this genre, taking only $16,000,000 on a $26 million budget. Few, however, even heard of Kline's next film, *Violets Are Blue . . .* (86), in which he and Sissy Spacek were high school sweethearts reunited when he is a small town editor and she an internationally-known photojournalist.

He was playing Hamlet when offered a role turned down by Harrison Ford, that of another newspaperman, Donald Woods, in *Cry Freedom!* (87). Woods was the white South African who went to bat for the black victim of Apartheid, Steve Biko (Denzel Washington), and since Biko was the lesser of the two roles, Kline drew back admirably, handing every scene he could to Washington. It could be that the necessarily awkward script

A Fish Called Wanda *(88)*
was a British comedy
which harked back to the
days when every other
British comedy was about
incompetent crooks: its
huge worldwide success
may have betokened
nostalgia for the past – or
that many wanted to catch
John Cleese in his re-run
of Basil Fawlty. That the
film was enjoyable was
mainly due to Kline, who
went cheerfully OTT as
crazy Otto. With him is
Jamie Lee Curtis.

was one reason for the film's failure, at least in the US. There, there might have been resentment that the British mogul Richard Attenborough had been given a huge amount of American money, $29 million, to make a film on a matter of seemingly little concern to white Americans. It took less than $3 million, and was snubbed at Oscar-time. Yet it was nobly, affectingly, done, a large statement on an iniquitous system and, when about Woods, a tribute to a man who put his principles above his country. Attenborough said of Kline that he was 'a complex character, a total chameleon – and an engaging and bewitching man. He can charm the birds off the trees, but he is also terribly shy.'

By contrast, Kline's next film was mediocre and a huge success. John Cleese, who had been in *Silverado*, offered him a supporting role in a vehicle for himself, *A Fish Called Wanda* (88), a British comedy which took over $29 million at the US box-office. Directed by an Ealing veteran, Charles Crichton, its humour harked back to those days, when every other movie crook was as thick as two planks. As one of them, the extrovert and phoney Otto, Kline seized his chance and did his least interesting screen work to date; he was rewarded with a Best Supporting Oscar. More rewardingly he did 'Much Ado About Nothing' opposite Blythe Danner for the Shakespeare Festival: his Benedick, said Les-lie Bennetts in the 'New York Times', 'immediately displays the dazzling physical virtuosity that has so often characterized his performances . . . [his] comedic flair for the antics of self-important swashbucklers has long delighted New York audiences; his Benedick may be brilliant, but he is also vain and hilariously foolish.'

Kline did *The January Man* (89) for writer John Patrick Shanley playing a New York fireman recruited into detective work because his eccentric mind works best that way. He himself called the piece 'a murder mystery-comedy thriller-*film noir*-absurdist-theatrical-naturalistic mess', and the last word was opera-tive for critics, who did not recommend it. He considered playing the Bogart role in *White Hunter, Black Heart*, but instead decided to do *I Love You to Death* (90), a *comédie noire* directed by Kasdan, in which he plays a New York Italian restaurateur whose infidelity to his wife (Tracey Ullman) causes her family to try to murder him. His own wife, Phoebe Cates, has an unbilled guest spot as a girl he tries to pick up. The film was not well received, making that two duds in a row as a star actor. As it came out he directed his own 'Hamlet' in Central Park, a performance rapturously received, and televised in November.

Next up: *Soapdish* (91), with Sally Field, to be followed by *The Mambo Kings Play Songs of Love.*

KRIS KRISTOFFERSON

Kris Kristofferson was the first big male star to sport a beard – but then, it suited the times, like his denims and open-necked shirts and the guitar he carried. He was famous first as a singer–concert artist and recording star, a little bit older than most as these things go, but boyish-looking despite the beard. The background was impossibly romantic – Rhodes scholar and army officer on one hand, and janitor and barman on the other, with stints as football-player, prize-fighter, helicopter pilot and writer. This was the new lifestyle in excess; but had he not written 'Help Me Make It Through the Night'? And was there not a drinking problem? Well, this nice man shared his problems with us; we might help him make it through the night, but he looked so . . . relaxed and relaxing, so confident and masculine in a profession of nonentities.

To fill in the details: he was born in Brownsville, Texas, in 1936, and was a Phi Beta Kappa scholar at Pomona College before going on to Oxford, where he had his first experience as a pop singer under the name of Kris Carson. After his stint in the army he drifted – finally in the direction of Nashville, where in 1965 he began composing and singing his own songs. He was moderately well known when Dennis Hopper asked him to be in a film he made as a result of his involvement with *Easy Rider* called *The Last Movie* (71), an apt title, for the handful who saw it thought it was trying to kill the cinema; among the abstraction was something about a film-unit in Mexico, and Kristofferson had a very brief role playing himself. He starred opposite Gene Hackman in *Cisco Pike* (72), as a washed-up pop singer hounded by him, and what quality the film had came from his personality and his songs. Seemingly typecast, he was the teddy-bearish out-of-work musician who had absconded with George Segal's wife in *Blume in Love* (73), but one who could see more potential was Sam Peckinpah, who cast him as Billy in *Pat Garrett and Billy the Kid*, opposite James Coburn. It was originally to have been directed by Monte Hellman, with Marlon Brando and Jon Voight. When Brando turned it down, Robert Redford agreed to do it, provided Sam Shepard played Billy. It was then shelved until MGM offered it to Peckinpah, who saw a chance to re-create his old West as dirty and dangerous, as it surely was. Alas, a plot was still missing: the two protagonists mill around, having adventures, sleeping with whores, and there is no great urgency about their meeting up. When they do, nothing much happens, which was why MGM cut its running time from 121

minutes to 80; but then the original editors, Roger Spottiswoode and Garth Craven, were permitted to restore the length to 106 minutes. In 1986 Peckinpah's original version was released to theatres, and it worked magnificently.

Peckinpah used Kristofferson again in *Bring Me the Head of Alfredo Garcia* (74), which he also wrote, with a little assistance. The command of the title is issued by a Mexican general whose daughter has been seduced, and it devolves upon a down-and-out pianist-bartender via three thugs (Helmut Dantine, Gig Young, Robert Webber). The pianist is played by Warren Oates, a tower of strength in a performance as beautifully judged as – well, the photography. Kristofferson has a supporting role, as a motor-cyclist intent on rape. 'Please don't,' whimpers the girl (Isela Vega), but when he takes her in his arms she responds as if there was no tomorrow. In a Peckinpah film, once a whore always a whore? At this point the film starts to go downhill, but till then it had looked like a masterpiece, reflective and elegaic: a real Jekyll and Hyde of a movie. The reception of both films proved, alas, that there was no longer an audience for this director's brand of myth-making. Thus Kristofferson was little known for his movie work till comforting Ellen Burstyn in the very popular *Alice Doesn't Live Here Anymore*: he was typecast, and she couldn't have deserved a better fate.

He was, in that film, what most ladies in the audience would have liked to come home to, but he had other ideas about his career and played a villain again: in *Vigilante Force* (76), a Vietnam veteran who, called in as town-tamer, proceeds to wade in corruption to the extent of murder. Not much was heard of the film, but too much was heard of *The Sailor Who Fell from Grace with the Sea*, after a fairly graphic restaging of the sex scenes in 'Playboy': but since the lady concerned, Sarah Miles, was not worth a dead match at the box-office, few bothered to go and see it. In any case, the transference of Mishima's novel of sexual obsession from Japan to Devon was not one of the industry's better ideas. Nor was it a good idea to remake *A Star is Born*, especially with Barbra Streisand, and since they fought throughout filming, Kristofferson may have regretted it; but he was very much liked as an over-the-hill rock star awash with booze. The experience, he said, made him go on the wagon, but there had been reports of concerts when he had not performed well; a 1977 tour with his wife (since 1973), Rita Coolidge, was, however, another matter, and very successful.

In films he and Burt Reynolds were football-players, buddies chasing the same girl

(Jill Clayburgh) in Michael Ritchie's *Semi-Tough* (77); and he and Ali McGraw were in the semi-tough *Convoy* (78) directed by Peckinpah: he was the leader of the convoy, Rubber Duck (as he was called). These films, not very impressive then, represent all that is crude-commercial in the movies of the time, respectively buddy-buddy aimlessness and auto-bashing mindlessness, with above-average directors, anodyne leading ladies and good ol' boy free-spirited heroes whose ethics are little more admirable than the rednecks they are up against. Since Reynolds was riding high at the time, the first took $24,940,000 and the second did $9,500,000 (on a budget of $11 million). Kristofferson should then have started *Hanover Street* in Britain with Geneviève Bujold, but called off at the last minute after reputedly watching one of his movies on TV: he denied this, explaining that he wanted to devote more time to music. 'When I walked away from that movie it was as big a surprise to me as anybody, but I got a feeling I haven't had since I quit the army . . . I had been doing so much, one film after another, with concert tours in betweeen. I fooled myself that I could do everything by working a little harder, but I had really burned myself out.' Earlier, he had said, 'Acting is what I enjoy and do best', but at this point he maintained that he did not care whether he made another movie. *Sans* beard and booze ('I'd just as soon drink gasoline as go back to it'), this minstrel toured, to be lured back into acting soon enough, as a sharecropper battling against a former slave, now in the Senate – Mohammad Ali, whose brief acting career was formally terminated herewith. This was a four-hour mini, *Freedom Road* (79), adapted from the 1944 novel by Howard Fast and directed by Jan Kadar, best known for *The Shop on the High Street*, who died soon thereafter. He was to have supervised a version for foreign cinemas, but foreign cinemas were not interested.

And then came *Heaven's Gate* (80), which left Kristofferson shaken, though it would have felled a lesser man. The saga of this débâcle is told in the book, 'Final Cut', by Stephen Bach, head of production of United Artists at the time, and every one of its 400 pages is an indictment of Michael Cimino, who wrote and directed. The movie concerned an incident in the settlement of the West known as the Johnson County War, when the immigrant population took up arms against the cattle barons. Kristofferson was cast as a Wyoming marshal on the side of the people, on the understanding that it was his appeal which had brought audiences to *Convoy*, despite 'contemptuous reviews': 'There might have been more desirable star names,' wrote Bach, 'but none that wouldn't have distended the budget.' They agreed to a fee of $850,000 plus 10 per cent of the profits, which did not conflict with a total cost of $7,500,000. That would encompass some other names – Jeff Bridges, Christopher Walken, Joseph Cotten – but not such box-office sureties as Jane Fonda or Diane Keaton, wanted for the female lead, since Cimino had promised Kristofferson top-billing; the role went to the ill-cast Isabelle Huppert. In Cimino's quest for perfection and self-aggrandisement (he had just won a couple of Oscars for *The Deer Hunter*), the budget escalated to $36 million, a sum only exceeded by *Cleopatra*, *Star Trek* and *Superman*. At a preview Bach said, 'Kristofferson was no pop idol, here, no supporting actor; he held the screen, a mature, weary man who has seen unpleasant things and expects to see more. At moments he recalled Gary Cooper,' some consolation when the company felt it was on a hiding to nowhere. As indeed it was: 'an unqualified disaster,' said the 'New York Times', one of the kinder reviews. The film took $1,500,000 in its first week and was then withdrawn to find a less gruelling running-time. It reopened in April 1981 to even worse notices and no business whatsoever. There were attempts by some, especially in Europe, to see the film as a triumph of personal vision over Hollywood's commercialism, and if they care to sit through the thing again it is entirely what they deserve. The film's failure brought UA to the market-place and, it could be claimed, it hasn't been the same since.

A clean-shaven Kristofferson teamed with Jane Fonda for *Rollover* (81), directed by Alan J. Pakula, who described it as 'American baroque.' It deals with two characters who believe themselves capable of controlling their worlds [till they] discover that they are themselves being manipulated.' Kristofferson was a banker and Fonda an ex-movie star involved in the world of high finance – a milieu which may have scared general audiences, though with rentals of $6,700,000 this film is hardly the failure it was always said to be. As a thriller, this has at its centre a superb idea: the two chief characters find that the only people they can trust are each other, and for very good reasons they cannot do so. Kristofferson later admitted that he felt 'vulnerable', unnatural without his beard. At all events, his name was associated with two failures, and he was to confess later that there were no offers of work for three years. He changed his agent (and in 1983 married for the third time, Lisa Meyers, a former law student), and found a job opposite Marlo Thomas in a telemovie, *The Lost Honor of Kathryn Beck* (84), an Americanization of the Heinrich Böll novel filmed as *Die Verlorene Ehre der Katharina Blum*. He played the anarchist (Jürgen Prochnow in the original) whose association with the heroine brings her to the attention of police and press. *Flashpoint* partnered him and the always excellent Treat Williams as Texas border patrolmen who stumble over a cache of money from a long-ago crime: a lackadaisical, predictable thriller which did little business. Then Kristofferson supported Willie Nelson in Alan Rudolph's *Songwriter* – ironically, since Nelson arrived in movies, like

himself, after success as a country singer. This is what they both played, with Nelson calling on old chum Kris to help him out when he has trouble with a greedy backer. As it happened, Nelson was not to have a movie career, while Kristofferson, after that hiatus, was to work almost nonstop but with a lower profile than before, in television and often in movies outside the mainstream.

For Rudolph he appeared in one of that director's more typical, undernourished, works, *Trouble in Mind* (85), about various drifters and gangland types in LA. He was an ex-con, an ex-cop imprisoned for taking the law into his own hands, taking up again with the equally world-weary Geneviève Bujold and becoming involved with the problems of Keith Carradine and his bimbo wife, Lori Singer. Kristofferson was really too good for a film which, by juxtaposing the mundane and the lurid, discloses itself as seeing life only through a movie prism: for he was perhaps the most natural actor since Spencer Tracy. All the more pity, perhaps, that he turned to television: *The Last Days of Frank and Jesse James* (86), as Jesse, with the top-billed Johnny Cash (who in 1969 had had a big success with Kristofferson's song, 'Sunday Morning Coming Down') as Frank and with Nelson in a small role, for NBC; *Blood and Orchids*, as a detective in Hawaii whose attempts to get at the truth are frustrated because a navy wife (Sean Young) has been ordered to lie, by her mother (Jane Alexander), about being raped, a four-hour mini for CBS; *Stagecoach*, in John Wayne's old role, with the top-billed Nelson as Doc and Cash as the marshal, for CBS; and *Amerika* (87), as an ex-presidential candidate, now a resistance worker in a USA ruled by the Russians. This one caused much controversy, not least because it lasted over fourteen hours and cost $41 million – which brought back only $22 million in fees from advertisers.

He made two more attempts to prove that the Western was not dead: *The Trackers* (88), directed by John Guillermin, as a retired Indian scout, and *Dead or Alive*, as an avenger on the track of a psychotic religious fanatic (Scott Wilson). The first was made for television; the second turned up on HBO when there was no cinema interest. That, too, was the fate of *Big-Top Pee-wee*, which Randal Kleiser directed; *Pee-wee's Big Adventure* had attracted the curious, to the tune of $18,100,000, so Paramount gave the naif farmboy a bigger budget, $15 million and Kristofferson as co-star – as ringmaster of the visiting circus – but a return of only $7 million indicated that Pee-wee (Paul Reubens) had lost his appeal even quicker than his obvious predecessor, Harry Langdon. Kristofferson had no better luck the following year: *Welcome Home* (89), Franklin Shaffner's last film, had the actor as a POW, presumed dead, who returns to find his wife (JoBeth Williams) happily married; and *Millennium* found him investigating an aircrash and becoming involved with Cheryl Ladd, leader of some martial women of 1,000 years in the future. Poor reviews and co-stars of minimal appeal meant losses respectively for Columbia ($400,000 returned on a $14 million outlay) and 20th-Century-Fox ($2,400,000 on $15 million).

The next two found him on familiar territory: *Pair of Aces* (90) for television, as a widowed Texas Ranger in pursuit of a killer of high-school cheerleaders, and *Perfume of the Cyclone*, an independent production, as a Chicago cop in search of his daughter who has disappeared in the Caribbean. He also appeared in *Sandino*, directed by the distinguished Chilean, Miguel Littin, in a co-production with Spain, a biographical study of the revolutionary leader Augusto Sandino (Joaquim de Almeida); Kristofferson played an American journalist friend. He said recently: 'Acting in films is probably one of the most boring jobs you can do because you're working five minutes and then you're off for an hour. A pilot described to me one time what flying was. He said: "It's hours of boredom interrupted by moments of stark terror." That's acting.' Nevertheless he continues to be prolific: *Helena* with Peter O'Toole, *Ryder*, and *Tipperary* with Drew Barrymore are all in the pipeline.

JESSICA LANGE

Put simply, Jessica Lange is one of the finest actresses Hollywood has found since its great days. 'Her commercial clout, like that of her colleagues Sally Field, Jane Fonda and her Virginia neighbor Sissy Spacek, seems to be on a precipice,' wrote Fred Schruers in 'Premiere' magazine in January 1990, as the second of two Lange films came out in two months . . . Hollywood can be harsh on its failures, as Lange found when she started out, but an actress of Fonda's quality works regularly, despite box-office setbacks, because she can be relied upon to give a performance which will be good, if not outstanding. Lange has not had a successful box-office career, but she should be around equally long.

She was born in Cloquet, Minnesota, in 1949, and attended that state's university; she became involved in acting while there and left to join an experimental underground theatre in New York. She studied mime in Paris for two years before returning to New York, where she took drama lessons, while sometimes working in a Greenwich Village bar and modelling. In 1970 she married a Spaniard, Paco Grande, whom she had met in college and who accompanied her to Paris; the later divorce found her making alimony payments to him. Meanwhile, a friend of his made a short in which she appeared, *Home Is Where the Heart Is*. Dino De Laurentiis found her not in this but via the Wilhelmina modelling agency and she was one of the many who tested for the Fay Wray role in his remake of *King Kong* (76). In the critical mauling the film received, she went generally unnoticed, but seeing it now it is hard to understand why – for she had looks, sexiness and a winning way with a comic line, as when she notes that a movie saved her life (during the shipwreck): she hadn't wanted to see *Deep Throat* and had been up on deck when the explosion occurred. De Laurentiis had put her under exclusive contract for seven years and said no, she says, to the few offers there were for her services. She began a relationship with the dancer Mikhail Baryshnikov and met director-choreographer Bob Fosse, who offered her a supporting role in his autobiographical *All That Jazz* (79), but that took a long time to get started. She appeared in bridal white in some of its more pretentious sequences (of which there were many), turning out to be the angel of death at the end.

She had to sue De Laurentiis to get out of her contract, but nothing more interesting was available than *How to Beat the High Cost of Living* (80), a suburban heist caper in which her partners-in-crime were Susan St James and Jane Curtin (who stole the film); Richard Benjamin was Lange's husband. Director Bob Rafelson selected her for the new version of *The Postman Always Rings Twice* (81) for 'a certain natural sexuality, as opposed to a kind of imposed, artificial acting'. As it happened, the film was too glum, too much a comment on the Depression years, too much an attempt to capture the *amour fou* aspect of the Visconti version – *Ossessione* – and too far from James M. Cain's clever piece of pulp fiction. Jack Nicholson was the drifter who chanced by to seduce Cora (Lange) away from her slob of a husband, but they were both so seedy themselves that it is a relief when she takes a comb to her hair. Their sexual sparring was steamy but not to be compared to that in the Visconti. Still, Lange indicated a disturbing presence and a more versatile screen presence than Streep, Dunaway and Jill Clayburgh, who seemed to have been sharing the leading roles for American film actresses.

It was said that everyone from Jane Fonda downwards had shown an interest in playing

Jessica Lange, right, in one of her few movie-roles in which she looks reasonably like her off-screen self, Tootsie *(82), for which she also won an Oscar. She says that she has, as an actress, a weakness for disguise, because it leads her further from herself and into character: so we have obliged in the other still. Below, she is the hard-working farmer's wife in* Country *(84), which she co-produced.*

Frances (82), that is Frances Farmer, the Hollywood star whose career had ended in arrests for drunken driving and who had subsequently spent her life in mental homes. Lange went after the role with a vengeance but it was no cinch, although the director was to be Graeme Clifford, who had been the editor on *Postman*; but Lange was cast after meeting one of the film's producers, Mel Brooks. She plays Farmer as a jolly, uncomplicated woman whom fate treated badly, never striking a pose nor demanding sympathy – and the chief reason why this film ranked high among Hollywood biopics (though given the others that is not a high recommendation). Kim Stanley, playing Farmer's mother, said of Lange, 'She is such a good, hard worker. And very talented. You haven't seen the end of that yet. She is the *real* article, that lady. And I loved working with her.' It was Ms Stanley who told Lange to follow-up quickly with a comedy role, and she hastened into *Tootsie*, in fact released a month earlier; she played the rather dumb soap opera co-star of Dustin Hoffman, who despite his 'sex-change' sets out to win her from the producer, Dabney Colman. The two films brought Oscar nominations, and she won Best Supporting Actress for this one, letting Best Actress go to Streep. The New

York critics had already voted her their Best Supporting Actress.

On *Frances* Lange had met the actor-playwright Sam Shepard, beginning a lasting relationship which has brought her her third and fourth children. They co-starred in *Country* (84), which Lange co-produced, the tale of an Ohio family having difficulty making a living. It was one of three bucolic tales which came along almost simultaneously, the others being *The River* and *Places of the Heart*, both of which Lange had turned down. Hal Ashby was to have directed her and Shepard, but was replaced by William Witliff (who had written the screenplay), but Lange replaced him with Richard Pearce after some days of shooting. The result was the most satisfactory of the trio – all of which, incidentally, brought Oscar nominations for their leading actresses, with Sally Field beating Lange and Sissy Spacek on the great night itself. Lange made one of her rare television appearances at this time, co-starring with Tommy Lee Jones in 'Cat on a Hot Tin Roof'.

In Spacek's film *The Coalminer's Daughter*, about Loretta Lynn, the role of Patsy Cline was taken by Beverly D'Angelo, who hoped to play it in the Cline biopic, *Sweet Dreams* (85), which was also produced by Bernard Schwartz: but she realized, she said, that there was little hope of doing so once Lange showed interest in the role. Like the Lynn film, this showed the corrosive effects of fame on people of limited intelligence, but it was dullish in comparison, as directed by Karel Reisz. The critic David Robinson wrote that Lange 'is exceptional: her Patsy Cline is open, extrovert, optimistic; and when she's mad she's really mad. Lange can suggest a whole crowd of muddled emotions battling for possession of her; and she conveys uncannily the look of a first-time mother regarding her small miracle.' With Spacek and Diane Keaton she played sisters in Bruce Beresford's *Crimes of the Heart* (86), and as the failed Hollywood singer who had returned home she gave the piece a truth which it lacked elsewhere. Shepard played her ex-lover and they worked together again on *Far North* (88), originally envisaged by her as a quick job to be done on cable TV. Shepard wrote it, not too plausibly, and he made his debut, somewhat self-consciously, as a director; Lange played his wife, a city girl returning to visit her father (Charles Durning). The film's reception by the public was cool, to put it kindly, but there was no warmer reaction to *Everybody's All American*, expected to be a big success as directed by Taylor Hackford. Lange played a vapid Southern belle who learns responsibility while her husband (Dennis Quaid) realizes that fame as a football player is not every-

thing; the film was retitled *When I Fall in Love* for some foreign markets.

Lange was little luckier with *Music Box* (89), though it did bring her an Oscar nomination and such notices as Adrian Turner's in '20/20', who called it 'by far the best thing she has done', and Bruce Williamson's, in 'Playboy', who referred to her 'bone deep, bruising star turn'; she played a Chicago lawyer defending her immigrant father (Armin Mueller-Stahl) against charges of Nazi atrocities in Hungary during the war (strictly speaking, he is accused of lying when applying for naturalization papers and is now to be extradited). Joe Eszterhas's script worked well as a thriller, though you would have to be indulgent about the discoveries so surprisingly made by Lange when seeking the truth, but the courtroom scenes are as tense and serious as we expect from this director, Costa-Gavros, and the hints that the American right is not out of sympathy with the Nazi regime do not come amiss. Paul Brickman's *Men Don't Leave* (90) was a loose remake of *La Vie Continue*, with Lange as a mother coping with the death of a husband and, later, the new man (Arless Howard); she made the character 'a moving and sympathetic figure', said Janel Maslin in the 'New York Times', adding that 'the film gets by mostly on Ms Lange's exceptional ability to hold an audience's attention'. She was certainly at her impressive best, but the film was not a great success. She next appears in *The Stick Wife* for Universal; her 'special relationship' with Orion finds her co-producing *Blue Sky* (91), in which she stars with Tommy Lee Jones, with Tony Richardson directing, after which she co-stars with Robert De Niro and Nick Nolte in a remake of *Cape Fear*.

Interviewed in 1990 she admitted that her

Jessica Lange is probably regarded as the best actress in Hollywood today, but she has in recent years appeared in too many rather downbeat movies to possess a commanding position. She has chosen realism at the expense of glamour, which has not hurt her prestige but it hasn't helped her box-office. None of these films has been more than moderately successful, but they were all honorable efforts – such as Men Don't Leave *(90), about a recently-widowed woman and her two children, Chris O'Donnell, left, and Charlie Kosmo.*

recent roles had been somewhat drab, but then 'I've done dramatic character parts. I haven't done traditional romantic leading lady roles. My choices have come from wanting to push my limits. Each time I choose a role it's to touch parts of me I haven't explored before as an actress.' She also said that she liked to look as different as possible, 'because I like the whole process of disguise – moving into a character who is far away from me.' And this 'may be due to a certain sense of privacy . . . I see it as dangerous when people are thrown into the public eye for who they are. I think it takes a toll on people, professionally and privately.'

VICTOR LANOUX

'France's New Film Idol Is a Cuddly Bear,' said the 'New York Times' in 1978, and it was not the best introduction to an actor of extraordinary talent. True, outside France Lanoux was best known for his amiable hero in *Cousin, Cousine* – and true, it was that which made him a star in France after a decade in films. The French tend to like best not the suave gigolo types of American, Italian or German movies but the sort of homely guy you wouldn't notice if he sat at the next bar-stool – Jouvet, Raimu, Harry Baur, Gabin, Fernandel, Bourvil, de Funès, Belmondo. They like him best in comedy, which helps to keep him human – otherwise, like Gabin and Belmondo they become *monstres sacrés*, and ossify. Lanoux, over forty, can be jowly and paunchy, but the point is that he has a greater range than most European film actors since the young Belmondo.

He was born in Paris in 1936, and evacuated for the war; he returned to Paris at the age of ten, and since he was a poor pupil he left school at fourteen to become an apprentice varnisher. A number of other jobs followed, till at nineteen he found himself on the Simca assembly-line; he went from that to the Algerian War as a parachutist, and returned wounded – which persuaded his father to ask a friend to give him a humble job at the Studio de Billancourt. That experience encouraged him to learn acting by correspondence course, which he quickly realized was hopeless, so he joined a real course; but as odd-job man, since he had no money. Circa 1961 he met Pierre Richard, who was looking for a partner for his cabaret act, and for some years they worked together and wrote sketches – including a season at the Bobino and a tour of 'Le Gorille'. They split when René Allio caught the act and chose Lanoux for a key role in *La Vieille Dame Indigne* (65), as the grandson of

the old lady (Sylvie), gradually coming round to seeing her point of view. That led to a star role in *La Vie Normale*, as a former detainee in a concentration camp whose selfish mother destroys his relationship with the (lady) doctor curing his nervous breakdown: but that was not shown till 1967 – without success. However, Georges Wilson of the Théâtre National Populaire saw the Allio film and engaged him to play Laertes in 'Hamlet'; with the TNP he also did 'La Folle de Chaillot', and then he had a three-year run as star of 'Illusion Comique' – as well as a supporting role in some jet-set whimsy, *Tu Seras Terriblement Gentille* (68). He had another leading stage role, in 'Le Cheval Evanoui' by Françoise Sagan, and during this time wrote two plays, 'Le Péril Bleu' and 'Le Tourniquet'; he returned to films in a supporting role in a heist thriller with Serge Reggiani and Marcel Bozzufi, *Trois Milliards dans l'Ascenseur* (72).

His film career proper began with a good role as Jean Gabin's son in *L'Affaire Dominici* (73), and after living next door to Marthe Keller in a comedy about a young commuter couple, *Elle Court, Elle Court la Banlieue*, he was with Gabin again in *Deux Hommes dans la Ville*. In 1974 the public saw him only on TV, but the following year five Lanoux films were released, starting with Yves Boisset's enjoyable *Dupont Lajoie* (75), a dual study of the French – *en vacances* and as racialists: Lanoux as an ex-parachutist was one of the first to jump to the conclusion that an Arab migrant worker was the murderer. A second film with Boisset, *Folle à Tuer*, found him as a crooked chauffeur who smokes cigarettes through a Dunhill holder and who boasts of raping eighty-six women after threatening them with a vial of vitriol. This was an excellent thriller in its own right, about a kidnapping and the distraught governess (Marlène Jobert): but it was Lanoux who gave it an edge – the best villain in French movies since Jules Berry, and perhaps excelling him in self-satisfaction. He was to observe later that one of the prerogatives of stardom was the opportunity to play unsympathetic star roles, citing Berry as his predecessor.

He was a happy-go-lucky dance-instructor in *Cousin, Cousine*, having an adulterous affair with Marie-Christine Barrault. The movie was a huge success in France, since it provided the French with the view that they like of themselves – sexy, anti-hypocrisy and anti-bourgeois, once given the chance. It was also much liked in the US, and probably brought back patrons who had been put off French movies by later Godard – which may be the best that can be said for it, plus the fact that it made Lanoux a star name. Meanwhile, he had already done supporting roles in *La*

Morte d'un Guide, an ORTF mountain drama which found its way into cinemas, and Granier-Deferre's *Adieu Poulet*, an adroit cop melodrama with Lino Ventura as the investigator and Lanoux as a shady, ruthless politician. Yves Robert's *Un Eléphant ça Trompe Enormément* (76) was about four ageing *copains* who were not quite as 'together' as they thought they were – Lanoux was the philandering one surprised when his wife upped and left: retitled *Pardon Mon Affaire* in Britain and the US, it appealed to the same audiences as *Cousin, Cousine*. Lanoux was a chauffeur again in *Une Femme à sa Fenêtre*, a Greek revolutionary who gets involved with Romy Schneider and the diplomatic set: but the film didn't give him a chance.

His two next films, however, provided chances, and he took them magnificently. Both Bruno Gantillon's *Servante et Maîtresse* (77) and Michel Drach's *Le Passé Simple* were refreshing variations on that tired old genre, the puzzle picture – and both were underrated. Gantillon's film concerned role-reversing in the manner of Genêt, with Lanoux as the dilettante forced into increased humiliation by his former maid and mistress, Andrea Ferreol; Drach's film starred his wife, Marie-José Nat, as an amnesiac fearful of unexplained incidents and the behaviour of husband Lanoux. Neither film suggested the Lanoux as lauded in the 'New York Times', but his range astonished – these men had fear and temper, pathos and an occasional kindness and note of humour. The roles, clearly, had been seen in earlier puzzle films, but never so quietly and spectacularly well acted.

He had a third good movie that year, Claude Berri's *Un Moment d'Egarement*, set sunnily on the Côte d'Azur, where he and Jean-Pierre Marielle have gone for a holiday with their teenage daughters: and it is Lanoux's daughter who begins a clandestine affair with Marielle, who wants to end it before she does. The film works because the playing of both actors is superlative. *Nous Irons Tous au Paradis* (78) was a sequel explained by its foreign title, *Pardon Mon Affaire, Too*; and *La Carapate* was also a comedy, reuniting Lanoux with Richard for a series of adventures, respectively as an escaped convict and the lawyer who had unsuccessfully defended him. Lanoux was again at his formidable best in Etienne Perier's *Un Si Joli Village* (79) as a wealthy factory-worker suspected of murdering his wife. The *juge* (Jean Carmet) making enquiries is cold-shouldered by the workers, and it seems that Lanoux will get away with it – if, that is, he did it. Again this actor is a splendid villain, monstrously arrogant, and yet it is easy to see why he is respected and loved (by his mis-

tress). As the new doctor in town, he acquits himself honourably in *Les Chiens*, with Gérard Depardieu, but the new town in this thriller by Alain Jessua was inspired by *Alphaville* and everything else – including the plot-line – is purloined from *Invasion of the Body-Snatchers*. Changing tone and tack, Lanoux was a bespectacled Jewish father (and son) in a dry and amusing study of a family reunion, Peter Kassovitz's *Au Bout du Bout du Banc*.

Jean-Marie Poiré's *Retour en Force* (80) detailed the deception and disillusionment available to a released prisoner (Lanoux), including his wife's affair with another man (Pierre Mondy). Switching again, Lanoux moved to the other side of the law, a Paris cop unscrupulous in his methods when investigat-

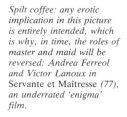

Spilt coffee: any erotic implication in this picture is entirely intended, which is why, in time, the roles of master and maid will be reversed: Andrea Ferreol and Victor Lanoux in Servante et Maîtresse *(77), an underrated 'enigma' film.*

In the films for which we best know Victor Lanoux he has played pleasant, rather shambling men, but it is a matter of record that he is the best French villain since Jules Berry in the pre-War period, capable of making any audience throw rocks at the screen. One of his best is in Un Si Joli Village *(79): he is probably a wife-murderer and is certainly the chief employer in the village – which is why making enquiries is a tough job for the inspector, Jean Carmet.*

ing drug-trafficking in a small town: clearly *Une Sale Affaire* (81), with Jobert. He was also the producer, and it was a big success. He remained a top cop for a comedy, *La Revanche*, which begins with the cheerful idea that his wife (Annie Girardot) writes *policiers* which are widely thought to be his work. Then: *Boulevard des Assassins* (82), another unsympathetic role, as the mayor of a small town in the south of France, and *Y-a-t-il un Français dans la Salle?*, as a politician of advanced years. Cops again: he and Jean Rochefort in Michel Vianey's *Un Dimanche de Flics* (83), much respected and about to retire but tempted when they come across a cache of drugs and money. Lanoux was a cynical, corrupt Swiss war profiteer in *Stella*, a Faustian tale with Thierry Lhermitte as a youngster influenced into collaborating after falling in love with the Jewish Nicole Garcia. After that, Paris theatregoers could see Lanoux in the title-role of 'Grand-père' – a role which came easily to him, he said, as he had three children of his own.

He was a good-humoured Paris aristocrat in the all-star *Louisiana* (84), available to the French as a three-hour movie and to Americans as a six-hour mini. A troubled production history had director Etienne Perier succeeded by Jacques Demy, who was replaced by Philippe de Broca. As a police inspector he pursued the *Voleurs dans la Nuit*, and was involved with crime again in Lee Marvin's French film, *Canicule*. And again in Yannick Bellon's *La Triche*, as a happily married Bordeaux police investigator whose bisexuality has been contained till he meets, in the course of his enquiries, a young jazz musician. A busy year concluded with Jean-Loup Hubert's *La Smala*, a delicious comedy in which Lanoux is a father coping with several children after his wife leaves him. Because of 'Grand-père', there was only one Lanoux film the following year, *National Lampoon's European Vacation* (85), as the thief who causes complications for Chevy Chase and family. This was a supporting role, as was that of Catherine Deneuve's ex-husband in *Le Lieu du Crime* (86), which gave him special billing and hardly a role at all. He played Philip Marlowe in a telefilm, *La Nuit du Flingueur*, and returned to the stage in 'Voisin, Voisine'. Sylvain Madigan's *Sale Destin!* (87) cast Lanoux as a butcher whose well-ordered life goes wrong when his prostitute mistress demands 60 million francs for compromising photographs, which he has no intention of paying: an engaging black comedy.

With decreased activity he did two supporting roles, an ex-cop, stepfather to the star, Eric Blanc, in *L'Invité Surprise* (89), a comedy directed by Georges Lautner, and the

Grand Inquisitor in a grandiose film about Goldoni and Vivaldi, *Venezia Rosso Sangue*. Most of his peers and colleagues had regularly worked in the peninsula, but he had held out till then. In 1990 he appeared in *Simon Mène l'Enguête*, an episode of a police series, 'Renseignements Généraux'.

SHELLEY LONG

As any addict of 'Cheers' will tell you – and was there ever a sitcom more addictive? – Shelley Long is a delectable comedienne, and Hollywood has certainly seen a number of them. In the past, that is: there aren't many around today to match Carole Lombard, Myrna Loy, Claudette Colbert or Jean Arthur, to whom Ryan O'Neal obliquely compares her in *Irreconcilable Differences* (what does he see in her? she asks, and he replies, 'The same as Jimmy Stewart saw in Jean Arthur').

She was born in 1949 in Fort Wayne, Indiana, the daughter of a schoolteacher. She majored in drama at Northwestern University and first found a degree of renown in a local television magazine show, 'Sorting It Out', on which she was co-host and associate producer. That experience tempted her to think that she should specialize in comedy, so she joined Chicago's Second City Improvisational Troupe. Arriving in Los Angeles meant steady employment, if in supporting roles: *The Cracker Factory* (79) for television, with Natalie Wood; *A Small Circle of Friends* (80), a dumb campus comedy; *The Promise of Love* for television, with Valerie Bertinelli; *Caveman*, a uniquely horrible prehistoric comedy with Ringo Starr in the title-role; and *The Princess and the Cabbie* (81), again for TV with Bertinelli in the star role. In most of these Long was a squeaky-clean college-type, but her rather patrician manner, thought director Ron Howard, could make something amusing out of a hooker in *Night Shift* (82) even if, halfway through, she abandons sleazy underwear to be a perfect heroine, the attainable for a confused Henry Winkler. It was an act good enough to bear repeating, so she helped Tom Cruise in *Losin' It* (83) down Mexico way.

These were Long's most prominent roles yet, but she was to become type-cast in something very different, the pretentious, dippy, culture-hungry barmaid, Diane, in 'Cheers', which began in 1982 – not that she was puritanical, because (every now and then) she desired its owner, the libidinous jock Sam Malone (Ted Danson), as much as she despised him. The relationship echoed two

Shelley Long and Bette Midler in Outrageous Fortune *(87), which began amusingly, as the snobbish, priggish Long is plagued by Midler, a good-hearted slob. They discover that their men have both gone missing and then that 'he' is the same man, and that's good for a laugh. But there were precious few more to come.*

classic partnerships, Powell–Loy and Tracy–Hepburn, and as far as technique and heart were concerned, this teaming was not to be found in arrears. The role brought her an Emmy and two Golden Globes, but not – incredibly (or so some people thought) – a chance to do something similar with Danson on the big screen. She returned to that, i.e. comedy, with the charming, funny *Irreconcilable Differences* (84), paired with O'Neal as a couple making it unhappily to the top of the Hollywood jungle. The film's indifferent box-office performance confined her to dealing out drinks in the Boston bar 'Cheers', professionally speaking, till *The Money Pit* (86), in which she watched, aghast, as Tom Hanks attempts to rebuild a decaying country mansion. Returns there were (financial) but few laughs, a situation reprised with *Outrageous Fortune* (87), in which she repeated her 'Cheers' persona, as an earnest young actress partnered with a slob, Bette Midler, looking for the heel they both loved. But the wit and invention of the TV series has given way to four-letter words, with a consequent deterioration of Long's once formidable way with a line. 'Right now,' she said, 'a Shelley Long picture is basically a comedy. I know that, and that's what people expect. I don't want to mess with that concept right now. I think it's going to grow and change as we go along.'

This statement was not only premature, but it ignored the deplorable state of the genre. Said the critic Neil Sinyard, writing in the

October edition that year of 'Photoplay': 'Anyone who saw the 50-year-old classic *Stage Door* on television recently must have been struck by the fact that it had more funny lines than you can find in an entire year of current comedy. Wit seems to have been supplanted by special effects (*Ghostbusters*), vulgarity (*Police Academy*) or by stars like Eddie Murphy and Rodney Dangerfield whose presence is inserted into what are called "vehi-

Shelley Long in Hello Again *(88), another comedy with an engaging idea: she dies, but returns to earth to find that she hasn't been as much missed as she had considered she should be.*

cles" – i.e. projects so feeble that, without the star's input, they would be unable to move even with a back-wind and going downhill.' 'Cheers' had, and has, over its innumerable years, the wit for which Sinyard and others yearn, and it is deeply ironic that Long, in deciding to leave it, as her five-year contract expired, should accept inferior material, simply because this was 'cinema'; and that is a first, incidentally, for no player before Long had had the choice of exchanging superior television for rotten movies. She did, and she blew it.

Now, talking of the comediennes of the past, *Hello Again* (88) was conceived by its writer, Susan Isaacs, 'as a Carole Lombard screwball comedy', with Long as an accident-prone suburban housewife who returns to earth in the manner of Sleeping Beauty to find that her husband has married her best friend and that her teenage son no longer needs her. And so on. Frank Perry produced and directed, opting for farce instead of satire – and since the film was made at Disney, we may be sure that its various committees approved this approach. After their success with *Outrageous Fortune*, they had every reason to suppose that Long's name billed alone above the title was sufficient box-office allure – and indeed, the film pulled in a nifty $8,965,000 despite mixed notices – and a word-of-mouth which was almost wholly unfavourable. At a cost of $18 million Weintraub produced *Troop Beverly Hills* (89), in which Long was a pampered, fussy housewife whose daughter persuades her to take charge of a troupe of boy scouts when her marriage goes on the rocks: a box-office haul of $3,600,000 did not help this financially troubled company. The film was amusing, and deserved better.

She had bad luck with the next two. *Don't Tell Her It's Me* (90) was a callow, boorish comedy about a romantic novelist (Long) intent on turning her wimpy brother (Steve Guttenberg) into a stud, a 'whirling vortex of desire.' *Shattered* was a drama about a woman who, after her marriage has broken up, begins to abuse her child, only to reveal to the therapist (Tom Conti) whom she knows she needs, that she herself was abused as a child. Hemdale, which produced the first, could not overcome poor reviews, while New World, in financial difficulties, sent the second direct to video. In 1990 she signed a year's contract with Ron Howard's company. Long may surprise us. She said once: 'I used to be afraid to play anything less than a brilliant, ambitious, articulate woman because I wanted women to always be regarded that way.' This isn't Diane Chambers speaking, or is it? 'Acting asked a lot of me. I was using the good

parts of myself and connecting with myself internally in ways that I don't always do out in the world'; 'my work is an important priority to me and Bruce's work is to him, so it had to be done [working 12 hours a day shortly after becoming a mother]. We both felt very strongly that the happier I am with my work the more I'll be able to bring to my role as mother.' The husband she refers to is Bruce Tyson, a financial analyst.

ROB LOWE

He is (or was?) '*le nouveau seducteur americain*' to 'Ciné-Revue', for an interview which quoted him as saying that having good looks was almost like an affliction as far as movies were concerned. To be young and beautiful was once a prerogative for movie stardom, but if those requirements went out of fashion, it was only by chance. When he and some other youngsters – Matt Dillon, Tom Cruise, Ralph Macchio, Emilio Estevez, Patrick Swayze, Sean Penn – erupted around the same time they were dubbed 'the brat pack', which was useful for magazines like 'People', which had a new generation to sell. When 'New York' magazine analysed their appeal and success, Tom Cruise came out well, as did Timothy Hutton, 'The Only One with an Oscar' (Best Supporting for *Ordinary People*). Lowe was 'The Most Beautiful Face'. That's what the guy said: he's been trying to live it down.

He was born in 1964 in either Charlottesville, Virginia ('Motion Picture Almanack') or Dayton, Ohio ('Film Review'). What is certain is that his family moved to Los Angeles when he was twelve, and some earlier experience on stage and in local television led to two After-School Specials, 'Schoolboy Father' and 'A Matter of Time'. He played Eileen Brennan's son in an ABC sitcom, 'A New Kind of Family' (79) and also did two pilots which went nowhere, 'Mean Jeans' and 'Thrills and Chills'. He was first noted in a strong role on television – but what may be regarded as his first movie – *Thursday's Child* (82), in the title-role, as the son of Gena Rowlands and Don Murray, a seventeen-year-old whose need for a transplant causes a family crisis. David Lowell Rich directed for CBS, who postponed transmission from this December to February the following year. A month later Lowe was on the big screen with several other youngsters, including most of those listed above, in Coppola's 'cult youth drama', *The Outsiders* (83). Lowe was billed fifth, as Soda-Pop.

He was a schoolboy seduced by an older woman (Jacqueline Bisset) in *Class*, but as that was something the film did not have, he did not become *The Graduate* for a new generation. Still, some young spectators liked the film, but few cared for *The Hotel New Hampshire* (84), in which he was the son of the hotelier (Beau Bridges) and lover of both Nastassja Kinski, who was Susie the Bear, and Jodie Foster, who played his sister. Lowe was top-billed in both – over some much more experienced players. *Oxford Blues* was all his – plus a bit of Julian Sands as his British buddy – and he was welcome to it. Few went to it, but most of them would have recognized a rip-off of *A Yank at Oxford*, in which Robert Taylor was also an arrogant American who doesn't make friends or influence people until he has wowed them with his rowing skills. Ally Sheedy played the girl from back home who always looked like a better bet than patrician Amanda Pays with whom he has been dallying. Only two of Lowe's films had done well, *The Outsiders* and *Class*, but *St Elmo's Fire* (85) reunited him with friends from both casts and other members of the brat pack, in all: Estevez, Andrew McCarthy, Demi Moore, Judd Nelson, Ally Sheedy and Mare Winningham, with Lowe making up seven college graduates facing up to life in the cold, cold world. Actually, it was just another of the myriad teenage pics around at this time, and one of the less substantial, if you can believe that; but with a gross of over $17 million it was Lowe's biggest success to date. He wore his hair long and an ear-ring, a saxophone player and a philanderer whose marriage had come unstuck and who is in hospital for drunken driving. A nice chap, all the same, or so the piece maintained.

Then he was *Youngblood* (86), an ice-hockey player who is seduced by his nympho-maniac landlady and who finds true love with his coach's daughter. He was also an exhibitionist, walking about clad only in a jockstrap, but what's a jockstrap for if not for both glamour and a giggle in teen movies? As for 'About Last Night', it was about, said the ads, 'men, women, choices, sex, ambition, moving in, no sex, risk, underwear, friendship, career moves, strategy, commitment, love, fun, breaking up, making up, bedtime, last night . . .' a claim that looked somewhat desperate (and there was no underwear to be seen, though perhaps it was worn). They would probably have got more people in if they had kept the original title of David Mamet's play, 'Sexual Perversity in Chicago', but it was thought that some newspapers would not accept ads – while it might also have suggested life among the same-sex set. Lowe and Demi Moore in fact meet in what might be a Singles bar, and they take it from there, with help and hindrance from their friends, James Belushi

and Elizabeth Perkins. They joke all the time, inasmuch as they must cloak their uncertainties – sex is the only certainty – in play. Seldom have movies been as accurate on the way lovers test each other, on coping with the loss of privacy, on accepting that there was a previous existence, on never being sure that this one will last, on whether to make the ultimate commitment: the only thing was, Mamet's play was about much older lovers, hence its title, a couple who between them had had too many relationships but still had not learnt enough to make this one work. Provided that you accepted the producers' belief that movie audiences were not interested in older lovers, this film worked quite nicely as directed by Edward Zwick, and it made a very pleasing $16 million.

In order to be accepted as a serious actor, Lowe accepted fourth-billing and a subsidiary role in Daniel Petrie's *Square Dance* (87), a bucolic drama about a thirteen-year-old (Winona Ryder), her grandfather (Jason Robards) and mother (Jane Alexander). Lowe was the mentally retarded violin-playing

Rob Lowe in Square Dance *(87), as an emotionally disturbed youngster who becomes a love object for a growing girl, played by Winona Ryder.*

Lowe, as handsome a lout as movies have had since Robert Taylor, has difficulty in living down his looks: but it becomes easier as his range widens, and he was notably fine in Masquerade *(88), as a seemingly wealthy beach-boy who is up to no good.*

boy the girl gets a crush on. The film did little for Lowe – or much business – but he stretched himself again in Bob Swaim's *Masquerade* (88) as either a wealthy playboy or, as one character calls him, 'a two-dollar gigolo'. Meg Tilly is the wealthy girl who falls for him hook, line and singer, not knowing (as we do) that he is in the employ of the malevolent stepfather who lives off her wealth. The film took $6,800,000, but since none of Lowe's starring vehicles have figured on 'Variety''s lists of 'Big Buck' movies, it is clear that they have all been modestly budgeted, accommodating his salary of a reported $400,000–$600,000. That would be a reasonable figure for one of his renown, which could not have been hurt by reported romances with Princess Stephanie of Monaco and Fawn Hall of Washington notoriety. Peter Bogdanovich's *Illegally Yours* was one of those films swept aside as its producers, the De Laurentiis Entertainment Group, faced financial difficulties; Lowe played a juryman who recognizes in the defendant a schoolboy crush, and thus sets about proving that she is innocent.

He was himself involved with the law when cited as using 'his celebrity status as an inducement to engage in sexual intercourse, sodomy and multiple party sexual activity for his immediate sexual gratification, and for the purpose of making pornographic films of those activities' – the latest in the ever-recurring Hollywood sex scandals, and perhaps the funniest. What the silly man had done was to have invited two girls, sixteen and twenty-two, to his room at the Atlanta Hilton while in that city for a political rally; he had apparently set up his videocamera and, after falling asleep, been in no position to stop them when the two wronged women made off with the evidence. This was in July 1988; the case was filed by a Mrs Parsons, mother of the younger girl, in May 1989, after what Lowe's attorneys described as attempt to 'extort the actor before going public in the suit'. Arsenio Hall observed that at last 'Rob Lowe has made a movie everyone wants to see', but what was not funny was the prospect of a twenty-year prison sentence ending Lowe's career. Found guilty, he might have been fined $100,000, and in fact he did lose financially because the Japanese company Suzuki had paid him $500,000 for a commercial and claimed that they could no longer use it. Still, they waited till after the case was dismissed before asking for their money back. Lowe was ordered to put in twenty hours of community service in LA, since he was technically guilty.

Lowe's one film during this period was *Bad Influence* (90), a Faustian tale in which he was a baby-faced schizoid leading yuppie James Spader into trouble, including videotaping him while having sex in downtown LA. Transworld produced, and Moshe Diamant, the company's co-chairman, explained: 'In terms of box-office, we'd been thinking Tom Cruise, Kevin Costner. In real terms, we'd been looking at a higher caliber of actor than Lowe – Nick Cage, Robert Downey. With Rob, the question was, "Does the personality eclipse the talent?"' What turned the trick was that Lowe's name could sell the film overseas. Curtis Hanson directed on a modest $7 million budget, and the film took more than that in its first ten days in release, but it did not do substantial business, perhaps because he should have stayed away from videotapes . . . And he might have done, since he thought originally that they wanted him for the Spader role, and he let himself be talked into the other one. Next up: *Helena (a Woman With a Dream)* with F. Murray Abraham; *Team 6* (the fourth retitling during production of this sea drama) for Menahem Golan; and *If the Shoe Fits*, made in Paris with Jennifer Grey. In February 1991 he is scheduled to play Brick in 'Cat on a Hot Tin Roof' in New Orleans.

MADONNA

As *Dick Tracy* opened to a breathlessly expectant world, Miss Madonna's publicity machine worked overtime. Alternatively, here was a woman of genuine talent, beauty and mystery about whom everyone was curious. There is another supposition, and the most likely, that she was the nearest the movies had now got to a sex symbol and was *ergo* of fascination *per se*. The last to get the treatment was Joan Collins, who had been *passée* for thirty years anyway, but a television soap had brought her new fame. These were desperate times. Marilyn Monroe, dead for thirty years, was still in everyone's consciousness. Why Madonna? She is an actress of small talent. She embarked on a concert tour to coincide with publicity for the film, and although that was a sell-out, her career as a movie star – which was what she desperately wanted to be – had consistently failed to get off the ground. Of course, *Dick Tracy* was an event: its cost was high, its ad budget was huge and Disney was into marketing the film in a way that vanquished its fifty years of selling Mickey Mouse. Madonna's romance with her co-star, Warren Beatty, was such a foregone conclusion as to be newsworthy. He was Hollywood's leading stud, and since she dressed like a hooker he automatically found her irresistible. Among the acres of newsprint devoted to *him* at this time it could be learnt that although he disliked press intrusion into his private life his name was seldom linked with a nobody. A well publicized affair with Madonna could only be beneficial for business; it hardly matters if, in life, they never spoke off the set. With people more intoxicated with their own fame (*why* does she want to be a film star?) than with what talent they have to offer, it is hard to care one way or the other. What's depressing is that the hacks think we do. And what is even more depressing is that we are not talking only of the tabloids, for whom celebrities like Madonna are common coinage.

She was born, Madonna Louise Veronica Ciccone, in Bay City, near Detroit, Michigan, in 1958, the third child in a family of eight, into a strict Italian Catholic environment. Her mother died when she was either five or seven (bios of the lady are not notable for their consistency), and she was educated at a convent school. One source says she planned on becoming a nun; most of the others, quoting the lady herself, agree that she was determined to be noticed as much as possible, whether by hanging upside down on the bars of the gym in coloured underwear or dressing like a floozie – 'Only because we knew our parents didn't like it.' She studied at the University of Michigan – certainly dance for three terms, though perhaps also art history and music theory. According to one source, she arrived in New York and told a cab-driver to take her where the action was, and to another she won a scholarship to the Alvin Ailey American Dance Theater. She auditioned for a job in a Paris disco, but quickly grew tired of that; back in New York she modelled nude for photographers and art classes, and made her movie debut in a soft porn feature, *A Certain Sacrifice* (79). After that she became a waitress, throwing in some dance routines for customer delectation, tearing at her leotard 'just to get myself noticed . . . Everybody knows I'm a bad girl.'

With two brothers she formed the Breakfast Club, but it was a demo-tape of one of her own songs which led to a recording contract in 1982. She had had several disco successes by the time she was approached to make another movie, but her brief appearance singing 'Crazy for You' does not indicate that audiences would be interested in her. The picture was *Vision Quest* (85), Harold Becker directed, and it starred Matthew Modine as a mixed-up high school student. *Desperately Seeking Susan*, usually given as her debut, was released two months later. She had auditioned for the director, Susan Seidelman, for the role of Susan, which was not the lead but it was crucial – since there is a contract out for her, and the heat is on when the would-be killer mistakes a bored New Jersey housewife (Rosanna Arquette) for Susan. This is an old plot: the bourgeois housewife who by chance gets caught up in mayhem – and romance – such as she never imagined. There were several original flourishes, not least the character of Susan, living off her wits and sex and not giving a damn what anyone thinks. As her concert costumes also make clear, she may be the first artist outside a porn movie to cater to masculine appreciation of garter-belts, but they look as though they came from the bargain basement of a sex-shop; with her punk trimmings she looked as though she had been dragged through a hedge backwards. It

Griffin Dunne, John Mills and Madonna in Who's That Girl? *(87). 'Who cares?' was the response of one critic (as mentioned in the text, but a good joke is always worth repeating).*

The Club Ritz on New Year's Eve: Dick Tracy *(90), with which Madonna's film fortunes finally turned around.*

was not a propitious day for sex on the screen, nor for a film career, since she had little screen presence or acting ability.

Still, since she was certainly noticed in it, she could take some credit for its take of over $10 million. A screen career seemed a possibility when she married Sean Penn, but their co-starring venture, *Shanghai Surprise* (86), was laughed off the screen. Their off-set antics found them the sobriquet 'The Poison Penns', with more bad publicity for both when Penn left her bound and gagged over New Year's Eve in 1988 (unsurprisingly, they were divorced a while later). In the meantime, she had starred with Griffin Dunne in James Foley's *Who's That Girl?* (87), a comedy in which she makes life hell for him while on parole and seeking the guy who framed her. 'Who's that girl? Who cares?' said one critic, Alan Frank, cruelly prophesying the world's reaction. In the wake of this second disaster her production company, Siren Films, moved from Universal to Columbia in a two-year development deal which gave them first refusal of any projects. Announced but not made: *Blessing in Disguise*; *Three of Hearts*, a lesbian drama with Robert Downey Jr and perhaps Demi Moore and Elizabeth McGovern; and, at 20th Century-Fox, a remake of *The Blue Angel*. While the film industry hesitated, Madonna struck: the unlucky one was David Mamet, who had written a play, 'Speed-the-Plough'. She said, 'I pursued it like a motherfucker . . . The character is so unlike me, dresses so unlike me, takes shit so unlike me. That's what I had to do because people kept on saying, she's just playing herself.' After some hesitation Mamet cast her, as secretary to a Hollywood mogul, and she did the play for six months alongside Joe Mantegna and Ron Silver. Her notices did not salute a blazing new actress, but were cautiously welcoming.

She did another movie, well cast at last as one of Damon Runyon's dolls, *Bloodhounds of Broadway* (89), left on the shelf when its producing company, Vestron, had financial difficulties. Columbia took over distribution but could not get many bookings. In 1990 'Variety' reported that Siren Films 'was booted off the Columbia lot' after its agreement had expired. She reputedly turned down the role Michelle Pfeiffer played in *The Fabulous Baker Boys* and was herself turned down for *The Godfather III* on the grounds that she would make Robert De Niro (who was then going to do it) look too old. Vamping Beatty in *Dick Tracy* (90) may just prevent her from becoming the Anna Sten *de nos jours*. That may have to be the climax of an extraordinary decade for Madonna, called 'the most famous woman in the world' by

'Rolling Stone'. 'For me it was super-stardom from the word go,' she said in 1983 to Luca Brasi, who celebrated the opening of *Batman* with this comment in the 'Sunday Correspondent': '[she] still inspires an astonishing amount of simpering fascination. By all the rules she should be despised by the arbiters of What is Hip, but so cannily has she played her game for eight years that people admire the brazenness which offends in others . . . there is the little question of her musical talent. That she cannot sing to save her life, and quite rightly felt terrified at the prospect of singing three Stephen Sondheim songs on the *Dick Tracy* soundtrack, is something with which only the most besotted fan would argue.' (Apparently Sondheim owed Beatty a favour.) This journalist mentions 'a trite monologue' in 'Vogue', listing Madonna as the latest of the blonde icons of film and pop history, from Dietrich to Debbie Harry – as appropriated by the star herself in her stage act. She intends to extend this process, threatening us with – just what the world needs – a remake of *Some Like It Hot*. In the meantime, due to the cautiously warm notices for her in *Dick Tracy*, she has no less than four movies lined up: the 1991 Woody Allen treat (so far untitled); *Soapdish*, with Sally Field; *Blessing in Disguise* reactivated, from her own production company; and *Leda and the Swan*. She is also reported to be the lead in *Evita*, a property which Disney has bought from the ailing Weintraub.

JOHN MALKOVICH

The best thing he ever heard about actors, said John Malkovich, was David Lean's comment that 'they are lovely to go to dinner with but they can be a bit of a nuisance on the set.' Malkovich also explained that he wasn't really a film actor: 'I probably know a lot more technically than most film actors about lenses and lights and things like that, but basically to be effective I need the sequence of events behind me. I get that in the theatre every night, which I find freeing in a way.' He also said of the theatre company he founded: 'What we were doing was better, that's all. We started out to try and do good work for its own sake. That has nothing to do with theatre in New York. Yeah, they want to do good work once they're doing it, but basically it's more to do with where that'll get them. That's perfectly natural, but not necessarily acceptable or right. If you did a good play in New York you got a little lead spot on "Kojak". That's not for me.' And: 'Generally you act in movies because you are too lazy to

act in theatre, or you can't, or you want a lot of money, or you want to be really famous.' He qualified on the money question, he admitted, but went on: 'And at times it's been an opportunity to work with some really good people. But I like to do things for myself, and on film you have a lot more people bothering you. If a cinematographer has his walkie-talkie on to cue a light during a difficult scene he'll hear from me and it won't be charming. You have to force yourself to be mean.' Malkovich talks about acting because that is what he does for a living. He isn't, like half the stars in movies today, a former stand-up comic whose need to be a movie star is so great that that is what he is. He is an anachronism – because, as it happens, he doesn't have movie-star looks; but he may be the most talented man now making pictures.

He was born in Benton, Illinois, in 1953, to a father who was the son of Yugoslav immigrants and who himself became a publisher and a director of the State Conservation Department. Young Malkovich went to Illinois State University in Normal, Ill., where he initially studied sociology and music, but changed to theatre for his degree. He had acted at college and formed the idea of his own company, to be led by himself and Gary Sinise. They called themselves Steppenwolf, and the first Steppenwolf Theater, in 1976, was in the basement of a church that was rented for $10 a month. Six years later, the co-operative of thirteen people moved to their third home, a proper theatre, though it had at one time been a chocolate factory. In that time they had mounted sixty plays, twenty of them directed by Malkovich; among those in which he appeared are 'The Lovers', 'The Glass Menagerie', 'The Birthday Party', 'Of Mice and Men' (as Lennie) and 'No Man's Land'. He also did small roles in two telefilms, *Word of Honor* (81) and *American Dream*, an experience which caused him to think about breaking away from Steppenwolf. In 1982 Steppenwolf decided to take their production of Sam Shepard's 'True West' to New York, where Malkovich won the Obie Award for his performance. As a result he was simultaneously offered the role of Biff in 'Death of a Salesman' on Broadway, with Dustin Hoffman, and a role in *Places of the Heart* (84). He preferred the play to the movie, but was disinclined to do it for a whole year; Hoffman was happy to accommodate him as far as rehearsals were concerned, and sent him off to the movie – to be made by Robert Benton, who had directed Hoffman to his Oscar-winning performance in *Kramer vs Kramer*. What Malkovich was to play in Mr Benton's bucolic piece with Sally Field was a blind man, and he was one of the few since movies began to do so with conviction. (Probably the worst depiction of blindness in movies is Michèle Morgan in *La Symphonie Pastorale*, looking steadily before her.) Malkovich constantly moved his head and his eyes as the blind do, trying to catch something in a shaft of light. It was a brave and moving performance.

Two months later he erupted into *The Killing Fields*, as the tearaway photographer colleague of journalist Sam Waterston. He did the play with Hoffman, and while doing so directed Lanford Wilson's 'Balm in Gilead' off-Broadway, to be rewarded by a clutch of prizes. After the play had duplicated its New York success in Chicago, he went to Greece to make *Eleni* (85) under the direction of Peter Yates, with a screenplay by Steve Tesich from the book by Nicolas Gage. Gage, later an investigative reporter on the 'New York Times', had left Greece as a boy, when his mother was executed in the Civil War in 1948; he had gone back in a spirit of revenge, with autobiographical passages about mother and his childhood which he acknowledged were partly fictional. These became flashbacks in the film, with Kate Nelligan as Gage's mother; Glenn Headly, Malkovich's own wife, had a small role as his wife in the film: for he was the obsessed Gage, giving the part more than it needed. 'I thought I was pretty bad,' he said later, and there were few who disagreed. If he planned a career as a leading man on screen, the film's failure was a setback. In New York he directed Raul Julia in 'Arms and the Man', and he played Biff again in Volker Schlöndorff's television version of *Death of a Salesman*, shown in some cinemas overseas. Hoffman and the author, Arthur Miller, had been astonished to see Malkovich seeking out the poetic aspect of Biff. Seeing this movie, one cannot imagine that the role has been better played. This is Biff, raw, boisterous, sensitive, the elder brother and the disappointed son. His performance later won him an Emmy.

He had a dual role in *Making Mr Right* (87), as a scientist and the robot, due to be sent out in space, he has designed in his own image – and one with more sex appeal than himself for, sure enough, there is a girl (Ann Magnusson) to fall in love with him. Malkovich was grateful to the director, Susan Seidelman, for giving him a shot at comedy, because the film 'is really a lot closer to the way I see myself than much of the serious work I've done.' He is a delight in both roles, but there the delights end. It was the first film this director made after her promising debut with *Desperately Seeking Susan*, when she was still being given the benefit of the doubt. Malkovich had a superior talent in Paul Newman, directing his wife Joanne Woodward in *The Glass Mena-gerie*, but coming little closer to making it really cinematic than Schlöndorff had done with Miller's play. This was by Tennessee Williams, and he let it speak for itself, with four superb performances. Malkovich played the autobiographical Tom and for perhaps the first time this was not a piece about a timid girl, and her mother's hopes for her, but about a boy recalling his past. Because of this actor's strength, his angular gestures (just enough to suggest he is gay), his quiet gaze, it is a study of a youth who is unhappy and at home. Malkovich completed the year in another classy autobiographical production, *Empire of the Sun*, directed by Steven Spielberg from J.G. Ballard's novel based on his experiences in China during the war. Most of the time he was in a Detention Centre, and here in the film is Malkovich carrying on like William Holden in *Stalag 17*, but less amusingly. Indeed, it was an arid epic, going nowhere slowly, and even Malkovich's wheeler-dealer was of little interest. He said later that he didn't care for the book, or Tom Stoppard's script, that Spielberg was 'warm' and Stoppard 'cold', and that from those opposing stand-points they thought that they could get an interesting performance from someone described as 'a major talent that could put something into the role which wasn't there in the writing. I couldn't.' At this point he returned to Broadway when Lanford Wilson's play 'Burn This' transferred from the Circle Rep, taking over the leading role from Cotter Smith, who was more threatening and ambiguous. Malkovich played for laughs, of which this amiable piece had already enough.

When Sinise was given the chance to direct a movie, *Miles From Home* (88) with Richard Gere, Malkovich put in a guest appearance, as Barry Maxwell, the 'Rolling Stone' reporter who turned the Roberts brothers into national heroes. Christopher Hampton, author of the original play, chose him for the film of *Dangerous Liaisons* (88). He was certainly a name, unlike Alan Rickman, who had created the role. Malkovich, after paying tribute to Rickman's 'magnificent' performance in *Die Hard*, had not liked his interpretation in the play – and, in any case, knew he would do it differently. His Valmont is a rake who has somewhat tired of debauchery, but cannot resist the challenge offered – just as de Laclos had it, at greater length, in the book. You could call him vulpine, but in 'Newsweek' David Ansen said his 'snaky charm is both droll and potent', while in the 'New York Times' Vincent Canby pointed out that 'Malkovich's intelligence and strength shape the audience's response.' Also on display this season was *The Accidental Tourist*, with himself and Phyllis Carlyle credited as executive

'Acting to die for' said one London critic when John Malkovich appeared on stage in that city in 1990: moviegoers had already come to the same conclusion. Malkovich in Places in the Heart *(84), top left, as the blind man; in* The Killing Fields *(84), top right as the spaced-out photojournalist; in* Eleni *(85), bottom left, as* New York Times *reporter Nicolas Gage; and as the decadent aristocrat Valmont in* Dangerous Liaisons *(88).*

Malkovich and Debra Winger in The Sheltering Sky, *based on the novel by Paul Bowles which finally came to the screen, after several failed attempts, in 1990.*

film was warmly received. With three films in the can: *Queen's Logic* (90), *The Sheltering Sky* with Debra Winger and *The Object of Beauty* with Andie MacDowell, he decided to try 'Burn This' with a London audience, and the small, suburban Hampstead Theatre obliged. The notices for the play itself were only fair, but those for Malkovich ensured that, transferred to the West End for a limited run, it would play to capacity for every performance. After London, he plays a clown in Woody Allen's new film (91), so far untitled, and the returns to Britain to do a play for the BBC, Harold Pinter's 'Old Times'; and in 1991 he will probably make his debut as a movie director.

London's critics were certain that no American actor since Brando had had such an electrifying and powerful presence. It may be hoped that movies and he will serve each other well, but, as Alan Arkin most recently proved, no amount of talent can compensate for the lack of conventional movie-star looks. In Arkin's case the good offers simply dried up in middle age, but Malkovich can be striking in looks, if not handsome. He can always find a handy toupee, as he has for most of his movie roles since the first two. 'For a long time I played brooding, James Dean types,' he said. 'I was kind of relieved when my hair fell out and I didn't have to do that any more.'

STEVE MARTIN

Steve Martin is in the great tradition of American funny men. It includes one genius, Buster Keaton, and several others of rare talent, including W.C. Fields and Groucho Marx. Like Fields and Keaton, he is often responsible for his own material. This is true of several of his rivals today, and the adjective which best suits him, 'manic', can also be applied to many of them. Why, then, is he so far in front? Let us say that Robin Williams is out there with him, and what they both possess is a quality common in the great age of stars but little known today, charm. But when he is manic, obsessed, his whole body is contorted; he is like something demented. He has heart and he has innocence, which is why his cry that he's a wild and crazy guy has so much resonance. Unlike many of the others who began their careers as stand-up comics, he has mastered physical comedy. It took him a month to work out the walk he uses in *All of Me* – not that it shows. He has ease. He said, 'Someone once described me as a guy who saw Fred Astaire and said, "I can do that."' Nevertheless, the films he chooses to

producers for Warners: some while previously, while working a production partnership, she had recommended Ann Tyler's novel as a vehicle for himself – and they had followed through, but with Lawrence Kasdan directing William Hurt in the leading role. He didn't like the result, but had not interfered after choosing Kasdan as the director; he liked Hurt's performance but thought both women 'disastrous', Kathleen Turner because she was miscast, and Geena Davis because she was unable to play what the role required, 'the pain of grief'.

He turned down the role eventually played by Timothy Dalton in *The King's Whore*, and left the cast of *Crazy People* when Tony Bill replaced its writer, Mitch Markowitz, who was making his directorial debut. Malkovich said that he was depressed, partly due to the break-up of his marriage (and that was partly due to an affair with Michelle Pfeiffer, one of his co-stars in *Dangerous Liaisons*). He also explained: 'If it had been really fun or something, it would have been right to start all over. I just didn't feel like it, really.' No mention was made of how much material was usable for the two weeks Malkovich had been on the film, but he was later to clarify the situation: 'You become uninsurable for a while. How can you expect people to invest ten or twenty million dollars in your work if you then suddenly decide you don't like it . . . I probably wouldn't do it again no matter how much I hated something.' He was replaced by the 'available' Dudley Moore, which is not the same thing at all; and even with Moore the do may require him to act up outrageously, and the results are correspondingly rewarding.

He was born in Waco, Texas, in 1945, and had his first contact with show business while living in California just along the way from Disneyland. He got after-school work there, selling guide-books and working in Merlin's Magic Workshop. He took the opportunity to study Wally Boag, whose vaudeville act consisted of making animals from balloons, and Christopher Fair, a juggler. Apart from teaching himself magic, juggling and the banjo he acted with an amateur theatre group. Betweenwhiles he studied symbolic logic at Long Beach State University. He moved into show business proper as a writer for 'The Smother Brothers Comedy Show'; he also wrote television material for Glen Campbell, Pat Paulsen and Sonny and Cher. During this period, Bill McEuen, whom he had known at school, became his manager, and they agreed that Martin should not be providing other people with material for the rest of his life. McEuen also managed the Nitty Gritty Dirt Band, so Martin became their opening act. He did this for other rock groups, 'a total drug casualty,' he admitted later. 'I had a beard and long hair. I wore a turquoise squash-blossom necklace and a conch-shell belt. . .' He decided he had had enough of this after two years, and changed his image to open for a middle-of-the-road group, The Carpenters.

The first time he headlined on his own was in Coconut Grove, Florida, and when he received a rave in the 'Miami Herald' he knew he was on his way. He started to appear on Johnny Carson's 'Tonight Show' in 1973 and was in 'Saturday Night Live' (76). McEuen had taken dozens of recordings of Martin's acts, and he sold an assembly to Warner Bros, which became a bestselling album, 'Let's Get Laid'. With that under his belt, Martin began to do SRO business in some of the country's biggest halls. McEuen arranged for David Picker, then head of Paramount, to catch his act in San Francisco. Paramount offered a contract, and put him into a short which he had written himself, *The Absent-Minded Waiter* (77). But, he said later, Paramount hated the deal and cancelled it when Picker left. They let him keep the short, which he successfully entered for an Academy Award nomination, and the $50,000 they had paid for a feature screenplay. He took it over to Universal, who immediately green-lighted it. Meanwhile he was one of several guest stars in *Sergeant Pepper's Lonely Hearts Club Band* (78), Robert Stigwood's failed attempt to have the world watch the Bee Gees horsing around to music by the Beatles. He was one of several names appearing briefly as themselves in a documentary on The Who, *The Kids Are Alright* (79) and again in *The Muppet Movie*, in which he was an insolent waiter.

That film-script, written by Martin and Carl Gottlieb (with an assist on the screenplay itself by Michael Elias) became *The Jerk*, with Carl Reiner in the director's chair. It traded on much of Martin's stage material, including the line, 'I was born a poor black child' – for Martin was a white foundling, guileless, ignorant and clumsy, brought up in a family of black Mississippi share-croppers. Told the truth about himself, he says, 'You means I'm gonna *stay* this colour?' despairingly before going out in the big world to examine his white inheritance. His adventures sharply divided the critics, some of whom found it patronizing and meandering. In truth, Martin seemed to be emulating Mel Brooks, even to using Brooks' worst gag, the knee in the groin. The public however, was in no doubt: the movie took almost $43 million on an outlay of $4,500,000. Seeing it again years later, Martin observed that he yelled too much, but 'it's a great first film'. He did not know what he wanted to do next: not *The Jerk 2*, nor his stand-up act – but that was what he did, reluctantly, and 'very depressed'. He was in Las Vegas when his agent sent him the screenplay of *Pennies From Heaven* (81), which director Herbert Ross had persuaded MGM to buy after seeing the BBC series. The original author, Dennis Potter, had Americanized it without making any improvement, and it remained a dreary, uninvolving story about a travelling salesman who, during the Depression, commits adultery with a schoolteacher who later becomes a hooker. Potter's use of the records of the time, to which the stars mimed, showed that he understood the songs as little as he did the period – but where Bob Hoskins in the original was loud and out of joint, Martin was likely and ingenuous. With his hair sleeked down and dyed dark (from its white-grey), he looked like a composite of the crooners of the thirties. Hoofing, he and/or Bernadette Peters (who was also in *The Jerk*) made this disaster bearable and sometimes more than that. The numbers were often lavish, staged with the old Hollywood pizzazz – one reason the film cost $22 million. Given the reviews, the film was lucky to take $3,600,000.

It also proved to Martin that he could have a career in movies. *Dead Men Don't Wear Plaid* (82) was written by him, Reiner (who also directed) and George Gipe, after a discussion on whether a movie could be built around old film-clips. In this one the clips are inserted – into a cod Chandleresque story, so Martin may be seen chatting with Davis, Stanwyck, Bergman and other ladies of the

Steve Martin looking content, and why not? – because he's The Man With Two Brains *(83). One of them is in a jar, and he's pretty obsessive about it.*

his guide is Charles Grodin who, as so often, runs away with the film. Arthur Hiller directed from a novel by Bruce Jay Friedman, adapted by Neil Simon.

After three failures, Martin 'didn't know what to do, what kind of movie to make, or if I was even going to make a movie.' Thus he hesitated when Reiner sent him the screenplay of *All of Me*. Martin perhaps wanted to avoid the 'anything goes' humour which characterizes much of Reiner's work, but this time he had a well-tailored script by Phil Alden Robinson, based on a novel by Ed Davis, 'Me Two'. The premise is that due to a metaphysical mishap a conscientious lawyer (Martin) finds his body inhabited by a recently deceased rich bitch (Lily Tomlin). It's a situation Thorne Smith would have revelled in, but in matters of sex this film is even more timid than the 1940 film of his *Turnabout*. It is also bland when it might have been mordant, which may be why it did poorly overseas. But it turned the trick for Martin in the US, where the New York Critics Circle voted him the Year's Best Actor and where it took $15,220,000 on a $12 million budget. Playing a pawn in the machinations of Tomlin (to get into the right body) and Martin (to get rid of her) is the English actress, Victoria Tennant, whom Martin married in 1986. Meanwhile he did a guest spot, as an ageless matinee idol, in *Movers and Shakers* (85), written and co-produced by Grodin, who had been trying to get this made for years; Grodin also starred in this supposed satire on a Hollywood studio trying to wrench a script out of a book called 'Sex in Love'. *Three Amigos* (86) starts with a splendid idea: Martin, Chevy Chase and Martin Short are Hollywood cowboys who, sacked by their studio, wander south of the border to find that they are expected to be as dirty and dangerous as they are on the screen. Martin wrote the script with Lorne Michaels and Randy Newman, whose excellent parody songs include one for a Singing Bush. Martin was disappointed by the result; he had wanted 'a big, dumb comedy. A lot of laughs, a lot of big, dumb situations. It became more of an action picture', adding on another occasion that he would like to remake it without John Landis, who directed.

Frank Oz directed *Little Shop of Horrors*, based on the musical in turn based on the 1960 film of Roger Corman. Rick Moranis was top-billed and Martin did an extended cameo as Dr Orin Scrivello, DDS (Drop Dead Sadist), a demented dentist whose biggest hang-up is Elvis Presley. He said he 'liked the bigness of that character and his complete stupidity-with-confidence' – the latter is a quality he had had in his act and he thought it 'a great thing' to play. Throughout these films Martin

film noir, while he kept his hair dark in order to be front-of-face for Bogart, Fred MacMurray and so on. It was a one-time gimmick, but enjoyable, returing $11,500,000 on its $10 million budget. The same team collaborated on the not dissimilar *The Man With Two Brains* (83), inasmuch as it's a send-up of mad doctor movies. Martin plays Dr Hfuhruhurr, a brilliant brain surgeon, who goes to Vienna with his new, already contemptuous wife (Kathleen Turner), to meed his idol (David Warner) in his Frankenstein-like laboratory. For a while the combination of sex comedy, black comedy and spoof becomes too rich and yet undernourishing, but Martin's dogged presence, eliding now and then to paranoia, is very taking. The film cost $10 million, but took only $4,600,000, which was why it went direct to video in most territories – as did *The Lonely Guy* (84), after returning only $2,300,000 of its $14 million budget. The title-role provided Martin with a change of pace, as a meek man who discovers others as lonely as he after being thrown out by his girlfriend;

had shown indications of wanting to grow up, to move out of the current Hollywood mode of comedy, careless, crude and usually borrowed – often from the peaks of the screwball era, which many of today's players fail to understand. He did so with one bound in *Roxanne* (87), one of the few comedies of the past twenty years which the past masters might have appreciated, not least for its affectionate portrait of small town life, a staple of Hollywood comedy from the 1920s through to the 40s. Martin himself wrote and co-produced this modernized version of 'Cyrano de Bergerac', giving a beautifully judged performance as the big-nosed romantic, here the town's chief fire-officer. He gave himself only one line which Woody Allen might have written for himself, and you wanted to shout with joy that it wasn't Allen saying it. It was also the first time Martin had worked with a first-rate director, Fred Schepisi, who gave full value to an already funny script. Daryl Hannah played the title-role and Rick Rossevich was excellent as the stricken swain for whom Martin first woos her. Later, when asked whether he was 'upset or surprised' when his work on this film failed to receive a single Oscar nomination, he replied, 'Yes on both counts.' Many other people were astounded, and although the film did only moderately well at the American box-office – it took $18,240,000 on a budget of $13 million – it proved to be his breakthough picture in overseas markets.

Planes, Trains and Automobiles is, as the title suggests, about getting from one place to another – but the snag is that the travelling companions are an unwilling odd couple, a buttoned-down collar ad exec (Martin) and a

slob (John Candy): if you like, just, Ollie to Martin's Stan. As written and directed by John Hughes, it rolls along merrily, though driving the wrong way on a freeway or in a burning car do not come high on the list of amusing situations. Because of the high cost of shooting on a variety of locations, the budget was $28 million, which translated into $22,100,000 at the wickets. *Dirty Rotten Scoundrels* (88) began life as a project to co-star Mick Jagger and David Bowie, a remake of the 1964 *Bedtime Story* with Marlon

Chevy Chase, Steve Martin and Martin Short as the Three Amigos *(86), real-life movie star cowboys who, forced to be cowboys in real life, prove inept at it. The American ads were something like this, but when the film failed to take off, the distributor elsewhere simply removed their pants and relocated their gun-belts around their garters. And the three amigos were too dumb to notice.*

All smiles for the moment: fellow-travellers – by chance, that is – Steve Martin and John Candy in Planes, Trains and Automobiles *(87): and as they proceed from one to the other, over half of America, Mr Martin's patience will wear very thin. Candy is far from the ideal travelling companion.*

Brando and David Niven. The matter rested when United Artists failed to prise the rights from Universal. Eddie Murphy was interested, but Paramount (owner of his exclusive services and at that point less inclined to humour his whims than later) was not. Frank Oz sent the screenplay to Martin about the time it was discovered that the rights had reverted to Stanley Shapiro, producer and co-writer of the original. Martin accepted the Niven role, the more suave of the two con-men, and Bill Murray was set to play Brando's old part. When he withdrew, Martin switched roles, with John Cleese and then Michael Caine set to play the Englishman. Said Martin: 'The toughest thing for me . . . was not allowing Michael Caine to get the upper hand with me. Michael's extremely charming, has worked with everyone and gives great lunch. After listening to him tell me terrific stories over lunch, I'd have to remember this man's character is trying to beat me at a con game.' If this situation created tension it was to the movie's advantage, for it is an almost constant delight, which could *not* be said of the original. Caine has the required smugness, but it is an assumed smugness, not a real one; he does not have that oily, hesitant quality which marked Niven's approach to comedy. Martin is magnificent, more addictive than ever: in the first place he can make idiocy (in pretending to be Caine's royal, but retarded, younger brother) funny, he can make larceny funny – well, anything: there had not been many things in movies for years as enjoyable as his expressions, from horrified to admiring, as he realizes that Caine is besting him. He gives little whoops of joy as he himself triumphs, but nothing becomes him as much as his attempts to look calm and not desperate when he can do nothing after (literally) immobilizing himself. The film, mostly shot on the Riviera, cost $19 million (including Martin's fee of $5 million), which was bettered by only $200,000 when the returns were in. In contrast, Ron Howard's acceptable but unexceptional *Parenthood* (89) cost $20 million but took $48,600,000. A panorama of family life, it kept Martin at the centre, but his role as a happily married husband and father did not make great demands on an immense talent. Still, said Peter Travers in 'Rolling Stone', it's a 'performance of solid gold'. Before the film came out he appeared in New York with Robin Williams in 'Waiting for Godot', directed by Mike Nichols. He was reunited with director Herbert Ross for *My Blue Heaven* (90), as a slick Mafia boss with a mop of black curly hair. The plot, as written by Nora Ephron, has him hiding away while being 'rehabilitated' by a nerdish FBI agent –

the role for which Martin was first cast. The role of the gangster was offered to Danny DeVito, who turned it down, and to Arnold Schwarzenegger, who didn't bother to reply. Ephron persuaded Martin to take it on, with Rick Moranis cast as the nerd. The result, though only moderately well-received, managed to take over $22 million in its first two months in release. Next up: *LA Story* (91) with his wife, from his own script; and *Pinsky*.

Bette Midler

'Fuck 'em if they can't take a joke' is, says Bette Midler, her motto; and a lot of people feel that way about her. She could never be described as vulnerable, and as a singer she was raunchy, outrageous and extreme – deliberately tacky, as she said herself. You might feel glad she was not a cold automaton like Barbra Streisand or Diana Ross, but a lady who didn't take herself seriously. 'I always wanted to stand out,' she said. 'I didn't want to be just another girl singer.' Later she said, 'To be a true legend, you can't do it just in music.' So we have her in movies, cast for type (one assumes) as a pushy extrovert. When the material is good, she is effective, if far from the form of the great comediennes of the past; when it is not, her idiosyncrasies, her brashness and her assertiveness can be rather grating. Perhaps, like Mae West, she should write her own dialogue. When in 1990 she sued the Ford Motor Company for using an imitation (done by one of her erstwhile back-up singers) in a commercial, she observed, 'I do have my standards. They're low, but I have them.'

She was born in Paterson, New Jersey, in 1945; her father was a house-painter. The family moved to Honolulu where, she says, they were the only Jewish people for miles. She studied drama at the University of Hawaii for a year before dropping out; for a while she packed pineapples. Heaven seemed to come when she was selected for a bit in *Hawaii* (66), as a missionary's sick wife, but nothing happened when she followed the production to Hollywood. She went to New York, where she was a typist, a store-clerk and a go-go dancer. She eventually landed a role in the chorus in 'Fiddler on the Roof', graduating to the role of one of Tevye's granddaughters after three weeks. But fame was to come in a gay bath-house: the boys in the bath-towels liked her act – 'flash and trash' she called it. 'The Divine Miss M', she styled herself, and she made an album called that. The gay men egged or cheered her on for quite a while, during which time Aaron Russo became her agent (and her lover). He decided that she should be on the stage and on television, and she scored a notable success in an off-Broadway revue, 'Clams on a Half Shell' (75) which brought her a Tony award. She began to appear on television and won an Emmy for a Special, 'Ol' Red Hair is Back'. She wanted more than anything to be in movies, so Russo approached 20th-Century-Fox about a musical: but there had not been a successful one since *Cabaret* in 1972. He proposed instead a dramatic film based on the self-destructive life of Janis Joplin, but instead of Joplin's songs there would be much borrowed from Midler's act. Russo even managed a co-producer credit on *The Rose* (79), which Mark Rydell directed, but even more astutely he got Bo Goldman to work on the screenplay, which has the flip dialogue absolutely right. Except for one maudlin scene (on the telephone), Midler is outstanding, never playing for sympathy. With a take of just over $19 million (it had cost $4,500,000) and the lady nominated for an Oscar (she lost to Sally Field), there was every reason to suppose that a brilliant movie career lay before her. Warners released a concert film, *Divine Madness* (80), filmed over a four-day period in the Pasadena Civic Auditorium with Michael Ritchie as director. She exuded sass and self-confidence, but most sensitive souls would have turned off and put on 'Judy at Carnegie Hall'. It was never expected to be a blockbuster, but the take of less than $2 million may be one reason why there were, in Midler's own words, no further offers.

Rescue came when director Don Siegel invited her to star in *Jinxed* (82), a film that lived up to its title. 'I'd let my wife, children and animals starve before I'd subject myself to something like that again,' said Siegel later. Ken Wahl, co-starring, said: 'There were problems. In one scene I have to hit her in the face, and I thought we could save some money on sound effects here . . . There were epic battles going on, not just with me but with everybody. We come from different worlds. Bette seems to enjoy being unhappy, and she's very abusive, both physically and verbally. When at one point Don Siegel told her about something or other, she shouted something about knowing how to act. He said, "But at least I'm prettier than you", and she hit him.' Wahl played a blackjack dealer who gets his revenge on a small-time gambler (Rip Torn) by stealing his mistress (Midler), in what was not overall a bad movie. It was a disaster at the box-office; amid a rash of personal troubles including a break with Russo and a breakdown, one thing was clear: as far as Hollywood was concerned, Bette had blown it.

She met and married Martin von Haselberg, born in Argentina, raised in Germany and educated in Britain, and known as Harry Kipper when he does a 'performance' turn. She was terrified that she wouldn't work again, and resolved to be a very good girl if and when she did. Motherhood followed and then rescue, from an unusual quarter – Disney. Except for its animated cartoons, its recent films for children had failed miserably. So it started a company, Touchstone, to make more adult films, and when the mild *Splash* tickled America's funny-bone word was out for more Touchstone comedies. Midler claims that Disney turned to her because she was known for her ability to make people laugh,

Bette Midler in full swing – which is something to see, though these days she restricts her performing to acting. This still is from her concert film, Divine Madness *(80).*

but Nick Nolte, she and Richard Dreyfuss were names not then hugely in demand; nor were the more recent credits of writer-director Paul Mazursky likely to stun you. (He called his leads 'Betty Ford's children', a reference to some well-publicized problems with drink and drugs.) *Down and Out in Beverly Hills* (86) was a re-working of a much superior film, Renoir's *Boudu Sauvé des Eaux*, given a title to remind some of George Orwell and a current picture with Eddie Murphy. Few other major stars would have wanted Midler's role, that of a klutzy Jewish lady with too much money, an uptight arse and a habit of calling up radio psychologists. With many chances she did not make her very funny, but the film attracted a dreamy $28,277,000 at the box-office. She was much better in *Ruthless People*, which also borrowed an old theme – from *Too Many Crooks* – of a kidnapped shrewish wife whose husband (Danny DeVito) refuses to pay the ransom money. Again modestly budgeted, the film took an even dreamier $31,443,000. Midler was billed fourth, on the understanding that blame is shared for a failure or placed on the first-billed star. She was due to be second, to Shelley Long, on *Outrageous Fortune* (87), but confidence in the script caused her to renegotiate for top-billing. And she was welcome to it, for this was a careless, disintegrating comedy about two aspiring actresses, a slob and a prig (guess who played which), who have a series of wild-goose chases while looking for their mutual lover. The director, Arthur Hiller, said: 'In any given situation Bette can show you fifteen different ways to do it. You're spoiled for choice.' The film took $22,647,000 at the box-office. When she went out to tub-thump, she claimed an exclusive Disney pact as her own producer, with full artistic control and a right to top-billing, plus a contradictory freedom to work for other studios (but this is the new Hollywood, and 'exclusive' probably means that Disney wants her unless something fabulous is offered from outside).

She teamed up with Lily Tomlin (they were 'The planet's two most gifted performing females,' according to Richard Corliss in 'Time' magazine) for *Big Business* (88), in which they were sets of twins separated at birth, but reunited. Playing a naive Southern girl and a hard-headed executive, Midler tended to overshadow the more talented Tomlin, despite rather obvious material. A box-office figure of $17,768,000 was, if not really big business, very good, and $24,882,000 for *Beaches* was even better. If movie stars were rated one out of ten, she said on a TV talkshow, 'I'd be 55.' And her box-office rating gave her the right to say it. The

film was a through-the-years tale of a friendship between opposites – a brash Bronx Jewish loudmouth who struggles along in show business, and an upright WASP type (Barbara Hershey) who becomes a lawyer. It was Midler's third vehicle in which she had starred with another woman opposite her, and she said, 'Enough already'; it was also her first serious role, if you like, since *The Rose*. She set her sights on another one, so flashy that they attract Oscars – Stella Dallas, who was dated when first played by Belle Bennett in 1925. A little updating of this mother-love tale in 1937 for Barbara Stanwyck did no harm, but this *Stella* (90) was frankly ridiculous – as, for instance, refusing her seducer when he offers to make an honest woman out of her. She, of course, is not as classy as he, from the other side of the tracks, as they used to say. Janet Maslin in the 'New York Times' said that despite such inconsistencies, added to the flaws of Olive Higgins Prouty's old novel, 'Ms Midler's performance manages to be both involving and wildly inconsistent.' One of her real and unheralded talents, said Maslin, 'is for camouflage, and her exuberance is most helpful in overshadowing the inconvenient aspects of this story,' and she concluded that she was 'right to tackle this role with spirit, gumption and absolutely no shame.' Despite critical put-downs the film had taken over $19 million in its first three months, justifying those Disney executives who had extended the 'exclusive' contract by four films before it had been publicly shown.

She was Disney's biggest star, it was widely said, since Mickey Mouse; as this foul-mouthed, former fag-hag said: 'If Walt was alive he probably wouldn't have let me on the lot.' Next along the line: *Scenes From a Mall* with Woody Allen, and *For the Boys* (91), singing to the troops through three wars.

LIZA MINNELLI

A while back the 'New York Times' did a full-page piece on Liza Minnelli which, like all early pieces on Liza Minnelli, had a lot about Mama: the difference this time was that Mama was not identified. The paper had clearly decided that there couldn't be one among its readers who did not know who Mama was. There are several reasons for this, not least of which was her decision to enter Mama's field – singer-actress; and in that field Mama was the greatest of her time. Liza's singing voice, we note at once, is not so melodious – even when she is not shouting, which, to be fair, is required by much of the material she chooses. (She said that she wanted to be a dancer, but parts are more open for singers.) Comparisons must be made – that is a cross Minnelli has to bear, though it might have been easier had she not reached her mother's eminence. Mother has always been a cross to bear, since childhood, with nervous breakdowns, the pill-popping, the career-reversals and occasional poverty. Gerold Frank's otherwise grave-stomping biography, 'Judy', contains some touching pictures of Liza coping. She paid off Garland's debts after her death, and she has always spoken of her with the fondest love and warmth. She said once, 'My mother gave me my drive, guts and integrity, but most of all my humor,' adding, 'My father gave me my dreams.'

Father was Vincente Minnelli, like Garland an MGM employee. Liza was born in 1946 in Los Angeles, and as a tot played her mother's daughter in the final scene of *In the Good Old Summertime* (49). She remained with her mother after the divorce, and reckons that she attended twenty-two different schools, which would include New York and London: at one in Scarsdale she played the lead in 'The Diary of Anne Frank.' After a short stint at the Sorbonne, she attacked show business in New York, and was offered the lead in an off-Broadway revival of 'Best Foot Forward' (63). Since childhood she had sometimes been brought out on to Mama's stage; now she appeared on her TV programme, and they co-starred together in two concerts at the London Palladium (64). The following year she was in a so-so Broadway show, 'Flora the Red Menace', and collected a Tony Award – the youngest actress ever to win one. She wanted to go into films, and landed a role as Albert Finney's American secretary in *Charlie Bubbles* (67), and her wistful, flip twenty minutes made bearable for a time this sour tale. Encouraged by her mother, she married, for the first time – Peter Allen, the Australian-born night-club entertainer; and she herself was singing in clubs and arenas – including the Olympia in Paris: a film of that performance indicated that she was losing much of her gaucheness and simultaneously gaining in control. In films she proved a natural – irresistible as she immodestly chased student Wendell Burton in *The Sterile Cuckoo* (69). Wrote John Coleman in the 'New Statesman': 'Hers is a performance, a remarkable one. Mostly all nose and bared gums and febrile chat, the last person in the world one would allow an acquaintanceship to be struck up with, this girl is not her mother's daughter for nothing. In one spot, on the telephone, when the boy is trying to fend her off, you can shut your eyes and those pure Garland plangencies, the old heart-jerking intonations, take

you over. Opening your eyes, you see some very fine acting is going on, too.' As the scarred girl in the household of misfits in *Tell Me That You Love Me, Junie Moon* (70), she confirmed the impression, but the film was another in Otto Preminger's line of duds.

Sally Bowles in *Cabaret* (72) had been played inadequately in the New York production, and magnificently (at least, late in the run) in London – by Judi Dench; the London production also had the best of Emcees, Barry Dennan – but the film went to the New York one, Joel Grey. No one who saw the London 'Cabaret' could have liked the film too much, since the book had been amateurishly hacked about, and some of the best songs cut, but Bob Fosse's direction dazzled, and the now American Sally was also pretty terrific – eager, kooky, revelling in her 'divine decadence, darling', friendly and often pathetic with her funny little mouse face. For this performance Minnelli won a Best Actress Oscar – and a very popular one, though Diana Ross was disappointed that she did not get greater recognition for her playing in *Lady Sings the Blues*. The film's success was such that Minnelli stayed with public performing while waiting for the right film. Then she chose badly – twice. *Lucky Lady* (75) concerned a *ménage à trois* – the others were Gene Hackman and Burt Reynolds – up to no good in the days of Prohibition; troubled location-shooting sent costs up to over $12 million, and the reviews soon ensured that not much of that would be got back. Blamed were the screenplay and the direction of Stanley Donen (with whom Minnelli and Reynolds quarrelled over the revised ending). *A Matter of Time* (76) was directed by another alumnus of MGM musicals, Minnelli *père*, who blamed AIP for re-cutting the material; but 'Variety''s reviewer, noting a second flop in a row for Liza, observed that all her film career needed was a good director. For the record, she played a French housemaid whose fantasies are indulged by fading beauty Ingrid Bergman.

Thus with Martin Scorsese's *New York, New York* (77), as 'Village Voice' put it, 'Liza's film career is on the line. If it flops, she'll be a one-picture movie star. While she is still regarded as roughly third in audience appeal behind Barbra Streisand and Diana Ross, it's a fast track, what with Faye Dunaway, Jane Fonda, Lily Tomlin, Tatum O'Neal et al moving up.' Well: the press killed audience interest in the previous two films, and though it was in general kinder to this effort, it was clear once you were watching it that Minnelli's performance as a band-singer was its only redeeming feature; but since, once the band-singer became a star she was

Cabaret *(72) was an above-average screen musical, constructed from an even better stage original: it was set in Berlin in the early 30s, which explains Liza Minnelli's rather outré get-up. Despite its success, Hollywood deemed that musicals were not in favour – as* New York, New York *(77) seemed to prove: but then, telling it like it was about a couple during the big band era was not a very cheerful idea. Playing sax in the background is Robert De Niro.*

modelling herself on Judy Garland, it still left a nasty taste in the mouth. We knew that Liza could not help cracking a line like her mother or looking as plaintive, but imitation as a singer was ill advised. Since we all hoped that she would have a happier life than Garland's, it was saddening around this time to read in an interview that she was fully prepared to put her career before her private life. Her second marriage – to Jack Haley Jr – went phffft, supposedly because of her relationship with Scorsese; and there have been a number of other romantic figures over the years – including Desi Arnaz Jr and Peter Sellers, to both of whom she was briefly engaged.

In 1977 she appeared in 'The Act', a sort-of-play built around a night-club act. The high prices (highest yet in Broadway legit) and respectable run proved beyond doubt the lady's appeal – as did SRO business at equally ridiculous prices at the London Palladium in 1978. Another Tony Award for 'The Act' confirmed her position and in 1979 she married its stage manager, Mark Gero – one reason being because she was pregnant by him. However, this pregnancy miscarried, as did two others during the next two years, despite cancellation of work in order to rest.

In 1979 she also appeared briefly and temporarily as Lillian Hellman in the off-Broadway production of 'Are You Now or Have You Ever Been?', in which she had invested; earlier, without publicity, she had subbed for Gwen Verdon in 'Chicago' – the work, incidentally, of the composer-lyricist team of John Kander and Fred Ebb, responsible for 'Flora the Red Menace', 'Cabaret' and special material for the Minnelli TV specials. There was talk of its becoming a film with herself and Goldie Hawn. That could well have been the good film she needed, but musicals were deemed to be too expensive and not sure-fire at the box-office. Curiously she was in a gigantic success, *Arthur* (81), as the kookie shoplifter who takes a wealthy playboy (Dudley Moore) away from his stuffy bride-to-be. Success was thought to be due to the exchanges between the playboy and his butler (John Gielgud), showing that this austere fellow was a good guy at heart, which is why he tolerates the unorthodox vulgarian for whom he works – a role for which Gielgud won a Best Supporting Oscar: a fit reward for one of the glories of the English stage when slumming. He and Moore made many other movies; the best that Minnelli could find was a guest-appearance in *The Muppets Take Manhattan* (84). Kander and Ebb wrote a musical for her and Chita Rivera, 'The Rink', about the relationship between mother-and-daughter entertainers. It ran until Minnelli checked out of it and into the Betty Ford Clinic for detoxification. She had been addicted to Valium since the time of her mother's funeral, and later to alcohol. She said later: 'You see, I loved giving it up, which is very strange. But I was so relieved that there was something physically wrong with me [a chemical dependence on drugs] instead of being so over-nervous I was going crazy.'

Recovered, she appeared in a telemovie, *A Time to Live* (85), based on fact, as a mother coping with a son with muscular dystrophy and the subsequent strains on her marriage. This brought her a Golden Globe award as Best Actress, and when she appeared at the London Palladium the following year she told reporters that she planned to make more films – but a reunion with Burt Reynolds, *Rent-a-Dick* (88), in which she played a hooker, quickly disappeared. She was in a three-part one-hour telemovie, *Sam Found Out*, which brought her nice notices, but another big screen reunion, with Mr Moore, *Arthur 2: on the Rocks*, received anything but a warm welcome. The original had taken $42 million, but 'Cuddly Dudley' had become 'Deadly Dudley' at the box-office in the interim. Like Minnelli, he sorely needed a successful movie, but a return of $7,500,000 on a $19 million budget did not provide it. Surely more talented than he, she was nevertheless ill-advised to still talk and carry on – at forty-something – like a wide-eyed adolescent. She has since confined herself to the concert circuit, with an undiminishing appeal. Her special appeal within the movie world has found her as presenter, compère or entertainer at most Oscar ceremonies, but she refused to sing 'Over the Rainbow' at the 1990 function. 'No one can sing it better than my mother,' she observed, leaving the job open to Diana Ross, who proved that no one could sing it worse.

She returned to film in *Stepping Out* (91), directed by Lewis Gilbert from a play which ran for a long time in London's West End.

RICK MORANIS

In rediscovering comedy – the films of the seventies were not very funny (especially the comedies) – Hollywood has found itself some individual comic talents, and Rick Moranis is among the best of them, small, nerdish, bespectacled and desperate.

He was born in Toronto in 1954 into a family of 'suburban, middle-class, aspiring professionals'. Show business, he decided, was something associated with the country across the border, but he liked it; the closest he thought he might ever get to it was working

in local television, as an engineer. While
doing so he was given his own show, which
went out in the small hours. He started
performing live, and in 1975 went to Los
Angeles with the intention of becoming a
stand-up comedian. But, he discovered, he
could not get employment without an agent,
and without an agent no one was willing to
employ him. Five weeks later he was back in
Toronto, where there was an offer – from
Dave Thomas, then starring in 'Second City
Television', at that point in its third season
with CBC. He impersonated Woody Allen
and a mad Hollywood producer, as well as
one-half of the beer-guzzling McKenzie
brothers, Bob and Doug, with Thomas. NBC
networked the show in the US in 1981, and in
1982 and 1983 Moranis won Emmys for his
comedy writing. He and Thomas put their
infamous brothers on an album, 'The Great
White North', which went Gold, and they
decided also to immortalize them on film, in
Strange Brew (83), which they also wrote and
directed. Also in the cast was Max von Sydow,
conferring a definite respectability, but he
could not help the film to repeat its Canadian
success elsewhere.

Moranis was then invited to Hollywood by
director Walter Hill, whose *48 Hrs* had just
made a star out of Eddie Murphy. Looking for
another free-wheeling talent to add comic
edge, he told Moranis that he could impro-
vise, but *Streets of Fire* (84) was chastening.
'It was a dreadful experience', he said, 'but it
taught me a lesson about how to select films
and about who to trust and what to believe of
what they tell you.' He played the cynical
lover and manager of the kidnapped rock-
singer (Diane Lane), inevitably losing her to
the Lochinvar (Michael Pare) who sets out to
rescue her. A fellow-countryman, director
Ivan Reitman, offered him a prime role in
Ghostbusters, as Sigourney Weaver's neighbour, an oddly-accoutred, diminutive accountant who is chased from his own party by a
hellhound – which is what he turns into. The
role as written was not much, but Moranis was
able to 'rewrite everything, but all actors did';
he had also learned a bit already about scene-
stealing, and the film's success brought him
plenty of offers. By the time the film came out
he had already done *The Wild Life*, a sort of
follow-up to *Fast Times at Ridgemont High*,
with the same writer, Cameron Crewe, and
producer, Art Linson, doubling here as director. This one shows its hustling high school
graduate (Eric Stoltz) moving out into the
world of Reaganomics and encountering
Moranis, a GQ-type at 'Fashion Dynasty' who
fancies himself a wow with the heroine. The
offers were all for nerdy roles, but with a
hundred scripts coming in, he waited. And

finally, wisely, took on two cameo roles, as
Morty the mimic, one of the many hangers-on
hoping for a share of *Brewster's Millions* (85),
and as chief of public relations in the *Head
Office* (86). As one of those guests at *Club
Paradise* he also seized his chance, as one
whose unprepossessing appearance does not
limit his unbounded confidence in attracting
the opposite sex. In one of the film's more
amusing moments (of which there were few),
he and his chum smoke a joint to impress two
girls, who promptly pass it on to the jocks they
are with. So where was he in the hierarchy of
Hollywood funnymen? – somewhere impre-
cise, since he had appeared in only one
popular film, *Ghostbusters*.

The failure of this last, which was resound-
ing, left him prey to Mel Brooks, hoping to
shore up his own unsure comic talent with
other funny men, in *Spaceballs* (87): Moranis
was the commander of the largest spaceship in
the universe, a bumbling pipsqueak. He was
the only, the perfect, casting possible for *Little
Shop of Horrors*, a musical fable based on a
stage hit in turn based on an old camp movie.
After all, the employee at the little shop can
only recoil in horror as its glory, a huge plant,
turns voracious for his enemies. What to do
between panic about the unthinkable and sit
back to accept the inevitable? Moranis's
perfectly pitched performance should have

*Rick Moranis, an amiable
young man who finally hit
it big with* Honey I Shrunk
the Kids, *the surprise
blockbuster of 1989. A
year later Moranis
observed that he was
subsequently sent 'scripts I
was totally wrong for, but
at least I'm able to work
with a level of actor,
director and material that I
hadn't been offered
previously.'*

brought in further offers, but again, he waited – to be rewarded by the role which really made him, the hapless father who has to confess *Honey I Shrunk the Kids* (89). This hare-brained comedy, a combination of 'Gulliver's Travels' and *The Incredible Shrinking Man*, proved irresistible to world audiences, who in the US/Canada alone returned $71,100,000 to Disney on a $22 million investment. Simultaneously, Moranis was in *Ghostbusters II*, and the funniest person in that sequel, and in *Parenthood*, as Steve Martin's pretentious brother-in-law, trying to bring up his baby daughter as a genius. Well, genius is what it takes to steal a film from Mr Martin, and Moranis just about managed it.

Starring in three, count 'em, three gigantic hits in one year, can't be bad, but when Moranis demanded $2 million to star in the sequel to *Honey I Shrunk the Kids*, Disney replied that they would happily replace him with Martin Short. 'Variety' reported that any other studio would have agreed to his demands. Meanwhile, he co-starred with Martin in *My Blue Heaven* (90), as a junior FBI clerk trying to settle a Mafia mobster (Martin) into a new lifestyle, and with more scenes together than in *Parenthood* they proved a more successful comedy team than many of the last few years. That could not be said of Moranis and Billy Crystal, for Moranis left the cast of *City Slickers* during shooting 'for personal reasons', to be replaced by Daniel Stern; Crystal is also the producer. Future plans include *Sibling Rivalry* with Dennis Quaid, and *How I Got in College*, with Harold Ramis. He has 'two young kids and I'd never see them at all if I directed . . . But for the time being it's wonderful to be someone who makes people laugh.' One of the curiosities of his appeal is that, by virtue of his looks, he might be just another Woody Allen clone, but he has a temperament which is more vivid than that of those who have gone before him. He knows his admirers and detractors are equal, and he understands them both. That's rare.

EDDIE MURPHY

Eddie Murphy is the only indisputable heir to Clark Gable. This young upstart is the King of Hollywood, unassailable, made popular by public demand. Like Gable he dominates the screen with his ease and confidence, less an actor than a personality the camera loves. He's cool, keen, generous, hip, flip and contemptuous of all authority; four-letter words come as naturally to him as breathing.

Above all, his hooded eyes reveal that he thinks the world ridiculous and funny, which may be why he is gloriously alive, with the ability to make his movies seem better than they are. The significant difference between him and Gable is that where Gable led the field of stars Murphy virtually had the place to himself. For a while he was the only guaranteed box-office attraction in the world. He knew it and took advantage of it, and then he was not quite so big.

He was born in Brooklyn in 1961 to a middle-class family (his father was a cop). At fifteen he went on stage at the Roosevelt Youth Center on Long Island and never looked back; after graduating, he walked into New York's Comic Strip club and so impressed the owners, Robert Wachs and Richard Tienkin, that they became his managers. At nineteen he auditioned for 'Saturday Night Live', seeking replacements as its stars moved on. Murphy stayed with the show for four years, introducing such characters as huckster Velvet Jones, Little Richard Simmons and Grumpy Gumpy; by the time he left he was said to be earning $30,000 a show. At Paramount Lawrence Gordon paid him $200,000 to star in *48 Hrs* (82), and Paramount has been reluctant to let him go ever since. Walter Hill directed this thriller, which top-billed Nick Nolte as a San Francisco cop who springs a con from San Quentin to help him track down two killers. Murphy took the film, 'the beautifully tailored, street-honed young fast-talker, whether patronizing big Nolte rotten, yuk-yukking away in mock-coon mirth, or (his set-piece) riotously humiliating a country and western bar crowded with menacing rednecks who respond to a flashed badge' (John Coleman in 'New Statesman'). The film took $30,328,000.

Murphy got $300,000 for *Trading Places* (83), a property originally designed for his idol, Richard Pryor, and Gene Wilder. It found him being sprung from jail again, as a beggar (pretending to be a blind and legless Vietnam vet) who changes places with a self-satisfied Philadelphia yuppie (Dan Aykroyd) at the whim of two old men (Don Ameche, Ralph Bellamy). This cruel comedy needed a Billy Wilder and got John Landis, who snatched at it instead of shaping it, but it still took $40,600,000. Paramount accordingly were happy to pay Murphy $1 million for ten days' work on *Best Defense* (84), though that sum was added to the studio's investment in this dismal Dudley Moore comedy, bringing it in at $18 million. The box-office return was only $10,500,000, but it would have been infinitely less without Murphy's participation – which was, it was laughingly clear, added only after the original film had been finished.

Eddie Murphy in Beverly Hills Cop *(84) and its sequel,* Beverly Hills Cop II *(87). The first of these shot him into the stratosphere – and much has happened to him since then. Perhaps too much.*

Moore played the inventor of a supertank and the 'Strategic Guest Star' (as Murphy was billed) drove it in trials in Kuwait.

On his first day as president of Paramount, Michael Eisner was stopped for speeding: so he decided to make a film about Los Angeles policemen. Three writers and seventeen drafts later, Martin Brest directed *Beverly Hills Cop*, originally planned for Mickey Rourke (who went off to do *The Pope of Greenwich Village* when filming was delayed). Then Sylvester Stallone changed his mind – fortunately for us and Paramount, who saw their $14 million investment return $108 million in the domestic market alone. What *Dirty Harry* was to Eastwood and *Bullitt* to Steve McQueen (both, incidentally, on the San Francisco force) this was to Murphy – though he was actually a Detroit cop who had seconded himself to LA to solve the murder of a pal, in the course of which he has many a brush with the local police. When he's fazed, as when told the price of a foolish piece of modern art, he yells out in falsetto, 'Get the fuck outa here', and there probably isn't a funnier moment in all 80s cinema. His fee has been said to be $4,500,000 plus a percentage, but if this is so an exclusive agreement of five films for $15 million seems unlikely, and that was what Paramount then announced: what was certain was that the man was a star the world over and Paramount wanted him exclusively. The studio fretted while he chose not to film – so 1985 was only big inasmuch as revenues continued to flow in from *Cop*. He returned after a two-year absence in *The Golden Child* (86), meant originally for Mel Gibson, who was lucky to miss out on this preposterous adventure directed by the once-estimable Michael Ritchie. Murphy played an LA investigator who specializes in finding missing children – and this one is a princeling who has disappeared somewhere in the Orient. What was clear was that Murphy saw himself in James Bond mood, a super hero, perhaps fallible and foolish, but determined to do what a man's gotta do. One report says his salary was $6,500,000; the film cost $25 million and took $39,700,000 at the US box-office.

Beverly Hills Cop II (87) cost $28 million and raked in $80,900,000, though the press liked it no better. The director Tony Scott had just given Paramount a big hit in *Top Gun*, and he applied his hi-tech flashy visuals to a story not worth telling in the first place. The original had humour and this had none, but the combination of Murphy and Scott said much about Paramount's ambitions at that time. Murphy disliked the script and improvised, and that, plus his often-late arrivals on set, did not make for a happy atmosphere. His fee was reported to be $8,500,000, but the

more reliable 'Variety' gave it as $7 million in reporting that it was the only film made under his previous contract for five films. He refused to apologize for breaking that contract, said 'Variety'. 'He dismissed such morality as "from the old school".' The contract which replaced it included development plans for his own two television companies. 'Variety' said it was for five films, but gave no salary details other than that the sum was likely to be less than the $16 million recently paid to Sylvester Stallone. A few months later 'Forbes' magazine gave the sum as $25 million for six films. Whatever it was he was on profit participation. Murphy's worth to Paramount was demonstrated when they released *Raw* aka *Eddie Murphy Raw*, a record of his stand-up act as filmed live at the Felt Forum in New York and directed, at Murphy's request, by Robert Townsend, whose *Hollywood Shuffle* contained a couple of jokes at Murphy's expense. *Raw* collected $24,800,000, putting it way in front of similar ventures by Richard Pryor and Bette Midler – and despite reviews such as this in 'Variety': 'Mostly it will be women who find his routine offensive and him a most unappealing misogynist.' Whether Murphy retained a sense of humour off the lot is debatable, given reports of an obsequious retinue and a palatial life-style – and an ego which was no longer merely commanding but dominant. Well, why not? – since he was reputed to have earned $27 million during the year; he was also the plaintiff in a paternity suit.

Coming to America (88) was directed by John Landis, with whom Murphy had 'artistic differences'. Landis said, 'Eddie is an immensely overpowering talent, But if you can imagine a nuclear plant, that energy is productive as long as it's contained. And if Eddie's not contained, he's gonna blow.' The plot found Murphy as a wealthy African prince who gets a job in a New York hamburger joint; James Earl Jones played his father and Arsenio Hall his travelling companion – and he, like Murphy, played several cameo roles as well. Murphy was also credited with the original story, but Art Buchwald recognized a number of similarities with a story which he had submitted to Paramount, and sued for breach of contract. Paramount, as its lawyers well knew, could have settled out of court and saved everyone much aggro: but that would be a tacit admission that Murphy was in the wrong. He was not named in the suit and was not called to testify. Hall went to the witness stand to verify that he and Murphy had thought up the story together; he also claimed that Murphy was generous and free of ego – which raised the question as to why he had not shared the story credit with Hall. At the outcome, Buchwald and producer Alain Bernheim were awarded $250,000 plus 19 per cent of the film's net profits. It had taken $65 million in rentals in the US, which translates to $125 million worldwide – but, Paramount claimed, there were no profits (when there were, Murphy would be getting 15 per cent of them). As of December 1989 the film was still posting a deficit of $18 million, given the cost of advertising, prints, etc. The budget had amounted to $39 million, approximately one-third of which went to Eddie Murphy Productions, including the following: $8 million for acting, $200,000 writing fee, $500,000 'producer's package', $1 million for travelling and housing expenses for Murphy and retinue (including huge lunch-bills at McDonald's for the extras and a 24-hour on-call limo for Murphy himself) plus another $1,700,000 'overhead', which turned out to be 25 per cent of the $6,800,000 paid to Murphy in 1987 in order that he could resign to negotiate the latest contract (the sum was to be spread over four pictures).

Earlier in his career Murphy had remarked that Paramount had so much money bound up in him that they would not put him into a bad movie. The truth was now, of course, that Paramount now did what he told them. And certainly *Harlem Nights* (89) was a bad movie. 'This disaster area is the work of one man,' said Richard T. Jameson in 'Seven Days'. 'A vanity production,' 'Variety' called it. Said the credits: 'Paramount Pictures presents in association with Eddie Murphy Productions, a film by Eddie Murphy. Starring Eddie Murphy . . . Executive producer Eddie Murphy. Written and directed by Eddie Murphy'. At the premiere, 'Why not Written by Eddie Murphy, Directed by Eddie Murphy?'

shouted a man at the back. 'That would have looked silly,' said a woman a few rows away. Most people thought Murphy looked silly in this tale of the Harlem gangland wars of the 30s, playing Richard Pryor's adopted son; 'LA Weekly' found him scandalously bad, 'carrying on like a talk-show guest whenever he isn't trying to milk ugly laughs.' But in the 'New York Times', Vincent Canby came to his rescue: 'Though [it] is nothing if not a Murphy work, the star gives a subdued performance. He looks great – all talc and Brilliantine and jazzy period clothes – but the very contemporary Murphy personality is held in check most of the time. It's not easy being the king . . . This is no update of the sort of arrogantly unfunny, self-referential films made by Frank Sinatra and his Rat Pack pals in the 1960s. At the center of *Harlem Nights* is one of the great young talents of the day in the process of seeing just how far he can go.' Whether Paramount was happy with a handful of good notices is doubtful, for the film had a negative cost of $30 million, to which was added another $20 million in advertising and prints. The domestic take was only $35 million, and if Murphy's preceding film was not in profit it was doubtful whether this one could be. There was also a flurry of lawsuits: the actress Michael Michele Williams sued after being dropped from filming, blaming Murphy's 'sexual harassment', while Tienkin and Wachs split, leaving Wachs in command of Murphy's affairs and Tienkin accepting an out-of-court settlement. And a writer, Michael Greene, sued for $35 million after recognizing 'over 100 similarities that just popped off the screen' – from a script he had written for Murphy and Pryor at the request of the William Morris agency, who had rejected it without returning any copies. As a postscript we might note that Pryor, with whom Murphy had long hoped to work, went on record to the effect that he did not consider Murphy to be a generous performer.

In October 1989 the 'New York Times' reckoned that Tom Cruise had replaced Murphy as 'the world's biggest movie star', but he was still No. 2. *Another 48 Hrs* (90) found Murphy now billed above Nolte, and that was virtually the only change, for this was less a sequel than a remake. In the 'New York Times' Canby had lost patience: '. . . he has developed some of the same maddening mannerisms that marked Frank Sinatra's performances in the Rat Pack movies. He speaks dialogue as if he hadn't time to figure out what it meant . . . It's a lazy, unresponsive performance.' In Britain Anne Billson in the 'Sunday Correspondent' was no kinder: 'His return to the role highlights his failure to add a single trick to his repertoire in the interim:

Nick Nolte and Eddie Murphy in Another 48 Hrs *(90), a sequel to their first co-starring venture in 1982. In the 'New York Times' Vincent Canby noted 'the difference between Eddie Murphy the young television actor making a terrifically engaging movie debut, and Eddie Murphy the 1990 supernova, the star of seven films that have earned more than one billion dollars around the world.' But, warned Canby, this is 'as much a star vehicle as* The Georgeous Hussy *once was for Joan Crawford. The Crawford name isn't idly evoked. You have to go back to the old M-G-M days to find movies that, with every gesture, let the audience know it was watching a star.'*

eight years later, the motormouth delivery and *hyuk hyuk* laugh have used up most of their credit.' It cost $38 million and took over $80 million, trailing *Days of Thunder, Back to the Future III, Die Hard 2* and *Total Recall* among the summer's action blockbusters. It had been another difficult film to make, with director Hill shooting round Murphy due to his 'tardiness'. This might be because he and Wachs wanted to force Paramount into a better deal, or so said the 'sources' quoted by 'Variety'. Before shooting started, Murphy had told 'Playboy' that he had 'a *horrible* deal at Paramount. Absolutely', and that when he had made the three pictures due he would move to 'whoever's gonna give me the most lucrative deal.' Among the bones of contention was *Beverly Hills Cop III*, for, as 'Variety' put it, 'with their handy new Paramount deal in pocket, it is only logical that they were keen to get the third *Cop* picture ready to go.' Wachs insisted that the project was stymied because there was no script, but from Paramount's point of view big money would go missing if it was cancelled altogether. In these sequel-infested times it was received industry wisdom that while each did less well than the one before, they could, if carefully budgeted, still ensure a healthier take than an unknown quantity. 'The trick with a talent like Eddie Murphy is to make sure he gets the right movies,' said an executive at another studio. 'If he isn't careful, he could be the next Burt Reynolds.'

BILL MURRAY

Bill Murray's speciality as a stand-up performer was to be insincerely sincere; he might come on as ever such a nice guy, but he was always a louse underneath. Playing on television his sleazy saloon singers and make-out artists, he was one of life's losers, never able to get along with anybody; in an executive suit you know he's got there by foul means rather than fair. As far as real life is concerned, he has got there partly by being at the centre of the 'Saturday Night Live' Mafia.

He was born in Wilmette, a suburb of Chicago, in 1950, of Irish Catholic stock, the fifth of nine children; his father was a lumber salesman. According to him, he was kicked out of the Boy Scouts and the Little League, and at the age of twenty he was busted for the possession of 8½ pounds of marijuana at O'Hara Airport. Turning to a more respectable occupation, he joined his brother, Brian Doyle-Murray, in Chicago's Second City company, specializing in improvised comedy, and then he followed him to New York, where he

was working on 'The National Lampoon Hour' for radio. He joined him on the show, and they were both in an off-Broadway offshoot, 'The National Lampoon Show' (75), which was staged by Ivan Reitman. He was seen in that by Howard Cosell, who asked him to be in his television show, 'Saturday Night Live with Howard Cosell' which, since it featured kiddie and animal acts, by definition had little to do with the 'Saturday Night Live' that followed, the NBC show produced by Lorne Michaels. Michaels certainly leaned heavily on 'The National Lampoon Show', for Murray – who replaced Chevy Chase as anchor-man – was working with such other alumni as his brother, John Belushi, Gilda Radner and Harold Ramis. Most of them were involved with *Jungle Burger* (79) aka *Shame of the Jungle*, a Franco–Belgian cartoon made four years earlier, which was reconstructed by two 'Saturday Night Live' writers and redubbed by its comics. Films, clearly, were where Murray was headed, for Reitman was directing *Meatballs*, on which Ramis was one of the writers. Filmed for cheapness in Reitman's native Canada, it was pretty low-budget in every other department, including humour and intelligence: but, then, it had no further ambition than to relocate last year's big hit, *National Lampoon's Animal House*, inside a summer camp, in which the top-billed Murray was Tripper, the eccentric chief counsellor. Those who shamelessly backed this wretched thing had more than their just rewards, with over $19 million at the domestic box-office.

Murray attempted to redeem himself by playing the 'gonzo' journalist Dr Hunter S. Thompson in Art Linson's *Where the Buffalo Roam* (80), but instead of being a tribute to a certain type of dynamic journalism it was merely hack work, and a box-office disaster. Ramis made his directing debut on *Caddyshack*, more of campus high jinks – at least, that was their level – set in a country club. Chevy Chase was top-billed, with Murray in a supporting role as maniacal assistant greensman whose obsession with killing the gophers ranks far above his concern for the golfers. Yet more of same: *Stripes* (81), directed by Reitman, co-scripted by Ramis, who also played the buddy of Murray, a no-hoper transformed by the army after almost wrecking it. Despite dire reviews that took in over $40 million for Columbia, who now regarded Murray as a major star. But there was nothing they, or anyone else, could do about *Loose Shoes*, a spoof of coming attractions, which had sat on the shelf for three years before finding a few apathetic patrons. Columbia asked Murray to step into *Tootsie* (82), partly to prevent its becoming the major disaster

Columbia issued this picture of Bill Murray when they both had much to smile about: he had just done a stint in Tootsie *(82) and was about to go into another big success,* Ghostbusters. *The relationship would end unhappily the following year when the remake of* The Razor's Edge *flopped.*

Bill Murray as the president of a television network and Alfre Woodard as his secretary in Scrooged *(88), an updating of Dicken's 'A Christmas Carol'.*

tering on the way some unlikely people, including Aykroyd, Murray, Eddie Fisher, Imogene Coca, Paul Rogers and Mort Sahl. It was little seen and neither was the remake of *The Razor's Edge*, a long-held dream of Murray, who wrote the screenplay with John Byrum. Wildly overplotted and overlong, it found in Murray a blank centre, a man in search of a meaning in life. According to most sources, Murray had agreed to do *Ghostbusters* only if this was part of the same deal, but what is certain is that Columbia regretted their participation, not bothering to open the film in many markets after it returned only $2,750,000 on an estimated budget of $13 million. After taking a supporting role in *Little Shop of Horrors* (86), Murray 'felt it necessary to back off for a bit', so he spent six months in France and another six building a house.

During his absence David Puttnam arrived as production head at Columbia. While speaking at a Chamber of Commerce lunch, he cited Robert Redford as one of the industry's exemplars (because his Sundance Institute has trained movie-makers and put financing into some films); Bill Murray, he said, 'exemplifies an actor who makes millions off movies, but gives nothing back to his art' – or so the 'New York Post' reported. Letters flew back and forth between lawyers, and Puttnam issued a denial. Murray himself said later: 'I think it was hysterical that Puttnam singled me out as an example of an old Hollywood baron or something . . . I'm a Hollywood outsider, and I could have gone along with a lot of what he was saying. You know, I don't do lousy movies and I don't do material I don't believe in, and that to me is giving something back to Hollywood. I'm not really a guy to bitch and moan about at all.' Meanwhile, Mike Ovitz of CAA declined to discuss *Ghostbusters II* with Puttnam; he knew that it could be the only large financial success associated with Puttnam during his regime – and that would have to be over, it was reported, before he would permit his clients to report to begin production.

predicted – and he did so, if unbilled, most amusing as Dustin Hoffman's flatmate, an aspiring dramatist with a pretentious line in conversation. Reitman directed *Ghostbusters* (84), written by Dan Aykroyd and Ramis for themselves and John Belushi. When Belushi died of a drug overdose in 1982, the role of the third ghostbuster was offered to Murray – who, ironically, was the funniest of the trio. The film, which cost an unfunny $32 million, took a very exciting $130,100,000.

Michaels, turning from television, produced *Nothing Lasts Forever*, written and directed by another 'SNL' regular, Tom Schiller. Zach Galligan starred, having adventures in a future New York and on the moon, encoun-

Murray, meanwhile, was looking for a come-back vehicle, and for a while settled on *Air America*, in which he and Sean Connery would play pilots; while he hesitated the producers talked to Kevin Costner, who was just becoming hot; but the film was eventually made with Robert Downey Jr and Mel Gibson. Murray had turned down *The Witches of Eastwick*; at this time he declined the Dustin Hoffman role in *Rain Man* and he expressed no interest in playing the title-role in *Batman*. He eventually settled on *Scrooged* (88), a screenplay by two of his 'SNL' writers, Mitch Glazer and Michael O'Donoghue. They

seemed the ideal choice, since this modern, Americanized version of 'A Christmas Carol' was merely a series of skits, as a mean TV network boss reforms after getting the Christmas message. It was difficult to know which was more dispiriting, Murray's attempts to turn the thing into a one-man show, or the sentimentality which threatened to engulf it. Since it garnered $31,500,000, Paramount could regard it as a success, though in fact it had cost $32 million, of which Murray was paid $8 million. The named director was Richard Donner, but Murray was reckoned to be the boss – and at that salary, who wouldn't be? No matter that 'Variety' called it 'appallingly unfunny'. There were no salary demands on *Ghostbusters II* (89) – Puttman was now safely back in Britain – because Ovitz packaged his client on profit participation: Murray, Aykroyd, Ramis and Reitman (Sigourney Weaver, not an Ovitz client, was also important in the cast). The cost was $37 million and the proceeds well down from last time at $61,000,000: and since a further $20 million had been spent on prints and advertising, that did not leave much for a five-way split . . . Overall, it was a much sprightlier movie, and much more suitable for children – at whom the ad campaign was partially aimed. Murray returned to Warners for *Quick Change* (90) written and directed by Howard Franklin from the same source as Belmondo's recent *Holdup*. That was set in Toronto; this transferred the action to Manhattan, with Murray as a local guy who, fed-up, enlists a pal (Randy Quaid) and his girlfriend (Geena Davis) into taking part in a bank heist. That 'was easy' said the ads, 'but getting out of New York was a nightmare'. The ads listed Murray as co-director as well as co-producer, which came as no surprise to Quaid, since he had remarked to the press that the film had two directors instead of the expected one. The film took over $15 million in its three months in release, but 'Variety' referred to it as a failure, adding that it almost certainly meant the end of stars controlling ad campaigns. Murray soon found himself at Touchstone, co-starring with Richard Dreyfuss in *What About Bob?* (91).

Murray married his wife Margaret (Mickey) while making *Stripes*, and they live with their two children in New York City and upstate Sneden's Landing.

JACK NICHOLSON

Just as the economic and social climate of Broadway produced the theatre enterprises known collectively as 'off-Broadway', so in the late 50s and 60s there grew up what might be called 'fringe-Hollywood' – not quite 'underground', but with a clear demarcation line between its product and that of the major studios. The films churned out were the Cinderellas of the industry, though none of them went to the ball. They had in common only low budgets – some of them minuscule – with the usual concomitant, the desire for a quick buck. Some of them had ideas and energy, much of it misdirected. A few of them featured Jack Nicholson, the only major actor to emerge from this outer-stage into the bright Hollywood spotlight. As soon, indeed, as he appeared in *Easy Rider*, half-way through, there was no question that here was an authentic star – the noun might be wrong, but this was a player of enormous charm and magnetism. As long as he was on screen, he diverted attention from the two leading players, Peter Fonda and Dennis Hopper. They represented, perhaps better than any, the new breed of Hollywood player; and Nicholson, willy-nilly, represented the sort of personality we are stuck with until the day that all men are flat, alike and automated.

He was born in Neptune, New Jersey, in 1937, and began acting in high school. Before going on to college, he spent a year with his sister in Los Angeles – and never went back. Instead, he got a job as an office-boy in MGM's cartoon department, and started to study with a professional group, the Players Ring Theater. He did some TV work, 'Matinée Theater', and was seen on the stage by Roger Corman, prolific producer-director of Z movies like *Attack of the Crab Monsters* and *Teenage Caveman*. Producing only, he gave Nicholson the lead in a fifty-nine minute quickie he was making for Allied Artists, *The Cry Baby Killer* (58), and it was not at all bad – about a teenager who shoots two guys who have beaten him up and then barricades himself in a storeroom with a couple of hostages. This led to another teenage drama, *Too Soon to Love* (60), which offered the surprising conclusion that parental neglect causes them to do it. In *The Wild Ride* he is a hoodlum responsible for the deaths of several cops. Then Irving Lerner signed him to play Weary Reilly, one of the chums of *Studs Lonigan*, from the James Farrell novel about a young Chicagoan (Christopher Knight) during the Depression. The film was heavily flawed by errors in casting and direction, and failed to justify its low budget. Low budgets were something Nicholson was accustomed to, but this was a United Artists release; its failure condemned him to more of Corman's drive-in movies, like *Little Shop of Horrors*, filmed in two days: 'about a guy who crosses a Venus fly-trap with some gigantic plant. He plant. He winds up feeding people to it.' Nicholson explained later. He played a masochist who gets his kicks in the dentist's chair. *The Broken Land* (63) was a Western about three escaped cons (he was one) who seek revenge on the sheriff who had unjustly gaoled them. It was made by 20th-Century-Fox's B-unit, the last such unit existing in Hollywood.

He returned to Corman to play the lead as the juvenile in a couple of his junky horror films. *The Raven* (63), as Peter Lorre's son, gritting his teeth like Pinocchio's Lampwick (undoubtedly a sketch for his performance in *The Witches of Eastwick*), and *The Terror*, more restrained as a Napoleonic officer. The first of these was sponsored by AIP, but the second was a three-day effort, using the props and costumes left over from the earlier film; also involved in the production were Francis Coppola and Monte Hellman. Then again, he was with 20th's B-unit for *Thunder Island*, but only as co-writer (with Don Devlin, who later wrote *Loving*), an above-average B about a Latin-American political group which hires a hit man (Gene Nelson). He then had his second brush with 'legitimate' Hollywood, as one of the shipmates of *Ensign Pulver* (64), who was Robert Walker Jr (and not, as in *Mister Roberts*, Jack Lemmon).

With 20th's B-unit again he was in the Philippines for a couple directed by Hellman, *Back Door to Hell*, as a GI in this drama about a wartime reconnaissance, and *Flight to Fury* (66), some escapism about vanished treasure. Filmed back to back, they were released a while apart, to no success, even by the modest standards at which they aimed. Nicholson and Hellman, with backing by Corman, looked for something more commercial and co-produced two Westerns, *Ride in the Whirlwind* and *The Shooting*. Hellman directed and Nicholson, gaining confidence, starred – as well as promoting both at various festivals, but as he ruefully said, all they got for a year's work was $1,400. Neither film was seen in the US, till by an odd sequence of circumstances they were sold to television – despite some acclaim in France, the home of lost movie causes. Nicholson wrote the first, about two wandering cowboys, and the second – the better of the two – was penned by Adrien Joyce. When this arrived in Britain in 1971 there were complaints that it was pretentious and incoherent, but there was also some admiration, not for the plot (about an ill-mixed quartet trudging across the Utah desert, with Nicholson as a hired gun) but for the atmosphere of this particular part of the West – lonely, cruel and menacing.

Discouraged, he had a look in on Corman's *The St Valentine's Day Massacre* (67), with one line as the driver of a getaway car. And he accepted a role in a piece of vicious trivia called *Hell's Angels on Wheels* (67), as a nonconformist member of the gang called 'Poet'. 'Variety' said his contribution was made up 'mostly of variations on a grin' – and, indeed, even when the films he made were reviewed (usually in some obscure publication) his acting was seldom commented upon. He turned again to writing; the screenplay of *The Trip*, produced and directed by Corman, with Peter Fonda, Susan Strasberg and Dennis Hopper, a drama about drug-taking which had some censorship problems. It is, in the end, probably more *for* than *against* (according to 'Time' magazine, Nicholson had been smoking pot every day for fifteen years). He then wrote *Head* (68), for a pop group called the Monkees. He loves it, he says; 'the best rock'n'roll movie ever made', but 'Variety' called it ﹍ 'silly psychedelic pastiche aimed at youth'. Actually, it's great fun; Bob Rafelson directed, and the two men co-produced. He also wrote *Psych-Out*, and appeared in it – as the leader of a rock combo who pals up with a deaf girl searching Haight Ashbury for her brother.

He might have escaped from this trough when he was approached to play C.W. Moss in *Bonnie and Clyde*, but in the end it was decided that he and star Warren Beatty looked too much alike; he did escape it when Rip Torn bowed out of *Easy Rider* (69). He just happened to be there, he said. Peter Fonda produced and Dennis Hopper directed, and they both starred, as two drop-outs who take off cross-country with some dope, and then cash, stashed away on their motor-cycles. Nicholson played the drunken hick-town lawyer they take on with them half-way along the route. The character was not new to movies – the weak, wealthy, spoilt Southern boy – but there were some new touches: he wears dude clothes of a decade ago; he's stuck in a job he hates, and, most of all, Nicholson conveyed the liberating sense of freedom as he threw it all away to hare off with his hippie friends. There are several other reasons why the film was superior to other motor-cycle films: it was better made and had a deep-seated romantic appeal. Its eventual huge box-office success shook Hollywood by the ears, and more than any other it was instanced as an example of the 'new' American film – though in the end its influence was much less than expected.

Armed with a Best Supporting Oscar nomination (and he should have won), Nicholson played (he had been offered the part much earlier) Barbra Streisand's brother in *On A Clear Day You Can See Forever* (70). 'All I am in the movie is bad,' he said, agreeing with

'A man went looking for America and couldn't find it anywhere' was the slogan used for Easy Rider *(69). The man who went looking was Peter Fonda and one of the things he found was Jack Nicholson – who promptly stole the film from him and his co-star, Dennis Hopper.*

the critics. His part was cut, including his singing of the title-song, which is a pity – for not long after the film was premiered he was probably a bigger box-office attraction than either of the above-title stars, Yves Montand and Streisand. This was due to *Five Easy Pieces*. The producers of *Easy Rider* proposed a starring film to Nicholson, and gathered round him old friends Rafelson to direct and Adrien Joyce to write it – and she based the chief character partly on Nicholson himself and partly on her dead brother. Nicholson said the film was 'an honest statement about where a lot of people are who cannot act out their crisis to a successful conclusion'. It was much more than that (it was also the best American film for years: the New York Critics voted it their Best Film of 1970); it was also one of the few American films about class, and one of the best to take a look at family relationships. Nicholson was a drifter, an oil-rigger shacked up with a clinging, sluttish waitress (Karen Black), and idling his time in bowling alleys. Circumstances take him back

to the family, which turns out to be resolutely middle class, cultured and intellectual; in the end, he abandons both environments to try for an unknown other. And his performance was one of the great charismatic ones.

The same company gave him a chance to direct – *Drive, He Said* (70), another film about youth and not generally considered a success. Then he was in Mike Nichols's *Carnal Knowledge* (71), written by Jules Feiffer, which detailed the disillusioning sexual odysseys of two college buddies (Art Garfunkel was the other) over a twenty-year span – and in considerable and graphic detail: an obsessed film which was not remotely as clever as it ought it was. Judith Crist said Nicholson was 'superlative'; Hollis Alpert called him 'superb'.

Unlike stars of the past, Nicholson had no hang-ups about taking small parts. He chose to do one – that of Tuesday Weld's arrogant lover in Henry Jaglom's *A Safe Place*, after which he rejoined director Rafelson for *The King of Marvin Gardens* (72): and he had no

*A gallery of Nicholson.
1) Five Easy Pieces (70);
2) Carnal Knowledge (71);
3) The Last Detail (73)
with Randy Quaid;* 4) The
Fortune *(75) with Stockard
Channing and Warren
Beatty;* 5) Missouri Breaks
*(77), on set with Marlon
Brando;* 6) Batman *(89);
and* 7) The Two Jakes
(90), the sequel to
Chinatown *which he
directed himself.*

hang-ups about star salaries, for at the time he could command $500,000 and he took the Screen Actors Guild minimum for this because he realized the subject was difficult. Neither film was very popular, but whereas Jaglom's abstract mess made Nicholson's previous worst seem like a masterpiece, Rafelson's, though also elliptical, had some marvellous things in it – including Nicholson as a jaded DJ who becomes enmeshed in the maelstrom caused by the schemes of his brother (Bruce Dern). Still, it was a dip in Nicholson's fortunes, till he was restored to grace by a very fine film indeed, Hal Ashby's version of a Robert Towne screenplay, *The Last Detail* (73). The best thing about it, said Vincent Canby in the 'New York Times', 'is the opportunity it provides Jack Nicholson to play the role of Signalman First Class Buddusky who, with Gunner's Mate First Class Muhall (Otis Young), is the well-meaning escort to the remarkably docile prisoner . . . [His] performance is big, intense, so full of gradations of mood that it becomes virtually a guide to a certain kind of muddled, well-meaning behavior.' It established, Canby went on, Nicholson as a youngish character actor 'at the head of a line that includes Al Pacino, Dustin Hoffman, James Caan and Robert Duvall'; and he concluded, 'Good film actors simply behave. They act natural. You can't see what they're up to. You can see what Nicholson is up to, but it's rather like hearing a musician in top form. You know there are mechanics involved and this awareness enhances the joy in the accomplishment.' At Cannes, Nicholson was Best Actor; he was at last Best Actor for the New York Critics for his private eye in a 30s thriller, *Chinatown* (74), another Towne script, this time directed by Roman Polanski. It brought Nicholson into the box-office ten at No. 8, and raised his salary to $750,000 plus a percentage.

The next year began well, dipped, and ended triumphantly. For the second film running, he was up to his ears in mystery: Antonioni's *The Passenger/Professione Reporter* (75). He explained both it and his work to the 'Guardian': 'Antonioni says he just tries to make something beautiful because truth is beautiful and beauty is truth. That's what I'm really into. I like making beautiful things. Maybe that sounds ridiculous but when I choose a film to do, it's because it interests me in that way rather than any other. I look at every character I play on the screen as being completely separate. You can say most of them are outsiders, but it's hard today to think of any character in a film who isn't an outsider. All I ask is that they relate to the truth in some way.' He sang, as a Harley Street specialist, in *Tommy*, a supporting role

which he did because he wanted to work with Ken Russell – and this 'rock opera' was that director's only successful film in years. He fought with Warren Beatty over Stockard Channing in Nichols's unsuccessful *The Fortune*, losing his pants and dignity with great style. He needed madder things to do, for in moments of triumph this frizzy-haired small-time con-man was very funny indeed. There were similar moments in *One Flew Over the Cuckoo's Nest*, battling with the formidable nurse (Louise Fletcher) as the one inmate to her measure; and audiences vocally and vociferally enjoyed this *loufoque* study of life in a mental hospital. Milos Foreman directed with all the skill of his Czech films, and there were a number of Oscars, including Best Actor to Nicholson, following a second consecutive New York critics' same. It made almost $60 million, which was very nice money at that time – especially for Nicholson, whose percentage was reckoned to have earned him a great deal of money. In his guest-starring role as the union leader in Kazan's *The Last Tycoon* (76), he briefly brought the film to life.

Among the films he turned down at this period are *The Sting*, *The Great Gatsby*, *Bound for Glory*, *Coming Home*, *Apocalypse Now*, *The China Syndrome* (the Jack Lemmon role) and *The Godfather* – because he did not have a scene with Brando. He's the one to beat, he once observed, and he did get a chance to work with Brando in Arthur Penn's *The Missouri Breaks* (77). Brando, at his most self-indulgent, let Nicholson walk all over him – and Nicholson, said John Simon, was the only person to emerge 'unscathed' from what was a very strong venture, a messy rangers vs rustlers tale, with Nicholson the leader of the first group. Both actors were paid $1,250,000, with Brando on a slightly higher percentage – but since the film took only $6,752,000 – perhaps half of what it had cost – there was no further money forthcoming. Notwithstanding, Nicholson promptly made another Western, *Goin' South* (78), which he himself directed. And it is like him – jovial, self-regarding, talented and absolutely refusing to take itself seriously. As gallows-bait saved by a pioneer woman (Mary Steenburgen) – who marries him so that he will work down her mine – Nicholson does his best to imitate George 'Gabby' Hayes, wild of eye and hair, manic. But he's like Olivier or Jouvet, testing, trying to see how far he dare go; he never draws back, but he's miles from a Robert Newton, hamming because he knows no better, or Burt Lancaster, letting us in on the joke (as in another comic Western, *The Scalp-hunters*). The film took $4,766,000, considerably less than it cost. There is little, however, in favour of Nicholson's wild, monotonous performance as a psycho in *The Shin-ing* (80), or indeed the enterprise as a whole. He jumped at the chance of working in Britain with the once-esteemed Stanley Kubrick, working from what would seem to be a particularly rubbishy novel by Stephen King. Nicholson played a winter caretaker in a deserted Colorado hotel who, unhinged by visions, chases his wife (Shelley Duval) and small son with an axe for a rousing climax. A number of hallucinations on everyone's part permitted Kubrick to cheat in the plotting. It cost £18 million and although it took just over $30 million was regarded by the industry as a failure, partly because most of that was taken in the first two weeks, before word-of-mouth confirmed the critics' opinions.

Nicholson returned to work for Rafelson in *The Postman Always Rings Twice* (81), play-ing a seedy drifter whose steamy affair with Jessica Lange leads speedily to the murder of her much older husband. The way to film James M. Cain's thriller was to concentrate on the twists, but this misconceived treatment made it into a dirge of the Depression. The film cost $12 million and took $6,070,000. Nicholson did not carry *Reds*, but had a guest-role as a hard-drinking Eugene O'Neill, locked in a *ménage à trois* with Beatty and Diane Keaton at one point: he took the film from them whenever he appeared. He again proved himself one helluva good actor in *The Border* (82), playing a border guard sucked into corruption (on the matter of illegal immigration), both because it pervades the very air and because his wife (Valerie Perrine) is loading the house with goods bought on credit. He is just an ordinary guy in shades, moustached and with thinning hair, laconic, and not much worried that he's a good guy turned bad. As directed by Tony Richardson, the film climbed well over budget to end up costing $22 million: poor notices brought it in at only $4,587,000. When Burt Reynolds relinquished the role of the hard-drinking, pot-bellied ex-astronaut in James L. Brooks's *Terms of Endearment* (83), Nicholson seized on it like a terrier, offering some very funny scenes with Shirley MacLaine, playing the neighbour he seduces. Brooks took Oscars for Best Picture, Best Director (not bad, when it's your first time out) and Best Screenplay from another medium; author Larry McMurtry, despite his eminence, was not one of the names contractually in the ads, but we may suppose considerable adaptation, for the Nicholson role did not appear in the original. Though this was not again a film he was required to carry, its high $50,250,000 rentals may be credited in part to his performance; the budget had been $13 million. The New York Critics named him the year's Best

Supporting Actor, as did the Oscar voters: accepting the golden statuette, he said that he hoped to be back for many more. He has since said that he hopes to collect more Oscars than Walt Disney.

His marriage in 1961 to actress Sandra Knight had lasted only five years. The high profile inescapable for a star of his renown meant that the other ladies in his life were well documented. The longest-lasting would seem to be Anjelica Huston, who had had a supporting role in *The Postman Always Rings Twice*. He had acted with her father John in *Chinatown*, and he proceeded to join both Hustons now for *Prizzi's Honor* (85), with John directing and Anjelica again in support. Partly because of Huston's illness – this was his penultimate movie – it was carefully budgeted, at $16 million, with most partici-pants on a percentage. Said Richard Condon, author of the original novel: 'I had a better percentage until two weeks before filming started, when Jack announced the deal he wanted. The backers said they couldn't pay it, so anyone who had a percentage had to give up part of it. Jack had $4,500,000 against 15 per cent of the gross. You can't reach out for greed better than that.' The film made back only $13 million, despite warm notices, effec-tively not admitting that as an underworld thriller it did not begin to compete with some earlier films of Huston's, e.g. *The Asphalt Jungle*. But what success it had may be

Jack Nicholson in One Flew Over the Cuckoo's Nest *(75), which won him the first of his two Oscars. He once said he intended to win more than Walt Disney – and, for a start, the New York critics have chosen him their Best Actor six times (on one occasion for three films).*

attributed to Nicholson, who won an unprecedented fifth Best Actor award from the New York critics. He played a Mafia hit-man who tangles with the wife (Kathleen Turner, who co-starred) of the man he has been sent to kill. With hooded eyes and balding hair, he was Huston's best interpreter of the underworld since Bogart.

If Nicholson's star was again high in the ascendant, matters on set, as it were, were not too happy. Financing could not be found for *The Mosquito Coast* (later made with Harrison Ford). Earlier, *Roadshow*, a project for himself and Timothy Hutton, to be directed by Martin Ritt and then Richard Brooks, moved over to Burt Reynolds (but was never made). And a sequel to *Chinatown* called *The Two Jakes* called it a day before shooting began. Robert Towne had written a script for which Dustin Hoffman would be partnered with Nicholson; when Hoffman dropped out, Paramount could not proceed without Towne and Nicholson, who owned one-half of the Gittes character so as to prevent the studio building a television series around him. The Hoffman role was rewritten to suit Robert Evans, who had produced *Chinatown*, but whose initial experience in Hollywood had been as an actor. Because Paramount had already spent so much in development (that figure was estimated at $4 million when the film was abandoned), Towne, Evans and Nicholson agreed to waive any upfront fees in order to keep within a reasonable budget. But Towne, who was to direct, disliked Evans's tests: what he wanted, he said, was not Evans's acting, but as he was in life; to make matters worse, it was reported that Evans was behaving 'like Faye Dunaway', whose temperament on the previous film still made her colleagues squirm. Although Nicholson's friendship with Towne went back a long way, he declared that he would not make the film without Evans. A last-minute high-level conference failed to reach agreement; the crew, assembled the following day for the start of principal photography, found there was nothing to shoot.

Meanwhile, the New York actor, Mandy Patinkin, was not happy on the set of Mike Nichols's *Heartburn* (86), a triangle tale set among Washington's smart set, with Meryl Streep as the wronged woman. Nicholson took over, making light work of the initial romance and the move to adultery, but when he begins to disappear from the action there is little of interest to sustain it. The result (see Streep) did not recover its budget, but Nicholson had a neat success with *The Witches of Eastwick* (87), which cost $27 million and took $31,800,000. George Miller directed from John Updike's novel, which had been considerably vulgarized. Nicholson played a Don Juan who does not seduce but who believes that his conquests are ready for a rather special screw. What goes on in his home is not unlike the more *outré* Fellini extravaganzas till it opts for *Exorcist* excrescences. The result is not taking but, to give the devil his due, not boring either. It allowed Nicholson to add some grotesqueries to the character he played in *The Shining*. A second film with Streep, *Ironweed*, proved disastrous, as few wanted to spend much time with the bums of the Depression. The director was Hector Babenco. Whether Nicholson could still cut it after these unrewarding outings was a question wonderfully answered by James L. Brooks's *Broadcast News* (88), in an unbilled cameo as a famous TV anchorman: he has the charisma and the false bonhomie, but mainly, since we see him only in glimpses, he impresses because he exudes a self-satisfied, cruel arrogance. For these three performances he was again the year's Best Actor for the New York Critics. *Ironweed* marked his ninth Oscar nomination, a record beaten among actors only by Laurence Olivier.

Jon Peters, one of the producers of *The Witches of Eastwick*, found Nicholson less than responsive when it was suggested that he play the villain, The Joker, in *Batman* (89). Undoubtedly, one of the incentives was money, though his contract specified billing over Michael Keaton, who was playing Batman. So much has been written about what Nicholson was paid and earned from the film that the facts have been obscured. What is certain is that it cost $50 million, to which was added half as much again in advertising and publicity, perhaps a new high; its domestic rentals were over $150,000,000, making it the fourth-highest grossing movie in the history of the industry (and small-screen rights went to NBC with no pre-cable deals, for $30 million for a first screening in 1992). Nicholson was on a percentage which included merchandizing sub-rights, and whether he was paid nothing up-front, $6 million or $11 million (all of which have been reported) his most likely earnings would seem to be in the $60 million range. Whether it was otherwise worth doing is another matter. The director, Tim Burton, congratulated himself on restoring the darker aspect of the first Batman strip cartoons, but what was on the screen was irredeemably second-rate, only fumbling towards the exuberance and magic of the first three *Superman* films. Nicholson was, said Jack Kroll in 'Newsweek', 'a one-man theatre of evil', but other critics complained that he went over the top. Yes, but in this sort of thing, who cares?

He directed as well as starred in the re-activated *The Two Jakes* (90), originally set to open in December 1989, but now postponed a year due to 'production difficulties'. Harvey Keitel has the Evans role on a budget of $19 million, with Nicholson about $5 million, plus 10 per cent of the gross receipts. The reviews were warm, but the film disappeared from 'Variety's weekly box-office report at just under $10 million. The cast of the film also includes Rebecca Broussard, who just recently had his baby. Actress Susan Anspach has named him as the father of her son Caleb, but he says that he has not had the chance to discover whether this is true. What is true, he says, is the comment often made to him by Elmer Valentine, who owns the Whisky a Go-Go nightclub: 'Jack, you're one of the good guys. A lot of people score and they don't know it. We scored, and we know it.'

Next up: *Sleepwalker* (91), to be directed by Alan Parker in Greece, and *The Death of Napoleon*.

PHILIPPE NOIRET

'I get the parts that might in the past have gone to Raimu, Louis Jouvet and Michel Simon,' said Philippe Noiret. On another occasion he observed that receiving awards was 'better than a kick in the ass. But at my age, when someone tells you you're the best European actor, you know better.' Yes, *mon cher*, but if you are heir to Raimu, Jouvet, Simon – and one would add Harry Baur – you have to be the best *something*. You stand with four of the greatest actors who ever lived, and you are not overshadowed by them.

Noiret was born in Lille in 1930, and he could not think of anything else to do while at school than act. He began his professional life walking on with Jean Vilar's Théâtre National Populaire, with similar brief appearances during the day, as it were, in *Gigi* (48), *Olivia* (51) and *Agence Matrimoniale*. His roles with the TNP got bigger, and he was a notable Sir Toby Belch in 'Twelfth Night' when he was only twenty-two. Agnès Varda was the TNP's photographer, and when she decided to direct a feature film, *La Pointe Courte* (55) she selected Noiret (when her original choice suddenly fell out) for one of the two leads, a fisherman trying to patch up his shaky marriage. Silvia Montfort is the wife, and the film – which is derivative of Italian models – returns to the couple between documentary footage of the fishers of Sète. The film had little success, but Noiret began to work in television, predictably as Cyrano de Bergerac, but also as Macbeth. He realized that his round, hangdog face and spaniel eyes condemned him to being a character actor, and,

despite leads with the TNP, accepted that his work in films would be in supporting roles.

He did little more than look in on *Ravissante* (60), but did have a role of substance in Louis Malle's *Zazie dans le Métro*, as the troublesome child's colourful uncle, a female impersonator who is married to the ravishing Albertine (Carla Marlier). He headed well down the cast-list in *Le Capitaine Fracasse* (61), who was Jean Marais, but had a fair role supporting Annie Girardot in Jean Delanoy's thriller, *Le Rendez-vous*. Then: *Les Amours Célèbres*, in the Belmondo episode, as Louis XIV; René Clair's *Tout l'Or du Monde*, as a property tycoon trying to cheat a country bumpkin (Bourvil); *Comme un Poisson dans l'Eau* (62); and *Le Crime ne Paie pas*, in the episode with Michèle Morgan and Pierre Brasseur. Although he showed a brisk wit, when he got the chance, he was not really noticed in any of these. But he had a fine chance as the wronged husband in Franju's fine version of a Mauriac novel, *Thérèse Desqueyroux*, giving evidence in favour of his wife (Emmanuelle Riva) who had tried to murder him, but who exacts revenge by keeping her confined to her room. He himself married Monique Chaumette, whom he had met at the TNP, not long after the film was finished.

After *Ballade pour un Voyou* and *Clémentine Chérie* (63), he was Cyrano in Abel Gance's flop *Cyrano and D'Artagnan*. He then made the first of several trips to Italy,

Philippe Noiret as a young man, in Agnès Varda's La Pointe Courte (55) with Silvia Montfort as his wife.

this time to appear in *Le Massagiatrici*. He returned to star roles, but whether they were worth having is another matter: Maurice Cloche's tear-jerker, *La Porteuse de Pain*, opposite a wronged Suzanne Flon; and Hervé Bromberger's *Mort, où est ta Victoire?* (64). He supported Jean Gabin in *Monsieur*, as the male head of the feckless family which Gabin protects while working as their butler, However, Noiret returned to first billing in Yves Robert's *Les Copains* (65) – the others were Pierre Mondy, Claude Rich, Christian Marin, Jacques Balutin, Guy Bedos and Michel Lonsdale, sharing a taste for wine, Mozart and practical jokes. In his first English-language film, *Lady L*, he played a client of Sophia Loren, who claims that he is a Minister when they are found in bed together (and he was dubbed by the director, Peter Ustinov). Jean-Paul Rappeneau's joyous *La Vie de Château* (66) gave him a by now familiar role, that of the husband with a dissatisfied wife (Catherine Deneuve), younger and prettier than he; it was set in Normandy during the summer of 1944 and the plot finds them harbouring a member of the Maquis while the German army is billeted on them. Billed only below Deneuve and Brasseur, Noiret was not yet entirely happy with leading roles – at least, this was the last he would play for some time.

He was the television interviewer who asked *Qui Êtes-vous, Polly Magoo?* of an American model working in Paris in this intended satire written and directed by William Klein, and a gynaecologist supporting Gina Lollobrigida and Louis Jourdan in Delannoy's *Les Sultans*, in which she gets jealous after seeing him (Jourdan) with his daughter. He made: *Le Voyage du Père*, a vehicle for Fernandel; *Tendre Voyou*, ditto Belmondo; *Night of the Generals*, as a detective enquiring into the affairs of Peter O'Toole; René Allio's *L'Une et l'Autre* (67), as confidant and fellow-actor to the heroine, Malka Ribovska; and De Sica's awful sketch picture, *Woman Times Seven/Sept Fois Femme*, admitting to his wife (Shirley MacLaine) that he has hired a detective (Michael Caine) to follow her. He had a splendid return to the leading role in Robert's *Alexandre le Bienheureux*, as a farmer whose laziness begins to be contagious, but was then clobbered with Bernard T. Michel's mistaken version of Benjamin Constant's novel *Adolphe, ou l'Âge Tendre* – to wit, he is the neighbour who allows his mistress (Ulla Jacobsson) to be in the film of that book within the film. He was in another of Klein's unsuccessful ventures, *Mister Freedom* (68), as Moujik Man, the sworn enemy of the title-character (John Abbey), the member of an American racist,

American racist, right-wing group sent to educate the French politically: once again Klein's comic-strip approach robbed the point of any of its jokes. Noiret had made this in the midst of several English-language films, all of which were released later: Michael Relph's foolish spoof, *The Assassination Bureau* (69), as a corrupt Government minister; Hitchcock's *Topaz*, on crutches (because he had broken his leg) as a French official who is also a Russian agent; and Cukor's *Justine*, as the unfortunate diplomat Pombal, resolutely hetero but in drag at the carnival ball to revenge himself on a rival.

He returned to France to two leading roles: Robert's *Clerambard*, a charming fable about a mean old sourpuss, living in a run-down château and hated by his family, who reforms after reading a life of St Francis of Assisi; and Philippe de Broca's *Les Caprices de Marie* (70), top-billed as one of the villagers, though the plot centres on the local beauty queen (Marthe Keller) and her new, wealthy American husband (Bert Convy), who rebuilds the village on the Hudson. Noiret had one of his best roles abroad in *Murphy's War* (71), as the timid French oil-engineer who joins Peter O'Toole in his adventures (for a while). He joined his distinguished predecessors – not only Jouvet, etc., but Gabin and Lino Ventura – in playing a weary but determined police inspector in Edouard Molinaro's *Les Aveux les Plus Doux*, with Roger Hanin as his partner. *Time for Loving* (72) was a three-part film directed by Christopher Miles and written by Jean Anouilh about finding time for sex in Paris, with Mark Burns and Mel Ferrer having trouble in the first two episodes and Noiret in the third, because of the demands of wife, mother and mistress. Annie Girardot was *La Vieille Fille*, staying at a run-down resort hotel near the Spanish border, one much beneath her, and Noiret was the insensitive fellow guest who can't or won't see that she wants to keep herself to herself. Or does she? These players together wrought magic for director Jean-Pierre Blanc, an industry unknown who had got backing after sending the script to Girardot.

Then: Edmond Free's *Le Trèfle a Cinq Feuilles*, with Liselotte Pulver forming an odd couple caring for some parasitic eccentrics who haven't the least regard for their financial difficulties; Molinaro's *La Mandarine*, a reunion with Girardot, as her husband, so despised by her mother (Madeleine Renaud) that she encourages her to flirt with the Englishman (Murray Head) who is also the lover of their daughter; Manlio Scarpelli's *Siamo Tutti in Libertà Provvisoria*, which was so bad that it was never shown in France; Yves Boisset's *L'Attentat*, based on the Ben Barka affair, in superb form as the unctious television personality masterminding the kidnapping (and there were equally compelling studies in villainy by Michel Piccoli and Michel Bouquet); and Marco Ferreri's self-indulgent comedy about compulsive eaters, *La Grande Bouffe* (73), with Marcello Mastroianni, Ugo Tognazzi and Michel Piccoli, all billed above him, as the others. Henri Graziani's remake of the novel by Jules Renard (the third screen version), *Poil de Carotte*, was co-written by him and Maurice Pialat, with an emphasis on the discord in the family rather than on the child ill-treated by his mother and neglected by his father; as the latter, Noiret gave one of his most deeply felt performances, almost eclipsing memories of Baur in Duvivier's 1932 version. After playing the head of French Intelligence in Henri Verneuil's English-language *Le Serpent/The Serpent*, he returned to Ferreri for another of his inept grotesqueries, *Touche Pas à la Femme Blanche* (74), with Mastroianni as General Custer and Piccoli as Buffalo Bill. This time Noiret was billed above the latter and Tognazzi, who was again in the cast.

If Noiret's two films with Ferreri are an aberration for someone who had almost always chosen quality material, it must be said that Ferreri had a reputation on his home ground and in France, if not elsewhere, and *La Grande Bouffe* – almost alone of his films – was a hit in the international market. By virtue of his work with Buñuel, especially, Piccoli was probably better known than Noiret in that market; but not since Marcel Dalio or Claude Dauphin had any French character actor worked so often in British or American. On his home ground Noiret was a more important actor than either of those predecessors, and at this point he was overtaking Piccoli in popularity – certainly after Belmondo, and perhaps ranking with Yves Montand as the most sought-after 'older' actor. For over fifteen years the directors who had dominated French film-making were those swept in on the *nouvelle vague* – and Noiret had worked with none of these, except with Malle at the beginning. For the sort of roles that Noiret might have played, Chabrol preferred Michel Bouquet; with the exception of the Jean Desailly role in *La Peau Douce* it is difficult to see where Noiret might have fitted into Truffaut's small universe; and he himself said that although he admired the films of Jean-Luc Godard, he never would have worked with him, for Godard 'works out of conflict. My taste is for harmony and teamwork.'

While the first dazzling successes of the *nouvelle vague* had thrown most of the previous generation of directors out of work, Noiret preferred to work with those who had come up since, not concerned with their precepts. This is a generalization, for de Broca was of that generation, and his best work is certainly preferable to the worst of Godard, Truffaut or Chabrol, all of whom had proved as variable as those directors whose work they had disliked when they were critics. What is certain is that Bertrand Tavernier disliked the *nouvelle vague* and looked back on older traditions. Noiret was the star of his first feature, and would call on him time and again, as with Kurosawa/Mifune, Ray/Chatterjee, Bergman/von Sydow (even if few would put Tavernier at the same eminence). Thus, for him Noiret was *L'Horloger de Saint-Paul*, the clockmaker of a suburb of Lyons, facing up to the fact that his son is on the run from the police. The screenplay was written, from a novel by Simenon, by the distinguished pre-*nouvelle vague* team of Jean Aurenche and Pierre Bost. Showing in Paris at the same time (as was also the last Ferreri) was Pierre Tchernia's *Les Gaspards*, with Noiret taking second-billing to that great bore of the French cinema, the monotonous Michel Serrault who, in the plot, looks for his disappeared daughter in the Paris underworld, where he discovers a slightly mad community with Noiret as its uncrowned king.

Marco Pico's *Un Nuage entre les Dents* teamed him with Pierre Richard, as a successful tabloid team of journalist and photographer who embark on an enquiry into a mass kidnapping of schoolchildren in fact organized by Richard's young son. It was well received but not very popular – and the reverse was true of Robert Enrico's *Le Secret*, with Noiret as a kindly, obtuse writer living in seclusion with his wife (Marlene Jobert) till a mental patient (Jean-Louis Trintignant) intrudes upon them. Alain Robbe-Grillet's *Le Jeu avec le Feu* (75) was high tosh, and Noiret got himself into a second bad one, Tavernier's second (and worst) film, *Que la Fête Commence*, a rambling and supposedly funny look at the court and Paris of the Regent, Philippe d'Orléans (Noiret). It opened to good notices in France, which brought it a New York opening, but the same distributor did not try to chance it in Britain. Already committed to these, Noiret turned down *Three Days of the Condor*, but the role was then offered to Max von Sydow which, he said, was honour enough. Returning to Enrico, he gave one of his most moving performances as an army surgeon who, in 1944, sets out in revenge after discovering that the Germans have massacred his family: *Le Vieux Fusil*, for which he was awarded the César for Best Actor. Then he crossed the Alps again to join Tognazzi, Gastone Moschin and Duilio del Prete, the four friends of *Amici Miei* who enjoy provoking trouble. Mario Monicelli took over the direction after the death of Pietro Germi, and it was hard to see in this crude piece that he had ever been a craftsman of distinction; Noiret played a small-time crime journalist whose upright son despises him and his sloppiness.

Tavernier returned to form with *Le Juge et l'Assassin* (76), which also gave Noiret one of his best roles as the *juge*, a petty official obsessed with the apprehension of a mass murderer (Michel Galabru) because he sees in it his way to the *Légion d'Honneur* and national fame. After Jacques Renard's *Monsieur Albert*, he crossed the Alps again for *Il Commune Senso del Pudore*, directed by Alberto Sordi, but the film did not make the journey in the opposite direction. Both *Une Femme à sa Fenêtre*, directed by Pierre Granier-Deferre from a novel by Pierre Drieu la Rochelle, and *Il Deserto dei Tartari*, directed by Valerio Zurlini from one by Dino Buzzati, were ambitious French–Italian co-productions, set respectively amid the diplomatic corps in Athens in 1936 and an outpost of the Austro–Hungarian Empire some years earlier. The first was basically a vehicle for Romy Schneider; the second gave Noiret a cameo role as a visiting general among an all-star cast (von Sydow, Trintignant, Fernando Rey, Vittorio Gassmann, Francisco Rabal). He was also in fine company (Fred Astaire, Peter Ustinov, Charlotte Rampling) as a hotel guest in Boisset's Irish whimsy-whamsy, *Purple Taxi*/*Le Taxi Mauve* (77), about which no words could be too unkind; but the reverse is true of de Broca's delicious *Tendre Poulet*, in which he is an unworldly professor at the Sorbonne and Girardot a top *flic* who were at college together: meeting up again, they fall in love while despising the other's profession. As charming as they are unpretentious, they are one of the screen's great teams. Between the two movies Noiret began work on Enrico's *Coup de Foudre*, but it was abandoned.

He followed with: René Richon's *La Barricade du Point du Jour* (78), a drama of the Commune with a name-cast, of which he was the biggest, but in a guest role, as a poet; Ted Kotcheff's *Who is Killing the Great Chefs of Europe?*, as one of them, a specialist in pressed duck; Jean-Pierre Mocky's *Le Témoin*, as a wealthy Reims banker and art-lover who invites an Italian friend (Alberto Sordi) to stay, but who finds himself investigating a murder instead of restoring the cathedral murals; Sergio Citti's *Due Pezzi di Pane* (79), as a street musician who doesn't know that he is sharing his mistress with his partner (Gassman); Jacques Grand-Juan's *Rue du Pied-de-Grue*; *On a Volé la Cuisse de*

Jupiter (80), de Broca's welcome sequel to *Tendre Poulet*, with our stars chasing after a piece of stolen archaeology while on honeymoon in Greece; Tavernier's *Une Semaine de Vacances*, repeating his role from *L'Horloger de Saint-Paul* for one sequence only of this study of a schoolteacher (Nathalie Baye); and Enrico's *Pile ou Face*, as a provincial cop investigating the suicide or murder of a mean little man (Serrault) living in the same building. He then did two of his best films. Francesco Rosi's *Tre Fratelli* (81) is a detailed, affectionate look at a Southern family as they gather from afar for the death of their mother – the Judge (Noiret) from Rome, the teacher (Vittorio Mezzogiorno) from Naples, and the factory-worker (Michele Placido) from Turin. Their father was played by one of Noiret's greatest predecessors, Charles Vanel, near to ending a film career which had begun in 1912.

The other film may be Noiret's best – it is certainly superb entertainment and perhaps the best that Tavernier has done, *Coup de Torchon*, based on a novel by Jim Thompson, 'Pop. 1280', with the action transferred to French West Africa in 1938. Noiret is the police chief, noted for indolence and for not being notably effective; his wife (Stephane Audran) despises him and is carrying on with the lodger (Eddy Mitchell) almost before his eyes. Stung one day by a comment of a colleague (Guy Marchand), he shoots two tramps and then a drunk, whose wife (Isabelle Huppert) is so grateful that she offers a quick fuck. After that, Laurent Heynemann's *Il Faut Tuer Birgitt Haas* seemed ordinary, a murder mystery which starts out with Noiret as the mysterious chief of a bureau for counter-espionage. Granier-Deferre offered him another first-class outing, on *L'Étoile du Nord* (82), which brought him to Brussels to stay at the boarding-house run by Simone Signoret, who is fascinated by his tales of life in Egypt, but the other guests think that he may be the perpetrator of the much discussed murder on the eponymous train of the title. The original story was by Simenon, and Noiret has fun with the role, as ever when playing a man of mystery, enjoying the laziness, the stubbornness, the boasting and the hint of fawning. *Amici Miei Atto II* (83) was a sequel, called for by the popular success of the first; de Broca's *L'Africain* was Noiret's first film with Deneuve since *La Vie de Château*, playing an unhappy couple who meet up again in Africa to quarrel over a stretch of land, which he wants for elephants and she for the Club Méditerranée; and *L'Ami de Vincent* was his second film for Granier-Deferre. His fourth film that year was a merry tale of the arrival of the Americans in Algeria in 1943, *Le Grand Carnaval*,

to be greeted by the mayor (Noiret) and the proprietor (Hanin) of the town's largest bar, who dreams of a lucrative trade in the black market. Noiret did only guest appearances in his next two films: the epic *Fort Saganne* (84) as the *bête noir* of its hero, Gérard Depardieu; and *Aurora*, as the doctor once loved by Sophia Loren and who could be the father of her baby. This last was made for American television. He had one of his biggest successes ever with *Les Ripoux*, written for him and Thierry Lhermitte by Claude Zidi, whose burlesques hitherto had marked him as one of the worst French directors ever. He made

amends with this gorgeous comedy which paired honest upright cop Lhermitte with one (Noiret) who knew every trick of the trade – and the dirtier they were the more he relished them. And the verb will do for Noiret's handling of the role.

Souvenirs Souvenirs was set in Paris in 1962, when Christophe Malavoy was trying to resurrect his career as a pop star after serving in Algeria and his brother (Pierre-Loup Rajot) is idling instead of studying; Jobert, Girardot, Claude Brasseur were in to support, along with Noiret, briefly as the headmaster. Nadine Trintignant's *L'Été Prochain* (85) was

Noiret in four of his biggest successes: 1) with Emmanuelle Riva in Franju's Thérèse Desqueyroux *(62); 2) with Annie Girardot in* Tendre Poulet *(77); 3) with Isabelle Huppert in* Coup de Torchon *(81); and 4) with Thierry Lhermitte in* Les Ripoux *(84).*

an ineffective family drama with Noiret as the dying patriarch: Claudia Cardinale was his wife and the director's husband, Jean, was a son-in-law. In Monicelli's *Speriamo che sia Femmina* (86) Noiret is a feckless count, married to Liv Ullman. He finally linked up with Chabrol for *Masques* (87), to play a conceited television personality who invites a would-be biographer (Robert Renucci) to his château. The result is never anything but a Chabrol film: when setting the scene he reminds us of the time when he was a master of suspense, but as the twists get sillier and sillier the film itself reminds us of the junk he has churned out since. Noiret's role was one he could play backwards, a man of great ego but with an intelligence not as bright as his fame: but in the circumstances he becomes as irritating as the film itself. He was more rewardingly employed in Giuliano Montaldo's appealing version of Giorgio Bassani's novella, *Gli Occhiali d'Oro*, set in a suspicious Ferrara in 1938, playing a kindly but lonely bachelor doctor who is befriended by some youngsters, one of whom is poorer and better-looking than the others; he foolishly takes him to the resort patronised by most of the local townsfolk, and is ostracised by them after a jealous fit in the hotel. Alone, one boy (Rupert Everett) continues to visit him, in what may be the best movie about homosexuality in that far-off period. Still picking carefully, Noiret came up with his fourth film for Granier-Deferre and one of the director's finest: *Noyade Interdite*, sent back to the dead little resort where he grew up, to lead a murder enquiry – and notably differ with a local colleague (Marchand). Noiret took a tumble, however, with Zeffirelli's *Il Giovane Toscanini*/*Young Toscanini* (88), if in a guest role, as the lover of prima donna Elizabeth Taylor: jeered at the Venice Festival, it has hardly surfaced since.

Throughout his career as a star actor only about 50 per cent of Noiret's films had been *widely* seen abroad: and since foreign art-house audiences had queued to see *Coup de Torchon* only *L'Étoile du Nord* and *Les Ripoux* had found foreign distribution on a large scale. For that, festival exposure is useful and Noiret had shown himself distinctly disinclined to make the sort of fodder which delights the donkeys who seem to make up the selection committees of the major festivals (and this is not the place to list some of the excellent films turned down over the years). But the next one found worldwide acceptance after being seen at Cannes: Giuseppe Tornatore's *Nuovo Cinema Paradiso* (89) was a nostalgic hymn to the great days of cinemagoing, with Noiret as a Sicilian projectionist who had imbued a small boy (Salvatore

Cascio) with his own love of movies. As in his last trip to Italy, for *Gli Occhiali d'Oro*, he gave a rigorous and moving performance despite some surrounding sentiment. Gianfranco Mingozzi's *Il Frullo del Passero* (89) was an erotic romance in which he thought he was past love till he meets a much younger woman (Ornella Mutti); and Richard Lester's *Return of the Musketeers* was a flop – not that that hurt Noiret, who had a few appearances as Cardinal Mazzarin. Tavernier's *La Vie et Rien d'Autre* was a grandiose, artifical but impressive study of a veteran soldier who in 1920 is obsessed with putting names to the corpses found at Verdun, so that the word would never forget the obscene numbers of the slaughtered. In this last role, in particular, Noiret was never more authoritative, as always finding any hint of humour in the dialogue to honour it with a wry smile. He won a Best Actor César for it, and because it was his hundredth film invited, as rarely, the press to meet him. He brushed aside comments in the press to the effect that he was a national treasure, but who was he to disagree? He also observed that if he has confidence in a director's talent, if he had a sense of humour and is honest and open, 'I'm easy to work with.' He also said that he had never cared for himself physically, but he had learnt from Gabin to let his defects work for him. And he remarked that once he was working, once he had 'fixed' his appearance for the role, he lived in a hotel entirely cut off from daily life.

He was effective in Rosi's tale of the Mafia, *Dimenticare Palermo* (90), but it was only a guest role, as the hotel manager; simultaneously he was on view in an eagerly awaited sequel, *Les Ripoux Contre les Ripoux*. *Monsieur Albert* had a Carnésque flavour, with Noiret as a petty crook who hides out with an army buddy and brings tragedy to all three when he falls in love with his mistress (Dominique Labourier). *Nuovo Cinema Paradiso II* was another sequel. *Faux et Usage de Faux* was inspired by what the French call *'l'affaire Ajar'*, when the Goncourt-winning Romain Gary won another for a novel under the pseudonym Emile Ajar. Noiret played the writer and Robin Renucci is the young cousin whose name he 'borrows'. He then joined Depardieu and Jean-Pierre Marielle in a film based on Marcel Aymé's novel, *Uranus*.

NICK NOLTE

Every now and then Nolte has his picture taken with his hair combed, in a shirt and tie, but most of the time he stares defiantly back at the camera, looking like an unmade bed.

His appearance, indeed, is easy to align with the personality, as portrayed in the movie magazines, of a wild man given to roistering. Then, he has made a number of forgettable action movies, so that overall there is much to obscure the fact that he is a fine screen actor.

He was born in Omaha, Nebraska, in 1940, to a father who was an irrigation project engineer. He was also on the Iowa State football team, giving young Nolte an ambition as he attended five different colleges in the mid-West; he was also adept at wrestling, baseball, sprinting, basketball and baseball, and hoped to have a career as a jock. Because most of his mother's family were academics or administrators, and he found them smug, he set his sights in the opposite direction. At one point he was put on probation for selling counterfeit draft cards, but he said later that he was not so much anti-war as anti-authority. It was while at Pasadena City College that he discovered he wanted to be an actor, after a friend had taken him to the Playhouse. For a while he did various jobs in Los Angeles, including one with a steel construction company. There were other aspiring actors in the city attending drama classes and hoping for the big break, but Nolte decided he would seek experience of legitimate theatre in the sticks. He said later that if you wanted to play Biff in 'Death of a Salesman' and Osborne's 'Luther' while still in your twenties, that was your best chance of doing so. For ten years he toured throughout the mid-West, appearing in some 150 productions. He was in Phoenix, Arizona, in 1973 starring in 'The Last Pad', when it was seen by its author, William Inge. He was so pleased with the production that he arranged a transfer to the Westport Playhouse in Los Angeles. It opened there the night Inge committed suicide, which did not hurt a run of several months. Nolte received several offers from television, starting with a role in 'Medical Center' and followed by small roles in movies for that medium: *Winter Kill* (74); *The California Kid*, which starred Vic Morrow as a psychotic (modern) sheriff and Martin Sheen as his victim (and Sheen's own brother, Joseph Estevez, had a small role as his brother); *Death Sentence* with Cloris Leachman as a juror when he is on trial for murdering his wife; and *The Runaway Barge* (75) with Bo Hopkins.

His first film proper was *Return to Macon County*, a sequel to *Macon County Line*, in which he and Don Johnson were the most prominent of several kids involved with drag-races and crime. It was not seen by enough people to elicit further movie offers, but television was offering a star part in a mini-series, *Rich Man Poor Man* (76), based on Irwin Shaw's novel. It followed the adven-

Nick Nolte has never managed to trail clouds of glory, but he can be relied upon to give a solid and, where necessary, a sympathetic performance. He 'is as terrific as ever' said the British critic Ann Billson in 1990, and most reviewers and industry professionals would agree.

tures of two brothers (the other was Peter Strauss) over many years – too many, in fact – and was sufficiently popular to spawn a sequel, *Rich Man Poor Man: Book Two*. Since Nolte had been killed at the end of Book One, the plan was for him to play his own son, but he considered this exploitation and refused, confident that his new-found fame would bring further offers. He waited a year – till a handsome hulk was wanted for *The Deep* (77), an expensive project about treasure under the sea also starring Robert Shaw, with whom Nolte wanted to work. Shaw attacked his role with macho gusto, coming off less well from a silly enterprise than Nolte, who stood around looking vaguely concerned, usually with the equally unclothed and even prettier Jacqueline Bisset. He was sufficiently impressive – physically – to be offered the role of Superman, but he turned it down to do *Who'll Stop the Rain* (78) for director Karel Reisz. When a film starts changing its title it's a cinch that no one loves it, and this was also around for a while as *The Dog Soldiers*. Either way it was a confused and confusing piece about two Vietnam veterans (the other was Michael Moriarty) peddling heroin, which it sees about as dangerous as lemon sherbet. Still, Nolte received a flush of fine notices, including this from David Denby: 'an actor I never expected to praise gives a smashing performance . . . he creates an aura of danger and physical power that takes you back to the young Burt Lancaster and even to Brando. And he's a lot less pretentious than either of those fellows.'

With one movie success and one failure, Nolte set his sights on an exposé of the life of a football pro, *North Dallas Forty* (79), based on a 1973 novel by Peter Gent. Unable to secure the rights, he nevertheless wrote a screenplay with a friend, Hal Hauser, which he submitted to Paramount – who said yes to the project and to him, but who commissioned a new script by Gent and Frank Yablans and Ted Kotcheff, producer and director respectively. The film was so downbeat – the hero was drug-addled for most of its length – that devotees of the game 'might prefer to see it swept under the Astroturf' (Lawrence Van Gelder in the 'New York Times'). Nolte's innate gentle nature was still discernible within the character, as it was again in two further failures, *Heart Beat* with Sissy Spacek, as Neal Cassady, husband to her and friend to Jack Kerouac; and *Cannery Row* (82) based on Steinbeck's novel, with Debra Winger, as a baseball player turned marine biologist.

Hollywood has often given up on gifted players with no box-office clout, but it persevered with Nolte – and not surprisingly, given his superb job in the Steinbeck film. Paramount was rewarded with huge returns when he played a detective in Walter Hill's *48 Hrs*, even though those were mostly due to his co-

Much of Cannery Row *(82) is indigestible because it's taken too faithfully from Steinbeck's novel. In the book, the marine biologist trying to forget his past and the wanderer-cum-hooker are not especially convincing: but touched by the talent and truth of Nolte and Debra Winger their every scene together is very special.*

star, the debuting Eddie Murphy. Roger Spottiswoode was one of the writers, and he cast Nolte in *Under Fire* (83), his first film as a director. Nolte played a news photographer in what is perhaps the best movie about the current turmoil in Latin-America, but when fine reviews helped it to bring in less than $4 million, he was clearly not a box-office proposition. Arthur Hiller's *Teachers* (84), a hellish look at that profession, did not change that view. Neither did *The Ultimate Solution of Grace Quigley*, another of Nolte's films to be re-titled, in this case several times, usually emerging as a mere *Grace Quigley*. Grace was played by Katharine Hepburn, who was grateful to Nolte for getting this long-nurtured project off the ground – for the subject was of doubtful appeal, that of an old lady who recruits a young hit-man in her quest for euthanasia. She was not too enthusiastic, however, when he turned up late and hung-over one morning: 'I hear you've been drunk in every gutter in town,' she said acidly.

Nolte's drinking – and his career – was taken in hand by his third wife, Becky Linger, whom he married in 1984. He was previously wed in 1966 and 1978, between which he lived with Karen Ecklund, who sued unsuccessfully for $4,500,000 'palimony', for the help she had given him in his career. Linger's guidance had almost immediate effect, for Nolte had the biggest success of his career in what might be termed the title-role in *Down and Out in Beverly Hills* (86), with Richard Dreyfuss and Bette Midler. Intermittently over the years he had proved to be an unmatchable action hero, but this time out he was an endearing stumble-bum. Disney produced, and its president, Jeffrey Katzenberg, called Nolte 'a really major star, one of the two or three most sought-after leading men in the industry'. This was unquestionably true, since he was paid $2,500,000 for *Extreme Prejudice* (87), in which he was a Texas Ranger battling it out with a flamboyant drug baron, once an old pal, Powers Boothe (one of his cronies in real life). 'I got a feeling,' says Nolte, 'that the next time we run into each other there's going to be a killing' – and, yes, the body-count was idiotically high, as might be guessed from the credentials: Carolco, the *Rambo* lot, produced, with Walter Hill directing from a story co-written by John Milius, but the public wasn't doing the same seeking-out as the industry. There were no *Rambo* crowds, however, and the film took a derisory $4,300,000, but that looked good beside the less than $1 million taken by *Weeds*, in which Nolte was a hardened con whose life changes when he writes a play which becomes a big hit on the outside.

He had better luck returning to Disney, for

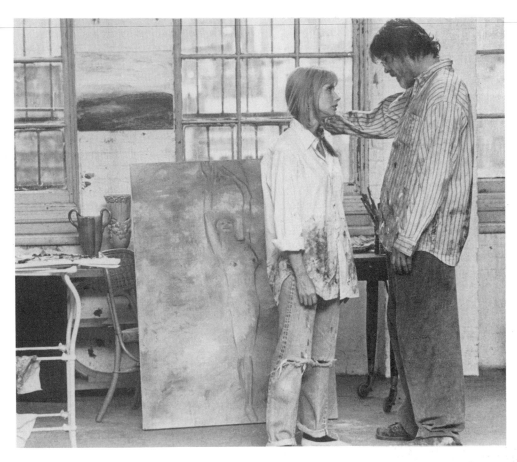

*Rosanna Arquette and
Nick Nolte in 'Life
Lesson', in which he
played a successful,
middle-aged painter in
rageing form, frustrated in
his love for the girl
(Rosanna Arquette).
Martin Scorsese directed it
as one of the three* New
York Stories *(89), but
despite an equally pointed
contribution by Woody
Allen, the public showed
no keener interest than in
the past in omnibus
movies*

Three Fugitives (89) was a well-liked comedy in which he was a tough ex-con held hostage by an inexperienced bank robber (Martin Short). It cost $17 million and grossed $18,500,000. At the same studio *New York Stories* cost $19 million but took only $4,700,000. The blame for this could be spread several ways – on to Martin Scorsese, for instance, and Francis Coppola and Woody Allen, for each directed one of the stories. Nolte was in the Scorsese piece, one of the two good ones, playing an expressionist painter obsessed to the point of dementia with his apprentice, Rosanna Arquette. She said: 'According to the press, Nick's been down and out in every gutter in New York. But he's the most professional actor I've ever worked with in my life.' Judging from the publicity during shooting – did every journo in the world get a freebie trip to Sarawak? – much was expected of *Farewell to the King*. Writer-director John Milius had dreamed for almost twenty years of filming Pierre Schoendoerffer's novel, and Nolte was ideal casting to play its protagonist, a wild man of Borneo, a US deserter (in the book, an Irishman) in the Second World War who unites the jungle tribes to wage guerilla war on the Japanese.

But, as Geoff Andrew put it in 'Time Out', 'this being a Milius movie, ensuing events centre around a soppy macho romanticism.' The reward for that was approximately $1 million at the ticket windows, one-third of Nolte's reputed salary on a $17 million budget. The combination of director Reisz, an Arthur Miller screenplay, Nolte and Debra Winger was equally disastrous: *Everybody Wins* (90) was prophetically mistitled.

But suddenly it looks as though Katzenberg had been right: *Q and A* found Nolte on outstanding form as a corrupt cop, bewildering a young and honest one. The film took $15 million almost immediately and was a hit for the director, Sidney Lumet, who needed one (his fast-working methods are one of the reasons the budget was a mere $8 million). He said: 'Isn't Nick just the best? I really think Nick is turning into one of the finest actors we've got.' *Another 48 Hrs*, a reunion with Hill and Murphy, was a more expected success. Next: *The Prince of Tides* (91), with Barbra Streisand, in a role once meant for Robert Redford, till he lost interest; *Cape Fear*, with Robert De Niro and Jessica Lange; and possibly *The Crew*, directed by Antonioni.

AL PACINO

'I guess I'm not a real movie star, in the sense of being a personality,' said Al Pacino once. 'People hardly ever recognize me in public' – or at other times, he admitted ruefully, they mistook him for Dustin Hoffman. He is less puckish, more soulful than Hoffman, but consequently we tend to lose him – which has been a distinct advantage in the best films that he has made, *Serpico* and *Dog Day Afternoon*. Both were based on actual events, and were made by Sidney Lumet on New York locations, both took what seemed to be a documentary approach to their subjects, so that the people came out rather like us – not movie people, 'characters' or heroes, but the people you ride with on the subway. It helped, too, that Pacino did not seem to be acting; but one left the cinema with an impression of a first-rate talent.

He was born in East Harlem in 1940, of Sicilian parentage; his parents divorced when he was two, and he was brought up by his mother and by grandparents in the Bronx. He dropped out of the High School for Performing Arts when he was seventeen, but studied

Al Pacino with Marlon Brando, son and father, in The Godfather *(72). In the old days they would have called the sequel 'Son of the Godfather' but it emerged as* The Godfather – Part II. *The fact that far fewer people went to see it, despite equally warm notices, might tell us something about the popularity of the first film.*

acting again, and began appearing off-Broadway. He also did, he said, any number of menial tasks between engagements. In 1966 he appeared in the first production of 'The Indian Wants the Bronx', as a sadistic punk, and when he played the role again he won the Obie (Best Actor Off Broadway) award. That opened up movies, and he played a gigolo in an unsuccessful soap-opera vehicle for Patty Duke, *Me, Natalie* (69); and was on Broadway in 'Does the Tiger Wear a Necktie?', winning a Tony for his performance as a sadistic drug-ridden psychotic. There were more drugs in Jerry Schatzberg's *The Panic in Needle Park* (71): he was a small-time crook and Kitty Winn was the girl who got hooked with him – but the public was by no means as interested in addiction as Hollywood supposed (this was one of several films on the subject) and few saw it. A great many people saw *The Godfather* (72): he had gone to Coppola after the role of the son who succeeds, growing from callow kid to the new godfather. The film's own success made him a star; but meanwhile he went to Boston to appear with a small company in 'The Basic Training of Pavlo Hummel' and 'Richard III'.

Schatzberg's *Scarecrow* (73) co-starred Pacino with Gene Hackman, but he was not exactly a box-office draw – though the reviews killed it. As 'Playboy' said: 'Pacino's open, vulnerable, tragi-comic performance turns out to be the only plus mark for a movie filled with the kind of gutter magic that made *Midnight Cowboy*'s losers so winning.' *Serpico* had been a New York cop of unorthodox bent who thought his fellow-officers had betrayed him, and wrote a book about it. Lumet took the view that there was no point in filming it unless we believed every word, and he did an even better job on *Dog Day Afternoon* (75), in which Pacino moved to the other side of the law – as a gay who decides to rob a bank in order to pay for his lover's sex-change operation. The first took $14,600,000, and the second, $22,500,000.

Between the two came *The Godfather: Part II* (74), in which Robert De Niro played Brando as a young man, and therefore Pacino's father. De Niro is another actor audiences can confuse with Pacino: both, here, were impeccable, but the film itself needed someone bigger, of more stature, at its centre – c.f. Gian Maria Volonte in Rosi's concurrent and otherwise muddled *Lucky Luciano*. And what are we to make of *Bobby Deerfield* (77)? – a favourite Hollywood project (it was announced for Paul Newman) which died the death after lethal reviews. Pacino was a Grand Prix driver who falls for well-born Florentine Marthe Keller, who like the heroine of *Love Story* – too much like, in fact – has an

Al Pacino on the other side
of the law in Serpico (73),
one of the two factual tales
– the other was Dog Day
Afternoon – about New
York's Finest in which
Sidney Lumet directed him
during the early 70s.

incurable disease. Well, best just to say that
no one's reputation was enhanced. Such
would also seem to be the case with Pacino's
'Richard III', taken to Broadway. However,
one obstacle to a prolific film career would
seem to be Pacino's salary demands. Since he
went into the box-office ten at No. 9 in 1974,
Paramount were not ill advised to pay him
$500,000 for the second *Godfather*, plus a
percentage: and he was No. 3 in 1975 and No.
7 in 1976. But he was said to have earned
more than a million dollars for his Grand Prix
stunt, and that couldn't be given away.

At this point he was due to make *Born on
the Fourth of July*. Martin Bregman, his agent
(he also handles Alan Alda) and producer,
bought the rights to the autobiography by Ron
Kovic (already known in Hollywood, for he
had been a technical adviser on *Coming
Home*) and had set up a deal with Orion to
distribute, with Daniel Petrie directing Oliver
Stone's script; but when the German financing
fell through the rights reverted to Universal,
who hesitated because the budget was $6
million, the subject was tricky (see Tom
Cruise) and Pacino of uncertain box-office
worth. Pacino got cold feet and the project fell
through when he decided to do . . . *And
Justice for All* (79) for producer-director
Norman Jewison. He might be considered a
liability in this, playing a lawyer, streetwise
and wild-eyed, a man supposedly of integrity,
but this was something he could not suggest.
The film was not too well received (it
deserved better), but Pacino was certainly not

a liability at the box-office for, solo-starred, it
attracted a healthy $14,500,000. *Cruising* (80)
turned in only $6,788,000 on a budget of $10
million, but then gays picketed cinemas –
though why, it was difficult to see: for Pacino,
playing a straight undercover cop searching
for the Central Park murderer of some homo-
sexuals, discovers not only that he likes
hunting the killer but having sex with men as
well. William Friedkin directed this exploita-
tive movie based on a novel published in 1971,

Which side is he on this
time? – as he enters a gay
bar to mingle with the
leather crowd. That's easy,
he's an undercover cop,
investigating a series of
murders of gay men:
Cruising (80). Rubbished
by the gay crowd, it has in
fact an extraordinary
ending, in which Pacino
keeps a rendezvous which
will end either in death or
sex. Or both.

but which claims in the credits, rather oddly, to have been based on some actual events of 1979. Pacino plays his badly-written role with strength and feeling; it was brave of him to take it on after so many others had turned it down, including Roy Scheider and Robert De Niro. He was badly served again by the writer, in this case Israel Horowitz, on *Author Author* (82), about a Broadway playwright who begins an affair with his leading lady (Dyan Cannon), partly because his wife (Tuesday Weld) is also having one. Arthur Hiller directed, rather well, this son of *Kramer vs Kramer*, to which the only response could be awful awful. It cost $11 million and took only $7,500,000. Brian De Palma's overlong, excessive variations on some old themes, *Scarface* (83), cost $31 million and managed a take of $23,330,000. As the Cuban immigrant determined to be tsar of the drug racket, Pacino was coaxed into caricature, eventually becoming as tiresome as the violence.

But what really sent him down was a potted history of the American *Revolution* (85), a subject which had traditionally failed since the early Silent days. The jinx was expected to be broken by the combination of Pacino and Hugh Hudson, then riding high after *Chariots of Fire* and *Greystoke*, but this failed at every conceivable level, including Pacino as a fur-trapper 'with an all-purpose Celtic accent' (Philip French in the 'Observer'). It cost $28 million and disappeared from American cinemas without taking even $1 million; it was expected to do better in Britain, because it was filmed there and because Hudson was British. The critics as quickly dispatched it, and the star was left with egg on his face because the ad campaign had featured a dignified 'Pacino', thus presenting him as a star so big he didn't need a first name. His fee had been $3 million plus expenses and the services of a cook and a secretary.

In 1981 he had appeared off-Broadway in a revival of David Mamet's play 'American Buffalo', which he did on Broadway in 1983 and later in London. The short-lived Cannon company announced a film of it with Pacino, as well as a remake of the Italian film we know as *Investigation of a Citizen Above Suspicion* and *La Brava*, after Dustin Hoffman had walked away from that. Like most of Cannon's projects, none of these came to fruition, but it is probable that Cannon was one of the few companies which would take a risk with Pacino. His cause could not have been helped when William Goldman's 1983 memoir became a bestseller, 'Adventures in the Screen Trade', for he told of Pacino needlessly keeping the hundred-strong crew of *Author Author* waiting in 'subfreezing weather' and then striding off the set when

reprimanded by Hiller, 'as gentlemanly a director as any now operating'. Bregman, the producer of *Serpico*, *Dog Day Afternoon* and *Scarface*, announced two films for Pacino in 1987, *Rififi* and *Vito*. Neither was made and it is probable that Bregman thought it best to continue to let Pacino lie low after some much-publicized failures. 'Pacino's a schmuck,' Oliver Stone told 'People' magazine. 'His career went into the toilet', but then he was bitter about the cancellation of *Born on the Fourth of July*. In 1989 producer Elliott Kastner sued Pacino for $6 million for backing away from *Carlito's Way*, and Pacino countersued for $4 million for the damage to his reputation.

Questioned about his absence from the screen, Pacino refers to 'my own picture, *The Local Stigmatic*, unseen publicly except for a week's showings at the Museum of Modern Art'. In the spring of 1988 he appeared in New York as Mark Antony in 'Julius Caesar' with John McMartin in the title-role and Martin Sheen as Brutus. Bregman slipped Pacino back into view in another cop movie, and it was a job to which the actor needed no adjusting. His Frank Keller in *Sea of Love* (89) is Serpico years on – alcoholic, disillusioned, shambling and nearing retirement; as directed by Harold Becker he was believable, enmeshed in a good plot about a personal column with ads inviting sexual encounters which ended up only too fatally for the men concerned. Ellen Barkin was sensationally sexy as the suspect whom Pacino falls for in this unsettling thriller, and audiences flocked to see their steamy love scenes, which brought in $27,500,000 on a $25 million budget. Pacino was also one of the guest stars under heavy make-up in *Dick Tracy* (90), which brought him the best notices of his career. 'Pacino's performance is heavyweight hilarity of a high order,' said Vicent Canby in the 'New York Times', 'His Big Boy Caprice, wearing a crazed expression and a maroon greatcoat, is a mad mixture of Scarface, Richard III and Groucho Marx.' David Ansen in 'Newsweek' wrote, 'Pacino, never known for comedy and almost unrecognisable under his make-up, turns Big Boy into a memorably funny slime-ball, issuing commands in gutteral spurts, his words trying to keep pace with his twisted, overheated thoughts.' That was a high, after which he was reunited with Coppola for the dangerously expensive *The Godfather: Part III*. The first agreed budget of $32 million was exceeded, despite filming in Italy to keep costs down, but it rose steeply. Pacino was on a fee of $8 million and an additional $500,000 for each day of re-shooting: and there were fifteen of these in September, in New York, but he was required for only six of them. The result is, Paramount hopes, its big Christmas film. Almost twenty years ago Part I did a then-phenomenal $85 million, but Part II took only $30 million . . . Only? Yes, but that mean a lot of people weren't curious about the fortunes of the Corleone clan. Hopefully, this time will be different.

DOLLY PARTON

'I sort of patterned my look from storybooks and the trash in our home-town . . . They were the town whores, but I didn't know that. They had tight skirts and really colorful clothes, high-heeled shoes and bleached hair and make-up and red fingernail polish. I thought they were just beautiful,' said Dolly Parton, of her appearance, which might be that of your local hooker or the lonely but friendly girl in the hotel bar. 'What are the first two things you notice about her?' goes one line, though it is an adaptation of an ad slogan for Jane Russell. When she wants to, she can look like a real lady, and a mighty purty one. She has not made many movies, but those few reveal a jolly girl with oomph and presence – if not, so far, much range. She is not an American original like Mae West, who invented herself, for, as Parton once said, she based her looks on others and her singing is little different from the other Country and Western female singers. But perhaps she

could, like West, write her own scripts. Once, when asked how long it took to do her hair, she replied, 'I don't know, honey, I'm never there.' (She has also admitted that the appearance is useful when she wants to be incognito: for without the wig and the make-up nobody recognizes her.)

She also said: 'I'm a message of hope – my whole life is. If I could make it, so can anybody. Sometimes I think I have more guts than talent.' Looking as she does, with her background, she looks dangerously like an invention of Al Capp. She was born in 1946 in Sevier, a town in the Great Smoky Mountains of Tennessee, the fourth of twelve children, to 'dirt-poor' farming stock. She started writing songs as a child, was singing on the radio at ten, and at thirteen she cut her first record, 'Puppy Love'. When she left school she headed for Nashville, but fame was not to come till 1967, when she became a regular on 'The Porter Wagoner T.C. and Road Show'. Her records were selling, she was earning $60,000 a year, and she began to be the most popular female singer on the C & W circuit. She was also married – to Carl Dean, an asphalt worker whom she met on her first day in Nashville. They remain married, though he is never seen with her publicly. Some reports have described the marriage as 'bizarre', since they are separated much of the time. She retorts: 'We are just very independent. He loves me to death. I'm

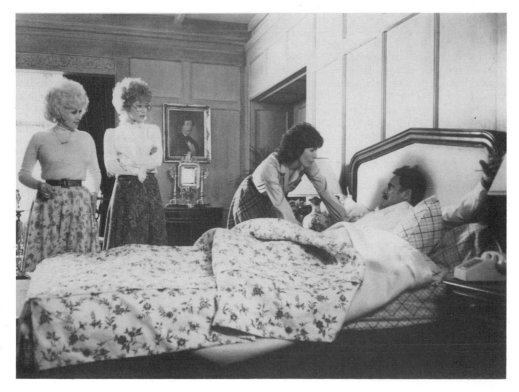

Dolly Parton, Jane Fonda and Lily Tomlin caring for Dabney Coleman in Nine to Five *(80), but he doesn't seem to be enjoying it – for a good reason: he is their prisoner. It's his reward for being an MCP (male chauvinst pig).*

Dolly Parton in The Best Little Whorehouse in Texas *(82). She ran it: who else?*

persona she had created for herself she would have to restrict her appearances, because she tended to overwhelm the material. A co-starring job with another star of Reynolds's clout seemed a good idea and she teamed up with Sylvester Stallone to make *Rhinestone* (84), the tale of a cabbie who is taught to give out with song by a C & W singer. Alas, the combination was the reverse of box-office dynamite. Parton consoled herself with the fact that at a fee of $4 million she was doing well: it was $2 million less than Stallone was paid, but $2 million more than was being paid to Meryl Streep, reckoned to be the second-highest-paid female star at the time. She returned to television in a film, *A Smoky Mountain Christmas* (86), a re-vamping (can you credit this?) of the story of Snow-White, which she also co-wrote.

And she was on television in 1987 with 'Dolly' on Sunday nights at 9, expected to be ABC's hit of the season: it bowed at fifth in the Nielsen ratings but had slipped to 43rd place within six weeks, representing a loss of 11,800,000 million homes. Parton continued to tour and to supervise improvements to 'Dollywood', the theme park near her home in Tennessee, in which she has invested some of her money. When films called again, she got billing below Sally Field but above Shirley MacLaine – in *Steel Magnolias* (89), playing the carefree mistress of the town's beauty parlour. It was nice to have her back.

his best friend. We have a lot of respect . . . We are not together all the time, but we're together more than the press would lead you to believe.'

She came into films when the producers wanted to widen the appeal of a Jane Fonda vehicle, *Nine to Five* (80): from television and cabaret they brought the comedienne, Lily Tomlin, but there was a third important distaff role to be cast: the secretary of the boss (Dabney Coleman), a girl so damn sexy that he doesn't believe she means no when she says no – the film's premise, for they kidnap him as punishment. Parton's performance in the role was much liked, and she had a hit record singing the title-song. The same director, Colin Higgins, gave Parton a co-starring role in the film version of a long-running Broadway musical, *The Best Little Whorehouse in Texas* (82): the songs suited her and so did the part, that of a brothel madam whose lover is the town sheriff. He was played by Burt Reynolds, and the film did sufficiently well to suggest that Parton had a movie career before her. She knew that if she wanted to retain the

SEAN PENN

Penn is the 'Peck's Bad Boy' of the movies, noted for temperament on the set, which naturally is reported, since his dislike of the press is well known. 'As far as audiences go,' he admitted in 1988, 'I think at this point I'm much more known as Madonna's husband who hits photographers more than as an actor.' He agreed that his popularity among Hollywood's powerful figures was not total, but he will be in business as long as there is a demand for actors with power, individuality and range.

He was born in 1960 in Burbank, California, to Eileen Ryan, a former actress, and Leo Penn, a film and television director. At Santa Monica High School he acted in and directed films in Super-8; at the age of nineteen he acted professionally for the first time, in the television series 'Barnaby Jones'. He did not find this challenging, so he bought a one-way ticket to New York, where he auditioned twice for a role in Kevin Helan's play 'Heartland'. His notices in it brought him the offer of a TV movie, *The Killing of Randy Webster* (81), in which he was fourth-billed; Hal Holbrook starred in this true story of a father trying to prove that his son was 'framed' by the cops who killed him. This led to the offer to play Timothy Hutton's roommate in *Taps* (81), a performance sufficiently liked to put Penn among the young actors most in demand. He was top-billed in Amy Heckerling's *Fast Times at Ridgemont High* (82), a considerable cut above the other teen movies of the period, as written by Cameron Crowe, who offered Universal an exposé on the strength of returning anonymously to high school as a student. Those in this movie hang around the mall swopping details of sexual antics – or, in the case of Penn, who made the piece memorable, as a spaced-out lame-brain on grass. The film did a handy $15,700,000, but few of its followers bothered with Rick Rosenthal's *Bad Boys* (83), a remarkably old-fashioned piece about juvenile delinquency set mainly in a prison for those practising it: Penn was the chief of them, a Mick who went to the bad because his mom liked entertaining men in the bath. He played a no-good again, but was no better served by a much better director: for Louis Malle's *Crackers* (84) was a laughless, aimless and noisy remake of *I Soliti Ignoti*. Penn supported Donald Sutherland and Jack Warden, but returned to top-billing with *Racing With the Moon*, another teen movie – though the difference this time was that it was set during the war, though if they had removed the vintage songs from the soundtrack you would hardly have known it. Richard Benjamin, who directed, was around at that time; Steven Kloves, who wrote it, was not, and this was his first screenplay to be filmed out of three written since leaving UCLA in 1961. The plot has Penn whiling away his time before joining the Marines and falling in love with Elizabeth McGovern, whom he wrongly thinks is very rich. Their off-screen relationship was not reflected in their scenes together, but he plays with an abrasive charm. The director remarked that he was 'a truth machine'.

John Schlesinger was more forthcoming: 'He's quite difficult, he really gets into the skin of the character he's playing. And as his character resists all authority, he naturally hated me, and I must say the feeling was reciprocated, although I think he's marvellous in the film.' It was called *The Falcon and the Snowman* (85), based on a true case in which a CIA man was so incensed by what he learns from the files of its involvement round the world – including its role in bringing down Gough Whitlam's left-wing government in Australia – that he offers the information to the Russians. Timothy Hutton played the CIA

man and Penn was the hophead, a fast-talking little runt, who acts as the go-between in Mexico City. It was a hip movie for the post-hippy generation, positing on the one hand decent and/or playful youngsters vs a cynical manipulative authority: but audiences were hip to it only to the tune of $7,720,000. They did not care at all for *At Close Range* (86), which might be comment enough on the flashy style employed by the second-time director, James Foley. But within that was a good story, also based on fact, of two poor Pennsylvania half-brothers who discover that the father (Christopher Walken) they hardly knew is a major criminal and who decide to imitate him till they learn better – or, rather, are disposed of so that they cannot bear witness. Walken was wonderfully malevolent, while Penn and brother Christopher went through many a manifestation of teenage angst.

On the soundtrack was a song performed by Madonna, Penn's wife, whose expressed desire to be a movie star has been often reported. They discovered a script at Hand-Made, about which the company was not too keen, but their interest caused *Shanghai Surprise* to go into production with Jim

Sean Penn and his then-wife, Madonna, in Shanghai Surprise *(86), which tried and failed to duplicate the larkiness of 30s adventure films (it was set back then). There were no surprises when, after dreadful reviews, no one (well, not many) wanted to see it.*

Goddard directing. He said his points of department were *The African Queen*, *His Girl Friday* and *Casablanca*, but these were influences undetectable in the result, a hokey but tired account of a missionary (Madonna) and a ne'er-do-well American salesman (Penn) tackling some baddies mixed up in the opium trade. Said the producer, George Harrison: 'We didn't know all the trouble they were going to cause us. In hindsight, I wouldn't have bothered. I don't think it was totally their fault either – I think something about the whole package wasn't right . . . What I was doing, basically, was sitting down talking to Sean Penn and Madonna all the time. Sean was in the difficult position of being Mr Madonna, and that really bugged him. He'd been punching out at the press, so they were really after him. Relentless, really. But Sean and Madonna caused a lot of their own problems by falling for it.' With critics and in cinemas, the film was an absolute disaster: if Madonna had a concert following it certainly was not interested in seeing this movie. When in February 1987 'People' magazine published a Hollywood issue, it listed Penn as the actor most readers least expected to be around in twenty years time, with 23 per cent of the vote, with Stallone as his nearest contender, at 9 per cent.

Since Penn had demonstrated a large talent as an actor, this animosity can only be explained by the behaviour of the Penns, as reported in the press (they were soon to split up), and doubtless the strength of feeling contributed to the failure of his two 1986 films. Nothing was heard of any Penn plans and he sensibly lay low till the maverick director Dennis Hopper teamed him with Robert Duvall for a cop thriller, *Colors* (88), which proved that in the right film the public would go to see Penn. That was a matter to be questioned again when *Casualties of War* (89) recouped only $7,400,000 of its $25 million budget. It was for the most part well received, but the reputation of the director, Brian De Palma, was not such that spectators thought him capable of making a serious statement on the Vietnam War, as written (beautifully) by David Mamet; it may be that there had simply been too many films on that particular subject – and who could have foreseen that this was the best of them? Michael J. Fox and Penn trained strenuously for their roles, which would take them on a sortie through the jungle with three other soldiers. Penn was the corporal who takes prisoner a native villager whose task is to service the men; Fox was the only one of the five to find this degrading and to argue against it at the risk of his life. Penn had his best screen role and he seized on it, providing a portrait of mindless evil, cocky and swaggering, as hateful a villain as the screen has seen

In bringing his career back from the abyss (see previous caption) Penn was lucky to be cast in Brian De Palma's coruscating film about the Vietnam conflict, Casualties of War *(89). The director was equally blessed, for Penn gave a brilliant performance as one of the most vicious men of war since Attila the Hun.*

since the 1921 *Tol'able David*. He followed it by teaming up with Robert De Niro in a would-be comedy, *We're No Angels*, playing convicts who disguise themselves as priests.

He had a guest-spot, sporting a pony-tail, in *Cool Blue* (90), turning up in a bar at the end to lecture Woody Harrelson (of 'Cheers') on bad behaviour, and he had special billing for his appearance in *Judgement in Berlin*, based on the case of three East Germans who hijacked a plane to defect to the West in 1978. Because of the element of terrorism, they were tried by a judge (in the film, Martin Sheen) under American jurisdiction. Penn played the key witness, an inarticulate student who had also fled oppression, and he did so magnificently – as coached by his father, who wrote the screenplay and directed. *State of Grace* was a much-liked gangster movie in which Penn played a hard-drinking Irish-American who returns to New York to become involved in big-time crime. He was paid $2,500,000, a high fee in view of the fact that it managed to take only $1,652,000 in four weeks on the 'Variety' chart (as research-ed from key city dates: the real figure might be 25 per cent higher). As writer and director he is making *Indian Runner* (91), but he won't be starring in it: Charles Bronson and Sandy Dennis will.

VALERIE PERRINE

Now, Valerie Perrine. Terrific-looking. Sexy as all-get-out. First-rate actress. Something wrong here, because she has not been all that prolific.

She was born in Galveston, Texas, in 1944, the daughter of an army officer and a former showgirl with Earl Carroll's Vanities. She grew up partly in Japan, where her father was stationed, and made her first stage appearance at the age of three in a Shinto festival. As an 'army brat' she found herself seldom in the same school for long, but the family eventually settled in Scottsdale, Arizona. She entered the University of Arizona, but was so restless during the first year that she auditioned as a dancer, on the strength of the ballet-and-tap lessons that her mother had made her take. This was in Las Vegas, however, which has known connoisseurs in the audience, so they started her in the back row. She got fed up with that after a month, but when a year in Scottsdale provided no solution to the problem of what to do she returned to Vegas, where she was a showgirl at the Desert Inn. She ended up as one of the three leading dancers at the Stardust Hotel, dressed in little but feathers, rhinestones and

fantastic head-dresses. She stayed eight years, she said, for the pay ($800 a week) – though it was hard work, two shows every day and three on Saturdays. She was to observe later that she was unprepared for movies, because she was too busy to see any.

Love, by her own account, was a welcome diversion, and it took her to Paris when one of her lovers was offered a job dancing there. She left him after a while and eventually found herself virtually penniless in New York – and in Los Angeles, if it comes to that. But at a Hollywood party she met an agent, Robert Walker, whom she considered not the typical Hollywood-agent type; he was enchanted by her looks and vivacity, qualities Universal were looking for as they auditioned two hundred girls to play a movie starlet in *Slaughterhouse-5* (72). He decided that she should be one of them, and Universal was delighted: she was put under long-term contract, and she made a sparkling debut in the film, directed by George Roy Hill from the novel by Kurt Vonnegut Jr. Much of its concept is resistible, such as its hero (Michael Sacks) as a modern Everyman, and it does go round the bend a bit to make its pacifist points; but Perrine gave it a lovely ending as the starlet who ends up with said hero on another planet, the mother of his baby. The company put her in one of its telemovies, *The Couple Takes a Wife*, as the wife employed by Bill Bixby and Paula Prentiss to house-keep, which she does only too well – and too prettily. She was loaned to 20th-Century-Fox to play a groupie who falls for racing-driver Jeff Bridges in *The Last American Hero* (73) and then to United Artists for *Lenny* (74),

Some people think that Valerie Perrine has more sex-appeal and sheer talent than anyone since Marilyn Monroe, and she certainly makes some contenders to that lady's crown look rather shoddy. We have had far too few opportunities to judge her, but she was sensational in Lenny (75), as that gentleman's wife. He – the comedian Lenny Bruce – was played by Dustin Hoffman.

that is, Lenny Bruce. Dustin Hoffman played that role, and she was merely tremendous as his lesbian-junkie wife, at first loyally standing by him and then confused as he self-destructs. Among the several awards for this performance was one from the New York critics.

Universal did not care to capitalize on this, and she was off the screen for 18 months, returning as the second half of the title, *W.C. Fields and Me* (76), that is, Fields's mistress Carlotta. This was one of the weakest of a rightly scorned semi-genre, the Hollywood biopic, as directed by Arthur Hiller; and Rod Steiger was miscast as the Great Man. Perrine and he did not get on, as was clear from the satisfactory assassination job she did on him when interviewed. Her propensity for speaking her mind is one of the reasons why she has not been more prolific. Certainly she left Universal at this point, but then the two pictures she had made there had hardly been a whammy with the public. She was in another dud, *Mr Billion* (78), with which 20th hoped to make a Hollywood star out of Italy's popular Terence Hill. He played an Italian garage-mechanic racing across the US to inherit, but he won't get the estate unless he signs an agreement within twenty days. Perrine was the detective hired to guard him (against the baddies who want him to lose), and Jonathan Kaplan was the director of this rather tired entertainment. She was Lillian Lorraine, the Broadway star, in *Ziegfeld: the Man and his Women* with Paul Shenar in the title-role, for television. That year she decorated *Superman*, as crony of the evil Gene Hackman. She was 'excellent' (critic Tim Pulleine) as one of the several ladies in the life of *The Magician of Lublin* (79), who was Alan Arkin – a married woman having an affair with him; but the film itself, directed by Menaham Golan, was not for the discerning, or even the non-discerning. Lustre considerably dimmed, she supported Jane Fonda and Robert Redford in *The Electric Horseman* – because, went the publicity, 'of the sensitivity and the quality of the part and the chance to work with Redford'. Maybe; all that can be said is that he matched her only in their scenes together, and that playing a Vegas showgirl (his ex-wife) could not have presented her with any difficulty.

She supported Robert Mitchum in the Canadian *Agency*, which had a few test engagements, and little more, in 1981, and in the meantime had the misfortune to be embroiled in *Can't Stop the Music* (80), rooming with songwriter Steve Guttenberg and giving up modelling to promote his songs – which means having them sung by the Village People, a group who capitalized (whatever their private orientation) on being

gay stereotypes. This made her a gays' moll, sort-of, which couldn't have displeased her, because she once said that she adored gays 'because they like dick and so do I'. In an interview at this time she said wistfully that she would like to be more successful, because she would be offered better roles, adding that she had only made two good films, *Slaughterhouse-5* and *Lenny*. She had high hopes, after making *Superman II*, of Tony Richardson's *The Border* (82), in which she was Jack Nicholson's cheap, spendthrift wife: but it was not a success, although she (and he too) was splendid in it. On television around the same time she played the mother of *Marian Rose White*, a child consigned to care because she has cruelly abandoned her. Television provided her with further work: *Malibu* (83), one of the thirteen billed names in this glam mini (others: Eva Marie Saint, Kim Novak); and *When Your Lover Leaves*, starring as a divorcée who has to start a new life when her boyfriend returns to his wife. She was also in a series, 'Leo and Liz in Beverly Hills'.

She dallied with a wife-troubled Michael Caine in the British *Water* (85) – and working with him, she declared, had been a joy (implying: unlike some others). She also said at this time, 'If there were ten good women's roles every year I'd do every one of them, but as there are only one or two and Meryl Streep gets them both, I'll get on with something else.' This meant a supporting role in Amy Jones's *Maid to Order* (87), a vehicle for Ally Sheedy, an heiress who – à la *Trading Places* – has to skivvy for an ostentatious couple in Malibu, roles played superbly by herself and Dick Shawn. She was not seen again till *Una Casa a Roma* (89), an Italian mini in which she was an American who turns out her unfaithful husband and turns her home into a pensione. *Bright Angel* (90) was written by Richard Ford from his stories, and directed by Michael Fields in his feature debut: it took a fresh look at an old subject, young lovers involved in crime, with Dermot Mulroney as the young protagonist. Perrine, who was billed fourth, had only a brief role at the beginning, separating from the boy's father, Sam Shepard. Perhaps *Hit Man* (91), with Morgan Freeman, will give her the success needed to re-establish herself. Hollywood was looking again at some of the talents it had misused or under-employed, and her name should be at the head of the list.

MICHELLE PFEIFFER

She has ice-blue eyes, which may be why writer-director Robert Towne thinks: 'You're constantly wondering what's underneath this almost [Grace] Kelly-like cool.' She would seem to have a greater range than Kelly, which would make her a surer survivor than Daryl Hannah and Kim Basinger, who are now getting the roles she has turned down.

She was born in Orange County, California, in 1957 of Swiss–Swedish–Dutch–German stock, the second daughter of four children; her father was a contractor working on air-conditioning and electric appliances. She took a theatre course in high school, but after that became a checkout assistant at a supermarket. Her hairdresser had asked her about modelling, and not long thereafter she was Miss Orange County. She failed to go on to becoming Miss LA, but she had acquired an agent to handle her for commercials and was taking acting lessons. She walked into the office of actors' agent John LaRocca, inviting herself to become his client; he arranged for her to receive a SAG card and a job with one line in television's 'Fantasy Island' (79), from which she went into the series based on *National Lampoon's Animal House*, 'Delta House', in a role so small she was billed only as 'The Bombshell'. LaRocca got her her first movie job, if only for television, supporting Earl Holliman in *The Solitary Man*, after which she played Susannah York as a younger woman in an independent picture, *Falling in Love Again* (80). Other small roles followed, in *Hollywood Knights*, as a car hop, and *Charlie Chan and the Curse of the Dragon Queen* (81), as a wealthy bimbo at a party. But these were not the sorts of roles she craved, so she left LaRocca and signed with the much more important William Morris Agency.

The effect was immediate, and she was all over television towards the end of the year: in a short-lived series, 'B.A.D. Cats'; in the television remake of *Splendor in the Grass*, as the wild sister of the hero, and in *Callie and Son*, fifth-billed in this vehicle for Lindsay Wagner. She was upped to second-billing in a true story filmed for TV, *The Children Nobody Wanted*, as one of them, adopted by Missouri bachelor Tom Butterfield, whose mission in life was to provide shelter for homeless youngsters. Butterfield, played in the film by Fredric Lehne, was also the associate producer. Pfeiffer heard that the producers of *Grease 2* (82) were looking for a female lead, so she auditioned for Patricia Birch, who was directing. She played the chief of the Pink Ladies and was delightful – sweet and funny. The complete failure of the film was a severe setback, and there were no offers, so she began taking acting classes with Peggy Feury. She set her sights on the role of the classy blonde who becomes drug-addicted

If (see previous entry) sexy and talented ladies are in short supply, try Michelle Pfeiffer, here, in the two roles in which we have most admired her: in Dangerous Liaisons *(88), as the virtuous aristocrat who is the prey of the debauched Valmont, and* The Fabulous Baker Boys *(89), as Susie Diamond, the vocalist whose way with a song is better than her voice.*

after marrying Al Pacino in *Scarface* (83); the director, Brian De Palma, however, was not interested in seeing her: but after what she called a four months' fight she got the role, and that led to John Landis casting her in *Into the Night* (85), as the mysterious blonde who jumps into Jeff Goldblum's car and who can't, or won't, explain why she is up to her neck in mayhem. She had the perfect charismatic blonde beauty needed, but was less lucky with *Ladyhawke*, cursed by an evil bishop so that she has to spend the days befeathered on the arm of her beloved (Rutger Hauer), who changes to a wolf each night just as she returns to normal. Together 20th-Century-Fox and Warner Bros spent $21 million on this fantasy, to see a mere $7,900,000 trickle back.

Promise first turned to achievement with Alan Alda's *Sweet Liberty* (86) as the melting, pliant, breathless young ingénue of the film being made within the film: but who, off the set, proves to be an ambitious, mercenary bitch who uses all around her in her quest for perfection. Landis was one of several directors credited on *Amazon Women on the Moon* (87), as was Pfeiffer's husband, Peter Horton, whom she had met at acting school. They were to split up at about this time, and this film could not have been one of the fonder memories of the marriage, an unfunny series of skits and parodies which had sat on the shelf for a year. Still, Pfeiffer had only a cameo role. She played a star again in *Nautica Jackson*, one of six one-hour 'Tales From the Hollywood Hills', an Anglo–American joint venture. This one, based on a story by John O'Hara, found Pfeiffer as a sought-after commodity realizing that there was little more to her life than that. As an actress she marked time as one of *The Witches of Eastwick*, the abandoned mother of six children who attracts Jack Nicholson. She did not care for the finished film, but later acknowledged that its success enabled her to pick and choose her roles. Cher, who was also in it, said: 'When I first met her I thought she was very sweet and maybe too sweet, too nice. But it's all part of someone who has a definite purpose, who's a lot stronger than even she knows sometimes. It's not possible to mess with her and come out on top.'

Pfeiffer was on fine form again as a bubbly-headed brunette in Jonathan Demme's *Married to the Mob* (88) – but trying to escape it with an FBI man (Matthew Modine), while her dead husband's Mafia boss (Dean Stockwell) hopes not to give her the chance. She shared a *Tequila Sunrise* with Mel Gibson and Kurt Russell in this thriller directed by Robert Towne, playing a restaurateur with a line in sardonic quips. Immediately on completion she went into *Dangerous Liaisons*, whose

director, Stephen Frears, had wondered whether she would not appear too lightweight beside Glenn Close and John Malkovich: but Demme assured him that that was unlikely. In the event her role as the virtuous Madame de Tourville only confirmed her ability to take on chameleon colours, as did her self-confident kook joining up with *The Fabulous Baker Boys* (89), Jeff and Beau Bridges, lounge pianists, as their vocalist. Much was made of her sexy 'Makin' Whoopee', atop a piano, but it was not going to make anyone forget Rita Hayworth in *Gilda*, even if Pfeiffer did her own singing. 'Pfeiffer has never been more alluring,' said David Ansen in 'Newsweek', 'She is slinky, brittle perfection.' The New York critics voted it the year's Best Female Performance and in London BAFTA thought her Best Supporting Actress. Before the film came out, she stretched herself by playing Shakespeare in New York's Central Park: she was Olivia in 'Twelfth Night', with Jeff Goldblum and Mary Elizabeth Mastrantonio.

Her salary was now reckoned to be $1 million per film, She appeared opposite Sean Connery in *The Russia House* (90) and turned down a role in *The Bonfire of the Vanities* because she was already committed to an inter-racial romance, *Love Field*, with Jonathan Kaplan directing. She wanted José Feliciano for her co-star, but Paramount insisted on Denzel Washington, who backed away. 'So much for star power' said 'Premiere' magazine, as Paramount let the project go to Orion, for whom Dennis Haysbert would be the male lead. She is due to co-star with Al Pacino in *Frankie and Johnny in the Clair-de-Lune* (91).

RICHARD PRYOR

Richard Pryor is a prodigiously talented man whom movies have tamed – somewhat. He is most at home as a stand-up entertainer, or rather, one who perches on a bar-stool in shirtsleeves with a natty bow-tie, a can of beer in his hand, 'mother-fuckerin'' about life's indignities and injustices. He is, said 'Newsweek', 'the man who took the jackhammer profanity of the black underclass and turned it into a scathing, hilarious street poetry.' Among black actors, he ranks somewhere in the hierarchy between Sidney Poitier and Eddie Murphy, both chronologically and in personality – oh, never with Sidney's solemnity, but less vulgar and raucous than Murphy, and more manic. He has not, unhappily, had the opportunities of either, but he can move when given the chance.

He was born in Peoria, Illinois, in 1940, into

a milieu which gave him much of his material – not, it would seem, growing up in his grandmother's brothel (as he has claimed), but in the middle of the red-light district. At the age of seven he was a habitué of the Famous Door, hanging in with the band after hours and meeting such visiting firemen as Count Basie, Louis Armstrong and Duke Ellington. At the age of twelve he appeared in a community production of 'Rumpelstiltskin', which furthered his taste for show business; but in the meantime he racked balls in his grandfather's pool-hall or drove trucks for his father's construction company. At eighteen he joined the army, and for two years – spent mainly with an airborne division in Germany – he experienced the extreme racism still then prevalent. Back in Peoria he emceed and told jokes at Harold's Club, which he left with a troupe of female impersonators. By 1963 he was a regular at the Café Wha in Greenwich Village in New York; he gradually developed his nightclub act, often improvising. Television would claim him, either for chat-shows or for his routines, though the going was hardly smooth, for on occasion he walked out of live shows and there were battles with sponsors over his spiel; he did – and admitted he did – use the medium to air his views on racial hatred and prejudice. However, booked once to appear on 'The Ed Sullivan Show', which went out live, he did not bother to turn up. He arrived in movies courtesy of one of Hollywood's tired old hands, the producer William Castle, who felt that movies were the right place to be for Sid Caesar now that his popularity on television had waned; he put Caesar into two medium-budget vehicles, surrounded by several other names, most of whom were associated with comedy. Thus Pryor was billed sixth in *The Busy Body* (67), as an ineffective detective whom Caesar meets in the course of his exploits. The film was not a success (neither was the other one, *The Spirit is Willing*).

In 1967 he was busted for possessing an ounce of marijuana, and he was later fined $75,000 on assault charges, after attacking the desk clerk of his West Hollywood apartment building and also, with a knife and fork, its owner. In 1968 he married for the fourth (but not the last) time – and these hiccups in his private life were one reason why he was billed as Richard 'Cactus' Pryor when he became one of Colonel John Wayne's brigade in *The Green Berets* (68). He was better served as a black leader, Stanley X, in a tired tale of youth rebellion, *Wild in the Streets*, but not by *You've Got to Walk It Like You Talk It or You'll Lose That Beat*, as a wino who stumbles into a men's room to lecture the star, Zalman King. That one stayed on the shelf for a while,

receiving less than a muted welcome when it surfaced in 1971. The cinema was not exactly taking Pryor to its bosom, so he made a movie for television: *The Young Lawyers* (69), as one of two black musicians accused of beating up a racist cab-driver. But movies were where he wanted to be, and in 1970 he walked out of his act while appearing at the Aladdin in Las Vegas when he suddenly realized that he loathed what he was doing; he drove home to Los Angeles and shortly afterwards moved to Berkeley to be removed from the atmosphere of show business – and who could blame him after yet another unfortunate credit? This was *The Phynx* (70) a horrible ragbag featuring mixed comics, directed by an unqualified Lee H. Katzin. The few curious about the title might like to know it refers to the 'Finks', some rock musicians picked by the Government to go behind the Iron Curtain to rescue some entertainers, most of whom were passé Hollywood names playing themselves. Pryor himself much preferred *Carter's Army*, made for television, in which he was a cowardly medic, one of an all-black company led by a redneck captain (Stephen Boyd). *Dynamite Chicken* (71) was a 'multi-media mosaic' put together by the humorist Ernest Pintoff, which examined modern pop-culture, including such icons as Marilyn Monroe and (from the sublime to the ridiculous) Andy Warhol; Pryor, top-billed, was one of two people being interviewed throughout – the other was Paul Krassner – offering radical comments on any number of topics from religion to hamburgers. This was another movie which had stayed awhile on the shelf. It was reissued in 1982 on the strength of Pryor's name, but did not find an audience.

Pryor's record career began to take off at this time. He had had one issued, 'Richard Pryor', in 1968, but it had been tailored for Bill Cosby's audience; now Laff Records issued 'Craps (After Hours)' in which Pryor was permitted to be less inhibited. It was the first of twelve albums for the company, while two years later he was also to sign with Reprise, with a winner the first time out, 'That Nigger's Crazy', which won a Grammy as the best Comedy Recording of the year. Studio biographies usually cite *Lady Sings the Blues* (72) as his movie debut, since those other films had either got nowhere or he had not been noticed: in this one, directed by Sydney J. Furie, he was 'Piano Man', a combination of several men who had been so vital in the life and career of Billie Holliday, played by the plastic Diana Ross. As the script had it, he was also her alter ego and was third-billed for so being. Although Poitier had supposedly opened up movies for black talent, the next few years were hit and miss, with:

Wattstax (73), a documentary on that district of Los Angeles, in which Pryor's monologues provided the high points; *The Mack*, a violent blaxploitation piece about warring black pimps (he was one) and hookers in Oakland; Furie's *Hit!*, another such, in which he is an engineer recruited by Billy Dee Williams to go to France to hunt down those who had supplied drugs to his dead daughter; and James B. Harris's *Some Call it Loving*, a bafflingly pretentious reworking of 'Cinderella', mixing jazz, lesbos and carny, in which he literally intruded as a graffiti artist dying of drink and drugs.

That was a busy year, for Pryor was also writing scripts for 'Sanford and Son', 'The Flip Wilson Show' and two specials for Lily Tomlin, which won him an Emmy award; he was also working on a screenplay for himself, *Black Stranger*, based partly on an old horror movie, *White Zombie*, in which he would be a black cowboy dabbling in the occult. When he could not get backing he decided that he had been blacklisted, but did not drop the idea, for when Mel Brooks approached him to work on the screenplay of *Blazing Saddles* (74), he penned a blazing part for himself as a black sheriff. And lo, he *had* been blacklisted: Warners originally told Brooks that Pryor could not sustain a leading role, but later admitted that they thought him unreliable, that he might walk out with the film unfinished. The role went to Cleavon Little, an artist about whom he was later publicly scornful – nor was he any kinder about Brooks, whom he considered had betrayed him. As an actor, the best he could find to do was Poitier's *Uptown Saturday Night*, which starred Poitier and Bill Cosby as married gadabouts: Pryor, as a cynical private eye, was one of several talented black actors – Harry Belafonte, Roscoe Lee Browne, Calvin Lockhart, Flip Wilson – in cameo roles. *Adios Amigo* (75) also starred a black actor who directed too, Fred Williamson, patsy to con-man Pryor, who regarded this spoof-Western as a consolation for not appearing in *Blazing Saddles*, but, unlike that, it lit no fires at the box-office. Williamson, a former football-player, also wrote the thing and produced – and between 1974 and 1983 he would chalk up no less than seventeen movies, on all of which he posed a quadruple threat, for they were all as amateurish as this one (the later ones were chiefly spaghetti Westerns, or gangster pics).

The concentration of black talent in some of these movies is a curious phenomenon, implying that they might not draw white audiences but that black people might crowd in to see all their favourites together. From Paul Robeson onwards till the time of Poitier, Hollywood recognized such talents as Lena Horne and the Nicholas Brothers, but did not use them enough, even in musicals. *The Bingo Long Travelling All-Stars & Motor Kings* (76) had a personable star in Billy Dee Williams, a superb actor in James Earl Jones and a marvellous comic in Pryor: but for once they were well used, not in stereotypical thrown-together thriller or comedy, but in a probing comedy-drama about being black in a white man's world. Set in 1939, it tells of a makeshift but all-star baseball team trying to make it independently while all the stops are against them. John Badham directed, taking over from Steven Spielberg, on Georgia locations, from a factual novel by William Brashler, with Pryor outstanding, even in this cast, as a player obsessed with the idea of infiltrating one of whities' teams as a Red Indian or a Cuban. Brashler said of Pryor that he 'could be instantly cruel, goading, unmerciful' – which he might not have experienced if Pryor had turned down the role, as he originally intended. After the Williamson film, he had been approached by an Atlanta-based lawyer, David McCoy Franklin, who also handled Cicily Tyson and Roberta Flack; he believed that Pryor could become a major star if handled properly, advising him to accept the Badham film; Pryor had turned it down because he was tired of being co-star or supporting player, but Franklin pointed out that the role, like that of 'Piano Man', was going to stay in the minds of the audience. He argued similarly in favour of Michael Schultz's *Car Wash*, which was something else, but invigorating, as it followed a day-in-the-life of same: not all those working there were black, and Pryor was not one of them but a swinging hot gospeller. Of his next movie he said that he didn't care for the script, but 'took the role for the same reason I did most of my other movies. Because nobody offered me anything else.' It was the movie which would prove that Franklin was right about his box-office potential.

Whereas his two earlier movies that year had taken only just over $4 million each, despite warm reviews, Arthur Hiller's *Silver Streak* took over $30 million, and that was not because of any box-office clout carried by the top-billed Gene Wilder or Jill Clayburgh. No, the public enjoyed this exercise in Hitchcockery written by Colin Higgins, in which a thousand and one nasty or baffling things happen on a train to a mild publisher (Wilder) and his sleep-in chum (Clayburgh). The *best* thing to happen, two-thirds into the picture, is the eruption of Pryor as a dude, to become companion-in-peril from then on. Universal, which had produced the two other films, had noted a favourable response to Pryor, and agreed with Franklin about his potential: the studio was prepared to offer him $1 million for each of four years, during which it had first refusal rights to six films Pryor would be making. Among those the studio offered to him were *Animal Farm*, a remake of *Arsenic and Old Lace* and *The Sting II*, the latter as a co-starring vehicle for him and Lily Tomlin. 20th-Century-Fox, meanwhile, were anxious to get Pryor into another film immediately, and proposed a black *Cyrano de Bergerac*, set on Haiti; he and Franklin looked more favourably on this project, but it stalled when they could not agree on a director. Warners were also taking another look at Pryor, whom *Silver Streak* had made *persona* very *grata*; so Franklin did another multi-million-dollar deal giving Warners first look at anything Universal passed on.

And it was at Warners that Pryor made his first movie as an undoubted star. He was attracted to the role of Wendell Scott, the first black racing-driver, in *Greased Lightning* (77), but the result was unworthy of both his new status and Scott. Presumably because it was set just after the war the black members of the cast seem to be imitating Stepin Fetchit: or perhaps Schultz, directing, lost control, but it nevertheless did $7,800,000 at the box-office. With the same director, *Which Way is Up?* took $8,600,000, which does not reflect the fact that the public was getting three Pryors for the price of one: for he played an orange-picker, a priest and a dirty old man. Some people did not get any Pryor at all, since Universal looked at the foreign returns of *Greased Lightning* (released by Warners) and decided to distribute it in only selected markets. The thought occurs that if it was anything like the dreaded Lina Wertmuller's *The Seduction of Mimi*, of which it was a loose remake, 'twas no deprivation.

Blue Collar (78) is a story of union corruption as it affects three factory workers, written and directed by Paul Schrader (his first movie in the latter capacity). They are Harvey Keitel, Yaphet Kotto and Pryor, with virtually no reference throughout to colour – and only when they get high on coke in a cat-house is it implied that Keitel is a black-lover. Pryor, who has attempted to screw the Internal Revenue, plays for laughs, but otherwise this is a serious picture – and perhaps his best, working to a dénouement not unlike *On the Waterfront*, but in the end to a much better one. However, this movie lacks the power of that one and it failed dismally to draw an audience. So there was little consolation for the agonies of filming, causing Pryor to observe years later that he still hated his co-stars and the director, who observed then that Pryor's trouble was that he 'does something pathological and very dramatic to remind

everyone that he is black first and big second'. The screenplay, incidentally, might have been biographical, since Pryor had been imprisoned for ten days in 1974 for non-payment of taxes, while his cocaine habit was said to cost $100 a day (and it was one which Franklin did not expect to break).

The Wiz cost $24 million and took only $13,500,000, but that was not the fault of Pryor, very funny in the title-role, or Michael Jackson or Nipsey Russell, superb as the Straw Man and the Tin Man respectively, or Lena Horne, popping up as the Good Fairy. On Broadway this black musical version of Frank Baum's old tale had survived memories of *The Wizard of Oz* and Judy Garland. Universal, worried about the cost, put the film in the hands of Motown, producers of *Lady Sings the Blues*; Diana Ross, who had an 'in' at Motown, asked for Garland's old role. Not only was she much too old, but, like Barbra Streisand (who also remade one of Garland's greatest films), she is the antithesis of Garland

Richard Pryor in Brewster's Millions *(85). A farce about a man who has to give away a small fortune in order to lay claim to a larger one, it first had Broadway audiences rolling in the aisles in 1906 (and even earlier it had been a novel). Edward Abeles, who played the role then, was the first screen Brewster in 1914. We can't speak for him, but we do know the other screen Brewsters: Fatty Arbuckle (1921), Bebe Daniels (1927; Paramount had given the role a sex-change), Jack Buchanan (1935) and Dennis O'Keefe (1945) – and arguably Pryor brought more to the role. But the film itself was rather flat champagne.*

– hard and bland, where she was wistful, sensitive, intense, vulnerable and witty; where Garland's voice had colour and character, hers has neither. When she is on the screen, the film is very bad indeed; when she is not, it is often magical – a consolation to the director perhaps, Sidney Lumet and designer Tony Walton.

A third movie that year was promising, *California Suite*, directed by Herbert Ross from a script by Neil Simon, with all-star couples inhabiting four hotel suites. Two of these were Pryor and Bill Cosby as doctors, vacationing with their wives, but any dignity conferred by the medical profession was undone by Simon, who provided only unfunny slapstick. The self-explanatory *Richard Pryor Live in Concert* (79) was sufficiently successful to rate a follow-up, *Richard Pryor Is Back Live in Concert* later in the year, but some of it was a rip-off; in the meantime the public could sample him in a cameo in *The Muppet Movie*, as a balloon-vendor. The next year began horribly, back with assorted comics in two supposedly comic biblicals, *Wholly Moses!* (80), starring Dudley Moore as a pharaoh, and *In God We Trust*, directed, co-written by and starring Marty Feldman, as God. Poitier directed Pryor's reunion with Gene Wilder, *Stir Crazy*, which has the two of them in various misadventures before landing in jail. It took over $58 million at the box-office. but only Pryor's looks of fear, trepidation and apprehension prevent it from being a totally unrewarding experience. Far better was *Bustin' Loose* (81), directed by Oz Scott, in which he and Miss Tyson are an odd couple, sneaky ex-con and prim schoolmarm, taking some kids across country – to the tune of $15,400,000 at the box-office. He was one of the producers, as he was again on *Richard Pryor Live on the Sunset Strip* (82), which may be why the audience is seen to be hysterical, even when the jokes are not particularly funny. It was during this period that he sustained a hideous accident, to find his body half-burned, reputedly while free-basing cocaine. Not amusing would be most people's verdict on the scatology in *Some Kind of Hero*, which was not in James Kirkwood's original novel, but gone is the POW homosexuality presumably more offensive or wrong for the Pryor image. Otherwise, as directed by Michael Pressman, this is a decent study of a Vietnam veteran (not black in the book) adjusting to life back in the US. At the box-office this was only a mild hero, with a take of $11 million, but Richard Donner's *The Toy* took $24,700,000, which isn't kids' stuff – though the story was, as millionaire Jackie Gleason hires Pryor, a penniless writer, as a plaything for his spoilt son. It was a remake of *Le Jouet*, which had starred Pierre Richard.

He was brought into *Superman III* (83) to keep it light, and he has many splendid moments as an unemployed dishwasher who becomes a computer expert and thus one of Superman's enemies. It did magnificent business (see Christopher Reeve) but the $7,200,000 brought in by *Richard Pryor Here and Now* seemed to indicate that his concert days on film were over. Had he made *Arsenic and Old Lace*, we might have had the chance to compare him with Cary Grant as a farceur, for he has the ability of all the great screen clowns (Keaton, being Silent and unsmiling, is the exception) to find new colours in the range of his voice and in his expressions: so to that extent it was satisfying to find him in a remake of one of the classic farces, *Brewster's Millions* (85), the one about the man who has to spend a huge fortune very quickly in order to inherit a larger one. The esteemed Walter Hill directed, it took $19,900,000 (just $100,000 less than it cost), but it was fairly laboured stuff. *Jo Jo Dancer Your Life is Calling* (86) cost $14 million and took a mere $8 million, a more important blow to Pryor's self-esteem, since he also wrote and produced it from an autobiographical script co-written by himself. There was a further failure with *Critical Condition* (87), which cost $14,000,000 and took only $8,900,000; Michael Apted directed this thin comedy about a con-man who takes over a prison hospital. *See No Evil Hear No Evil* (89) proved again that Wilder was a draw if teamed with Pryor, but he was no funnier: he played a deaf man and Pryor was blind in a comedy which pitted them against some killers and the New York police. It proved that previous film-makers had been wise to avoid human affliction as a subject for comedy; it cost $18 million and took in $20,100,000. Then Pryor was teamed with Eddie Murphy in the latter's ego-trip, *Harlem Nights*, as the older con from whom Murphy learns his tricks. Pryor (see Murphy) did not find it an overwhelmingly pleasant experience. He is reunited with Wilder for *Another You* (91).

CHRISTOPHER REEVE

Hollywood's obsession in the last few decades with comic-strip heroes has not provided audiences with any enlightening experiences, and for every Batman there has been a Flash Gordon, for each Dick Tracy a Lone Ranger. Still, movies never were all uplift and 'tis unlikely that they will ever be. That being so, the Superman movies of Christopher Reeve have provided as much sheer high spirits and fun as anything outside the best Disney cartoons – and they owe much of their success to Reeve, handsomely embodying the Man of Steel and his naif alter ego, Clark Kent. Reeve's Superman makes him well named, a perfect thing in an imperfect world.

Reeve was born in New York City in 1952 to parents of some eminence in their own fields – journalist Barbara Johnson and Franklin Reeve, editor of 'Poetry Magazine', lecturer at Yale and Wesleyan universities, and an expert on Russian language and affairs. When his parents divorced, young Reeve acquired a step-family of several brothers and sisters and a father who was a stockbroker. He made his first stage appear-

ance with the McCarter Theater Company in Princeton, New Jersey, at the age of nine, and within a few years was determined to pursue a career on the stage. Accordingly he enrolled at the Juilliard School in New York after graduating in English from Cornell University, under whose auspices he travelled to Europe to continue his studies, which meant backstage work in Glasgow, in London with Olivier's National (where he coached most of the cast for their accents in 'The Front Page') and in Paris with the Comédie Française. Returning to the States, he studied in John Houseman's advanced programme at the Juilliard while appearing in a daytime soap for two years, 'Love of Life' – but nobody loved him, he recalled later, for he played a smoothie married simultaneously to two women. He toured with Celeste Holm in 'The Irregular Verb to Love' and appeared in stock, as Aeneas in 'Troilus and Cressida', as Macheath in 'The Beggar's Opera', among others, and he toured with the New York City school in the leading role of Molière's 'The Love Cure'. He made his Broadway debut as Katharine Hepburn's grandson in Enid Bagnold's 'A Matter of Gravity' (76), which led to a small movie role as an officer in a naval drama starring Charlton Heston, *Gray Lady Down* (78). He had been seen in the Bagnold play by producers Pierre Spengler and Ilya Salkind, who were looking for their Superman, so while appearing off-Broadway in 'My Life' at the prestigious Circle Rep he was given time off to fly to London to audition, one of many actors to do so. At 6 feet 4 inches he was the right height, but he had to undergo a crash-course at the gym to develop the right muscles in the right places. Reeve was signed after Marlon Brando, who would play his father, and Gene Hackman, who would be his arch-enemy Lex Luthor.

As the film has it, *Superman* (78) is sent from Krypton, when that planet is to be destroyed, to Earth, where, growing up, his strength amazes those whom he thinks are his parents. Grown, he has superhuman powers and an ability to fly, abilities he uses in fighting evil. Among those he helps are Lois Lane (Margot Kidder), a reporter who does not recognize him in the timid, clumsy Clark Kent who works with her on the newspaper. After a pretentious, almost interminable sequence on Krypton, the film begins to take off, and it soars as Superman flies. As directed by Richard Donner, this is a smashing, often magical entertainment, as the public realized, for its dangerous budget of $55 million turned into $82,800,000 at the box-office. Reeve's performance was sufficiently liked for it to propel him to the front rank of movie actors, so Rastar-Universal starred him in *Somewhere*

'You'll believe a man can fly' said the ads for Superman, *and when he did, with Margot Kidder, the effect was as magical as anything in movie history. He, of course, was Christopher Reeve, in the event the only conceivable man-of-steel, and this still is, in fact, from* Superman II *(80).*

in Time (80) as a writer who wills himself back to 1912 to relive an affair he had then with an actress (Jane Seymour). It was broken up then in *Maytime*-fashion by an impresario, played by Christopher Plummer in John Barrymore-like fashion. Otherwise it is an anaemic, misconceived piece of whimsy as directed by Jeannot Szwarc from a story by Richard Matheson – with the evident exception of Reeve, who is touching as the bewildered lover, and its setting, the Grand Hotel, Mackimac Island, in Michigan. Release had been delayed in the hope that it might benefit from the anticipation regarding the second *Superman*, but it had disappeared before then, with a take of only $4,400,000. Much of *Superman II* had been filmed alongside the first one, and a flurry of legal actions (or threats thereof) preceded the filming of extra material to make it feature-length. Reeve successfully negotiated a huge salary rise plus a percentage from the $250,000 he had been paid for the original, unlike Brando, who was simply written out of the sequel, because his fee was too high to allow for any increase in the budget. Reeve was critical of this man-oeuvring, calling it an 'appalling' decision made for economic rather than artistic reasons; the producers he found 'unworthy, devious and

unfortunate as people'. Donner, he said was 'the only one who kept things from being done in a shabby way and kept our morale high'. Richard Lester, 'creative consultant' on the first, was the credited director of the second, and Reeve was forced to accept him because his contract was ready signed. In the event he 'liked and respected him'; he praised his skill and his ability to inject Donner's material into what he was shooting (Hackman, top-billed, never returned to film with Lester). The way the thing was produced, he concluded, 'is the lowest you can go without actually cheating' – though he approved of the result, which is equally outstanding – perhaps a little lighter, with the cheering conceit that Superman is now a national hero. It cost $54 million to make and took in $65,100,000.

During this period Reeve returned to the stage, to play Hildy in 'The Front Page' in the Williamstown Theater Festival, in which he had appeared as a teenager; he has tried to return for each subsequent season, and has been seen in 'The Greeks', 'Holiday' and 'The Royal Family', among others. He was also faithful to the Circle Rep, returning at this time to be a homosexual Vietnam veteran in a wheelchair for their production of Lanford Wilson's 'Fifth of July', which transferred to

Broadway. He returned to movies in *Death-trap* (82), Sidney Lumet's version of a Broadway thriller by Ira Levin, which starts with a successful playwright (Michael Caine) suggesting a collaboration with a student (Reeve) at one of his seminars; by the time it finishes, a wife (Dyan Cannon) is dead, one or other of the men or both are revealed to be gay, and their games with each other have turned lethal. It was not much to get worked up about, and audiences didn't, so that its long Broadway run was transformed into a mere $9 million at the box-office. Lumet explained that he had chosen Reeve for the role because of his Superman; 'Reeve's timing – and humour – had to be just about perfect to make the character come off.' To which might be added that Olivier himself could not have brought off *Monsignor*, which was Hollywood socking it to the Church again, with Reeve as a priest who takes to the black market in the belief that money should be diverted from crime to a Better Cause. The setting was Rome in 1945, and Frank Perry directed from a screenplay which demonstrated that Abraham Polonsky and Wendell Mayes had both seen better days.

If Reeve was only a modest actor in such roles he was splendid as Clark Kent and merely charismatic as Superman: which *Superman III* (83) proved again. Although Richard Pryor was brought in for comedy relief, Lester as director attempted to make it more 'earthbound', as he put it, and he managed to keep the budget down to $35 million without its being conspicuously less spectacular than its predecessors: but with rentals amounting to only $37,200,000, a continuation seemed in doubt. Reeve had been contractually bound to play the role in two sequels, if the producers had so desired – as they had. Later he observed: 'It's a nice image, and if I'm still remembered for it in twenty years' time you won't find me knocking it. It hasn't been the end of the road for my career. I've lived an adventurous life and there's still plenty of good other roles waiting to be played.' One of these would be Basil Ransome, the struggling young lawyer from Mississippi who finds himself adrift among *The Bostonians* (84), at least as conceived by Henry James in his novel: in that, if translated well, he would muddy the waters between a prospective bride (Madeleine Potter) and her self-appointed guardian (Vanessa Redgrave), whose feelings may not be at all maternal. But as adapted by Ruth Prawer Jhabvala, Ransome has been flattened into an ordinary leading man, while James Ivory is not the director to ensure that Reeve looked more than vaguely in period. He had been approached for the role through his grand-

mother, and had taken only $100,000, one-tenth of his usual salary, for prestige and a percentage of the profits, but there was little going on either account. Miss Redgrave did persuade him to appear in London with her in another James piece, as adapted by and for her father some years earlier, 'The Aspern Papers'.

Reflecting an off-screen hobby, Reeve played the lead in *The Aviator* (85), ferrying mail across the US in 1918; when his boss (Jack Warden) believes that passengers could be more lucrative he has him fly a troublesome girl (Rosanna Arquette) to Idaho, but they crash. So did the film; badly directed by George Miller and poorly written, it did little or no business. Reeve was accordingly better employed as a television Vronsky in an adulterous affair with Jacqueline Bisset, *Anna Karenina*, but a two-picture contract with Cannon did him little good. He was strongly attracted to *Street Smart* (87), which gave him the chance to play another reporter – even weaker than Clark Kent and smarmy into the bargain. As written by David Freeman from his own experience, Reeve is a journo who makes up a story about a pimp, only to find the DA using it as evidence to prosecute a real-life one (Morgan Freeman). Cannon Releasing allowed the film to die, but it had not been much helped by the direction of Jerry Schatzberg. In the interim, another second-string director, Jeannot Szwarc, had given Salkind a failure, *Supergirl*, in 1984. It

Almost unrecognisable without his Superman kiss-curl, Christopher Reeve in sombre mood in The Bostonians *(84).*

could be claimed that Helen Slater was much less suitable for the role than Reeve as her male counterpart; and it was one which he was to do again, with reservations. Cannon were producing *Superman IV – The Quest for Peace*, since the Salkinds had sold them the rights; Warners, whose financial input into the first three had been considerable, now coughed up only a little, but they agreed to distribute – a more promising prospect than Cannon. Reeve's price for donning his blue leotard again was control over the script, written by Lawrence Konner and Mark Rosenthal. What he could not control were the cheesy Special Effects, though given Cannon's reputation these should not have surprised him. Sidney J. Furie directed, not battling enough (though he tried) for quality as Donner and Lester had done. The film still cost as much as Part 3 of the saga, i.e. $35 million, but in the wake of disastrous reviews only $8,100,000 was returned at the box-office. The public had seen three super Supermans and did not care to experience a poor one. Hackman, Kidder and Reeve were spared poor notices – indeed, 'Reeve could not be better,' said critic Alan Frank – but it was a sad finish to the best of the comic-strip movies.

Three failures had a bad effect on Reeve's career, and he accepted the role of Kathleen Turner's fiancé in *Switching Channels* (88), a remake of *His Girl Friday* – and can you imagine anyone wanting to play one of Ralph Bellamy's sad sack 'other man' roles? He was fine in it, but only likeable in a mini-series, *The Great Escape II: The Untold Story*. In 1989 he played Leontes in an off-Broadway production of 'The Winter's Tale', and then he returned to TV for a movie, *The Rose and the Jackal* (90), effectively playing Allan Pinkerton, the gruff Scotsman who started the detective agency during the Civil War, more or less at the request of the Government. We shall next see him in *So Help me God!* with Raul Julia, and *The Midnight Spy*, being directed in Poland by Witold Orzechowski. Either might restore him to the eminence in which many people would like to find him.

He lives in New York and London with Gae Exton, the mother of their two sons.

BURT REYNOLDS

In these days of frequently lousy movies it's always good to be reassured that Hollywood doesn't change: they're all out to make a quick buck. John Schlesinger once said 'The "Flavour of the Month Club" mentality of many producers, whereby they try to guess public tastes, is hard to cope with', and from Schlesinger's point of view he would probably have been happier in the days of the great impresarios, who knew what they wanted (when they heard about it). It has always been open season and an open game on stars: the studios declined and the star-system fell apart, but then it was discovered that the industry was more dependent than ever on stars, if, now, just a handful. Thus, since Newman, Redford and McQueen could not go on forever, who would be taking their places? Every half-bit favourite from TV was tested; certain actors were thrown at the public in film after film, without discernable result; and all the time the next big star was there, and he had been, for more than a decade. From Richard Dix via Wayne and Bogart to Jack Nicholson, that was usually the case, but with Burt Reynolds it can't be said that he sneaked up on us: he was pretty noisy about it.

For one thing, he did a lot of talk-shows: he was such a witty and volatile guest that they asked him to turn host. With huge glee he told Merv Griffin's audience that his current (dramatic) series had been axed, adding that he had now the distinction of being cancelled at various times by the three major networks. There was no pomposity, no bull, about Burt: that was the start of the 'good-ol'-boy' image, and it was 'very calculating. I thought that I could get on television and say, "Hey, my last picture was a turkey", and people would find it funny.' So, there was a much publicized relationship with yesteryear's American sweetheart, Dinah Shore, a good few years older than he, and that nude centrefold in 'Cosmopolitan' (posing nude hadn't hurt Marilyn Monroe either). And he appeared in one film in nun's habit, fully moustached. This was a macho-guy who didn't take himself seriously. Gable and Cagney hadn't, and the public still worshipped them, and who now had a kind word for the solemn, self-absorbed and serious male idols of the late 40s and 50s? Says Robert Aldrich, who directed him in *Hustle*: 'Behind that false humor and false modesty is a bright man who's paid his dues. People think he's Charley Charm, but that's only part of it. Burt is a strong-willed, self-centered businessman; he does what serves Burt, and he should.' Such comments didn't hurt Mary Pickford, either.

He was born in 1936 in Palm Beach, the son of the police chief. At college his chief interest was football, and he was about to sign with the Baltimore Colts when a car-smash damaged his knee; with the insurance money he went to New York, where he got the acting bug, but he went home again – to act at the Palm Beach Junior College, which resulted in a scholarship to the Hyde Park Playhouse in

New York. After a spell in stock, he was in the New York City Center production of 'Mister Roberts', starring Charlton Heston, and that led to small roles in TV, notably in 'M Squad'. He was second lead to Darren McGavin in 'Riverboat', and later joined the long-running 'Gunsmoke' to play an Indian blacksmith; he refused a 20th-Century-Fox contract (in order to stay in drama school in New York) and was dropped by Universal. During this time he obtained small roles in two movies, *Angel Baby* (61), which earned him $15,000, an independent production about evangelism, starring George Hamilton, and *Armored Command*, at Allied Artists with Howard Keel, in which he was an opportunist GI scrapping with sergeant Earl Holliman over foreign agent Tina Louise. Before quitting 'Gunsmoke' in 1966 he had been married to British-born actress Judy Carne, and had starred in a duff B, *Last Message From Saigon* (65) as a CIA agent. There was an offer from Italy for a spaghetti Western, *Navajo Joe* (66), in the title-role (he has, via a grandmother, Cherokee blood), but that was an experience he later called 'one of the most dreadful' of his life; there had been a number of Indian roles earlier on TV, and he was offered a series, 'Hawk', about one who was a modern cop. It did not run; neither did a one-hour pilot, 'Lassiter' (68), and he was no luckier with three movies: *Fade In*, a tale of movie-making with Barbara Loden which failed to get any bookings (but it was later sold to TV on his name); *Impasse* (69), a caper movie set in the Philippines; and *Shark!*, a US–Mexican co-production written and directed by the dreaded Samuel Fuller (who disowned the final cut), about treasure-hunters and the title threat thereto. There was another short-lived TV series, 'Dan August', and finally a major (well, almost) Hollywood movie, *100 Rifles*, so he did not mind dipping to third-billing – as a half-breed Mexican bank-robber pursued by Jim Brown and Raquel Welch. At United Artists, producers Jules Levy and Arthur Gardner liked him well enough to give him the title-role in *Sam Whiskey*, an itinerant gambler who involves himself in a Western version of *Rififi–Topkapi*. At this time he was getting $150,000, ten times the amount he had been paid for his first movie. This is already the Reynolds image, waiting to be burnished: Burt the jerk, only too fallible behind his long cigar, boasting but bested, diving for sunken treasure in longjohns with a coal-scuttle over his head. As entertainment, however, the film does not compare with two TV movies: *Run, Simon, Run* (70), in which he was a wronged Indian planning revenge on the reservation; and *Hunters Are For Killing*, in which he was

an ex-con on a visit to his home town. Enraptured by his image in *Sam Whiskey*, he turned down *M-A-S-H* to do another abysmal movie, *Skulduggery*, at Universal, in which he and Susan Clark discovered a lost New Guinean tribe; he also turned down the role of an Indian in *Tell Them Willie Boy Is Here* because it carried a four-picture contract.

Then came Miss Shore and the talk-show days, and on one he met the editor of 'Cosmopolitan', who asked him to bare his all, or nearly, for her lady readers. Reynolds said that he knew that this would make him famous, but it might also render him infamous or a joke: but, he reckoned, his talent was strong enough to counteract the notoriety, and he also had a very good film in the can. This was *Deliverance* (72), in which he and Jon Voight headed an urban team of four on a backwoods river-trip which turns nightmarish. It was a film of quality, and Reynolds was finally launched as a fully-fledged Hollywood star. He played a detective in a joky cop comedy – this was the one with the nun-drag – *Fuzz*, on the trail of Yul Brynner; and was in a sketch in Woody Allen's *Everything You Always Wanted to Know About Sex But Were Afraid to Ask*, directing copulation from inside the body. The *Shamus* (73) was him, a private eye; *White Lightning* was moonshine in this Deep South melodrama produced by Gardner and Levy; and *The Man Who Loved Cat Dancing* was – well, Cat Dancing was an Indian (not Reynolds), and no one loved this especially dreary Western. The female lead, Sarah Miles, was involved in a location scandal when her manager killed himself, and it was thought that that was what killed it at the box-office: MGM therefore held it up for two years before letting it into Britain, but reception for Miles and film was no warmer.

That Reynolds still had a way to go was evidenced when he mentioned that he was still getting scripts turned down by Redford, McQueen and Newman – as he said when he explained why he turned down the role of James Bond: it was 'a rough decision to take', but he felt unable to equal Sean Connery in the role. Anyway, the public offered only a cool welcome to the next two, *The Mean Machine* (74) and *W. W. and the Dixie Dance Kings* (75); Aldrich directed the former, a vicious yarn about an ex-football pro and the effect of his presence in prison, and John Avildsen directed the latter, some high jinks about a con-man leading a troupe to Grand Old Opry. The music changed to Cole Porter for *At Long Last Love*, Peter Bogdanovich's doomed attempt at a lighthearted 30s-style musical: it hadn't enough class, despite the songs and the sets, but Reynolds supplied some as a bored millionaire – as well as the moustache clipped à la Clark Gable (Reynolds was the first actor to turn down *Gable and Lombard*; it was offered to Steve McQueen and Ali McGraw, and to Warren Beatty, who agreed to do the script if the names were changed). Unlike many of his peers, he is unafraid of changing his image, of taking on challenges, of trying to 'grow' as an actor, and to that extent his millionaire in Bogdanovich's film was a success; but he could not do much with the nice Frisco cop in *Hustle*, since he was unable to suggest any sort of neurosis which might explain why his live-in companion (Catherine Deneuve) was a high-class callgirl. He produced with Aldrich, who also directed: his usual job of trying to attract attention at all costs, including credibility. The film is one of the Reynolds 'stiffs' which 'Variety' later assessed as nevertheless able to draw big ratings on TV; indeed, this actor's popularity stayed in abeyance through some more flops. Since *At Long Last Love* had been a joy to make, but had died, he himself expected great things of *Lucky Lady*, since the location shooting had been a 'nightmare'; but this supposedly lighthearted adventure (with Liza Minnelli) of the 20s lost most of its near-$13 million investment. The *White Lightning* team produced *Gator* (76), a sequel, with Reynolds again playing the

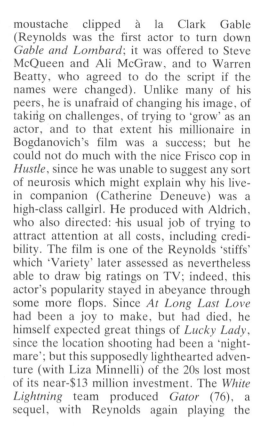

Burt Reynolds and Ryan O'Neal in Nickelodeon *(76), Peter Bogdanovich's botched hommage to the pioneers of the Silver Screen. O'Neal played a director and Reynolds a star – in his case, as if to the manner born, since he loved being a movie star. And he worked very hard to achieve it.*

happy-go-lucky moonshiner Gator McGlusky, and himself directing – at a combined fee of $600,000, plus 10 per cent after break-even, and then 40 per cent to 50 per cent of the profits: but not with conspicuously successful results. *Nickelodeon* was another of Bogdanovich's concepts, and Reynolds was a green country boy who becomes a Silent star under the tutelage of Ryan O'Neal: some cutting might have helped.

Smokey and the Bandit (77) got only marginally better reviews, but this was the movie the public had been waiting for; dismissed in New York and other urban centres, it began to build till at the end of the year 'Variety' offered its domestic gross at over $58,900,000, and third position at the box-office, after *Star Wars* and *Rocky*. It had cost only $4 million, and was hardly more than an extended car chase; and the director, Hal Needham, hadn't made a film before. He was a stunt-man, and had met Reynolds on the 'Riverboat' series; he had stunted for him since – though Reynolds does many of his own stunts – and Reynolds had in the past tried to get him a job in the director's chair. Surprisingly fresh on a number of worn themes, the film owed its popularity, it was agreed, to Reynolds, and he came in fourth among the box-office stars. He shared a 'Time' cover with Clint Eastwood, and, said Philip French in the 'Observer', he 'finally establishes himself as one of the most remarkable comic talents in the American cinema, an immaculate performer with superb timing and an ability to suggest rare depths of intelligence and emotion.' The film under discussion was Michael Ritchie's *Semi-Tough*, a satirical look at professional football and, in passing, a number of contemporary obsessions; Kris Kristofferson was Reynolds's team-mate and rival in love.

In life (it seems) Reynolds is something of a hypochondriac, so as he had kidded his images over the years he acted in and directed *The End* (78), about 'a shady real estate man who learns he has only a year to live'. That's how Frank Rich saw it in 'Time', adding that the man 'is a jerk. Since the movie is a mess, Reynolds cannot win' and that the actor is miscast: 'Sonny seems to be a Jewish neurotic, but Reynolds's many talents do not include an ability to impersonate Woody Allen.' Rich also pointed out his 'gallantry' and 'generosity' to his fellow-players – try and find that in those male stars of the 50s – and concluded that Reynolds devotees would not buy it; they did not, and it was nevertheless a shame, for Reynolds had boldly put his film-persona on the line – a fact half-appreciated by John Coleman in the 'New Statesman', referring first to 'this bland grinner, to the dim many the 70s echo of Cary Grant.' Needham directed *Hooper*, which was about – what else? – stunting in Hollywood. That was the Reynolds in 1978 that the public wanted to see, and despite the onslaught of John Travolta he was No. 1 at the box-office; his co-star, as in *Smokey*, was his off-screen companion, Sally Field. In 1979 they acted together in 'The Rainmaker' at the Burt Reynolds Dinner Theater, which he had opened in his home town.

He remained miffed that he had been second choice for roles which had won Oscars for the guys who had nabbed them – Jack Nicholson and *One Flew Over the Cuckoo's Nest* and, more recently, Jon Voight and *Coming Home*, observing that Nicholson's Oscar nomination (for *The Last Detail*) and Voight's friendship with Jane Fonda had been factors in his losing them. He decided that his career needed a more serious picture, and *Starting Over* (79) was chosen, one of several films about divorce which followed in the wake of *Kramer vs Kramer*. Candice Bergen leaves him to do her own thing, and he takes up with Jill Clayburgh – none too easily. As directed by Alan J. Pakula, it could not make up its mind whether it wanted to be a hard look at the subject or a Burt Reynolds comedy, but its take of $19,100,000 – following the $20,600,000 for *The End* – proved that Reynolds was still a potent name at the turnstiles. In order to get the film finished he had forgone director-approval on *Rough Cut* (80), only to find that producer David Merrick had sacked Don Siegel, to replace him by Peter Hunt. Siegel was reinstated, but this once reliable director did only hack-work on a script which deserved no better. Reynolds was a jewel-thief operating in Britain, Lesley-Anne Down his accomplice and David Niven the Scotland Yard man engaged in tracking them down; at one point he does an impersonation of Cary Grant, and Miss Down said to him (off-camera), 'You're *not* Cary Grant. You're doing *Tony Curtis* doing Cary Grant.' The film took only $10 million at the wickets on a budget of $14 million. Needham directed *Smokey and the Bandit II*, which did $38,900,000, a falling off from the original but no matter, and *The Cannonball Run* (81), which took $36,800,000 on a cost of $18 million. Reynolds's salaries were respectively $2 million and $5 million (for just three weeks' work) – and $5 million was the sum named when Paramount sued 20th-Century-Fox for taking him away from them to do this film. It turned out to be a loose remake of Roger Corman's 1976 *Cannonball* and also an attempt to yoke *The Great Race* with *It's a Mad, Mad, Mad, Mad World*, as ill-assorted couples try to get from one place to another, double-crossing all the while and besting

Reynolds in Smokey and the Bandit *(77), one of the films with which he got very lucky. Which is to say, like most of his vehicles, it wasn't very good, but it was one of many which took the public's fancy. But no one could complain about the way Sally Field, as here, partnered him.*

various rednecks. Reynolds's romantic interest was Farrah Fawcett, and they were supported by the likes of Roger Moore, Dean Martin and Sammy Davis Jr in guest-roles.

Needing a relief from such moronic capers (as who wouldn't?) Reynolds played a swinging bachelor with *Paternity* leanings for Paramount, who had scheduled this for him after *Rough Cut*: one reason he had chosen to do other films in the interim was because he had not been sure that the role was right for him – even if he had the most lavish wardrobe since the heyday of Joan Crawford – and he was proved right when the film took only $8,500,000. His third film that year, *Sharkey's Machine*, found him as a vice-cop pitted him against underworld boss Vittorio Gassmann, when he falls for one of Gassmann's hookers (Rachel Ward, a role originally meant for Sally Field): daft stuff, but a return of $18,400,000 on a budget of $17,500,000 was not to be laughed at. Reynolds also directed, disclosing a somewhat unsettling penchant for sleaze. His career seemed to move in an exciting direction when he made *The Best Little Whorehouse in Texas* (82), based on a

Reynolds in The End *(78), as a hypochondriac gloomily pondering his fate. That's how the UA publicity people originally captioned this still. We might now consider that he was contemplating the decline of his movie fortunes.*

Broadway musical, if only because Dolly Parton wanted him to give up boxer-shorts for a jockey-slip. There was also a song for jocks in jock-straps (in the shower-room) and a dance for girls in garter-belts (in a brothel), between which we were offered a tame tale of a sheriff (Reynolds) trying to close down a brothel while enamoured of its madam. Possibly the outré ingredients contributed to the film's earnings of $47,300,000 on a budget of $35 million. Reynolds looked as dispirited as any man would when his girl said she didn't like his underwear, but he was back on form with Goldie Hawn as *Best Friends*, two Hollywoods screenwriters who decide to marry after several years of collaboration. This was a sweet comedy, as written by Valerie Curtin and Barry Levinson and directed by Norman Jewison, all of whom have much fun at the expense of the film industry. The film made back $19 million, exactly what it cost. It would be Reynolds's last decent film in a long while.

He was offered the role for which Jack Nicholson won an Oscar in *Terms of Endearment*, but he was already committed to *Stroker Ace* (83), which found him once again as a car-racer. That it was all too familiar seemed certain when it returned only $8,900,000 on an investment of $14 million. Still, it must have been fun to make, since the director, Needham, had been living with Reynolds for some time, and the leading lady, Loni Anderson, would become the second Mrs Reynolds – that is, after he made headlines in 1985 when he announced during

a TV talk-show that he had not got AIDS. He was on sounder cinematic ground with *The Man Who Loved Women*, Blake Edwards's remake of a Truffaut film in which Charles Denner had played the lead. Reynolds was more convincing than he as a compulsive womanizer, but when he did his scenes with Julie Andrews, as his psychiatrist, it was clear that this was a potentially great team with the wrong material. Said 'Variety': 'There's an unpleasant feeling for about an hour that the film is never going to get started, followed by the equally unpleasant feeling that it may never end.' To avoid the awkward option of having two Reynolds films play against each other in the Christmas season, Warners opened *Cannonball Run II* in Japan, postponing its US release till the following year – but to little avail. Described by 'Variety' as 'a combination of arrogance and cynicism', it took a poor $14,600,000, on a $17 million budget, but that was an improvement on the Edwards film, which cost $19 million and took only $4,800,000. No way was Reynolds going to entrust his next venture to Edwards (as initially planned), a co-starring feature with Eastwood, his contender for the box-office crown a while earlier. Therefore, 'creative differences' were cited when Edwards withdrew from *City Heat* (84), with Richard Benjamin taking over: the two stars played ex-comrades-in-arms, now rivals, in this tale of gangland wars in Kansas City in 1934. They were both powerhouse – these were still the good days – and it made $21 million (on a $25 million budget) very quickly; but it dropped out of sight equally swiftly.

Retribution was swift – for someone who acknowledgedly watched several Clark Gable movies every week and who saw himself as 'the sort of unsophisticated Cary Grant of the 1980s'. Reynolds offered only mechanisms, and *Stick* (85), which he also directed, was a trial for even the most indulgent of cinemagoers: he managed to get some old-style lyricism in the love scenes with Candice Bergen, but the rest of it was horribly old hat, as ex-con Reynolds sought to avenge the death of an old chum and bring down some big-time drug-dealers. It had all been considerably more exciting in Elmore Leonard's original novel. What the film needed to work was Bogart's soul-weariness in *High Sierra*, said David Denby in 'New York' magazine, 'but Reynolds can't create a character; he constantly violates the feelings we have about Stick and replaces them by the feelings we've always had about Burt Reynolds. He's smiley-cute and clever, practically winking to the audience in complicity, and none of this has anything to do with the character of Stick.' The film cost $22 million and realized only

$3,400,000. Reynolds, more than anyone of his generation – including Eastwood – had hitched his wagon to the star vehicle, and it wouldn't budge. Ill-health made him turn down the Richard Gere part in Lumet's *Power*, and conceivably the role of a devious power-crazy manipulator might have revived public interest in him. He himself observed, 'The public never tires of a particular character. Look at John Wayne, who always did the same thing. Look at Bob Hope, or Mae West, for that matter.' *Heat* (87) engendered some interest in the press when Reynolds got involved in a fisticuffs session with the director, Dick Richards, who sued for $25 million, but that publicity did not bring the people in. It was the first Reynolds film to go out via an independent since *Shark!* in 1969. William Goldman scripted, without distinction, a tale about a Las Vegas tough guy (Reynolds) helping an ex-girlfriend avenge a beating-up. *Malone* concerned an ex-CIA man trying to stop a megalomaniac (Cliff Robertson) from achieving power. Orion distributed, and it beat *Heat*, which didn't break the million-dollar barrier of 'Variety''s chart: but it took only $1,200,000, which put it near to the bottom of the list. Both budgets were probably in the $10-12 million, and Reynolds was said to be still getting $3 million a picture.

If he thought 1987 was bad, worse was to come. First there was *Rent-a-Cop* (88), a reunion with Liza Minnelli who was helping him, a detective, to find the real culprit of the crime for which he was busted. 'Reynolds looks bored and is boring here,' said 'Variety', 'with an ill-fitting toupee that is downright embarrassing from one close-up angle'; and then the film literally died at the box-office. He seemed to be in luck when Michael Caine was detained on *Jaws 4*, because what he needed, above all, was to get away from the over-familiar thick-ear Reynolds melodramas. The film concerned was a comedy, *Switching Channels*, in fact a remake of *His Girl Friday*, with himself in the Grant role. The supposedly 'hot' Kathleen Turner was in the Russell role – and taking top-billing – with support from another strongish name, Christopher Reeve: but the film cost $18 million and took only $3,800,000. Poor reviews did not help, and Reynolds could console himself, too, that it was his first film for some time not to go direct to video overseas. That fate awaited *Physical Evidence* (89) with Theresa Russell, in which he was a drunken cop who wakes up to find himself the chief suspect in a murder investigation. Reynolds himself thought the role a new departure, because for the first time he was playing a loser, and one who is basically unsympathetic: but there was no new departure at the box-office. Michael Crichton

directed, but, said the 'Guardian's' Derek Malcolm, 'the script alone would stop a bison in its tracks.' It cost $17 million and took only $1,500,000.

He returned to television, as 'B.L. Stryker', a cop series which alternated with two others, one with Peter Falk and the other with Lou Gossett; and he changed his image by wearing a grey wig instead of a black one in *Breaking In*, a gentle comedy directed by Bill Forsyth and written by John Sayles – about an ageing thief teaching a new one the tricks of the trade. As the film came out he observed that he saw a new career for himself as a character actor. Because his career was in trouble he had accepted the Screen Actors Guild scale, and taken only $1,511 a week, plus 10 per cent of the gross. The budget therefore was kept to a manageable $6 million, but with a take of only $700,000 it did not seem that the public was curious about Reynolds in his new guise. 'I'm trying to do things now that are not just fun, but are a challenge to me. Now, more than ever, I want to use some of this stuff inside me,' he said. He played another supporting role in *Modern Love* (90), an autobiographical film produced, written, and directed by and starring, Robby Benson, who appeared with Reynolds in *The End* and *Rent-a-Cop*. The players worked for scale in this independent production in which Reynolds, billed fifth, played Robby's father-in-law. In a movie world dominated by *Total Recall* and other movies which ten years earlier might have been offered to Reynolds, this quickly disappeared. He was being offered many, including one with Sally Field, Disney's *Wild Hearts Can't Be Broken* and *Indian Runner*. He said he was far too busy to bother, as he started a 30-minute TV series, 'Evening Shade'. He also planned to direct *Alby's House of Bondage*, but not to star. Asked whether he had taken for granted, or been jaded about, his time as king of the box-office he replied ambiguously, 'Sure I did. I was proud of that achievement, but I didn't relish it. I would now – and how! Just being among the top ten is a big thrill. But times change, and you can't always figure the public . . .' No doubt he has his adherents when his films are scheduled on 'The Late Show', but if Clark Gable is on another channel, which will you be watching?

MICKEY ROURKE

Mickey Rourke is drawn to roles in which he has to appear seedy, slovenly, debauched, dangerous and always intense – and some of these qualities he has in life. 'I don't give two fucks about who goes to see [my movies] or who has anything to say about them,' he says. 'They pay me good money, and that's what it's about for me right now – getting paid to do a job.' He often says 'fuck' on the screen, too; he takes his shades on and off with regularity; and he smokes a lot.

He was born in 1956 in Schnectady, New York, of Scots-Irish descent, to a father who was an undertaker and bodybuilder and who separated from his wife when the boy was seven. With his mother, brother and sister he moved to Miami, where he acquired five tough step-brothers. It was their teasing, he said, which helped turn him into a street-fighter; he was an amateur boxer known as 'Mick the Slasher' for a while, but after a friend persuaded him to appear in an amateur production of a play by Jean Genet, 'Death-watch', he decided to be an actor. He went to Chicago, where a small company offered him an apprenticeship building sets. He did not care for that, so moved on to New York to

study under Susan Seacat at Lee Strasberg's school, supporting himself in odd jobs which ranged from selling pretzels and ice-cream on the sidewalk to nightclub bouncer and furniture mover. An admired role in the school's production of 'Richard III' encouraged him to try Hollywood, where he auditioned 78 times before getting a job, obtaining small roles in Spielberg's *1941* (79) and Cimino's *Heaven's Gate* (80). Before the second of these was shown, he had had prime roles in three telemovies: *City of Fear*, which starred David Janssen as a reporter, fourth-billed as a psychotic killer based on 'Son of Sam'; *Act of Love*, third-billed as Ron Howard's brother, as a paraplegic (after an accident), whom he begs to kill him; and *Rape and Marriage – the Rideout Case*, top-billed in this story, based on fact, as the husband sued for rape by his wife (Linda Hamilton).

He was first noticed in cinemas in Kasdan's *Body Heat* (81), as the punk employed by William Hurt to make the bomb, and he was in a second excellent showcase when Barry Levinson cast him as one of the five young companions in *Diner* (82) – the smart-talking one who works in a hairdressing saloon and studies law in the evenings to impress the girls. A nod as Best Supporting Actor from the National Society of Film Critics did no harm at all, nor did talk of a new Brando and a new James Dean. But Nicolas Roeg's *Eureka* (83) was of little help, since it had only a few sporadic bookings. Rourke was a lawyer. Francis Coppola cast him as 'Motor-cycle Boy', the worldly innocent, in *Rumble-fish* (83), the second of his two absurd teenage films taken from the novels of S.E. Hinton. Matt Dillon had a bigger role, as the younger brother who hangs on his every word, but the film set a pattern for the films in which Rourke would star thereafter: it lost money (it cost $10 million and took only $1,282,000).

In Stuart Rosenberg's *The Pope of Green-wich Village* (84) he was a cousin – to Eric Roberts, who leads him into a heap of trouble including blackmail, robbery and lesser matters. It cost $8 million and took $2,563,000. Cimino invited him back, as star now, for a thriller set in Chinatown, as a dedicated cop trying to cleanse the place of its drug-runners: *Year of the Dragon* (85) cost $24 million and took only $7,331,000 – but then many members of the press found it hardly less reprehensible than *Heaven's Gate*. This did nothing – on the contrary – to eliminate Rourke's contempt for critics. He was a wealthy commodity broker with designer stubble in Adrian Lyne's steamy *9½ Weeks* (86), playing kinky games with an art dealer (Kim Basinger) till she has become his sexual slave: despite much comment on its content, that brought in only

Mickey Rourke in Barfly *(87), one of the several sleazy dramas he has made which have failed to make any impact at the box-office.*

$2,500,000 on a $17 million outlay. Lyne observed that it was not an easy film to make, since Rourke often arrived on the set in the morning 'hanging in rags . . . You have this low-life bravado there, but then again he's a really sensitive, shy guy as well.' Lyne did not care for Rourke's entourage and it is one constant of Rourke's interviews that mention is made of the fact that he is accompanied by a somewhat older minder.

Oh well, perhaps Alan Parker's *Angel Heart* (87) would be the break-through, what with Robert De Niro in support and Rourke as a private-eye in a thriller with many of the trappings of *film noir*. It was set in 1955, when even run-down private-eyes did not go around with five days' stubble on their faces; it cost $18 million and returned $6,500,000. Parker observed that 'Working with Mickey is a nightmare. He's very dangerous on the set because you never know what he's going to do. But out of that comes a fantastic spontaniety.' Rourke looked the same, if fatter, in *Barfly*, directed by Barbet Schroeder who, not being Parker, was unable to prevent the affectation in Rourke's performance. But then this was a smug low-life movie, as taken from some autobiographical writings by Charles Bukowski, who mightily approved of Rourke and the way he played a character based upon himself. The film cost Cannon $3 million and it took $1,380,000. He then played an IRA gunman who, disillusioned with violence, agrees to one last killing in order to obtain a passport: Mike Hodges directed *A Prayer for the Dying* in Britain from the novel by Jack Higgins. It cost the equivalent of $6 million, but the Goldwyn Company, which had the US rights, saw a return on their investment of only $568,500.

Rourke played a boxer in *Homeboy* (88), from his own script, which Michael Seresin directed. In May 1989 he sued the producer, Elliott Kastner, for $5,200,000 in compensation and $3 million punitive damages for not being paid or being granted the approval rights as called for in his contract: the details were disclosed of a fee of $100,000 (i.e. much less than the $2 million claimed by some sources) plus $100,000 for the script. That is virtually all that has been heard of this venture, which went direct to video in the US and which in Britain was dismissed by the critic Tim Pulleine as a 'laborious exercise in low-life melodrama [and] very much a vehicle for Mickey Rourke, whose strenuously mannered performance unwisely vies for comparison with Marlon Brando in his heyday.' The cast included his estranged wife, Debra Feuer, whom he had met not long after first arriving in Los Angeles. Little was heard, either, of *Francesco* (89), a biography of St Francis of

Assisi made in Spain in which Rourke has the title-role – but then the director is Liliana Cavani, whose name does not automatically inspire foreign sales. One of the British tabloids reported that he had donated part of his fee to 'causes in Northern Ireland', which did him no good at all; nor were matters improved when he explained that he had given the money not to the IRA, but to Joe Doherty, 'a prisoner in New York City'. Rourke is the one name constantly attached to *The Crew*, which should mark the return to the screen of a much more talented Italian director, Antonioni, but two other projects for Rourke were stalled – the life of Al Capone and the life of Jerry Lee Lewis, *Great Balls of Fire*, which was made with Dennis Quaid instead.

The contract for *Homeboy* had been drawn up in June 1986, before it was clear that Rourke had little drawing power, but it was strange at this stage to find a major company, Tri-Star, sinking $20 million into *Johnny Handsome* as a star vehicle for Rourke. He played a badly disfigured petty crook who, transformed by plastic surgery, seeks revenge on those who have wronged him. True, Walter Hill directed, but his box-office record was far from unblemished: in the event the film took $2,600,000. It was reported in the trade press, none too confidently, that Rourke's lack of appeal on his home ground was compensated for by his following in France – and that, anyway, though people did not care to see his films in cinemas they hired them on video, which was why he was still being paid a large salary.

Wild Orchid (90) advertised itself as 'coming from the creators of *9½ Weeks*', which you would have thought warning enough. One of the co-writers and co-producers of that film, Zalman King, had in the interim been at it again, also directing, with the equally execrable *Two Moon Junction*, but perseverence can pay off, as Russ Meyer and John Waters have shown, in this field of schlock exploitation. King's speciality is soft porn, and it paid off for him on this occasion, for over $11 million came into the box-office, Rourke's best achiever in a long while. He was more than slightly ridiculous, however, as a frightfully rich, enigmatic stranger with a bandana, necklace, ear-ring and Harley Davidson, bewitching Jacqueline Bisset's new business lawyer, Carre Otis. It is clear from the start that he'll bed her sooner or later – and it's later. 'This is', said one contemptuous critic, 'the longest film ever made about foreplay'. Pictures of the pair of them appeared in 'Playboy' in compromising garb and situation, and Rourke sued the producers, Vision International, who countersued on the grounds that he and Otis refused to film certain scenes and had not permitted certain pictures to appear for publicity. Cynics might connect this controversy with the film's lively box-office performance, but *9½ Weeks* had generated far more publicity to less avail. Now it's a return to Cimino, who remade *The Desperate Hours*, with Rourke in the Bogart role. Apart from the question of Cimino's fitness for the job, there is the matter of filling Bogart's shoes. There may be actors around who can do this, but Rourke is emphatically not one of them. It opened in the US to virtually unanimous hostile reviews, but managed a not-too-desperate $1,600,000 in its first week. Help may be at hand in the person of Simon Wincer, fresh from his triumph with *Quigley Down Under*, for he is directing Rourke and Don Johnson in *Harley Davidson and the Marlboro Man* (91).

THERESA RUSSELL

Theresa Russell is a major talent, an entrancing actress, who chooses to make an above-average number of bad films.

She was born in San Diego in 1957. Her parents – 'original California hippies', she called them – divorced when she was six, and her mother's second marriage broke up when she was eleven. At fourteen, while at Burbank High School, she had an offer to do some modelling and at sixteen she left home, to live with a primal therapist who encouraged his patients to scream their way to a cure. She had been bitten by the acting bug in school, and so enrolled in Lee Strasberg's school in Los Angeles, figuring that if she didn't make it she 'was young enough to take a course at something else'. At some point she made the acquaintance of producer Sam Spiegel, who urged director Elia Kazan to cast her in *The Last Tycoon* (76) – because, in Kazan's opinion, he had failed to get her into bed but had not given up hope (Kazan in his memoir: 'the truth is that most men of imagination and passion in the arts tend to use their power over young women – and young men – to this end. It's life-loving and inevitable'). So Kazan took a gamble on an untried talent, feeling that her virtues would outweigh the disadvantages, and he fought for her when Spiegel wanted her replaced. Russell's Cecelia, the daughter of movie tycoon Robert Mitchum – and the book's narrator – did show inexperience, but she had a cool, mysterious quality which suggested a star in the making.

After beginning in such prestigious company she hesitated over her next film, selecting *Straight Time* (78) when Dustin Hoffman

chose her after seeing the Kazan film. She was the middle-class girl at the job agency who begins an affair with con-on-parole Hoffman – which reminded many that in the old movies gangsters usually aspired to someone like Loretta Young, classy and lovely. She then appeared in a mini-series about Watergate, *Blind Ambition* (79), as the wife of the lawyer John Dean (Martin Sheen) but turned down a role in *The Empire Strikes Back* (presumably: she said *Star Wars*, but that had appeared two years previously), because she 'didn't think a futuristic space fantasy would be right for me'. The next film-maker to come calling was the Britisher, Nicolas Roeg, for *Bad Timing* (80), the usual Roeg bummer, pointless and pretentious at the same time. Russell, as an American living in Vienna, is pursued by a professor (Art Garfunkel) of psychology, who goes a bit berserk when he finds that she is married to a mysterious gay man (Denholm Elliott). Once when Garfunkel is leaving her she tears off her panties and screams: 'You want it? Fuck me now'. So he does. On the stairs. And he does so again when she's either dead or dying (but not on the stairs). All to a subtext of Freud (of course), Klimt, Pinter's 'Niemandsland', Theda Bara and Billie Holliday. Russell, according to her own testimony, pursued Roeg and married him, thus ensuring that she got into another lousy movie, *Eureka* (83), playing the married daughter of a wealthy Canadian (Gene Hackman), both of them involved in a sensational murder case, based on fact.

It could be simply stated that Roeg's films do not get shown in the US, despite American names, some American money or a pre-production deal; it would be truer to say that there is usually a reluctance to show them, and that they they usually turn up much later for a couple of duff weeks at one of the less fastidious art-houses. Russell, anyway, was a virtually unknown quantity when she returned to Hollywood to play the drug-addicted Sophie in the remake of *The Razor's Edge* (84) opposite Bill Murray. Anne Baxter had won an Academy Award in the same role, and while there were no Oscars going for this lumpy effort it was clear that Russell's performance transcended script and direction. Roeg's *Insignificance* (85) was, of course, wrongly named, for with the irony marking all his work it was all deeply significant – about what, however, it was hard to tell. It was even harder to stay in the cinema. Russell was an actress based on Marilyn Monroe, while Gary Busey was a Joe diMaggio clone and Tony Curtis was got up to look like Senator McCarthy. Russell finally managed to appear in a movie made by a director of talent, Bob

Rafelson's *Black Widow* (87) – and she was sensational in it, as good as any of the great femmes fatales of the past. Naturally she was in the title-role, as a wealthy woman whose husbands have a habit of dying; she was particularly clever towards the end, when she begins to realize that federal agent Debra Winger may be on to her.

Aria was a project of producer Don Boyd, who persuaded ten directors to take any piece of operatic music of their choice and put a piece of film to it as either appropriate or inspired. Roeg chose an aria from Verdi's 'Un Ballo in Maschera', accompanied by a tale of an assassination attempt on King Zog of Albania in 1931. Russell played King Zog – of course. For the record the other directors were Charles Sturridge, Jean-Luc Godard, Julian Temple, Bruce Beresford, Robert Altman, Franc Roddam, Ken Russell, Derek Jarman and Bill Bryden – a couple of whom, on previous evidence, should have known better, but only genius could have got the rest packed into the same bloody awful mess. It did few people any harm – except those who saw it – for it disappeared with record speed. Russell was receiving other offers, but she did not want to leave the children, or to take them with her, in view of the location work involved. But it was *en famille* when she and Roeg went to North Carolina to make *Track 29* (88), from a script by Dennis Potter. She explained: 'Gary Oldman plays my son/lover. It's a black comedy about people not wanting to grow up, about mental breakdown. With Nic and Potter what are you going to get? Either something exciting or a load of rubbish.' The answer was a foregone conclusion for one critic who had not dreamed of seeing it, and he recalls smugly listening as a group of his peers argued as to which of them had loathed it most. Joseph Losey was to have directed it with Vanessa Redgrave in 1983, when financing fell through. For the record, Russell, playing vulgar and much older than her years, is sexually frustrated – her husband (Christopher Lloyd) appears to get his rocks off playing with his train-set – and traumatized by the death of her son, whom she thinks is incarnate in a cockney stranger, one who pretends to smoke her tampons and uses her diaphragm as a hat for a doll. It is not that such things should not be seen in this day and age, but that they are put on screen by people without the least discernible sense of humour. Russell was then to have done *Chicago Loop* with Roeg, specially written by Paul Theroux, but that was never made – perhaps because Roeg's box-office record was not one to attract investors.

She decided instead to appear in two films the public might actually want to see, so she

Theresa Russell as you might find her in one of the films directed by her husband, Nicolas Roeg, Bad Timing (80), and in Bob Rafelson's Black Widow (87), one of the few films she has made which have enabled her to demonstrate both talent and beauty.

played a chic defence attorney in Michael Crichton's *Physical Evidence* (89), working on behalf of a down-and-out ex cop, Burt Reynolds: but this was one of those Reynolds dogs which rolled over and died. She was no luckier with *Impulse* (90), in which she was a sexually repressed LA cop who goes on the streets, but strictly in the line of duty. 'Sometimes, working vice, it excites me,' she says. 'I wonder what it would be like to lose control.' It was directed by Sondra Locke, who had clearly learnt only the wrong things from the Eastwood movies in which she had appeared. It really is too bad.

The Roegs now live in the US, where he directed an unadmired telefilm of *Sweet Bird of Youth* with Elizabeth Taylor. In the meantime, it's out of the frying-pan and into the fire, for Ken Russell (no relation) is directing her in *Whore* (91), which she follows with *Kafka*, co-starring Jeremy Irons. Roeg is scheduled to direct his wife again in *Cold Heaven*, with John Travolta, about a married woman out of control because she is having an affair.

MARIANNE SÄGEBRECHT

Bagdad Café begins in the worst art-house manner, with coloured filters over the lens, which seldom look at anything straight on. Nor is the plot too taking: a middle-aged German couple quarrel in the middle of the Arizona desert, and the wife, left at the roadside with her case, goes to stay at the only place she can find – a run-down café run by some squabbling black people in the middle of nowhere; and nowhere is what it deserves. It is run by the bad-tempered Brenda, who decides that she does not like the lady, Jasmine Münchgstettner, any more than Jasmine likes her. Jasmine is shy, introverted, a stranger in a strange land; she looks awful in every way, with her pot hat and shapeless clothes – but she responds to gestures of friendship with a moue of pleasure, in a voice as small and feminine as her figure is not. She finds that she has taken the wrong suitcase, but then she has been doing the wrong thing all her life – when, that is, she has had to take any decision herself. It may be that only one choice is open to her, to spend the rest of her life in this dump. Sitting alone and forlorn in her room, she is afraid to do anything at all; but she is, after all, German, and the room is in disorder. She starts to clean it. And thus did audiences fall in love with a remarkable lady, Marianne Sägebrecht.

She was born in 1945 in Starnberg in Bavaria, but lived in Munich from the age of fifteen. Her father was killed in the last week of the war, and the stepfather she acquired at the age of seven was half-Jewish, a survivor of the concentration camps, who took against her because she was pure German; as a child she read as much as she could about the Nazis' treatment of the Jews, and she dyed her hair red to show solidarity with the gypsy children in the village of Bachhausen, where she was growing up. Also there she had a backyard theatre, and later was a member of the drama group at high school; but after leaving she trained as a medical laboratory assistant, while also studying photography. In 1964 she married, and in 1970, while assistant to a neuro-psychiatrist, conceived the idea of inviting her friends round for exceptional meals with some improvised – or rehearsed – theatricals on the side. The following year she and her husband took the opportunity to manage a cabaret-revue venue in her native town, which they did for three years. They were divorced in 1974 and she became assistant photography editor on 'Colours' magazine. A year later she became manageress of 'Mutti Bräu', a meeting-place for artists; she worked for a while in the 'Marienkafter' in Schwabing (the artists' quarter of Munich) and in 1977 conceived and founded 'Opera Curiosa', which was a combination of cabaret and review. In her own words: 'With the help of my magic wand I produced an eclectic mixture of ballet dancers, acrobats, street singers, strippers, clowns, body-builders, "world champion snuff-takers", opera singers and unknowns displaying their talents.' The 'company' – in all, over 180 performers – taped two shows for television, and played in Hamburg and Berlin during the four years of its existence. During this period, Martin Sperr, whom Sägebrecht had known at the 'Mutti Bräu', offered her a role in 'Adèle Spitzeder' (79), which he was putting on at the Studio-Theater in Munich; he himself played the title-role and she played a prostitute who at various times pretends to be both a peasant and an opera singer.

In the audience one night was the film director Percy Adlon, who offered her the role of Frau Sanchez in a television film, *Herr Kischott* (80), his free adaptation of 'Don Quixote' as transferred to a Bavarian setting. Two years later she formed another cabaret group and accepted the Schwabing artistic prize for her work with 'Opera Curiosa'; she worked diversely in cabaret and theatre over the next few years, but in the meantime made her film debut proper in Adlon's *Die Schaukel* (83), a study of an unorthodox Munich family in the 1880s, in a small role as a trinket-seller. She had also worked for Adlon as his stills photographer, and he had realized that she had a certain quality which could be effectively used in a star role. *Zuckerbaby* (85) was written for her, a touching tale of an overweight and lonely undertaker's assistant who sets out with great determination to win and woo the driver of the subway train which takes her to work. To do this she must discover his identity and then his weaknesses, as well as make up in other ways for her figure. It turns out that he is married, but this turns out to be no obstacle, till his wife returns from a trip out of town . . . The film's reception would lead to an offer from Hollywood, but in the meantime Sägebrecht played one of the customers at a male strip-club on the Hamburg waterfront, in *Crazy Boys* (87), directed by Peter Kern. What humour there was was restricted to the girth of the customers' bodies, which was not enough to gain the film many bookings, said 'Variety''s reviewer, adding that Sägebrecht achieved her laughs through her ability rather than her size.

Adlon's second vehicle for Sägebrecht was *Bagdad Café*, or to give it its original title, *Out of Rosenheim*, a reference to the couple's home town. Adlon wrote it with his wife; it is in English, and Jack Palance co-stars as a onetime Hollywood hand who now paints, and who develops a fondness for the lonely German lady. The piece is mysterious – and beautifully acted – but it is soon clear as Jasmine blossoms that she is the Ugly Duckling, an unlikely person to bring beauty and happiness. To that extent it shares a theme with its contemporary, *Babette's Feast*, but to say how she does so might be giving too much away, except to say that one line, 'It's magic time', may be taken literally. The Hollywood film was Paul Mazursky's *Moon Over Parador* (88), with Richard Dreyfuss, in which she had a small role as the German-born housekeeper to, and formerly the nurse of, a South American dictator. Adlon's third vehicle for Sägebrecht, *Rosalie Goes Shopping* (89), is set in Arkansas, and she is married to a pilot (Brad Davis), with a large family, mostly grown up. The way she goes shopping is on credit or with complex schemes with credit cards, which go unexplained. Adlon explained that he put together many observations on American life while writing the script, but they have not meshed. The result is a dog's dinner of little nourishment, not to be mentioned in the same breath as the two earlier films: their incipient cuteness has burgeoned, their wayward humour has gone haywire and the piece carries no conviction. It did, however, draw this tribute in the 'New York Times' by Janet Maslin: 'It would be difficult to say where Mr Adlon would be without the incomparable Ms Sägebrecht, the star of his earlier films and the shrewd yet beatific center

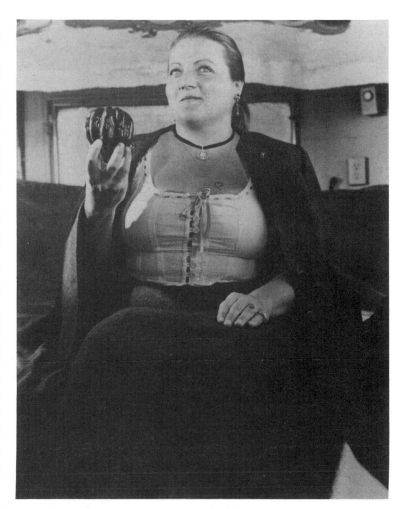

Marianne Sägebrecht in Bagdad Café *(87), in which Jack Palance and the world fell in love with her. Maybe that's an exaggeration, but those who saw Percy Adlon's film were in thrall to her – and just to prove to any who didn't see it that she can be as attractive in person as in personality, here she is in* Rosalie Goes Shopping *(89) – but it was not, alas for her or Herr Adler, a worthy follow-up.*

of this one. With her doll's features and her feisty, oversized body, this actress is as physically startling as she is temperamentally unique. Someone else might have made Rosalie more abrasive or her motives more identifiably anti-establishment, thus heightening the cultural condescension of desolate, merchandise-mad Americana. But Ms Sägebrecht is so disarming, so serenely tough and so utterly unclassifiable that her presence works real magic.'

At this point she decided to end the partnership with Adlon, admitting later that he was not very pleased; as her friend, he did not think she had been unwise. She declined to appear in a US television series based on *Bagdad Café*, which would co-star Jean Stapleton as Jasmine and Whoopi Goldberg as Brenda (played so well originally by CCH Pounder). She accepted the role of the German housekeeper in Danny DeVito's *The War of the Roses* (89), but declined another, in Penny Marshall's *Awakenings*, 'because it is not my destiny'. Her American agent, she reported, was 'very angry' that she had not taken the opportunity of the TV series and five years in the US to become internationally famous. But, she said, she did not want to spend five years in the US. They disagreed again over *Martha und Ich* (90), which would mark the first film in Europe for Jiri Weiss since he had fled at the time of the Soviet invasion of Czechoslovakia of 1968. 'There's not enough Holocaust in it,' they advised her. 'Don't accept it unless they've got Ben Kingsley as well.' The role was played by Michel Piccoli, and there were fond notices for both players when the film was shown at the Venice Festival. Piccoli plays a role based on Weiss's uncle in this Czech-Franco-German co-production in which Sägebrecht beautifully plays the housekeeper whom he marries, and who follows him to the ghetto in Prague when the authorities start to follow the Nazi line on Jews.

ARNOLD SCHWARZENEGGER

'You're the king,' people keep telling Arnold (let's stop at that) throughout *Pumping Iron*, and he doesn't disagree. The film is a documentary about body-building, centred on himself, a hymn to him, and he clearly thinks that everyone seeing it will be only too happy to worship at the shrine of his sculptured torso. Praise is compulsory, his due. But although he has presence and some humour, there was seldom a less likely movie star. His Austrian-accented voice has (or had) difficulty with a line of more than three words. His

huge mass of a body makes him move awkwardly, and move he must since he is an action man, not to be found in the lounge sweet-talking the ladies. Every so often he is seen in a suit and tie, looking handsome and anomalous, for he threatens to break out of it like King Kong. Having big muscles would seem a dubious virtue to anyone but the most dedicated jock (Clive James once described him as 'looking like a condom filled with walnuts'), since the hours spent acquiring them would seem to consist of numbing hours of boredom in the gym – not, however, to Arnie, who says, 'Bodybuilding is like coming, like having sex with a woman. In a gym I'm coming all the time.' He said that in *Pumping Iron*, and also this, about competitors, that he will book one into a room, 'and that night he will never forget . . . I mean, I will talk him into bed.' Perhaps there is there a clue that he is not 100 per cent hetero, and perhaps some fans feel that by virtue of his passion for body-building he is androgynous, which would appear to be an attractive commodity in today's market. He appears to be enjoying himself immensely and who can blame him? – those hours in the gym have made him a movie star, the ultimate goal of the narcissist.

Still, the popularity of this hulk gives pause, for it is much greater than that achieved by such Neanderthal predecessors as Johnny Weissmuller or Victor Mature – or even Steve Reeves, another noted for his pectorals before his performance (and Arnold's own boyhood idol). Could it be coincidence that it happened in an era when action cinema was dominated by Sylvester Stallone? He is 'angry at hearing my name mentioned in the same breath . . . Stallone uses body doubles for some of the close-ups in his movies. I don't. One, my ego wouldn't let me. And two, I don't need a stand-in because there's nobody around with a better body than mine. Nobody.' Humour, he says, 'is the thing that separates me from Stallone, Eastwood and [Chuck] Norris. I spend hours dreaming up funny lines. I like to have all this intensity and then all of a sudden a funny line to make everyone relax.' It is true, of course, he is a much cheerier screen presence than Stallone: but then who isn't?

He was born in 1947 in the village of Thal, just outside Graz, Austria, the son of a policeman who was also a champion at ice-curling. He believes it was because of his father that he sought to be recognized and admired from an early age: 'I always put myself up there on the screen with my favourites – like John Wayne, Burt Lancaster, Kirk Douglas . . .' He said that money did not interest him, but he considered how much money another of his idols, Reg Park, had made from constructing a magnificent body, so at the age of fifteen he set out to do the same. He was befriended by a former Mr Austria, who took him to his first body-building championships, when he decided he would one day be Mr Universe (which he achieved). He won his first international title, 'Junior Mr Europe', at the age of eighteen, in Stuttgart, and till he retired from competition was 'Mr Universe' five times and 'Mr Olympia' seven (or vice versa). A return to the muscle-flexing ring in Melbourne for a last successful try for 'Mr Olympia' in 1980 was filmed and issued on cassette as *The Comeback*.

In 1968 he had come to the attention of Joe Weider, the publisher of 'Muscle and Fitness', who brought him to the US along with his friend Franco Columbu. Dubbed 'the Austrian Oak', he entered a contest in Florida and allowed Weider to set the two of them up in Santa Monica. They began to invest in real estate with money earned from a mail-order body-building enterprise named for an 'Arnold Strong' and it was under this name that Arnold made his first movie, *Hercules Goes Bananas* (69), later retitled *Hercules in New York*, an idiotic adventure in a which a dubbed and peplum-clad Arnie rushes about Manhattan. It is hard to see under either title, and one report says that Arnold played comic relief to the lead, 'Arnold Stang'. He studied business and economics at the University of Wisconsin. In 1972 he was seen at a contest by a free-lance photographer, George Butler, who with his partner, Charles Gaines, took him up and packaged him 'with extraordinary finesse', as Teresa Carpenter put it in her 'Premiere' profile. He was put to modelling, to taking ballet lessons, to being photographed by Robert Mappleforth and to acting again, in television's *The Streets of San Francisco* and in Robert Altman's *The Long Goodbye* (73) in a small silent role as a hood who beats up Elliott Gould. He was unbilled, but still Arnold Strong, a name he was about to drop. He says that he began to take speech lessons after Lucille Ball offered him a role in a TV movie, *Happy Anniversary and Goodbye* (75).

Gaines had written a novel which Bob Rafelson prepared to film, *Stay Hungry* (76); he prevailed upon an unwilling Rafelson to see Arnold, who charmed him enough to cast him as a body-builder, an ex-Mr Austria, who befriends the hero, Jeff Bridges. In the book, Arnold's role had been the primary one but for the film it became a major supporting one; and several critics praised Arnold's gentle performance. Few thought he was acting material, so Butler and Gaines waited for their own film of the book, *Pumping Iron*

(77), a documentary based on the manual which they had persuaded Arnold to write (and which Simon and Schuster published in 1974). Although the reception accorded the movie seemed to confirm the trio's belief in Arnold's charisma, Hollywood remained unimpressed till Hal Needham cast him as the hero, 'The Handsome Stranger', pitted against *The Villain* (79), Kirk Douglas in this 'Road Runner'-type Western which became *Cactus Jack* in some territories after flopping in the US. Arnold had another star role on TV in *The Jayne Mansfield Story* (80), as that lady's muscle-bound husband, Mickey Hargitay; Loni Anderson was Jayne.

There were still no further takers for the moment for Arnold the Actor, and Dino De Laurentiis turned him down for the title-role in *Flash Gordon*. Despite its failure, De Laurentiis was prepared to go ahead with another comic-strip-like adventure, *Conan the Barbarian* (82), conceivably because the director, John Milius, had a certain prestige (the then little-known Oliver Stone wrote the script). Milius insisted on Arnold, leaving the acting to the supporting cast headed by James Earl Jones and Max von Sydow. As a vengeance-seeking warrior, Arnold looked and acted like a barn door, but this two hours

Arnold Schwarzenegger in Conan the Barbarian *(81). In 1990 Ian Penman analysed his appeal in the 'Sunday Correspondent': 'But where once even Eastwood posed questions of borderline morality, Schwarzenegger is pure destruction. He is almost a new genre in himself – bits of Comix, bits of Cyberpunk, bits of the Vigilante and the Unstoppable It (*Hallowe'en, Friday Thirteenth*) genres.'*

Schwarzenegger in Commando *(85). In the earlier* Terminator *Penman wrote of him: 'He is utterly essential for the role [of robotic dependability] – but also utterly disposable [as] the skeletal robotic framework takes over. There is no revenge or pleasure in his killing and no justification. He is just a killing machine – bad, but used to fill the film with mega-killing hardware.'*

break-through film, believing that audiences saw him adding some humour to his lines, which he was required to do deadpan. The truth is that this picture was in the *Mad Max– Blade Runner* mould and well-done for what it was: its domestic take was $17 million (on a budget of $6,500,000) which meant that Arnold's three starring movies had all done more than respectably. In a Hollywood desperate for certified success no one balked as his fee doubled, especially when *Commando* (85) looked like picking up the Rambo fans, as ex-commando Arnold tears round half South America in search of his daughter, taking on dozens of deadly opponents at the same time. He hacks off the arm of one with a chainsaw and then hits him over the head with it. The writer of this amusing little scene – the whole film – was Steve E. de Souza, who has been employed to write 'zingers' since for Arnold, who already knew that he wanted to turn to comedy. The film's take was $17 million, so everyone looked the other way when *Red Sonja* bombed. Fleischer directed, from a pulp story by Robert E. Howard, creator of Conan. Arnold played it safe by being this Conan-clone, pitted in this similar tale against an evil queen – played by Brigitte Nielsen – against whom he seeks revenge. *Raw Deal* (86) did somewhat better, taking just over $7 million, but the critics remained cold to Arnold; neither did they like this thriller about an ex-FBI agent, now a small-town sheriff, who goes undercover to tackle the Mafia.

In 1986 he married Maria Shriver, niece of politician Edward Kennedy, after a courtship which began at some time after their first meeting in 1977; they maintain separate residences. His fee had gone from $2 million early in the year to $5 million, a price justified by John McTiernan's *Predator* (87), which cost $25 million and took $31 million – though why is anyone's guess. The plot has Arnold being called in when some bigwigs disappear in the jungle: he and his handful of chums come across a village, which they pulverize: ten minutes of people being blown up and burnt alive – and that's before the alien arrives – do not justify the director's claim that he was making 'a Saturday afternoon adventure movie', though, as Ralph Novak said in 'People', no one going to it would expect *Blithe Spirit*: the star, he observed, 'has little to do but flex, glare and shoot. He manages to be likeable nonetheless.' *The Running Man* was a loose remake of Yves Boisset's *Prix de Danger* and originally meant for Christopher Reeve: despite this, it was Schwarzenegger-formula stuff, set in the future, with our hero as a competitor in the ultimate television game-show, having to defend himself against

of primeval savagery and swordplay drew enough cinemagoers on its home ground for them to cough up a collective $21,700,000, which was $700,000 less than it had cost. Having had many worse failures, De Laurentiis was accordingly looking for a success and felt happier to be with a devil he knew: *Conan the Destroyer* (84) cost $18 million and although it took only $14,300,000, there was much more red ink in other De Laurentiis ledger books. Richard Fleischer directed.

Critics predicted that Arnold would never make the Best Actor line-up: he was the least likely candidate for major stardom since Rin Tin Tin. Few expected him to outlast *Conan*, including De Laurentiis who, he said 'sort of sneered' when Arnold told him that he did not intend to do a third. However, director James Cameron cast him as *The Terminator*, half-man half-robot, who is sent back from the future to the present to murder a seemingly innocent woman: nothing can stop him. Arnold himself looks back on this as his a panel of deadly enemies. It cost $31 million and took $16 million. With this one his fee had gone to $10 million, which may be why *Red Heat* (88) cost $30 million; it took the same as its predecessor. Walter Hill directed this thriller about a Russian cop (Arnold), known as 'Iron Jaw' who teams up with his American equivalent (James Belushi) to drive some ruthless drug-dealers from the streets of Chicago. Ivan Reitman directed *Twins* after Arnold had told him he wished to work with him; Reitman got together several writers, who came up with a plot about the perfect man, as conceived from several geniuses: the only trouble is, he has a twin brother, Danny DeVito, without a single one of his advantages. Another wheeze made Arnold a virgin, having his first love scene, and he commented that he usually romanced guns and grenades. DeVito observed of him that he was 'very kind and gentle . . . nothing like his crush-you-like-a-bug persona'. The casting of these two is a funny idea ('Only their mother can tell them apart', went the ad-line), and if the result – like Arnold's performance – is amiable rather than uproarious the public adored it. With a domestic take of over $57 million (at a cost of $17 million) it was Arnold's biggest success to date. The deal arranged gave him little up front, but 17.5 per cent of any profits, with a further 17.5 per cent shared equally between DeVito and Reitman. Arnie's take was reckoned to be $20 million (i.e. from the worldwide grosses) and it may be said that he worked very hard for it; he is co-operative, helpful and professional; he is also willing to tub-thump for his films, sending millions of flowers to the secretaries of talk-show hosts all over the country. He is unlikely to spend his future as a light comedian: 'Today, you have to think about the video market, domestic release, foreign release and TV and cable. Action heroes usually satisfy all those needs. That's really where the money is.'

This remark is perceptive enough to prove one prevailing aspect of the Schwarzenegger publicity, that his investments and his work on body-building had made him independently wealthy before he found film stardom. Could he be the ultimate fulfilment of the American dream? Ruthless, handsome, wealthy – and an immigrant, too. The touching emphasis on his superman abilities would seem to be confirmed when *Total Recall* (90) was announced with a budget of $54 million and the news, reported in the 'New York Times' in January of that year, that Universal had offered him 50 per cent of the profits on any film he made for them. It was also reported that an English journalist had researched his Austrian past for a biography, and that

Arnold was trying to buy the company planning to publish it. *Total Recall*, anyway, was an old project whose time had finally come. David Cronenberg was to have made it for M-G-M with Richard Dreyfuss in 1984, but changed his mind. Schwarzenegger was to have made it in the 2-picture deal with De Laurentiis, which included *Raw Deal*, but dropped out because he could not get director approval. In 1987 Bruce Beresford was to have directed it with Patrick Swayze (q.v.), but De Laurentiis went bankrupt: Arnold moved at once and asked Carolco, for whom he was then making *Red Heat*, to buy it for him. It eventually came his way, and then our way, eagerly awaited and heavily promoted: Paul Verhoeven, who directed, had made a reputation with the not-dissimilar *Robocop*, and the screenplay was 'inspired' by a short story by one of the most ingenious of

Schwarzenegger in Red Heat *(88). 'In him we see the glorification of weaponry . . . He is the Germanic Übermensch, Tarzan gone technical. Films with military budgets appeal to an illiterate, cynical, powerless sub-class, whose belief in the redemptive power of hardware admits no moral grey zones.' (Penman).*

SF writers, Philip K. Dick, 'We Can Remember It for You Wholesale'. Amid the usual booms and bangs, Arnie can be seen as a humble construction worker of the twenty-first century who dreams of Mars, to which he eventually gets himself sent for many a shock, including the fact that he may not even be who he thinks he is. Arnold's salary was said to be $10 million and later $13 million; after four months on release it had taken over $118 million – yet this was less than expectations had hoped.

Schwarzenegger then had the depressing choice of *The Terminator 2: Judgement Day* (91), and *Predator 2*, but chose the former on condition that James Cameron again directed, ceding the other film to Danny Glover. He then began another comedy, *Kindergarten Cop*, for which he and Reitman would again take a cut of the profits.

TOM SELLECK

Onwards and upwards from Milton Berle, few television stars have made the transition to the big screen. If you catch Tom Selleck in anything he did for TV as a young man, there is little to distinguish him from any other young male hopeful – personable enough, hunky, but with no more personality than such Hollywood actors of the 50s as, oh say, Ray Danton and Richard Egan. He did not change much when stardom found him, or vice versa, but his new-found confidence and enthusiasm were winning. He was tall and so macho, but he didn't take himself seriously – which, indeed, it would have been foolish to do with that rather high-pitched, squeaky voice. That and his Castro-clone moustache do not suggest an unassailable virility. He is like no one else in the history of stardom, and therein lies his appeal. 'He's the biggest boy scout in America', as his co-star (in 'Magnum') John Hillerman puts it.

He was born in Detroit in 1945, the son of a real estate investor, but he grew up in the San Fernando Valley, near Los Angeles; in his teens he won a basketball scholarship to the University of Southern California. Work beckoned in the form of modelling, making commercials for Pepsi-Cola, Salem and Revlon; and when he was picked out of the audience of television's 'The Dating Game' he was seen by a talent scout, who arranged a contract at 20th-Century-Fox. Nothing came of that, but he appeared in fifteen episodes of 'Bracken's World', a soap starring Leslie Neilsen, and occasionally in another screened in the daytime, 'The Young and the Restless'. Mae West saw him in a Pepsi commercial and cast him as a stud in *Myra Breckinridge* (70).

He had been seen earlier in the year in a movie for TV starring Arthur Kennedy as an insurance investigator, *The Movie Murderer*, third-billed as a cop. At Fox, director Russ Meyer chose him to play a small role as a publisher in *The Seven Minutes* (71), based on Irving Wallace's novel about a pornography trial. These modest credits led to the offer of a leading role, but in a cheapjack film about witches (his wife was one of them, or seemed to be), *Daughters of Satan* (72). Few saw it, as was the fate of another exploitation piece, *Terminal Island* (73). He headed way down the cast-list for a TV movie, *A Case of Rape* (74) starring Elizabeth Montgomery, and in cinema movies could be briefly glimpsed under a tin hat in *Midway* (76). Working unpaid for him was publicist Esme Chandler, an old Hollywood hand, who would be rewarded by helping him guide his career and enjoying his subsequent fame, by sitting in on all his interviews (her only other remaining client is Sam Elliott, also better renowned for looks than ability, and also first known through his television work). He was fourth-billed in *Most Wanted Man*, a pilot for a short-lived Robert Stack series, and he had a good role as an engineer whom Barry Sullivan attempts to blackmail in order to get a contract, in *The Washington Affair* (77), but that had to wait for showings till after Selleck became famous. Not that audiences were anxious to have it, for the plot had been available eleven years earlier as *Intimacy*, under the same director, Victor Stoloff. Selleck made another TV movie, *Superdome* (78) and had a goodish small role in Michael Crichton's thriller, *Coma*, as a cheerful sick football player. He also found himself in two episodes of 'The Rockford Files', working with James Garner who, he said, gave him a standard to which to aspire.

His break came with a totally unnecessary telemovie, *Returning Home* (79), a shortened remake of *The Best Years of Our Life*, in the Dana Andrews role: for this led to two more starring roles for that medium, in a mini-series, *Louis L'Amour's 'The Sacketts'*, in which he, Sam Elliott and Jeffrey Osterhage were pioneer brothers, and *The Concrete Cowboys*, a thriller in which he and Jerry Reed were good ol' boys in Nashville. When that one became a series, Geoffrey Lewis played Selleck's role, for he himself was tapped to star in one, by Universal, who had signed him to a contract for that purpose. He did seven pilots before 'Magnum, P.I.', which CBS picked up. Simultaneously he was the first choice from two hundred for the role Harrison Ford eventually played in *Raiders of the Lost Ark*. George Lucas held up shooting for five weeks while negotiating with CBS to release Selleck: it didn't happen and in the end the film was finished before Selleck was called back to 'Magnum', for shooting on that was delayed due to an actors' official strike. Other movies he had to pass on included *Rich and Famous*, *The Cannonball Run* (in the role Sammy Davis Jr played) and *Victor/Victoria* (Garner's role), but he did find time to do two for television: *Divorce Wars* (82), playing a Seattle divorce lawyer whose own marriage – to Jane Curtin – is falling apart, and *Louis L'Amour's 'The Shadow Riders'*, reunited with his brothers of that writer's earlier TV sage-brush saga.

Playing detective Tom Magnum, the Hawaii P.I., made Selleck internationally famous. It revealed a genial personality rather than great thespian abilities, and he showed due concern for his limitations in returning to the cinema as star: indeed *High Road to China* (83) followed the *Raiders of the Lost Ark* formula, with Selleck setting out from Istanbul in the late 20s. Golden Harvest produced, at a cost of $20 million, with $15,500,000 at the domestic box-office and some smashing returns overseas. Golden Harvest was also involved in *Lassiter* (84), which found Selleck as an American gentleman thief in London just before the Second World War: this cost considerably less, which was just as well since it checked in at only $9 million in the US. And

Tom Selleck lost Raiders of the Lost Ark *because of his commitment to 'Magnum P.I.', so when he returned to movies – as a star – he did so in a very similar film,* High Road to China *(83). That and his other films of that time were only moderate successes at best, and it was thought that that was because he insisted on playing himself, or his 'Magnum' personality, bumbling, amiable and unthreatening. Given that, this film was an appealing adventure tale with one excellent credential – at one point it had been on the schedule of director John Huston.*

Selleck's second shot at movie stardom, Lassiter *(84) was no more demanding than the first – for audiences, that is. He again had to do a fair number of stunts, including a chase over a roof and an escape via overhead wires Chasing him were Nazi agents, apparently abundant in London just before the outbreak of the War. With him is Jane Seymour.*

when Crichton's *Runaway* failed – Selleck was a future cop hunting down rebel robots – it looked as though Selleck's screen career was halted. In 1985 he was married for the second time, to a British dancer called Jillie Mack, who had been in 'Cats'.

'Magnum' continued, and 'Magnum''s fees, which were $4,800,000 a year or $220,000 per episode. His screen career was rescued, as with so many others, by Disney, who teamed him with Ted Danson, a TV star who had not yet played the lead in a movie, and Steve Guttenberg, who had starred in some popular films without sharing much credit for their success: they played swinging bachelors whose lifestyle is hampered by an infant, *Three Men and a Baby* (87). This was a jolly, broad remake of *Trois Hommes et un Couffin*, whose writer-director Coline Serrau was originally to have helmed for Disney. That Leonard Nimoy took over may be one of the reasons why the budget of $18 million was high by the standards of this cost-conscious studio, which watched as a happy $82,300,000 poured into its coffers. With that sort of box-office success he could take his pick of offers and no longer needed 'Magnum', whose producers considered it had had a long and useful life. It finished amicably in 1988; no one pointed out that in 1985 Selleck's contract was said to have had five more years to run.

He was said to be getting $2 million each for his next two films, both of which he carried (i.e. without a co-star of his standing) and both of which took $9 million domestic. The bad news is that Warners poured $20 million into *Her Alibi* (89) and Disney $17 million into *An Innocent Man*. Bruce Beresford directed the first, a likeable comedy about a supposedly suave writer of thrillers who becomes involved in the sort of plot he might have written, and Peter Yates directed the second, a clichéd prison drama. The press was enthusiastic about neither, and the 'New York Times' did a laconic note on the Yates film: 'The star, a handsome, strapping and very mild-mannered actor, manages to overplay the early nice-guy scenes and underplay the later ones, in which his character is supposed to turn tough.' Or, as Mark Kermode put it in 'Time Out', 'Selleck is the real villain, portraying his transformation from wide-eyed innocent to hardened man-of-the-world by changing from clean-shaven mop-top to stubbly slicked-backed, with reflecting shades to boot! Laughable.' This was the first of four features on a non-exclusive pact with Disney which gives him the option of developing others.

His fee in 1990 is said to be $4 million per film. Whether or not, *Hard Rain* (90) and *Quigley Down Under* have kept him busy.

The second was originally intended for Steve McQueen or Clint Eastwood before Selleck, then it was dropped because Westerns were thought to be unpopular. The project was revived again after the success of the mini-series *Lonesome Dove*, with the same director, Simon Wincer. He is an Australian, and the film, as the title implies, is set in his native country, with Selleck as an American sharp-shooter arriving to work for rancher Alan Rickman, who tells him that his job is to kill off the aborigines as a matter of state policy. From this there develops several classic situations, with Selleck giving his best showing yet in movies. Then he returns to Disney, Danson and Guttenberg for *Three Man and a Little Lady*, directed by Emile Ardolino, of *Dirty Dancing* fame. Ardolino explained that the bachelors' motto of the earlier film had been: 'So many women, so little time', but with age and the baby growing up they matured, with Selleck involved in a romance with Nancy Travis. After that he makes *Tokyo Diamond* (91), about an American baseball pro working for a Japanese team.

MAGGIE SMITH

To the British, there is currently no more delectable comedienne in the world than Maggie Smith. She cares little for films, so the bulk of her work has been confined to the stage, with occasional forays into TV. As with Vanessa Redgrave (whom she doesn't resemble one jot) theatre critics do not so much review her work as write her love-letters. Ronald Bryden wrote in the 'Observer' in 1969: 'Will it be possible [in the future] to convey the quality which indisputably now makes her a great comedienne? Her effects are not of the kind critics can analyse.' Yet, unlike the fabled stars of the past, she is earth-bound; she is innocent and vulnerable and very much afraid of being found out. She lives on a perpetual knife edge of inadequacy, from which she distracts us, hopefully, by prattling on in what is normally a series of *non sequiturs* (or at least sounds like them). When she is on a winning streak she cannot disguise her glee – though even then she's likely to go pale with self-doubt. She's too canny not to know she's pathetic and funny. This sense of humour seems to desert her as she turns increasingly to drama; but the touch and the timing remain as sure.

She was born in Ilford, a town in the eastern outlying regions of London, in 1934, and was schooled at Oxford, where her father was a pathologist at the University. She joined the Playhouse company in that city and did walk-ons; her first important part was when OUDS borrowed her to play Viola in 'Twelfth Night'. But when she left the Playhouse her talents were diverted to revue – in 'Cakes and Ale' in Edinburgh and several at London's Water-gate. Leonard Sillman saw her and engaged her for his New York 'New Faces' (56). When she returned to London she co-starred with Kenneth Williams in another revue, 'Share My Lettuce', and was put under contract by Ealing, who featured her in a very ordinary crime drama, *Nowhere to Go* (58), in a straight part, as a restless young socialite who befriends crook George Nader. She wasn't very good. When Ealing closed down, her contract was sold to MGM and Associated British, but none of them, she said later, knew what to do with her, and they finally dropped her. Meanwhile, she joined the Old Vic Company (1959–60), then on its last legs, but only her Maggie in 'What Every Woman Knows' was generously received. She played opposite Olivier in 'Rhinoceros' (60), taking over from Joan Plowright; and got her first critical raves for her performance as the waif in Anouilh's 'The Rehearsal' (61) in Bristol and London. Her Dumb Dora portrayals in Shaffer's double-bill 'The Private Eye' and 'The Public Ear' brought her the 'Evening Standard' Drama award; and she won more awards as 'Mary Mary' the following year.

She was an undoubted West End star, so why she chose to do a featured-role, as a French model, in a mediocre comedy, *Go to Blazes* (62), is anybody's guess. However, she then did the multi-starred, big-budgeted *The V.I.P.s* (63), as Richard Burton's mousy secretary, and stole every scene from him, as he predicted she would. Olivier invited her to join the newly formed National Theatre, and she somewhat reluctantly took the plunge (she had envisaged a career in comedy). Among the plays: 'Othello', 'The Recruiting Officer', 'The Master Builder', 'Hay Fever' (as Myra), 'Much Ado' (as Beatrice), 'Black Comedy', 'Miss Julie' and 'Trelawney of the Wells'. In films she did a cameo in *The Pumpkin Eater* (64) as Anne Bancroft's garrulous and lazy lodger, probably the funniest ten minutes of the cinema year; and in *Young Cassidy* (65) she was, somewhat less effective as the timid beloved of Rod Taylor. Nor is her Desde-mona in the awkward film of *Othello* likely to be remembered among her achievements. In *The Honey Pot* (67) Susan Hayward, Capu-cine and Edie Adams got the glamour and better billing, but she got Cliff Robertson at the end, a better part and the notices – even if the role was a variation on the one she had done in *The V.I.P.s*. She played another secretary – Peter Ustinov's – in *Hot Millions* (68), and for the first time in a full-length part

on screen was able to demonstrate the sort of comedy at which she excelled. Said Ustinov: 'I'd have to really search my memory to find any actress to equal her, and after a long time I'd probably have to give up.'

But real international acclaim came with *The Prime of Miss Jean Brodie* (69), a transcription of Muriel Spark's novel which Vanessa Redgrave had done on the stage, a tale of a Scottish teacher of the 30s with a Fascist bent and an obsessive hold on her 'gels'. The wry comic tone of the play became drawn-out movie sentiment and, in the cir-cumstances, the actress offered only a sketch of Miss Brodie. But in the US Vincent Canby in the 'New York Times' found her 'stagger-ing' and Arthur Knight in the 'Saturday Review' thought 'to play such a role is a major achievement for any actress. Maggie Smith does more. Her Miss Brodie is so human, winsome and appealing.' Some months later,

Admirers of Maggie Smith (and those who had seen Vanessa Redgrave in the stage version) were divided on the merits of The Prime of Miss Jean Brodie *(69) – but she still won an Oscar for her performance. Co-starring, as a fellow-teacher, was her then husband Robert Stephens.*

Why anyone should want to film the dated, pallid, cliché-ridden mysteries of Agatha Christie is itself a mystery, but several movie versions have attracted many star names, if ageing ones: Death on the Nile (78) with, from left to right, David Niven, George Kennedy, Peter Ustinov (as the detective Hercule Poirot), Lois Chiles, Simon MacCorkindale, Bette Davis, Jack Warden, Maggie Smith (as Davis's travelling companion), Angela Lansbury and I.S. Johar.

Only intermittently have Maggie Smith's extraordinary comic skills been seen in films: using them in California Suite (78) she stole the film from her numerous co-stars and was the only aspect of the film about which every critic was unanimous.

when asked about further movie offers, she said, 'Quite honestly, not a murmur.' Then she won the Best Actress Oscar, and the BFA Best Actress award.

By that time she was heavily engaged at the National. She had left it to do 'The Country Wife', but with the National had done both 'The Beaux' Stratagem' and 'The Three Sisters' in Los Angeles just before the Oscar ceremony. In London she added Hedda Gabler to her repertoire; then returned to Los Angeles with her husband, Robert Stephens (also a National player), to do 'Design for Living'. For Alan J. Pakula she made *Love and Pain and the Whole Damn Thing* (73), about a prim English woman who finds love in Spain with an equally introverted young American (Timothy Bottoms); also filmed in that country was *Travels With My Aunt*, directed by George Cukor from a novel by Graham Greene. The latter had been intended for Katharine Hepburn (till she disagreed with MGM on the script), and since the role was clearly too old for Smith, her performance was not well received. Neither were either of the films, and they consequently did not do well, thus ending industry enchantment with this actress. Further, there was some carping from theatre critics when she did 'Private Lives' and 'Slap'; and she, over-sensitive perhaps, took herself off to Stratford, Ontario, where she acted for the next several years – e.g. Cleopatra and Millamant in 1976, Lady Macbeth in 1978. Her presence there brought the press from all over the world, and her notices were as good as ever. In between seasons she was one of several names in some starry movies: *Murder By Death* (76), in the role modelled on Nora Charles; *Death on the Nile* (78), as Bette Davis's bitchy spinster companion; and *California Suite*, in the episode with Michael Caine. 'Smith gives her best screen performance ever in the role of a hard-drinking, hard-talking actress who arrives in Beverly Hills for Oscar night,' said Frank Rich in 'Time' magazine – a view in which most viewers concurred; and it brought the actress a popular Best Supporting Oscar.

Except for the interiors of *Death on the Nile* she had not worked in Britain for a long while when she took over from Diana Rigg in 'Night and Day', but then she was already contracted to do the play in New York. In 1980 she played the title-role in 'Virginia' (Woolf) in Stratford, Ontario, and returned to the London stage in the same play. Then she concentrated on films for a while: *Clash of the Titans* (81) in a brief role as a goddess, but the screenplay was written by her (second) husband, Beverly Cross; the Merchant–Ivory *Quartet*, as the painter wife of Alan Bates,

expatriates living in Paris in the 20s; *Evil Under the Sun* (82), from an Agatha Christie tale, as a former showgirl running the hotel where the murder(s) take place; *The Missionary*, as a charitable milady with an uncontrollable passion for the priest (Michael Palin) she has invited to stay; *Better Late Than Never* (83), as a governess whose charge is fought over by David Niven and Art Carney; and *Lily in Love*/*Jatszan Kell* (85) aka *Double Play*, as an actress in this US–Hungarian version of Molnar's 'The Guardsman', which can think itself lucky it was not mentioned in the credits. Christopher Plummer was at his most embarrassing as the husband who disguises himself to woo his wife all over again. These last two films had difficulty finding bookings, as she seems to have expected, for she looked bored throughout.

The tonic she needed came with *A Private Function*, written by Alan Bennett, a comedy about a Yorkshire town celebrating the wedding of Princess Elizabeth and Philip Mountbatten. Given the best dialogue she had had in ages, Smith seized upon it, offering a portrait of a monstrous provincial snob, both hideously self-righteous and afraid she will be found out. She won the BAFTA award as Best Actress and returned to Merchant–Ivory for *A Room With a View* (86), to play the spinster who chaperones its heroine to Florence. On the stage she was in 'The Way of the World' and, among other plays, Peter Shaffer's 'Lettice and Lovage', which after a long London run she took to New York in 1990. Her only film during this period was *The Lonely Passion of Judith Hearne* (87), based on Brian Moore's novel, once destined for Katharine Hepburn and later Deborah Kerr. Judith Hearne is a shy Irish spinster with a secret drinking habit, a lady who conceives a passion for an Irish-American visitor (Bob Hoskins); too low-key, as directed by Jack Clayton, it achieved only limited showings. When she leaves 'Lettice and Lovage' she is scheduled to film Chekov's *The Cherry Orchard* (91) opposite Bob Hoskins, under the direction of Lindsay Anderson.

SISSY SPACEK

When invited in her declining years to name the best young actresses, Bette Davis would pause as if to suggest that the young stars of today could not compete with those in her time. Then she would say, as if magnanimously, 'Sissy Spacek'. Few would deny that Spacek is a sensitive and intelligent actress, but one supposes Davis liked her because, like her, she has to work hard to make up for her

Sissy Spacek in Badlands *(73), as the wispy country girl who goes on the run with her lover after he has murdered her father. Terrence Malick directed this haunting movie (and one other before deciding, alas for us, that the film industry was just too exhausting a place to be).*

some visiting firemen: Marvin is attracted to her, and a contrast was meant between the big shambling man and this wisp of a girl. The film was a deserved failure, so that she did not really make any impact till *Badlands* (73), cast as another country girl – one who watches her young lover (Martin Sheen) shoot her father (Warren Oates) before going off on a shooting spree with him. These characters were based on Charles Starkweather and Carol Fugate, who were active in Nebraska in 1958; the film was written and directed by Terrence Malick, who had had so poor an experience with his screenplay for *Pocket Money* that he had managed to get this financed independently. It cost $350,000, and Warners bought the distribution rights for $900,000 after a showing at the New York Film Festival.

Earlier that year she had appeared in a TV movie, *The Girls of Huntingdon House*, as one of the unwed mothers being taught school therein by Shirley Jones, who becomes unsettled thereby. She was relatively healthy as one of *The Migrants* (74), third-billed after Cloris Leachman and Ron Howard, but it was based on a story by Tennessee Williams. Rather oddly, since she was an established actress, she was the (credited) set decorator on Brian De Palma's *Phantom of the Paradise*, working for production designer Jack Fisk, whom she married at this time. Again for television she was *Katherine* (75), pampered by pa Art Carney till she becomes a revolutionary not unlike Patty Hearst.

Having now established a corner in unsettling, rather fey, young women, she caught the attention of Brian De Palma, who cast her in the title-role of *Carrie* (76). This one required her to acquire telekinetic powers after having her first period, burning people up, literally, and dying with her mother's carving-knife stuck into her. She was not quite back to normal as the kooky housekeeper forced on Keith Carradine in Alan Rudolph's *Welcome to L.A.* Rudolph's mentor, Robert Altman, then put her into *Three Women* (77) with Shelley Duvall. Spacek was the new intern in a rehabilitation home for the elderly, and Duvall another who befriends her; the third woman was Janice Rule, who was pregnant in the plot. Altman had conceived the film while dreaming, and on waking designated it as a star vehicle for Spacek and Duvall: both are superb, but otherwise the thing is of nightmarish badness.

She remained off the screen for two years, because all she was offered were sisters of Carrie. She returned in an excellent role, that of Carolyn Cassady, the lady who completed the *ménage à trois* with Jack Kerouac (John Heard) and her husband Neal (Nick Nolte): *Heart Beat* (79), but writer-director John

lack of looks. But whereas Davis would use the whole palette, even in uninteresting roles, Ms Spacek seems to favour only shades of grey. She has a shy smile and a wistful expression; she is very good at panic and looks of concern, but she certainly does not look as though she has the stamina for Hollywood longevity.

She was born in 1949 in Quitman, Texas, a town so small that it did not even have a cinema. Her father was an agent for the Department of Agriculture. With her brother Robbie on banjo she performed at local dances; he died of leukaemia when she was seventeen, so that when she told her parents that she wanted to try her luck in New York, they told her to live her life to the fullest. She stayed with her cousin, Rip Torn, and his wife, Geraldine Page, through whom she got a walk-on job in Andy Warhol's *Trash* (70); she also studied acting with Lee Strasberg, but later said, 'The best method for me is to become a blank page'. She appeared on television in 'The Waltons' and 'The Rookies', among others; Michael Ritchie auditioned her for *Prime Cut* (72), in support of Lee Marvin and Gene Hackman, but in the pivotal supporting role as a naif country girl who has somehow been rounded up, with several others, to satisfy the sexual tastes of

Byrum seemed oddly ill at ease with the beat generation and the book by Ms Cassady which was cited as his source material. Thus far Spacek had not appeared in a popular film, but that was changed when she played the *Coal Miner's Daughter* (80), the story of Country and Western singer Loretta Lynn. Aided by Michael Apted's direction and perceptive screenplay by Tom Rickman, it told of a couple – Tommy Lee Jones was the husband – not over-endowed with intelligence or well equipped to deal with fame. Spacek had to move from backwoods child to busty song queen, which she did with such discretion that she was awarded a well-deserved Best Actress Oscar. The film did so well in its first year, before the Oscar, taking $36 million, that Universal accorded Spacek the privileges of stardom – the promotion of her husband to director. *Raggedy Man* (81) proved Fisk more than adequate to the task; it also proved that he did not want to stretch his wife too far. She played a wartime divorcée who is endangered by two simple-minded siblings when they become jealous of the new man (Eric Roberts) in her life. Spacek said she saw the film as a feminist statement, but it is doubtful whether anyone else did. Anyway, the result is not a combination of *Carrie* and *Coal Miner's Daughter*, but was clearly meant to please those who had liked both. Given the difference in quality of the two films, such individuals were likely to be rare, or else the Fisks had a more inflated idea of her box-office value than most people.

So it proved: Universal did not bother to open this nice film in many territories.

The studio was luckier with *Missing* (82) – Costa-Gavras directed this tense political thriller, pitting her against her right-wing father-in-law (Jack Lemmon) for a sturdy performance. Despite excellent reviews, the film performed only modestly, taking in just over $7,800,000, but at just over $5,100,000 *The River* (84) did even less well than one rival, *Country*, and much less well than the other – *Places in the Heart* – despite the presence of the supposedly potent Mel Gibson. The film showed a commitment to the earth such as the screen hasn't experienced since Dovzhenko, but it seldom convinced one that poor folks should so go against the system. It was Spacek's last film for Universal.

There were some major talents involved on *Marie* (85), including director Roger Donaldson and writer John Briley, working from a true story set down by Peter Maas: it told of a battered bride who in 1958 finds herself moving up the political pole in Nashville, not realizing – at the start, anyway – that she is being used for some devious politicking. Spacek, eyes shining, is determined to beat the system, but she sometimes seems to be in a Burt Reynolds movie. *The Great McGinty* was funnier and more pungent. Fisk directed another pleasing but minor film, *Violets are Blue* (86), in which Mrs F played an international photojournalist reunited with her high school sweetheart, Kevin Kline; and then she spent a night telling her mother (Anne Bancroft) why she was intent on committing suicide in *'Night Mother*, a stagey version of Marsha Norman's play which, like its predecessor, went direct to video in most territories. It has something in common with the next, that both were based on plays which were Pulitzer-prized without showing why. This second film was *Crimes of the Heart*, in which she and Jessica Lange and Diane Keaton were sisters. She was the one who went on making lemonade after shooting her husband.

She was off the screen for some time, probably not missed – which no one would have said of Davis at the same age. *The Long Walk Home* (90) sat on the shelf for a while when its production company, New Visions, had financial difficulties; when shown, it turned out to be an above-average drama about civil rights with Spacek as a wealthy lady sympathetic to the cause, and Whoopi Goldberg as her maid. But there was not, alas, a big audience for the film. Spacek was then supposed to do *The Plastic Nightmare* opposite William Hurt, but it went ahead with Tom Berenger, retitled *Shattered*. Next: *Hard Promises* (91), directed by Lee Grant and co-starring William Petersen.

Sissy Spacek as Country and Western singer Loretta Lynn in Coal Miner's Daughter *(80), an unexpectedly fresh look at the old business of rags to riches. It brought Spacek a Best Actress Oscar.*

SYLVESTER STALLONE

To some, Sylvester Stallone is 'truly an all-time great . . . the *most* remarkable and gifted actor that the Seventies have produced'; to others he is 'an obnoxious, talentless "personality"' – or so went the text of two letters in 'Playboy' after he had been interviewed, which was all part of the Stallone overkill. After starring in one film, he was voted the No. 1 box-office star in the US, and that had not happened to Gable or Wayne *or* anybody before; but just as surely as John Q. Public went to that, he did not want to know about the next two. The trouble was, we knew too much about him. To that one 'Playboy' correspondent, 'His rags-to-riches story is truly an inspiration to anyone who has ever wanted that million-to-one shot', but to others it looked like arrogance, especially when we had read it six times in six different journals. And then the disappointment at not getting the Best Actor Oscar – well, we saw that on TV. It is easy to be sceptical. Russell Davies explained it in the 'Observer': *Rocky*, he said, 'the film he has written, hawked about, and now won prizes and a fortune with, is just a publicity man's extension of the face – and Stallone is his own publicity man. Improbable Hulk writes Movie! Amazing Feat of Intellectual Concentration by Hulk. Oscars for Hulk Pic! So wrapped up is Stallone (he allows us to think) in his own idea of himself as monster that he even dubs the boxer he plays in the film, Rocky Balboa, with the mock-boastful sobriquet "The Italian Stallion" – the Italian for stallion being, of course, *Stallone*. I doubt if there has been anything like it in promotion before; it's as though Frankenstein's creation, still wearing his outsize skull, surgical stitches and a bolt through the neck, had turned up at the studios with a new monster-script of his own under his arm.' The public rooted for Rocky and then Rambo; all these years later the jury is out on whether they like the man behind them.

He was born in that part of New York known as Hell's Kitchen, the son of a Sicilian immigrant, in 1946; from the age of five onwards he lived in Maryland and, after the divorce of his parents, in Philadelphia. He was a difficult pupil, often expelled, and he finally went to a special college; for a time he toured around in Europe, including a spell at the American School of Switzerland as a bouncer. That was more the type of job he was to do when he returned to New York, though the aim was to become an actor. He got to play a minotaur in Picasso's play, 'Desire Caught by the Tail', in the Bronx, and was in a sexploitation movie that was never released, *Party at Kitty and Studs*, as Studs'. He did do an unbilled bit as a hoodlum in *Bananas* (71), but there is nothing else on record. In 1973 he and his wife decided to try Hollywood, and he did make a Western, *Rebel*, which was so bad that it was shelved. No one would take it on the strength of his name until 1989, when it turned up on video, much chopped about and retitled *A Man Called . . . Rainbo*. In 1990 a hitherto unknown Stallone film, *Rebel*, was released in Britain, claiming an unlikely production date of 1980; for the record Stallone played an idealist caught between his girlfriend and a terrorist movement. He also landed a role as one of the gang in *The Lords of Flatbush* (74), and in addition was given an 'Additional Dialogue' credit. It was an attractive performance of a punk-like 50s kid, all brawn and no brain, a permanent sneer and drooped-over eyes set uncertainly in a white punch-bag of a face. At least, it was attractive as long as Stallone seemed to be satirizing punkdom, but it can only be said that it led to no further leads: he plummeted to almost the bottom of the cast-list on *The Prisoner of Second Avenue*, as one of those who made Jack Lemmon's life a misery – a hoodlum in the park bent on picking pockets. He did have another good role in *Capone* (75), as that gentleman's lieutenant, the one who betrays him. There was another one in *Death Race 2000*, as David Carradine's loud-mouthed rival, but he had only a small role in *Farewell My Lovely*, as one of the thugs.

The publicity story on *Rocky* (76) was that a virtually penniless Stallone had submitted it to United Artists and had insisted on playing the lead. The less glamorous truth is that he had already sold an autobiographical screenplay called *Hell's Kitchen* to the producer Ed Pressman for $250,000. Chartoff and Winkler, producing for UA, tried to buy it, and when he wouldn't sell, they commissioned another script from Stallone – and that became *Rocky*. Pressman found the two screenplays similar enough to sue, but his lawyer found a way to get him something of the action. 'I guess I can take credit for semi-discovering Sylvester Stallone,' said Pressman, 'for what it's worth.' Anyway, according to the publicity, UA wanted *Rocky* so much that they were prepared to pay Stallone $315,000 for the script, but when he insisted on playing the lead they restricted the budget to $1 million. That meant in turn that the Writers' Guild could not object if the script was sold for only $20,000, but for starring in the film Stallone was to receive a 10 per cent profit participation. Since the picture took over $56 million everyone did very nicely, while in the meantime previews were so favourable that UA signed Stallone to a five-picture contract. By Stallone's own admission *Rocky* was an

Look upon this image and on this. Rocky and Rambo, or is it the other way around, tough guys as played incessantly by Sylvester Stallone – partly because the public doesn't turn up in sufficient numbers to see him in anything else. Of his sixteen films to date, ten have failed to pass the $10 million mark in domestic rentals, yet in 1990 he signed a deal with Carolco, for fees ranging from $12 million to $17 million. As the song said, 'Nice work if you can get it', but do we really need Rambo IV, *which the deal also calls for? These two stills are actually from* Rocky II *(79) and* Rambo III *(88).*

attempt to recapture the optimism of the films of the past: Rocky was a loser who wanted to be a winner, a Philadelphia guy who is only ambitious enough to want to go the distance. John Avildsen directed, and the film and he won Oscars.

There was no kudos going for *'F.I.S.T.'* (78), directed by Norman Jewison and co-written by Stallone and Joe Estzerhas, from a story by the latter. The title is an acronym for a fictional trade union based on the teamsters, with Stallone as the rebel idealist who becomes the corrupt leader with a white streak in his hair. His self-absorbed performance broke neither the monotony nor the pervading air of smugness – a sort of admire-us-we're-not-taking-sides attitude. Stallone was now ready for *Hell's Kitchen*, retitled *Paradise Alley*, with Pressman no longer involved now that Stallone was a force in the industry. Stallone had made some changes to the earlier screenplay and he now also directed. It is set in 1946 and it's all about how three brothers decide they'll get out of Hell's Kitchen by going into the wrestling racket. William Goldman in his memoir describes the first of this pair as 'a big-budget film and a disappointment'; the second is 'a disaster, but at least a low-budget one'. The takes were respectively $9,176,684 and $4,213,255. Still, *Rocky II* (79) took over $42 million despite poor notices, such as that of Frank Rich in 'Time' magazine, who called it 'the most solemn example of self-deification since Barbra Streisand's *A Star is Born*.' Stallone directed, but Bruce Malmuth made the superior *Nighthawks* (81), the story of two New York cops – the other was Billy Dee Williams – hunting an international terrorist. It took only just over $7 million and John Huston's *Victory* only just over $4 million: Stallone played an American POW who wants to join the soccer team and, under control, showed a certain likeable quality. But it was clearly time to return to Rocky.

At the time of the second of the series he was said to have asked for $2 million plus 15 per cent of the profits. The first word on *Rocky III* (82) was that he would get the same participation but one million more up front. Goldman in his book quotes $10 million and cites Stallone's flops with the comment: 'Have you ever heard such madness? Probably the largest amount ever paid a performer in the entire history of the civilized world. Isn't that insanity?' It was reported that UA had refused to pay that sum and had agreed to $7 million for Stallone's combined skills as actor, writer and director. He himself announced that he had turned down $8 million on the ground that he didn't want to play Rocky for ever. He did not play in a remake of *A*

Streetcar Named Desire which producer Martin Poll bought for him and then cancelled; neither did he make *The Godfather III* as writer, producer, director or star, all of which he was supposed to be. He did play Rambo, an ex-Green Beret, in Ted Kotcheff's *First Blood*, using military tactics as he escaped the wallies trying to catch him. He says at the end: 'I want what every guy who came [to Vietnam] and spilled his guts wants – for our country to love *us* as much as we loved it.' And David Denby in 'New York' magazine observed: 'The proud Rambo never tells anyone that he's a vet, that he's been through hell. Stallone, who in any case can barely deliver a line, gets by with his smoldering, heavy-lidded stare, his sleepy, primal-man beauty.' The first of these 1982 movies cost $17 million and took over $66 million; the second cost $14 million and took over $22 million – in itself a good figure, for the film was much ridiculed and criticized for its violence by people who had not seen it. The figures dumbfounded observers who felt that Stallone had little to offer as an actor and would soon be gone. He himself said around this time that he would one day be the second actor president.

He directed, but did not appear in, a John Travolta vehicle, *Staying Alive* (83), and both of them were attacked by its writer, Norman Wexler, who said that they had turned his script into 'a cliché-ridden, teenybopper picture. It's succeeding [at the box-office] despite Stallone . . . vacuous, impoverished, crass and crude. Stallone's religion is show business narcissism.' Sometimes it looked more like minting money: he and Dolly Parton got $6 million and $4 million respectively for *Rhinestone* (84), which included her advice on the screenplay, credited to him and Phil Alden Robinson. Four weeks into shooting director Don Zimmerman was replaced by Bob Clark and the budget eventually worked out at a hefty $28 million; but this supposedly light-hearted jape about a New York cab driver being taught to sing Country and Western took only just over $12 million. 20th-Century-Fox, which produced, was not happy at all and Paramount cancelled as 'too costly' a plan to co-star Stallone and Eddie Murphy in *50-50*. However, two old friends were waiting profitably: *Rambo: First Blood Part II* (85) brought in over $78 million on an outlay of $25,500,000 and *Rocky IV* did $76 million on a budget of $30 million. Carolco, which had produced the first Rambo, complained that Orion had not listened to them on the marketing of that one, so they took this one to Tri-Star, who did, to the satisfaction of all concerned – well, not quite, for David Morrell, who wrote the novel on which *First Blood* was based, had refused to have anything to do with this second episode; having seen the film, he called it 'a cartoon. On military bases they show it as a comedy; a guy I know in the Marines told me that at his base they were rolling in the aisles, hysterical.' When the film's director, James Cameron, was asked how much of that film was his own work, he replied, 'The politics are Stallone's, the action's mine. He was responsible for that extra bit of flag-waving American patriotism.' President Reagan approved, and having watched Rambo's shoot-first-and-argue-later tactics, observed that he would know what to do 'next time' when terrorists took Americans hostage. Oh, Stallone was patriotic all right, for *Rocky IV* gave him a Russian opponent – allowing Stallone 'to fight and win a war that hasn't yet been declared – World War III,' as Vincent Canby put it in the 'New York Times'.

His first marriage had ended messily in 1972, with mutual recriminations and a divorce settlement of $32 million. In 1985 he married model and singer Brigitte Nielsen, who told the press that she had come from her native Denmark to do expressly that. He also gave her roles in two films, *Rocky IV* and the one that followed. Stallone's mother publicly called her 'a gold-digger' and when the marriage broke up twenty months later claimed to have seen her in bed with another woman. Nielsen had signed a pre-nuptial agreement, so that she couldn't collect as his first wife had done: there was a $2 million out-of-court settlement, plus another $2 million to make no comment on the marriage.

Cannon, struggling to become a major supplier, had been negotiating for two years with Stallone because it felt that they spoke the same language: with Warners participating on finance for release rights, now that Stallone had proved himself still a hot number, the company made *Cobra* (86) and *Over the Top* (87). The first concerned a rampaging policeman who believes himself the cure for all crime; Stallone's own screenplay is based on a superior crime novel by Paula Gosling which has been ruined in the process: her British publishers were not sure how to react when told they could not associate the film with the book, while her American publisher found that their agreement with Warners prevented a reissue while Stallone's own novelization went on sale – but then, the announcement might be true that the film was based in part on the script he had written for *Beverly Hills Cop* when he was scheduled to appear in that. The second concerned a bull-headed truckie fighting for control of his kid, and the screenplay by Stallone and Stirling Silliphant was said to be based on Nielsen's

attempts to get her son out of Denmark. In the event, neither had any discernible merit, but the first managed $28 million on a $24 million budget; however any profits were swallowed up by the second, which cost $25 million and took only $8,300,000. His fee for each was $12 million (with participation), and 'People' magazine, noting that that had doubled since *Rhinestone*, looked at its loss of $16 million and wondered whether the next one would lose $32 million. 'People' had to eat its words, but that was small consolation for Cannon – or Stallone, who discovered again that the public had little interest in him unless he was bashing around killing enemies. He had agreed to a sequel to *Cobra*, but none was forthcoming: otherwise he was committed exclusively to United Artists for six years, to make ten films of which he would star in five. The only certainty was *Stoner*, which was never made, while there was unlikely to be another *Rocky*, for he had no further ideas – which most people thought was apparent after the first.

Carolco announced its intention of buying into Stallone's UA contract and its willingness to pay $100-125 million for the video and foreign rights to the first two Rambo pictures, which Stallone owned. It was announced that his White Eagle Productions had secured his release from his exclusive deal with UA and that he had signed a deal with Carolco, to release through Tri-Star – an agreement which did not include any further Rambos. His fee for the current one, *Rambo III* (88), was given by one source as $12 million, by yet another as $16 million and another as $20 million, the latter figure a cash advance against a percentage of the gross: whichever, the budget escalated from $32 million to $58 million, a new record for an American film. Later in the year *Who Framed Roger Rabbit?* would cost even more, but whereas that earned over $81 million in the US, this did only $28 million. The second-unit dirctor, Peter Macdonald, replaced Russell Mulcahy as director after some weeks of shooting, at which point there had to be replacements for several other key members of the crew, including the cameraman and the costume designer: to no avail, for this daft anti-Soviet action pic was no better than its predecessors. In fact, Stallone was now something of a joke, if – gratifyingly to himself – an expensive one. He diversified, playing a convict in *Lock Up* (89), 'which meets most expectations,' said 'Variety', 'for those who don't care if their warrior is even more charmless, violent and glum.' It was 'so ghastly,' said Baz Bamigboye in the (London) 'Daily Mail', 'that I felt incarceration would have been preferable to seeing [it].' 'Far too much of the film,' said Stephen Holden in the

'New York Times', 'is taken up worshipping his jaw-line and well-oiled torso.' He didn't direct, however: John Flynn did. Filming was delayed while Stallone was hospitalized for an overdose of steroids, pushing the budget to $17 million. It took $8 million. *Tango and Cash*, in which he and Kurt Russell are buddy-buddy LA cops, was another troubled shoot, with Andrei Konchalovsky – though he still was credited – replaced as director by Albert Magnoli (who had made *Purple Rain*). The result is estimated by 'Variety' to have an eventual haul of around $25 million, which continues this odd, extravagant saga, for its budget of $55 million became $75 million when the price of prints and advertising was added.

Many of the stills issued of this film show Stallone in glasses – you know, the new Stallone, the intellectual one. He told 'American Film', 'I know I've been playing these monosyllabic sides of beef, but you get caught up in it . . . I really don't have a defense. I have to admit it . . . I'm not a right-wing jingoistic human being. Rambo is.' Commenting on this, the 'Dallas Morning News' observed, 'In a way, it's difficult to not be impressed by the level of denial required to spend years getting rich by producing one of the most reprehensibly manipulative, intellectually bankrupt bodies of work in recent history, and then turning around to moan about how sensitive and misunderstood you are.' Stallone told interviewers that he wanted to escape his image, and that he had written a screenplay about Edgar Allen Poe which he would like someone of the calibre of Kubrick to direct. Who needed *Rocky V* (90)? – not the critics, anyway. *Dead Reckoning*, a futuristic tale, would seem to be the same old Stallone stuff, and it was to have been followed by a life of Puccini – which would, said Stallone, 'be the perfect role to make people realize I am not a dumb idiot who kills people.' This may have been pushed into limbo when Stallone decided to do a comedy, *Oscar* (91), originally meant for Danny DeVito.

Eddie Murphy said that Stallone told him: 'They dress you up; they put make-up on you; and you go out and they make millions and millions on you and you get a little bit of it. When you get old, they get someone else to do your job and it's over. We're whores.' Whoredom? Don't blame Stallone: if a poor player can make that sort of money it must be a pleasure to be a whore. It must also be agreeable to look at the record: two Stallone films are among the thirty top-grossing films of the 70s, three more among the twenty top-grossing films of the 80s and another three in the first hundred. Harrison Ford's record is better, but he is not considered the prime factor in the success of some of his films. Like it or not, Stallone dominated movie stardom in the 80s over all the other stars of the time.

MERYL STREEP

Meryl Streep once lived with the actor John Cazale, who, she said, called her 'the delicious robot'. He thought, she admitted, 'that I acted quite perfectly, but without the least feeling.' She is, said Cher, who appeared with her in *Silkwood*, 'an acting machine in the same sense that a shark is a killing machine. That's what she was born to be.' Some have felt less kindly about that. 'Streep in action is like being asked to admire the inside of a watch when actually all one needs to know is the time,' wrote Chris Petit in 'Time Out', 'Her tick-tock precision is so self-contained, so wrapped up in its own technique that her performances are no more than the cleverest impersonations, quite detached from the rest of the movie. Movie is a good word to expose Streep's limitations: she does not move, emotionally or physically. Each rustle and sigh might be carefully worked out for its individual effect, but added up it smacks of acting by numbers.' 'Think of la Streep, and you invariably think of her fragrant garden of abundant blooming accents,' said Tom Hibbert in 'Empire'. 'By putting on another frightwig and plucking some fresh vocal inflections – *voilà!* – she is transformed into yet another of her tense and neurotic martyr woman creations (though all the annoying little trademarks and mannerisms, the pained smile and the fussy nods of the head, the wiping of the pointy nose, the determination not to be seen in any way as glamorous stay *exactly* the same from performance to performance).' To put it more succinctly, she's dead boring.

She was born in 1949 in Summit, New Jersey, and was drawn to acting from an early age – a school 'Oklahoma!' and the lead in 'Miss Julie' while at Vassar, where she originally went to study music. She spent her senior year on an exchange scheme with Dartmouth, studying the theatre, and then entered the Yale Drama School. She went from that, in 1975, to the O'Neill Playwrights' Conference in Waterford, Connecticut, to appear in five plays, and made her professional debut that year in 'Trelawny of the Wells' for Joseph Papp. The following year she joined Papp's Shakespeare Festival Company to appear in 'Measure for Measure' (Isabella to Cazale's Angelo) and 'Henry V' and, in 1976, Kate in 'The Taming of the Shrew'. In

1977 she was in a production of 'The Cherry Orchard' at the Lincoln Center and in the Chelsea Theater Center's revival of the Brecht–Weill 'Happy End', which transferred to Broadway, the only time to date she has played the Great White Way; but she was in the Phoenix Theater productions of Arthur Miller's 'A Memory of Two Mondays' and Tennessee Williams's '27 Wagons Full of Cotton'.

She made her film debut, for television, as the wife of a hockey-player, Michael Moriarty, in *The Deadliest Season* (77), and it was her ambition which brings about his downfall. The role, however, was not large, nor was that in Fred Zinnemann's *Julia*, when she was billed seventh as one of Jane Fonda's friends, Anne Marie. For television, she was in the 9½-hour mini-series, *Holocaust* (78), playing a Catholic girl who marries James Woods, who is Jewish. It was multi-nominated for Emmy awards, and Streep was one of the winners. She also appeared in a TV play by Wendy Wasserstein, 'Uncommon Women and Others', concerning some Mount Holyoke graduates meeting up for a reunion lunch seven years later; also in the cast were Jill Eikenberry and the splendid Swoosie Kurtz, both of whom were in the studio when the play was repeated in 1990: the subject under discussion was the progress of the cast in the intervening years. Her role in *The Deer Hunter* was originally small, and she took it to be with Cazale, whose last picture it would be: she played his girl, attracted to Robert De Niro, and director Michael Cimino invited her to build it up. The film was rubbish, but high profile rubbish, winning several Oscars, and a nomination for Best Supporting Actress did her no harm at all. Cazale died of leukaemia and Streep married a sculptor, Don Gummer, a few months later.

She gave the same smug, mannered, febrile, glib performance in quick succession, in: *Manhattan* (79), as the wife who leaves Woody Allen for another woman; *The Seduction of Joe Tynan*, as Alan Alda's research assistant, encouraging him to commit adultery; and Robert Benton's *Kramer vs Kramer*, as the ex-wife battling Dustin Hoffman for custody of their child. She was hateful in this, as she was supposed to be, and in an earlier Hollywood would have given Gail Patrick a run for her money, eternally cast as 'the other woman'; but she won a Best Supporting Actress Oscar and then the title-role in one of the year's most prestigious productions, *The French Lieutenant's Woman* (81). Karel Reisz directed from a Harold Pinter script which reduced the brilliant Victorian pastiche of John Fowles's novel to a dignified romance and replaced the commentary with a miscalcu-

lated modern story about actors playing in a film of it. Jeremy Irons, hot from 'Brideshead Revisited', was the man and Streep the enigmatic woman, robbed of mystery as interpreted: but she does look stricken and haunted, though that may have had something to do with her brave stab at an English accent. The effect was of an elaborate con-job, and many of the people who flocked to it seemed to think so: for Streep's next film, Benton's *Still of the Night* (82), attracted less than $4 million on a $10 million budget. She was again a woman of mystery, but this time in the Hitchcock manner, attracting Roy Scheider even though he thinks she may be a murderess. She was certainly not the cause of the film's failure, and with *Sophie's Choice* her name was again on everybody's lips. Alan J. Pakula directed this study of disillusion, as a young Southern boy shares the affair of two

Meryl Streep in Sophie's Choice *(82), which amply demonstrated her three expressions – smiling, sulking and, when required to do anything else, looking stricken. She won an Oscar against four superior talents: Julie Andrews (Victor/Victoria), Jessica Lange (Frances), Sissy Spacek (Missing) and Debra Winger (An Officer and a Gentleman). Simultaneously Ms Lange did win a Supporting Oscar for Tootsie, which might account for her fine performance in Frances being passed over.*

others in the same boarding house, Kevin Kline and Streep, playing a Polish Catholic survivor of Auschwitz. At the Oscars, she beat out Jessica Lange, who was up for *Frances*, and that must be the Academy's silliest choice since 1944, when an ordinary performance (in *Gaslight*) by Ingrid Bergman beat a brilliant one (in *Double Indemnity*) by Barbara Stanwyck. As Elia Kazan remarked, Lange is one of those creatures the camera loves, but Streep is merely an ideal drama school actress. She did, however, give a good performance by her own standards in what for her was a character role, Karen in *Silkwood* (83), the nuclear power station worker who was killed in a suspicious car crash in 1974 after threatening to expose its health hazards. The project had originally been developed by Jane Fonda, who dropped it reluctantly, and only partially because she had been involved in another movie about the dangers of nuclear power, *The China Syndrome*. Streep dropped a consonant or so, chain-smoked and wore cheap clothes: she did not get under the skin of the character, as did Sally Field in the not dissimilar *Norma Rae*, but it was a terrifying movie as directed by Mike Nichols, and very popular.

Falling in Love (84), however, only managed to take under $6 million on a $12 million outlay. Streep and Robert De Niro were Connecticut commuters who begin an affair after a brief encounter (yes, that *Brief Encounter*) in a New York bookstore. Being major stars, they were expected to transform this old-hat material with their charm and their truth, but neither had the first quality and even his talent could bring little to the second. Streep's fee was $2 million, and *Plenty* (85) took just $441,685 more than that at the American box-office on a budget of $10 million. This British film, directed by Fred Schepisi, was based on a play by David Hare, whose stated aim is to 'try to show the English their history': in this case this was from the War to the Suez crisis as experienced by one tiresome, neurotic upper-class lady. The history he was taught at school, said Hare, was 'phoney and corrupting', which would be adjectives to describe this film were it of any merit. On stage with Kate Nelligan it seemed to have a little, if not much; with Streep, smirking and sulking, it had none. Her fee went up to $4 million for *Out of Africa*, and was justified when it took over $43 million on a cost of $30 million. There were nine Oscars, including those for Best Picture and Best Direction (Sydney Pollack), but not much satisfaction to be had beyond some pretty views and the performance of Klaus-Maria Brandauer as Streep's husband. She played the writer Karen Blixen, on whose memoir, it

Klaus-Maria Brandauer and Meryl Streep, Danish-aristocratic husband and wife, in Out of Africa *(84), which enabled this actress to get another of her fabled accents into gear. He, Brandauer, stole every scene and when he is shunted into the background – in favour of her lover, Robert Redford – the film is little more than a pretty travelogue.*

was based, and her Danish accent was much admired except in Denmark; Robert Redford played her lover, as vacuous as she but much prettier (she emphasized the Baroness's frumpishness).

Heartburn (86) was also autobiographical, as directed by Nichols from the novel by Nora Ephron based on the break-up of her marriage to the journalist Carl Bernstein. Jack Nicholson played that role; Streep again proved herself the Virginia Mayo *de nos jours*, laughing and crying on cue without showing the least involvement; and the film took $11,800,000 on a budget of $20 million. Her fee was again $4 million, and *Ironweed* (87), again with Nicholson, took less than that at the box-office. It cost $27 million. Hector Babenco directed the screenplay by William Kennedy, from his novel, and Streep was a bag lady of the Depression years. She did one of her renowned accents, Australian this time, in Schepisi's *A Cry in the Dark* (88; Australian title: *Evil Angels*), more true-life stuff, with Sam Neill, playing Lindy Chamberlain, whose baby was killed by a dingo but who was put on trial for her murder. It was a strong film, notably pointed on the ethics of the press, but the public did not want to know: it cost $15 million and took only $2,500,000 at the American box-office. The New York critics judged her the year's Best Actress and so she was when the Australian film awards were announced; they also named it the Best Film. A poll of fifty-four critics instituted by the magazine 'American Film' in 1989 found Streep the Best Acress of the decade, but then they also considered *Raging Bull* the Best Film. Nicholson was Best Actor, and about this time Streep gave a notably foul-mouthed interview to 'Premiere', in which she complained that Nicholson had got $11 million for *Batman*: if she asked for that, she said, they would laugh at her, implying that Nicholson could get away with it because he was a man.

Well, no. It's a question of talent. Streep had been the darling of some critics, but the public knew better. She had another failure with *She-Devil* (89) directed by Susan Seidelman from the novel by Fay Weldon, concerning a glamorous marriage-wrecker (Streep) who takes a nice man (Ed Begley Jr) from his fat, slobbish wife – played by Roseanne Barr, then riding high with her own television series. Said New York's 'Seven Days': 'La Streep wears the air of repressed panic she habitually dons when required to do comedy and throws herself around as if she were on the stage, squeezing her face ostentatiously into the spoiled sourpuss and kittenish seductress her constricted role requires.' The cost, according to 'Variety' and including publicity and advertising, was $27 million: the box-office return was only $6 million. She then did *Postcards From the Edge* (90), more autobiography, this time from Carrie Fisher, whose mother, sort-of – Debbie Reynolds – was played by Shirley MacLaine. Streep did a real mechanic's job on the heroine's problems with drugs and the fast life, but a four-week total of $26,608,000 does suggest she has broken her box-office jinx – admittedly with a 'name' director, Mike Nichols and a cast also including Gene Hackman, Richard Dreyfuss and Dennis Quaid. Streep was then scheduled to do the often off-and-on screen version of the musical *Evita*, more closely identified with it than the other actresses mentioned hitherto. When she withdrew due to 'personal reasons' (she claimed exhaustion) a report in the 'New York Times' said, 'things came to a boil in mid-September when Ms Streep kept escalating her salary demands'. She would not, of course, be the only star of her generation who over-estimated her commercial value – and she was still in demand, for despite 'exhaustion' she went almost immediately into Albert Brooks's *Defending Your Life*. Neither of these films had been shown when she whined at a meeting of the Screen Actors Guild that there were no longer any roles available for actresses. No one has heard Glenn Close or Jessica Lange complaining.

She was one of the few to make an impact in films in the 80s. She has been called a great actress, but we shall let the critic John Simon have the last word (even if he was discussing another player, Wendy Makenna): 'It is a capital offense for an actor (unless the part calles for it) to exude smugness: the more so for one who has nothing to be smug about.'

PATRICK SWAYZE

Mr Swayze is eloquent on the effects of one hit film: 'It's amazing how one movie can blow the lid off. Suddenly everybody in the world wants to be your buddy.' And: 'You have to keep yourself to yourself, otherwise you'd go insane. Sometimes I wonder what is this monster I've created for myself, but really I'm happy as a goose.' Of all the requests for interviews and job offers, including making records and an exercise video: 'It's insanity. After *Dirty Dancing*, everything was keying in to Patrick Swayze swinging his butt. That's not what I'm about. I don't listen to any of that sex symbol bull. The trick is not to believe it. If other people want to, that's up to them. The adulation gets embarrassing.' And: 'Don't put your dreams in a box and take them out once a year to check them out before packing them away again. If you're content to wait your chance, you might wait forever.' All the same . . .

Patrick was born in Houston, Texas, in 1952 to Patsy Swayze, who would later run the Houston Jazz/Ballet Company and choreograph *Urban Cowboy*. After winning a gymnastics scholarship to the city's San Jacinto College, he won another (scholarship, that is) to study dance in New York and made his debut as a dancer in 'Disney on Parade' as Prince Charming. In the company was a former pupil of his mother, Lisa Niemi, whom he married a few years later. He made his New York debut as a dancer in 'Goodtime Charley' and later took over the role of Danny Zuko in the long-running 'Grease', His first movie role was small, in *Skatetown USA* (79), a roller-disco fantasy which starred Scott Baio and Flip Wilson, but he was seen to advantage in a telemovie, *The Comeback Kid* (80), as one of several underprivileged youths being coached by a once-big baseball pitcher (John Ritter), and he was one of the younger generation when a grizzled bikers' band celebrate a reunion in *Return of the Rebels* (81). Also on TV, but starring, he was one of *The Renegades* (82), a bunch of young toughs recruited by a cop to prevent crime. This was the pilot for a series which he did not do, having had better offers for cinema movies, *The Outsiders* (83), playing the elder brother of Pony Boy (C. Thomas Howell), and *Uncommon Valor*, as a high-handed ex-GI who antagonizes the unit established by a colonel (Gene Hackman) to find his son, who has been missing since the Vietnam War.

He and Howell were reunited for two more youth movies which were released simultaneously, *Grandview USA* (84) and *Red Dawn*. They were not much alike, however, as directed respectively by Randal Kleiser and John Milius: the first was a small-town tale centred on a demolition-derby and the second was a violent tale of youngsters who turn guerilla warriors in the wake of a Soviet invasion. The first starred Jamie Leigh Curtis, but Swayze was top-billed in the second. Neither effort was of a quality likely to attract anyone of sensibility, and the same may be said of *Pigs vs Freaks*, but that's an odd one all right. It originated as an award-winning short written by Jack Epps Jr, shown in 1970. Expanded to a feature in 1980, directed by Dick Lowry, it starred a bearded Tony Randall as coach for the juvenile delinquents who are to play football against the town's cops. You don't need to be told which side Swayze was on. Anyway, after sitting on the shelf, it turned up on TV at this time, retitled *Off Sides*. It was in this medium that Swayze attained fame as the young lover of the divided families in the Civil War mini, *North*

and South (85), based on the novel by John Jakes. Another novel by Jakes formed the basis of another mini, *North and South Book II* (86) which, garnered with such names as Olivia de Havilland, James Stewart and Jean Simmons, delivered in the ratings game.

Youngblood put him back on the big screen, but he was in support of Rob Lowe in this teen movie, as his rival on the ice-hockey team and taking the film from him each time they were on screen together. He was ready for big movie stardom – of a sort: for *Dirty Dancing* (87) cost only $5 million and its producers, Vestron, were more noted for video deals than film-making. It is set back-when in a resort hotel in the Catskills, where the show-off dance instructor (Swayze) falls for a plainjane (Jennifer Gray) despite parental disapproval, and he wins her, despite ingredients – the missing wallet and the unwilling alibi – which have been around since Mrs Henry Wood. This would not have passed muster in the Mickey-and-Judy days, but at that time films were targeted at family audiences and not merely teeny-boppers. This young hero services married women, but when he sleeps with his girl it's true love, and they're 'better people' because of it. The combination of 60s music and old-fashioned morality is not unendearing in its simple way, and we should not forget the lyrical views: but then the whole thing had been programmed – not in the Hollywood computer, but by talented people wanting a foothold: director Emile Ardolino and writer–co-producer Linda Gottlieb. Who would have thought, thirty years after the James Dean era, that a hero would wear braces to keep up his pants? – but he has black leather too, and sleek black pants. Swayze, smooth, blond, with a certain virility, cockiness, became a star, but he was not the sole reason the film took $25 million at the box-office.

He was then scheduled to make *Total Recall* in Australia under the direction of Bruce Beresford, for the De Laurentiis Group, but insufficient funding was available (which could not have displeased Arnold Schwarzenegger, who had already seen the script and decided that it was for him). And Swayze was doubly unlucky, for very few went to see him as *Tiger Warsaw* (88), who shoots at his dad, thus scuppering his sister's wedding plans and who would seem bent on doing the same to her second attempt when he returns fifteen years later. Still, he refused to do *Dirty Dancing II*, even at a fee of $5 million, because his demand for quality all the way could not be met – the sort of integrity which must make him very isolated in Tinsel Town. As he said: 'I've struggled too long and too hard in this business to give less than 100 per

cent.' When Vestron went bankrupt in 1990 with only that one success out of more than forty failures, 'Variety' reported the matter a little differently. Swayze did not want to make a sequel unless it was written by Gottlieb, who was not interested in repeating herself: but as she and Swayze were wooed, to that fee, huge for him, no one seems to have bothered about his co-star, Ms Gray, who thought there was too big a gap between the fee offered to Swayze and the $500,000 Vestron were prepared to pay her. On that *Dirty Dancing II* foundered, but with a sequel-crazy industry there is still reason to be grateful to Swayze, who did not, after all, lie.

He also said, when asked why he had chosen to make *Road House* (89): 'If you do nothing but art films, you're gonna get your vote cancelled . . . and I worked hard to get as much violence taken out of the film as possible.' Joel Silver, the producer of *Lethal Weapon*, had clearly ordered some similarities here, as Swayze swings into town as a 'cooler', i.e. a security expert specializing in taming rowdy drinking-places. Here he is up against gang boss Ben Gazzara, but he has kung fu skills and an amiable mentor in Sam Elliott.

Swayze, as slyly self-aware as Mel Gibson and Danny Glover and equally adept at suggesting a slight send-up, is also a superior action hero, but the film returned only $12,400,000 of its $19 million budget. The figures on *Next of Kin* were also fairly brutal – a $7 million return on a budget of $12 million. Still, Warner Bros did not press-show the film, a sure sign of a stinker. Swayze played a hillbilly cop who has long dreamed of revenging his brother's death in the jungle of Chicago, and John Irvin, who directed, commented that he had the ability to seem 'streetwise, while holding on to his small-town beliefs.'

So there was a question-mark over the name of a man too hastily termed 'a megastar' after *Dirty Dancing*, but it was triumphantly answered by *Ghost* (90), which took over $163 million in just over three months of release, potentially overtaking *Pretty Woman* at over $175 million – but that at over seven months on general release. With steam left in both, they should have no difficulty in attaining rank in the Top Ten most successful films of all time. He played the title-role, desperate to return from the dead because he knows his widow (Demi Moore) is in danger; as the

Patrick Swayze and Jennifer Grey in Dirty Dancing *(87), which has the distinction of being the only successful film made by the video Company, (Vestron) during its foray into film-making.*

Swayze and Demi Moore in Ghost *(90), a hit of such proportions that it makes the money taken* Dirty Dancing *look like loose change. They played a couple separated by death: and since he knows that she is to be killed in the same way as he was, he tries to prevent that in spectral form.*

medium who helps him to do so, Whoopi Goldberg also reversed her almost disastrous movie track record. As for Swayze, he followed Richard Gere and John Travolta in proving that that 'heart-throb' and 'hunk' reputation was one thing, but getting into a good movie is the name of the game. He was committed to *Point Break* (91) before *Ghost* burst through the ectoplasm, but its promoters would have breathed a little easier. In the film he will play an FBI agent hot on the trail of bankrobbers. After that: *Double Fault*, a psychological thriller which 20th Century-Fox have brought for him.

JOHN TRAVOLTA

The Robert Stigwood Organization is to cinema what McDonald's is to cuisine: just as there is a large public for junk-food, so there is for 'Tommy', 'Jesus Christ Superstar', 'Evita' and two of the first three movies of John Travolta. It's no use complaining; and it's no use saying that it's all a question of promotion, because what the public doesn't like it doesn't buy – as Stigwood discovered with some of his other (heavily-publicized) enterprises. All the same, it is depressing. Rock-fanciers dislike most of the records wafted by RSO's methods into the No. 1 spot (a phrase in itself depressing), and even if we sympathize with efforts to break down Hollywood resistance to rock, we cannot find cheering the spread of the methods of the

record industry. However, Hollywood certainly did not yelp when the media went to town on Travolta – when he achieved the twin pinnacles of the American dream, a 'Time' magazine cover and the 'Playboy' interview, both within months of becoming famous. In the reams written about this rather bland young man, it is said that RSO decided that with Elvis Presley dead America needed a new hero – which overlooks the fact that Presley's fans were middle-aged, along with him. But movies certainly needed a young hero. Audiences had grown younger, and the stars – well, they hadn't grown younger. *Saturday Night Fever* was just what they were waiting for. It might have been assembled by computers fed by teenage opinion polls. 'No one,' Travolta told 'Playboy', 'thought it was bullshit. It was just cold, it was hard language, it was hard-driving, it was *real*. Everything had a cold reality to it' . . . and one can only say that if he believes that, he'll believe anything. However, among the bits borrowed from other adolescent dreams – *American Graffiti, Rebel Without a Cause* – was something movies have ever overlooked: the nine-to-five guy with nothing to look forward to beyond his Saturday night date. Preparing for that, this guy had his one truthful scene, preening before the mirror and squirting on the after-shave: he might have been any young man over the last forty years. At that point he almost began to justify some of the publicity, and, yes, he did move well on the disco-floor.

His very ordinariness may be his salvation.

In the old days, those who pined to be movie stars longed for the glamour: now, we know the life isn't very glamorous but it is, conversely, very easy to be famous. TV personalities and rock stars prove you don't need talent to achieve it. You need, maybe, a show-business family and a Colonel Parker-like promoter. Travolta's mother had been part of a radio singing group called 'The Sunshine Sisters', and his father – a semi-pro football player and tyre salesman – encouraged both her and the six children, of whom only one didn't go into show business (and even he, it's said, is hooked). John was born in Englewood, New Jersey, in 1954; at the age of nine he was in a local production of 'Who'll Save the Plowboy?'; before dropping out of school he had studied dancing under Fred Kelly (Gene's brother), and at sixteen he moved across the Hudson to Manhattan, where he lived with a sister. Within a year he had had small roles in revivals of 'Gypsy' and 'Bye Bye Birdie', and had attracted the attention of an agent-manager, Bob LeMond, who got him jobs in commercials, in TV ('The Rookies', 'Owen Marshall', 'Medical Center'), and in

two other musicals, 'Grease' (as Doody) and 'Over Here!' He had already been passed over for a small role in *The Panic in Needle Park*; during this time he failed to get a part in *The Last Detail*, but he did have one line in *The Devil's Rain* (75). LeMond turned down a small role in 'The Ritz' in favour of an attempt on Hollywood, and landed him a supporting role in a TV series on school life, 'Welcome Back, Kotter'. The star was Gabriel Kaplan, but audiences were soon rooting for the dumb but sexy Vinnie Barbarino (Travolta); and before the first episode had aired, Brian De Palma had cast him in *Carrie* (76), as the long-haired boyfriend of one of Carrie's friends (Nancy Allen). He was approached to do a role in *Days of Heaven*, but the 'Kotter' schedule would not permit it; at the end of the season he was able to do a TV movie, *The Boy in the Plastic Bubble*, in the title-role, an afflicted youngster who falls in love with the girl next door; the director was Randall Kleiser, and Travolta's mother was played by Diana Hyland, who became very much a part of Travolta's life till she died of cancer in 1977.

John Travolta and Dona Pescow in Saturday Night Fever (77), *a movie so outstandingly popular that he became one of the icons of the seventies – like the Beatles in the sixties or James Dean in the fifties. Or like Humphrey Bogart in the forties or Clark Gable in the thirties.*

Allan Carr, a Hollywood impresario, owned the rights to 'Grease', a long-running but critically dismissed Broadway show about high school kids of the 50s; he saw Travolta in 'Kotter', and a deal was made with Stigwood whereby they became partners in the film version of 'Grease', and Stigwood offered a three-picture contract to Travolta worth $1 million-plus. Simultaneously the screenplay of *Saturday Night Fever* (77) was worked up from an article in 'New York' magazine, and since it had clearly more potential than the uninspired shenanigans of *Grease* (78), it was made first. The former got mediocre notices, and the latter extremely poor ones, but both confounded today's rule that the only movies to succeed are those with press approval, for at the end of 1978 they had swamped all competition of recent years, except *Star Wars* and *Close Encounters of the Third Kind*. The acres of newsprint expended on Travolta were certainly responsible for drumming up the curious, but despite the magazine articles, etc. that multiplied, glorifying him alone, it was difficult to find anyone, even the under-tens who seemed to constitute much of the audience, more than mildly enthusiastic. Here are three British reviews of *Grease*: 'Despite all the promotional ballyhoo around the fact that this is the second film to star John Travolta . . . it is brutally apparent that it might well be his last: the whole of that wet-lipped, dreamy-eyes personality is diffused of any real power by a narrative framework which can barely support itself, never mind him' ('Sunday Telegraph'); 'Travolta still radiates that sense of dangerous innocence and spring-heel jackanapery that impales the eye. But if this ragbag of remnants dyed in Day-glo had been his first starring film, I do not believe the Empire [the cinema] would have been under siege last Wednesday night' ('Sunday Times'); 'The insipid Olivia Newton-John is dull when playing the shy virgin and blush-making when acting the sexy leather-clad siren to win her Dean-age swain. The object of her affections, the incipient J.D. with the over-groomed D.A., Danny, is played by John Travolta, a simpering figure from a Mad Magazine parody of *West Side Story*, who seems almost embarrassed by an awareness of his limited talent' ('Observer'). *Fever* was directed by John Badham, after Stigwood sacked Avildsen, reputedly the day he was nominated for his *Rocky* Oscar; *Grease* was directed by Kleiser.

Travolta's third RSO movie was made at his suggestion, after seeing Lily Tomlin's one-woman show. It made as much sense as Elizabeth Taylor and Kermit the Frog, or Milton Berle and Dolly Parton. Would you believe, a tale of passion? – *The Graduate*

crossed with *Love Story*? Tomlin's longtime friend and collaborator, Jane Wagnor, wrote and directed, and came in for most of the stick: the reviews were lethal, and *Moment by Moment* fell by the wayside. It made money for Stigwood, since it cost $5 million, and he sold distribution rights to Universal (Paramount released the other two) for $8 million. Its failure was presumably why exhibitors voted Travolta behind Burt Reynolds as box-office champ in '78. Still, according to 'Saturday Night Live' producer Lorne Michaels, 'John is the perfect star for the 70s. He has this strange androgynous quality, this all-pervasive sexuality. Men don't find him terribly threatening. And women, well . . .' He didn't finish. Well, indeed.

Travolta had signed with Orion for two movies at a fee of $3 million each. The first was announced as *American Gigolo*, which the trade thought an uneasy choice after a well-published flop. He himself was afraid that the older woman–younger man aspect would echo the failure of that – and director Paul Schrader was not happy when Travolta wanted to rework the dialogue till he was more comfortable with it. A family bereavement was said to be the reason for opting out, and the role went to Richard Gere, said to be the first choice before Travolta got 'hot'. Travolta's first film for Orion was James Bridges's *Urban Cowboy* (90), playing an oilfield worker who meets and falls in love with Debra Winger in a tacky C & W bar, but for whom marriage is another matter altogether. The film's gross of $23,810,000 suggested – indeed shouted – that Travolta should not be written off, but a second film for De Palma, *Blow Out* (81) cost $18 million and stopped taking money at $7,600,000. It was typical of the films De Palma was then making, a confused, manipulative and derivative (of *Blow-Up*, as the title seems to acknowledge) thriller built round a Philadelphia sound-engineer who discovers that his tapes seem to contain evidence of a political assassination. 'I saved your life,' he says to the sole witness (Karen Allen), 'The least you can do is have a drink with me.' He is to save her life again and battle with many meanies to get at the truth: but Travolta's way of showing a man driven, obsessed, is to be boringly bland throughout. Travolta was then offered *An Officer and a Gentleman*, written with him in mind, but he decided that he needed a 'light' picture at this stage and Gere again took the role. *Night Shift* was also offered, but that role went to Henry Winkler, for Travolta played it doubly safe by doing a sequel.

Staying Alive (83) at least had the virtue of not calling itself *Saturday Night Fever II*, but that, as it happened, was the only one it possessed – though a take of over $33 million is still a lot of lettuce, even if that was a good way below the original (but not a bad return on an $18 million budget). The Tony Manero character is the only thing the two films have in common: he has become a gypsy, a Broadway dancer, who drops his regular girl (Cynthia Rhodes) for the stuck-up broad (Finola Hughes) who has the lead in the show. Travolta is immensely photogenic, and the director, Sylvester Stallone, who knows something about star appeal, lets the camera dwell on his large eyes, his large cheekbones, his large mouth; he lets the guy move. The film presents the Stallone philosophy, as propounded in *Rocky*, of how the little man can make it with a combination of perseverance and luck – provided he sticks to his kind and doesn't tangle with rich kids. The *Two of a Kind* were Travolta and Olivia Newton-John, reunited for a puerile whimsy in which they redeem the world just as the Supreme Being is considering a second Flood; they meet when he's attempting to rob the bank in which she is a teller – and that is the high point. What made matters worse was that it 'has all the earmarks of a bargain basement job', as 'Variety' put it – as if Travolta was rejecting the evidence and accepting the word of those who called him a flash in the pan. The $12 million the film took can only be due to his drawing power, for both the film and his co-star were slaughtered by the critics. She did not help matters by telling the press that he was afraid of women, going on to express the opinion that his friendship with Diana Hyland was entirely due to ambition, because she was much better known; Hyland, she added, had introduced him to Stigwood.

In all events, *Perfect* (85) was intended as a new departure, as directed by James Bridges and co-written by him and a 'Rolling Stone' reporter, Aaron Latham, who had written an exposé of Californian health clubs. Since Travolta plays an investigative 'Rolling Stone' reporter we might have expected something like *Five Star Final*: what we get is the same old Travolta vehicle, with him doing his aerobic thing in the health clubs, photographed and cut in such a way that he and the teacher (Jamie Lee Curtis) might almost be fucking. 'What's wrong in wanting to be perfect? What's wrong in wanting to be loved?' she asks, and the questions set up all sorts of resonances, about the film, the plot and the characters, all of a crippling banality. The movie, which had cost $19 million, took a far from perfect $6,112,000. The sharp-eyed may spot way down the cast list the name of Paul Baressi, who in 1990 told the press that he had been Travolta's lover for two years. By that time Travolta was again a name to conjure with, but the years between were sticky.

His manager during this period was Mike Ovitz of CAA, who had also advised him not to make *Splash* because Warren Beatty planned a similar film, *Mermaid*, which was never made. Travolta left the agency and took stock; he decided that he was being blamed for each mega-budget disaster – and since many of the attacks were personal he dropped his plan to direct a film called *Greenwich* (in which, however, he did not plan to appear). He lowered his salary demand to $1,750,000 upfront and accepted three medium budget films, to be made with the minimum of publicity. Reviewing *The Experts* (89), 'Variety' referred to these three as 'come-back' films, implying that there was little future for Travolta if the other two were as bad as this – and admittedly it had been on the shelf for a couple of years. Supposedly a comedy, it had two streetwise New Yorkers – the other was Arye Gross – kidnapped by the Russkies to advise them on modern America in order to train their spies. It went direct to video in most countries, and the 'Variety' review of *Look Who's Talking* suggested that that might be too kind a fate in this case. Amy Heckerling's film cost $8 million and it took the remarkable figure of $134 million in its first eight months in release. This is almost certainly not because of the gimmick of a baby which speaks with Bruce Willis's voice, but to a traditional romance in which it takes the heroine till the fade-out to realize that the man for her is the one the audience chose for her at the outset. She is an accountant (Kirstie Alley), made pregnant by her wealthy executive lover (George Segal), who reneges on his promise to marry her because he is going through a 'selfish' phase. The staff at the hospital think the cabbie (Travolta) who brought her is her husband, and he takes to popping in to play surrogate father while she searches among a bunch of nerds and wimps to find someone from her own class to marry her. Absence had put a little weight on Travolta, without sharpening either his personality or sense of comedy: but he was perfectly amiable, and the piece could not have been the success it was had spectators not been rooting for him.

Everyone was talking about Travolta, and much more now is riding on two films in the can: *The Tender* (90), in which he plays an alcoholic father, and *Chains of Gold*, in which he is an ad executive who becomes a social worker involved with teenage drug addiction. The first came out to sink without trace, and the second remained on the shelf (till this writing) after its producer, New Line, collapsed. Maybe no one wants to take it over, which would mean that Travolta is not so hot after all. But he can never be written off again, even if *Look Who's Talking Too* does not come up to expectations. Next up: *Midnight Rider*.

KATHLEEN TURNER

Kathleen Turner is among the dozen bankable actresses in Hollywood, with a good track record and a sheaf of good notices to her credit. She is versatile, handsome and appealing without having much of the individuality of the great women stars of the past.

She was born in 1954 in Springfield, Missouri, to a mother who was a native of that state and a father in the diplomatic service, which is why she grew up in Canada, Cuba, Venezuela and Britain. When he died, when she was eighteen, the family returned to Missouri and she enrolled in Southwestern State University. The actress Tess Harper, who knew her as a fellow-pupil, said, 'She was

Kathleen Turner in Romancing the Stone *(84), as an author of romances – which is a gag of sorts, for what happens to her, up the Amazon with Michael Douglas, is supposed to be even more far-fetched than the things she writes about.*

the most determined person I'd ever met. Unlike the rest of us, she had a game plan.' This took her to the University of Maryland, where she continued to act in college productions, and then to New York, where she found herself an agent and live-in companion, David Guc, who got her work in commercials while she waited on tables. A real job was not long in coming, in a soap opera, 'The Doctors'. She made her Broadway debut in 'Gemini' in 1978, and went on to play, among other roles, Titania and Hippolyta in an Arena production of 'A Midsummer Night's Dream'. She auditioned for the role in *Body Heat* (81) which made her a star, replying, 'This sure is a friendly town' after a stranger has asked her, 'Hey lady, you wanna fuck?' He is a seedy lawyer (William Hurt), and not only do they fuck so much and so often that he cries off for a while, but he is involved in a scheme to rid her of her middle-aged husband (Richard Crenna). Under the direction of Lawrence Kasdan, Turner is convincing and confident, but the role needs a Stanwyck, a Bacall, or even a Lizabeth Scott.

Nothing worthwhile seemed to be coming along, so she accepted *The Man With Two Brains* (83), playing the girl who takes up with Steve Martin after her wayward behaviour has given her sugar-daddy a heart attack. 'I was a typical dumb-bell girlfriend,' she said later, 'and being – I felt – wasted in a silly and secondary role. But I'd work with Steve again in a minute. On a more equitable basis, of course.' She auditioned again, for the role of the novelist who shares Michael Douglas's Amazonian adventures in *Romancing The Stone* (84), a success of such proportions that she could write her own ticket. But a couple were already in the can. In Philippe Mora's *A Breed Apart* she ran the local store while conservationist Rutger Hauer and mountaineer Powers Boothe went to battle over the eggs of a bald-headed eagle for which bald-headed Donald Pleasance was prepared to pay plenty big cash. In Ken Russell's *Crimes of Passion* she was a dowdy designer by day who dons leather and blond wig at night to be China Blue, dominatrix – and particularly dominating Anthony Perkins. Later she said, 'Now either he is a very convincing actor, or he is an eerie man. But I did not feel that comfortable around him.' He may have felt the same about her, for he said that she had 'strong opinions, lots of energy. She's direct, which can be interpreted as brusque, and she doesn't like to waste time, which can be viewed by the fainthearted as impatience.' The first of these two films had a few screenings before going straight to video; audiences of the second should have been so lucky, though Turner herself feels that it contains some of her best work. She was, in fact, better served by *Prizzi's Honor* (85), which she accepted for the chance to work with director John Huston and co-star Jack Nicholson: she and he played hit-persons for a Mafia family who marry but, understandably, do not trust each other.

With one big critical success, her first film, and a very popular one, *Romancing the Stone*, her relationship with Guc fell apart. 'When I started to feel my power,' she said, 'the balance didn't work': but he remained her agent. She married someone who presumably did not mind her power, Jay Weiss, a New York developer, and baulked at a sequel to the film which had given her that power. 20th-Century-Fox threatened a $25 million lawsuit, so she was reunited with Douglas for *The Jewel of the Nile*. The film was successful enough for her to feel easy about a third instalment, should there be one, for movie-making is about making it, and who knows? – 'in a few years time I might be second-billed to someone no one has heard of today'. She was billed below Douglas, but was the sole star of *Peggy Sue Got Married* (86), replacing Debra Winger who bowed out after an accident. Douglas advised her against taking the role, because she would be playing mothers soon enough. But this Peggy Sue is only maternal for a while, because she gets knocked out at a class reunion and is able to recall her youth while knowing what the future holds: so why does she marry the wimp (Nicolas Cage) who 'won't go all the way' instead of the free spirit who deflowers her on the river bank? Francis Coppola directed this mild, disintegrating whimsy. *Julia and Julia* (87), directed in Italy by Peter Del Monte in 'high-definition video', seemed to offer the sort of prime role this actress was seeking. She played a woman in crisis, torn between two different dreams or realities, in one of which she is being unfaithful with Sting, and in the other worried about the husband (Gabriel Byrne), a corpse on their wedding day. Video was the obvious destination for this one, while *Switching Channels* (88) was only too aptly named – and if, having done so, you found *His Girl Friday* on another one, you would not want to switch back: for this was a remake, and Turner was only adequate in the role in which Rosalind Russell had been sensational. Her co-star was Burt Reynolds, but he was of little help (see Reynolds) at the box-offce.

She was the voice of Jessica, sexy wife of a bunny *extraordinaire* in *Who Framed Roger Rabbit?*, and then the wife of William Hurt in *The Accidental Tourist*, which reunited them with writer-director Kasdan. It was only a supporting role, and not a very sympathetic one, dumping him on whim and wanting him

back again in the same fashion. Reunited with Douglas, they were an ideal couple – affluent, well appointed - till the day she says, 'When I watch you sleeping, when I see you eating, when I look at you now, I want to smash your face in.' Thus begins *The War of the Roses* (89), but this time (see Douglas) there was no discord at the box-office. The role had been offered to her four years earlier, when the couple's children had been much younger; but, as she said, there was no way to make either character sympathetic if they allowed the kids to be destroyed. She was childless – since that is one of the points of the play – in a revival of Tennessee Williams's 'Cat on a Hot Tin Roof', which she took to success on Broadway in 1990. In preparation were two films which she would produce herself, *A Flag for Sunrise* and *Hardboiled*, in which she would play a detective. The second of these was cancelled, when it was announced that she would play a detective in a film for A.N. Other, *Warshawski* (91), the first of a series.

N.B. Her favourite novel is 'Portrait of a Lady' by Henry James, and any actress who loves that particular book deserves to play Isabel Archer. She may not be quite right for the role, but what a film it might make!

JON VOIGHT

'It's nice that people like you are around,' says Jennifer Salt to Jon Voight in *The Revolutionary*. We have not had too many chances to echo her sentiments, but his performance in *Midnight Cowboy* is one of the best ever in an American film. Peter Evans in 'Cosmopolitan' suggested that he had created a classic figure to stand with Captain Bligh, Rhett Butler and *Streetcar*'s Stanley Kowalski. Brando, at least, is a good comparison, for Voight's Joe Buck, the midnight cowboy, was the best portrayal of stupidity on the screen since Brando's in *On the Waterfront*. It's not an easy thing to do, and only a fine actor could do it: suggest a low IQ, a retarded mentality – at the same time conducting an audience into the labyrinthine ways of that calf's brain behind the bland, handsome young face. For Joe Buck was a Texas stud, with ambitions exclusively connected with his crotch: in a sublimely innocent way he thought he would get ahead by hustling.

Anyone who had doubts as to what extent this was acting – and Voight's triumph is indicated by the fact that many did – might well look at his background and his other work. He is the son of a Yonkers golf pro, and was born in that New York suburb in 1939. One of his brothers is a university lecturer; his father wanted him to follow a career on the

Jon Voight

links but after graduating from the Catholic University of America in Washington, DC, he joined a stock company in Vermont. In New York he studied under Stanford Meisner; then returned to Vermont to play leading roles, including Happy in 'Death of a Salesman'. He first appeared on Broadway in 'The Sound of Music' (59), as the telegraph-boy who becomes a Nazi – and he married the girl with whom he sang the duet; after that he toured with Howard Keel in 'Camelot' and got jobs in TV, notably in 'Cimarron Strip' and 'Gunsmoke'. He also acted off-Broadway, including 'A View From the Bridge' on which Dustin Hoffman was assistant director; and won a 'Theater World' award when he appeared on Broadway in 'That Summer That Fall'. There was a film offer, to play one of Robert Ryan's cattle-rustling gang in *The House of the Gun* (67); and a better one, for *The Russians Are Coming The Russians Are Coming* – but John Philip Law did that, since Voight instead accepted *Frank's Greatest Adventure*, which he followed with another unsuccessful independent venture, *Out of It*. The former was filmed in Chicago and shown at Cannes in 1967 – the debunking of some American myths, with Voight as a smiling hick who is killed and then reincarnated as Superman and Superman's terrible twin. Paramount looked at it and said no; after the success of *Midnight Cowboy* United Artists bought both films and

gave them limited showings, with the first of them rechristened *Fearless Frank*. The second was much the better, as written and directed by Paul Williams, a satire on life in a smart Long Island high school. Said 'Playboy': 'Voight limns a shrewdly funny character study of a jock-strapping football star – a stud so self-conscious about the power and glory within his Man-Tanned loins that he all but limps.'

Midnight Cowboy (69) was directed by John Schlesinger from a novel by James Leo Herlihy, with a screenplay by Waldo Salt. Schlesinger was on the point of signing Michael Sarrazin when Salt's daughter Jennifer saw Voight in Pinter's 'The Dwarfs'. (She was later described as Voight's companion; later again he had another unsuccessful marriage.) Voight's performance brought him the New York Critics' award as the year's Best Actor (but the Oscar went to John Wayne for a sentimentally acclaimed performance). The praise which greeted Voight's performance enabled him to pick his own parts: 'I wanted to be an actor,' he said. 'They wanted me to be a superstar' – so he decided to do a supporting role in *Catch-22* (70), as the almighty wheeler-dealer Milo Minderbinder. He turned down *Love Story*, and with Paul Williams again writing and directing he chose to play *The Revolutionary* – a performance which elicited the adjective 'miraculous' from

Jon Voight as the Midnight Cowboy *(69), a sad story of a smalltown hustler convinced that his body is the sole equipment he'll need to make it in New York – sad, and very successful. It made a lot of money and won a Best Picture Oscar.*

Tom Milne (in the 'MFB'), and one certainly to rank with that in *Midnight Cowboy*: he was a student of good intent and bumbling brain, looking so hard for a left-wing cause to espouse that he loses or mislays the distinction between revolution and anarchy. It was a brilliant film, perceptive and witty on such matters as the bourgeoisie and the generation-gap: its stance was presumably disliked by some critics, who allowed it to pass virtually unnoticed: on its merits it should have attracted the same (huge) public of *One Flew Over the Cuckoo's Nest* a few years later.

Its public failure gave pause to Warners, for whom Voight was making two films. They were pretty sure of *Deliverance* (72), directed by John Boorman, since the book had been a bestseller – and the film was extremely successful; he was again excellent – in an unshowy part, that of a decent urban man trying to cope with the nightmarish mysteries and mores of the backwoods. After three years of delay – an experience Voight described as 'searing' – *The All-American Boy* (73) was released, and the few who bothered might have seen Voight as a small-town boy dreaming of becoming an Olympic boxer. There were better reviews, but only slightly better business for Martin Ritt's *Conrack* (74), the tale – based on a true story – of an idealistic Southerner who decides to teach young black children. In Britain, impeccably accented, he played a German newspaperman who becomes a fanatical Nazi-hunter in *The Odessa File*, but except for him there were only unappreciative reviews for Ronald Neame's film of Frederick Forsyth's bestseller. With three failures, he was not in demand in Hollywood, but he did get Hollywood financing into Maximilian Schell's *Der Richter und Sein Henkel/The End of the Game* (75), but there were no American takers for the film itself. And *Accident of War*, made for director Peter Collinson, never seems to have been publicly shown. During these years he had acted on the West Coast in 'Romeo and Juliet', 'A Streetcar Named Desire' and 'Hamlet', and had collaborated on three unproduced screenplays; he had also acquired a reputation for being unreliable, as 'Newsweek' later put it: 'a notorious maverick who had made a series of box-office flops [and] had walked off two productions and made waves on others': one film he was scheduled to do at this time – 1976 – was Boorman's *Exorcist II: The Heretic*. His respectability as an actor was compensation for his lack of pulling power: the film was a foreseen hit, and Warner's wanted the good reviews not accorded the first *Exorcist*. At the last minute Richard Burton took over – which is as well, since the film did fail. A flop that Voight had turned down was *Lucky Lady*, in 1975.

The come-back film was *Coming Home*

Coming Home *(78) marked the come-back of Jon Voight; his performance in this earned him an Oscar.*

(78), concerning a young wife (Jane Fonda) and her involvement with two Vietnam veterans – her husband (Bruce Dern), a gung-ho Marine officer, and the gentle paraplegic (Voight) with whom she falls in love. Jerome Hellman (who had produced *Midnight Cowboy*) had assigned Voight to the role of the husband, which was the third role of importance; Voight got the bigger role only when it was turned down by Jack Nicholson, Al Pacino and Sylvester Stallone. It won him the Grand Prix at the Cannes festival, Best Actor awards from the New York critics and the Academy (an Oscar). It also reminded Hollywood of his exceptional ability to get inside the skin of a role, and it consequently brought him another 'important' role – that of *The Champ* (79), in Zeffirelli's version of an old Wallace Beery vehicle. In discussing his reasons for remaking it, Zeffirelli sneered at *The China Syndrome* and *Kramer vs Kramer*, which has a similar plot to this one – and much less sentimentality. Ricky Shroder is the child being fought over and Faye Dunaway is the ex-wife who wants him. What quality the film has is in Voight's amazing performance, creating a character where none exists in the writing – the modest, not-too-bright ex-pug living for his kid. The film took a healthy $12,615,000, but that was considerably less than *Kramer*.

On receiving his Oscar, Voight signed to do two films for Orion, co-productions with his own company. He also co-wrote *Lookin' To Get Out* and starred with Ann-Margret under Hal Ashby's direction in 1980; they play a couple who con their way to Las Vegas to make a killing at the tables. Orion and UA took a look and sold it to Lorimar and Paramount, who shelved it till late 1982, when 'Variety' noted 'Grim B.O. outlook'. And so it proved. It had cost $17 million and it took $300,000. The second film for Orion was not made. Instead, Voight and his co-producer, Robert Schaffel, took their next venture to CBS Theatrical (as they termed themselves, to differentiate from an earlier sortie into film-making): *Table for Five* (83), which was supposed to provide an 'off-beat, vulnerable part' for Voight, as a father taking his three young kids on a Mediterranean cruise. Both producers were divorced, as were the writer David Seltzer and director Robert Lieberman. The publicity claimed: 'The four of us divorcees kicked around ideas a lot and eventually it all came together as a cohesive, personal story.' Perhaps that was the trouble: it was too slight and too cute. It was also too long at over two hours, but then CBS planned to turn it into a two-and-a-half-hour special if it was a success in cinemas. It was not, and CBS cancelled a plan to star Voight in *The Raoul Wallenburg Story*.

Runaway Train (85) was directed for Cannon by Andrei Konchalovsky on top form, from a screenplay originally by Kurosawa: alone on said train are two escaped prisoners, Voight and Eric Roberts, as it moves through some unearthly scenery for some thrills unencountered in the cinema since Buster Keaton's *The General*. The man who had been Joe Buck had no trouble with the dese, dems and dose of this old lag, but few went to see him. In *Desert Bloom* Voight gave another outstanding portrait of the inarticulate – the heroine's moody stepfather, who runs a rundown gas-station, who has a gammy leg (because of a war wound) and who has a number of psychological problems. There was nothing of Joe Buck here, for this man is a nasty bit of work, if bewildered by his own fits of temper. Voight's was the only name among the cast, even if his was not the largest role. Both films failed almost completely after decent notices. It could be argued that the first film offered merely one single situation and that few cared about the subject of the second, a girl growing up in Arizona at the time of the A-bomb tests. He didn't film again till *Eternity* (90), produced and directed by Steven Paul, and written by his mother, Dorothy Koster Paul, together with Voight. This preachy melodrama was not an ideal vehicle for a comeback, especially when dealing with reincarnation – though Voight himself was on fine form as do-gooder opposing evil capitalist Armand Assante. What cannot be argued is that Voight has a greater talent than Richard Dreyfuss, Richard Gere, John Travolta and Al Pacino, all of whom found renewed success after a string of failures: not only do they lack Voight's versatility, but they do not seem such genial fellows with whom to spend a couple of screen hours.

DENZEL WASHINGTON

Denzel Washington does not care to be considered the successor to Sidney Poitier, but the bottom line is that there have been many between the two who have seen true screen stardom elude them because there are only so many roles for black actors – at least, of this skill and sensitivity. We are not talking here of those who can eat up the screen.

He was born in 1954 in Mount Vernon, New York, a comfortable suburb, to a father who was a minister and a mother who ran beauty shops. His original intention was to become a doctor, but while studying at Fordham University switched to journalism – which he also decided he did not want to do, for after acting in summer camp he concentrated on that in his last year, going on to study with the American Conservatory Theater in San Francisco. After testing the waters in Los Angeles he went to New York, where he appeared in 'Coriolanus' for Joseph Papp's Shakespeare in the Park. He then moved off-Broadway and won the Audelco Award for one of his early appearances, playing Malcolm X in 'When the Chickens Come Home to Roost', and he also appeared in 'The Mighty Gents' and 'Ceremonies in Dark Old Men'. He had already been seen to advantage in two telefilms, *Wilma* (77), as the childhood sweetheart of Wilma Rudolph (Shirley Jo Finney), who overcame physical handicaps to run in the 1960 Rome Olympics, and *Flesh and Blood* (79), as a buddy of Tom Berenger. He entered movies proper via Michael Schultz's *Carbon Copy* (81), an alliance of old hands, including producer Carter de Haven and co-writer Stanley Shapiro, who with the director had come up with a tired screenplay in which Washington walks into the office of a highly-paid executive (George Segal) and says, 'Hi Dad'. He wants a home for the summer, which is provided by Segal's snobbish wife, unaware of the boy's identity. Father and son, when all is discovered, are reduced to penury and eventually separate – but are reunited after Dad learns that the boy is a medical student. 'I saw a black,' he says. 'I didn't see a doctor. I saw a short-order cook.' It could be argued, despite that line or because of it, that Washington was being forced to play one of the old stereotyped roles, but he acquitted himself honourably in a piece that was overall patronizing.

In 1982 he began his stint in TV's superior hospital comedy series, 'St Elsewhere', as Dr Philip Chandler, but that did allow time for other work, such as another telefilm, *License to Kill* (84), a treatise on drunk-driving with James Farentino and Don Murray. That year he also appeared with Alfre Woodard in the LA production of 'Split Second' and in Norman Jewison's *A Soldier's Story*, which, as 'A Soldier's Play', had brought him an Obie award two years earlier when performing it with the Negro Ensemble Company. The star of the film was Howard E. Rollins Jr, playing an officer who arrives to investigate a murder on an army installation in Louisiana in 1944 – to the consternation of the other officers and to the delight of his fellow-blacks. One of them had been the victim, and Washington, bespectacled and articulate, was one of the suspects. Because Jewison had also made *In the Heat of the Night*, every reviewer mentioned it: this was as much a study of service life as of the tensions between the races, but although Charles Fuller had adapted his own

George Segal played a happy and successful executive whose life-style is destroyed when young Denzel Washington walks into his office and says 'Hi Dad'. Washington made his cinema debut in the film, Carbon Copy *(81), which he later refused to discuss. It's not a particularly good film, but it is certainly against racial prejudice.*

play, some force had vanished between stage and screen. Washington had another excellent supppording role in Sidney Lumet's *Power* (86) as a vicious political manipulator, and he starred in a television movie, *The George McKenna Story*, as the principal of a run-down drug-ridden LA school who so totally transformed it that he enjoyed a degree of national fame. The director was Eric Laneuville, one of Washington's co-stars in 'St Elsewhere'.

When no African or British black actor was deemed suitable for *Cry Freedom!* (87), director Richard Attenborough chose Washington to play the South African activist Steven Biko, who was murdered in police custody. Universal might have been pleased, since Washington's fame from TV might help at the box-office; Attenborough tactfully implied that it needed an actor of Washington's accomplishment to play a difficult role, but the truth perhaps was that Washington had some of the charisma needed to make Biko's following credible. Kevin Kline (q.v.) was equally sound in the other leading role, and these two performances alone should have helped this exciting, noble film to a better box-office fate. As 'St Elsewhere' finally ended, Washington was able to appear on Broadway, in 'Checkmates', and to star in a British film, as a Britisher, who after years with a crack paratroop outfit – fighting in the Falklands and Belfast – returns to a decayed inner-city housing estate and a host of problems related to it: *For Queen and Country* (89), somewhat dourly directed by Martin Stellman. Washing-

There was much criticism of Richard Attenborough when he chose Washington to portray the South American activist Steve Biko in Cry Freedom! *(87) – for he was not a big name in his native America, and there were surely British or African blacks able to play the role. So there were, agreed Attenborough, but he had been unable to find one with the necessary charisma.*

Washington co-starred with Bob Hoskins in *Heart Condition* (90), which – like *Carbon Copy*, which he refuses to discuss – examines racial prejudice in the form of comedy, when his reincarnation makes havoc for a bigot, Hoskins. He had become associated with too many serious pictures and felt this one might do its job, once he had made known his objection to aspects of the script: 'I suggest changes on all my films,' he said significantly, 'I'm getting braver with every film.' He should have made a few suggestions to Spike Lee, a notably uneven (black) writer-director, whose *Mo' Better Blues* was one of his weaker efforts; Lee also appeared in it, having cast Washington as a jazz musician who takes his art too seriously. Washington turned down *Love Field* with Michelle Pfeiffer, to appear in *Mississippi Masala* with Sarita Choudhury, directed by Mira Nair, the American-domiciled Indian-born director of *Salaam Bombay*. Then he is due to appear in *Disappearing Acts* with Whitney Huston. He is married with two children.

SIGOURNEY WEAVER

'I think when I see an actress performing in a film and it seems to be directed specifically at men then that strikes me as less inspiring than women who are acting for themselves, or even for other women,' says Sigourney Weaver. 'That's why I admire great Europeans like Garbo and Dietrich who seem to combine their intelligence with their bodily allure so well, and not feel a problem, seem almost immune to the effect they're having. We seem less comfortable. Very beautiful American actresses, say someone like Candy Bergen, are prone to pooh-poohing any suggestions that they *even* arouse men.' These observations bear witness to the 'intelligence' mentioned in most profiles of and interviews with the lady, and if she keeps these in a press-book she will find ample evidence of her own effect on men.

She was christened Susan, but took the name 'Sigourney' from 'The Great Gatsby', when she was in her teens, as more suited to the image she wanted to project. For there are strong show-business antecedents: her father is Pat Weaver, former NBC president, and her mother is the English-born actress, Elizabeth Inglis. Susan was born in New York City in 1949. She read English at Stanford University till she dropped out to work in an Israeli kibbutz, after which she studied drama at Yale (where she appeared in the chorus of 'The Frogs' with Meryl Streep). During the first of these educational experiences she is

ton was then *The Mighty Quinn*, which had started out as *Finding Maubee* with Robert Towsend in his role. After reading the notices, Towsend must have been glad that he was well out of it, for this was a sluggish murder mystery, without suspense. A pity, since there were some bright ideas in this tale of a moralistic Caribbean chief of police, Quinn, looking for a boyhood chum who is now the island's most notorious figure and perhaps a murderer. The good film Washington deserved – and needed – was *Glory*, directed by Edward Zwick with Matthew Broderick as the commander of a black regiment during the Civil War. It also brought Washington a Best Supporting Oscar for his fine performance as the runaway slave who is unjustly whipped for desertion. Morgan Freeman gave an equally powerful performance as a fellow-soldier, and was one of Washington's rivals for the Oscar, for his performance in *Driving Miss Daisy*.

supposed to have lived in a tree-house with a boyfriend and to have dressed in elf-outfits knitted by herself on a machine; during the second, one tutor defended her by saying, 'You don't get rid of a Greek goddess because she doesn't dress well.' Her height (5 feet 11 inches) was one reason for so many rejections when she auditioned for roles; she was advised to try Bloomingdales instead – and indeed was wondering whether she would make it as a bank-teller when she was taken on as understudy for another tall actress, Ingrid Bergman, in 'The Constant Wife' (74). Her father had given her a long list of contacts, but these were of little help. Already she had appeared very much off-Broadway in 'Titanic', in 'Gemini' by Albert Innaurato, whom she had known at Yale, and in 'Das Lusitania Songspiel', a Brecht parody improvised with Christopher Durang, another fellow-student. Durang wrote a play for her, 'A History of the American Film', but she was turned down for it: it is a truly terrible play, but this particular rejection she took hard. She did find work in a television soap opera, 'Somerset', and she auditioned for a small role in *Annie Hall* (77), which she relinquished for a stage part: Woody Allen insisted that she do at least a walk-on, but 'Unless you know my raincoat, you'll miss me.'

Television again drew her away from experimental off-Broadway plays and 'lousy' notices, in the form of an eight-part series, 'The Best of Families', about aristocratic women; and it was not long after that that she received the script of *Alien* (79), to be directed by Ridley Scott. The film's producers had seen her in a play and got in touch with her: 'The script seemed like an old chestnut, so I put on some very high-heeled boots – after all, who cares if I looked like Jackie Onassis in space – and went along to read for the part.' The publicity line has it that such actresses as Jane Fonda and Faye Dunaway had been considered, and that Weaver was interviewed for the role only two weeks before shooting was to begin: what was missing was the information that an SF horror movie was unlikely to attract a name actress. The role, after all, was that of an astronaut, one of several attacked in their spacecraft by a mysterious force which, when seen, is stomach-churning (or meant to be). Weaver was really too good for the role, but rather stilted in one that might have been meant for her, a television reporter from a cultured background in Peter Yates's *Eyewitness* (81) aka *The Janitor*, with William Hurt. Between the two films, a friend of her father, Hume Cronyn, had introduced her to a powerful agent, Sam Cohn of ICM. He could not help when she was turned down for other roles

because of her height – nor, in the case of *Urban Cowboy*, because she was too old. She turned down a chance to co-star with Luciano Pavarotti in *Yes, Giorgio* because she refused to appear only as an accessory to the male lead (and, in doing so, avoided appearing in one of the greatest flops in movie history). And Cohn advised her to turn down *Body Heat* because of the sex scenes required by the script.

Her third film – and her third for 20th-Century-Fox – should have been *Lone Star*, based on a play by actor-playwright James McClure, who had been her companion since they had appeared together off-Broadway in 'New Jerusalem' in 1979; but 20th cancelled the project three weeks before shooting was due to start. Instead she went to the Far East to play an attaché at the British Embassy in Peter Weir's *The Year of Living Dangerously* (82), opposite Mel Gibson. She said later: 'It was a happy experience. Mel Gibson was quite happy for me to wear four-inch heels if I wanted, and Peter Weir gave me a sense of film I hadn't had before. He also indicated that I have some kind of strength on screen.' Yes, and ease as well, but she was not so interesting again in *The Deal of the Century* (83), involved with Chevy Chase, as the widow of a would-be weapons merchant. It was her introduction to screen comedy, but did not reflect any great strengths in that direction. She set her sights on the role of Jack Nicholson's wife in Martin Ritt's *Road House*, but it went to Diane Keaton – till the project was cancelled. Had she done it, Weaver might have lost out on a gigantic box-office hit, *Ghostbusters* (84), in which she was a preppy classical musician living in Central Park West, where eggs come popping out of their shells to fry of their own volition on the counter-top. Her affair with McClure had broken up not long after she had appeared in 'Old Times' in Williamstown, Mass., in 1981, when it was directed by Jim Simpson. She and Simpson were married in 1984, and two years later he directed her as Portia in an off-Broadway production of 'The Merchant of Venice'. After noting a Broadway appearance with William Hurt in 'Hurlyburly' during this period, we find her filming more frequently, encouraged by her husband.

She also admitted that she enjoyed making her movies in bunches, so that if one failed, another might be a hit. She disliked *Une Femme ou Deux* (85), with Gérard Depardieu, and later would refer to it only as 'that French film'. She was not at first too happy about a sequel, *Aliens* (86), but 20th thought her essential – or, if you like, unavoidable, since most of the other astronauts had been killed off. However, she spoke warmly of

Sigourney Weaver when she was having trouble with the supernatural and decided to call in the Ghostbusters (84). What with multiplying ghostbusters and aliens, she hasn't had too many chances to show her skills in more, er, important dramas.

James Cameron, who directed, and later said that she enjoyed the responsibility of carrying it. Conversely, she had high hopes for *Half Moon Street* because she liked the Paul Theroux novel on which it was based. It featured her as an American academic down on her luck in London who finds the world's oldest profession is an answer to her problems; she also finds a high-ranking diplomat (Michael Caine) and a nest of spies. The result she found 'a great disappointment because Bob Swaim, the director, allowed himself to lose control of the film. He didn't fight for the original; he changed my character into this humourless looker with brains that had nothing to do with my idea [of her and the book]'. She also noted that Swaim had had to argue with the backers, and that a good producer could have prevented him from dissipating his energy in that way.

Gorillas in the Mist (88) was a co-production between Warners and Universal, partly because both were preparing projects on the same subject, and partly because filming in isolated parts of Africa was likely to prove expensive – and, in fact, the film cost $22 million. The title is taken from the memoir by Dian Fossey, who left her native America to study the threatened gorilla species of central Africa. In the event she became their guardian, making enemies galore among local traders and the natives who sell to them. She did not discourage the view that she was a witch, and by the time the colony of apes had grown, she had become obsessive: when one is killed she goes berserk, and in 1985 she was murdered, with no one arrested for the crime. The producers' first choice was Jessica Lange, who was pregnant, but they had little difficulty in deciding which leading actress could project the required strength and determination: Weaver. They gave her a brief and unconvincing romance with a photographer (Bryan Brown) and did no more than suggest she became a bit cranky. Michael Apted did a fine job of directing, for absorbing but not outstanding results. Healthy reviews helped it to a gross of $12 million. Among them: 'Sigourney Weaver's best and boldest role. She is incandescent' (Peter Travers, 'People' magazine); 'Sigourney Weaver's towering performance is awesome. It's a stunning piece of work' (Philip Wuntch, 'Dallas Morning News'). She followed with what amounted to a supporting role in *Working Girl*, in which Melanie Griffith would emulate her in order to get a man (Harrison Ford) and get ahead – something Griffith can do, for Weaver is in hospital after a skiing accident. But for Weaver this was a clever career move – all-class in the first part and all-bitch after discovering Griffith's duplicity. Less sympathetic than Melanie Griffith, an enchanting heroine, you remembered her equally.

Ghostbusters II (89) was the expected sequel. Said co-star Bill Murray: 'She's a good actress and everything, but she works in Method and we don't. I'd literally pick her upside-down before every take, tickle her, do anything to shake her body up so that she'd be loose. You'd see her mind working, see *this huge skull* working and I'd go, oh God, here's trouble! With comedy that's deadly. She's very, very considerate of the crew . . . She has a very strong will.' She said she was doing the piece 'as a tribute to the precious innocence of Bill Murray, a performer who is fresh and loose in a way most of us could never be. Yesterday for some reason he kept spitting hairballs at me on the set, like a cat would. The director had to tell him to stop doing that, but Bill thinks I'm too stiff and is continually freaking me out on the set . . . I'm not doing [it] for the dramatic challenge, that's for sure; in fact I don't think the producers wanted me to play the part all over again at all. But it's a fun thing to do; kids love it.' Her reputed fee was $1 million. She was to have done *The Handmaid's Tale*, but was pregnant, ceding her role to Natasha Richardson. Another sequel, *Aliens III* (91), was offered, and she agreed to do it if she could work on the script. In the meantime, in 1990, she and several other leading participants in *Aliens* sued 20th Century-Fox for their percentage of the profits; hers, at 10 per cent, was higher than the other claimants.

ROBIN WILLIAMS

Robin Williams is not the only one to be suprised that his film career was so long getting off the ground. He had made a considerable reputation as an out-of-synch, off-the-wall stand-up comedian. In 1986 he said, 'I guess if I'd listened to my agents and managers, who keep saying I should play someone like myself, by now I'd have a built-in audience.' In 1987 he did do so, and the rest is history.

He was born in Chicago in 1952, the son of an executive of the Ford Motor Company. The family travelled a lot when he was a child and as a consequence he seldom had friends for long: loneliness, he has said, caused him to make up conversations with imaginary characters. While living in Marin County he entered Claremont Men's College to study political science; he discovered that he preferred acting and transferred to the Juilliard School in New York on full scholarship. He stayed three years without responding too well; but it was when he failed to get an acting job in San Francisco that he started doing stand-up comedy. In Los Angeles he did so at the Comedy Store, while studying the 'art' of it with Harvey Lembeck. Larry Brezner saw him at the workshop and became his manager, getting him a job in the unsuccessful revival of Rowan and Martin's 'Laugh-In' (76). He also got him an engagement to guest-star as the extraterrestrial misfit, Mork, in one episode of 'Happy Days' – and that was so well received that Williams was hired for a series, 'Mork and Mindy'.

He made his film debut in a star role, not perhaps because he was an exceptional talent, but because that role was not easy to cast, the sour-tempered braggart sailor of the animated cartoons, *Popeye* (80). As producers of the original cartoons, Paramount owned the rights, and because the public was responding to *Superman* and other 'ephemera' of that period the company decided to give Popeye another whirl – live-action this time. It hired a prestigious director and writer, Robert Altman and Jules Feiffer respectively, and for its expertise in this field, they invited Disney to co-produce. The whole venture was misconceived, but the public liked it well enough to return $24,600,000 on a $20 million investment. Shelley Duvall played Olive Oyl. The film did nothing for Williams, who was off the screen till *The World According to Garp* (82) which, as directed by George Roy Hill, at least reduced the excesses of John Irving's pseudo-Günter Grass novel. It emerged – surprisingly, given the source – as a civilized entertainment, with Williams giving a warm, unpretentious performance as Garp, the kindly, well-meaning, ordinary guy coping with the eccentricities of his mother (Glenn Close) and, among others, a transvestite friend (John Lithgow). It cost $17 million and took a respectable $14,700,000, but it did nothing to establish Williams as a movie man. Nor did Michael Ritchie's *The Survivors* (83), who were an enthusiastic him and a tired Walter Matthau, in danger of their lives after

Robin Williams in The World According to Garp *(82), one of several films he made which demonstrated his attractive personality and sense of humour, but which were not in themselves attractive enough to draw a large public.*

True stardom, for Williams, had to wait till Good Morning, Vietnam *(87), and it came with a vengeance – doubtless because he was playing someone, a disc-jockey in fact, who was able to speak with the authentic Williams voice, that is, incorporating the sort of material he used in his stage act.*

identifying a crook. This smudged satire on a gun-crazy society – Ritchie used to be much sharper – cost $14 million and returned only half of that sum in the domestic market; as it went direct to video in most foreign outlets little more came in. Williams was a bushy-bearded Russian musician who defects in Paul Mazursky's *Moscow on the Hudson* (84), which did a nice $12,300,000 – but it was not too nice, since it had cost $13 million. Since his performance was the film's chief merit, it could be said that he was at last on his way.

Well, no. The next three were lost, almost without trace: Roger Spottiswoode's *The Best of Times* (86), with Kurt Russell, and Williams bespectacled as a bank vice-president intent on rewriting history by restaging a football game which he flubbed some years before; *Seize the Day*, Saul Bellow's novel filmed for television, in which he is a salesman in the 50s up to his neck in a mid-life crisis after his marriage has come apart; and *Club Paradise*, as a Chicago fireman staying there, in the Caribbean, in this ramshackle comedy. It cost $15 million and returned only $6,900,000. And then came *Good Morning, Vietnam* (87). If that was not the breakthrough, Williams said himself, they were making an expensive travel film. Ben Moses, a TV producer, had written a script based on an army disc-jockey, Adrian Cronauer, who broke every rule in the book. Brezner com-

missioned a new screenplay from Mitch Markowitz that would incorporate much of Williams's stage act; and Barry Levinson, for once not directing one of his own scripts, let Williams have his head. During this time the project left Paramount, which wanted a straight comedy, 'Animal House in Vietnam', for Disney, which saw its investment of $14 million make a return of $58,100,000. Williams, more manic and much further out than the real Cronauer, offered a very festival of himself, spieling on before the mike, moving from one-liners to impersonation to speculation and reflection, on matters from Nixon to lesbians to *The Wizard of Oz*. Around him was a simple-minded plot about why the Americans should not be in Vietnam, but that didn't matter.

The world fell in love with Williams, and so did Disney. *Dead Poets Society* (89) was to have been directed by Jeff Kanew, who wanted Alec Baldwin or Liam Neeson for the lead. Disney offered it to Dustin Hoffman, who demanded one rewrite too many. Williams accepted the leading role, that of a teacher with unorthodox methods: '*Carpe diem*, lads! Seize the day. Make your lives extraordinary!' When director Peter Weir came aboard, they agreed that a teacher should not be a performer, but at the same time Weir simply 'loaded the camera and let him take over. It was crazy and chaotic and very, very funny.' He was also able to get from Williams something, he said, that he hadn't shown on screen since *Garp*, 'the openness and confidence of someone with nothing to lose'. The reviews were not wholly favourable, but the film brought in $38 million in the US on a $20 million budget; it was a big hit the world over – and in France, for instance, one of the most successful American films in years.

The image presented by Williams in these two films, short-haired and healthy, is not entirely consistent with the shambling, scruffy one of his 'act'. This has had several airings, growing the while, on record and on television. When HBO televised 'On Location: Robin Williams – An Evening at the Met' in 1986, John Leonard in 'New York' magazine quoted Norman Mailer on Nixon, 'He walks like a puppet more curious than most human beings, for all the strings are pulled by a hand within his own head' – which, he said, was true of Williams, who '*does* jerk around while the hand in the head thinks funny things . . . He needs an audience, like a huge therapy group, to make him real. In this he resembles Mailer more than Nixon: shaman, stuntman, Quixotic, paranoid, exorcist, gyroscope, mainlining on contradictions. Unlike Mailer and Nixon, of course, he has a sense of humour. It's ferocious.'

By his own admission Williams started this period partying, womanizing and taking drugs; but he gave up drugs after the death of John Belushi (he was one of the last people to see him) and because of a sense of responsibility towards his son. In his stage act he says, 'Cocaine, wooh. What a wonderful drug. Anything that makes you paranoid or impotent, give me more of that.' His marriage broke up in 1986 and he now lives with Marsha Garces. 'Right now I'm moving through my personal life like a haemophiliac in a razor factory,' he observed. They live near San Francisco and not in Los Angeles,

After Good Morning, Vietnam, Dead Poets Society *(89) provided Williams with a double-whammy, a second international hit. In France, for instance, its takings exceeded those of any American film for as long as most young cinemagoers could remember.*

because 'the trouble with the place is that if you don't have people there that will grind you down, then you just start whirling.'

In 1989 he and Steve Martin, with F. Murray Abraham, did a sold-out limited run of 'Waiting for Godot' in New York. *Cadillac Man* (90), directed by Roger Donaldson, found him as a smarmy, callous womanizing car salesman, and despite poor notices it attracted over $27 million within its first three months of release. The general consensus was that it was fine as long as it kept Williams front and centre, but fell off with the introduction of his co-star, Tim Robbins, a jealous husband threatening death and destruction because of his philandering. Next along: *Awakenings*, (91) with Robert De Niro and *The Fisher King* with Jeff Bridges. There is probably no more sought-after actor in Hollywood, and other future movies may include *Good Morning Chicago*, a life of Lech Walesa, a sequel to *Moscow on the Hudson* in which Williams returns to the Russian capital and a stint as the villain opposite Batman. Also: Barry Levinson's *Toys* and *Hook*, with Dustin Hoffman, as the grandson of Peter Pan.

BRUCE WILLIS

There ought to be something to explain the fever surrounding this capable but not very prepossessing actor, since his short film career quickly made him a millionaire. He is readily available to the press and he has made a couple of very successful films, but there is something odd about the whole shebang: for instance, his is the baby's voice in *Look Who's Talking*, a mediocre film which does not depend on that fact, other than as a gimmick. It was a big success, but the voice was not individual enough – nor was it given much in the way of humour to say – and yet there can barely be anyone in the cinemagoing world who does not know who is doing the talking.

He was born in Germany in 1955 to a soldier who had married a local girl. He was brought up in New Jersey, where his father worked as a mechanic, and he became a security guard, earning four dollars an hour. His first experience in show business was playing harmonica with a band called Loose Goose, about which time he attended Montclair State College, where he appeared in 'Cat on a Hot Tin Roof'. He managed to get a small part in an off-Broadway play, 'Heaven and Earth' (77), but was more lucratively employed tending bar in a nightclub, Kamikaze, and modelling Levi's 501 jeans in TV commercials. In 1979 he found a job in a play,

'Railroad Bill', which required one of the cast to play a harmonica; he played five other characters as well. And he found brief appearances in three movies made in New York, *The First Deadly Sin* (80), *Prince of the City* (81) and *The Verdict* (82). In the first of these he can be recognized passing Frank Sinatra in a restaurant doorway, but he was deleted from the final print of the other two. There were also small roles in 'Hart to Hart' and 'Miami Vice'. In 1984 he took over the important role of Eddie for the last hundred performances of Sam Shepard's 'Fool for Love', which brought him Triad Artists as his agents. They arranged for him to fly to Los Angeles to audition for the role of Madonna's boyfriend in *Desperately Seeking Susan*. He was unsuccessful, but while there also auditioned for a series, 'Moonlighting': and thus it came to be. He co-starred with a one-time Hollywood name, Cybill Shepherd, as his glamorous partner in this detective series, smirking and batting one-liners at each other. Willis's brusque self-confidence seemed as far inferior to Tom Selleck as Selleck himself is to Clark Gable. The subtext to each week's mystery story was that although they bitched each other and quarrelled, they were sexually attracted: eventually they became lovers and much of the zip went out of the series. Ms Shepherd was increasingly at odds with its creator, Glenn Gordon Caron, and when ABC supported her instead of him, he left. The atmosphere after that, Willis admitted, was apathetic, with the stars' absence from occasional episodes leading to poor ratings. He was not sorry when ABC decided to cancel after the fourth season.

The division between movie stars and television stars, he also said, was almost unbridgeable, but the president of Tri-Star, Jeff Sagansky, decided that he was a cinch for the big screen: 'We went after him hard. What sets Willis apart from most TV actors is that he has a quality of danger and intensity – it's something all great movie stars possess.' Not only that: they were prepared to pay him $3 million a picture. They did not care to film *Bandits*, the Elmore Leonard novel which he had optioned, reportedly for $500,000. More probably that would have been the *eventual* price, but despite the fact that 'every studio in town wants to produce it', none did so, either during the period of Willis's option or since. Its plot, concerning an ex-con and IRA money meant for the Contras in Nicaragua, would presumably have capitalized on Willis's 'qualities of danger and intensity', but Tri-Star and writer-director Blake Edwards decided to go for that rather doubtful comedic streak that Willis had exhibited in his battles with Ms Shepherd. 'Blake is a master of sophisticated

Bruce Willis in action. Die Hard *(88) and* Die Hard 2 *(90). The same thing really, but more people turned up for the second episode, thus ensuring* Die Hard 3. *As one industry wag put it, the first was a re-vamp of* The Towering Inferno, *the second of* Airport, *so the third will have to be a new version of* Beyond the Posiedon Adventure.

comedy,' said Willis, 'and that's what we do on the TV series.' Alas, neither the series nor *Blind Date* (87) bears out this contention, and although Willis 'had a ball working with Blake', that was not an experience shared by the audience as they watched a sober financial analyst (him) cope with an inebriated bimbette (Kim Basinger). Although the film was widely reported to be a failure, a return of $15 million (on an $18 million investment) means that quite a lot of people left their television sets to see it.

Certainly, with a bestselling Motown record, 'The Return of Bruno' (singing, not playing the harmonica; Bruno is what his mates call him), auspices were good for another comedy for Edwards and Tri-Star, *Sunset* (88), a title which referred to Hollywood's boulevard. In this wheeze James Garner played Wyatt Earp and Willis was Tom Mix, the Western star of the Silents, noted for his physical prowess and natty outfits. It was ill-advised casting, since Willis lacked both Mix's looks and his charisma. Garner took the notices, but few took themselves to the film, which returned only $2 million of its $19 million cost. It was widely reported that the industry scoffed when 20th Century-Fox offered Willis $5 million for *Die Hard*, sending the budget soaring to $28 million. 20th needed a success more than somewhat, for *Cocoon* had been its only really big one since *Return of the Jedi* in 1983, and *Die Hard* looked as if it might well provide one, with its spectacular action – a combination of the one-of-a-kind *The Towering*

Inferno and that best-of-its-kind, *Dog Day Afternoon*. Willis played a New York cop who arrives in LA at Christmas to visit his estranged wife (Bonnie Bedelia), to find her and the staff of the Nakatomi Corporation held hostage in a deserted skyscraper by terrorists intent on stealing $600 million in bonds. Willis, in hiding for most of the time, has to have Superman-ish powers of resource and strength to outwit them, not to mention being able to walk sockless over a floor of broken glass – cheap, but effective. Although the screenplay is credited to Jeb Stuart and Steven E. de Souza, from a novel by Roderick Thorpe, the result gives the impression of having been written by a committee; but directed by John McTiernan, the thrills are undeniable, with pluses in two outstanding villains – Alan Rickman (the mastermind) and Alexander Godunov (his psychopathic henchman). Willis proved to have the right determined, gritty quality – easy to believe in him as a nose-to-the-grindstone cop – and 20th-Century-Fox breathed more freely as the film proceeded to bring in $36 million. Willis's name had been deliberately omitted from the initial ads on the grounds of his being a liability, but when the studio now offered him $8 million for a sequel, no one was any longer laughing.

According to the director, Norman Jewison, Willis did not get an astronomical sum for *In Country* (89), since they were trying to keep the budget to $14 million (it ended up at $18 million), and in the actor's own words, 'It's a story I wanted to be part of . . . It's about the recovery of this nation from the Vietnam War.' The piece, set in a small Kentucky town, tells of a girl (Emily Lloyd) who, curious about her father's death in the war, turns to her uncle, another veteran, shell-shocked and cynical. Willis, bearded and sad-eyed, was far from the sleazy sexiness of his private eye in 'Moonlighting'. The film took only $1,600,000 at the box-office, and if Willis was on a percentage he would have to look instead to *Look Who's Talking*, which was expected to bring him – on a minute profit participation – between $8 and 10 million. The sequel of his great success was at one point to have been called *Die Harder*, but with even greater originality they came up with *Die Hard 2* (dubbed 'Die Harder') (90), and since we are on statistics, it cost $62 million, an increase over its original budget of $40 million. The director this time was Renny Harlin, a Finn with little Hollywood experience, with a screenplay by de Souza and Doug Richard-Richardson which pushed Thorpe's hero into the events of a different novel altogether, '58 Minutes' by Walter Wager. Those events concern terrorists planning to seize Dulles Airport to free a foreign dictator (Franco Nero), and the refusal of the authorities to believe Willis when he tells them, meaning that he has to act alone. 'Willis has become a convincing action star but often flounders in the film's softer moments,' said 'Variety', 'When he has to bellow his wife's name near the end it sounds like a bad parody of *A Streetcar Named Desire*, producing one of the film's few unintentional chuckles.' It turned out to be one of the most attractive action films in the summer market, taking $105 million in its first 50 days in release (beaten only by *Total Recall*).

Willis's salary goes down to $5 million on *The Bonfire of the Vanities*, partly because it's a prestige production and partly because that is the sum being paid to the top-billed Tom Hanks; Melanie Griffith is getting $3 million. After that we shall see *Mortal Thoughts* co-starring Demi Moore, whom Willis married in 1987, directed by Alan Rudolph (who took over when Claude Kerven left after 'creative differences'); and *Hudson Hawke* (91) with Andie McDowell (who replaced Isabelle Adjani, who replaced Isabella Rossellini after Adjani's Oscar nomination for *Camille Claudel* had supposedly made her a bigger 'name' in the American market). This went well over budget during production, the second Willis-Joel Silver film to do so (Silver was one of the producers of Die Hard 2). After that: *Billy Bathgate* with Dustin Hoffman, then *The Last Boy Scout*.

DEBRA WINGER

She is vibrant and determined. She has a sense of humour. And she has inspired one of the neatest recent tributes from a critic to a star: 'Most big-name actresses in Hollywood these days either look like they're stuck in some other decade (Keaton) or they look like, well, big-name actresses (Streep). Winger is someone who is alive in 1988, the girl down the hall from yours. She's for real' (Louis Menand, reviewing *Betrayed* in New York's 'Seven Days' magazine).

She was born in 1957 in Cleveland, Ohio, into a Hungarian-Jewish orthodox family, the proprietor of the Winger Brothers Meat Company. The Wingers moved to Los Angeles, and after graduating at the age of fifteen she took the money she had saved working as a waitress and went to Israel, where she worked on a kibbutz and joined the army. At nineteen she was paralysed after a fall sustained while working as a teenage troll at Magic Mountain amusement park, with the threat of remaining blind and crippled throughout her life. She vowed that if she recovered she would become an actress, and did so with apparent ease – in a police documentary demonstrating the sexual perils of hitch-hiking, which led in turn to commercials and small parts in television, including most notably that of Lynda Carter's sister in the series, 'Wonder Woman'. Miss Carter was, chronologically, the first of many colleagues to earn Winger's contempt: she 'was just a mannequin – only concerned with the way she looked and the fact that I wouldn't wear the same eye make-up as she did. The whole thing was a nightmare.' She quit after two episodes, despite a six-year contract: the producers demanded that she honour it, and her lawyers got her out of it only because the show switched networks.

Meanwhile, she was cast in a sleazy movie, *Slumber Party '57* (77) as one of a group of girls relating their sexual exploits in flashback. This led to a supporting role in a telemovie, *Special Olympics* (78), in which Charles Durning played a widower trying to keep his family together. *French Postcards* (79) was a sort of *American Graffiti* abroad (the two films shared the same writers) about a group of students vacationing in France. Director James Bridges then cast her opposite John Travolta in *Urban Cowboy* (80), as the hardworking girl he marries after meeting her in a bar. She said later: 'I loved it. It was the opening of everything for me because of the way Jim Bridges worked: the freedom, the collaboration, the end product. It was a slice of life, that movie. I'm real proud of it.' She was called upon to replace Raquel Welch in the arty-misplaced *Cannery Row* (82) with Nick Nolte, which might look like desperation, for it is hard to think of two actresses less alike; but it is also difficult to imagine why the producers felt that Welch could bring any conviction to the world of John Steinbeck. Winger was much better casting as the drifter-hooker, but few people saw the film. The reverse is true of *An Officer and a Gentleman*, in which she was a factory worker aspiring to marry one of them, Richard Gere. He she found 'a brick wall. He keeps saying nice things about me, and I don't know the man so I shouldn't say mean things about him, but [the film] was a real bad time for all of us. We did whatever we had to do to survive. The producer was the only living person I had contact with, and he was a real pig.' The director, Taylor Hackford, she added, was 'an animal'.

She was in another big success, James L. Brooks's *Terms of Endearment* (83), as Shirley MacLaine's daughter who dies of cancer. In the film they didn't like each other too much, a situation repeated off the set; when

Debra Winger in her two most successful movies to date, An Officer and a Gentleman *(81) and* Legal Eagles *(86). Her habit of speaking her mind has not endeared her to many in an industry which cannot afford to ignore her talent for tearing up the screen.*

MacLaine won her Oscar, her acceptance speech referred to Winger's 'turbulent brilliance'. But she rapped with co-star Jack Nicholson, who said of her: 'She's real smart, very dedicated, extremely resourceful about her work. You put up with her contentiousness because there is always something at the bottom. You get something you wouldn't get unless you took the trip with her. The girl's got boom.' She herself admitted: 'I do admit to being challenging, but it's always for the work, it's never personal. I will walk out on a scene if it's all lit and ready to go but it's not happening. Just because we're on schedule is no reason to shoot bad acting. Someone once said to me, "You're inconsiderate." And I said, "Inconsiderate? Bad acting is the ultimate inconsideration." It's a collective slap to a million faces at the same time.'

Certainly Bridges was anxious to work with her again, and *Mike's Murder* (84) had started out as a vehicle to showcase her abilities, playing a mousy bank-teller who falls heavily for a sexy lug – and who steps out of character to investigate his killing in some of the seedier joints of LA. It had been filmed two years earlier and in the meantime had been much tampered with: but to little avail, for it went quickly to video in its country of origin and was unseen in many others. She was not happily cast, but she was more assured and appealing than she had yet been in *Legal Eagles* (86), as defence lawyer for a client (Darryl Hannah) who is being prosecuted by assistant DA Robert Redford. They were not Hepburn and Tracy, but she eyed him always with a yen, gently underplaying. Again she didn't care for the director, Ivan Reitman, nor the experience: 'I don't regret doing it, but I don't think it stands on its own against good films. It was a nightmare to make. Shooting was supposed to be ten weeks, and it went on for four months. And it was fat – almost $40 million – and, politically, I'm opposed to that kind of money unless it's an epic. I took my salary and left.' The film had been prepared for Dustin Hoffman and Bill Murray, and when she accepted it it was to play Murray's role, with a sex-change; later she discovered that she, Reitman and Redford had been sold to Universal as a package, which caused her to rebel because she 'started to feel like commerce instead of an artist'. The agency was CAA, the most powerful in Hollywood, but she left only temporarily. A year later the producer Martin Ransihoff wanted to get her, Dan Aykroyd and Bill Murray as a package for *Switching Channels*, but none of them was interested and CAA passed on supplying replacements because Universal had been burned with *Legal Eagles*, which took only $27,700,000 and thus was red in the ledger books.

Winger's talent seemed to grow with each movie, and she was especially effective in Bob Rafelson's *Black Widow* (87) as an employee of the justice department who goes sleuthing when she connects a series of murders to the widow (Theresa Russell) of their victims. The film has her as one of the boys, a slob who would love to be as chic as her prey, if she only knew how. The film took in a very decent $11,500,000. She was one of several guest stars in Alan Rudolph's uncharacteristic *Made in Heaven*, playing a male angel. The stars were Kelly McGillis and Timothy Hutton, to whom Winger was then married (they had lived together before tying the knot in 1985, but separated in 1989).

In Costa-Gavras's *Betrayed* (88) Winger played another of her strong ladies, an undercover cop who sleeps with the handsome Fascist (Tom Berenger) on whom she is trying to pin a rather nasty racial murder. Maybe they were thinking of *Vertigo*, in which another cop was sexually drawn to his victim, but there were indeed a number of inconsistencies in Joe Eszterhas's script, which is why this one does not rank with the director's best films. Winger missed Brooks's *Broadcast News* because she was pregnant, as well as *Postcards From the Edge*, which was postponed. She returned to the screen in a real bummer, *Everybody Wins* (90), in which she was a schizoid who turns out to have been a notorious floozie. Among the other losers were Nolte and Arthur Miller, whose screenplay emerged under Karel Reisz's direction as incredibly old-fashioned; the result, said 'Variety', was 'virtually unreleasable'. Matters did not improve with *The Sheltering Sky*, though it co-stars John Malkovich and is based on Paul Bowles's superb novel of an American couple adrift in North Africa: the director in this case is Bernardo Bertolucci, who is not, alas, the one this material deserves.

JAMES WOODS

Said James Woods, contemplating his twentieth year as an actor: 'The risk now is to invest my time and energy in real life and not get swamped by attaining the fantasy I always wanted – being a big movie star.' He said this to Aljean Harmetz of the 'New York Times', who reported that he was unusual among today's players in not having a business manager. The lesson would seem to be that without a business manager or conventional good looks it takes twenty years, or almost, to become a star. He may feel that that's better late than never, and so may we. There are too few actors of his intensity and versatility.

He was born in Ogden, Utah, in 1947, the son of a US army officer, and of Irish Catholic stock on his mother's side. For a while he saw life from married quarters in various states till the family settled in Warwick, Rhode Island, where he attended high school. A friend persuaded him to try out for the school production of 'The Little Foxes', and he made his debut with his arm in a sling (because of an accident) and grey hair and moustache. Nominated to the Air Force Academy because he had the highest test-scores in Rhode Island, he went instead on full scholarship to study political science at the Massachusetts Institute of Technology in Boston, where, while studying, he managed to participate in thirty local productions. During his last semester he quit, because, 'It dawned on me, wouldn't it be great to do something you love for the rest of your life?' He arrived in New York in 1968 and almost immediately got a job in the chorus line of 'South Pacific', alongside John Savage. He was not there for long, but on Broadway in 'Borstal Boy', which was followed by the role of Indian bearer in 'Conduct Unbecoming'. He auditioned for a third British play, 'Saved', before its director, Alan Schneider, who was looking for someone to take over the lead. It brought him three awards, including an Obie and the Clarence Derwent Award for Most Promising Actor. He also appeared in 'The Trial of the Catonsville Nine' (71), 'Moonchildren' (72), 'Green Julia' and Jean Kerr's 'Finishing Touches' (73). In 1971 he appeared on a Hallmark Hall of Fame presentation with Joanne Woodward, 'All the Way Home'.

He made his film debut in *The Visitors* (72), a little-known film made by a well-known director, Elia Kazan. Kazan, who loved film-making but loathed Hollywood, decided to go for a low-budget – $175,000 – effort with minimum union involvement. He shot in 16mm in and around his own Connecticut home (which housed many of the participants during filming) with his son Chris as scenarist and co-producer. The subject, taken from a newspaper item, concerned two Vietnam veterans who turn up at the home of a former buddy who had given evidence against them when charged with raping and killing a native girl. Kazan had 'found the joy of film-making again', but the reaction to it was patchy, and United Artists, which had it for distribution, did not feel inclined to push it. It did not play in many markets, and Woods, as one of the guilty GIs, was one of the few young actors not to benefit from his association with one of the cinema's premier talents. However, he learnt this from Kazan: 'You must love every character you play and find something about

him that you care about.' His roles in movies gave him little footage in which to experience this: *Footsteps*, starring Richard Crenna as a football coach, as a reporter; *A Great American Tragedy*, also for television, with George Kennedy as a man on the dole; *The Way We Were* (73), as Barbra Streisand's college boyfriend; *Night Moves* (75), as a movie stuntman, ex-boyfriend of the girl whose whereabouts Gene Hackman has to discover; and two more for TV, *Foster and Laurie*, who were Perry King and Dorian Harewood as New York cops, as a drug addict; and *F. Scott Fitzgerald in Hollywood* (76), with Tuesday Weld and Jason Miller.

Alex and the Gypsy provided him with his first good movie role since the Kazan film, as Jack Lemmon's neurotic bail-bondsman assistant, and he was well-noticed as the assistant DA in a TV movie with Bette Davis, *The Disappearance of Aimée*. He was an army captain in *Raid on Entebbe* (77), the better of the two films made on this subject, for TV in the US and cinemas overseas; then the BBC came after him for *Billion-Dollar Bubble*, playing a computer expert in this docudrama (though the word hadn't been invented then) on the Equity Funding insurance scandal in the US. For five weeks' shooting he was paid what he earned for half a day on his last telefilm, but he thought the experience far more worthwhile. The BBC threw it away in its 'Horizon' slot, but it was bought by Time-Life Television for the US; and it was his calling-card till *Holocaust* (78), a mini-series in which he was the tortured Jewish artist husband of Meryl Streep. He said he felt no sense of commitment from the producers, and that he 'thought it was a bit of a soap opera when I first read the script. But it was also an important issue, and given the low quality of American television, [it] was like Shakespeare.' He added that many survivors of the concentration camps had told him that the fact that the world was more aware of what had happened atoned for the inaccuracies, and he was proud that, because of the series, the West German government extended their statute of limitations on war crimes. On another level, the project gave Woods the chance to work with Ian Holm, whom he had idolized since seeing him on Broadway in 'The Homecoming'.

Just prior to that he had been seen to advantage as one of *The Choirboys* (77), tenth-billed as one of ten LA cops so called for their raunchy, drunken escapades, indulged in to relieve the tensions of the job. Woods was the one who bungled while trying to arrest two hookers at the same time. He also thought the film a vulgarization of Joseph Wambaugh's book, and was given the opportunity of leaving without pay when he mentioned this to director Robert Aldrich. Three more telefilms followed: *The Gift of Love* (78), a version of O. Henry's story, 'The Gift of the Magi', with Marie Osmond and Timothy Bottoms; *The Incredible Journey of Doctor Meg Laurence* (79) with Jane Wyman; and *And Your Name is Jonah*, starring with Sally Struthers as a New York couple who discover that their small son is deaf rather than mentally retarded, as originally diagnosed. Among the others not liking *The Choirboys*, and there were many, was the author, who decided to exercise tight control over the filming of another of his novels, *The Onion Field*. He chose the little-known director, Harold Becker, and let his wife talk him into casting Woods as the violent and disturbed Greg Powell, who one night in 1963 shot a Los Angeles cop in an onion field. The film is basically about the traumas of the partner (John Savage) who escaped slaughter, and how he coped as Powell's appeals dragged on through the Californian courts. Because the film was starless and perceived to be relentlessly grim, it took only $4,300,000, in comparison to the $6,850,000 of those police academy *Choirboys*; but anyone chancing upon it on television is guaranteed to be riveted for over two hours.

'Brilliant, just brilliant,' said Wambaugh of Woods. 'The only intelligent actor I've ever met' – which may be why Woods did a cameo in the next Wambaugh–Becker film, *The Black Marble* (80), as a busking violinist serenading the improbable lovers, Robert Foxworth and Paula Prentiss. But if *Holocaust* and *The Onion Field* had made Woods a name, he seemed an unlikely guy to carry a picture: so the best he could do was as William Hurt's Vietnam chum in *Eyewitness* (81), quirky and a born loser, who is also a murder suspect. He starred and played the title-role in *Fast-Walking* (82), a prison guard hired as a hit-man when politician Robert Hooks is on the line; James B. Harris wrote and directed, and it was only too well named as far as the box-office was concerned. Neither was there a warm welcome for Ted Kotcheff's *Split Image*, in which a college athlete (Michael O'Keefe) falles for a girl (Karen Allen) and is drawn into a cult headed by a weirdo (Peter Fonda); Woods was the deprogrammer hired by his dad (Brian Dennehy) to lure him back. He had a big role which he played dynamically – but in the reduced circumstances of a muddled horror film written and directed (in Canada) by David Cronenberg, *Videodrome* (83). It starts promisingly, as a TV cable director (Woods) finds himself monitoring a mysterious rival channel submitting porn; it gets better as he discovers that this has a hallucinatory effect, but after a while it is liable to lose the most patient viewer.

Woods returned to a supporting role in *Against All Odds* (84), as the neurotic bar-owner and big-time bookie who employs Jeff Bridges, but he had a lot of footage as Robert De Niro's gangster buddy in *Once Upon a Time in America* – so, however, did everyone else since the director, Sergio Leone, is as fond of length as he is of pretension. A further wasted credit was *Cat's Eye* (85), an assembly of three of Stephen King's derivative horror tales, with Woods in the first of these as a man so desperate to give up smoking that he allows a Mafia man (Alan King) to threaten reprisals on his family if he starts again. In Canada he appeared in *Joshua Then and Now*, as a Jewish writer who marries into a prominent WASP family despite also a father (Alan Arkin) who was a petty hood; based on a sprawling semi-autobiographical novel by Mordecai Richler, it was originally a mini-series cut to feature-length. In the tele-film *Badge of the Assassin* he was a police inspector on the trail of terrorists in New Orleans.

By this time Woods looked like being a younger version of Robert Duvall, much respected but precariously balanced between chief protagonist and lead support. This is not, of course, a bad position to be in, but Woods was easily more watchable, more rewarding, than the handful of Hollywood draws. He simply needed the right showcase, and that came along with *Salvador* (86). The star role had already been cast, that of journalist Richard Boyle, who scripted the film with its newish director, Oliver Stone. Woods was taken aboard to play his buddy, Dr Rock, but he convinced Stone that he was the only one who could play Boyle, so the star was dropped and James Belushi engaged to play Dr Rock. The film begins a little like *Easy Rider*, with Woods and Dr Rock joshing as they travel south; in Salvador fellow-journos are cynical and the American ambassador (Michael Murphy) tries to do the right thing by co-operating with the unprincipled bullies running the country. As someone says, you can't stop the march of history, and it is clear that the humanitarians, the left-wing guerillas in the hills, will prevail. Stone took *Dr Strangelove* as his model, using comedy to alleviate discussion of the unthinkable, and he has in Woods a man to risk danger to the point of paranoia. His admiration for the actor was justified, for Woods works fast and with such wit and intelligence that he can get away with both the polemic and the Perils of Pauline exploits. These may not have been as widely seen as those of Indiana Jones, but there was no longer any doubt that here was a major actor. However, as his next credit was another

TV movie, a year later, we must suppose he turned down offers in the interim as of no interest. Or, as he put it, 'I didn't sell out during the twenty years it took to get hot; I'm not going to sell out now.' Anyway, *Promise* was co-produced by James Garner, who toplined as a carefree bachelor who on the death of his mother has to care for his schizophrenic brother, Woods – who was awarded a Golden Globe and an Emmy for Best Actor.

Also for television he was on terrific form *In Love and War* (87), beautifully partnered by Jane Alexander – though they were separated for most of its length, because he, as a crack US naval pilot, was captured during a raid on North Vietnam. He had another splendid co-star in *Best Seller* – Brian Dennehy, who played an ex-cop novelist who fancies his writer's block can be cured by throwing his hand in with a psychopathic hit man (Woods), who hopes to use him to expose a murder racket. A good idea, rather obviously developed in Larry Cohen's script, though sharply directed by John Flynn. Despite their earlier failed venture, Wood and James B. Harris co-produced *Cop* (88), which Harris wrote and directed from a novel by James Ellroy. He had not done much better this time around, with coincidence piled upon coincidence as the maverick gent (Woods) of the title pursues a serial killer. Said the critic David Quinlan: 'You've got to hand it to James Woods. You can't take your eyes off this lethal actor on screen, even in a mediocre movie like this thriller, which runs like a Clint Eastwood reject of five years before. Who knows what the man might do if he learned to choose the right script!' Said Harris: 'Working with James is the most pleasurable experience I have had.' Said Lesley Ann Warren, who co-starred: 'I can count on two hands every actor I ever wanted to work with, and James Woods has always been one of the few . . . It was everything I thought it would be. He's inspired as an actor, and funny, provocative and smart as a person. He's tremendously aware of things like camera, lighting and continuity, and does know an amazing amount about the ins and outs of making a film.'

This knowledge did not help him in getting better movies, for the best that *The Boost* could do was to quickly become a camp classic, as Woods and his wife, Sean Young, succumb to California cocaine culture (though in the original novel, Ben Stein's ''Ludes', the cause of their destruction, was a much milder drug). It was just another movie, said Vincent Canby, 'about the awful things that addicted people do to themselves and to one another, whether they drink, sniff or shoot up'. Becker

directed, and Woods was passionately committed to it: 'The part was written to all my rhythms. It was a journey to the depths of my soul. Playing it was like being hit by a freight train. I was going full throttle on the edge of the envelope.' The film came and went quickly, taking less than $1 million, but was to leave a humdinger of a hangover – and to be much heard about in the headlines of the tabloid press. Not to digress, Woods had at one time a longstanding relationship with Jill Clayburgh but, as he ruefully remarked, it was not easy to sustain because she was much more famous – it was the time of *An Unmarried Woman* – and better off than he. He also said that he did not think actors and actresses could live together. In October 1987, while filming *The Boost*, he was living with Sarah Owen, co-owner of an LA fabric store, when she filed a report with the LAPD charging that he had held her at gunpoint at their

James Woods, who won't remind you of the matinée idols of the past. Unlike many in this book, he learnt his craft on the stage, and honed it in almost twenty years in movies. This one is Once Upon a Time in America *(84).*

shared home. The matter was dropped and the following January, after filming wrapped, they became engaged. Shortly afterwards Young began to talk publicly about her 'emotional involvement' with Woods, though she insisted that it did not become physical. Woods's only public comment on the relationship (in the December 1988 'Vogue') is, 'Does the word "nightmare" mean nothing to you?' But in August of that year he and Owen charged harassment in the Los Angeles Supreme Court, demanding restraint and damages of $2 million. The deposition accused Young of sending them 'photographs and graphic representations of violent acts, deceased persons, dead animals, gore, mutilation and other images specifically designed to cause [them] emotional distress.' Young was questioned by police about a mutilated doll left on Woods's doorstep, and while denying all the charges still managed to make reference to him and Owen when publicizing the film (on camera, in 'Entertainment Tonight', 'If you wanted to hurt me, Jimmy and Sarah, you did'). The matter did not reach the courts, but according to Young's lawyer, a settlement was reached.

Meanwhile, Woods was in Joseph Ruben's *True Believer* (89), as a burnt-out Civil Rights lawyer who gets his adrenalin running again when he has to re-open the case of an Asian in jail for a killing: Woods's own notices were as good as they ever were, but the film itself was only moderately received, returning Columbia only $3,700,000 on a $14 million budget. Woods was also much praised for his role as the founder of Alcoholics Anonymous in a telemovie, *My Name is Bill W*, but it was transmitted against *Guts and Glory: the Rise and Fall of Oliver North*, which vanquished it in the ratings, causing James Garner, who co-produced, to protest publicly against the

system. Woods still obviously needed a first-rate movie to establish his credentials for good and all; he needed a popular co-star and an admired director, both of them preferably with recent hits. So *Immediate Family* seemed to fit the bill, for Glenn Close was playing his wife, and the director was Jonathan Kaplan, fresh from *The Accused*. But this sentimental drama about a couple and the baby they adopt was universally panned and did poor business (see Close).

Woods can also be seen in a thriller, *Fighting Justice*, also starring Robert Downey Jr. They play opposing lawyers cleaning up Chinatown – respectively cynical and idealistic: this film first surfaced in Britain on video in October 1990.

Onwards and upwards: *Hills Like White Elephants* (90), from a Hemingway story, with Melanie Griffith, as a Hemingway-like hero, and 'as always, near perfection,' said 'Variety'. The film was one of three short stories which went out on HBO under the awkward title *Women and Men: Stories of Seduction* (the other two in this anthology were Dorothy Parker's *Dusk Before Fireworks*, directed by Ken Russell, and Mary McCarthy's *The Man in the Brooks Brothers Shirt*, directed by Fredric Raphael).

Perhaps *The Hard Way*, a co-starring venture with Michael J. Fox, will turn Woods's track at the box-office, though he is likely to blow Fox off the screen in the process: and the same could be said of Ted Danson, Kevin Kline and Gene Hackman, all mentioned earlier in connection with the role. It can be predicted that Woods will continue to be offered star roles, even if he continues to lack drawing-power, because he will win an Oscar one day. That may not be his ambition (he was nominated for *Salvador*), but Hollywood thinks Oscars equal prestige and profits.

TITLE CHANGES

Most title changes within the English language are taken care of in the text, so the following is chiefly a listing of foreign films with their English titles. In some cases the films were not shown in Britain or the US; in others they were known under their original title.

Blow Out, GB   *La Grande Bouffe*, Fr (75)
Breathless, US   *À Bout de Souffle*, Fr (60)

Cinema Paradiso, GB, US   *Nuovo Cinema Paradiso*, It (88)
Clean Slate, GB, US   *Coup de Torchon*, Fr (85)
Le Cop, GB   *Les Ripoux*, Fr (88)

Dear Detective, GB, US   *Tendre Poulet*, Fr (77)
Dog Day, US   *Canicule*, Fr (84)
The Dogs, GB   *Les Chiens*, Fr (79)

Evening Dress, GB   *Tenue de Soirée*, Fr (86)

Family Business, US   *L'Été Prochain*, Fr (85)
The French Conspiracy, US   *L'Attentat*, Fr (72)

Get Out Your Handkerchiefs, GB, US   *Préparez vos Mouchoirs*, Fr (78)
Going Places, US   *Les Valseuses*, Fr (74)
The Gold-rimmed Spectacles, US   *Gli Occhiali Oro*, It (87)

The Hidden Gun, US   *Le Vieux Fusil*, Fr (75)
How To Destroy the Reputation of the World's Greatest Secret Agent, GB   *Le Magnifique*, Fr (73)

The Janitor, GB   *Eyewitness*, US (81)

The Last Metro, GB, US   *Le Dérnier Métro*, Fr (80)
The Last Woman, GB, US   *L'Ultima Donna*, It (76)
Let Joy Reign Supreme, US   *Que la Fête Commence*, Fr (75)
Let's Hope it's a Girl, GB   *Speriamo che sia Femmina*, It
Life and Nothing But, GB, US   *La Vie et Rien d'Autre*, Fr

Making It, GB   *Les Valseuses*, Fr (74)
A Matter of Resistance, US   *La Vie de Château*, Fr (65)
Moon in the Gutter, GB, US   *La Lune dans le Caniveau*, Fr
My American Uncle, GB   *Mon Oncle d'Amérique*, Fr (80)
My New Partner, US   *Les Ripoux*, Fr (88)

The Northern Star, GB   *L'Étoile du Nord*, Fr (82)

One Wild Moment, US   *Un Moment d'Égarement*, Fr (77)

The Plot, GB   *L'Attentat*, Fr (72)
Pookie, GB   *The Sterile Cuckoo*, US (69)

The Return of Martin Guerre, GB, US   *Le Retour de Martin Guerre*, Fr (82)

Saigon, GB   *Off Limits*, US (88)
Scene of the Crime, US   *Le Lieu du Crime*, Fr (86)
A Strange Place to Meet, GB   *Drôle d'Endroit pour une Rencontre*, Fr (89)
A Summer Affair, GB   *Un Moment d'Égarement*, Fr (77)

Too Beautiful For You, US   *Trop Belle pour Toi*, Fr (89)
Too Many Chefs, GB   *Who Is Kiling the Great Chefs of Europe?*, US (78)

Under Satan's Sun, GB, US   *Sous le Soleil de Satan*, Fr (87)

The Woman Next Door, GB, US   *La Femme d'à Côté*, Fr (81)
A Woman or Two, GB, US   *Une Femme ou Deux*, Fr (85)